OREGON
End of the Trail

OREGON

END OF THE TRAIL

✦

*Compiled by Workers of the Writers' Program
of the Work Projects Administration
in the State of Oregon*

✦

AMERICAN GUIDE SERIES

ILLUSTRATED

BY THE PACIFIC

Sponsored by the Oregon State Board of Control

BINFORDS & MORT : *Publishers* : PORTLAND

Republished 1972
SOMERSET PUBLISHERS — a Division of Scholarly Press, Inc.
22929 Industrial Drive East, St. Clair Shores, Michigan 48080

Library of Congress Cataloging in Publication Data

Writers' Program. Oregon.
   Oregon: end of the trail.

   "Sponsored by the Oregon State Board of Control."
   Reprint of the 1940 ed., issued in series: American
guide series.
   Bibliography: p.
   1. Oregon--Description and travel--Guide-books.
I. Series: American guide series.
F874.3.W73 1972   917.95'04'4   72-84501
ISBN 0-403-02186-3

THE OREGON GUIDE is the major accomplishment of the Oregon Writers' Project of the WPA. More than the conventional guide book,
this volume attempts to present the history and heritage of Oregon as
well as its numerous points of interest and the contemporary scene.
Though designed to portray Oregon to visitors, it is also intended, as
it were, to present Oregon to Oregonians.

As Governor of the Commonwealth I am happy that this valuable
work is being made available to the citizens of Oregon and the nation.

(Signed) CHARLES A. SPRAGUE.

March 1, 1940

Preface

THE OREGON GUIDE is the product of many hands and minds working joyously, without hope of individual reward or recognition, to accomplish something of which by and large they are proud, and diffidently offering it to the public of travelers and scholars and general readers. In contributing this volume to the American Guide Series, the members of the Oregon Writers' Project of the Work Projects Administration, speak collectively and anonymously. Most of them would rather have had some small part in its creation, working as carpenters of language with words as tools, finding facts and fashioning them into sentences and paragraphs and chapters, than to have built a fast highway or an impressive public building. For, generally, the writer believes that long after the best road of his day has been supplanted by a straighter and wider one, and long after the highest building has crumbled with time or been blown to bits by air bombs, this book will remain. And the makers of this Guide have faith, too, that their book will survive; in the future, when it no longer fills a current need as a handbook for tourists, it will serve as a reference source well-thumbed by school children and cherished by scholars, as a treasure trove of history, a picture of a period, and as a fadeless film of a civilization.

It was easy to write about Oregon. The state has something that inspires not provincial patriotism but affection. California has climate; Iowa has corn; Massachusetts has history; Utah has religion; and New York has buildings and money and hustle and congestion; but that "lovely dappled up-and-down land called Oregon" has an ever-green beauty as seductive as the lotus of ancient myth.

It is not only the native son of pioneers who feels this affection for the land. The newcomer at first may smile at the attitude of Oregonians towards their scenery and their climate. But soon he will begin to refer to Mt. Hood as "our mountain"—significantly, not as "The Mountain," as Seattlites speak of Mt. Rainier. Soon he will try to purchase a home-site from which he can view it. And before a year of life in Oregon has passed, the sheer splendor of peaks and pines, the joy of shouting trout-filled mountain streams, the satisfying quiet of Douglas firs, the beauty of roses that bloom at Christmas, the vista of rolling wooded hills and meadows always lush and green, the scenic climax of a fiery sun sinking into earth's most majestic ocean—all will have become a part of his daily happiness, undefined and unrecognized in his consciousness, but something so vital that he can never again do without it. And he will even, as do the natives, find merit in the long winter of dismal skies and warm but chilling rains, calling himself a "webfoot" and stoutly proclaiming that he likes it—when all the while he means that he considers it poor sportsmanship to complain, since he knows that this is the annual tax he pays for eternal verdure, for trees and grass and ferns and ivy and hydrangeas and holly, and for the privilege of appreciating by contrast the short bright rainless summer cooled by the softest yet most invigorating northerly winds.

These tributes are generally inspired by only a part, not even a third part, of Oregon. Beyond the wall of the Cascades, which cuts the state into two sections sharply contrasting topographically, stretches a land whose character is that of the plateaus and deserts and mountains of the Rockies country. Yet even the climate of this eastern region has its enthusiasts, and has been thus described by Claire Warner Churchill: "It rains. It snows. It scorches. It droughts. It suspends itself in celestial moments of sheer clarity that hearten the soul. Whatever else it may do, it challenges rather than enervates. Rather than complacency it breeds philosophy."

So Oregon offers, it is claimed, the greatest variety of climate and scenery and vegetation of all the states.

It was this very diversity that occasioned a lively controversy in the selection of a subtitle for the Guide. In a public contest many Oregonians offered titles dripping with ardor. Such phrases as "The Land of Perpetual Spring" and "Land of the Midwinter Rose" were viewed by out-of-state critics with arched eye-brows as either un-factual or over-sentimental. Stolid history lovers suggesting "The Beaver State," were countered with the quip, "Why not call it the Rodent State so as not to discriminate against our rabbits and prairie dogs?" Others argued that the subtitle should derive from the state stone, which is agate, or the state bird, the meadow-lark, or even the state flower, the Oregon grape, which has an unromantic but highly practical history. Geographically-minded persons, aware that Portland is the farthest west of America's large cities, advised "Oregon—Farthest West." Another group wanted "Oregon—Nearest Japan," and their argument was political. Finally, an amateur artist drew a dust cover depicting the setting sun and proffered "The Sunset State."

And what of Oregon's future? It is, after all, only a few short years between the time when William Cullen Bryant wrote in one of his greatest poems about the primitive country "Where rolls the Oregon and hears no sound," and the present, when Bonneville Dam has made a great gash in beautiful Columbia Gorge, and when the greatest structure in history, Grand Coulee, looms portentously to the north. Oregon today is still the most unspoiled and most uncluttered spot in America—partly because the gold rushes of California and Alaska left it undisturbed. Soon, perhaps, it will be changed by the coming of Power, the inrolling of immigration from the dust bowl, the devastation of timber-cutting and forest fires, and the boosting activities of chambers of commerce. It may be regrettable to see this peaceful beautiful land transformed into a network of highways, clogged with cars and defaced with hot dog stands, the groves littered with tin cans and papers, the hills pock-marked with stumps, and the cities cursed with the slums that seem to accompany industrial progress.

The sons of Oregon today are tall and sturdy, and the complexion of the daughters is faintly like that of the native rose—a hue gained from living and playing in a pleasant outdoors. Will the sons of the impending industrial age be shorter and shrewder, and the daughters dependent for their beauty upon commodities sold in drug-stores; and will Oregonians become less appreciative of nature and rooted living and more avid and neurotic in the pursuit of wealth? These are some of the questions and misgivings in the minds of native Oregonians, including some of those who wrought the Oregon Guide.

Yet the writers of the Guide worked hard and gladly, though aware that their names would never be known. And only here can acknowledgment be made of their zeal and devotion. They were aided and encouraged by many citizens of Oregon who served as consultants, and by many institutions which gladly and courteously opened to them their stores of history and tradition and current fact. Among those who helped are: Leith Abbott, Dr. Burt Brown Barker, J. R. Beck, C. I. Buck, Dr. V. L. O. Chittick, Dr. R. C. Clark, H. L. Corbett, Dr. L. S. Cressman, Dr. H. C. Dake, Wm. L. Finley, George H. Flagg, Dr. James A. Gilbert, Frederick Goodrich, Mr. and Mrs. E. J. Griffith, Mrs. Charles A. Hart, M. T. Hoy, Herbert Lampman, Mrs. Katherine Lawton, Lewis A. McArthur, Roi Morin, Glen W. Neel, J. A. Ormandy, Dr. E. L. Packard, Jamieson Parker, Phil. Parrish, Professor

Morton E. Peck, Miss Nellie B. Pipes, Alfred Powers, Charles P. Pray, Ralph J. Reed, Professor Wm. A. Schoenfeld, Leslie Scott, Earl Snell, Dr. Warren D. Smith, V. D. Stanberry, Oswald West, F. B. Wire; also the State Library, the Portland Public Library, the Oregon Historical Society, the Portland Art Museum, the State Planning Board, the State Highway Commission, and the U. S. Forest Service.

T. J. EDMONDS, *State Supervisor.*

Contents

Part I. Past and Present

Part II. Cities and Towns

Part III. All Over Oregon

Part IV. Appendices

Illustrations

Maps

General Information

*(State map, showing highways, and maps
giving railroad, air, bus, and water transportation routes in pocket, inside back cover.)*

Railroads: Great Northern Ry. (GN), Northern Pacific Ry. (NP),
Southern Pacific Lines (SP), Union Pacific R. R. (UP), Spokane,
Portland & Seattle Ry. (SP&S), Oregon Electric Ry. (OE) (*see
TRANSPORTATION MAP.*)

Bus Lines: Pacific Greyhound Lines, Union Pacific Stages, North Coast
Transportation Co., Spokane, Portland & Seattle Transportation Co.,
Oregon Motor Stages, Mount Hood Stages, North Bank Highway
Stages, Boyd's Dollar Lines, Independent Stages, and Benjamin Franklin Line serve all but most remote sections. Pacific Greyhound and
North Coast are principal carriers N. and S., operating over US 99,
the former S. of Portland into California, the latter to Seattle and
points N. Union Pacific Stages and Spokane, Portland & Seattle line
(US 30), are chief lines E. and W., the former operating E. and the
latter W. from Portland: all lines listed above enter Portland; average
fare, 2c per mi. (*see TRANSPORTATION MAP*).

Air Lines: United Airlines (Vancouver, B. C., to San Diego) stops
at Portland and Medford; United Airlines (Portland, Pendleton, Salt
Lake City, Omaha, Chicago, New York) connection at Pendleton for
Spokane (*see TRANSPORTATION MAP*).

Waterways: Principal waterways are Columbia and Willamette Rivers.
Portland, on the Willamette, is a regular port of call for coastwise
vessels between Los Angeles, San Francisco, and Seattle and for combination freight and passenger vessels to the Orient, and to South
American, Atlantic Coast and European ports. Freight and passenger
river boats operate between Portland and Astoria, and Portland and
The Dalles.

Highways: Eight Federal highways, six of them transcontinental or with international connections. State highways connect all sections. State police patrol highways. No inspection of cars into Oregon, but cars from Oregon entering California undergo inspection for horticultural diseases. Water or gasoline scarcity possible only in high desert region of southeastern Oregon. Gasoline tax, 6c (*for highway routes, see STATE MAP*).

Motor Vehicle Laws (digest): No fixed speed limit, but no person shall drive at a speed inconsistent with prudent control of car; "indicated speeds," which are accepted as reasonable, are 45 m. p. h. on open highway, 25 m. p. m. in city residence districts, 20 m. p. h. in business districts and at intersections where vision is obscured, and 15 m. p. h. while passing school grounds. Speed in excess of 45 m. p. h. on open highways permitted, but driver operates at his own risk. State licenses not required of non-residents, but cars must be registered within 24 hrs. after entry into state; registration may be made with secretary of state or his agents, which include chambers of commerce and the American Automobile Assn.; no fee charged. State police supply information; they drive blue cars with state insignia on the doors and are easily recognized by their blue uniforms.

Headlights must conform with 8-point adjustment system. Accidents resulting in injury to person or property must be reported within 24 hrs. to nearest chief of police or sheriff. Minimum age for drivers 15 yrs., unless special permit has been granted. Full stop required while streetcars are loading or unloading passengers, except where safety zones have been established.

Unlawful: To drive while intoxicated, to carry any person on any external part of automobile, to coast in neutral, to park on paved or main-traveled portion of highway, to carry more than three persons over 12 on front seat, to pass streetcars on L., to display windshield stickers other than temporary licenses and registration tags.

Accommodations: Hotel accommodations are adequate; tourist camps along all main highways; U. S. Forest Service camps within forest areas; beach accommodations along US 101 at all seasons; eight dude ranches, the four most elaborate ones being in Baker and Wallowa Counties. At Portland, during Rose Festival in June, and Pacific International Stock Show in autumn; Salem, during State Fair in September; Pendleton, during Round-Up in September; and at Astoria, during Regatta in late summer, advance hotel accommodations should be arranged.

Climate and Equipment: Moderate temperatures prevail W. of Cascade Mountains; medium weight clothing sufficient the year around; topcoats needed in the valleys in all seasons but summer, and along Pacific Coast even in warmest weather; rain general during fall and winter, when water-proof clothes will be appreciated.

East of the Cascades temperatures are more extreme: summer days hot, nights cool; summer travel equipment should include mediumweight clothing; snow and sub-zero weather in winter.

Special outdoor clothing, cooking utensils, and bedding required for hiking and pack-horse trips; equipment available in any county seat town; drinking water wholesome and plentiful in Cascades and western Oregon, but water from rivers not recommended except in most primitive areas.

Recreational Areas: Thirteen national forests (*see STATE MAP*); of these, Wallowa, Mount Hood, Willamette, and Rogue River have primitive areas, all have recreational areas. Crater Lake National Park and Oregon Caves National Monument, both in southern Oregon, are other National playgrounds.

Recreational areas visited to best advantage in summer; guides available for primitive areas; any U. S. Forest Service headquarters or ranger will furnish information; national forest campers between July 1 and Sept. 30, except at improved campgrounds, required to obtain campfire permits from rangers and to carry ax, water container, and shovel; all campfires must be put out before camp is abandoned, or campers are liable to heavy fine; smoking while traveling in national forests forbidden except on paved or surfaced highways.

Poisonous Plants, Reptiles, Dangerous Animals, and Insects: Poison oak prevalent E. of Cascades and in valleys between Cascade and Coast Ranges; rattlesnakes only poisonous reptiles, not common but found occasionally E. of Cascades, in southern Willamette Valley, and southern Oregon; none has been found W. of Coast Range; bears, mountain lions, and timber wolves, found in the mountains, generally harmless unless molested.

Poisonous insects are the Rocky Mountain or Spotted Fever tick, found in cattle country of eastern Oregon from March to June; Black Widow spiders, active in late summer months, found occasionally around rock and lumber piles; mosquitoes attain pest proportions only in high Cascade forests when snow is melting in early summer.

State Liquor Laws: State controls liquor traffic; hard liquor purchasable only from state stores or agencies; permit, costing 50c and good for 1 yr., must be obtained by residents and visitors for purchases; hard liquor sold only in original packages and may not be consumed on premises; beer, ale, and unfortified wine may be purchased without a permit from privately owned and operated depots, licensed by the state, and may be consumed on the premises.

Fishing Laws: Nonresident angler's license, $3; special vacation license for two consecutive days, $1; unnaturalized persons must obtain $25 alien gun license before purchasing angling or hunting license; all persons 14 yrs. and more must have license to hunt or angle; licenses may be obtained from any county clerk, the State Game Commission, or its agents, usually drug and sporting-goods stores; complete copies of state game laws available at any agency.

Open season for trout, fixed by Oregon Game Commission, usually from April to November; bag limit, 15 lb. and 1 fish, but not to exceed 20 fish in 1 day; or 30 lb. and 1 fish, but not to exceed 40 fish in 7 consecutive days, except special bag limits for certain lakes and streams (for which see complete state game laws); for trout more than 10 in., season open all year in Pacific Ocean, its tidewaters, and Coast lakes.

Open season for salmon, 15 in. and more, entire year; bag limit salmon 20 in. and more, 3 such fish in any 1 day, but not to exceed 10 such fish in any 7 consecutive days; bag limit on 15 in. salmon, 15 lb. and 1 fish, but not to exceed 20 fish in any 1 day; salmon under 15 in. classified as trout and may be taken only as such.

Bass season open entire year except in Oswego Lake, where it runs from Apr. 5 to Oct. 31, both inclusive.

Crappies, catfish, perch, and sunfish seasons open all year except in certain waters, for which see complete state laws.

Hunting Laws: Nonresident's license $15 including deer tag; elk tag, $25 additional. Licenses may be obtained in same manner as fishing licenses (*see above*) ; open season for game animals and birds, all dates inclusive:

Bear: Entire year, except in Jackson, Josephine, and Klamath counties, where open season is Nov. 1 to Nov. 30. Buck deer, Sept. 20 to Oct. 25; bag limit, 2 Columbia blacktail deer or 1 mule deer having not less than 3 forked horns. Bull elk, having horns: Nov. 8 to Nov. 18. Chinese pheasants: Oct. 15 to Oct. 31 in most counties; bag limit 4 birds in 1 day, 8 in any 7 consecutive days, with 1 hen pheasant in bag of 8. Hungarian partridges: Oct. 15 to Oct. 31 in Wasco, Sherman, Morrow, and Wheeler counties; Sept. 15 to Nov. 15 in Malheur, Baker, Wallowa, Union, and Umatilla counties; bag limit 6 birds in 1 day, 12 in any consecutive 7 days. Quail: Oct. 15 to Oct. 31 in most counties except Klamath, where season is from Oct. 1 to Oct. 31, bag limit 10 birds in any consecutive 7 days. Grouse, native pheasants: Oct. 15 to Oct. 31 W. of Cascade Range summit, Sept. 10 to Sept. 30 in eastern Oregon, bag limit 4 birds in 1 day, or 8 in consecutive 7 days. Ducks, geese, brant, coots, Wilson snipe, or jacksnipes; Nov. 1 to Nov 30, bag limit on ducks 10 in 1 day or in possession at any one time, geese and brant 4 in 1 day or in possession at any one time, snipe 15 in 1 day or in possession at any one time.

Unlawful: To kill whitetail deer, sage hens, to hunt at night, to hunt on any game refuge, to hunt deer with dogs, to waste game wantonly, to shoot from public highway or railroad right-of-way, to hunt on lands without permission of owner and to lie in wait for deer at or near licks, to possess more than 30 lb. and 1 fish (trout) or more than 40 trout at one time. The provision as to trout, permits angler to have 1 fish in excess of 30 lb. provided the aggregate does not exceed 40 trout. (*In view of frequent changes in regulations tourists should check with latest editions of hunting and fishing laws.*)

Picking wild flowers is not forbidden in national forests, and timber may be removed from certain areas under a sustained yield system; but picking flowers along highways in national forests or in dedicated recreation districts is not allowed.

General Service for Tourists: A publication of value is the *Oregon Blue Book,* an official state publication, available in public libraries, or for sale by the Secretary of State, Salem, 25c per copy; chambers of commerce, state troopers, automobile associations, forest officers will supply information at any time.

No toll bridges or toll ferries within Oregon, but toll charges are made for interstate crossings at several points between Oregon and Washington. Three bridges and seven ferries cross Columbia River between Astoria and Umatilla, levying charges varying from 50c for car and all passengers to $1 for car and driver (*see Tours*). Travel over Interstate Bridge at Portland is free.

Calendar of Annual Events

Only events of general interest listed: for descriptions consult index. Many opening dates vary with the years and are placed in the week in which they usually occur.

JANUARY

Third week	at Kamela	La Grande Ski Tournament
Fourth week	at Government Camp	Cascade Ski Club Tournament
Fourth week	at Portland	Olympic Bowman League Shoot
Fourth week	at Eugene	Olympic Bowman League Shoot

FEBRUARY

Second Friday	Statewide	Arbor Day
Third week	at Government Camp	Winter Sports Carnival
Third week	at Government Camp	Pacific Northwest Slalom Tournament
Fourth week	at Government Camp	Champion Ski Jumps
Fourth week	at Vale	"El Campo" Celebration

MARCH

First week	at Portland	Salmon Fishing Derby
Third Sunday	at Prineville	Old Timers' Reunion
No fixed date	at Portland	Dog Show
Easter	at Portland	Easter Services in Mt. Tabor and Washington Parks

APRIL

No fixed date	at The Dalles	Indian Salmon Feast

MAY

First Sunday	at Champoeg	Oregon Founders' Day
First week	at Klamath Falls	Flower Show
Third week	at Milton	Pea Festival
Fourth week	at Klamath Falls	Upper Klamath Lake Regatta

JUNE

First week	at Lebanon	Strawberry Fair
First week	at Union	Eastern Oregon Livestock Show
First week	at Independence	Jersey Jubilee
Second week	at Canyon City	'62 Gold Rush Celebration
Second week	at Portland	Rose Festival
Second week	at Salem	Oregon Trapshooters' Association Meet
Second week	at Government Camp	Summer Ski Tournament
Second week	at Weston	Pioneer Picnic
Third week	at Brownsville	Pioneer Picnic
Third week	at Portland	Oregon Pioneer Assn. Celebration
Third or Fourth week	at Taft	Redhead Round-Up
Fourth week	at St. Helens	St. Hellions Days
No fixed date	at Sheridan	Phil Sheridan Day
No fixed date	at Gold Beach	Fat Lamb Show
No fixed date	at Beaverton	Flower Festival
No fixed date	at Newberg	Berry Festival
No fixed date	at Florence	Rhododendron Show

JULY

First week	at Hillsboro	Happy Days Celebration
First week	at Molalla	Buckaroo
First week	at Bend	Water Pageant
First week	at Klamath Falls	Rodeo
First week	at Vale	Rodeo
Second week	at Marshfield	Paul Bunyan Celebration
Third week (biennial)	at Oregon City	Frontier Days Celebration
Third week	at Portland	Fleet Week
Third week (every 3rd yr.)	at Eugene	Oregon Trail Pageant
Third week	at Tillamook	Tillamook Beaches Jubilee
Third week	at Hood River	American Legion Mt. Hood Climb
Third week	at Gearhart	Oregon Coast Golf Tournament
Third week	at Stayton	Santiam Spree

Third or Fourth week	at Baker	Mining Jubilee
Fourth week	at Grants Pass	Gladiolus Show
Fourth week	at Ocean Lake	Devil's Lake Regatta
No fixed date	at Corvallis	Pacific Northwest Horticultural Show
No fixed date	at Tillamook	March of Progress
No fixed date	at Portland	Outdoor Portland Symphony Concerts
No fixed date	at Coquille	Flower Show

AUGUST

First week	at Silverton	American Legion Baseball Playoff
First week	at Nyssa	Owyhee Canyon Days
First week	at Mount Angel	Flax Festival
Second week	at Bend	Flower Show
Third week (biennial)	at Oregon City	Territorial Days Celebration
Third Sunday	at Falls City	Old Timers' Picnic
Fourth week	at Ashland	Shakespearean Festival
Fourth week	at Independence	Hop Fiesta
No fixed date	at Portland	Outdoor Portland Symphony Concerts
Fourth week	at Astoria	Astoria Regatta

SEPTEMBER

First week	at Lakeview	Round-Up
First week	at Ontario	Stampede
First week	at The Dalles	Fort Dalles Frolic
First week	at Heppner	Rodeo
First week	at Salem	Oregon State Fair
First week	at Caves City	Miners' Jubilee
First week	at Prairie City	Round-Up
Third week	at Pendleton	Round-Up
Fourth week	at Enterprise	Race Meet and Rodeo
No fixed date	at Condon	Rodeo
No fixed date	at Siletz	Rodeo
No fixed date	at Monmouth	American Legion Hi-jinks

OCTOBER

First week	at Portland	Pacific International Livestock Show
No fixed date	at Milton-Freewater	Apple Show
No fixed date	at Newberg	Farm Products Show
No fixed date	at Merrill	Potato Show
No fixed date	at Dufur	Ex-Service Men's Reunion

NOVEMBER

| No fixed date | at Coquille | Corn Show |
| No fixed date | at Corvallis | State Horticultural Show |

DECEMBER

Second week	at Oakland	Northwestern Turkey Show
No fixed date	at Roseburg	Turkey Show
No fixed date	at Portland	Cat Show
Fourth week	at Simnasho	Indian New Year's Celebration

COUNTY AND DISTRICT FAIRS

AUGUST

No fixed date	at Gresham	Multnomah County Fair
No fixed date	at Tillamook	Tillamook County Fair
Last week	at Toledo	Lincoln County Fair
Last week	at Eugene	Lane County Fair
Fourth week	at Hermiston	Hermiston Project Fair

SEPTEMBER

First week	at Canby	Clackamas County Fair
First week	at Ontario	Malheur County Fair
First week	at Moro	Sherman County Fair
First week	at Dallas	Polk County Fair
First week	at Hillsboro	Washington County Fair
Second week	at Lakeview	Lake County and 4H Club Fair
Fourth week	at Redmond	Deschutes County Fair
Fourth week	at Enterprise	Wallowa County Fair
Fourth week	at La Grande	Union County Fair
No fixed date	at Woodburn	Community Fair
No fixed date	at Halfway	Baker County Fair
No fixed date	at St. Helens	Columbia County Fair
No fixed date	at Myrtle Point	Coos County Fair

No fixed date	at Gold Beach	Curry County Fair
No fixed date	at John Day	Grant County Fair
No fixed date	at Burns	Harney County Fair
No fixed date	at Gold Hill	Northwest Jackson County Fair
No fixed date	at Grants Pass	Josephine County Fair
No fixed date	at The Dalles	Northern Wasco County Fair
No fixed date	at Tygh Valley	Wasco County Fair

OCTOBER

| First week | at Prineville | Crook County Fair |

PIONEER ASSOCIATION MEETINGS

FEBRUARY

| Fourteenth | at Portland | Sons and Daughters of Oregon Pioneers |

MAY

| First Saturday | at The Dalles | Wasco County Association |
| Second week | at Hood River | Hood River County Association |

JUNE

First week	at Tillamook	Tillamook County Association
Second week	at Canyon City	Grant County Association
Second week	at Burns	Harney County Association
Third week	at Portland	Oregon State Pioneer Association
Third week	at Brownsville	Linn County Pioneer Association
Third Sunday	at Hillsboro	Washington County Association
No fixed date	at Weston	Umatilla County Association

JULY

Last Sunday	at Coquille	Coos County Association
Last Sunday	at Dayton	Yamhill County Association
Last Wednesday	at Enterprise	Wallowa County Association

AUGUST

First Sunday	at Prineville	Crook County Association
Third Sunday	at Toledo	Lincoln County Association
No fixed date	at Canyon City	Eastern Oregon Pioneer Association

SEPTEMBER

No fixed date   at Oregon City   McLoughlin Memorial
Association

OCTOBER

at Lexington   No fixed date   Morrow County Association

PART I.

Past and Present

Oregon Yesterday and Today

OREGONIANS pridefully point out that theirs is the only state for which a transcontinental highway is named. It is the Oregon Trail, which began at Independence, Missouri. Even yet there travel along US 30, which in part roughly approximates and in part coincides with the original trail, a continuous caravan of folk whose purposes parallel those of the pioneers who sought adventure, profit or release from economic pressure. This third objective they have realized, it is said, because the Trail's End State, although slow to respond to the impetus of prosperity, has been correspondingly resistant to the effects of depression.

Oregon's topography, as well as its location, has importantly affected its development. The ninth largest commonwealth, it is divided physically by the Cascade mountain range, and metaphysically by economic, political, and sociological Alps of infinitely greater magnitude. The Cascades cut the State into two unequal portions from the northern to the southern boundary lines. If the geologists are correct, the mountains owe their eminence to a terrific vulcanism that sent the great peaks hurtling up through the ooze and miasma of prehistoric Oregon. The disturbance gave the modern state a scenic grandeur that has exhausted even the superlatives of the gentlemen who write recreational brochures, but it walled eastern Oregon away from the humid winds, the warm rains of the coast, and turned most of the land, through countless aeons of slow dehydration, into a country of drought and distances, of grim and tortured mountains and high desert grown sparsely with stunted juniper and wind-blown sage.

The mountain range stood as a colossal veto of whatever motions the early eastern Oregon settlers might have made toward economic equality with the pioneers of the lush country west of the Cascades. It turned them, out of sheer necessity, into cattlemen and sheepmen and miners and "dry" farmers, just as more benign circumstances made western Oregon residents into lumbermen, dairymen, fishermen and farmers, and—in the more populous centers—into artisans and politicians and financiers. At once the hero and the villain of the early Oregon piece, the Cascade Range still imposes a dozen divergent viewpoints upon the modern State; and it is therefore unlikely, if not impossible, that there be any such thing as a typical Oregonian.

The history of the State has been an essay in dramatic counterpoint that did not in itself make for homogeneity. The epochal journey of Lewis and Clark into the wild country still stands as a monumental achievement. The explorers live as shining examples of men who had a difficult job to do, and who did it with resounding thoroughness. But, while they pried open the dark doorway to the unknown West, the reports that they brought back of the Oregon Country's teeming animal life opened the territory also to some precious scoundrels.

The fur traders who came after Lewis and Clark were as realistic in their approach to the country as were Cortez to Mexico and Pizzaro to Peru. They plagued the Indians with whiskey and social diseases, salted the very beaver skins with corruption, and yearned to be quit of the savage land as quickly as possible. The missionaries who followed were, in the main, devout if somewhat severe men who strove mightily to invest the natives in spirituality and trousers; but even among these a few learned to sing upon both sides of the Jordan, and to deal more briskly in real estate than in salvation. While the great overland migration to Oregon has been sanctified by tradition it seems foolish to presume that the covered wagons carried nothing but animated virtues into Oregon.

The great migration, as a matter of fact, contained every sort of human ingredient. Here came craftsmen from the Atlantic seaboard cities, uprooted by cheap labor from troubled Europe, journeying across the yellow Missouri, the great deserts and the towering mountains. So, also, came eastern farmers whose soil had worn thin from the sowings and reapings of two hundred years, doctors who lacked patients, lawyers who lacked clients. They came because they thought that they might better themselves and their families. No sane person would question their courage, or the hardihood of those who survived; but it is barely possible that they were not all either sunbonneted madonnas, or paragons of manhood jouncing westward with banjos on their knees.

The better of those who came may have lived longer. They certainly toiled harder, and they left the stamp of their fierce industry upon everything they touched. Had they been given time, had immigration ceased with them, they might have fused and welded the traits of a dozen eastern localities and produced something—a mode of speech, a style of architecture, a form of culture, or even a set of prejudices— uniquely their own. Subsequent waves of immigration, however, washed again and again over them, to warp the sober pattern of living that they laid down. The discovery of gold in southwestern Oregon and in the eastern portion of the State in the fifties and sixties brought the living prototypes of Bret Harte's fictions into the country by the thousands during the next two decades. The argonauts, like the Federal troops who came to fight a half dozen bloody Indian wars, had the irresponsibility of men who live lonely and dangerous lives anywhere, and they sowed their seed from Port Orford, on the southern Oregon coast, to the Wallowa foothills, on the State's northeastern boundary line. Veterans of Lee's shattered Army of the Confederacy, spared their horses by Grant at Appomattox, rode the starveling beasts into the country that had irked the Union commander as young lieutenant at Fort Vancouver years before, and men of his own victorious army pushed westward to settle side by side with their vanquished foes.

Then General Howard's troops blew out the last determined Indian resistance with a single gust of black powder smoke at Willow Springs in 1879, and eastern capitalists began to read some significance in the tumultuous Oregon scene. The transportation kings arrived, to wrestle for supremacy like embattled bulls, and while their methods may have shocked students of ethics, the shining rails went down, so that men along the Deschutes might ship some of the largest and finest potatoes in the world, and Jackson County fruit growers might find a market for their golden pears, and the lumber barons might hack at the State's timber resources. Lumberjacks from the thinning pine woods of Michigan swarmed into the Oregon wilds, just as in many cases their fathers before them had come into the Middle West from the hardwood forests of Maine, and the great epoch of Oregon lumbering was begun.

It is an interesting genealogical fact that the grandsons of Maine residents sometimes married the descendants of men who had come from that state a half century before; but there were not enough of these to make a Yankee sampler of Oregon. Swedes had come in too, and Norwegians; German and Bohemian immigrants were planting garden plots and pulling stumps as the forest wall receded. In Astoria Finnish fishermen adapted themselves to a climate less rigorous than that of their native land, while on the hills of southeastern Oregon, Spanish Basques were raising sheep, to the disgust of cattlemen who ruled like feudal lords over ranches larger than the lesser Balkan states.

The ranchers and the cowboys who served them, were as pungent a set of personalities as the North American continent ever knew. Their manner of living was Oregon's last link to the fabulous West that has vanished forever. Many of the cattlemen rode into the unmapped country with no other possessions than their rifles and blankets and the clothing that they wore. Their successful efforts to wring livelihoods from the hostile land is an unwritten epic of the frontier. Although the financial wizard, Henry Miller, might swallow their ranches eventually, they held things with a short rein while they lasted, and were quicker to resort to the rifle than to the courts of law. Some of them were pillars of rectitude who married early, begot large families, and grew gaunt and gray and old in sober monogamy. Others punished their livers with bad whiskey and pursued their amours in the Indian lodges as well as in the brothels of Pendleton and the settlements of the Klamath Basin. A woman tavern keeper on Applegate Creek in Jackson County wrote to her niece in 1854: "Em, I should like to have you here, but a young lady is so seldom seen here that you would be in dange of being taken by force."

This reckless era wore itself down with its own sheer animal vigor, and died, figuratively, in its tracks, like a spent bull. There followed the homesteading migration of the early 1900's when thousands of easterners settled upon lands that often failed to yield a living. Some of them ultimately beat their way back to the East, many found footholds in the productive soils of the western part of the State, and Oregon cities absorbed the rest. Then the World War was fought and finished, Oregon troops came back from overseas, and the State passed through the golden twenties and the lean nineteen-thirties to immediate time.

The forces of good and evil, as we know them, have hammered one another through every hour of the State's history. Balanced against debaucheries, failures and land frauds are the solid accomplishments of men and women who had honesty of purpose and vision, vast courage and friendliness, and generosity that sprang warm from their hearts.

Politically, the individual Oregonian may be certain that he understands himself, but he cannot always be so sure of his neighbors. Citizens of conservative opinion may declare solemnly that a staunch and inflexible conservatism is the bone and bowel and sinew of the State's body politic, but the body politic has never patiently endured a tightened belt, and there has been no lack of faithful followers to heed the chant of every economic muezzin from Henry George to Dr. Townsend. Throughout the State, a preponderantly conservative press voices at least an editorial approval of the status quo; but there is always a play of heat-lightning and a rumble of distant thunder along the political horizon, and champions of new causes emerge each year.

Oregon politics have been matters of both comedy and melodrama. The State was harshly dictatorial in its treatment of Chinese immigrants, with whose descendants the commonwealth now finds no quarrel; but it was also the first to introduce the initiative and referendum, and the breath of liberalism has never entirely failed. Unpredictable as are voters elsewhere, Oregonians sometimes make strange uses of their franchise. The Ku Klux Klan burned its fiery crosses over a hundred hills, and its propagandists sowed racial intolerance in every county of the state, but the Oregon electorate, unmoved by these activities, plodded to the polls and elected a Jewish governor. The voters of Salem enthusiastically accepting a plan for a new courthouse as proposed in a primary measure, marched forth at the general election to reject the tax levy with which the structure was to have been built. The general elections of November, 1938, found the Oregon electorate voting down a sales tax which was intended to have financed an extended old-age pension plan, approved in the preceding primary. The commonwealth's true political picture reads from Left to Right, with all deviations and all shades of opinion represented, and in the very vociferousness of dissenting voices, Oregon may count its democracy secure.

Oregonians have expressed themselves well in the fields of art, letters and music. Although Portland has been called the "Athens of the West," only a few persons are inclined to be disagreeably emphatic about the matter, or to make a fetish of culture. The State's painters and sculptors show strength and imagination and skill, and men and women employed by WPA have executed some of the most forthright work among contemporary artists. Oregon writers delve into a wealth of raw source material, and do well with what they withdraw and refine; and if it is not precisely true that there are more writers in Portland than in any other American city, as has been contended, there are at least an astonishing number of poets and novelists and journalists for so small a municipality. Besides these, there are sailors who come from the sea to write of what they have seen, and former lumberjacks who wade as zestfully into the world of letters as once they did into the Oregon mill-ponds.

All this promises well for a rich and full and native culture in the future, but it should not be supposed that the state has yet abandoned itself utterly to the refinements of the arts. The pulp magazines sell as well in Oregon as anywhere else, the cinema offers as many ineptitudes;

and while the Portland Junior Symphony, or the touring Monte Carlo Ballet, may attract large audiences to the Portland Auditorium, the beer halls are filled also with citizens who frankly prefer "swing" rhythms. Perhaps the greatest cultural achievement of the commonwealth is expressed by the fact that only one state, Iowa, has a greater degree of literacy, although higher education in Oregon was long retarded by persons opposed to any institutions more advanced than the most elementary of schools.

Pictorially Oregon is this: tidy white houses and church spires of the Willamette Valley settlements, like transplanted New England towns, among pastoral scenery warm and graceful as the landscapes of Innes; the Alice-through-the-looking-glass effect of a swift incredible geographic change that lifts the motorist out of lush green forests and over the wind-scoured ridgepole of the Cascades, and plummets him into a grim Never-Never land of broken rim-rock and bone-bare plains beyond the range; the lamplit frontier towns of eastern Oregon, the rolling, golden wheatlands, great ranches where booted and spurred men still ride; Crater Lake, with its unbelievably blue waters trapped forever in a shattered mountain peak; Newberry Crater, the Lava Fields and the Columbia Gorge; and the Wallowa Mountains where the last big-horn sheep in Oregon browse among mile-high lakes and meadows of alpine flowers. Or if the bird's-eye view is toward the west coast; a humid, forested, mountainous region, fronting the Pacific, to which it presents, abruptly, a precipitous escarpment, relieved here and there by long stretches of sand beaches, an occasional lumber port or fishing village, or a river mouth. Southward toward California the land rises in a jungle of ranges dented by narrow valleys where live and work miners and lumbermen.

If symbolism may be needed to complete the picture, let there be two symbols for Oregon: a pioneer of the covered wagon epoch, and beside him likewise grim and indomitable, the plodding figure of a modern farmer driven from middle-western soil by years of drought. Thousands of dust-bowl refugees have drifted into Oregon since 1930. If hunger and hardships and uncertainty are the essences of the pioneer tradition, they are a part of it already; and as the bearded early immigrants brought a first cohesion to the territory, these latter day American pioneers may strengthen that cohesion and make their own distinctive contribution to the future state.

Natural Setting

RUGGED coast line, sandy beaches, heavily timbered ranges, snow-capped peaks, broad river valleys, rough drainage basins, lava fields, gigantic geologic faults, and rolling upland plains cut by deep gorges, spread out in changing panoramas in this land of scenic surprises. Rugged masses, but slightly changed from the form of their volcanic origin, stand out in contrast to wide areas with lines softened by erosion.

Oregon is a land divided by great mountain barriers into regions of productive farms and desert wastes; it is a land of crowded habitations and scanty settlements, of lofty eminences and deep depressions, of isolated mountain-hemmed areas and open plains beyond the limit of vision, of deep lakes and barren playas, of rushing rivers and dry water courses, of dense forest undergrowth and park-like stands of timber.

The present State, formerly part of a vast area known as the Oregon country, is bounded on the north by the State of Washington, on the east by Idaho, on the south by Nevada and California, and on the west by the Pacific Ocean. Forming the larger part of its northern boundary line, the historic Columbia River gives the State somewhat the shape of a saddle, with its pommel near the river's mouth. The Snake River, with a rugged gorge deeper than the Grand Canyon of the Colorado, forms more than half of the eastern boundary. These two rivers, with the three hundred miles of coast, make more than two-thirds of Oregon's boundary line.

The state's extreme length, along the 124th meridian, is 280 miles; its extreme width, between Cape Blanco and the eastern boundary line, is 380 miles. Including 1,092 square miles of water surface, its total area is 96,699 square miles, making it the ninth largest state in the Union. With the exception of the far eastern portion, it lies in the Pacific Time Belt; and it embraces 36 counties.

The lofty and frosty-peaked Cascade Range divides Oregon into two unequal parts. To the east is the broad plains-plateau section; to the west, and comprising about one-third of the state's area, lies the more fully developed and more densely populated valley and coast section.

Although the dominating mass and altitude of the Cascade Range are responsible for major differences in climate, topography, and much else within the state, geographers subdivide Oregon into eight natural regions, or physiographic provinces, differing in soil, climate, plant life, and other characteristics. From west to east, these are the Coast, Southern Oregon, Willamette, Cascade, Deschutes-Columbia, Blue-Wallowa, Southeastern Lake, and Snake River regions.

The Coast Region, extending from the backbone of the Coast Range to the Pacific Ocean, is a long strip of less than 25 miles in average width. The Coast Range is low and rolling, with a mean elevation of less than 2,000 feet and occasional peaks up to 4,000 feet. Its western foothills leave but a narrow margin of coast plain, varying from a few miles wide to a complete break where precipitous promontories jut out into the ocean. Many streams rise in this range and flow westward into bays and estuaries or directly into the Pacific. Two southern rivers, the Umpqua and the Rogue, penetrate the Coast Range from the western slope of the Cascades. Seven of the streams are navigable for river craft from ten to thirty miles, and were once picturesquely active with steamboat commerce. A little stern-wheeler used to go up the deep but narrowing Coos until passengers on the deck could almost reach out and touch the damp and mossy walls on either side. A pioneer doctor at Florence, on the Siuslaw, owned a motor boat but no horse and buggy. Seven jetties have been built along the coast, but there are few good harbors. The old Spanish mariners passed them by, and Drake claimed that he anchored in a "bad bay." Rainfall averages about seventy-two inches annually, the climate is made mild by the closeness of the Pacific, and luxuriant vegetation, green the year around, affords a natural grassland for dairy farming along the lower valleys. Dairying, fishing, and lumbering are the principal industries. There are few railroads, but the region has a good network of highways, including the scenic Oregon Coast Highway, which roughly parallels the coast line for its entire distance. Astoria, Tillamook, Marshfield, and North Bend are the towns of major importance in this region.

The Southern Oregon Region, extending from the Calapooya Mountains southward to the state line between the Cascades and the Coast Range, is of rough topography, with heavily timbered mountainsides, dissected plateaus, and interior valleys of fine fruit, nut, and vegetable land. Portions of the Rogue River Valley are famous for pears and of the Umpqua River Valley for prunes, the former being raised largely with irrigation, the latter without. Game is plentiful in its many wilderness areas, and fish abound in its streams. It is one of the richest mineral regions in the state, and has abundant potential waterpower. Canning and preserving of fruits and vegetables, lumbering, and mining are the chief industrial activities. Roseburg, Grants Pass, Medford, and Ashland are the principal towns. A number of fine highways penetrate the region, but there will long remain many remote and primitive areas. Although the climate is varied, there are no extremes.

The Willamette Region comprises the famous Willamette Valley, a rectangular trough of level and rolling farm and timber lands, about one hundred and eighty miles long from the Columbia River to the Calapooya Mountains, and sixty miles wide from the Cascades to the Coast Range. The Willamette River and its tributaries drain the entire region, which has a widely diversified agriculture, the greatest commercial and industrial development in Oregon, and two-thirds of the state's population. Its particularly favorable soil and climatic conditions, and the availability of the Willamette and its tributaries for water transportation, made it the goal of most of the early immigrants. This early settlement and the region's natural advantages have maintained its position as the most important area of the State. Together with the Coast Region, it contains some of the finest stands of marketable timber now remaining in the United States, making lumbering an important industry. Manufacturing covers a wide variety of products, many of which have a national distribution. The region enjoys a mild climate and abundant rainfall, and has an excellent network of highways, railroads, waterways, and airways. Scenically, it is considered by many travelers to be one of the most beautiful in the West. Portland, Oregon City, Salem, Albany, Corvallis, and Eugene are the principal towns of the Willamette Valley.

The Cascade Region, extending along both sides of the Cascade Range, is an area of rugged grandeur. The western slope is the more precipitous, leading down into the Willamette, Umpqua, and Rogue River valleys. The eastern slope merges into a high plateau, which differs in climate and rainfall from the western slope because of the mountain barrier to the warm moisture-laden winds from the Pacific. Drainage is largely into the Deschutes River. Flora and fauna are distinctly, almost abruptly, different on the two slopes. With its mountain lakes and tumbling streams, the region has tremendous possibilities for irrigation and waterpower. Some irrigation developments have already been made, and a number of valley cities have power dams along the water-courses. It is an important grazing area. Lumbering flourishes, and immense stands of timber still await the saw. Of the 13,788,-802 acres of national forests in Oregon, more than one-third are in the Cascade Region. The two most important agricultural districts are Hood River County, in the extreme north, with its famous irrigated apple orchards, and Klamath County, in the extreme south, prolific in potatoes, barley, and dairy products. Increasing accessibility has caused extensive use of the region as a playground. Being near to Portland, Mount Hood is the main focus of recreation, although Crater Lake, the Three Sisters, and other attractive natural areas are becoming increasingly popular. The Klamath lakes and marshes are famous shooting grounds, and the Pacific Crest Trail along the backbone of the Cascades is a notable hiking and saddle route. Climate and rainfall vary with the slope and altitude. Klamath Falls and Hood River are the principal cities.

The Deschutes-Columbia Region is a great interior plateau between the Cascade Range and the Blue Mountains. Most of the northern boundary is the Columbia River. The entire course of the Deschutes River and most of the John Day River are within its boundaries. It is a country of rolling hills, interspersed with level stretches of valley and upland. It is situated in the great Columbia lava flow, said to be the largest and deepest in existence. Canyon walls, from fifteen hundred to two thousand feet in height, reveal as many as twenty superimposed flows. The climate is dry and hot in summer, moderately cold in winter, and the region has from ten to twenty inches of annual rainfall. Irrigation is practiced wherever conditions warrant, but dry farming predominates. The wide uncultivated sections support large herds of sheep and cattle. There are some magnificent pine forests, mostly in the foothills, and regional lumbering operations are carried on. The few towns are supported largely by trade in livestock and agricultural commodities, and by the manufacture of flour, lumber, and woolen products. There are several good highways, along with two main railroad lines and a number of branch lines. The Dalles, Bend, and Pendleton are the principal towns.

The Blue-Wallowa Region is an area of about twenty thousand square miles in the northeastern part of the state, with two great mountain masses—the Blue Mountains, with the reverse L of the Strawberry Range, and the Wallowa Mountains. The Blue Mountain section consists of rolling terrain, covered with park-like stands of timber; the other is rugged precipitous country, with beautiful mountain lakes and other striking scenery. The climate is less temperate than in the western part of the State, and the annual rainfall is from ten to twenty inches. The only farms are on the broad river bottoms, with livestock, wool, and hay as the most important products. There is much gold mining, principally by dredging. Parts of five national forests lie within the region. Industrial activity is restricted largely to lumbering, flour-making, and gold and copper refining. Highways are being extended as the recreational advantages of the region become more widely recognized. There is one main-line railroad. Baker and La Grande are the largest towns.

The Southeastern Lake Region, including the High Desert, gives a first impression of being an immense wasteland of little value for human use, but it has many undeveloped resources. It extends southward from the Blue-Wallowa Region to the southern state line and contains many lakes, some of which dry up altogether or shrink greatly during the summer. Even some of the larger lakes have been known to evaporate entirely, then fill again. A striking example of this is Goose Lake on the southern boundary. For years settlers had seen the weathered wagon ruts of early emigrant trains leading up to the lake shore, and continuing from the water's edge on the opposite shore, although the lake was too deep to ford. One of the emigrant-train pioneers was asked how the wagons got across. They didn't cross any lake, he said, in their journey. The mystery of the tracks remained; but years later the lake dried up, and there were the wagon ruts leading across its bed and connecting with those on the two shores. Precipitation in most parts of this region amounts to about 10 inches annually. Livestock, principally sheep, is the chief product, although some farm crops are raised in scattered sections, and there is some wild hay. Surface streams and underground water are both scanty. Minerals other than salts from the dry lake beds are rare. There are few improved highways and but one branch railroad. Although the area is generally treeless, portions of the Deschutes and Fremont National Forests have fair stands of pine, in which some lumbering is done. The population is sparse. Burns and Lakeview are the chief towns.

The Snake River Region is a strip along the eastern boundary of the State, consisting of an open plateau from thirty-five hundred to four thousand feet in altitude, with narrow and deeply-cut river valleys low ranges of mountains, detached buttes, rim-rock, and sagebrush plains. It is semi-arid, with only about ten inches of annual rainfall

The Vale and Owyhee irrigation projects have brought a considerable acreage into high agricultural productivity; and in other sections, such as the Jordan Valley, there are several smaller irrigation projects. The northern portion has a number of adequate highways and railroads, but in the south there has been little transportation development of any kind. The area has considerable mineral wealth, great herds of sheep and cattle, and some horses. Except in the irrigated sections, the population is very sparse. Ontario and Vale are the principal towns.

Altogether, Oregon has a geography of immense diversity and notable contrast. In what is now Lake County, in December, 1843, John C. Fremont ascended to an altitude of seven thousand feet amid snows and howling winds. Suddenly, from a rim, he looked down three thousand feet upon a lake, warm and smiling and margined with green trees and grass. He and his party on that December day picked their way down the declivity, from winter into summer. He named the two points Winter Rim and Summer Lake.

GEOLOGY AND PALEONTOLOGY

Two distinct bodies of land, washed by the primal sea, were the nuclei from which, at an extremely remote period of time, the present state of Oregon was formed. One of these was in what is now the Bald Mountain region of Baker County and the other in the present Klamath-Siskiyou area of southwestern Oregon. The subsequent geological history of the state is chiefly the story of their extension and topographic variation by elevation of the sea bed, by lava flows, by deposits of volcanic ash, and by erosion.

For millions of years these islands alone stood above the water, but during the Triassic period (one hundred and seventy to one hundred and ninety million years ago) the sea, while it still covered most of the present state, had become shallow around the Blue Mountains. Sedimentary beds of this period are found on the northern flanks of the Wallowa Mountains, and typical exposures are seen along Hurricane Creek, Eagle Creek, and Powder River. Rocks of the Jurassic period (one hundred and ten to one hundred and seventy million years ago) are widespread in both the Blue Mountain and the Klamath regions. Fossils of the flora of this period, found at Nichols in Douglas County, and consisting of conifers, cycads and ferns, point to a tropical climate for the region at that time.

At the close of the Jurassic period, or perhaps a little later, there was a great upheaval in the region. The low-lying land and adjacent sea bed were thrust up by forces below the earth's surface, and about the site of Baker became what were probably Oregon's first mountains; while the shallower sea bed, with its lime shales and volcanic rocks, became the Powder River Mountains.

At the opening of the Cretaceous period (sixty-five to one hundred and ten million years ago), sea surrounded the Klamath Mountains, flowing in from California over the site of Mount Shasta to what is now Douglas County and thence to the main ocean by a passage near the mouth of the Coquille River.

The close of the Cretaceous period saw the Blue and Klamath regions, with their accretions, separated by a sea dike that had been slowly rising out of the ocean bed from Lower California to the Aleutian Islands. The elevation of this barrier, the Sierra Nevada Range in California and the Cascade Range in Oregon and Washington, divided the State into two geologically, geographically, and climatically dissimilar parts. It made the region to the west a marine province, in which geologic changes were brought about by agencies existing in and emanating from the sea; it made the region to the east a continental province, the development of which was bound up with the large land mass of the continent.

Rising slowly, the dike shut out the sea from the interior and created three great drainage areas: one to the south, which in time became the Colorado River; one to the north, which in a later age formed the Columbia River Basin; and a third, in what is now southeastern Oregon, whose outlets were cut off and whose waters disappeared through evaporation. At the close of the Cretaceous period, the sea retreated and never again advanced farther than the present axis of the Cascades.

At the dawn of the Tertiary period or age of mammals, fifty million years ago, eastern Oregon was a region of lakes. The Blue Mountains and the Cascade hills were green with forests and beautiful with large flowering shrubs. Magnolia, cinnamon, and fig trees flourished. Sycamore, dogwood, and oak appeared. The Oregon grape, now the state flower, grew densely in the hills. Sequoias towered to imposing heights.

The earliest, or Eocene, epoch of the Tertiary period is represented by the first upthrust of the Coast Range, by the Monroe, Corvallis, and Albany hills, and by the Chehalem and Tillamook coal beds. The development of coal, however, was greatest along the Coos Bay coast. New land was forming in the next epoch, the Oligocene, as shown by the structures in the John Day Valley and in northwestern Oregon. In the former region these are sedimentary rocks known to geologists as the John Day series. Late in the same epoch or early in the Miocene, vast flows of lava, now known as the Columbia lava formation, began to well up from the earth. This was an age of volcanism, when the Cascade hills, later to become mountains, belched clouds of ashes that were carried eastward to take part in filling the great eastern Oregon lakes; when vents opened in hillsides to pour out gigantic rivers of molten rock that filled the lakes and valleys to the east and surrounded lofty mountain peaks with a sea of basalt; when the great plateau now encompassing most of Oregon from the west slope of the Cascades eastward was formed. The Blue and Wallowa Mountain ranges of today rise above the plateau, but the effect of their height is minimized by the thick strata of lava surrounding their bases. Geologists pronounce the formation to be one of the three greatest lava flows of the world. Twenty-five successive flows have been counted in the Deschutes Valley, and as many as twenty in the Columbia River canyon.

Changes other than volcanic were also taking place in the Miocene epoch. The Umpqua Valley was being elevated above sea level. The Calapooya Mountains, which had been rising late in the preceding epoch (as indicated by recovered shell fossils), were extending to join the slowly developing Coast Range, thus excluding the sea from what is now southwestern Oregon. Toward the middle of the epoch comparative quiet returned. The old animal life of the earlier epochs of the Tertiary period had perished, and new types succeeded. Forests blossomed in new glory. By the close of the epoch the Coast Range had formed a solid wall paralleling the Cascade hills, and the Willamette Valley had been elevated above the sea.

During the Pliocene epoch which followed, land was elevated over all the area of western United States. The Oregon coast extended many leagues farther west than it does today. A period of coastal depression followed, and land which once was mainland is now submerged far out at sea. Volcanic activity reappeared in the Cascades, and toward the end of the epoch there was great activity in mountain building both along the coast and in the Cascade region. It was then that the Cascades attained their great height, erected their superstructure of peaks and castles, and were crowned with snow. The barrier thus raised shut out from the interior the warm moisture-laden ocean winds, and turned the climate colder. By the middle of the following. or Pleistocene, epoch, the glacial age had come on.

Oregon was never under a continuous coat of ice during the Pleistocene epoch, as was much of continental North America. At this time glaciers formed on Mount Hood, Mount Jefferson, the Three Sisters, and sky-piercing Mount Mazama in southern Oregon, and were scattered through eastern Oregon and along the Columbia River gorge. Among the largest moraines is a lateral one on the east side of Wallowa Lake, in extreme northeastern Oregon. It is approximately six miles long, one-fourth of a mile wide, and between six hundred and seven hundred feet high.

An event of importance at the close of the ice age was the violent eruption of Mount Mazama, which either blew up, scattering its substance over the surrounding countryside, or collapsed and fell into its own crater. Perhaps both explosion and collapse occurred. This cataclysm resulted in the formation of the huge caldera now occupied by Crater Lake.

Another period of land depression followed, during which Oregon lost still more of its western coastal area. The Willamette Valley became a sound or fresh-water lake formed by the damming of the Columbia by ice, at which time water flowed 300 feet above the present level of Portland, 165 feet above that of Salem, and 115 feet above that of Albany. An important development of this period was the faulting in the Great Basin area of southeastern Oregon, when the imposing Steens and Abert Rim Mountains were formed.

During recent time, deposits found in Oregon have included stream gravels, silt washed from the valley sides, dunes along the coast and in the lake region of eastern Oregon, peat bogs in the coastal dune area, volcanic deposits in the Cascade Mountains, shore deposits along the beaches, and many others. The shifting dune sands damming sluggish streams have created a chain of beautiful fresh-water lakes along the ocean shore.

In many parts of the Cascade Mountains there are cinder cones that have the appearance of recent origin. Some of them may be not more than a hundred years old. The *Portland Oregonian* reported an eruption of Mount Hood as late as 1865.

Since 1862, when Dr. Thomas Condon, Oregon's noted pioneer geologist, discovered and made known to the world the now famous fossil beds of the John Day Valley, Oregon has been an important center for paleontological research. Exploration has been rewarded by yields of a number of the most highly prized specimens of prehistoric plant and animal life uncovered in the United States, and has revealed the fascinating story of Oregon's ancient eons. Plant life of the Pliocene epoch was not represented in Dr. Condon's finds; but in 1936 the discovery of flora fossils of that epoch, in the Deschutes River gorge nine miles west of Madras, filled the one gap existing in the record.

The oreodonts, an interesting group of animals now extinct, were formerly abundant in the lower lake region of the John Day Valley. Oreodonts ranged in size from that of a coyote to that of an elk. These animals had the molar teeth of a deer, the side teeth of a hog, and the incisors of a carnivore. Oreodonts, rhinoceroses, and peccaries are in the Condon collection of fossils. The well defined metacarpal bone of a camel was found in the gray stone of a former lake bed near The Dalles, and fossils found in other regions of the State indicate a probability that the camel once roamed much of the Pacific Northwest.

The fossil head of a seal found in 1906 and that of a giant sea turtle found embedded in sandstone near the Oregon coast in 1939 prove that these primitive species lived in that section when the ocean still covered western Oregon. Seal fossils have also been found in the Willamette Valley. In southeastern Oregon, in the vicinity of Silver (or Fossil) Lake, were discovered the fossil bones of a wide variety of birds. This region has also yielded the remains of a mylodon—a great sloth as large as a grizzly bear—four kinds of camel, a mammoth elephant, three species of primitive horse, and many smaller animals.

A notable fossil recovery was that of the mesohippus, a tiny three-toed horse, found in 1866 by men digging a well near the Snake River not far from Walla Walla in eastern Washington. Taken to The Dalles and given to Dr. Condon, who identified them, these bones brought attention to the "equus beds" of eastern Washington and Oregon.

The mastodon and mammoth have left abundant fossil remains in Oregon. A fine specimen of the broad-faced ox, precursor of the bison, was dredged from the Willamette River. Fossil remains of the ground sloth, though rare, have been found in Yamhill County and in the John Day Valley. Remains of the rhinoceros are plentiful in the large lake beds. The Suidae, or hog family, is represented in the lower lake regions by several species, the largest of which is the entelodont. Fossils of a musk deer and of the head of a primitive cat about the size of the present-day cougar were found in the north fork of the John Day River. This area also abounded in early ages with saber-toothed cats.

The dog of the Miocene epoch is represented in fossils indicating an animal about the size of the Newfoundland breed.

In the northeastern part of the state, and in the vicinity of Burns, Canyon City, and Prineville, various groups of important fossil shells of the Jurassic period have been found. In Baker and Crook Counties, and in the Siskiyou region of southern Oregon, the carboniferous rocks have yielded many interesting groups of fossil shells of the Paleozoic era. The trigonia, a bivalve shell of Cretaceous times, is abundant in both southern and northeastern parts of the state.

A group of marine shells of great interest to the geologist and paleontologist is that of the chambered cephalopods. Of highest rank in this group are the ammonites, which became extinct at the close of the Cretaceous period. Both the chambered nautilus and the ammonite have been found widely distributed in the rocks of the Siskiyou region. At Astoria and in the vicinity of Westport, the Columbia River, cutting into the Eocene belt, has exposed specimens of another beautiful shell fossil, the aturia.

Submerged groves of trees in the Columbia River near the Upper Cascades indicate that this river between the Cascades and The Dalles was more than twenty feet lower when these trees were living than it is today. These submerged forests are in a slow process of decay and are not "petrified," although they have been thus termed by some laymen. The upright position of the trees affords evidence that rising water covered them where they stood.

In Columbia Gorge, near Tanner Creek, were found fossil fragments of a leaf of the gingko tree, a beautiful species known previously only in sacred groves around the temples of China and Japan. Since discovery of these fragments, test plantings of gingko trees imported from Japan have been found to thrive in the vicinity of Portland. Near Goshen, on the Pacific Highway, is an assemblage of fossil leaves, entombed in fine-grained volcanic ash, resembling trees of the lower Oligocene epoch, whose counterparts now flourish in Central America and the Philippines. This evidence seems to establish unquestionably the existence of a tropical climate in the Oregon region at some remote time.

FLORA AND FAUNA

In the moist valleys, on the craggy mountains, and on the semi-arid deserts of Oregon, grow a multitude of flowers, ferns, grasses, shrubs, and trees. One authority lists more than two thousand species and subspecies that flourish within Oregon's 96,000 square miles.

Western Oregon offers a warm and sheltered conservatory for the development of plant growth. A large area is covered with Douglas fir, interspersed with cedar, yew and hemlock, while along the coast grow gigantic tideland spruce and contorted thickets of lodgepole pine. In the southern Cascades and in the Siskiyous, firs give place to the massive pillars of the sugar pine. Near the southern coast are extensive groves of Port Orford cedar, redwood, and the rare Oregon myrtle found nowhere else in America. Eastward of the Cascades are the widely distributed forests of yellow pine, lodgepole pine and Englemann spruce. On the desert uplands grows the western juniper, hardy and sparse, furnishing the only shade. In the valleys and on the adjacent hills of the Columbia, Willamette, Umpqua, Rogue and other rivers, appear numerous hardwoods and deciduous trees—oaks, maples, alders, willows, and those unsurpassed flowering trees, the red-barked madrona and the Pacific dogwood.

Along the sea beaches and on the wave-cut bluffs are verbenas and wild asters, tangled thickets of devil's club, laurel, sweet gale, and rhododendron, and watery sphagnum bogs lush with the cobra-leaved pitcher plant and the delicate sundew. In June, on the windy headland of Cape Blanco, a party of visitors picked sixteen varieties of flowers within a single acre.

In Oregon valleys great fields are seasonally blue with the wild flag, pastures are bright with buttercups, and the moist woods with violets, trilliums, and adder's-tongues. Alpine regions are deeply carpeted with sorrel, and orchids lend their pastel shades. Deeper in the forest grow the waxy Indian pipe, the blood-red snow plant, and the rare moccasin flower. In the Siskiyous are more than fifty plants found nowhere else in the world.

Both on the coast and in the interior valleys Scotch broom glows goldenly, but is regarded by farmers as a pest. In the spring and early summer, the wild currant's crimson flame, sweet syringa, ocean spray, and Douglas spirea form streamside thickets of riotous blossom; and the glossy-leaved Oregon grape, by its omnipresent neighborliness, justifies its selection as the State flower.

Eastward of the Cascades there is a decided topographical and botanical change. A hiker on a mountain trail will sometimes notice an almost knife-edge break between the two floras. A high inland plateau, broken by deep river canyons and small scattered mountain ranges, stretches away to the state's borders. This seeming waste is an empire of fertility

Sagebrush and juniper abound, and beneath their branches the sage lily develops in splendor. Along the bluffs of the Columbia, wild clover covers many dry hillsides, and distant fields take on a misty, purplish hue, like wafted smoke. Lupines and larkspurs tint the landscape for miles, while locoweeds, some of them of great beauty though of evil fame, are very abundant. Here, too, are the yellow-belled rice root, the blazing star, and the Lewisia and the Clarkia, named for the adventurers who discovered them.

Among early botanical explorers, besides Lewis and Clark, were Douglas, Nuttall, Pickering, Brackenridge, and Tolmie. Douglas relates that in hunting for cones of the sugar pine, after he had shot three specimens from a 300-foot tree, he was confronted by eight unfriendly Indians. By offering tobacco he induced them to aid him in securing a quantity of the cones. As they disappeared to comply with his request he snatched up his three cones and retreated to camp.

The flora of Oregon plays an important part in the Indian lore of the region. Nearly two hundred plants found place in the commercial, industrial, medical, culinary, and religious economy of the Northwest tribes. With the passing of winter, camps became active with preparation for the annual food gathering. Tribes migrated to the camas prairie, the wappato lake, or the wocus swamp, for the yearly harvest. Throughout the State there is a great variety of wild fruit, which formed a principal article of subsistence for the natives. A dozen varieties of berries, wild crab apple, plum, Oregon grape, ripened in their season. Bird-cherry, salal, and wild currant grew in profusion in forests and along the seashore. Nuts of various kinds were stored for the lean months, and seeds of numerous grasses and rushes added the important farinaceous element to the diet.

The Indians also utilized a great many varieties of nutritive roots. Camas, the most extensively used, is an onion-like bulb with a spiked cluster of blue flowers. In some parts of the State, great fields are azure in April with its bloom. Townsend says, "When boiled this little root is palatable, and somewhat resembles the taste of the common potato; the Indian mode of preparing it, however, is the best—that of fermenting it in pits underground, into which hot stones have been placed. It is suffered to remain in these pits several days; and when removed, is of a dark brown color . . . and sweet, like molasses. It is then made into large cakes . . . and slightly baked in the sun." Another root is the wappato, a marsh bulb growing in great quantity along the lowlands of the Columbia, on Chewaucan Marsh in Lake County, and in many other shallow lakes. This was one of the chief commercial roots of the tribes, much sought after by those whose country did not produce it. Numerous other roots lent variety to the diet—blue lupine, which, when baked, resembles the sweet potato; Chinook licorice, bitterroot, the tuber of the foxtail, wild turnip, lily bulbs, and onions.

A host of plants was included in the medical kit of the Indians. Roots of the wild poppy were used to allay toothache. The dried ripe fruit and the leaves of the scarlet sumac were made into a poultice for skin disease. A tea from the bark of the dogwood was imbibed for fevers and colds. Wild hops and witch hazel aided in the reduction of sprains and swellings, and rattlesnake plantain was efficacious for cuts and bruises. Oregon grape and sage brush, buckthorn and trillium, death camas and yarrow, false Solomon's seal and vervain, went into the pharmacopoeia of the tribes, while the juice of the deadly cowbane augmented the supply of rattlesnake virus as a poison for arrows.

Mats, baskets, nets, and cords were made of the fibres and leaves of grasses, nettles, Indian hemp, tough-leaved iris, milkweed, dogbane, and scores of other fibrous plants. Cedar was the favorite lumber tree, because of the ease of working the long, straight boles. Canoes, from the small one-man craft to those of sixty feet in length, were wrought from single cedars, while the great communal houses were made of huge slabs split from cedar logs and roofed with the bark. Drawing and casting nets were woven of silky grass, the fibrous roots of trees, or of the inner bark of the white cedar. Bows were usually made of yew or crab-apple wood, while arrows were shaped of the straight shoots of syringa or other tough stems. Fish weirs were made of willow, as were the frames of snowshoes. Fire blocks were of cedar and twirling sticks of the dried stems of sagebrush or manzanita.

Many of the Indians of Oregon still continue in this ancient economy. Each season the Klamaths reap the wocus seed from the yellow water lilies of Klamath Lake, the Warm Springs Indians journey into the mountains for the berry picking, and some tribes still dig the wild roots. On the Warm Springs Reservation a root festival is held in the spring and a huckleberry festival when the huckleberries ripen in late summer. These are thanksgiving feasts bringing out colorful costumes and consisting of dances, speeches, and religious ceremonies that are parts of a well defined ritual, the meaning of which is preserved in the tribal life.

Following the customs of their red neighbors, the pioneers drew a portion of their subsistence from the wilderness. Wild berries and fruits of all kinds went into the frontier larder, as well as many of the wild roots used by the Indians. One comestible of the early Oregon housewife was camas pie, a delicacy dwelt on reminiscently by more than one longbeard at pioneer gatherings. Miners' lettuce took the place of the cultivated vegetable, and so often did our forbears substitute the dried leaves of the *yerba buena* for "store tea" that the plant has become known by the common name of Oregon tea.

Not only did the pioneer draw heavily upon the floral resources of the State for food and shelter but his modern descendant continues to utilize these products extensively. Wild berries are gathered by the ton, chittam bark, digitalis or foxglove, and other medicinal plants are collected for the market, and flowers and shrubs are brought in from forest and crag for rock garden, park, or lawn.

The bird and animal life of Oregon is fully as varied as the plant life. Eliot lists over three hundred species: song birds, game birds, and birds of prey; mountain dwellers, valley dwellers, and dwellers by the sea. Perhaps a third of them are permanent residents, a third part-time residents, and a third transient visitors to the region. Great contrasts are found, for the dry eastern areas are incongruously intermingled with large marshlands and lakes. One may observe the aquatic antics of grebes, cormorants, pelicans (*see KLAMATH FALLS*), herons and coots, and almost simultaneously, on the high arid lands round about, catch glimpses of the great sage grouse, the sage thrasher, and the desert sparrow.

Best loved by Oregonians is the state bird, the western meadow lark, heard from fence or tree at almost any season of the year. Another favorite is the robin, abundant in field and garden, foraging in winter orchards, lighting the chill gray months with his song. The blackbird lingers through the year, his notes ringing in gay orchestration. Numerous also among the permanent residents are the willow goldfinches, the Oregon towhee, the chickadee, sparrow, and bluebirds.

Less frequently are seen the great blue heron, the killdeer, and the mountain quail; hawks and owls and the Oregon jay; the varied thrush or Alaska robin; the water ouzel of perfect song. Yearlong one may hear the drum of flicker or woodpecker, the hoarse caw of the crow, the screech owl's hoot. Along the seashore curve on swift wings, gulls, fulmers, petrels, and the myriad other dwellers of cliff and marsh. And, climaxing all, the great American eagle still sometimes flies darkly against the sky. A popular children's story is of a log schoolhouse on the Columbia, where, on the Fourth of July, an eagle swooped down, took in his talons the school flag that floated from the summit of a tall fir, and flew away with the banner over mountains, rivers, and valleys.

More than fifty summer residents return to Oregon after southern winters. The more numerous of these are the rufous humming bird, the russet-back and the hermit thrush, the swallows, warblers, and many finches. Among the shyer and less frequently encountered are the band-tailed pigeon and the mourning dove, the lazuli bunting and the western tanager, the Bullocks oriole and the clown-like chat, the horned lark and the magpie of Eastern Oregon, the sandpiper, and the plover, with scores of lesser birds. From the far north come many others for the winter months, including the ruby-crowned and the Sitka kinglet, the cedar and Bohemian waxwing, the junco, and a host of sparrows.

Foremost among the numerous game birds is the China pheasant, which was imported into the state in 1881, when twenty-six birds were turned loose in the Willamette Valley. This hardy stranger now receives the larger part of the sportsman's attention, thus giving the more timid birds—the ruffed and sooty grouse, the sage hen and lesser quails—a greater margin of hope for survival. The aquatic game birds, including the Canadian goose, the mallard, canvasback and wood duck and the teal, have greatly decreased but are now protected by stric· Federal laws.

With six more names this incomplete roll call must close—the Stellar jay, mythical demigod of the Chinook tribes, the sand-hill crane, the pelican, the whistling and trumpeter swan, the white heron. Plume hunters visited Malheur and Harney Lakes in 1898 and perpetrated a carnage that amounted almost to annihilation of the white heron, known to commerce as the snowy egret.

Many other winged inhabitants, worthy of description, must go even without mention. Pages would not suffice to list all the myriad swim mers and fliers that make up the vivid pageant of Oregon bird life.

Within the borders of Oregon there now live, or were formerly found, characteristic varieties of almost all North American temperate-zone mammals. Of the fur bearers it may be said that the state was founded on the value of their pelts. The sea otter is gone, and land otters are now scarce, but mink, bobcats, foxes, muskrats and racoons are still plentiful; and the beaver, for all the high hats to which he was a sacrifice in the old days, also remains. This gnawer, the backbone of the early fur trade, was once so plentiful in Oregon that Franchere, in 1812, took 450 skins of it and other animals on a 20-day trip up the Columbia from Astoria. In 1824, Peter Skene Ogden said of his seventy-one men equipped with 364 traps: "Each beaver trap last year in the Snake Country averaged 26 beavers. Was expected this hunt will be 14,000 beavers." Two years later in the Harney country, a band of six trappers averaged from fifty to sixty beavers a day. As late as 1860 many of the Eastern Oregon streams were "thronged with beavers," but later the animals were almost exterminated. During the last quarter century, however, due to rigid protective laws, they have increased in numbers until colonies are now found in many counties of the State.

The king of the Oregon forests is the cougar, and in many sections still lives the black bear, venerated by the early Indians and reverently called "grandfather." Some tribal myths taught that the bear was the ancestor of all Indians. In rare instances is found the fierce grizzly or silvertip, the great "white bear" of Lewis and Clark.

Most abundant among the larger animals are members of the deer family—the Columbian black-tailed of mountain and coastal forest; the larger mule deer, an inhabitant of the dryer Eastern Oregon sections; elk or wapiti in the Wallowa region and the coast mountains; and, in the extreme southeast part of the State, some of the largest remaining herds of pronghorns or American antelope, graceful and fleet.

In the southeast, also, numerous skeletal remains of the buffalo have been found, and small bands of bighorn or Rocky Mountain sheep still inhabit the wild crags of the Wallowa Range.

The Cascade timber wolf continues in some numbers, but the chief representative of the wolf clan is the shy and crafty coyote.

Oregon has a number of interesting smaller animals. The porcupine is common in almost all sections at high altitudes, as is the peculiar mountain beaver or sewellel, not a true beaver but a burrowing rodent, which seems to have no very close allies elsewhere in the world. Woodland sections are inhabited by varieties of wood rats, called by the natives "pack" or "trade" rats because of their predilection for carrying off small articles and leaving in their stead a pine cone, a nut, or a shiny pebble as apparent compensation. At very high altitudes lives the pika—little chief hare or cony—rock-inhabiting creatures that gather and dry large amounts of "hay" for winter provender. Chipmunks. squirrels, hares, and rabbits are numerous. Jackrabbits in the sage lands. like the stars above, frustrate all census takers because they "count too high." An Italian settler in Eastern Oregon left the country and gave gastronomic reasons for doing so: "I no like da Eastern Org. No sphagett, no macarone, too mucha jacka-da-rab."

The coastal headlands and rocky promontories present many interesting glimpses of the life habits of seals and sea lions, and the rocks, wave-washed and scarred, harbor a marine fauna that is of interest to scientist and common observer alike.

Oregon snakes consist mostly of the harmless garter snakes, the King snakes, and the Pacific bull snakes. The deadly rattler is now confined largely to the dryer eastern counties.

The fishes of the state are of three types—those living entirely within the salt waters of the Pacific; the migratory fish which spend most of their life in the sea but enter the rivers to spawn; and the fresh-water fish living in lakes and rivers. Of the first, the coast fisheries of halibut, herring, pilchards, and other lesser fish add greatly to the wealth of the state. Aside from this, sportsmen find profitable recreation in surf fishing.

Of the migratory fishes, the salmon is of first importance. Myriads of the five great species—the chum, the humpback, the silversides, the sockeye, and the royal chinook—travel up streams for great distances, those of the Columbia deep into the fastenesses of its mountainous watershed. The salmon is the chief commercial fish of the state. In marked contrast to the gigantic salmon is the smelt or eulachon, called anchovy by Lewis and Clark, and also known as candlefish because their small dried bodies, rich in oil, were formerly utilized as torches. Each spring they still run the Sandy River in countless thousands and are taken by Portlanders with bird cages, nets, and buckets.

The prince of all the fresh-water fishes is the great steelhead trout, the fighting spirit of which is so renowned that fishermen have crossed oceans and continents to pit their skill against its strength. All of the cold water streams of the State are well stocked with smaller trout, the principal ones being the rainbow, the cutthroat, the brook, and the Dolly Varden.

Bass, sunfish, and crappies have been introduced into most lowland streams, and give the angler abundant sport. Fishing for catfish furnishes contemplative recreation for whole families, particularly on Sauvie Island, where on Sundays the wooden bridges across the sluggish streams are double-lined with Portlanders. Of the plentiful suckers, especially noteworthy are the multiple varieties inhabiting the Klamath ·Lakes and river and adjacent waters. To the Klamath and Modoc Indians these were formerly a source of wealth second only to the great salmon runs.

A red fish that abounded fifty years ago in Wallowa Lake and Wallowa River has mysteriously disappeared. In early days white men found this food fish in almost limitless quantities in spawning season. It is said to have existed nowhere else except in one small body of water in Idaho. It was "probably a very small variety of salmon now extinct."

In the summer of 1937, visitors to Bonneville Dam saw the blocked migration of the Columbia River eels—it had never before been conceived that such countless masses of them inhabited this current. The new white concrete, in a wainscot reaching several feet above the water line, was dark and wet with spray, and this damp area was compactly fringed with eels, hanging like extensive drifts of kelp. Driven by their relentless upriver urge and obstructed by the temporarily closed floodgates, they attempted to scale the sheer and massive walls. Side by side and one below the other, they climbed up until they reached the dry portion of the masonry, upon which their bodies had no clinging suction. Then they slid down, leaving the ones below to try, then returning themselves to make the effort again and again. An eastern scholar came away disturbed and sick at the sight, and saying, "It is such a terrible demonstration of futility as to haunt the mind."

Salmon, "netted, hooked, trolled, speared, weired, scooped—salmon taken by various sleights of native skill—" composed the chief diet of the Columbia Indian tribes and was also a principal object of trade. Certain ceremonies were observed with the first fish taken: he was laid beside the water with head upstream and with salmonberries placed in his mouth; his meat was cut only with the grain; and "the hearts of all caught must be burned or eaten, and, on no account, be thrown into the water or eaten by a dog." The catches were cleaned by the women, dried and smoked, and often pulverized between two stones before being packed away in mats for trade or for winter consumption. Lewis and Clark described in great detail the fishing, curing, and packing, at Celilo Falls, where today remnants of the tribes continue to stand on the jagged rocks and spear the salmon in the rapids or dip them out with nets.

The natives also depended much on the sturgeon, and took many smaller varieties of fish to fill the winter larder. They trapped or shot wild fowl, and caught elk and deer in covered pits dug along favorite runways or feeding grounds.

The dress of the Columbia River Indians consisted principally of a robe fastened by a thong across the breast and made, usually, of the skins of cougars, wildcats, deer, bear, or elk. The most esteemed of the women's robes were made of strips of sea otter skin, interwoven with silk grass or the inner bark of the white cedar. The upriver Indians used the hides of elk and larger animals in the construction of their tepees.

The folklore and mythology of the Oregon Indians contains a veritable "key" to the fauna of the State. Their gods and demigods, their spirits of good and evil, took on the forms of birds and beasts, while their own origin was usually explained by naming some tribe of animals as their ancestors. The animal people, they said, were here first, before there were any real people.

The birds were always a source of wonder to the red men because of their musical songs and their ability to soar into the skyey regions where dwell the supernatural beings. The eagle was regarded with veneration and was the chief war symbol. The fierce electric storms raging on the high peaks were personified as incarnations of the mysterious "thunder bird." Bluejay was a mischievous, impish deity among the Chinooks. He was the buffoon of the gods, always playing pranks on others and as often as not becoming the victim of his own folly.

The chief animal deity of the Columbia tribes, however, was the coyote. He was the most important because when he was put to work by the chief Supernatural Being, he did more than any of the other animals to make the world a fit place in which to live.

NATURAL RESOURCES AND THEIR CONSERVATION

The fur of wild animals was the first natural resource of Oregon to be utilized by white men. It was the fur trade that brought this northwest coast region to the attention of the world. A hundred years ago beavers were abundant in every creek, river, and lake in the state. In 1812 it is said that a small group from Fort Astoria returned to the post after a twenty-day expedition with "450 skins of beaver and other animals of the furry tribe." As late as 1860 a traveler on the headwaters of the Deschutes reported that "every stream thronged with beaver."

Although fur was the first natural resource of Oregon it is by no means its most prominent, but the fur trade is still a stable part of the state's industry. Oregon is a green land of forests and grassy wilderness teeming with wild life; a land of rich-soiled valleys maturing to golden harvests; a land of minerals; of streams that hold a vast potential water power; of timbered areas immensely valuable for lumber.

Agricultural lands are the most important on the list of Oregon's many natural resources. Of the state's total land area of 61,188,489 acres, land in farms comprise 17,357,549 acres, according to the U. S. Agricultural census of 1935. There were in that year 64,826 individual farms which, with land and buildings, were valued at $448,711,757.

In 1934, 2,831,742 acres of crop land were harvested, while there was crop-failure on 280,426 acres. Idle or fallow crop land amounted to 1,085,286 acres; 723,585 acres were in plowable pasture; woodland pasture took in 2,778,314 acres; other pasture 8,536,677 acres; woodland, not pastured, 571,630 acres, and all other land in farms, 549,889 acres.

In general, eastern Oregon has the most extensive grain lands and the greatest grazing areas, while western Oregon is devoted to diversified farming and fruit growing. The use of agricultural land is steadily increasing. The growth of all land in farms between the years 1930 and 1935 was about 809,000 acres.

According to the U. S. Census of 1930 (the latest figures available) Oregon's population was 953,786. Persons gainfully occupied numbered 409,645. Of these, 81,879 were workers in agriculture, about 20% of the whole. The total farm population was 223,667. In 1935, according to the U.S. Agricultural Census, Oregon's total farm population had grown to 248,767, an increase of 25,100 or more than ten per cent. In the same year the value of products for all manufacturing industries was $265,437,000, while the estimated gross income from farm production (crops and livestock) was $99,800,000 and the cash income $89,300,000.

Next to agricultural lands in importance to Oregon are the forests. In 1935 (according to figures of the U. S. Forest Service and the U.S. Agricultural Census) of the state's 61,188,489 acres, a total of 28,217,000 acres were covered with forest. Of these forest areas, 19,278,160 acres were covered with saw-timber—trees of more than 12 inches in diameter inside the bark.

The total volume of saw-timber in Oregon in 1934 was 300,793 million feet, board measure. Of this, 137,043 million feet, or 46 per cent, were privately owned; 112,599 million feet, or 37 per cent, were in National Forests; and 51,151 million feet, or 17 per cent, were on other public or Indian lands. Privately owned saw-timber covered 10,756,447 acres; saw-timber in National Forests 5,481,163 acres; and saw-timber on other public and Indian lands 3,040,550 acres.

Of Oregon's 300,793 million feet of saw-timber, 213,114 million feet grew west of the Cascade mountains and consisted mainly of Douglas fir, West Coast hemlock, spruce and cedar; and 87,679 million feet grew east of the Cascades, with Ponderosa pine, Douglas and White fir, and Western larch the most important species.

Forests furnish the raw materials for Oregon's largest manufacturies: lumber, shingles, pulp and paper, veneers, plywood, doors, masts, spars and square timbers, besides supplying the special woods used in cooperage plants and for the making of furniture, wooden boxes, automobile bodies, ladders, etc. In 1929 some 50,000 persons were employed in forest industries, or about 12 per cent of all gainfully occupied. An estimated 300,000 people, a large proportion classified as rural non-farm, are directly or indirectly dependent for their living on forest activities and industries. The 1929 value of products from Oregon's forest industries was $181,231,473, while these products provided about two-thirds of the out-going freight tonnage.

In 1937, according to figures of the State Fish Commission, 27,689,-805 lbs. of fish were taken from Oregon waters, of which 26,578,712 lbs. were salmon, 522,620 shad, 472,121 smelt, 82,207 sturgeon and 24,145 lbs. bass. Of the salmon more than 16,000,000 lbs. were of the chinook variety, and the rest silversides, steelheads, bluebacks and chums. Of lesser commercial importance are cod, flounder, black snapper, tuna, crabs, clams, and oysters. The smelt were caught in the Columbia River, as were about 90 per cent of the salmon, while the remainder of the take came from bays and inlets of the Pacific Ocean and Oregon rivers emptying into them. The average yearly yield of Oregon fisheries (according to the U.S. Department of Commerce) is valued at some $2,500,000, while approximately 4,500 persons are employed in catching and handling the product.

Oregon (according to the State Department of Geology & Mineral Industries) produces in metals, gold, quicksilver, silver, copper, lead, zinc, and platinum, important in the order named, and in non-metals, stone, sand, gravel, cement, and clay, besides coal, diatomite, lime, pumice, and mineral waters. Production figures for 1938 were: metals $3,318,000; non-metals $5,500,000; total $8,818,000.

Production of metals in 1936, in detail, amounted to: gold $2,126,-355; quicksilver $329,750; silver $65,880; copper $52,808; lead $7,268; zinc $6,100; platinum (estimated) $2,100; total $2,590,261.

Oregon is second only to California in the production of quicksilver. Baker County leads in gold production. Next in rank are Josephine, Douglas, Coos and Curry counties. Copper comes from Josephine County. Southwestern Oregon has several chromite properties.

In spite of predatory loss and the 68,612 hunting and fishing licenses issued during 1938 by the State Game Commission (according to report by the U.S. Wildlife Bureau) big-game animals increased in numbers between 10 and 15 per cent.

Of deer ranging the state outside of National Forests there were in 1938 an estimated 135,000 mule and 60,000 blacktail, while in the National Forests there were 141,860 of all species. Elk in the state numbered 22,000 of which 19,000 were in the National Forests.

Predatory animals in National Forests were estimated to number as follows: coyotes 23,200; bobcats 8,500; lynx 1,260; cougar 660 and wolves 130.

According to the State Game Commission there were in Oregon in 1938 some 16 state hatcheries for the propagation of game fish, mostly trout of various species. Oregon is an all-year fishing country, meaning that there is an open season for some sort of game fish every month in the year. Game fish, which were threatened with depletion some years ago, are now increasing, through regulation as to catches, and through stocking. Fishing in tidal waters is permitted the year around.

Beside wildlife in National Forests in Oregon in 1938, the range afforded grazing for 82,547 privately owned cattle and 587,000 sheep.

Oregon's greatest power source is the energy of falling water. According to the report of the State Planning Board of 1936, 16,000 miles of streams hold 4,605,000 horsepower of potential energy available 90 per cent of the time, or third among states in potential electrical energy.

In 1889 the first long-distance transmission line in the world was constructed in Oregon, sending power 14 miles from a hydroelectric plant at Oregon City to Portland. In 1936 there was in the state 254,000 horsepower of installed hydroelectric capacity distributed among some 250 plants, large and small, privately owned and municipal and state. The total share of Oregon from the Bonneville project will ultimately reach 500,000 horsepower.

Besides power, the streams of Oregon furnish water for the reclamation of arid lands. Among the most important irrigation projects are the Owyhee and the Klamath. The Owyhee project, according to the U. S. Reclamation Service, embraces lands near the Owyhee and Snake rivers to the extent of 115,383 acres, of which 48,100 acres were irrigated in 1937.

The Klamath project provides for diversion of water from Upper Klamath Lake for the irrigation of about 40,000 acres east of Klamath Falls and for the reclaiming of 33,000 acres of the bed of Tule Lake and along Lost River. During 1937 about 51,468 acres were irrigated and 50,439 cropped, including pasture.

Oregon's recreational resources are unsurpassed in the United States. The green beauty of the country makes it constantly attractive, while the ever-varying contrasts of mountains, streams, and valleys holds continued surprise. There are in the state more than 1,000 lakes, many in settings that would make them famous for loveliness, were they better known.

The U. S. Forest Service has built trails and roads in all parts of the National Forests and dotted them with pleasant and well-equipped, sanitary camps for the convenience of visitors, campers, and sportsmen.

Conservation with a view to perpetuation of Oregon's natural wealth is the policy of both private and public interests. In the matter of agricultural lands and forest domains, federal and state agencies are working hand in hand with private owners for beneficial regulations as to use and preservation. Farm lands have come under scientific scrutiny as to crop possibilities; the public range has been placed under official control as to grazing; and the method long practiced in National Forests of selective cutting and leaving of seed-trees has been adopted by many private, forest-owning concerns.

A conservation program is being carried out by the Civilian Conservation Corps for the forest service. Among the important work completed by the enrollees of some 17 camps in National Forests from April 1933 to July 1937 were: 3,488 miles of truck trails; 3,593 miles of telephone lines; 227 lookout houses and towers; 1,240,681 acres of rodent control work; 327,691 man-days of fighting forest fires; and 764,775 acres of insect pest control.

A conservation plan of the utmost concern to Oregon is the Willamette River Basin Project, authorized by Congress June 28, 1938. Preliminary mapping was done during the years 1935 to 1939, by U. S. Army Engineers. The project embraces flood control, which is vitally needed, the storage of water for irrigation, the development of water power, and the improvement and deepening of stream channels for commerce. Millions of dollars will be expended over a period of six to ten years; reservoirs will be built to insure water for agricultural lands, and modern locks will be constructed at Willamette Falls near Oregon City. Actual work on three storage reservoirs is planned to begin in 1940, and to be completed before the end of 1941.

Indians

ARCHEOLOGICAL research has revealed evidences of numerous successive cultures in many parts of Oregon. Surviving the wear of centuries on canyon walls and cliffs are rude designs daubed in red ochre or outlined in primitive carving. Although often the subject of fanciful interpretation, most of these pictographs and petroglyphs are devoid of symbolic or esoteric meaning, being merely the groping efforts of prehistoric man to give graphic expression to his experience. Burial mounds in irregular patterns mark the places where the dead, with their crude artifacts, lie buried. Along the coast, numerous kitchen middens—heaps of shells, bone and stone fragments, and miscellaneous refuse, overgrown with grass and trees—indicate the existence of prehistoric homes. Where the Coast Highway cuts through such a kitchen midden, as it does at several places, varying levels or strata in the heap are revealed, denoting successive occupations of the locality.

Stone and obsidian weapons and bone fragments, frequently discovered beneath layers of lava or volcanic ash, indicate human existence in Oregon at a remote period. Near Abert Lake in Lake County, and at the base of Hart Mountain in Warner Valley, are excellent examples of prehistoric painting and carving. A local legend associates Abert Rim with the retreat of an "Indian army" that ended in a plunge over the cliff, at the foot of which are scattered many relics. Near The Dalles, Arlington, and Forest Grove, and in the Cascadia Caves, are diverse examples of prehistoric pictorial representations. The Linn County mounds, the Deschutes region, the Malheur and Catlow Caves in Harney County, and numerous other sites, have yielded weapons, utensils, and other Indian artifacts.

The Indians who inhabited Oregon at the coming of the first white men were members of twelve distinct linguistic families. Along the south side of the Columbia, from its mouth to the Cascades, the Chinookans held sway. Important branches of this family were the Clatsops, who lived along the river to Tongue Point and along the coast to Tillamook Head, and the Cathlamets, who dwelt a short distance farther up the river; while numerous bands on Sauvie Island and about the mouth of the Willamette were known by the collective name of Multnomahs. The Clackamas tribe lived in the Clackamas Valley and about the falls of the Willamette. In all, some 36 tribes of the Chinookan family occupied the south shore of the Columbia, and as many others dwelt near the north bank.

The Athapascans occupied two widely separated regions. On the Clatskanie and upper Nehalem Rivers lived the Tlatskanai, a warlike tribe. It is said that the early Hudson's Bay Company trappers did not dare to traverse their lands in a group of fewer than 60 armed men. In southwestern Oregon dwelt the other Athapascans—the Tututni, the Upper Coquilles, the Chastacostas, and the Chetcoes. Also in the southwestern region were the Umpquas and the Siuslaws, who together form a separate family.

The Salishan family, although more numerous north of the Columbia, was represented south of that river by the Tillamooks and the Siletz. The Yakonians, consisting of the Yaquina and the Alseas, lived on the two bays thus named; and on Coos Bay and the lower Coquille dwelt the three tribes of the small Kusan family.

One of the most important families was the Kalapooyan. This numerous people occupied the whole of the Willamette Valley above the falls, practiced flattening of the head, and lived on game and roots. A dozen tribes of this family inhabited the Willamette region at the coming of the white man. The Atfalati or Tualati, numbering more than 30 bands, occupied the beautiful and fertile Tualatin Valley. Other tribes of this group were the Yamhills, the Chemeketas, and the Santiams.

The southern part of Oregon was occupied by divisions of three families: the powerful Klamath and Modoc tribes of the Lutuamians or Sahaptians, the Takelmans of the upper Rogue River, and two "spillovers" from California—the Shastas and Karoks of the Hokan family.

The upper Columbia River country was the home of other Sahaptians. The greater part of this family lived in eastern Washington and the Lewis River district of Idaho; but four tribes, the Willewah branch of the Nez Perces, the Umatillahs, the Teninos of the Deschutes River, and the Tyighs of the Tygh Valley, inhabited the uplands of eastern Oregon. The Waiilatpuan branch was represented by the powerful Cayuse or "horse" Indians, dwelling on the headwaters of the Umatilla, the Walla Walla, and the Grande Ronde Rivers. A small offshoot of this branch had in times past wandered over the Cascades into western

Oregon, and under the name of Molallas lived along the Molalla River. Over the high desert country of the southeastern region roamed the nomadic Snake and Paiute tribes of the Shoshoneans.

Intercourse between the various tribes and later with the white men made it necessary for the Indians to supplement their many dialects with a common language. Among merchant Indians at the mouth of the Columbia there grew up a pidgin language based upon Chinook, and later intermixed with French and English words. This language became known as Chinook jargon, and was widely used by all tribes, as well as by the early settlers, traders, and missionaries. When the Indians were removed to reservations, many who had not adopted the jargon were obliged to learn it in order to speak with their neighbors.

The local customs of Indians in the western valleys and coast region differed greatly from those of the interior. The western tribes, because of the density of the forests, usually traveled by canoe. They subsisted chiefly on salmon, roots, and berries. The opening of the salmon season in June was attended with great formality. The first salmon caught was sacred, and was eaten ceremonially in a long-established ritual intended to propitiate the salmon and insure future runs. Before the arrival of the whites, the coastal Indians were scantily clad. The men went entirely naked in summer, and the women wore a flimsy skirt of cedar bark fiber or grasses. In winter, the men wore a robe made of skins reaching to the middle of the thigh; the women added to their costume a similar robe reaching to the waist; or either might wear a fiber cape.

Among the Chinooks, distinctions of rank extended to burial. The bodies of slaves were tossed into the river or gotten rid of in some other way, while the free born were carefully prepared for box, vault, tree, or canoe burial, and were honored with rituals of mourning which included periods of wailing during a certain length of time, cutting the hair, and refraining from mentioning the name of the dead. Entombment varied according to the tribe and locality. Columbia River Indians utilized Memaloose Island near The Dalles, Coffin Rock near the mouth of the Cowlitz River, and other islands and promontories, with ceremonial dressing and storing of bones. The coast Indians used canoes supported on decorated scaffolds, and placed the head toward the west so that the departed spirit might more easily find its way to *Memaloose Illahee,* or the land of the dead, which lay somewhere toward the setting sun. Valley Indians often placed their dead, wrapped in skins, in the forks of trees.

The houses of the western Oregon Indians were of the communal type, from 40 to 60 feet long and 20 feet wide, constructed of large cedar planks and roofed with bark or boards. The interior walls of these great lodges, scattered in clusters along the coast, the Columbia, and the lower Willamette, were tiered with bunks. Along the middle of the floor ran a firepit, the smoke escaping through a gap left along the ridgepole of the roof. Men, women, children, and dogs mingled in the dusky interior. These houses were put together with lashings, and when fleas and other vermin became intolerable the houses were dismantled and the planks removed to a new location, supposedly leaving the fleas behind.

The Indians of river and coast were skilled in fashioning canoes. Each of these was made from a single log, their size varying from the small craft capable of sustaining only one person to the great war canoe in which as many as 60 warriors might safely put to sea. For these graceful vessels, cedar and spruce were usually preferred, though fir was also used.

The native bow, like the canoe, was beautifully and skillfully formed. It was generally made of yew or crab-apple wood. The string was a piece of dried seal-gut or deer-sinew, or consisted of twisted bark. The arrows, about a yard long, were made of arrow-wood or cedar. Household utensils included baskets of cedar root fiber or tough grasses often woven so closely as to be watertight, and stone mortars and pestles for pulverizing seeds and wild grains. The principal art displayed was in the carvings on house posts and canoe figureheads, and in the fashioning of woven mats and baskets. Basketry was a highly developed art, many examples of which, richly colored with intricate and pleasing designs, today grace museums or are offered for sale in Indian curio stores.

The culture of the northeastern Oregon tribes had undergone a definite change a few decades before the invasion of the whites. Through the introduction of the horse they had become a more or less nomadic people. The Snakes, Nez Perces, and Cayuses counted their wealth in horses, and because they were thus free to move about they evolved a culture based largely on the chase and warfare. Buckskin ornamented with dyed porcupine quills formed their dress, their moccasins, and their shelters, and skins dressed with the fur intact made their robes and blankets. Game, supplemented by roots and berries, was their food.

The Shoshonean culture of the southeast plateau was of a lower order, owing to the nature of the barren and forbidding country. The Klamath and Modoc culture, influenced by the same factors but modified by the *tules* (reeds) and *wocus* (yellow water lily) of the Klamath and Tule Lake marshes, presented a definite departure from the culture in other sections of Oregon. The Klamaths and Modocs have been termed "pit Indians" because their dwellings were little more than roofed-over pits sunk about four feet below the surface of the ground. These houses appeared as mounds of earth about six feet high, with a circular hole two and a half feet in diameter at the top, from which a ladder led down into the circular space below. The interior was 20 feet across, with sleeping bunks and arrangements for storing dried meats, seeds, acorns, and roots. The whole was substantially built, the roof being of poles covered with rushes and with earth taken from the pit beneath. On hooks from the rush-lined ceiling hung bags and baskets, laden with such luxuries as dried grasshoppers and berries. About the bunks hung the skins of deer and other game.

The dress of the women consisted of a skirt of deerskin thongs fastened to a braided belt; the men wore breechclouts of deerskin, and the children went entirely naked. When grasshoppers were abundant the Indians scoured the valleys, gathered the insects in great quantities by driving them into pits, and made preparations for a feast. A fire was kindled in one of the pits, and after the latter had been thoroughly heated the harvest was dropped in, covered with damp *tules* and hot stones, and baked. Prepared in this fashion the insects were eaten with great relish. They were also powdered and mixed with *wocus* meal in a kind of bread baked in the ashes.

All tribes believed in an existence after death, and in a soul that inhabited the body yet was distinct from the vital principle and capable of leaving the body in dreams, faints, and trances, though if it stayed away too long the body died. Other living things were also similarly endowed. So it was that a canoe builder deferentially addressed the tree from which he obtained his log, as though it were a conscious personality, and a fisherman spoke apologetically to the first catch of the season as he took it from the water.

Creation myths varied from tribe to tribe. The creation of men and animals was ascribed by one to *Echanum,* the fire spirit, by some to Coyote, the transformer, who is given credit for creating the tribes from the legs, head, belly, and body of his vanquished enemy, the beaver. Stories of Coyote and Thunderbird were common to many tribes. The Thunderbird was ruler of the storm, avenger, originator of numerous taboos, and creator of volcanic activity. Coyote in a hundred grotesque forms was the hero of many roguish stories, emphasizing his trickery, selfishness, and prurience, and the source of rigid taboos regarding foods, domestic economy, and ceremonial observance.

Legends were invented by the Indians to explain the origin and form of many geographic features. The story of Loowit, a beautiful Indian girl, who was the subject of a quarrel between rival lovers, and who dwelt on the natural rock Bridge of the Gods which once spanned the Columbia River at the Cascades, tells of the destruction of the bridge and of Loowit's transformation into Mount St. Helens, while her lovers became Mount Adams and Mount Hood. Another legend has it that Neahkahnie Mountain on the coast reached its present form from a single blow of the hatchet of Coyote, who built a fire on the mountainside, heated rocks and threw them into the sea, where the seething waters grew into waves that have been crashing against the shore ever since. Mitchell Point, once called the "Storm King" by the Indians, was believed by them to have been built to part the storm clouds that hurried up the Columbia.

In 1938, Oregon's surviving Indian population was distributed as follows: Klamath Reservation, 1,201; Warm Springs Reservation, 1,094; Umatilla Reservation, 1,117; Siletz River district, 1,140; and on the public domain, 2,220. The population on the Umatilla Reservation is composed of Cayuse, Nez Perce, and Walla Walla tribes, with many full bloods and many mixed breeds, all of whom speak the Nez Perce language. Wascos, Teninos, and Paiutes are chiefly concentrated on the Warm Springs Reservation. Klamaths, Modocs, Yahooskins, Snakes, Shastas, and Pit River Indians are gathered on the Klamath Reservation. Rogues (or Tututinis), Chetcos, Tillamooks, and other mixed tribal remnants dwell in the Siletz River region. There is an independent village of Paiutes a few miles north of Burns.

The Indians living on reservations dress in much the same way as their white neighbors, live in the same kind of houses, and carry on the same domestic and industrial pursuits. Their native handicrafts include tanning and decorating of skins, fabrication of baskets, beadwork on buckskin, and the making of cornhusk bags and mats. Each reservation is served by church mission schools or by the public school system of the State, the only government Indian schools being on the Warm Springs Reservation and at Chemawa near Salem.

Four canneries care for the output from 5,000 acres of upland peas on the Umatilla Reservation, and on the Klamath Reservation contracts between Indian owners and commercial interests have resulted in the cutting and marketing of much timber. Fine horses, cattle, hay, and grain are produced. All land has been allotted, and a business committee for each reservation has superseded tribal government.

Although Oregon Indians have abandoned most of their tribal ways, at times drums still throb above the music and words of tribal songs and busy feet pattern the ceremonial dances. The salmon festival on the Columbia River is generally held in secret each year; but the annual root feast at Simnasho in the spring, and the Warm Springs and Klamath Reservation huckleberry feasts in the fall, are open to the public.

The Umatilla Indians form an encampment at the Pendleton Round-up and participate in the parade and Westward Ho pageant. The Round-up, though colorful, is not a true picture of Indian life, but a dramatized version of what the Indian thinks the white man wants to see. As many as 2,000 natives in ceremonial trappings participate as paid performers.

History

THE earliest explorers along the coast of what is now the State of Oregon were Juan Rodriguez Cabrillo, a Portuguese in the service of Spain, and his chief pilot Bartolome Ferrelo, who are believed to have sailed up from Mexico as far as 44° north in 1542-3. About the same latitude was reached in 1579 by Sir Francis Drake, who there abandoned his search for a northern passage to England and turned the prow of his *Golden Hind* southward. Whether the Spanish navigator Sebastian Viscaino sailed farther north than the 42nd parallel on his voyage of 1602 is a moot question, though one of his ships under Martin d'Aguilar proceeded another degree or two northward and reported the entrance to a river or strait not far from Cape Blanco.

A century and three-quarters elapsed before further discoveries of importance were made. The Spaniards Perez in 1774, Heceta on two voyages in 1774 and 1775, and Bodega in 1775 sailed along all or most of the present Oregon coast, and on his second voyage Heceta noted evidences of a great river in the northern region. In 1778 the English navigator Captain James Cook, seeking (as Drake had sought) a northern sea passage from the Pacific to the Atlantic, reached from the south what is now Vancouver Island and anchored for several weeks in a fine harbor to which he later gave the name of Nootka Sound. Here he traded with the Indians for furs, and learned much about their life and customs.

Ten years later another Englishman, Captain John Meares, fitted out a naval expedition in search of the great river that Heceta had reported in 1775. Entering the broad mouth of the present Columbia, he decided that this was no more than a large bay and departed after naming the entrance Deception Bay and the promontory on the north Cape Disappointment. It remained for an American sea captain and trader, Robert Gray of Boston, to verify the existence of the hitherto legendary "River of the West." In company with Captain John Kendrick, Gray made a trading voyage to the Pacific in 1788; and the two ships commanded by these men, the *Columbia* and the *Lady Washington,* were the first American vessels to visit the northwest coast. On a second voyage from Boston, in the *Columbia,* Gray again visited this region and entered the long-sought river on May 11, 1792, sailing for several miles upstream, trading with the natives, and making notes about the surrounding country. Before leaving, he named the river the Columbia, after the first ship to anchor in its inland waters. Five months later, Lieut. William R. Broughton, an English naval officer under Captain George Vancouver's command, explored the river for nearly a hundred miles inland, sighted and named Mount Hood on October 29, and formally claimed the region for Great Britain on the grounds that (though he knew of Gray's earlier visit) "the subjects of no other civilized nation or state had ever entered this river before."

For a good many years both before and after Gray's verification of its existence, the river was commonly referred to as the Ouragon, Oregan, Origan, or Oregon. As early as 1765, Major Robert Rogers, commanding an English post in the upper Mississippi Valley, petitioned King George III for permission to conduct an exploring party to the Pacific Ocean by way of the river "called by the Indians Ouragon." As now spelled, the name first appeared in Jonathan Carver's *Travels in Interior Parts of America,* published 1778, in a reference to "the River Oregon, or the River of the West, that falls into the Pacific Ocean at the straits of Anian." Carver states that he got the name from the Indians, and most authorities believe it is derived from the Sautee word *oragan,* meaning a birchbark dish. It remained unfamiliar to the public at large until William Cullen Bryant popularized and perpetuated it by the reference in his poem "Thanatopsis," published in 1817:

> Or lose thyself in the continuous woods
> Where rolls the Oregon, and hears no sound
> Save its own dashings.

As the river was long known as the Oregon, so the vast northwest territory of which it was one of the most prominent geographical features acquired the name of "the Oregon country" or "the Oregon territory." The region thus designated originally comprised all the land between the Rocky Mountains and the Pacific Ocean, from the vaguely delimited border of the great Spanish Southwest to the equally vague delimitations of British America and the Russian possessions on the north. By the Treaty of Florida in 1819, the southern boundary was fixed at the 42nd parallel; and in 1846, Great Britain and the United States agreed to a northern boundary along the 49th parallel. From the area of more than 300,000 square miles within these boundaries were later carved the present States of Oregon, Washington, and Idaho, in their entirety, and Montana and Wyoming in considerable part.

Into this immense wilderness, inhabited only by scattered tribes of Indians, came the American explorers Meriwether Lewis and William Clark, heading an expedition authorized by President Jefferson and Congress "to explore the Missouri River, & such principal streams of it, as, by its course & communication with the waters of the Pacific Ocean, may offer the most direct & practicable water communication across this continent, for the purposes of commerce." Starting up the Missouri on May 14, 1804, the party reached the headwaters of the Columbia in October of the following year, journeyed down the river to arrive at Cape Disappointment in November, and passed the winter in a rude log fort which they named Fort Clatsop, after a neighboring Indian tribe. In the spring they began the homeward journey, reaching St. Louis on September 23, 1806.

The accounts of this expedition, the first to be made by white men across the Oregon country, aroused widespread interest, particularly in the immense opportunities for fur-trading offered by the northwest region. In 1806 a British trading post was set up by Simon Fraser of the North West Company, on what later came to be known as Fraser's Lake, near the 54th parallel. But the first post in the Columbia River region was that established by members of John Jacob Astor's Pacific Fur Company in 1811 at Astoria, close to the log fort in which Lewis and Clark had passed the winter of 1805-6. One group of Astor's company sailed from New York around Cape Horn, arriving in March 1811 at the mouth of the Columbia, where eight members of the party lost their lives in an unskilful attempt to enter the river. Another group took the overland route and arrived about a year later. After disembarking the men who built the post at Astoria, the ship in which the first party had arrived proceeded northward along the coast to trade with the Indians, and very soon thereafter was destroyed with a loss of more than 20 lives in a surprise attack by hostile natives.

The fur-trading operations at Astoria were scarcely well under way before war broke out between Great Britain and the United States, and early in 1813 the Astorians received information that a British naval force was on its way to take possession of the mouth of the Columbia. This news was brought by agents of the North West Company, who offered to buy the entire establishment of Astoria at a reasonable valuation. Fearing confiscation if he delayed matters, the American factor accepted this offer, and the post was renamed Fort George by its new owners.

Astoria was restored to American ownership in 1818, and the United States and Great Britain agreed to a ten-years' joint occupancy of the Oregon country. Spanish claims in the nebulous southern area were eliminated a year later, when the southern boundary was fixed at the 42nd parallel; and Russia in 1824 renounced all interests below 54° 40' north latitude. After its purchase of Astoria in 1813, the North West Company continued to control the Oregon fur trade until 1821, when it was merged with its British rival the Hudson's Bay Company. Soon thereafter, American trappers and traders began to push westward beyond the Rockies into the rich domain of the British traffic, and their frequent clashes with men of the Hudson's Bay Company together with the beginnings of organized immigration brought the vexed question of sovereignty over the Oregon country increasingly to the fore. By the late 1830's many Americans were demanding in bellicose tone that Great Britain should relinquish all jurisdiction south of 54° 40', and "Fifty-four forty or fight" proved a popular slogan in Polk's compaign for the presidency. The issue was finally settled in 1846, when the two countries compromised on a boundary along the 49th parallel, and the Oregon country between that and the 42nd parallel on the south became undisputed American soil.

The treaty of joint control was in effect when Dr. John McLoughlin destined to be the most powerful individual in the territory for 20 years, came down the Columbia to Fort George. Appointed Chief Factor of the Hudson's Bay Company in 1824, within a year he built Fort Vancouver on the north bank of the Columbia River, a few miles east of the mouth of the Willamette. Six-feet-two, beaver-hatted, already white-haired at 40, McLoughlin knew how to control his half-wild white trappers; he made beaver-hunting vassals of the Indians and for a long time succeeded in crushing all competition—though many of his competitors were given places in the Georgian mahogany chairs at his table. With Fort Vancouver as the capital, he was king of a vast domain stretching from California to Alaska and from the Rocky Mountains to the sea.

Jedediah Smith, a Yankee trader, reached Oregon by way of California in 1828. Indians near the mouth of the Umpqua had attacked his party, killing all but himself and three companions, and taking his furs. McLoughlin sent an expedition to secure the pelts, which he then bought from Smith with the understanding that the Yankee should thenceforth stay out of Oregon.

Nathaniel J. Wyeth of Boston came to the Columbia in 1832 with the intention of starting a salmon fishery and packing plant. After returning to the east coast in 1833, he came again to the Oregon country in 1834 and established Fort William on Sauvie Island. With Wyeth's second company were the Methodist clergyman Jason Lee and his nephew Daniel Lee, the first of many missionaries to come to the Northwest. They proposed to educate and Christianize the Indians, and for this purpose they established in 1835 a Methodist mission station and school in the Willamette Valley. The School was taken over in 1844 by the Oregon Institute (now Willamette University), organized in 1842. Other missionaries arrived, among them Dr. Marcus Whitman and Henry Spalding in 1836.

Until early in the 1840's there was no local government in the Oregon territory except that of the Hudson's Bay Company which exercised feudal rights derived from the British Crown. McLoughlin enjoyed the protection of British laws in the conduct of his company's affairs, but Americans in the territory were for the most part ignored by successive administrations at Washington. However, the missionaries formulated regulations for themselves as well as for the Indians over whom they assumed charge, and their leadership was accepted in a large measure by the independent American settlers.

The Lees were discouraged by the indifference of the Indians to religious salvation, but in letters to friends in the East they extolled the wild western country, thus supplementing the publicity given to the territory by Hall J. Kelley, a Boston schoolmaster who was one of the first propagandists for Oregon. Jason Lee, on the first of two trips to the Atlantic coast, presented a memorial to Congress asking for the Government's protection of its citizens in Oregon. Meanwhile, American settlers were finding their way into the Willamette Valley. The "Peoria Party" came in 1839, a few more arrived in 1840, and about 40 adults and children in 1841. In 1842 Whitman made a difficult winter ride across the Continent on missionary matters and also to enlist homeseekers and invoke governmental aid in the settlement of the Oregon country. That year a larger immigration came across the plains, and in 1843 the first considerable wagon train made the long and trying journey over the Oregon Trail. Thenceforward the population rapidly and steadily increased.

Despite his misgivings concerning the effect of their arrival on the business of the Hudson's Bay Company, Dr. McLoughlin had aided the newcomers with credit and counsel. In 1845, however, the company forced him to resign and his influence upon the development of the region came to an end.

Life in the Oregon country was crude in the extreme, but despite its difficulties, it was not without its favorable aspects. Pioneers hewed their cabins and barns from the forest, and took their food from the newly tilled ground or from the surrounding wilderness. The climate was mild, and farm animals required little outlay for stabling or winter feeding. The scarcity of money was a great inconvenience, somewhat mitigated by the issue of what were known as "Ermatinger money" and "Abernethy money," the use of wheat and peltry as mediums of exchange, and the coinage of "beaver money" at Oregon City. Chiefly unfavorable to peace of mind in this life of primitive self-sufficiency were the inevitable isolation and ever-present fear of the Indians. Of these, the former was perhaps the harder to endure.

Attempts to form an organized government in Oregon antedated the settlement of the boundary question by several years. When Jason Lee went east in 1838, he carried a paper signed by 36 settlers petitioning Congress for Oregon's admission to the Union. In the next year, the Reverend David Leslie and about 70 others presented a similar petition asking for "the civil institutions of the American Republic" and "the high privilege of American citizenship." Congress, however, was hesitant to act because of possible trouble with Great Britain, and the Americans in Oregon became restless while awaiting a decision. Plans for a provisional government became a matter of active discussion when, early in 1841, Jason Lee made an earnest speech on the subject. Very soon thereafter an event occurred which hastened the efforts to organize. This was the death of Ewing Young, who owned a great part of the Chehalem Valley and a large herd of Spanish cattle which he had driven north from California. In the absence of a will and any legal heirs, arrangements were made at his funeral to call a mass meeting of Oregon's inhabitants south of the Columbia River for the purposes of appointing officers to administer his estate and to form some sort of provisional local government. At this meeting, held February 17 and 18, 1841, at the Methodist Mission in the Willamette Valley, a "Supreme Judge, with Probate powers" and several minor court officers were elected, and it was resolved "that a committee be chosen to form a constitution, and draft a code of laws."

At an adjourned meeting held four months later, it was moved "that the committee be advised to confer with the commander of the American Exploring Squadron now in the Columbia river, concerning the propriety of forming a provisional government in Oregon." The naval commander, Capt. Charles Wilkes, and his fellow officers were definitely opposed to the settlers' plans, and assured the people that soon they would doubtless be placed under jurisdiction of the United States government. The arrival in September 1842 of an official sub-agent of Indian affairs, who contended that his office was equivalent to that of Governor of the Territory, served further to retard the movement for setting up a local government.

Several isolated Indian outrages, however, and the threat of a concerted Indian attack upon the American settlement in the Willamette Valley led the inhabitants of that region to meet at Champoeg on May 2, 1843, "for the purpose of taking steps to organize themselves into a civic community, and provide themselves with the protection secured by the enforcement of law and order." On July 5 of the same year the settlers again assembled at Champoeg and adopted "articles of compact" as well as a detailed "organic law" based largely upon the laws of Iowa. The provisional government thus organized was confirmed and came into effect as the result of a special election held on July 25, 1845. George Abernethy was chosen Governor, and remained so by re-election throughout the three years of provisional government.

President Polk attempted to secure a territorial government for the region before his term expired. On August 14, 1848, more than two years after the boundary dispute was settled, and as the climax of a 24-hour debate; a dilatory Congress passed the bill admitting Oregon as a territory. President Polk signed the bill the next day and then proceeded to appoint Territorial officers, including General Joseph Lane, of Indiana, as Governor, and Joseph L. Meek as United States marshall. Meek had gone to Washington to report the Whitman massacre, and to function as a self-styled "Envoy extraordinary and minister plenipotentiary from the Republic of Oregon to the Court of the United States." He returned by way of Indiana to inform General Lane of his appointment, and the two hurried to the Northwest, reaching Oregon City by boat and proclaiming the Territorial government on March 3, 1849, the day before Polk went out of office.

The new Territory of Oregon embraced all of the original Oregon country between the 42nd and 49th parallels from the Rockies to the Pacific. It was reduced to the confines of the present State of Oregon in 1853, when the rest of the original area was organized as the Territory of Washington. From this latter, in turn, the eastern portion was detached in 1863, to form the largest part of the Territory of Idaho.

With the discovery of gold in California in 1848, Oregon farmers, soldiers, tradesmen, and officials joined in the mad rush to the gold fields. Within a few months two-thirds of Oregon's adult male population had left for California. Many of the stampeders acquired quick and easy fortunes, returning with as much as thirty or forty thousand dollars in gold dust and nuggets. This new-found wealth was badly needed; debts were paid, farms improved, houses built. And in addition to the gold-rushers who became well-to-do, those who remained at home also prospered. The miners in California required food, lumber, and other supplies, and they turned to neighboring Oregon for them. The price of wheat soared to $4 a bushel, flour to $15 a barrel, and lumber to $100 a thousand feet. Oregon began to take on an atmosphere of well-being. Log cabins gave way to comfortable dwellings of the New England and southern type; many of these are still standing today.

The Indian population of the Oregon country, estimated at about 27,000 in 1845, was comparatively peaceful throughout the domination of McLoughlin. But the rising tide of immigration in the 1840's filled the red men with apprehension and resentment, increased by wanton invasions of Indian rights by unprincipled whites. In November 1847 a band of Cayuses attacked the Presbyterian mission near the site of Walla Walla, killed Dr. Marcus Whitman, his wife, and 12 others, and burnt all the buildings. The settlers immediately declared war upon the Cayuse tribe, and after several battles the Indians were routed and their villages destroyed. Another campaign, marked by a sharp engagement at Battle Rock and desultory skirmishes in other places, began against the Rogue Indians in 1851. Although Governor Joseph Lane effected a treaty with them at Table Rock, attacks and reprisals continued until 1855, when Jackson County volunteers massacred 23 Indians, including old men, women, and children. This act drove the Indians into a frenzy of resentment; they appeared everywhere, killing the settlers and driving off their cattle. Culminating a year of bitter struggle, the final battle of the campaign was fought at Oak Flat, on the Illinois River, June 26, 1856. Three days later, Chief John surrendered, and was subsequently imprisoned at Alcatraz. Meanwhile a similar war had raged in eastern Oregon, but the defeat of the Spokane nation on September 1, 1858, and the execution of 16 Indians by Colonel Wright, brought the hostilities to an end.

During the Territorial period, social and economic conditions in

Oregon improved rapidly. Numerous ships discharged and loaded cargoes in the harbors, gold was discovered in several southwestern counties, and roads and bridges were constructed. More than a score of academies and two universities came into existence. A fire destroyed the state house at Salem on December 30, 1855, and the seat of government was moved to Corvallis; but the legislature, meeting in the latter city in 1856, decided to transfer the capital back to Salem, where it has since remained.

The slavery controversy retarded the movement toward statehood, presenting the main obstacle to unity at the constitutional convention in 1857. Finally a determination of the issue was left to a popular vote to be taken concurrently with the vote on the constitution itself. At a special election on November 9, 1857, the people ratified the document and defeated by a large majority the proposal to permit slave-holding. The largest majority of all, however, was given to an article prohibiting the admission of free negroes into Oregon. Though this provision was a dead letter for many years, only in 1926 was it taken out of the constitution.

The bill granting statehood to Oregon was signed by President Buchanan on February 14, 1859, but the news did not reach Portland until March 15. By noon of the next day the announcement found its way to Oregon City, where it aroused little excitement. "A few persons talked about it with languid interest," said Harvey Scott, "and wondered when the government of the state would be set in motion." But Stephen Senter of Oregon City, feeling the news ought to be speeded to Salem, undertook to act as messenger, and like Paul Revere rode over miry roads and through swollen streams, spreading the tidings that Oregon was a State. The legislature was convoked and the organization of the state government completed on May 16, 1859.

The brilliant and ambitious Edward Dickinson Baker came up from California to stump the State for his old friend Lincoln and for himself as United States Senator. Eloquent beyond most Pacific coast public men of his time or since, he caused the congregated pioneers to wonder that such glorious speech could come from mortal mouth. He was elected, but soon joined the Army and made a final dramatic appearance before the Senate in a colonel's uniform. He was killed in the early months of the Civil War while leading a charge at Ball's Bluff. Little Willie Lincoln at the White House commemorated him in a poem, and the city of Baker and Baker County were named for him.

In general, Oregon's part in the Civil War was confined in the main to protecting the frontier from marauding bands of Indians. Governor Whiteaker proved dilatory in responding to President Lincoln's call for volunteers; and after waiting until September of 1861 for the Governor to act, Colonel Wright, who commanded the United States forces within the State, requisitioned a volunteer troop of cavalry for three years' service against the Indians in eastern Oregon. By 1862 there were six companies in the field, forming a regiment known as the First Oregon Cavalry. This unit, in addition to its service against the Indians, held in check the Knights of the Golden Circle, a secret order which opposed the war. There was a good deal of secession sentiment in the state, and several seditious newspapers were suppressed during the conflict.

Within a few years after the Civil War, Oregon was plunged into Indian troubles that continued intermittently for more than a decade. The Modocs went on the warpath in 1872, when attempts were made to force them onto the Klamath reservation. A mere handful of warriors, under the leadership of "Captain Jack," they retreated to the lava beds near Tule Lake, California, and there held out against a large force of United States soldiers, upon whom they inflicted defeat after defeat with little loss to themselves. They resisted until the courageous chieftain was captured and hanged, after he and some of his band had treacherously assassinated General E. R. S. Canby and an associate during a parley on April 11, 1873.

In 1877, the younger Chief Joseph of the Nez Perces, incensed at the government's attempt to deprive his people of the beautiful Wallowa Valley, refused to be moved to an Idaho reservation. Several regiments of United States troops were dispatched to force him into obedience. After a number of sharp engagements and a retreat of a thousand miles across Idaho and Montana, ending about fifty miles from the Canadian border, Joseph was compelled to surrender. It is reported that he raised his hand above his head and said: "From where the sun now stands, I will fight no more forever." This great Indian warrior died in 1904 and was buried at the foot of Wallowa Lake, in the heart of the mountains he loved so well.

Soon after the close of the Nez Perce war, the Paiutes and Bannocks spread such terror throughout eastern and central Oregon that in 1878 the white farmers began moving into towns or erecting block houses for protection. This outbreak, however, was short-lived, and by 1880 the Indian troubles in Oregon were for the most part ended.

With the completion of the Union Pacific to Promontory Point, Utah, in 1869, and construction of a connecting line to Portland in the early 1880's, a new era of population growth and economic expansion began for Oregon. Homesteads were established in the more isolated sections, and the eastern plains and ranges were utilized for large-scale production of wheat and livestock. Industries for processing the materials from forests and farms came into being. Steamship as well as railroad commerce developed at a rapid rate. The *Sally Brown,* sailing from Portland to Liverpool in 1868, carried the first full cargo of Oregon wheat ever to be exported; since then Portland has become one of the more important wheat-shipping ports of the world. In the three decades between 1870 and 1900, the State's population increased from 90,923 to 413,526. Impressive evidence of a century's advance was presented in the Lewis and Clark Centennial Exposition, held at Portland in 1905.

The second Regiment of Oregon's National Guard was the first unit of the American expeditionary force to support Admiral Dewey at Manila, in the Spanish-American War of 1898. The regiment took part in several engagements with the Spanish, and remained in the Philippines throughout the campaign against Aguinaldo.

Oregonians were among the first American troops in active overseas service during the World War, taking part with distinction in the engagements at Chateau Thierry, Belleau Wood, St. Mihiel, Cambrai, Argonne Forest, and elsewhere. In the total of 44,166 Oregon men enrolled in the American forces, more than 1,000 deaths were recorded, and 355 were cited or decorated for distinguished service.

In the march of political and social progress, as expressed in legislative enactments and constitutional amendments, Oregon has kept well abreast of her sister States. The Australian ballot system was introduced in 1891, and a year later William S. U'Ren of Portland began an extensive campaign that resulted in adoption by the state of the initiative and referendum in 1902, the direct primary in 1904, and the recall in 1908. Other progressive steps were taken with the adoption of woman suffrage in 1912, workmen's compensation and widows' pensions in 1913, compulsory education in 1921, and a system of people's utility districts in 1930.

Nothing in recent Oregon history is of greater significance for the future than the construction by the Federal government of Bonneville Dam and lock on the Columbia River 42 miles east of Portland. Begun in 1933 and now (1940) nearly completed, this $70,000,000 project will supply hydro-electric power to a huge area in the Columbia River region and will permit navigation by ocean-going vessels as far east as The Dalles.

With only 13,294 inhabitants in 1850, Oregon has developed into a modern State of more than a million population, and its possibilities for future development are as bright as those of any commonwealth in the Union.

Agriculture

THE first independent and successful American farmer in Oregon was Ewing Young, erstwhile fur-trader, who came in 1834 and in the following year had crops growing and cattle grazing on the rich acreage of the Chehalem Valley. Before his arrival, various ventures in agriculture had been attempted, the earliest being by Nathan Winship and his crew of the *Albatross,* who brought hogs and goats and did some planting along the lower Columbia River bottoms in 1810. This experiment was flooded out, and a year later the Astor expedition brought hogs, sheep, and cattle, and planted vegetables at Fort Astoria. Dr. John McLoughlin, of the Hudson's Bay Company, started a farm at Fort Vancouver in 1825; and three years later he placed Etienne Lucier, one of his trappers, who had become superannuated, on a tract of land at the present site of East Portland. In 1829, James Bates established a farm on Scappoose Plain, and three years later John Ball began wheat growing in the Willamette Valley. These men were share-croppers for the fur company. In 1835, Nathaniel Wyeth brought cattle, hogs, and goats, with grain and garden seeds, to Sauvie Island, but later relinquished the land to Dr. McLoughlin, who established a dairy on the island under the supervision of Jean Baptiste Sauvie.

Favorable reports concerning the fertile valleys of Oregon brought a trickle of eastern farmers into the new and unclaimed country in the late 1830's. Thereafter, immigration increased rapidly, until the trickle became a stream and then a flood. The cry of "Free land!" echoed back over the Oregon Trail, and the route became crowded with long processions of covered wagons.

Wheat was the pioneers' first and principal crop. Many of the early homeseekers arrived in the Willamette country destitute, and Dr. McLoughlin, partly with an eye to future profit and the enhancing of British influence, staked them to clothing, tools, and seed-wheat, to be repaid in kind, so that thousands of settlers were at length in debt to him. In 1846 more than 160,000 bushels of wheat were produced in the Oregon country. By an act of the provisional government, wheat was declared legal tender and had a standard value of $1 a bushel. With the rush of the gold-seekers to California, the price soared to $6 a bushel, and by 1849 more than 50 ships had entered the Columbia River seeking supplies of grain. This export commerce provided the economic foundation for building towns and seaports, laying out wagon roads, establishing steamship lines, and constructing railways. For the next half century the Willamette Valley, with its brown loams and silty clay soils, was predominantly "wheat country."

In 1861, gold was discovered in eastern Oregon and backtrailing farmers, attracted by the possibility of finding fertile land near the new diggins, followed the influx of miners to the region. Town sites were staked out and agricultural development began. River steamers plying the Columbia hastened the movement of farmers to the inland plateaus and sagebrush plains. The first wheat grown in this portion of the state, was harvested in 1863 by Andrew Kilgore in Umatilla County. Within a few years, wheat was being sown over a large area of eastern Oregon. Shipping centers sprang up along the river; and when, in the early 1880's, the railroad came through, wheat-growing developed wherever the soil was suitable and shipping possible.

It was inevitable that this extensive single-crop production should make for exhaustion of the light basaltic soils and a consequent decrease in the yield. In time it became necessary to reduce the seeded acreage and to try various plans for restoring fertility. Summer fallowing or dust mulching, a method whereby half of each ranch remains unseeded in alternate years, is now generally adopted, and wheat still remains the principal crop in Oregon. Production in 1937 was 20,424,000 bushels, valued at $18,263,000 or slightly more than 30 per cent of the combined income from all crops in the state. The average yield from the 993,000 acres harvested was 20.6 bushels an acre.

Present-day wheat ranching in the rolling country of eastern Oregon is a highly-mechanized industry. Each spring, tractor-drawn gang-plows, harrows, and drills prepare and seed the moist earth. In late summer, great combines move over the vast fields, reaping and threshing, in a golden haze of chaff and straw, and leaving at measured intervals bags of wheat stacked behind them. Day and night, trucks haul the grain to towering elevators in nearby towns, or to freight sidings and warehouses, for shipment by rail or water to flour mills and export markets.

Of other grains than wheat, the principal crops in 1937 were oats, 10,360,000 bushels, harvested from 280,000 acres; barley, 4,160,000 bushels, from 130,000 acres; corn, 2,178,000 bushels, from 66,000 acres;

and rye, 600,000 bushels, from 48,000 acres. In the same year, such forage crops as clover, timothy, and alfalfa yielded a combined total of 1,428,000 tons, cut from 806,000 acres. Tame hay is now grown on a much greater acreage than wheat; and 242,000 tons of wild hay were cut in 1937 from 220,000 acres, principally in mountain valleys east of the Cascade range and in the Klamath and Harney basins.

From the time farming began at Fort Astoria until 1828, when enough wheat was raised to support the inhabitants, potatoes were the main substitute for bread. As settlement increased and spread it was found that certain portions of the Oregon country were peculiarly adapted to potato culture, notably the Deschutes region, with a soil of volcanic ash and loamy sand, the Klamath Falls district of fine sandy loam, and the sandy silt and humus of Coos County, on the coast. In 1937 Oregon produced 7,840,000 bushels of potatoes on 49,000 acres, or an average of 160 bushels an acre.

There is scarcely a vegetable known to the temperate zone that does not thrive in Oregon. Every ranch has its home garden and truck farming is an important commercial activity in certain parts of the state, particularly on acreage near large towns. Onions head the list of truck garden products, 660,000 sacks being marketed in 1937. Green celery is a close second, with a 1937 output of 234,000 crates, grown chiefly in the middle Columbia and Willamette Valley. Cantaloupes from Douglas and Wasco Counties are of a superior grade.

Describing the Oregon country as he saw it in 1845, the Reverend Gustavus Hines wrote: "Apples, peaches, and other kinds of fruit, flourish, as far as they have been cultivated; and from present appearances, it is quite likely that the time is not far distant, when the country will be well supplied with the various kinds of fruit which grow in the Middle States." The first extensive planting of fruit trees was done at Milwaukie in 1847 by William Meek and the Lewelling brothers, who brought some 800 seedlings and a few grafted trees over the Oregon Trail in boxes fitted inside their covered wagons. The venture paid well. The first box of apples placed on sale in Portland realized $75, and in 1851 four boxes were sold in San Francisco for $500. Seth Lewelling set out the earliest Italian prune orchard in 1858; and the brothers developed a number of distinctive fruit varieties now well known in Oregon—among them the Black Republican, Lincoln, and Bing cherries, the Golden prune, and the Lewelling grape.

Fruit growing has become one of Oregon's major economic activities. Hood River apples, Rogue River pears, The Dalles cherries, and Willamette Valley prunes are famed throughout America and Europe. Only one other state (California) produces more prunes than Oregon, the 1937 yield being 43,000 tons, valued at $1,414,000. Other principal fruit crops of the same year were apples, 3,763,000 bushels, valued at $3,010,000; pears, 3,621,000 bushels, valued at $2,350,000; cherries, 124,000 tons, valued at $1,525,000; grapes, 2,100 tons, valued at $69,300; and peaches, 241,000 bushels, valued at $2,892,000.

Strawberries, raspberries, currants, youngberries, loganberries, and evergreen blackberries thrive in various sections, though the best crops are produced in the moist western valleys. Strawberries constitute the most important item in this list, the 1937 crop amounting to 1,050,000 crates, was raised on 14,000 acres (an average yield of 75 crates to the acre), and valued at $3,518,000. Cranberries have long grown wild, principally on peat-bog land along the coast, but are now profitably cultivated over a large acreage.

Nuts of various kinds, chiefly English walnuts, and filberts, are raised, especially on the sandy loams and "red hill" lands of the Willamette and Tualatin Valleys, one of the few regions of the world adapted to filbert culture. There are approximately 9,000 acres of filbert orchards in Oregon, or 85 per cent of the national total, and about 14,000 acres of bearing walnut trees.

Hops are among the principal agricultural products of the Willamette Valley. High green-hung hop trellises cover thousands of acres in Marion County. Although over-production in recent years has reduced the value of the crop, Oregon continues to produce more hops than any other state in the Union. The value of the 1937 crop exceeded $4,000,000.

Wild flax grew in Oregon before the first white men came, and has been grown there almost continually from the beginning of settlement, but not until recent years has a consistent effort been made to utilize the product commercially. In 1915 a flax plant was established at the state penitentiary; and recently the Federal Government, through the Works Progress Administration, assisted in constructing scutching plants and mills. In 1935, more than 2,000 acres were planted to flax. About 2,000,000 pounds of fiber are annually produced at the state plant.

Seed production provides the farmers of Oregon with some three million dollars of annual income. Nearly a million pounds of alsike clover seed, sown as a soil-restoring rotation crop in wheat growing areas, are marketed annually; and west of the mountains, vegetable seeds are produced on an extensive scale.

Ornamental nursery stock yields almost a million dollars each year for Multnomah County nurserymen alone. Field-grown roses are shipped out of the state in carload lots. Daffodil, tulip, and gladioli farms are numerous in western Oregon, and hothouses with thousands of feet under glass supply cut flowers and bulbs to local and national markets.

Until 1837 the only cattle in the Oregon country belonged to the Hudson's Bay Company, which supplied milk to the settlers but refused to sell any part of its stock to them. With the object of breaking up this monopoly, a group of prominent men in the Willamette Valley, headed by Jason Lee and Ewing Young, organized an expedition to California "to purchase and drive to Oregon a band of neat cattle for the supply of the settlers." The expedition sailed early in February 1837 on the U. S. brig *Loriot,* commanded by William A. Slacum, and returned overland a few months later with some 600 head of cattle and a number of horses, which were distributed among the settlers. The supply of livestock was considerably augmented in 1841, when Joseph Gale and others built the sloop *Star of Oregon* and sailed it from the Columbia River to San Francisco, where they traded their vessel for cattle, horses, mules, and sheep, which they drove north over the wilderness trails to Oregon. Soon thereafter the long "cow columns" of the eastern emigrants began to arrive in the Willamette Valley, and the future of one of Oregon's principal economic resources was permanently assured.

By the early 1870's, cattle ranching had become a firmly established and highly profitable activity in the vast range lands of central and southeastern Oregon. For the next two decades, cattle had almost free run of this semi-arid plateau country, where the bunchgrass grew stirrup-high; and the unfenced area of Harney County in particular contained some of the most extensive ranches and largest herds in the West. But it was not long before sheepmen began to compete for the open range, and violent friction ensued between them and the cattle barons. Sheep were maliciously slaughtered, and their owners retaliated by burning the stacks, barns, and houses of the cattlemen. Into the feud was injected another element inimical to both sheep and cattle ranchers —the invasion of homesteaders with their fences and land-speculators with their townsites. The outcome was defeat for the hitherto dominant cattle kings, restriction of their rights, and a gradual decrease in the size of their herds. However, Harney County has remained a prominent cattle region, and Oregon as a whole is still an important cattle state.

In an estimated total of 945,000 head of cattle in Oregon at the beginning of 1937, nearly 260,000 were cows and heifers kept for milk —a notable contrast to the first little herd, owned by the Hudson's Bay Company, which browsed the moist levels of Sauvie Island more than a century ago. Adjacent to the principal cities and towns are many dairy farms and creameries. The Tillamook, Coos Bay, and other coastal areas, with their perennial green pasturage, are ideal dairying regions, and the irrigated Klamath basin is also an important field.

The first sheep successfully driven across the plains were brought to Oregon in 1844 by Joshua Shaw and his son. Saxon and Spanish merinos were introduced in 1848, and purebred merinos in 1851. The earliest herds were confined to the western region, particularly the Willamette Valley, but by 1860 many had been established in eastern Oregon. As the favorable climate and range conditions became better known, sheepmen from California and Australia swarmed into the State, and by 1893 the herds had increased to two and a half million head. After rising to 3,319,000 in 1930, the number declined to an estimated total of 2,245,000 at the beginning of 1937. Besides the marketing of mutton, a large annual clip of wool is sold. The 1937 production was more than 17,000,000 pounds, the average weight per fleece being 8½ pounds. Shipping of wool began in 1862, when the surplus clip of that year, amounting to 100,000 pounds, was sent from the Willamette Valley to New England. Many settlers brought goats with them across the plains, but commercial goat-raising is a comparatively recent enterprise. The most prevalent breed is the Angora, valued for its mohair wool. Today more than half of the mohair wool produced in the United States comes from Oregon.

Every pioneer farmer raised hogs to provide fat for soap, candles, and cooking, and meat for his table. Purebred swine were brought to the state in 1868, after which the importation of fine hogs became common. The number of hogs on Oregon farms at the beginning of 1937 was estimated at 242,000 as against only 169,000 in 1935.

Poultry has always been indispensable in Oregon farm life, since the first leghorns were introduced in 1834. Not until the present century, however, were eggs and poultry produced on a large scale. The temperate Willamette Valley is a favored area. Commercial turkey raising is comparatively new, but with its favorable summer climate and freedom from disease the state has already become an important producing area.

In 1935 there were 64,826 individual farms in Oregon occupying

17,358,000 acres or 28.4 per cent of the state's entire land area, and with a collective value for land and buildings of $448,712,000. Of these farms, 17,206 were under 20 acres each in size, 30,498 were under 50 acres, 40,782 were under 100 acres, and 3,046 comprised 1,000 acres or more; the average acreage per farm being 267.8. In the combined farm area, about 3,100,000 acres were used for crops and about 12,000,000 acres consisted of pasture land. Of the total number of farms, 50,046 were operated by full or part owners, 715 by managers, and 14,065 by tenants. The total farm population numbered 248,767; and of the persons working on farms, family labor accounted for 83,102 and hired help for 15,287. Considerably more than 25,000 farm operators worked part time to pay off their farms during the year. Farms to the number of 29,740 or 45.9 per cent of the total, were carrying a combined mortgage debt of $119,670,000.

Although much sub-marginal land cultivated during boom years in the "high desert" of south central Oregon, and in the remote hill regions elsewhere, is now abandoned, the total acreage of land in farms increased 50 per cent in the quarter-century from 1910 to 1935 and more than 22 per cent in the decade of 1925-35. Yet the total value of land and buildings declined sharply—from $675,213,000 in 1920 and $630,828,000 in 1930 to $448,712,000 in 1935. The number of mortgaged farms decreased from 51.5 per cent of the total in 1930 to 45.9 per cent in 1935, with an accompanying decrease of nearly $2,500,000 in the total farm mortgage debt. The number of farms operated by tenants increased from 9,790 in 1930 to 14,065 in 1935; and in the latter year 21.7 per cent of the total number of farms and 17.1 per cent of all land in farms were under tenant operation.

Government irrigation projects in the Owyhee, Klamath, Umatilla, Vale, and three other districts have done much to increase the agricultural resources of Oregon. More than a million acres are now under irrigation in the state. Summer irrigation is rapidly supplementing normal winter rainfall in portions of the Willamette and Hood River Valleys.

The State Agricultural College at Corvallis, founded 1868, has played a role of incalculable importance in Oregon's agricultural activities. Besides the specialized training given to thousands of young men and women, it conducts experimental farms in various parts of the state, maintains a radio broadcasting station, publishes numerous bulletins, and contributes in numerous other ways to the improvement of farming and the conditions of farm life in general. A state agricultural experiment station has assisted Oregon farmers for more than 50 years, and the first quarter-century of farm agent work in the state was celebrated in 1937. The State Agricultural Society, founded 1854, was the first of several state-wide organizations of farmers, the most important of which is now the Oregon unit of the National Grange. The annual State Fair at Salem and Pacific International Livestock Exposition at Portland are attended by farmers and stock breeders from every part of Oregon.

Industry, Commerce and Labor

INDUSTRY AND COMMERCE: Timber is the dominant factor in Oregon's industrial and commercial life, and activities connected with it spread over all but the grasslands and the high plateaus in the southeastern section. So important is timber and its products that there is hardly a community, in western Oregon at least, whose prosperity does not depend upon it. Even the state's tax-supported schools derive a good portion of their income from the forests. The importance of the industry is symbolized in the state shield, which the founding fathers inscribed with a forest and a ship.

Water-powered mills, with up-and-down mulay saws, cut the boards for Oregon's earliest frame houses. The first steam-driven mill, with a circular saw, was built in Portland in 1850, while teams of oxen were busy hauling logs down skidroads which are now Portland streets. Along the shores of the Columbia, inland as far as Hood River, were great stands of timber. Here the lumber industry had its first real beginnings. Skidroads were pushed from the river banks into the dense forest. Over these the bull teams, driven by swaggering bullwhackers, hauled the big butts to water, where they were made into rafts and floated down to the mills.

By 1890, when the exhaustion of the forests of the Great Lakes region was in sight, Oregon began to be prominent as a lumber state. The lumberjacks followed the timber west. It is common to find loggers in Oregon today whose fathers helped cut the pine of Michigan, and whose grandfathers helped fell and saw the spruce of Maine.

Timber owners and sawmill operators, too, came from the lake states to Oregon and built mills in the Willamette Valley and pushed logging railroads into the foothills. The Coos and Tillamook Bay districts were developed. When, later, lumber operators from the southern states arrived, because the timber there was giving out, they found Oregon forest land mostly taken up.

Shortly after 1900, widespread corruption in the lumber industry was exposed in the great Oregon Timber Fraud cases. Men grew wealthy by acquiring forest areas through a system of "dummies", names of non-existent people or of persons who for a few dollars signed fraudulent homestead applications. A happy outcome was the setting aside later of thousands of acres of forest, formerly public domain and open to home-steading, to form national reserves within the state.

In eastern Oregon the lumber industry was slower in starting but once begun it gathered great speed. There the timber is mainly pine. Some of the largest sawmills in the world are now located at Burns, Bend, and Klamath Falls. Others are near Baker and La Grande.

Waste has marked the lumber industry throughout its history, but today pulp and paper manufacturing, which takes care of much lumber refuse, seems to be developing into a major aspect of the lumber industry. Furniture making, utilizing Oregon oak, alder, maple and walnut, is growing in importance. Several hundred persons in the Coos Bay area are employed in making novelties from myrtlewood. In Marsh-field and Coquille the manufacture of battery separators from the acid-proof Port Orford cedar is a leading industry. This unique wood is also used in airplane construction. In general, the utilization of forest prod-ucts is greater in the pine than in the fir regions. One reason is that pine is easier to "work" than fir. Much low-grade pine goes into box "shooks", the pieces from which boxes are made. One pine mill furnishes all the curtain rollers used by a large manufacturer of automobiles. Small pieces of pine are made into toys. One mill specializes in ironing boards.

Until 1930 the tendency was towards larger and larger sawmills. Some of the pine mills in Bend and Klamath Falls have a rated eight-hour capacity of 300,000 feet of lumber. A fir mill at Marshfield has a capacity of 650,000 feet in the same space of time. Of late years, however, because of the depression and because of the increased overhead costs in large mills when on curtailed production, and because of the loss of the European market for heavy timbers, few large mills have been built. Instead, many cutting only from 10,000 to 50,000 feet a shift have gone into operation, using logs hauled on trucks which have sup-planted logging railroads.

The income from forest products in Oregon is about 177 million dollars annually. Some 40,000 persons are employed who receive in wages and salaries approximately 56 million dollars.

Fishing is still an important industry in Oregon, particularly so on the Columbia River at Astoria, at Warrenton, and at The Dalles; and on the Pacific Coast at Tillamook, Newport, Reedsport, and the cities on Coos Bay. Salmon is the leading catch, with halibut, pilchards, cod, steelhead trout, shad, and oysters important in the order named.

The salmon-wheels in the Columbia River, a few of which are still standing, are reminders of a past made obsolete by law. Formerly thousands of salmon were taken in these ingenious contraptions. However, horse-seining is still done on the lower river, where teams, neck deep in water, pull in nets filled with struggling fish. The animals, most of them old discarded work-horses, seem to be rejuvenated by the brine. Astoria is the largest fish-canning center in the state. From here a fleet of boats puts out to troll or seine in the river, or off the coast. For the past few years the catching and processing of pilchards for oil and fertilizer have become important activities during a two-month season at Astoria and Coos Bay. This industry is so new that no reliable data on it have as yet been collected. However, in 1936, a tax of 50 cents per ton on pilchards taken in Oregon waters netted about $35,000. The annual yield of all Oregon fisheries is about 25,000,000 pounds, valued at over $2,600,000. The pilchard products are used locally and along the Pacific Coast; salmon and allied products, canned, smoked, dried, or kippered, are shipped to all parts of the world.

From mining, Oregon receives a small but steady income. Gold, copper, silver, and lead rank in the order named. Mercury production equals that of gold in value, or about $350,000 annually. Three thousand persons are engaged in the production of minerals in the state, and the total income is approximately $4,500,000 a year. Gold was Oregon's earliest mineral discovery. In eastern and southern parts of the state prospectors are still active in the mountains and along streams. Tales of "lost" mines persist as part of local folklore. In Curry, Baker, Jackson and Josephine counties are many ruins of "ghost towns," built hurriedly and as swiftly abandoned and forgotten.

Manufacturing in Oregon has made slow but steady progress. The lumber industry plays the role of a general stimulant through its demand for logging locomotives, donkey-engines, steel cables, blocks and timber-cutting tools, much of which equipment is made in the state. In Portland a factory, in business since 1887, builds 13,000 stoves and 2,500 furnaces a year. Another plant specializes in automatic stokers that are sold all over the world. Still another makes 2,000,000 tin cans annually to meet the demands of the local fruit and fish-canning industries. Woolen goods have been made since earliest days. Though wool in great quantities and of excellent grade is still produced in the state, the industry has lagged somewhat in late years.

Oregon grows a fine grade of flax fiber, yet mills have come and gone for fifty years. In 1935 an Oregon Flax Committee was appointed to investigate the industry and make recommendations. In October of that year the Works Progress Administration consented to earmark money to build three flax-processing plants in the state. In December the Agricultural Adjustment Administration granted a federal subsidy of $5 a ton to flax growers. Committees which were granted WPA funds for plants, furnished land and contributed cash to the enterprise, while farmers and business men, backed by their bankers, organized cooperatives. The state engaged experts to supervise construction of the plants and to help the cooperatives get started. The WPA agreed to construct the plants and run them for one year, whereupon the state assumed responsibility.

Oregon exports, like the state's commerce in general, depend on the activity of the timber industry, which in turn influences agriculture. The bulk of water-borne shipments consists of lumber, flour, wheat, paper, and canned goods, including salmon, in the order named. Next in rank are logs, apples, dried fruits, pulp-wood, hides and leather; then plywood, cereals, doors, milk, vegetables, cheese, and butter. Cattle, sheep, horses, and hogs on the hoof, poultry and poultry products, and wool in the raw, are shipped chiefly by freight car.

The total commerce of the Port of Portland, Oregon's chief commercial terminal, which handles by far the largest share of the state's shipments, was 7,353,378 tons in 1938. Some 1717 vessels entered and cleared, carrying a tonnage of 5,556,535 tons. Total port commerce value in 1938 was $273,258,096. Commerce along the inland waterways and by train, truck and electric line, with shipments from Tillamook and Coos bays, added vastly to the state's commercial figures.

The Bonneville dam on the Columbia, forty miles east of Portland, completed by the Federal Government in 1937, had an immediate capacity of 115,250 horsepower, and foundations for 576,000 additional horsepower. This gave inestimable impetus to Oregon industry and commerce. The largest development to date (1940) is that of the American Aluminum Company that has purchased a 300 acre site and has scheduled the opening of a plant in 1941. Public Utility Districts for use of Bonneville power are being organized in many parts of the state, and many private companies are negotiating for the use of power from the dam.

LABOR: Romantic historians of the great migration to Oregon have woven a stirring tale of a land-hungry yeomanry carving an empire out of the wilderness. The covered wagons, however, brought with them also a number of mechanics and artisans driven from their homes by chaotic industrial conditions in the East. In Europe the great period of unrest following the Napoleonic Wars set in motion a wave of emigration that flooded America's Atlantic seaboard with thousands of indigent workers. Wage scales toppled and standards of living fell as the Europeans entered every field of labor.

American workers, faced with the specters of unemployment and poverty, chose westward migration. By the middle of the century the trek to the Northwest was under way. In the wagon trains were Oregon's first printers. These men carried pamphlets of craft unionism among their gear, and became the pioneers of the Oregon labor movement. From Oregon and Washington territories they came in 1853 to Portland, then a town of about 1,000 inhabitants, and organized a Typographical Society along the lines of the successful National Typographical Union formed in the East in 1850. Portland soon became an important shipping point, and in 1868 the longshoremen set up their Portland Protective Union. This was Oregon's second labor association.

Meanwhile there had arisen the problem of competitive Chinese labor which was to harry the white workers of Oregon for many years. Driven out of California by anti-Chinese feeling, the Orientals flocked north as far as Portland. The Burlingame Treaty, ratified in 1867, which opened the country to coolies recruited for railroad construction, greatly increased the number of yellow laborers. A crowded labor market resulted, followed by decreased wages, at a time of rising living costs.

White laborers, threatened with the loss of their jobs, responded by boycotting those who employed the Asiatics. Feeling ran high and for the first time in Oregon a line was sharply drawn between those for and against Orientals. Political destinies were shaped by the conflict, which was fought out in the decades following, industry as a whole staunchly favoring the low-wage coolie labor, and the white workers forming organizations to effect its exclusion. In 1886 the anti-Chinese agitation was at its height. Mayor Gates of Portland called a meeting of protest in favor of the Chinese, but Sylvester Pennoyer took over the meeting and declared that the Chinese must go. Partly because of his stand on this question he was elected governor of the state at the following election. Heroic attempts were made to organize a central labor body which might better handle the issue, but a confusion of economic and political aims prevented united action.

Finally, however, labor did draw itself together within a framework

URAL, U. S. POST OFFICE, ONTARIO

OREGON TRAIL IN 1843

DISCOVERY OF THE COLUMBIA RIVER

ASTORIA IN 18

DEL PALMER HOUSE, DAYTON

LADD AND REED FARM, REEDVILLE

UMATILLA, 1864

ATTLE RANCH

OWYHEE PROJECT FARM

MAIN INTAKE KLAMATH COUNTY PROJECT

IRRIGATED FIELD, OWYHEE PROJECT

ENTRAL OREGON SHEEP **RANCH**

CENTRAL OREGON SHEEP HERDER

OREGON STATE CAPITOL, SALEM

DAYTON FARM FAMILY LABOR CAMP

FARM BOY

DIANS FISHING FOR SALMON, 1856

COLUMBIA RIVER SALMON FISHERIES

PILCHARD FISHING FLEET

FISH NETS DRYIN

ERIAL VIEW, PORTLAND

AERIAL VIEW, OREGON STATE COLLEGE

OLD ADMINISTRATI
BUILDING, O.S.C

DEADY HALL,
U. OF O.

STATE FORESTRY BUILDING, SALEM

UNION STATION, PORTLAND

FIRST PRESBYTERIAN
CHURCH, PORTLAND

TEMPLE BETH ISRAEL
PORTLAND

of united craft associations. These weathered the panic of 1873, and by 1882 were ten in number. The unions learned to make use of the strike, and, although most walkouts were lost, some, among them the strike of the harnessmakers in 1889, gave union labor confidence and a measure of badly needed prestige.

The period between 1880 and 1890 was one of tremendous expansion in Oregon, and alternately harsh and kind to labor. As the Northern Pacific Railroad, completed in 1883, linked the state to the great industrial cities of the East, Portland grew from a town of 25,000 to a marketing and shipping center with three times that many people. Building construction reached unprecedented levels. Commodity prices continued to mount until the minor depression of 1884.

Samuel Gompers visiting Portland in 1883 had to raise his voice to make himself heard above the noise of the building operations in the booming city. But he achieved his purpose, that of leading Portland's 300 organized craftsmen into forming the Portland Federated Trades Assembly, the first central labor body in Oregon with a completely unified membership. The assembly found itself opposed by the Knights of Labor, James Sovereign's organization, established since 1880, which had 600 members. The two bodies, one committed to rigid crafts unionism, the other to the policy of including all craftsmen in the same organization, engaged in a struggle for control of all Portland labor. The Knights were temporarily left in possession of the field, and in 1885 the Portland Federated Trades Assembly was dissolved.

Although Congress passed the Chinese Exclusion Act in 1882, this legislation did not affect the Orientals already in the country. Their number was augmented by smugglers, who found the closed immigration channels easy to circumvent. Thus, during the depression of 1884, labor found itself, in spite of the exclusion law, competing with an ever increasing number of Asiatics. Knights of Labor organizers led Oregon's aroused workers to action and in 1885 a camp of Chinese coolies was attacked by a mob at Albina. Oregon's Governor called the militia, which refused to serve. More riots followed, an anti-Chinese convention was called together, the boycott was again invoked and for the first time in Oregon dynamite was used as a class-war weapon. As the result of these events the Knights of Labor dominated the situation when Samuel Gompers returned to Portland in 1887.

All attempts to revive the Portland Federated Trades Assembly, dead for two years, had failed, but Gompers, now representing the American Federation of Labor (formed the year before) succeeded in bringing the central body back to life. The A. F. of L. had only 250,000 members in the United States to pit against the Knights of Labor's national organization of 700,000 members, but the influence of the Knights was on the wane in Oregon, while that of the A. F. of L. now rose rapidly. In 1889 the Portland Federated Trades Assembly showed its strength through a boycott in favor of locked-out brewery workers. In 1890 the A. F. of L. called a general strike to obtain the eight-hour day, and Portland's union carpenters won their fight, though they had to submit to a wage-cut in return for victory.

The 1890's were not happy years for Oregon workers. The "hard times" of 1893-95 were levying a heavy toll upon the whole country, and the plight of organized labor in general was desperate. Oregon's unemployed grew in numbers, hunger marchers stormed Portland's city hall, and hungry men joined Coxey's Army. The state's railroad workers walked out in sympathy with Gene Debs' great transportation strike and lost their jobs when the strike failed.

In its struggle for existence the Portland Federated Trades Assembly clung to its A. F. of L. affiliation, and fought off the threat of the newly formed Central Labor Council for control of Oregon's workers. It called a state labor congress to devise means of relief, and again obtained undisputed leadership of the battered labor ranks, with new union charters granted.

The need of a state labor body had become apparent and in 1902, when 17 strikes disrupted Oregon industry, 175 delegates, representing about 10,000 workers, met in Portland and formed the Oregon Federation of Labor. The Federation stood for economic and political reform, and was largely instrumental in obtaining legislation for the establishment of the state bureau of labor in 1903. Made strong by the Federation, craft unionism felt more secure. Nothing now appeared to challenge the authority of the A. F. of L.

However, the idea of the One Big Union advocating that labor, to be effective, ought to set aside all distinctions of craft, color, sex and nationality, and unite in one coordinated body began to attract attention. This idea was reaffirmed by the Industrial Workers of the World, a revolutionary organization formed in Chicago in 1905. Soon the world was to hear much of the I. W. W., or the "Wobblies" as members were nicknamed.

The genius of the organization was "Big Bill" Haywood, a former miner who knew conditions in western mining and logging camps. The I. W. W. seemed peculiarly fitted to conditions in the Far West, and among the miners and lumberjacks of Oregon the influence of Haywood's organization was soon paramount. In 1907 that part of the state's lumber industry centering about Portland was paralyzed by the greatest strike in its history. The walk-out was brief, and although no recognition was gained, strikers pointed to increased wages and improved working conditions as results of the dispute.

The I. W. W. remained a power in the lumber industry until war measures in 1917, gave to its members all they were fighting for, including the eight-hour day, better sanitation and working conditions, and beds provided by operators so no man would have to carry his blankets on his back in order to obtain a job. With its objectives gone, the organization lost its militancy and dwindled. However, it came back again after the Armistice, when the threat of lowered wages and the return of the longer working day again menaced. Lumber and logging operators, with the aid of the 4L, first a war-measure organization and later a "Company Union," made strenuous war on the I. W. W., which in 1919 retaliated with a general strike. This was unsuccessful, and after much violence and bloodshed, and sharp division of sentiment among the lumber workers, the I. W. W. gradually lost footing.

The 4L—the Loyal Legion of Loggers and Lumbermen—was formed by the Federal Government through the War Board to do away with unrest and dissatisfaction in the lumber industry of the Pacific Coast, and thus to speed up the production to meet war-time needs. Barring nobody because of previous affiliations, it was organized in the summer of 1917 and soon included all persons in any manner engaged in camps or sawmills. As long as the government ran the 4L, peace was maintained between the workers and their employers. After the end of the war, however, most of the loggers as well as many of the sawmill workers dropped from the rolls. Members who remained belonged to the better paid categories among the lumber workers. After 1919 the Loyal Legion never possessed the confidence or support of the great mass of workers, and is regarded by many as having taken on the character of a "company union". The 4L continued to function in some sort of manner until, pressed by changing labor conditions, it reorganized under the name of the Industrial Employees Union, with an influence largely confined to the pine-producing districts.

In recent years only two major strikes have taken place in Oregon—the International Longshoremen's Association strike in 1934, for better conditions, and that of the Sawmill and Timber Workers' Union, in 1934-35. They were settled by the aid of Federal arbitration. Both disputes were tinged with the passions and prejudices of extremists on the sides of labor and capital alike, but led to improved working conditions and union recognition.

The Oregon Federation of Labor with a present membership of approximately 70,000 represents craft unionism in Oregon, with its corresponding purposes and motives. The idea of industrial unionism, or the vertical plan of organization as opposed to the horizontal, has been powerfully revived through the C.I.O. headed by John L. Lewis; and the late 1930's in Oregon have been marked by spectacular struggles between the two union systems. By initiative process a rigid anti-picketing law was adopted at the general election of 1938.

Transportation

IN the late spring of 1837 a little company of men and women, sent
out from Boston to reinforce the four lonely brethren at the Methodist mission station in the Willamette Valley, arrived in the lower
waters of the Columbia, after a voyage of ten months by way of Cape
Horn and the Sandwich Islands. Near the mouth of the Willamette
River they were met by Jason Lee, who had made the journey of 75
miles from the mission by canoe, and with him they paddled up the river
to the station. In mid-July two women among the newcomers were
united in marriage to Lee and his co-worker Cyrus Shepard. "As the
sickly season came on," according to a contemporary record, the newly-
married couples "performed two tours through the country, for the
benefit of their health." The first was a ten-days' journey on horseback,
southward along the Willamette River, eastward to the headwaters of
the Molalla, northward to Champoeg, and back to the mission. Very
shortly thereafter they set out on foot "to perform a land journey to
the Pacific coast," following a trail some 80 miles long from the valley
to the ocean that had been used by Indians and by retired Hudson's Bay
trappers. Though they found this route "exceedingly difficult, on account of the abruptness of the ascending and descending, and the numerous large trees that had fallen across it," the party arrived at the Pacific
in four days; and the same length of time was required "in crossing the
mountains, jumping the logs, fording the streams, and traveling over the
prairies" on the return. By the end of August they were back at the
Willamette station, "better qualified, from the improvement of their
health, to pursue the business of their calling."

Most of the common methods of travel available in the Oregon
country a century ago are represented in the above brief narrative—by
canoe on the waterways, by horseback in the valley bottoms and level
open country, afoot through the mountains and other forested areas over
narrow trails cut by Indians and trappers. With the coming of the
homeseekers, however, the principal trails were rapidly broadened into
roads. Thousands of immigrants in ox-drawn wagons, with their leaders

and guides on horseback, eventually fashioned a main route of travel from the lower Missouri River to the Willamette Valley. In its far western course this route traversed the northeastern corner of what is now the State of Oregon, entering from the valley of the Snake River near the latter's confluence with the Malheur, and continuing past the sites of Baker, La Grande, and Pendleton to the junction of the Walla Walla River with the Columbia. This latter point was the end of the original Oregon Trail, the rest of the journey being accomplished by boat and portage down the Columbia. But in 1843 a roadway was broken along the south bank of that river as far west as The Dalles; and in the following year a route came into use from the site of La Grande over the Blue Mountains to the Umatilla, along the latter to the Columbia, and thence to The Dalles. From this point westward, the river provided the only means of transportation until 1845, when Samuel Barlow and Philip Foster cut a crude wagon road through the forests and over the precipitous slopes south of Mount Hood to Willamette Falls at the site of Oregon City. In 1846 they improved the grades and secured a toll franchise. Travelers using this road of 85 miles in length paid tolls of $5 a wagon and $1 for each head of livestock. Today part of the course is followed by the Mount Hood Loop Highway.

A second road, completed in 1846, led into the Willamette region by way of the Malheur River valley and the Klamath country, thence through the mountains and northward to the upper Willamette. By this time relatively short stretches of primitive road had been constructed between various adjacent settlements not connected by waterways. Some of these were community affairs, built by the settlers to provide means of local intercourse; others were commercial enterprises, operating under toll franchise. By 1846 there was a wagon road from Portland to the fertile Tualatin Plains. Many of the early roads led to river landings where boat service was available. Bridges, too, began to be built. On May 8, 1850, according to a local record, "the court proceeded to let by public outcry the bridge across the river near Hillsborough immediately below the forks of Dary and McKays creek where the former Frame bridge stood"; and another bridge was built across the Yamhill River, at the site of Lafayette, in 1851.

Popular demands for adequate mail service hastened the transformation of trails into vehicular roadways. A stagecoach line began operations in 1851 up and down the Willamette Valley and to points in southern Oregon; this line was taken over by the Wells Fargo company four years later. In 1857 a Concord coach made the run of about 50 miles from Portland to Salem in one day. Larger vehicles, some of them drawn by six horses, came into use as the roads were gradually improved. During the early 1860's connections were established with California stage lines, and fast service was instituted to adjacent valley and mountain points.

Until well along toward the middle of the 19th century, freighting on the Columbia River was chiefly controlled by the Hudson's Bay Company, which operated fleets of large barges for carrying furs from the upper tributaries of the Columbia down to the company's general depot at Fort Vancouver, where the pelts were examined, dried, and packed for shipment to London. Each of these barges had a cargo capacity of five or six tons, and was manned by a crew of at least six French-Canadian or half-breed oarsmen. At the Cascades, the boats and their cargoes were carried across a short portage, while the rapids below were "shot" by the sturdy voyageurs. Many of the early homeseekers and their belongings were transported down the river in these barges. The Hudson's Bay Company long maintained a similar service on the Willamette River as well.

There were few steamboats on either river before 1850. In that year the *Columbia,* 90 feet long, was launched at Astoria and began operating on a semi-weekly schedule between Astoria and Oregon City, on the Willamette. This service was supplemented later in the same year by a larger vessel, the *Lot Whitcomb,* built and launched at Milwaukie, near Portland. Steamer service above the falls at Oregon City reached Salem in 1853 and Eugene in 1857. At Portland, ocean-going vessels loaded shipments for California, the Sandwich Islands, and eastern ports by way of Cape Horn.

Wagon wheels were still creaking over the mountain passes when pioneer promoters in the Northwest began to organize railroad companies. In the late 1850's, Joseph S. Ruckel and Harrison Olmstead gave Oregon its first rail service, selecting as their scene of operations the portage trail around the Cascades of the Columbia River. Here, in the summer of 1859, four and a half miles of wooden track were laid, between the site of Bonneville and what is now Cascade Locks; and over this track, mules and horses pulled trains of four or five small cars. A few months later the wooden rails were given a bearing surface of sheet iron, and the *Oregon Pony,* first steam locomotive to be built on the Pacific coast, began transporting amazed immigrants past the Cascades in a cloud of sparks and steam and smoke. The Union Transportation Company, later reorganized as the Oregon Steam Navigation

Company, also came into being in 1859. Starting operations with eight small river boats, it eventually acquired the portage railroad at the Cascades and another higher up along the Columbia between The Dalles and the mouth of the Deschutes River.

Oregon's railroad history begins with a project for a line from Oregon to connect with the railroad already built from California to the East. This intention resulted in plans for two lines, one from Portland up the east side of the Willamette River, the other on the west side. A group sponsoring each plan sought for land grants from the Federal Government, and a conflict developed between the "Eastsiders" and the "Westsiders" which involved much lobbying and trickery. In 1868 both broke ground for their lines. A Kentuckian, Ben Holladay, a picturesque character typical of the financiers of his time, thrust himself into this struggle and pushed the fortunes of the East Side road. The backers of the other line came at last to an agreement with Holladay that victory should go to the line that first completed twenty miles of track. Holladay won, and the rival road was sold to him. His road, the Oregon and California, had, however, been built only to Roseburg when, in 1873, financial difficulties blocked further construction.

Henry Villard, whose gift for organization was of much importance in the development of Oregon, was a German-American who had been a newspaper reporter in the 1859 gold rush to Colorado and in the Civil War. He had come to Oregon to represent German bond-holders in Holladay's enterprises. Villard took over the Oregon and California Railroad, and resumed the building of the line. It reached Ashland in 1884 and was extended over the Siskiyous to connect with San Francisco and the East in 1887, after Villard's control of it had ended.

Villard also acquired the Oregon Steam Navigation Company, which controlled traffic on the Columbia River, and, reorganizing it as the Oregon Railway and Navigation Company, began building a line on the Oregon bank of the Columbia, intending to link it with a road being built northwestward across Idaho by the Union Pacific. That road, however, refused to join its tracks with Villard's. With Eastern backing, Villard managed to gain control of the Northern Pacific, then being built from Minneapolis toward the West. Confronting this opposition, the Oregon Short Line (Union Pacific) and the O. R. & N. joined in 1884. Oregon now had its outlets to the East and to California.

The period from 1890 until well into the present century was one of almost continual railroad expansion in the state. With trunk lines established, branch lines were extended up many valleys where the settlers had relied on stagecoaches or steamboats. Astoria, the state's oldest city, had no railroad until 1898. Not until 1911 were coyotes on the high plateaus of central Oregon startled by steam whistles, and then the air was made doubly shrill by the construction race to Bend between the Hill and Harriman lines. Marshfield waited until April 5, 1918, to greet its first train. Burns, center of the cattle country, had to wait until 1924.

But the smell of gasoline was already heavy in the air. The good roads movement opposed at the outset by many who were to benefit most from it, was well under way by 1910. Auto travel demanded speedy and accessible highways. Presently the first of the one-man stage and truck lines appeared, automobiles that bumped over the still-dusty roads at 25 miles an hour, stopping anywhere and everywhere for passengers and freight, and delivering them to cities or remote mountain hamlets. Ribbons of asphalt, macadam, and concrete radiated from the more populous centers, and stretched out a few miles at a time across and up and down the state. The Columbia River Highway was begun and completed. The Pacific Highway became a hard-surface reality in 1932. By the end of 1939, there were almost 50,000 miles of road in the state, of which about 5,900 had medium or high type improvement.

Meanwhile the rail carriers were entering the bus and truck transport business and were pulling up rails that had outlasted their usefulness. Today, there are innumerable trucking lines, both interstate and intrastate. Much of the inland freight trade of Oregon's coast communities was first made possible by trucking companies, and the vast spaces of southeastern Oregon are still served entirely by motor.

Oregon was quick to grasp the significance of air transport. No sooner had stunt flying in crude planes become a part of state and county fair programs than adventurous individuals began buying machines for private use. Pastures near population centers became landing fields. As these pioneers showed the possibilities of flying, progressive cities started building airports. By 1936 there were 32 established airports in 31 cities. Three of these—Portland, Medford and Pendleton—are transcontinental lines and many of the others have been recognized as intrastate ports. There are also many emergency landing fields. In recent years the United States Forest Service has used planes for detecting and fighting forest fires.

The year 1936 saw the development of important Oregon airports, when the Works Progress Administration allocated one and one-half million dollars for their modernization and improvement. The new Portland airport was established on the Columbia River and the Medford, Pendleton, and Astoria ports were improved.

Some 60 steamboat lines, operating in the coastwise and intercoastal trade have ports of call in Astoria and Portland; with the early completion of improvement to the river channel below Bonneville Dam, The Dalles is expected to become an important deep-water port. A total of 7,763,683 tons of outgoing vessel freight crossed the Columbia River bar in 1934; rafted lumber reached 4,318,906 tons; a total of well over 12 million tons for the year.

Steamboating on the Columbia and lower Willamette Rivers is still carried on by a few combination stern-wheel freight and towboats, craft whose construction recalls the days when rivers were the chief lanes of commerce and travel. There are also three small passenger boats plying six times a week, between Portland and Astoria. They call at way ports on both sides of the river and a trip on one of them recalls the old steamboating days.

Racial Elements

OREGON'S racial background is principally American. The first
white inhabitants—the hunters and trappers, explorers, traders
and farmers of 1800 to 1820, were either American-born or American
in their general outlook, habits and ambitions. The Hudson's Bay Company, which established Fort Vancouver in 1824-25, though British-
controlled and in part British manned, employed many French-Canadians who, when their terms of service expired, settled on French Prairie
in Marion County, where their descendants can be found today. The
Hudson's Bay Company also prepared the way for the missionary settlers, zealous Americans who endeavored to improve the lot of the Oregon Indians.

In the wake of the Methodist missionaries, beginning about 1840, a
few American settlers began to cross the great plains, the number increasing until the first large immigration arrived in 1843. From then
on, almost every year showed a steady numerical increase, Missouri
being the leading contributor to the population flow. These settlers were
looking for economic opportunities more favorable than could be found
in the older sections of the country and, regardless of their diverse
national origins—German, English, Irish, Dutch, Scotch, Scandinavian,
French and Italian—they were already Americans in their general outlook, habits and ambitions.

During the 1850's gold hunters, adventurers and settlers drifted into
Oregon from California; merchants and mechanics, laborers and professional men arrived from New England, the eastern seaboard and the
Mississippi Basin, seeking more favorable economic opportunities than
could be found in those regions.

In 1860 Oregon had a population of 52,465, which increased by
decades—to 90,923; 174,768; 317,704; 413,536; 672,765; and 783,389,
bringing the 1930 population to 953,786. In 1860 the per cent of
foreign born was 9.8, which mounted to 18.0 per cent in 1890 and fell
again to 11.6 per cent in 1930. The increase of aliens corresponds to
the period of railroad construction when swarms of common laborers,

including Asiatics, were imported; and their decrease to the period of adjustment and changing economic conditions that followed. Of the 11.6 per cent of foreign born in Oregon in 1930, almost one-third came from English-speaking countries; 13,528 from Great Britain and North Ireland; 2,802 from the Irish Free State; and 17,946 from Canada.

Immigration to Oregon had two peaks—1880-90, when 142,936 people arrived, and 1900-10, when newcomers numbered 259,229. The first increase was largely due to the completion of the transcontinental railroads and the construction of local lines, affording easy transportation for settlers; while the second was in the main the result of the World's Fair held in Portland in 1905, which brought vast crowds of visitors, many of whom remained or returned later to the state to live; the development of irrigation which opened large tracts of land for settlement; and the modern exploitation of Oregon's great lumber resources, with the consequent growth of all business.

Of Oregon's 953,736 total population in 1930, 937,029 were white and 16,707 dark-skinned; 392,629 were born in the state and 450,667 in other states; and 110,440 were foreign-born. The native Oregonians, though less than half of the number of inhabitants, comprise, culturally and economically, the dominant elements in the state. The character of the early settlers has, in numberless instances, been inherited by their descendants, and pioneer names abound in the register of Oregon industrialists, merchants, bankers, agriculturists, and public and professional men. The thoroughly American character of Oregon's population is emphasized by the few exceptions to the rule. Only in isolated instances do groups of people maintain cultural habits that distinguish them from the majority. Among these are the Basques of the southeastern part of the state; the Germans of Aurora; the Finns and Scandinavians in and about Astoria; and the Chinese of Portland. Of Oregon's 110,440 foreign-born, 12,913 came from Germany; 5,507 from Finland; 22,033 from Denmark, Norway and Sweden, and 2,075 from China. The number of Basques is negligible. Japanese number 4,958, but they have adopted occidental customs to a surprising degree. The negroes, numbering 2,234, are prone to live in colonies. All children in Oregon, regardless of hue of skin, attend the same schools, and restrictions because of color in business or occupational activity are non-existent. Indians number 4,776, largely on reservations, the most important of which are the Klamath, Umatilla, and Warm Springs (*see INDIANS AND ARCHEOLOGY*). There remains a small sprinkling of Mexicans, Filipinos and Hindus, insignificant in numbers.

In Oregon, as in other states, there has been a shift in population from country to city. In 1890 the urban inhabitants constituted 26.8 per cent; in 1900, 32.2; in 1910, 45.6; in 1920, 49.9; and in 1930, 51.3 per cent. The total urban population in that year was 489,746, while the rural numbered 464,040. The tendency of urban centers to absorb the native-born rural citizen is, of course, a familiar phenomenon. The residence of the foreign-born, because of his occupation, is usually determined before he leaves his homeland. Most of the state's immigrants from England, Scotland, Wales, and the north of Ireland, flocked to Portland because they were there likely to find work at the industrial pursuits in which they were skilled. Similarly, a large portion of the immigrants from Scandinavia, Russia, Italy and Poland selected this city as their residence, largely because it afforded them the most promising chances to make a livelihood in ways to which they were accustomed. Immigrants from Denmark, the Netherlands, Switzerland and other agricultural countries, drifted to the dairy, fruit and farming districts by preference; while Finns, and to some degree Russians, Swedes and Norwegians, sought regions where fishing, lumbering and sailing were the principal occupations.

Among groups that differ from the rest of the population are the Basques of Malheur County. More than forty years ago an immigrant from the Basque provinces in Spain visited the Jordan valley in southeastern Oregon. He was a herdsman, and the sweep of country from Crane in Harney County to the Nevada line, reminded him of home in its promise of fine pasturage for sheep. He wrote about the region to his brother in Spain, who soon joined him. Thus was started an immigration that resulted in the establishment of several Basque communities.

The people are thrifty and energetic and have become prosperous. In manners they are courteous and pleasant, but reticent. They have to a great degree maintained the cultural habits of their native country. Besides English, most of them speak Spanish and their native tongue of Escuara. Their appearance is marked by clear olive complexions, dark eyes, fine teeth and red lips. With their Spanish love of color they enjoy wearing bright sashes and vests. It is not unusual to find a group of them gathered about an accordion or guitar player, singing and dancing as many generations of Basques have done before them.

The German community at Aurora, Clackamas County, dates from 1856. The year before, because of marked Indian hostilities, migration to Oregon had slowed down. A determined band of Germans, of Bethel,

Missouri, decided to brave the danger of conflict with the redskins, and set out on the long westward trek. They were threatened on several occasions but eventually arrived in the Willamette Valley.

They obtained land, settled down to an experiment in communal living, and named their colony Aurora. Farms were established, fields cleared, and crops and stock raised. Dwellings, a church, a community house, shops and stores took shape; also a school and a park. A band was organized, the finest in the state at the time. Being industrious and frugal, the colony thrived.

The community developed on a communistic-religious basis, though the details are not fully known. The products of farm and shop were placed in a storehouse from which all members drew supplies as needed. No money changed hands. So diversified were the talents of the colonists that their town was practically self-sustaining.

It flourished, a place apart, both as to vocational and recreational life, for more than twenty years. Its religious leader was Dr. William Keil, the colony worshipping in accordance with the inspirations he drew from the Bible. When he died in 1877, a process of disintegration began. In time, hastened by pressure from the outside world, the communal property was divided and members of the Aurora colony embarked on individual enterprises.

Finnish immigrants—and in some measure Scandinavian—were drawn to Astoria because of the fishing and sailing, the shipbuilding and lumbering, pursuits to which they were accustomed in the old country. There had been a time, about 1870, when transient American fishermen from California had done the fishing for the Astoria canneries and caused a small "Barbary Coast" to grow up. The newcomers from the north of Europe were a different class of people. They were eager to settle down as law-abiding citizens, save money and send for families left behind. Besides being excellent workmen, they were steady and industrious. Gradually Astoria developed a Finnish-Scandinavian atmosphere. In 1930 more than half the city's population of 10,349 were Finnish-Scandinavian born, or of Finnish or Scandinavian parentage, with a sprinkling of Russian stock.

Chinese immigration to Oregon began in 1850. In that year the scarcity of common labor, caused by the rush of able-bodied men to the California goldfields, became so acute that Asiatics were imported. The influx increased with the years and the construction of the railroads, beginning in 1862, brought the Chinese pouring into the state.

At first everybody was satisfied. The Chinese were patient workers, willing to toil long hours for small wages. But a reversal of feeling came with the completion of the first overland railroad in 1869. With swarms of coolie laborers released to compete with white laborers for jobs that were none too many, they were soon regarded as a menace by white workers in general all along the Pacific Coast. In Oregon the idle Chinese flocked to Portland, Oregon City, and other large towns.

For many years after 1870 anti-Chinese demonstrations were frequent. In Portland men met in open lots and harangued against the Orientals, while conservative newspapers defended them. Torch-light processions marched through the streets, carrying anti-Chinese banners. A committee of fifteen was chosen to notify the hated foreigners to "git up an' git." Masked men terrorized the Chinese by dynamiting their dwellings. Chinese lives were sacrificed and little done about it. The militia was finally called out to cope with the situation, but did no permanent good. It was only through the passing of the Chinese exclusion act in 1882 that violent race prejudice was finally appeased and the anti-Chinese feeling died down.

In Portland, as in other cities of the state where Chinese live today, they reside for the most part in a well-defined section. Portland's China-town is about two or three blocks wide and seven or eight long. Chinese is commonly spoken and Chinese dress frequently worn. Chinese funerals are still magnificent spectacles, and debts are still liquidated on the day of the Chinese New Year. However, these people are in general very quiet, peaceful and self-sufficient and ask only to be permitted to live as they see fit. With tong wars relegated to the past, the problems of work and business constitute their principal interests.

Oregon's 4,958 Japanese are engaged chiefly in farming, gardening and small commercial enterprises. A few are employed by industry or in hotels and restaurants. As farmers, their ambition to own land raised issues of national and international import. A quarter of a century ago early orchardists of the Hood River Valley hired Japanese laborers to clear land. The Oriental stump-diggers saved money and began to buy orchard land of their own, and to build homes. The act was resented and in 1917 a Hood River senator introduced a bill in the Oregon legislature, prohibiting Asiatics from owning land in the state.

The bill was withdrawn at the urgent request of the United States Department of State, for fear that it might have serious international consequences at a time when the country was on the verge of war in Europe. A later legislature, however, adopted the bill, following the example of California in this respect. In the meantime, a Hood River anti-Japanese association had been formed, and the Hood River Post of the American Legion had lent its influence toward prohibiting Japanese immigration to the United States. The American Legion Post carried the issue to the state convention, and the latter obtained endorsement of the principle at their national meeting in Minneapolis. This was the beginning of a movement which resulted in Congressional action prohibiting Japanese immigration.

Of late the anti-Japanese ownership laws of Oregon have been much nullified, because Japanese children, born in the United States and guaranteed citizenship by the Federal Constitution, have acquired land under white guardianship. Thus Japanese today successfully own land in Oregon and till it with profit since they are expert gardeners and orchardists.

The proportion of negroes to whites in Oregon was greatest in 1850. being then 1.6 per cent. The 1930 total of 2,234 negroes in the state is only 0.2 per cent of the inhabitants. In the pre-Civil War era negroes were brought to Oregon by wealthy southern immigrants in such large numbers that in June 1844, a law was enacted declaring all persons brought into the country as slaves must be removed in three years or become free. In 1857 the State Constitution provided that no free negroes might enter Oregon. This law was, however, more honored in the breach than in the observance, and has long been a dead letter.

Of Oregon's 2,234 negroes, more than half live in Portland, in a colony, for the most part, on the east bank of the Willamette. The men are chiefly employed as railroad porters. They have several churches of their own, as well as lodges and other organizations.

Tall Tales and Legends

CEDAR shakes, described as "shingles that are the same thickness at both ends," covered the log cabins of early Oregon. When Paul Bunyan's loggers roofed an Oregon bunkhouse with shakes, fog was so thick that they shingled forty feet into space before discovering they had passed the last rafter.

Paul Bunyan performed notable feats in Oregon, eclipsing the prowess of his famous predecessor Joe Paul, the Indian guide who lifted a barrel of lead from the floor to the trading post counter. He created Spencer's Butte, the Columbia River, and Crater Lake. Spencer's Butte, near Eugene, represents one wagon load of dirt, upset when Paul was making a road. The Columbia River was also something of an accident, being the deep, irregular furrow dug by Babe, the big blue ox, when he peevishly broke away with a plow and rushed headlong from the mountains to the sea. Into Crater Lake Paul dumped the last of the blue snow, where it melted and produced the azure phenomenon that greatly amazed early loggers.

Although Paul and Babe had ceased their exploits long before logging became important in Oregon, tales of "bull teams" continue to circulate. A bull-whacker for a logging company near Knappa found that sweet nothings, whispered in the oxen's ears, inspired them to prodigious feats, and he would race from one animal to another with his confidential endearments. In contrast was the far-reaching vituperation of Little Billy Ross, employed at Westport, whose voice could be heard for miles, and his stage-driving counterpart in Eastern Oregon, Whispering Thompson, whose ordinary conversational tones thundered across two counties.

Joe Gervais, descendant of an Astor boatman, gravely explained a Bunyanesque feat that he performed along the ocean. The Clatsops and Nehalems, a little tired of their constant warfare with each other, asked him to keep peace between them.

"I put the Clatsops at work on their side," he said, "and the Nehalems at work on the south, moving rocks and dirt. It was slow going because we had to have a solid rock foundation. That required patience to fit the rocks together and yet allow space through the center so that water forced in by the ocean waves would surge up through it and trickle down the mountains, to irrigate the trees which we intended to plant."

When Gervais sighted an elk, he gave directions to his hounds and paddled his canoe home as fast as he could. Scarcely reaching his cabin before the elk would lope into sight, closely followed by the dogs, he would shoot it at his door.

Animals figured largely in pioneer tall tales. A ravenous cougar met a hunter on a mountain trail. When it sprang, the man rammed his hand down its throat, caught it by the tail, deftly flipped it wrong side out, and it tickled itself to death. A bear with a thorn in its paw mutely begged and obtained aid from an Oregonian. Imagine his astonishment the next morning to discover that during the night the grateful animal had brought him two hams and a side of bacon. A farmer in Eastern Oregon, who missed first his hogs, then his ripened corn, learned that bears had killed and cured the hogs and had ricked the corn in a secluded place.

In primitive Curry County areas wild hogs enjoy their porcine Eden, each succeeding generation teaching its young to sleep with heads downhill so that they may escape faster when disturbed by hunters. The first man to discover Chinook salmon in the Columbia, caught 264 in a day and carried them across the river by walking on the backs of other fish. His greatest feat, however, was learning the Chinook jargon in 15 minutes from listening to salmon talk. Sheepherders claim that they rub tobacco juice in their eyes to keep awake during their long vigils. An erratic early-day sawmill in Union County received a cottonwood log, from which it cut seven thin boards and a wagonload of sawdust. Within three days, the hot sunshine so enlivened the boards that they warped themselves out of the lumber yard and were found a mile away in a neighbor's corral.

An inhabitant of the upper Rogue River, in passing down a narrow trail, shoved a huge boulder from his path. It crashed down the canyon, reached the bottom, and to his amazement, rolled up the other side. It poised on the crest then plunged down again, only to ascend to its original resting place. The native fled. Returning some weeks later, he discovered the rock had cut a new transverse canyon and was still crashing back and forth, as regular as a pendulum.

Frogs and snakes in Klamath County formerly made winter migrations to the south. The trek began in late September, snakes and frogs crawling and hopping along together in such numbers that the procession required two hours to pass a given point. Two long parallel ridges were formed, one of snakes and one of frogs. At ten in the morning a halt was called and a long rest taken. Lumped, entwined, and bunched together during their siesta, they made a mass two feet wide, a foot and a half high, and a mile and a half long. Just before marching formations were resumed, about two o'clock in the afternoon, the hungry snakes gulped down a few of their companion frogs.

During dog days in August a rattlesnake bit Luther King, later featured in Oregon newspapers as Rattlesnake King. The wound upon his leg healed quickly. Twenty years later, in August, the old scar became a running sore. By early September he was well again. The next year in early August the old sore reappeared accompanied by another. Each August thereafter all the old ones and a new one broke out. King believed that when the number of sores equalled the number of rattles, his affliction, which he called the "Serpent's curse," would be removed. The cumulative eruptions upon his leg had reached more than a dozen when he died.

As ingenious as these stories, are those of the labor-saving devices used by early Oregonians. A Lake Creek settler used mouse traps to catch crawfish, while an Umpqua pioneer placed his hog pen where daily tides filled a fish trap with sturgeon for the hogs' food. A southern Oregon farmer broke a breachy horse, not by mending his fallen fences, but by tying an iron nut to the animal's foretop in such a manner that it hit him between the eyes each time he tried to jump.

Other tales that sound incredible have had the backing of reliable report. In 1877 sea pigeons came into the Columbia River in such multitudes that they formed a winging column 15 miles long. A caterpillar migration in Lane County was of such proportions that a Southern Pacific train was stalled when the rails became slick from the quantities crushed. During a cold spell a rancher in the Coast Range could not understand the nightly commotion of his horses out in the barn until he found that shivering cougars, in search of comfort, had been sleeping in the manger. A Siskiyou hunter, who bugled with a cowhorn to disperse his 20 hounds after game, was much annoyed by the coming of the railroad, because his hounds, mistaking the locomotive's whistle for the horn, "would wander on wild chases like the foolish after snipe." In a canyon between Portland and its Cascade watershed the huge wooden pipeline was gnawed by beavers, which were undeterred by the interminable length of the log they set themselves to severing. A village merchant in the Blue Mountains sold, and still sells, snowshoes for horses. Forty feet of cowhide belting used by an early Eastern Oregon sawmill stretched so much that within a week 50 feet had been cut off by installment shortening and 40 feet were still left.

Oregonians of the settler period, like the native tribes before them, were tinged with melancholy, but, unlike the Indians, they trafficked very little with spooks. At Rickreall and a few other places in the Willamette Valley were haunted mills. In Benton County was a hollow locally known as Banshee Canyon tenanted by the ghost of Whitehouse, a suicide. From the old, long-vacated Yaquina Bay Lighthouse came cries from a throat that was not human and light from a place where no light was; it is now occupied as a lookout station by the Coast Guard. A young journalist, while on vacation in the high Cascades, was lured away from his sleeping companions at night by mountain Lorelei, and was never afterwards found, passing into "some sweet life that has no end

> Within the Cascades' inner walls,
>   Where nymphs beyond all fancy fair,
> Soothe him with siren madrigals
>   And deck him with their golden hair."

During the gold rush in Jackson County in the 1850's money to pay for the new courthouse was obtained from gold panned from the dirt excavated for the basement of the building. "Back yard" mines are still conducted in Jacksonville. One of the town's early churches was built on one night's receipts from the gambling houses. Hardworking men tossed away a year's or a season's earnings in a night at resorts which catered to their tastes. Bartenders swept pennies, proffered in change, to the sawdust floor with a gesture as grandiose as that with which they had tossed away their keys on opening day, a symbol that indicated that their place would never close.

Several accounts of buried wealth have caused much searching and digging. Letters, anchors, dots, and arrows on the rocks of Neah-kah-nie Mountain have long tantalized treasure hunters. Interviews with Indians during the period of settlement yielded varying and fantastic stories of shipwrecks, of a negro who was killed and interred with a chest on the mountain, and of slant-eyed Orientals and swaggering Spanish pirates. Pieces of oriental wood found on the shore, and tons of beeswax dug from the sands, have to a degree verified the stories of the wrecks.

Laurel Hill, on the old Barlow immigrant road near Mount Hood, also hides treasure, placed there by a highwayman who murdered his accomplice and buried their loot. Upon his deathbed the outlaw confessed to his son, who spent several summers trying to find the money, but discovered only the blazes on the cedar he had been directed to seek.

When two miners from the Randolph beach mines became apprehensive of robbery, they buried a five-gallon can of gold dust beneath a tree and left the country. Upon returning they found that a forest fire had swept the district. The can of gold, as yet undiscovered, has been sought for years.

The Blue Bucket Mines, said to be located on a swift central Oregon stream that is literally pebbled with gold nuggets, have been sought for seventy-five years. Emigrants, camping for the night on a hazardous section of Meek's Cut-off, fished in the stream. Yellow pebbles, taken from the stream bed, and hammered flat on wagon tires, served as sinkers in the swift current. Children filled a blue bucket with the stones but all were tossed aside as the train proceeded. Several years later, tales of the gold strikes in California renewed discussion of the yellow pebbles, and a wild rush to discover the Blue Bucket Mines ensued. They have never been discovered.

Aptness of description, sometimes with a jest, is evident in the names applied to pioneer Oregon localities. Some of this nomenclature persists, but much of it has been discarded by a more polite but less poetic era. Fair Play was so called from the fairness of its horse races. Lick Skillet and Scanty Grease have an obvious origin. Row River was named for neighborhood feuds; Soap Creek for bachelors who had no soap; and Ah Doon Hill for a Chinese who was shanghaied there. Hell's Canyon on Snake River, the deepest chasm in America, is as descriptive of wild grandeur as God's Valley in the Nehalem country is of peace.

Huckleberry Cakes and Venison

ASK an old pioneer about his first years in the Oregon country and a reminiscent light comes into his eyes. "Our first years in Oregon? Well, it wasn't so bad. There were venison, fish, and wild game. We had plenty of berries. Our principal dish was boiled wheat or hominy and milk. Used side bacon as a seasoning. Didn't have much salt in those days. Salt was so scarce it was often traded for its weight in gold. The Indians were fairly friendly. Taught us a lot. Oh, yes, my mother used to work pretty hard cooking for our big family, but she never seemed to mind the hardships."

Many an old-timer remembers the revolving table, a common sight in the homes of early settlers. It was a circular, homemade affair about six feet in diameter, like an ordinary table; but attached to a support in the center, about eight inches above the main surface, there was a smaller table-top that could be revolved by hand. Appetizing arrays of food used to grace these curious old tables—loaves of golden bread and plates of butter, brilliantly colored fruits and vegetables, cinnamon-brown gingerbread cakes, fruit pies with rich juices staining the crisp crust, head cheese, fresh or salted meat and fish.

Some of the dishes enjoyed by the pioneers of Oregon have not been prepared for many years; but the recipes for others are carefully preserved, and (with some adaptation to present-day methods and materials) are still followed by many housewives. In the former category is fern pie, thus referred to by George A. Waggoner in his *Stories of Old Oregon:*

At supper, among other things, we had what I feel assured but few mortals have ever tasted—fern pie. It was made of the tender and nutritious stalks of young ferns, and was very good. Thomas was surprised, but said the Lord was very wise, and had undoubtedly clothed the hills and valleys with the delicious plant in order that the coming generation might be supplied with food, and never be without a supply of good pie. . . . I believe these pies are now extinct, and their making a lost art, unless, happily, a recipe has been preserved among the early settlers of Sweet Home valley.

Prominent among the recipes that are still popular is the following, originated some 70 years ago by Mrs. John James Burton, an Oregon pioneer:

MEAT PANCAKES

To a cupful of cold meat add a few raisins, chop the mixture fine and season with salt, paprika, the pulp of a lemon, nutmeg, sugar, and 1 teaspoon of finely chopped pepper; add an egg and heat the mixture. 3 eggs, a pint of milk, and enough flour to make a thin batter. After beating thoroughly, drop the batter in large spoonfuls on a hot and well greased frying pan. As each cake browns on one side, place some of the meat mixture on it and fold the cake over the mixture. Then place the cakes in another pan containing a little meat-stock and butter, and steam from 5 to 10 minutes.

The wild fruits of the Northwest were much used in early days, as indeed they are now. The huckleberry, blackberry, Oregon grape, elderberry, and serviceberry provided a basis for many delectable dessert dishes. Here is an old recipe that is still much used:

HUCKLEBERRY GRIDDLE CAKES

Sift together 2 cups of flour, 1 teaspoon of salt, and 1½ teaspoons of baking powder. Combine with 1 beaten egg, 1½ cups of sour milk, and 1 teaspoon of soda. Then add 1 teaspoon of melted butter and 1 cup of huckleberries. Bake on hot greased griddle, and serve with syrup or thick huckleberry sauce.

An early western recipe for apple turnovers, named no doubt for some long-departed Mrs. McGinty of culinary prowess, runs as follows:

McGINTIES

Wash 1 pound of dried apples, removing bits of core and skin, and soak overnight. Next day stew in enough water to cover, and when soft run through a collander. Replace on stove, add enough brown sugar to make the fruit rich and sweet, and cook until thick; then cool and add 1½ tablespoons of ground cinnamon. Line a dripping-pan with pie crust, put in fruit mixture and cover with upper crust, gashing the latter slightly to let the steam escape. Press edges of crust together and bake—at first in a hot oven, then reducing the heat. When done cut into diamond-shaped portions, and serve hot with cream.

Sourdough biscuits and prospector's soup were known to every oldtimer who roamed the mountains, valleys, and plains of the West in search of some likely spot in which to stake a mining claim. This is the way they were commonly prepared:

SOURDOUGH BISCUITS

Mix 1 pint of flour and 1 teaspoon of salt with 1 pint of warm water or canned milk. Beat into a smooth batter, and keep in a warm place until well soured or fermented; then add another teaspoon of salt, 1½ teaspoons of soda dissolved in half a cup of tepid water, and enough flour to make the dough easy to handle. Knead thoroughly, until dough is no longer sticky, then cut up into biscuits and cook in a pan containing plenty of grease.

PROSPECTOR'S SOUP

Put 2 tablespoons of bacon fat and 3 tablespoons of flour into a saucepan, and stir over a medium fire until the flour is golden brown. Then add 1 quart of boiling water and a half a can of milk, stirring in slowly until smooth, and season with salt and pepper to taste. An onion may be added to improve the flavor.

Deer once roamed the Oregon woods in countless numbers, and the settler's meat supply was easily replenished at the expense of a charge of powder and lead. The favorite method of cooking venison was by roasting, a method which the housewife of today continues to follow.

ROAST VENISON

Rub a leg or saddle of venison with butter, wrap it in buttered paper and place in roasting pan. Make a thick paste of flour and water, and apply a half-inch coating of this to the paper. Put a pint of water in pan, cover the latter, and roast in a moderately slow oven, allowing 30 minutes of roasting time for each pound of meat and basting every 15 minutes after the first hour. Before serving remove paper wrapping and baste with a sauce of melted butter, flour, salt, and pepper.

Fish from the rivers and coastal waters provided a bountiful food supply for early Oregonians. The Indians depended largely on salmon for their sustenance throughout the year; and today, as for more than a century past, this fish is a staple delicacy. Fresh salmon, split lengthwise and slow-baked in a willow frame before an open fire, according to the Indian method of cooking, has a delicious flavor that modern grills and broilers fail to impart. An old recipe for preparing salt salmon, one that continues to be extensively used, is as follows:

SALT SALMON, PIONEER STYLE

Soak two pounds of salt salmon in fresh water overnight. Next day shred without peeling 6 or 8 potatoes, place the salmon and potatoes in a stew pan, cover with boiling water, and boil until the potatoes are done. Serve in a cream sauce.

A delicacy not to be found on any restaurant menu is smoked native or brook trout. Preparation of this *chef-d'oeuvre* assumes an ample supply (from 50 to 200 pounds) of freshly caught trout, since the time and labor required in the operations would not warrant dealing with a picayune quantity. The place should be in the mountains where plenty of the right variety of willow for smoking may be secured—Elk Lake, for example. The next step is to build a conical tepee or wickiup of stout green boughs covered with leaves. Then, from the nearby marshes or shores of the lake, loads of young willows are brought by canoe to the improvised smokehouse. When the fish have been suspended inside the structure, a subdued smoky fire of willow twigs is maintained for 24 hours—a task requiring energy, patience, and an optimism that is justified by the results. After the smoked trout are dressed with butter in a hot pan and cooked over glowing camp coals, the gourmand has only to take the final step and eat as heartily as he likes, while the rest of the catch can be conveniently shipped from the mountains to his home.

Coos Bay is noted for its Empire clams, which sometimes weigh four or five pounds each. The large necks of these clams can be split into sections after scraping off the rough outer skin; the sections are then well pounded, dipped in seasoned flour or cornmeal, and fried to a crisp brown. The Indian method of making clam chowder was to soak the clams overnight in a freshwater stream, and then throw them into a hollowed log containing water heated to the boiling point by hot stones. After they had opened, the clams were scraped from their shells and replaced in the water, together with chunks of jerked or smoked venison, dried wild onions, and wapato roots that the squaws had gathered in dry lake beds. An appetizing counterpart of this can be prepared today in a boiler over a driftwood fire, substituting bacon, potatoes, and ordinary onions for the now less accessible minor ingredients used by the Indians.

Another prized marine delicacy is the Columbia River smelt or eulachon (referred to by Lewis and Clark as the anchovy), which is caught in immense quantities each spring. These little oily fish are commonly fried in their own fat, but a favorite way of serving them on the Pacific coast is this:

Heat 2 tablespoons of olive oil or bacon grease in a skillet, and brown therein a small quantity of minced onions, garlic, and green pepper. Add a can of tomato sauce, and let simmer for 5 minutes; then add half a cup of vinegar and cook 2 minutes longer. Meanwhile dredge the smelt in flour, and fry until brown and tender. Place on platter, and pour the sauce over the fish.

It was old Peter McIntosh, a Canadian, who introduced the fine art of cheese-making to Tillamook County more than half a century ago, and Tillamook has been famous ever since for its American cheddar.

In his delightful book, *The Cheddar Box,* Dean Collins writes: "If you follow the trail of the history of cheese in the Pacific Northwest, outside the confines of Tillamook County into southern Oregon, you'll still find Peter McIntosh. . . . And if you'll sit in on a meeting of Alaska sourdoughs talking about the Klondike, you'll hear about McIntosh cheese, which was as yellow as the gold in Alaska, and at times commanded almost ounce for ounce in the mining camps." A delicious cheese sauce for boiled fish, especially halibut, has been originated by the Portland home economics expert, Mary Cullen. Her recipe runs as follows:

Melt 2 tablespoons of butter in the top of a double boiler, and add 1½ tablespoons of flour, half a teaspoon of salt, and a quarter teaspoon of pepper and paprika. Blend thoroughly, and add gradually 1½ cups of milk. Cook 10 minutes, stirring constantly, then add half a pound of cheese grated or cut into small pieces, and beat with an eggbeater until the cheese is melted. After draining the fish, pour the sauce over it and garnish with parsley and lemon.

In pioneer days, what is still known locally as "Oregon tea" was made by brewing the leaves of a shrub called by the Spaniards *yerba buena,* "the good herb." Parched and ground peas provided a substitute for coffee, when the latter could not be had.

Sports and Recreations

THE charms of Oregon have been sung since 1805 when Captain William Clark wrote his vivid description of its ocean shore, mountains, and streams. A few years later William Cullen Bryant in *Thanatopsis* celebrated the grandeur of its great river and its forests. Today hundreds of miles of highway penetrate the innermost fastnesses of the wilderness; and trails that were formerly seldom trodden have become all-year routes of travel.

The extension of good roads has coincided with a Federal program designed to conserve Oregon's resources for recreation. In 1897 the Federal government took over wide areas of forest land, and later created national forests and opened them to the public. In May 1902 Congress established Crater Lake National Park, and in July 1909 President Taft proclaimed the Oregon Caves a national monument. Within the past few years the U. S. Forest Service has set apart large tracts as recreational and wilderness areas. Its sustained-yield forest policy preserves these great playgrounds for perpetual public uses (*see NATIONAL FORESTS*).

Angling in the thousands of streams and lakes in all parts of Oregon is one of the state's chief sports. The cutthroat, the rainbow, the Dolly Varden, and the eastern brook trout are the principal game fish, but the one most sought after is the cutthroat, which starts upstream in March or April, when it is very susceptible to a bait of salmon eggs. In summer its taste turns to flies, with an all-season relish for royal coachman No. 10 and a less sustained appetite for March-brown, red-and-blue, upright, and grey hackle.

Men the world over have come to Oregon to fish for the steelhead, king of game fish, torpedo-like on the line. Flies, spinners, and crayfish tails are the enticements to make it strike. The Rogue and the Umpqua, its chief habitat, are at their best from July to October. The Deschutes is a famed trout stream in which flies are used exclusively during all seasons.

Rudyard Kipling has left an exciting account of a day on the Clackamas River, matching strength and wits with a battling salmon. The Willamette River below the falls at Oregon City is one of the few places in the world where a fisherman can sit in his boat and calmly wait for salmon to bite. This is possible because of the swift current that carries the lure into the face of the up-river bound salmon. The Columbia, the Nehalem, the Umpqua, and the Rogue have spring runs of Chinook salmon, which are usually lured by No. 4 spinners and wobblers. The autumn runs of Silverside salmon entice anglers to coastal streams and bays.

The State Game Commission maintains sixteen fish hatcheries in all parts of the state at which trout are propagated for the stocking of streams and lakes. At these hatcheries millions of fingerlings are developed each year.

In the lower Columbia and Willamette rivers and in the lakes and bayous of Sauvie Island are bass, crappie, catfish, blue gill, and perch. The Tualatin, the Long Tom, and the Yamhill rivers, as well as many coastal and mountain lakes, are stocked with bass. Many vacationists go deep-sea fishing in small vessels off the coast, or angle with pole and line from the sand or rocks for tom-cod, perch, sea-trout, and flounders. Each year the early spring smelt-runs attract great crowds of visitors to the banks of the Sandy.

At the opening of the hunting season, red-capped and red-shirted men flock to forest, mountain, or field. As many as 12,000 deer—the Columbian blacktailed in the western section and the mule-deer in the eastern and southeastern section of Oregon—are killed annually. Elk or Wapiti are hunted in the Wallowa and Blue Mountain region, but antelope are at present protected by law. On the Hart Mountain Antelope Preserve in the south central part of the state are great herds of this fleet little animal. Timber wolves are few but coyotes plentiful. Bounties have decreased the number of cougars and bobcats, but these animals have by no means entirely disappeared. Cinnamon and black bears are most numerous on the western slopes of the Cascades and in the Coast Range.

The State Game Commission operates five game farms from which are liberated yearly thousands of China and Mongolian pheasants. Geese and ducks are found in the entire drainage area of the Columbia and on the marshes and lakes of southeastern Oregon. In the western valleys and upland pastures are pheasants, quail, bobwhites, and Hungarian partridges, while blue and ruffed grouse inhabit most wooded sections of the state.

The Canyon Creek game refuge in Grant County has been reserved for bow and arrow hunters. Arrows are inspected for sharpness at a checking station near John Day.

Because of its many sky-piercing peaks and its leagues of forest trail, Oregon is especially appealing to the climber and hiker. There are many mountain-climbing organizations in the state: The Mazamas, the Wy'east Climbers, and the Trails Club of Portland; the Angoras of Astoria; the Obsidians of Eugene; the Chemeketans of Salem; the Skyliners of Bend; the Crag Rats of Hood River, and others, with more than 2,000 members in all. The peak of Mount Hood, with an average of 1,500 ascents a year, is second in mountain-climbing popularity in the world. Hundreds of foot and bridle-trails criss-cross the forested mountain regions. The Skyline Trail, that clings to the summit of the Cascade Range across the entire length of the state, is one of the Nation's most interesting hiking routes.

Thousands enjoy swimming and canoeing in Oregon lakes. Many own motor launches and cruise up and down the rivers and lakes of the state. Towns dotting the Oregon Coast draw throngs of tourists each year. The most popular are Seaside, Cannon Beach, Tillamook County and the Lincoln County beaches. Popular forms of recreation are surf bathing, clam digging, crab raking and netting, deep sea fishing, shell and agate collecting, tennis, and golf. Most Oregon cities have modern pools for residents and visitors.

An annual winter sports carnival is held at Mount Hood each year. The peak is only sixty miles from Portland, and Timberline Lodge, constructed in 1936 by the Works Progress Administration, located on its slope, is easily accessible by automobile and stage (*see MOUNT HOOD*).

Tobogganing, skiing, snowshoeing, and hiking are the main forms of winter recreation. Winter sports are also held at Three Sisters, west of Bend, in the Cascades east of Eugene and Albany, in the Blue Mountains near La Grande, the Anthony Lakes area near Baker, in the Siskiyous, and in many other sections.

The Pendleton Round-Up, a civic enterprise held in a mammoth arena, is representative of many of its type in the state. Competitive events include racing, broncho-breaking, roping, steer riding, and bulldogging. As a special feature of the Round-Up, Indians come in from the Umatilla Reservation to dance and to re-enact scenes which were once a grim reality to living members of the tribe. In the boxes around the arena many prominent figures of the Old West gather to watch the revival of activities in which they themselves once participated.

Tennis courts are found everywhere; the larger towns often provide municipal grounds, some of which are flood-lighted for night playing. Twenty-one free public courts in Portland are maintained by the city Bureau of Parks. In or adjacent to Portland are twenty-four golf links and "out-state" are sixty additional courses, most of them located in Western Oregon. Fees are moderate, ranging from 30c for nine holes to $2 a day.

The state has the usual round of interscholastic and inter-collegiate sports, as well as professional and semi-professional events. The Coliseum of Portland, ice-skating rink, is the home arena of the Buckaroos, members of the Pacific Northwest Hockey League. In summer the Multnomah Civic Stadium is nightly filled with an average of 7,500 dog-racing fans; about 400 greyhounds are brought to Portland for these events from kennels all over the United States. Racing and pari-mutual betting are legal in Oregon, and from these the state annually collects $60,000 in taxes. Horse races are features of the State Fair at Salem and of various county fairs.

Social Welfare

PIONEER Oregon had a simple formula of social welfare: work was provided for those who could work and aid for those who could not. Whatever latter-day society has added to the homespun tradition has been brought forward by trial and error methods in a state which still has vast unexploited natural resources and, theoretically at least, offers more opportunities than many other states.

If the present results of Oregon's efforts to provide aid for the indigent young and old, hospitalization for the physically and mentally ill, and rehabilitation for criminals may seem inadequate in some respects, it should be remembered that most of the state's present social welfare institutions are comparatively young, and were established to complement a robust pre-depression economy.

Few persons in the opulent 1920's anticipated the havoc that falling prices and dwindling markets might work upon Oregon's great lumbering and agricultural enterprises, or that "seasonal" work—long a convenient stop-gap measure for spring and summer unemployment—might fail to halt a rising tide of indigence, swollen by the migration of thousands of desperate persons from the drouth areas of the middle west. It is significant that the editor of a prominent newspaper recently questioned the necessity of organization among the unemployed, intimating that opportunity still knocked at every man's door in Oregon, even if not so loudly and insistently as some romanticists would have us believe. In Oregon, as elsewhere, the Federal Government has entered into the relief field upon a tremendous scale, and the number of the unemployed apparently makes the continuation of Federal aid imperative. The achievements of the Federal agencies—the WPA, PWA, NYA, and FSA—are a warm penumbra between the bright accomplishments of Oregonians who have striven to keep alive the best pioneer tradition of mutual help, and the darkness of insufficient relief, the thin slops provided on soup lines, and the county poor farms for the needy aged.

Until the beginning of the present decade, Oregon's legislative assemblies, drawn from a state with many diverse geographical sections and divergent economic problems, left most public welfare services to be performed by the counties, or by various private agencies. A legislative act of 1913, however, required that counties levy a tax providing assistance to mothers with dependent children. The state had early a workman's compensation act, faulty in the opinion of many persons, because of a clause which permits employers to reject the responsibilities of the measure. Old age pensions which seldom reach maximum payments of $30 a month have been declared inadequate by many sociologists. The state board of health, which has broad powers, cooperates with county and municipal agencies, and seldom operates locally, unless authorities refuse or neglect to enforce ordinances. The board has done yeoman service in Oregon's fight against disease, and its efficiency is reflected by the fact that the state has 9.2 hospital beds for every thousand of population, an enviable rating compared to the national standard of 4.6 beds per thousand.

The excellence of hospital facilities is perhaps the brightest tone of the Oregon social welfare spectrum. While many of the state's 72 hospitals, sanitariums, and related institutions with their total of 10,298 beds, are in Portland, there are modern hospitals in every section of the state except the most remote areas. On Marquam Hill in Portland are a notable group, consisting of the Doernbecher Memorial hospital for children, The United States Veterans hospital and the Multnomah County General hospital which houses the laboratory and class-rooms of the University of Oregon Medical school. Outstanding among denominational general hospitals in the city are: St. Vincent (Catholic), Good Samaritan (Protestant Episcopal), both of which maintain schools for nurses; Emanuel (Lutheran) and the Portland Sanitarium (Seventh Day Adventist). Other modern institutions include the Hahnemann Private Hospital, Portland Medical Hospital, Portland Convalescent Hospital, Sellwood General Hospital, Portland Eye, Ear, Nose and Throat Hospital, the Mountain View Sanitarium, the Portland Open Air Sanitarium, and the Shriners Hospital for crippled children. A cooperative hospital is in the process of organization.

Other hospitals of official nature in addition to the Multnomah County hospital and the Veterans institution are the Multnomah County Tuberculosis Pavillion, which cares for indigent persons, the Oregon State Tuberculosis hospital at Salem, a similar institution at The Dalles, and the Morningside hospital at Portland, maintained by the government for the care of mental patients from Alaska.

The Oregon Tuberculosis Association, supported by the sale of penny

Christmas seals, is interested in the eradication of tuberculosis by educational methods, early diagnosis, nursing service, promotion of preventive legislation and appropriations for clinical and hospital services. Mrs. Sadie Orr Dunbar for many years executive secretary of this organization is now (1940) on leave of absence as national president of the General Federation of Women's Clubs with headquarters at Washington, D. C. The tuberculosis death rate of Oregon has gradually been lessened until it is now among the lowest in the world.

Critics of the State declare that the high percentage of industrial accidents makes the maintenance of numerous hospitals necessary, but constantly diminishing epidemics and low infant and general mortality rates seem to indicate consistent and reasonably thorough efforts to safeguard and improve public health. Oregon has made conscientious attempts to check venereal diseases, through the establishment of clinics for the treatment of gonorrhea and syphilis, and through the passage of a law which requires physical examinations before marriage licenses can be obtained. The state's experiments in the field of cooperative medical care have attracted nation-wide attention, and thousands of persons belong to group health associations, which provide preventive medical service, surgery and hospitalization at low cost.

Conditions in the institutions for the mentally ill are less favorable. Both the Oregon State hospital at Salem and the Eastern Oregon State hospital at Pendleton are overcrowded, and the effect of economic cataclysm is evident in the steadily increasing number of commitments since 1930. These institutions supplanted—and improved—a system under which before the mentally ill were cared for under contract or by a private asylum in Portland. Both hospitals provide educational facilities, medical and dental care, and vocational therapy, as does also the Oregon Fairview Home for feeble-minded and epileptics, located near Salem.

Approximately 2000 children annually receive care in institutions supervised by the State Child Welfare Commission, whose functions, by act of the 1939 legislature, are being absorbed by the State Welfare Commission. The bright record for child welfare has been smudged occasionally by scandals arising from the efforts of certain institutions to regulate placements of orphaned or abandoned children for purposes of profit alone, but these are exceptional cases.

Portland with more than one-third of the state's population, has many child placement organizations, juvenile clinics, orphanages, foundling homes and shelters for unmarried mothers and their children. Outstanding is the Albertina Kerr Nursery Home which provides for babies of unmarried or abandoned mothers and for foundlings under five years of age. The Salvation Army offers similar services at its White Shield Home; the Volunteers of America provide an additional place of refuge for deserted or widowed mothers and their children; the Louise Home cares for delinquent girls and for young unmarried mothers and their infants, and also maintains a juvenile hospital for girls afflicted with venereal diseases. In the city and its vicinity there are a dozen institutions which shelter children from infancy to seventeen years of age. Many are non-sectarian; Catholic charitable activities in the Portland Arch Diocese are coordinated under one agency; the Jewish Shelter Home, cares for children between the ages of three and sixteen, and serves also as a placement bureau.

Portland offers social welfare services similar to those afforded in most other metropolitan cities. There are children's clinics, supervised playgrounds and recreational centers within the city, summer camps in the country to which are sent selected children and, occasionally, their mothers from the city's low rent districts. An outstanding contribution to child welfare in Portland is the Fire Department's "milk fund," supported by athletic events, which distributes milk to undernourished pupils in the public schools.

The Portland Community Chest, of which Ralph J. Reed has long been secretary, coordinates the activities of 44 charitable and philanthropic organizations, including many already mentioned here, and through its annual campaigns solicits all or a large portion of the funds upon which their operation depends. The Chest maintains the Portland Council of Social Agencies as a social service planning board representing public and private agencies of the county. Established in 1920, the Community Chest over-subscribed its quota in 1939. Its annual budget, in recent years fully subscribed by Portland citizens, provides for the full scope of activities usual in a Chest program.

The Portland City Bureau of Health maintains an emergency hospital for first aid at the Portland police headquarters. The Women's Protective Division of the Portland police department cooperates with the Bureau. The "Sunshine Division" of the Portland City Police Department has won acclaim by collecting new and used material for distribution to needy families. The Portland Fire Department "Toy and Joy Makers" repair annually great numbers of broken toys donated to the organization for distribution as Christmas gifts.

Oregon's Good Will Industries provide work and wages for aged and otherwise handicapped poor, collecting discarded articles which are refurbished and sold in stores throughout the city.

The Travelers' Aid Society functions in Portland as well as in other metropolitan areas. A legal aid committee of the Oregon Bar Association renders free legal assistance to indigent persons in Multnomah County, while the American Civil Liberties Union acts to safeguard constitutional rights of free speech and assembly.

The Multnomah County Health Unit provides skilled nursing in the home and conducts health education. Indigent soldiers in the county are provided for from the funds raised by a tax levy.

Fraternal orders have established many homes for their aged members in Portland. The Maccabees, the United Artisans, the Odd Fellows, Masonic Orders and the Eastern Star all maintain homes in the state. The Oregon-Washington Pythian Home also serves Oregon, though located at Vancouver, Washington. The Patton and the Mann Homes in Portland provide board and room and general care for men and women under 60. Grandma's Kitchen gives shelter to 300 homeless men and 50 indigent women, besides operating a salvage department and a working girls' home. The First Presbyterian Church Men's Resort in Portland maintains a free reading and writing room.

Operating in Portland are several agencies which give aid to different national groups. The National Association for the Advancement of Colored People is also active. The American National Red Cross has a number of county chapters in Oregon, the Multnomah County Chapter with 30,000 members being the largest and most active.

Oregon has the usual organizations classed as "character building" institutions including the Young Men's Christian Association, and the Young Women's Christian Association. The 4H Clubs and the Future Farmers of America are active throughout the state. Boy Scouts and Campfire Girls and Girl Scouts have many active troops.

In the field of penology, Oregon suffers from the lack of a modern and more commodious penitentiary, although the treatment of prisoners is generally humane, and the commonwealth's efforts to rehabilitate criminals equals those of penologists in many other states. Oregon's first penitentiary was established by legislative act of the territorial government in 1851. First located at Portland, it was moved to Salem in 1866.

On January 24, 1939, it housed 1071 inmates, of whom 10 were women. Convicts labor in a prison flax plant, which has developed into an important establishment with the largest scutching plant in the

United States, although regulations are imposed by many common-wealths and foreign nations against the importation of prison-made goods.

The prison magazine *Shadows* for two successive years (1936-1937) won the Walter F. Gries award, the "Pulitzer Prize of prison journal-ism." Its title page bears the legend: "A monthly magazine dedicated to those who would salvage rather than destroy," and its purpose is, "to give inmates an opportunity for self-expression; to encourage moral and intellectual improvement among the inmates; and to acquaint the public with the true status of the prisoner." The magazine is available to the general public at $1.00 per year.

The Oregon Prison Association, a private agency conducted by the Pacific Protective Society, does valuable work in maintaining the rights of prisoners and overseeing their welfare following release.

Oregon correctional institutions for youth stress rehabilitation rather than punishment. The Frazier Detention Home of Portland cares for delinquent boys committed by the Department of Domestic Relations. The Oregon State Training School for Boys near Woodburn receives boys 10 to 18 years old and gives them training in useful occupations. Girls from 12 to 25 classed as delinquent or incorrigible are sent to the State Industrial School for Girls at Salem. The school provides educational facilities, medical and dental care, and special vocational instruction.

Among the state agencies at Salem, directly or indirectly involved in social welfare are the State Board for Vocational Education, State Board of Eugenics, Oregon Mental Hygiene Society, State Welfare Commission, State Industrial Accident Commission, and the Unem-ployment Compensation Commission. Also near Salem is the School for the Deaf, which cares for children between the ages of 6 to 21 years who are unable to attend ordinary schools.

The School for the Blind at Salem provides special education for visually handicapped youth. The Blind Trade School includes in its curriculum, broom making, chair caning, and classes in Braille. Dormi-tories are provided for those living at the school, which is under the jurisdiction of the State Commission for the Blind and the Prevention of Blindness.

The broad program of the Work Projects Administration in Oregon has, through service projects, made substantial contributions to the social welfare of the state. More than fifteen hundred persons are em-ployed upon projects that have a wide range in variety and point of

utilitarian purpose. Through the services of a Readers' Project, blind persons are able to remain conversant with current events, or to hear such books or magazines as they prefer read to them in their homes. The WPA activities include survey studies, adult education projects, and a housekeeping unit, through which women are taught modern housekeeping methods. In addition, WPA units supervise installation, extension and revision of public records, and conduct six nursery schools in Portland and 21 throughout the state. Among other service projects are recreational leadership which supervises play in public parks and schools, the Library Aid Project and two units engaged in public health and hospital work; also classes in First Aid and Traffic Safety.

The NYA conducts classes in iron work, carpentry, photography, art, poster drawing, domestic science, clerical work, domestic service, and also trains library assistants. Classes are limited to those employed on the NYA program, but a number of clubs are being formed which will admit other youths to membership. A photography club, already active, meets three times a week, using the facilities of the NYA center.

The Farm Security Administration, another Federal agency intensely active in Oregon, has granted rural rehabilitation loans to more than 4000 families, made rehabilitation grants to another 4000 families, aided a hundred native families through one resettlement project, and a thousand families through community and cooperative services.

The Federal Government has been compelled to bear the major portions of Oregon's relief burden since the counties' facilities for aid proved inadequate during the early years of the depression. County relief budget almost trebled between 1929 and 1932 and even at present the county burden still remains heavy despite Government relief expenditures. The picture today is far from bright, Oregon differs very little in this respect from other states in the Union.

Education

THE first school in the Oregon country was conducted at Fort Vancouver for the half-breed children of the Hudson's Bay Company trappers. Its teacher was John Ball, a Dartmouth graduate who came west in 1832 with the first Wyeth party. Not wishing to accept free lodging from the factor, Dr. John McLoughlin, Ball asked for work and was assigned to teaching. Early in 1833 he was succeeded by another member of the Wyeth party, Solomon H. Smith, who taught for a year and a half, and then eloped with the Indian wife of the fort's baker. Thereafter, Smith taught in a school at French Prairie, and later established a school at Clatsop Plains. By the end of 1834, Jason Lee and his three co-workers in the newly-founded Methodist mission school at French Prairie were teaching the Indian and half-breed children of the region to read and write.

The pioneer schools of Oregon received little public support, but were usually maintained by individuals or church organizations. At the primary school conducted in Oregon City during the winter of 1853-4, tuition was free because Sidney Walter Moss, Oregon's first writer of fiction, paid most of the expenses. While some communities provided primitive schoolhouses, many of the early classes were held in settlers' cabins, where the teacher was often a pioneer mother or other person familiar with the rudiments of learning. Teachers in privately conducted schools that charged a fee were paid meager stipends, in addition to being "boarded around." Such a "rate bill" school was established in Portland as early as 1847. The tuition fees were commonly no less meager than the pay of the teachers. An announcement of the Lone Butte school, in Marion County, states in 1854: "One quarter taught at $5 per schollar. The other two quarters cost $4 per schollar each."

In the early agitation for free schools, a prominent part was taken by the Reverend George H. Atkinson, often referred to as "the father of public education in Oregon." But this agitation produced little in the way of concrete results until the Territory of Oregon was officially organized in 1849. Then, under the terms of the Nathan Dane Act, two sections of land in each township throughout the Territory were granted and reserved for sale to provide funds for educational purposes; and in his inaugural address to the first Territorial legislature, Governor Joseph Lane emphasized "the importance of adopting a system of common schools and providing the means of putting them in operation." Two months later the legislature accepted the land granted by Congress "for the support of the common schools," voted a two-mills school tax, specified certain requirements for administration of the educational system, and stipulated that every school should "be open and free to all children between the ages of four and twenty-one years."

According to the Federal census of 1850, the Territory of Oregon (then embracing all of the present States of Oregon, Washington, and Idaho, with parts of Montana and Wyoming) contained in that year only three public schools, with a total of 80 pupils under the supervision of four teachers, and with an annual income from all sources of less than $4,000. The "academies and other schools," conducted under private or denominational auspices, numbered 29, with 842 pupils and 44 teachers.

Public schools were opened at Portland, West Union, and Cornelius in 1851, and at Oregon City in 1855. At the end of the quarter-century following the adoption of Oregon's first school law, the State could boast of 530 public schools, with 860 teachers. The latter received an average monthly salary of $45.92 for men and $34.46 for women. Before 1900 the only high schools in the State were those at Portland, Astoria, Baker City, and The Dalles; but their number increased rapidly after 1901, when special provision was made for them as a part of the public educational system, and by 1910 the total had reached 115. Union high schools in rural districts were authorized in 1907, the first of such schools to open being one at Pleasant Hill, in Lane County.

The first book printed in Oregon was an abridged edition of Webster's Speller, issued from the *Oregon Spectator* press at Oregon City on February 1, 1847. But in the early years of settlement, very few textbooks were to be found in the Oregon country. Solomon Smith had only one school book at Fort Vancouver, and a single McGuffey Reader did duty for the entire school at Amity in 1848. The scanty supply of readers, spellers, and arithmetics brought by early immigrants was supplemented with almost every sort of available printed matter, including the Bible, books of verse, religious journals, and newspapers. Not until passage of the common school law of 1872 was a uniform system of textbooks adopted throughout the State.

A considerable portion of the three or four million acres comprised in the land grants for educational support found its way into the hands of private speculators, who paid only a nominal sum for their purchases. As a result, the amount each district received from the common school fund was small in the early years, and school taxes were reluctantly imposed upon settlers struggling to secure a foothold in the new country. Moreover, most of those settlers were accustomed to think of education as a denominational or private concern, as indeed it was for the most part until the late 1860's. Of the numerous academies, institutes, and seminaries established in Oregon during the first three or four decades of settlement, the earliest of all was the Oregon Institute, which in 1844 purchased the land and buildings of the Methodist mission school founded ten years earlier by Jason Lee and his nephew Daniel in the Willamette Valley at the present site of Salem. This eventually developed into Willamette University, the oldest institution of higher education in the far West. Other early denominational schools which formed the nuclei for present-day universities or colleges were Tualatin Academy (Congregational), founded at Forest Grove in 1848, now Pacific University; McMinnville College (Baptist), founded at McMinnville in 1857, now Linfield College; Albany Collegiate Institute (Presbyterian), founded at Albany in 1866, now Albany College; and Friends' Pacific Academy (Quaker), founded at Newberg in 1871, now Pacific College. The towns of Dallas and Jefferson had their originating centers in two of the early academies—La Creole Academic Institute and Jefferson Academy respectively, both established in the middle 1850's. Of the few pioneer educational institutions in eastern Oregon, the Blue Mountain University (Methodist), founded in 1875 at La Grande, was best known. Since the 1850's, Roman Catholic academies and institutes have been active in the State's educational life.

Corvallis College, founded at Corvallis in 1858 and for a time controlled by the Southern Methodist Church, was the precursor of Oregon State Agricultural College, opened under that name in 1868. The first graduating class, in 1870, consisted of four persons. This institution has since become one of the leading agricultural colleges of the country, with a faculty of 345 members and a student enrollment of 4,476 in 1938.

The University of Oregon, at Eugene, grew out of a land grant made in 1859 "to aid in the establishment of a university." Not until 1872, however, did the State legislature definitely provide for its creation, and the economic depression of the ensuing years delayed its completion until 1876. The first graduating class was that of 1878. The faculty list comprised 230 names and the student enrollment was 3,420 in 1938.

A separate department of higher education with an administrative chancellor now brings under unified control the Oregon State College, the University of Oregon, and the three State normal schools. The latter, which trace back to early teachers' institutes and to teacher-training courses in the academies and seminaries, comprise the Oregon College of Education at Monmouth, founded 1910; the Southern Oregon College of Education at Ashland, founded 1926; and the Eastern Oregon College of Education at La Grande, founded 1929.

Special schools for the blind, the deaf, and the mentally deficient are maintained by the State (*see SOCIAL WELFARE*). Vocational training is stressed in these institutions, as it is also in the Chemawa Indian School, established by the Federal government in 1880, near Salem.

In 1936, according to Federal statistics, the number of pupils enrolled in the public elementary and secondary schools of Oregon was 188,361. The teaching staff comprised 7,017 persons, who received an average annual salary of $1,154. The total expenditures for these schools amounted to $15,746,000, or a per capita of $15.48 with respect to the entire State population. The enrollment in private and parochial schools, excluding kindergartens, was 12,791; while that in universities, colleges (including junior colleges), and professional schools totaled 11,131.

That Oregon's education system has done efficient work is perhaps best attested by the fact that, according to the Federal census of 1930, only one other State (Iowa) had a lower percentage of illiteracy with respect to the total population. The Oregon rate was only one per cent, as against a national average for the continental United States of 4.3 per cent.

Federal and State agencies, either singly or in cooperation, have carried on noteworthy educational activities of a special sort during the recent depression years. The Federal Emergency Educational Program was initiated in 1933 by the Civil Works Administration. When the latter was dissolved, the program was in part continued with State emergency relief funds; and since the inception of the Works Progress Administration, it has been financed out of WPA appropriations.

Courses have been added from time to time, until the curriculum now includes cultural and vocational training in almost every important field. More than 3,000 alien residents have been prepared for American citizenship in special Americanization courses, and the elements of English reading and writing have been taught to more than 800. Incidental to the main objectives of the emergency educational program is its effectiveness in improving neighborhood relations and fostering community spirit through classroom contacts and an interchange of ideas. In 1936 the Portland Public Forums, one of ten national demonstration projects in adult civic education, achieved excellent results under joint sponsorship of the Federal government, through the Commissioner of Education, and the State WPA organization. Forums were conducted for eight months, with a total attendance of 100,418 persons.

Religion

THE harbingers of organized religion in Oregon were four Flathead Indians who in 1832, according to a contemporary chronicle, "performed a wearisome journey on foot to St. Louis, in Missouri, for the purpose of inquiring for the Christian's Book and the white man's God." When, in due course, news of this "wonderful event" appeared in eastern religious journals, "a general feeling of Christian sympathy was produced in all the churches of the land for these interesting heathen, and a proposition was made that the Missionary Board of the Methodist Episcopal Church proceed forthwith to establish a mission among the Flathead Indians."

Jason Lee, a Methodist clergyman engaged in spreading the Word among Indians in Canada, was chosen to set up the proposed mission. With his nephew Daniel (also a clergyman) and two lay workers, Cyrus Shepard and P. L. Edwards, Lee accompanied the second Wyeth expedition to the Oregon country, arriving at Fort Vancouver on September 15, 1834. Here, a fortnight later, he preached two sermons "to a congregation of English, Irish, French, half-caste, &c., which were the first sermons ever preached in the place, and doubtless the first that many of the people had ever heard." Upon the advice of Dr. John McLoughlin, chief factor of the Hudson's Bay Company, and "after much prayer for direction as to the place," it was decided to locate the mission in the lower Willamette Valley rather than in the Flathead country. Before the end of the year the little party had erected a rude log shelter some 75 miles up the Willamette River, at a place known as French Prairie, and had begun its labors "for the spiritual benefit of all the Indians, and the few French people who had settled in the country."

In the following year a Presbyterian clergyman, Samuel Parker, was sent out by the American Board of Commissioners for Foreign Missions, to explore the Oregon country with a view to selecting the most desirable site for a Presbyterian mission. With him came Dr. Marcus Whitman, appointed by the same body to work as a medical missionary among the Indians. But upon their arrival at the Snake River, Whitman decided to return East and to endeavor to persuade the Board into sending missionaries immediately to Oregon, without awaiting Parker's report. In 1836, Whitman made his second journey to the Northwest, accompanied by his wife, Mr. and Mrs. Henry Spalding, and W. H. Gray. Setting up a mission station at Waiilatpu, near the site of Walla Walla, he labored indefatigably here until late in 1847, when he and his wife with several others were killed in an Indian raid upon the station. Spalding established a mission among the Nez Perces in the Snake River Valley. Two years later, Daniel Lee and H. K. W. Perkins were assigned to missionary work at The Dalles. These three missions, with the earliest one of all at French Prairie in the Willamette Valley, were the outposts of Protestant Christianity in the Oregon country until the arrival in 1840 of the "great reinforcement" gathered by Jason Lee on a return visit to the East.

But the region was known to Jesuit missionaries long before the coming of the Methodists in 1834. Most of the French-Canadians employed by the Hudson's Bay Company were of the Roman Catholic faith, as was the company's chief factor, Dr. McLoughlin; and religious instruction in the little school at Fort Vancouver was in accordance with the tenets of that faith. The first church within the present limits of Oregon was a log structure erected by Roman Catholics at St. Paul (in what is now Marion County) in 1836, although mass was not celebrated there until three years later. Father Blanchet presided here after his arrival in 1838, and in 1844 he became archbishop of the Roman Catholic Church in Oregon, whose seat of authority was removed from Oregon City to Portland in 1862.

For the most part, the earliest settlers had neither time nor money to build churches, but they organized small congregations in a few scattered communities, which were served by itinerant preachers such as Robert Booth and Joab Powell, who are commemorated in a statue on the Capitol grounds at Salem. With the ever-rising tide of mass immigration after 1842, however, various Protestant denominations found it possible to erect their first houses of worship. The earliest of these was built by the Methodists at or near the site of Oregon City. Under date of Sunday, June 23, 1844, the Reverend Gustavus Hines has recorded that he "Preached to a congregation of about forty persons in the Methodist Church at the falls, and proved the truth of the Saviour's promise, 'Lo, I am with you.'" Other denominations that soon followed this example were the "Old School" Presbyterians at Clatsop, near the mouth of the Columbia, and the Disciples of Christ or Campbellites on the Yamhill River in Polk County, both in 1846; the Cumberland Presbyterians at Rickreall, Polk County, in 1848; the Episcopalians at Portland, in 1851.

Besides the "Old School" and Cumberland sects, two other Presbyterian bodies were represented in early Oregon—the Associate Presbyterians and the Associate Reformed Presbyterians, both dissenters from the Church of Scotland. These two merged in 1852, to form the United Presbyterian Church of Oregon, the first church body in North America organized under the name "United Presbyterians." The Baptists first organized at West Union in the Tualatin valley in 1844.

The earliest Jewish congregation in Oregon was that of Beth Israel, organized at Portland in 1859, although its synagogue was not built until some time later. The immigration from Germany and Scandinavia in the 1870's and 1880's brought many Lutherans, and this denomination is now prominently represented in the state. Japanese residents of Portland maintain a Buddhist temple in that city.

The religion preached in Oregon's early days was of an extremely fundamentalist character, promising salvation to the faithful and eternal damnation to the unbeliever. That this sort of religion still exists in some degree is evidenced by the Pentecostal and Four-Square Gospel denominations, whose rise is an interesting phenomenon of the past two decades. Religious prejudice was also evident in 1922, when Oregonians, stirred by appeals of the Ku Klux Klan, then active on the Pacific coast, sought unsuccessfully to do away with Catholic parochial education in the state.

"Somewhat over one-fourth of the total Oregon population belongs to some religious denomination. The leading denominations numerically are the Roman Catholic, Methodist Episcopal, Baptist, Disciples of Christ, Presbyterian, Congregational, Methodist Episcopal (South), and Protestant Episcopal."

Literature

A S is the case with most of the other states, the literature of Oregon may be said to begin with the accounts of the first explorers and travelers. In 1775, twenty years before the historic overland journey of Lewis and Clark, Captain Bruno Heceta, a Spanish navigator, sighted the Tillamook coast and recorded his impressions of its rugged outlines in his diary. Three years later the English Captain James Cook remarked in the log of his voyage to the Northwest that Sir Francis Drake had mentioned the severity of the climate hereabouts in June, whereas in March he found it mild enough; but ten days later Cook himself confessed that cold and snow prevailed along the coast later to be known as Oregon.

When Captain Robert Gray discovered the Columbia River in 1792, a log was kept by one of his young sailors, John Boit, Jr. Among other shrewd observations the lad noted the fine stature of the Indian males and the comeliness of the females. The Lewis and Clark journal, besides its historic significance, has great claim to literary value. With the reports concerning the trappers and traders of the Hudson's Bay Company, historical accounts began to be flavored with legend. And even the dry commercial records of the fur company helped Washington Irving vividly to reconstruct in *Astoria,* published in 1836, the setting of its far-reaching empire.

Jason Lee, the indefatigable Methodist missionary of the Willamette Valley, through his eloquence was able to interest Easterners—particularly the religious minded—in the primitive wonders of the Oregon region. His wife, Anna Marie Pittman, is credited with being Oregon's first poet. Her farewell poem to her husband, written in 1838 when he was starting east, is marked rather by intense conjugal devotion and pious fervor than by literary excellence.

During the same year the Reverend Samuel Parker, who had accompanied Dr. Marcus Whitman on his first trip to the Northwest, published a *Journal of an Exploring Tour Beyond the Rocky Mountains* (1835), which had an astonishing success for that time, selling some

1,500 copies within a few years after its issue. The author pointed out one of the early disadvantages of missionary work in the new Land of Canaan: "There is yet one important desideratum—the missionaries have no wives. Christian white women are very much needed to exert an influence over Indian females."

The career of the poet, Cincinnatus Heiner Miller (1841-1913) better known as Joaquin Miller, illustrates the vicissitudes and adventurousness of pioneer life. At the age of 13 he arrived in Eugene City in a covered wagon. Between 1855 and 1857 he lived with an Indian woman, by whom he had a child. After his Indian love affair he studied in Columbia College, Eugene; was class valedictorian and poet; then, successively, he taught school, practiced law, tried mining, rode the pony express, edited a newspaper, married, went into cattle raising, became a judge, printed his first volume of poems, *Specimens* (1868), in Portland, his second, *Joaquin, et al,* a year later, and in 1870 was divorced. Publication in 1871 of *Songs of the Sierras* in London made him famous. Thereafter his visits to Oregon were infrequent and his name was associated with California. A bit of a charlatan, Miller was a restless, spectacular, character, capable of writing an occasional poem with a vigorous lilt.

With Marcus Whitman on his famous trek in 1836 was the missionary historian, W. H. Gray, best remembered as the author of one of the first histories of the State. His *History of Oregon* (1870) is notable because it provided first-hand information (for many years he was Government inspector of the port of Astoria) of the region and also because it anticipated the work of Hubert Howe Bancroft.

The first comprehensive history of early Oregon was the work of Bancroft (1832-1918) and his little-known associates. Bancroft, a San Francisco publisher, set out to become the historian of the entire West. His grandiose plan came near enough to fruition to assume epic proportions. By 1868 he had accumulated more than 15,000 volumes relating to the West and during the ensuing years he employed a large staff of reporters and archivists to supplement his material. In this great work it is believed that he had the help of a dozen competent writers who never received credit for their share of it. His *History of the Northwest Coast* (1884) was a prelude to the richly documented two-volume *History of Oregon* (1886-88), in which source material on the State was finely combed. The *Oregon Historical Quarterly, IV,* contains an analysis of the contributions of his collaborators.

One of his associates, Frances Fuller Victor, was a remarkable literary personality, poet in her early youth in New York, and author of *The River of the West* (1870) and *All Over Oregon and Washington,* authoritative accounts of the Oregon territory. She worked on Bancroft's staff for eleven years and in this capacity wrote the *History of Oregon* (1886-88) as well as several other studies. Among her other works were a volume of poems and short stories, *The New Penelope* (1877), *Atlantis Arisen*: or, *Talks of a Tourist About Oregon and Washington,* and *The Early Indian Wars of Oregon* (1894). She died in 1902 in a Portland boarding house after several years of bitter poverty.

Francis Parkman's famous *Oregon Trail* first published as *The California and Oregon Trail* in 1849 belongs in this record, though it deals mainly with conditions at the eastern end of the trail. It should be read in connection with such volumes as W. J. Ghent's *Road to Oregon* (1929), *Early Far West* (1931), and *The Oregon Trail* (1939) by the Federal Writers' Project of the Works Progress Administration.

Judge Charles H. Carey, prominent in Portland's cultural activities, is one of the State's outstanding historians. His numerous historical works include a *History of Oregon* (1922) and a *General History of Oregon* (1935). Professor R. C. Clark, of the University of Oregon, was a scholarly historian of Texas and of Oregon; in 1925 he published a *History of Oregon* and in 1927 a *History of the Willamette Valley*. Other historians in special fields of State and local history include Bishop Edwin Vincent O'Hara, who wrote the *Pioneer Catholic History of Oregon* (1911-1925); Dr. Dan E. Clark, of the University of Oregon; and Professor Frederic G. Young, editor of the *Oregon Historical Quarterly* from 1900 to 1928, and author of numerous articles. In 1900 Professor Young rode a bicycle along the entire length of the Oregon Trail. A standard work is Horace S. Lyman's *History of Oregon: the Growth of an American State* (4 vols., 1903). Richard G. Montgomery has written *The White-Headed Eagle* (1934), an excellent biography of Dr. John McLoughlin. Philip H. Parrish published in 1931 *Before the Covered Wagon,* a collection of historical essays.

The Oregon pioneers, men and women, wrote copiously but rarely with any literary intent. Their memoirs are valuable source material for the historian and historical novelist. Such accounts as *A Day with the Cow Column* (1934) by Jesse Applegate, George A. Waggoner's *Stories of Old Oregon* (1905), T. T. Geer's *Fifty Years in Oregon*

(1912), and the *Autobiography of John Ball,* published as late as 1925, have a veracity that often escapes the authors of historical fiction.

The best of these volumes of reminiscences is *Cathlamet on the Columbia,* a small book of 119 pages, first published in 1906. Its author, Thomas Nelson Strong (1853-1927), spent his earliest boyhood playing with Indian children, then moved to Portland and later became a prominent attorney. Few books have shown so clearly "the influences of the surrounding forests, natives, and frontier," which, as Strong declared, molded his life. Of equal native vigor and honesty is *The Country Boy,* (1910) by Homer Davenport (1867-1912), the well-known cartoonist; a homely, humorous record of his boyhood in Silverton and the Waldo Hills. The State's more recent complexion is shown in George H. Putnam's *In the Oregon Country* (1915) and A. D. Pratt's *A Homesteader's Portfolio* (1922).

A year after Oregon was organized as a territory, the first novel, *The Prairie Flower, or, Adventures in the Far West,* was written in the new country. This novel was published in Cincinnati in 1849. Emerson Bennett was credited with its authorship, but there can be little doubt that it was motivated and mainly written by Sidney Walter Moss (1810-1901), a hotel-keeper of Oregon City. It was notable for its portrayal of early mountain characters and its salty trapper's dialect. Within a decade three more literary works appeared. W. L. Adams of Yamhill County wrote in 1852 a melodramatic satire in verse entitled *Treason, Stratagems and Spoils in Five Acts, by Breakspear,* which was first published serially in the Portland *Oregonian.* A second work was *Ruth Rover* (1854), a two-volume novel of the Oregon Trail and French Prairie life, by Margaret J. Bailey. In 1859 Abigail Scott Duniway (1835-1915), who later became the State's most brilliant champion of woman suffrage, published *Captain Gray's Company,* a fictional version of the overland journey of the first immigrants, marked by a somewhat barren realism.

A fictitious reconstruction of primitive life before the coming of the white man is found in one of Oregon's most popular novels, *The Bridge of the Gods,* published in 1890 by Frederic Homer Balch (1861-91). The theme of the story is the collapse of the legendary stone bridge which Indians believed once spanned the Columbia River at the Cascades. Although the time of the story is some 200 years ago, Balch gave his Indians an authentic touch of life through first-hand studies of the myths of the Columbia River Indians and visits with the redmen. In spite of its romantic flavor and somewhat sentimental style, the novel successfully recreates the feeling of a pagan, primitive world and has moments of genuine poignancy.

A novelist of the period of fur trading and exploration is Eva Emery Dye, of Oregon City. Her *McLoughlin and Old Oregon* (1900) is accepted by the reading public of the State with the same affection accorded *The Bridge of the Gods* and for a similar reason; it is filled with a sense of Oregon's historic background, especially that of the Hudson's Bay Company and its redoubtable factor. Her second book, *Stories of Oregon* (1900), suffered destruction during the printing, in the San Francisco earthquake and fire. In 1902 she turned to the Lewis and Clark expedition for *The Conquest: the True Story of Lewis and Clark.* Another book, *McDonald of Oregon* (1906), was based on the journal of that notable trader. In. *The Soul of America* (1933) she describes the influence of women in pioneer society.

Popular short-stories and numerous juveniles brought moderate wealth to John Fleming Wilson (1877-1922). His sea tales have achieved some fame and his *Tad Shelton, Boy Scout* (1913) has become part of the reading equipment of Oregon youngsters.

H. L. Davis strikes the modern note of pungent realism in his novel, *Honey in the Horn,* issued as the 1935 Harper prize novel. This gusty saga of homesteaders along the coast and on the "high desert" of eastern Oregon became a best seller and in 1936 received a Pulitzer award. Davis, in the manner of the younger generation, deflowers the sweeter legend of the heroic pioneers, seeing them as average humans and none too civilized in speech and customs.

Many of the newer novelists and short-story writers of the state are drawing on the rich sources of Oregon's historical, social, and industrial background for this material. Sheba Hargreaves and Sabra Conner have written historically authentic novels of pioneer days. Robert Ormond Case and Ernest Haycox have taken the range lands of the "high desert" as their domain and are producing colorful tales of the cattle era. Edison Marshall, prolific producer of popular fiction, has written a number of short stories of literary merit. Charles Alexander has done some excellent animal stories, among them *The Fang in the Forest* (1923) and *Bobbie, a Great Collie* (1926). Interpreters of Indian lore are Claire Warner Churchill, author of *Slave Wives of Nehalem* (1933) and *South of the Sunset* (1936), and Clarence Orvel Bunnell, writer of *Legends of the Klickitats* (1933). Anne Shannon Monroe has published several novels of the eastern Oregon range country, *Feelin' Fine* (1930), the life of William (Bill) Hanley, and a number of volumes of personal and inspirational essays.

Mary Jane Carr has written a number of children's books, the most popular of which is *Children of the Covered Wagon* (1934), and Theodore Ackland Harper is author of a dozen juvenile stories with scenes laid in Siberia, Mexico, and Oregon. Albert Richard Wetjen is a writer of sea stories and in two volumes, *Way For a Sailor* (1928) and *Fiddler's Green* (1931), has attained to literary excellence. James Stevens, formerly of Bend, has published *Homer in the Sagebrush* (1928), short stories of Oregon workers, but is best known for his Paul Bunyan legends, *Paul Bunyan* (1925) and the *Saginaw Paul Bunyan* (1932). Recent additions to Americana are Stewart H. Holbrook's *Holy Old Mackinaw* (1938), a natural history of the American lumberjack and *Iron Brew* (1939), the history of the iron industry.

Other prose writers who have contributed to the State's literary output are Vivien Bretherton, Eleanor Hammond, Alexander Hull, Laura Miller, Kay Cleaver Strahan, Elizabeth Lambert Wood, Ared White, and Richard L. Neuberger.

Of Oregon's poets, with the exception of Joaquin Miller, the best known is Edwin Markham, born at Oregon City in 1852, though his fame is based almost entirely on the polemical "Man With the Hoe," which was written at San Francisco in 1898. He published other volumes of poetry during his residence in New York and in 1927 he edited the *Book of Poetry*. Except for the fact of his birth in Oregon, the poet has had little connection with the State.

Minnie Myrtle Miller, ex-wife of Joaquin Miller, during the 1870's was a poet in her own right, composing in the early Victorian style. Sam L. Simpson (1846-99) wrote one popular piece, "Beautiful Willamette" (1868), that escapes the obscurity of his later verse.

Beloved poet of Oregon scenes is Ella Higginson, (b. ca. 1860) who began as a successful author of western short stories and by degrees became known as the author of several volumes of poetry, including *When the Birds Go North Again* (1898), *The Snow Pearls* (1897), and *The Vanishing Races and Other Poems* (1911). Her lyrics have tempted many composers and her songs have been rendered by Calve', Caruso, McCormack, and other singers.

Charles Erskine Scott Wood, for 35 years a Portland lawyer, is now living in California. His *Poet in the Desert* was published at Portland in 1915, but he is more widely known for the satirical *Heavenly Discourse* (1927) and *Earthly Discourse* (1937). During a long and active life Mr. Wood has boxed the compass from a conservative corporation counsel to a vigorous radical graced with humor.

One of the most gifted of Oregon's sons, John Reed (1887-1920) of Portland, finally devoted his talents to the cause of world revolution and received the unique distinction of burial at the foot of the Kremlin in Moscow, where his grave is an object of communist pilgrimage. As a young man and Harvard graduate he was a poet of distinction; the themes of *Sangar* (1912), *The Day in Bohemia* (1913), and *Tamburlane and Other Poems* (1916) in their virile imagery and lyrical abandon give little hint of the potential revolutionist in him. The rebellious motive becomes apparent in his graphic articles on Pancho Villa and on labor subjects in the *Metropolitan Magazine* in 1913 and 1914. Soon he was active in several strikes and wrote as an observer for the radical *Masses*. In 1917 he went to Russia. Intimacy with the leaders of the Russian Revolution resulted in his powerfully written *Red Russia* (1919) and the classic of the left, *Ten Days that Shook the World* (1919).

Mary Carolyn Davies, educated in Portland and later a resident of New York City, combines a sensitive lyrical gift with flashes of intuitive insight. Following the war poems, *The Drums in Our Street* (1918), oppressive with the tragedy of men fighting, came a one-act allegorical play, *The Slave With Two Faces* (1918), and other volumes of poetry, notably *Youth Riding* (1919) and a book of western verse, *The Skyline Trail* (1924).

A pure lyrical note is struck in the poetry of Hazel Hall (1886-1924). An invalid after her twelfth year, her failing eyesight later caused her to turn from doing needle work for her living to writing. Her poems, suggestive of the exquisite sensitivity of Emily Dickinson, appeared in such magazines as *Century, Yale Review,* and the *New Republic.* Her three published volumes are *Curtains* (1921), *Walkers* (1923) and *Cry of Time* (1928), a posthumous volume. Simplicity of statement and images that seem almost inevitable mark such poems as "Three Girls," selected by William Stanley Braithwaite as one of the five best poems of 1920.

A number of Portland poets have published books of literary value: Mable Holmes Parsons with *Pastels and Silhouettes* (1921) and *Listener's Room* (1940); Ethel Romig Fuller with *White Peaks and Green* (1928), and *Kitchen Sonnets* (1931); Ada Hastings Hedges with *Desert Poems* (1930); Eleanor Allen with *Seeds of Earth* (1933); Howard McKinley Corning with *These People* (1926) and *The Mountain in the*

Sky (1930); and Laurence Pratt with *A Saga of a Paper Mill* (1935) and *Harp of Water* (1939). Other contemporary poets who merit mention are Queene B. Lister, Charles Oluf Olsen, Walter Evans Kidd, Ben Hur Lampman, Courtland W. Matthews, Phyllis Morden, Borghild Lee, and Eleanor Hansen, all of Portland; Ernest G. Moll of Eugene who has published three volumes of verse; Lulu Piper Aiken of Ontario; Paul E. Tracy of Baker County, a plumber, who writes of the people of eastern Oregon; and Verne Bright of Aloha. Bright has written a book-length narrative poem, *Mountain Man,* of the early trapping period and the Oregon Trail, parts of which have appeared in the *Frontier and Midland* and the *North American Review*. These poets exhibit a feeling for their own locale that augurs well for the continued vitality of Oregon poetry.

Oregon journalism (*see NEWSPAPERS AND RADIO*) owes much to Harvey W. Scott, editor of the Portland *Oregonian* from 1877 to 1910, president of the Oregon Historical Society from 1898 to 1901, and author of many historical articles, collected in six volumes as *History of the Oregon Country* (1924).

A number of publishers have been active in Portland, producing books by indigenous authors. Among them were S. J. McCormick, George H. Himes, A. G. Walling, E. M. Waite, The J. K. Gill Co., F. W. Baltes and Co., and McArthur and Wood. At present the University Press of Eugene and Binfords and Mort of Portland are publishing many excellent books, mostly of a regional nature. The John Henry Nash Press at the University of Oregon prints books of fine format and typography.

Theater, Music and Art

THE history of fine art in Oregon is a brief one. Yet a good deal of art has been created in the state during the past fifty years. The early inspiration of this work was mainly the romantic interest aroused in artists of eastern communities by the primitive and frontier life of the Rockies and the regions beyond.

Among the settlers themselves the urge for self-expression most commonly found release in the singing of homely songs brought from the East and from Europe. Instrumental music for such occasions was largely provided by "fiddles" and accordians, many of which had first enlivened the camp-fire gatherings on the "road to Oregon," or had eased the nostalgia of gold-seeking miners in distant Eldorados. Only occasionally in the early decades was itinerant entertainment available. The visit, then, in 1855, of Stephen C. Massett, impersonator, singer, song writer, and globe trotter, journeying from San Francisco by boat, for readings and concerts at Astoria, Vancouver, Portland and other interior Oregon towns, today seems symbolic. While he was giving a concert in the small Salem courthouse, lighted by six tallow candles, all were dramatically extinguished by a gust of wind as he was singing "The Light of Other Days." At the close of his performance at Corvallis he was obliged to shake hands with half the frontier population before they would let him depart. Appreciation for the arts was inherent in Oregonians from the beginning.

Later, with the growth of settlement Oregon came into contact with the general development of art in America. Theaters were built in the larger towns, and applauding audiences, their eagerness for entertainment often exceeding their artistic discrimination, viewed the productions of the professional stage or listened to the voices and instruments of the world's great musicians. Symphony organizations and choral societies were organized, employing almost entirely local talent. Art museums came into being, their services supplementing the activities of the few artists who sojourned for a time amidst the western scene, or remained to settle among the native-born craftsmen.

By 1915 the state had become articulate in the truest sense. The physical scene was still unspoiled and grand. But now there was as much respect for the life of the people as for the beauty of the region, although as yet this "putting forth" was often tentative; the evidence was more of promise than of fulfillment, more traditional than native. Only from the perspective of the present does the achievement of the past twenty-five years in the field of the arts have significance. Today in Oregon the worthy work of the stage, the concert hall, and the art studio, professional and amateur, enjoys the recognition of a discerning patronage.

THE THEATER

The first known theatrical performance in the Oregon Country was given in 1846 by the crew of the British sloop *Modeste,* anchored in the Columbia River off Fort Vancouver. Settlers from many miles up the Willamette Valley made the journey to see the play, which, oddly enough, was a sophisticated drama, *Three Weeks of Marriage.* This production, like others that followed at rare intervals, was melodramatic in theme and treatment; virtue and vice were plainly marked and the moral heavily stressed. In reporting the performance *The Spectator* of Oregon City generously remarked that the actors "sustained their characters in the most creditable manner, that even had Will Shakespeare himself looked in he could not have said, nay . . ."

In 1855, in the gold camp of Browntown in Southern Oregon, the entrancing San Francisco child star, Lotta Crabtree, entertained the miners and was showered with coins and nuggets. However, when she returned in 1863, at the age of sixteen, she was hissed when she endeavored to sing patriotic airs declaring her loyalty to the North. "She faced a cold and relentless audience and they never gave her a hand," her manager related.

During the 50's the people of Oregon were entertained principally by mediocre minstrel troupes and one-ring circuses. In Portland, in 1858, the Stewart Theater housed a small company of players for the "better part of the season." After that the theater appears to have diminished in interest for the home-building Oregonians until 1861, when the Willamette Theater opened in Portland. Here in 1864 appeared "Julia Dean Hayes, for a limited number of nights." Her plays were *Othello, Hamlet, Romeo and Juliet,* and *The Man in the Iron Mask.* She interrupted her Portland engagement with several one-week stands at Salem. In the same year Mr. and Mrs. Charles Kean appeared with their Shakesperian company in the *Merchant of Venice*. A traveling troupe of players visiting Salem and other Willamette Valley towns in 1875 presented *Ten Nights in a Barroom*.

As Portland continued to grow, her interest in the theater grew also. In 1875 the New Market Theater, Oregon's first brick showhouse, was built at a cost of $100,000, and a truly gorgeous presentation of *Rip Van Winkle* was staged. Soon thereafter the Tivoli (1883), playing comic opera, and the Casino (1885), fitted with a bar and tables and playing cheap melodrama, were opened. The latter, under moral protest, was later reconstructed and renamed the New Park (1888). Thereafter grand opera, alternating with the lighter vein of Gilbert and Sullivan, was offered, with occasional productions of such melodramas as *The Creole* and the sensational *After Dark*. Portland's prominence as a mecca of the drama brought eager playgoers from as far away as San Francisco.

Traveling drama, however, reached its acme with the opening in February, 1890, of the Marquam Grand Opera House. The initial production was *Robin Hood*. In the two decades that followed, such pretentious shows as *Ben Hur,* the *Old Homestead,* and the *Count of Monte Cristo* made this house the center of Oregon's theatrical and social life. Here in 1893 James L. Corbett, the prize ring champion, played in *Gentleman Jack*. Great artists who performed at the Marquam Grand were Sarah Bernhardt, Frederick Warde, Sir Henry Irving, Ellen Terry, Edwin Booth, Lillian Russell, Julia Arthur, Nat Goodwin, James K. Hackett, John Drew, and many others. A galaxy of opera stars, including Modjeska, Melba, and Nordica, with supporting troupes, made Portland the entertainment center of the Northwest.

Portland's theatrical production reached its most extravagant attempt at realism during this period, when the road show *Blue Jeans* played the Marquam Grand. *Blue Jeans* was a melodrama with one scene laid in a sawmill, and since sawmills played a major part in Northwest life, its opening was well but critically attended. The promoters advertised this scene as "Mechanically Perfect in Every Detail." The stage "mill," however, proved to be merely a pitifully inept reproduction, and when the silk-hatted villain sneered at his brave but helpless victim about to be fed into it; "Die like a dog, you—," he was interrupted by a clear, bellowing voice from the audience: "Set your blocks or you won't get no clears outa that log." This advice was thoroughly justified, and the uproar which followed caused the manager to ring down the curtain for good on the Portland run of this play.

Meanwhile, as early as 1894, nearly a dozen other Oregon towns had built theaters, invariably termed opera houses. These exhibited road shows almost exclusively, with the occasional "great" of the legitimate stage taxing their usual 1000-seat capacity.

Early in the 1900's several small theaters came into being, presenting principally variety shows, burlesque, and "thrillers." This phase was a further development of the variety type of entertainment brought to Portland in 1889 by John Cordray, but now made acceptable for women as well as men. Straight vaudeville houses were opened under the management of Sullivan and Considine, Keating and Flood, and Alexander Pantages. On one occasion the latter presented Charles Chaplin in *A Night in a London Music Hall.*

These years saw also the forming in Portland of local stock companies playing New York successes. George L. Baker, responding to the trend of the times, organized the Baker Stock Company (1902). Forty-week seasons of stock were not unusual. Road shows continued to visit and when, later, the Columbia was opened, a packed house thrilled to the famous Mrs. Leslie Carter playing *Madame Du Barry.*

The first moving picture was shown in Portland, August 7, 1897. Soon thereafter small movie houses or "nickelodeons" sprang up in Portland and in other Oregon towns and became so popular that by 1915 the legitimate theater, competing with its most formidable entertainment rival, was operating at a loss. Nearly every small town in the state had a movie "palace," while the larger cities supported from three to six; Portland had more than twenty. As a consequence, theatricals suffered a much diminished patronage.

With the waning of the professional theater in the state, local self-expression in the field of amateur acting made a bid for public recognition. A dramatic class, begun under the auspices of the Portland Labor College and directed by Doris Smith, soon developed into the Labor College Players. The first group of its kind in the country, it produced such one-act plays as Davis' *Miss Civilization* and Yeats' *Land of Heart's Desire,* and was the inspirational medium for the founding of similar groups elsewhere.

Popular support waned, allowing the Labor College Players to die after a few years, but it was revived in 1925 with the forming of the Portland Civic Theater, until 1927 known as the Portland Art Theater. In 1929 this organization absorbed the locally popular Bess Whitcomb Players, an independent amateur group formed in 1927, and enlarged its activities. Self-supporting and nonprofit-making, the Civic

Theater has offered the public creditable and often distinctive productions, with such Broadway successes as O'Neil's *Anna Christie* and *Ah, Wilderness,* Coward's *Design for Living,* and Rice's *Judgment Day;* and has given amateur performances, sometimes while the shows were still running in New York. One-act play writing contests were conducted for local talent, and in 1931 a school of drama was added as a feature of the theater's activities. Dean Collins, teaching playwriting to large classes, also made adaptations of such universal favorites as *Alice in Wonderland,* and the *Christmas Carol.* The former had several presentations as an out-of-door Portland Rose Festival feature. In 1936 the Civic Theater school of drama came under the direction of the University of Oregon extension division. Since 1937 the Civic Theater Blue Room productions have supplemented the usual program of five stage productions each year.

Since the middle twenties Shakespearian drama seemingly has appealed most strongly to the Oregon play-going public, with visiting English troupes most loudly acclaimed. Local performances, however, have not been lacking. A civic Elizabethan theater maintained at Ashland since 1935 presents a yearly summer Shakespearean Festival. Under the direction of Angus L. Bowmar, of the Southern Oregon College of Education, such plays as *Hamlet* and the *Taming of the Shrew* are staged with professional actors carrying the leads, assisted by supporting casts of students. For one week four plays are given two performances each to audiences averaging seven hundred each evening. In 1937 and 1938 the Reed College Players and the Civic Theater Players jointly produced *Othello* in summer out-of-door performances.

For several decades dramatic pageants have been popular. Since the late twenties the Portland Rose Festival Association has staged mammoth productions at the Multnomah Stadium and the city parks, celebrating the symbolism of the rose, the city's chosen flower. These presentations, and the Oregon Trail Festival given periodically at Eugene, have been ably directed by Doris Smith and others prominent in the state's dramatic life. For a brief time around 1920 Portland's Chinatown had a Chinese theater.

Since 1936 the Federal Theater Project of the Works Progress Administration staged effectively Shakespeare's *Taming of the Shrew,* Langner's *Pursuit of Happiness,* and the three "living newspaper" plays, Arthur Arent's *Power,* and *One Third of a Nation,* and Sundgaard's *Spirochete.* Several of these and the children's fantasies, *Pinocchio* and *Hansel and Gretel,* were produced in the WPA Federal Theater, Portland, opened to the public in May 1938. Dance skits given at Timberline Lodge in 1937, depicting flax culture, Indian life, and other regional folk activities, were followed in 1938 by *Timberline Tintypes,* sketches portraying Oregon logger life. These performances were under the supervision of Bess Whitcomb, State Director of the Federal Theater Project. *Tapestry in Linen,* a play dealing with flax culture, was written by the project and staged at Mount Angel in the summer of 1937. Since its beginning in October 1936, the Portland unit played to an aggregate audience of 200,000; of this number, 83 per cent were admitted free of charge.

Oregon has had a few well-recognized playwrights. Jules Eckert Goodman, born at Gervais in 1876, received national acclaim in 1910 for his play *Mother,* and later was co-author of *Potash and Perlmutter.* Margaret Mayo, born at Salem in 1882 and first an actress, was the author of *Polly of the Circus* and other plays produced on Broadway. Among contemporary playwrights, Alice Henson Ernst is known for her dramas based on the Alaska gold rush and aspects of Indian life, published under the title of *High Country,* and Laura Miller for short folk plays locally produced. *Bloodstream,* by Frederick Schlick was produced at the Times Square Theatre in New York City in 1932, and his *The Man Who Broke His Heart* was released by Paramount in 1935 under the title of *Wharf Angel.* Sally Elliott Allen is known for studies in domestic life. Mrs. Allen, author of more than twenty one-act plays, in 1933 won the James B. Kerr award, offered by the Portland Civic Theater, for a three-act play, *What the Gulls Knew.* All of these writers have had one-act plays produced by little theater groups of the state.

The noted actress, Blanche Bates, was born in Portland in 1873 but three years later moved to San Francisco, where she made her first stage appearance in 1894. Earle Larrimore, Ona Munson, Mayo Methot, and Portland Hoffa, among contemporary players, were Portland born, and Clark Gable once resided in Oregon.

MUSIC

The French-Canadian voyageurs plying the Columbia River from 1818 until about 1845 enlivened their days and nights with gay songs in French patois, but the River of the West seems not to have had a chant peculiarly its own. A lusty song, "Fur Trader's Ballad," was sung amidst laughter and filled flagons on Yuletide occasions at old Fort Astoria, but what tunes the trappers may have sung on their long winter hunts are unknown. Stanzas adapted from the English and Irish poets and heard wherever a river threaded the Northern wilderness were sung by Narcissa Whitman, a particularly good singer, and Eliza Spalding, wives of the missionaries, upon their arrival in the Oregon Country in 1836. Most often heard were "Hail to the Chief," "At the Clear Running Fountain," and Thomas Moore's "Canadian Boat Song." The overland pioneers, as appears from countless references in old journals, brought with them texts and tunes from their homelands which they sang on almost every occasion. Only fragments remain of the covered-wagon ballads and homesteader minstrelsy. "Oh, Susannah," by Stephen Foster, was universally popular during the California gold rush and was soon carried into Oregon. But for the next few decades such songs of sentiment as "Annie of the Vale," "The Old Log Hut," "Sweet Genevieve," and "I Wandered by the Brookside," were most frequently heard, supplementing the countless religious songs found in the denominational hymnals.

As early as 1849 a program of vocal music was given at Oregon City by William Morgan, who had "given concerts in New York and other Eastern cities." Among the twelve numbers sung by him were such long-forgotten songs as "Pretty Star of the Night" and "The Ivy Green." For dances of that day, particularly the Christmas Ball held each year at Oregon City, music was furnished by the United States Army Band, stationed there with other military units to preserve order among the Indian tribes and the gold seekers turning northward from California. Pioneer Oregon had many singing groups, usually associated with religious organizations. In 1856 a chorus of young people trained at Oregon City journeyed to Portland and sang from the collection, *Floria's Festival,* and for a quarter-century pupils of the old Portland Academy sang in happy unison from *Merry Chimes,* a popular western song book. In the 1860's the Finck family at Aurora, organized the Aurora Band, which was soon very popular at fairs and political rallies throughout the Willamette Valley. Years later one of their number, Henry T. Finck, became known as a New York music critic and wrote the autobiographical *Adventures in the Golden Age of Music.* The DeMoss family, like troubadours of old, toured the state and surrounding country, singing to settler and city dweller alike.

As Oregon developed culturally, symphonic music began to make its appeal. The first known orchestral programs were given in Portland in 1868 and 1870 by a United States Infantry Band. In 1875 an amateur musical society was formed, and in 1882 the Orchestral Union was organized. This union with the newly-established Apollo Club gave a musical program in 1883 in a building which stood on the site of the present Municipal Auditorium.

Thereafter, musical activities in Portland grew in volume and interest. With a 160-voice chorus and a 25-piece orchestra, William H. Boyer conducted the first performance of Handel's *Messiah* on January 16, 1895. The following year the city was electrified by the initial visit of the great Sousa and his band. It was during these years, beginning with a concert on October 30, 1895, that the original Portland Symphony Orchestra, first conducted by W. H. Kinross, struggled into being. In 1902 and 1903, with Edgar E. Coursen directing, it played accompaniments for concerts given by the Willamette Valley Choral Union at Corvallis and Eugene. Organized in 1899, the Choral Union gave yearly festival concerts in principal towns throughout the Willamette Valley.

During these years the cowboy, the logger, the miner, and the itinerant ranch-hand sang or chanted as he labored, or when he gathered with his companions in the bunkhouse or around a campfire. None of their songs, however, were of local origin. In certain instances liberties of improvisation were taken with well-known compositions. Not until after 1900 was one of these songs, a refrain of the "road," given written record: "Portland County Jail" is included in Carl Sandburg's *American Songbag*.

The first "Music Day" in the history of expositions in the United States was given at Festival Hall, Lewis and Clark Exposition ground, Portland, in 1905; Frederick W. Goodrich was in charge. Three years later, at the Alaska-Yukon Exposition at Seattle, a Portland chorus sang Samuel Simpson's "Beautiful Willamette," composed by Father Dominic, O. S. B., of Mount Angel Abbey. The same composer's overture, "Call of the West," was played by the Portland Symphony Orchestra at a Portland concert, May 1, 1914.

The Portland Music Festival Association, after two years (1917-1918) of symphonic and choral music supremacy in the Northwest, under the leadership of Carl Denton and W. H. Boyer, suspended because of conditions brought on by the World War. Following the dedication of the Municipal Auditorium in 1918, the Portland Symphony Orchestra, which had previously played in theaters, opened an annual program of concerts that continued for twenty years. From 1925, guided by the distinguished conductor, Willem Van Hoogstraten, this 60-piece orchestra, recognized as one of the foremost in America, played both the established masters and contemporary composers. From 1923 to 1925, and again from 1929 to 1938, the Portland Choral Society, sometimes called the Portland Symphony Chorus, sang once yearly with the orchestra. Oratorios by Handel, Verdi, and Mendelssohn, among others, were given. In 1938 the Symphony management announced a two-year suspension of activities.

Beginning in 1919, Hal Webber pioneered in the development of children's orchestras. Under his stimulation the Portland Junior Symphony Orchestra was organized in 1925; conducted by Jacques Gershkovitch, it continues its noteworthy performances. In 1936 the Stadium Philharmonic Orchestra gave the first of its annual series of six outdoor summer concerts, or "Starlight Symphonies," with distinguished guest-conductors and soloists.

A few Oregon musicians, members of the Society of Oregon Composers, have had works produced by the Portland Symphony Orchestra, or have been accorded publication and production elsewhere. Among these are the former Portlander, Aaron Avshalomoff, for his suite "The Soul of Kin Sei"; Manuel Palacios, for "Entr'acte Valse" for strings, and the deceased Dominic Waedenschwiler, for the previously mentioned "Call of the West." Dent Mowrey, nationally known pianist of Portland, is the composer, among other symphonic pieces, of "Dance Americaine," and the tone poem "Gargoyles of Notre Dame." George Natanson and E. Bruce Knowlton, in the 1920's and early 1930's, produced operas and light operas, a few of them written by the producers. Some sacred music and a few popular songs have been locally composed, with pieces by Alexander Hull and L. W. Lewis among the most noteworthy. The Oregon State Song, "Oregon, My Oregon," was selected in competition in 1920; the words are by J. A. Buchanan, the music by Henry T. Murtagh.

The Oregon State Music Teachers' Association has long had a wide influence, and groups and societies for the study, composition, and enjoyment of music, vocal and instrumental, number more than two score. All of the principal ethnic groups—German, Norwegian, Swedish, Swiss—have large choral organizations, most of which center in Portland. All of the state's institutions of learning have ably directed music departments, and many have choruses or glee clubs, of which the University of Oregon Glee Club is the best known. Howard Barlow, the distinguished orchestra conductor, first lived and studied in Portland. A few dance bands originating in Portland, notably George Olsen's, are nationally known. Through the years nearly all of the great personages of concert or operatic fame have sung in Portland and elsewhere in the state.

Since 1936 the Federal Music Project of the Work Projects Administration has made band and orchestral music widely available to the public. Guided by Frederick W. Goodrich, State Director and Oregon's only member of the National Association of Orchestra Leaders, the project is supplying music for many civic occasions and, in the spring of 1940 revived symphonic music, which had been temporarily discontinued with the suspension of the Portland Symphony Orchestra in 1938. The orchestra is under the direction of Leslie Hodge. Since December 1936 the bands and orchestras of the Oregon Federal Music Project have played to audiences aggregating nearly three-quarters of a million persons, including 200,000 in the schools of the state.

ARTS AND HANDICRAFTS

Arts and handicrafts in the Oregon country began with the original inhabitants, the Indians. While none of the tribes of the region were blanket weavers, garmenting themselves in grasses, or in skins, whole or woven, all were basket makers, fashioning with withes and grasses waterproof containers. Into these, symbolic designs were worked: images of the thunderbird, the fire-crow, and the sun. Wooden bowls, a few bearing designs, were carved from cedar and other soft woods. Everywhere the bark house door-posts were carved and painted with tribal insignia for the protection of the dwellers. The Coast Indians reached a high level of art in the decoration of their canoes, often of great size, carved, inlaid, and colored with the images of whales and thunderbirds. Likewise, their grave-canoes, holding their dead in air in some riverside memaloose, were supported by frames decorated with meaningful triangles and circles in black and red. Centers for the fashioning of arrowheads and spear-heads, work in which the red craftsman took a pride of design, were maintained in many parts of the state. Still remaining, but gradually wasting from the surface rock on which they were carved, are the petroglyphs of the vanished tribesmen.

The earliest professional painter to bring art to Oregon was Lieutenant Henry Warre, sent by the British government to picture the Pacific Northwest. Oil paintings of Fort Vancouver and Oregon City, as they appeared in 1841, are of much interest today. Shortly thereafter a United States Army artist, his name now forgotten, accompanied a mounted rifle regiment and painted several excellent views of the Columbia River. In the 1830's John Mix Stanley did numerous sketches of both people and scenery. On his second tour, in the early 1850's, he painted portraits of such frontier personages as John McLoughlin, Peter Skene Ogden, and Amos Lovejoy.

A few skilled cabinet makers and allied craftsmen followed the covered wagons westward. Settling in the growing centers, these workmen-artists executed, painstakingly if somewhat imperfectly, much of the state's early household furniture. The German Aurora colony produced numerous pieces of able workmanship—spool beds, oak chests, woven-bottom chairs—now collectors' items. The members of this colony, and other craftsmen in Portland and Oregon City, fashioned architectural iron work of great beauty. Much of the pottery used by the pioneers was moulded and burned at the Buena Vista kilns, on the mid-Willamette River.

About 1880 Edward Espey's genius flowered briefly, leaving as his best creation the oil painting, *Repose,* now hanging in the Portland Public Library. Espey died at 29 and little is known of his career or his work. Toward the close of the century Cleveland Rockwell's marine views, notably the much-reproduced *Columbia River Bar,* found their way into many galleries and private collections.

Early contributions in the field of sculpture in Oregon came mainly from visiting artists attracted by the esthetic possibilities of Indian and western life. Hermon A. MacNeil, who had studied in Paris and Rome, made several trips to northern territories and reservations; his *Coming of the White Man,* an Indian group study, stands in Washington Park at Portland. Contemporaries of MacNeil were A. Phimister Proctor, represented by his monuments in Eugene and Portland, and Alice Cooper, whose life-size bronze of *Sacajawea,* the Shoshone Indian woman who guided the Lewis and Clark party, was unveiled in Portland in 1905. Two sculptured fountains of this period grace downtown Portland streets. The *Skidmore Fountain,* near the waterfront, was the work of Olin Levi Warner, who made an extensive tour through the West in the late 1880's. Between the Plaza Block and Lownsdale Square, the *Elk Fountain,* a bronze figure by Roland H. Perry, dedicated in 1900, stands where elk grazed in pre-pioneer days. In the early years of the Twentieth Century, Douglas Tilden, called "the most eminent sculptor of the Western Coast," completed his group study, *Soldiers' Monument,* dedicated to Oregon's Spanish-American War dead. It stands in Lownsdale Square.

Two native-born cartoonists came into prominence in the nineties. Homer Davenport (1867-1912), born near Silverton, won international attention by his vitriolic anti-Tammany cartoons of 1896 in the New York *Journal* and his Spanish-American war sketches of 1898. Frank Bowers, Davenport's cousin and a Silverton contemporary, also won notice as a New York cartoonist.

Public interest in art appreciation received its earliest encouragement in 1892, when the Portland Art Association was organized and an art museum opened on the second floor of the old City Library. Outgrowing these facilities in 1905, the first public art museum in the Pacific Northwest was built and art instruction to the public was begun. Here, for a quarter of a century, many students received instruction in various branches of art, some graduating to continue study elsewhere, a few winning national recognition. Meanwhile, an appreciative audience viewed the growing permanent and traveling exhibits, represented by a wide selection of American and Old World paintings of all schools.

The first decades of the present century saw a flowering of art in Oregon, although only a few of the local artists were native born. Soon after 1900 Charles Erskine Scott Wood, poet-lawyer, executed some excellent paintings in oils and water color. The impressionist, Childe Hassam of New England, visiting the state in 1908, painted forty canvasses of the "high desert" in the Blitzen River region of Harney County. Louis B. Akin (1872-1913), native-born, beginning an art career as a sign painter, devoted the concluding fifteen years of his life to portrayals of the Southwest Indians. The marine and landscape oils of Rockwell W. Carey, born near Salem in 1882, and C. C. McKim, who died in Portland in 1938, were prominent among artists of this period. Merle DeVore Johnson, born at Oregon City in 1874, studied at Stanford, going to New York in 1910 as an illustrator and cartoonist. He became a prominent authority on American first editions. He died in 1935.

Through the years the majority of Oregon artists have been exponents of open-air painting. In a desire to sympathetically portray the regional scene they have inclined toward realism. The airy lyricism of the landscapes of Clyde Leon Keller (b. 1872), who has worked in Portland since 1906, and of Anthony Euwer (b. 1877) of the same city since 1915 has aided in popularizing local pictorial art. Since 1912, Harry Wentz, born at The Dalles, has divided his creative efforts between teaching at the Portland Art Museum and painting water colors of Oregon's mountains and sea coast. Percy Manser, who has lived in the Hood River Valley since about 1920, has likewise painted mountain and coastal scenes much admired by Oregonians. During the 1920's Emil Jacques, Belgian artist, conducted a studio in Portland while teaching art at Portland (Columbia) University; he left his influence upon several local artists, and contributed nine panels to St. Mary's Cathedral. Coming to Oregon ten years ago from the range-lands of the Wyoming Rockies, C. S. Price (b. 1874), largely self-trained, and a friend of the cowboy artist, Charles Russell, has executed some noteworthy oils of life in this region. Two of his pioneer studies, done while employed on a Civil Works Administration art project in 1934, are on permanent display in the Portland Public Library; two others hang in the Senate Office Building and the United States Treasury Building, Washington, D. C.

Since 1915 at least three portrait painters of merit have lived in the state. Likenesses of Oregonians, painted by Sidney Bell (b. 1888) from 1915 to 1930, hang in New York and Washington galleries. Colista Dowling, a long-time resident, has painted portraits of many prominent Oregonians. Leonabel Jacobs, a former University of Oregon student, has painted likenesses of Mrs. Warren G. Harding and Mrs. Calvin Coolidge.

Other artists, native to the state or of extended residence, have expressed themselves in a variety of mediums and techniques. Born in Oregon were the three well-known magazine illustrators, Henry Raleigh (b. 1880), Fred Cooper (b. 1883), and Mahlon Blaine. Regional bird life has been recorded in colors by R. Bruce Horsfall (b. 1869) in numerous books and magazines. Wylong Fong, a young Chinese artist living in Portland some fifteen years ago, created vividly in oils but is best remembered for Oriental figure studies done with pastels on velvet. Phyllis Muirden, teaching art in Portland high schools, has executed some much-admired water colors.

At least four etchers may be claimed by the state. W. F. McIlwraith, a New Englander, made Portland his home for more than twenty years, returning to New York in 1939. His subjects were chiefly historical and marine, done in free and incisive lines and with rich tonal gradations. The highly-acclaimed architectural etchings of Louis Conrad Rosenberg, born in Portland in 1890, hang in the British Museum, the Royal Academy of Arts at Stockholm, and the Smithsonian Institute. Eyler Brown and Lloyd Reynolds, among younger craftsmen, have had notice beyond the state.

In 1924 monumental sculpture as a civic contribution again received recognition when Douglas Tilden's *Circuit Rider* was unveiled on the State Capitol grounds. The 10-foot bronze of *Abraham Lincoln,* mounted in the Portland Park Blocks, was sculptured by George Fite Waters in 1928. Gutzon Borglum's giant bronze of *Harvey W. Scott,* early editor of the Portland *Oregonian,* erected in 1933, looms atop Mount Tabor. The state's largest sculptural acquisition is the *Oregon Pioneer* statue, by Ulric Ellerhusen, which stands on the tower above the new State Capitol.

Within recent years a small group of sculptors have made their homes in Oregon. Native born was Roswell Dosch, whose talent had just begun to flower when his life was cut short in 1918 by influenza while serving as an officer in the World War. At that time he was head of the School of Applied Arts of the University of Oregon. Following him at this institution from 1921 to 1927 was Avard Fairbanks (b. 1897), now teaching at the University of Michigan. His brother, J. Leo Fairbanks (b. 1880), has been art instructor at Oregon State College since 1923. Both have done portrait busts, group studies, plaques, and architectural art work for both civic and private use. Adrien Voisin, after study in Paris and a period of residence in California, came to Oregon in 1931. He has done portrait busts of Indians and of prominent Oregonians and plaques of historical subjects. Gabriel Lavare, who also came from California in the early 1930's, is best known for his bas-reliefs—carvings over the three entrance doors and the *Mother and Child* medallion in the foyer of the new Oregon State Library, the lion and the lioness at the entrance to Washington Park, Portland—and for the Town Club fountain. Oliver L. Barrett, sculptor-teacher at the University of Oregon for the past five years, in 1939 executed the marine figure standing in the Battleship Oregon Memorial Park, Portland. Ralph Stackpole, born in Oregon in 1885, early removed to California and Paris and gained recognition as a portraitist in bronze. A new approach to sculpture is being made by Anna Keeney (b. 1898), now living in Chicago, who has just completed a large fountain for the Leander Stone School in that city. The artist uses glazed terra cotta forms set in solid stone for an entirely new effect. Miss Keeney studied sculpture under Avard Fairbanks at the University of Oregon, from which she graduated in 1928, remaining there as assistant instructor for two years. Her mother lives in Arlington, Oregon. Miss Keeney modeled the figure of the *Fallen Aviator,* at Condon, Oregon.

With exhibits and class rooms crowding the original Art Museum building, the first unit of a new and permanent structure was erected in 1932; a second unit was completed in 1939. Indubitably, the works shown at the Art Museum of such Europeans as Monet and Derain, and later of Picasso and Matisse—the latter two to a lesser extent—have influenced the subject matter and treatment of many contemporary artists. The experimental foreign techniques have modified somewhat the tendency of some state-loving artists to reproduce too literally what they saw around them. Also influencing art expression have been the art classes at the various schools of higher learning, notably the University of Oregon and the Oregon State College. The former institution has been most influential in sculpture. The University of Oregon Art Museum, erected within the last decade, houses, among other notable groups, the Murray Warner collection of Oriental art (*see EUGENE*).

Contemporary Oregon artists, many of them young, number more than two score, working in a variety of mediums and techniques. Charlotte Mish, Portland, is best known for her marines and landscapes in oil but has also done portraits. An example from the water colors of Edward Sewell represented Oregon at the "American Scene" Exhibition at Indianapolis in 1933. In 1935 Edgar Bohlman, a thirty-three year old native of Forest Grove, made his New York debut with paintings of cafe and street life done while living in Spain; the work displayed an interesting mixture of boldness and detail. Prior to this, in 1931, he designed the stage sets for the New York production of *The Venetian Glass Nephew*. After painting quietly in Portland for more than ten years, Darrel Austin, in 1938 exhibited in Hollywood and New York, winning acclaim for his oils of women and girls in green orchards executed in a rhythmic riot of color reminiscent of Van Gogh and Renoir. Maude Walling Wanker (b. 1882), with a photographic intent, has placed on canvas nearly all of the state's historical sites and buildings; a few less than one hundred paintings done since the summer of 1933. Albert Gerlach (b. 1884) of Portland is the designer of a number of art glass windows installed in churches, theaters, and halls in Oregon and Washington, while Bernard Francis Geiser is painting a series of murals for St. Mark's Episcopal Church, Portland. David McCosh (b. 1903) of the University of Oregon art department depicts in oils and water colors subjects of social significance, avoiding rigid formulae. His *Venita, Oregon,* done in oil, distinguished the small group of art works representing Oregon at the New York World's Fair in 1939. Among his staff colleagues, Andrew Vincent has been exhibited at the Chicago Art Institute.

Several contemporary artists are producing murals and easel paintings dealing with regional and social themes. The mural, *Early Mail Carriers of the West,* by Rockwell W. Carey, at the Newberg post office, and the two tempera panels by John Ballator, at the St. Johns post office, were executed under the sponsorship of the Section of Fine Arts of the United States Treasury Department. Under the guidance of the Civil Works Administration and the Works Progress Administration Art Projects, paintings and decorations in a wide variety of mediums, including glass mosaic and wood marquetry, have recently been produced for federal, county, and city buildings. Frontier and industrial subjects are most popular. WPA muralists include Amiee Gorham, Virginia Darce, Howard Sewell, and Edward Quigley; and in a diversified field the woodcuts of Charles E. Heaney, the lithographs of Kurt Fuerer, the wood carvings of Eric Lamade, and the wood marquetry of Martina Gangle deserve special mention.

Among the various enterprises of the Federal Arts Project is the metal work of O. B. Dawson, who, with a small crew of craftsmen, fashioned in 1937 the ornamental wrought iron gates for the University of Oregon Library and for the Memorial Union Building on the campus of the Oregon State College, and the grille and metal fittings in the Mount Hood Timberline Lodge. Skilled cabinet makers and other craftsmen also furnished the Lodge as a recreational center in a manner harmonious to the rugged natural scene. At Portland, a pottery kiln built as a WPA project and sponsored and maintained by the Arts and Crafts Society, offers its facilities free to the public. Cooperating with the Works Progress Administration, the Salem Federal Art Center came into being in the summer of 1938. The Center exhibits the works of living American artists, national and local, conducts a free art school, and offers public lectures. With the cooperation of sponsors in cities and towns near Salem, branch Federal Art Centers are planned, with exhibits, and classes taught from the Salem center. A similar art center, but more elaborately planned, is in prospect (1940) for Portland. State WPA Art Project activities have been in charge of Dr. Margery Hoffman Smith, Art Director, and Thomas Laman, Assistant Art Director.

Several organizations of artists, while promoting their own work, have fostered the development of talent and art appreciation in the state. The earliest of these, the Arts and Crafts Society, was founded in 1905 by Mrs. Lee Hoffman. In December 1929 the Oregon Society of Artists was formed, while the Oregon and Portland chapters of the American Artists Professional League were established in 1931. All of these groups hold annual or semi-annual exhibits. From 1930 until her death in 1936, Mrs. Harold Dickson Marsh was the state's most active exponent of organization among artists, and in 1934 was chairman of National Art Week, inaugurated by the League at her suggestion.

It must be admitted that the native conservatism of Oregonians has, until recent years, materially hindered experimentation and free expression among its artists. Today this restraining influence seems, happily, on the wane. Many artists, their viewpoints broadened by a realization of the social significance and the functional usages of art, are creating with broader regional meaning and wider universality.

Newspapers and Radio

THE *Oregon Spectator,* first newspaper published west of the Rocky Mountains, made its initial appearance on February 5, 1846, at Oregon City; it was issued by the Oregon Printing Association. With a swagger typical of that period, it flaunted on its banner, "Westward the Star of Empire Takes Its Way." Colonel William G. T'Vault, prominent in early Oregon newspaper history, was the first editor of the *Spectator,* but his aggressive nature balked at the association's rule against political discussions. T'Vault resigned after a few weeks and went to southern Oregon. He edited the *Umpqua Gazette* at Scottsburg after several years, and later moved the paper to Jacksonville under the name of the *Table Rock Sentinel.* Charged by his enemies at Jacksonville with harboring abolitionist sympathies, a heinous accusation in Oregon in those days, the doughty colonel declared, "If I thought there was one drop of abolition blood in my veins, I would cut it out." The statement silenced his critics.

Henry A. G. Lee, a descendant of the Virginia Lees, succeeded T'Vaul on the *Spectator,* and in turn was followed by George L. Curry, later Territorial governor. Curry, too, found the inhibition against political discussion irksome, and he resigned to found in Oregon City the *Free Press,* Oregon's second newspaper. The *Free Press,* issued first in March 1848, gave up the ghost when the gold rush emptied Oregon of its few printers.

The last of Oregon's three pre-Territorial publications, a 16-page magazine, was the *Oregon American and Evangelical Unionist,* begun June, 1848, and published and edited on Tualatin Plains by the Reverend John S. Griffin. The press that was installed for this magazine had been used in Oahu, Sandwich Islands, by the American Board of Commissioners for Foreign Missions for the printing of hymns, catechisms and gospels in the islanders' native tongue. It was later given to Dr. Marcus Whitman and the Reverend H. H. Spalding, Presbyterian missionaries in the Oregon country at Waiilatpu and Lapwai. The press arrived at Fort Vancouver in 1839 and was carried by canoe up the Columbia to the missions. A man named Turner, the first tramp printer in Oregon, operated the press at Lapwai, turning out hymns, Biblical passages, and educational tracts in the Nez Perce, Flathead and Spokane Indian languages. After eight issues, the *American* was suspended, because, according to Editor Griffin, somebody opposed to his views on the Whitman massacre bribed the printer to break his contract and go off to the California mines. The last number appeared in October, 1848.

Oregon's fourth newspaper, the *Western Star,* which was established to foster the growth of Milwaukie in the face of the rising settlement at Portland, began publication in November, 1850, with Lot Whitcomb, an aggressive local promoter at its head. He hired two young printers, Waterman and Davis, to run the press, and eventually became so indebted to them for unpaid wages that they owned the plant. In the dead of a May night in 1851 the new owners moved it on a flatboat to Portland. Milwaukie rose en masse. The men were accused of stealing the newspaper, but it developed that Whitcomb had actually sold it. Waterman and Davis explained that they moved the property at night to escape opposition, so high ran the feeling between the two towns. At Portland the *Western Star* became the *Oregon Weekly Times.*

A few months after the birth of the *Western Star,* two newspapers destined to exert great influence on Oregon affairs appeared. They were the *Weekly Oregonian,* established at Portland on December 4, 1850, and the *Oregon Statesman,* that began publication at Oregon City in March 1851. Both are still major publications, the former as the *Oregonian* at Portland and the latter under its original name at Salem. The *Oregonian* has been published as a daily for more than seventy-five years and the *Statesman* for a half-century.

In their early years these two newspapers were bitter rivals, but they have long since laid aside their enmities. The *Weekly Oregonian,* financed by Colonel W. W. Chapman and Stephen Coffin, was a Whig newspaper, and the *Oregon Statesman,* owned and edited by Asahel Bush, supported the principles of the Democratic party. After publishing his newspaper at Oregon City for a few years, Bush moved it to Salem, explaining the move by saying that business had not been good, but adding "Oregon City is not all of Oregon." At Salem the newspaper became the spokesman of the famed "Salem clique," an aggressive group of Democratic party leaders who exerted tremendous influence in the early days of the Territory.

The *Statesman* and the *Weekly Oregonian* battled over Oregon's admission to the Union, with the slavery question, thinly disguised at times, the real issue in the controversy. The former urged statehood, and the latter, under Thomas J. Dryer's editorship, opposed it, fearing that slavery would be imposed on the Territory by the National Government. Nine times in seven years the issue appeared in one form or another, and on four occasions it went to a vote of the people. The *Oregonian,* however, withdrew its opposition in the fourth election on the ground that under statehood the slavery issue would rest with the people and not with congress. This proved to be a decisive factor in the dispute, as the electorate finally voted for admission to the Union.

H. L. Pittock gained control of the *Weekly Oregonian* and converted it into a daily, the *Morning Oregonian,* in February, 1861. In 1877 Harvey W. Scott assumed the editorship, beginning a notable career in Pacific Northwest newspaperdom which continued until his death in 1910. In 1937 the name was changed to the *Oregonian.* In time the ownership and policy of the *Statesman* also changed, and it became a Republican newspaper.

While the *Weekly Oregonian* and the *Statesman* were fighting over statehood, the *Spectator* expired. But out of the wreck arose the Oregon City *Argus.* W. L. Adams, the founder, was an admirer of Abraham Lincoln, and he made the *Argus* the first distinctively Republican newspaper in Oregon if not on the Pacific Coast. Adams was a master of cutting invective, which he turned to good account against the Democratic leaders of his day. The editorial columns of the *Argus* under Adams, the *Table Rock Sentinel* under T'Vault, and the *Weekly Oregonian* under Dryer, reflected the tense condition of Oregon public opinion on the stormy issues of statehood and slavery. So bitter did the diatribes become that Oregon editorial expression of the period was referred to by newspapermen as "the Oregon style." This reached a climax during the Civil War, when the Federal Government suppressed five newspapers, two at Eugene, the others at Albany, Corvallis and Jacksonville, for their attacks upon President Lincoln's prosecution of the war. The *Eugene City Democratic Register,* one of the papers suspended, was at the time edited by Joaquin Miller. He revived it as the *Democratic Review* in 1863.

For two decades after the Civil War, Oregon newspaper history was strewn with the obituaries of new enterprises. Newspapers sprang up in all sections of the State, but lack of printers, want of capital, scarcity of news print, and difficulty in news transmission made the business hazardous.

Length of service and able editorial direction have established the *Oregonian* as a potent influence on Oregon thought. The Oregon *Journal,* established in 1902 at Portland by C. S. Jackson, is equally successful in moulding public opinion. Long a liberal Democratic newspaper, it is now independent, with Democratic sympathies. The *Journal* early attracted attention as a champion of Oregon's Initiative and Referendum, Recall, Direct Primary, and other progressive measures.

The *Telegram,* established in 1877 and for three decades owned by the *Morning Oregonian,* dominated the Portland afternoon daily field until after the *Journal* was born. Some of the most brilliant men in Pacific Northwest journalism were developed by the *Telegram.* A. C. McDonald, one of its early executives, died from the effects of a duel with James K. Mercer, editor of the Portland *Bee,* in the early 1880's. Mercer went to prison for fifteen years. Among the men who directed the *Telegram* in its heyday were Alfred D. Bowen, Clifford J. Owen, John F. Carroll, and Paul R. Kelty, later an editor of the *Oregonian.* Although owned by a Republican newspaper, the *Telegram* was usually Democratic in politics in order to keep competitors out of the field. In 1914 J. E. Wheeler and L. R. Wheeler, prominent Pacific Northwest lumbermen, bought the paper, but several unpopular campaigns, one being against the Ku Klux Klan, undermined its prestige and untoward circumstances plunged it into bankruptcy. C. H. Brockhagen, at that time publisher of a string of Pacific Coast newspapers, purchased it in 1927 with the backing of Herbert Fleishhacker, San Francisco capitalist. Under the editorship of Lester Adams it began to recoup its political fortunes, and in 1930 it was victorious in a campaign for the public ownership of water-power. In 1931, however, the *Telegram* was sold to the Portland *News,* a Scripps-Canfield newspaper. In the merger the personality of the historic paper was lost, and nothing remained of it in the *News-Telegram* but the name. Two Oregon newspapers have won national recognition in recent years. In 1934 the *Medford Mail Tribune* received the Pulitzer award for its campaign against political corruption and in 1937 Quincy Scott, cartoonist of the Portland *Oregonian* was awarded honorable mention.

Despite the consolidation of Oregon newspaper properties in the past few decades, there remain 208 newspapers in the State, of which twenty-eight are dailies and 180 are weeklies. The weekly newspapers maintain, on the whole, high standards and a number have won national recognition by their excellence.

RADIO: The growth of radio facilities among people who once depended upon stagecoach and pony express to bring their news has been rapid and widespread. Today, with a population numbering fewer than a million persons, Oregon has more than 500 licensed amateur radio stations, fourteen commercial broadcasting stations, and two non-commercial stations. It is estimated that more than 172,000 homes in the State are equipped with radio receiving sets.

Radio does not appear to jeopardize newspaper prosperity, and it thrives in Oregon without opposition from the Fourth Estate. Oregon's two largest newspapers are substantially interested in broadcasting stations, the *Oregonian* owning Stations KEX and KGW, members of the NBC red and blue networks respectively, and the Oregon *Journal* holding a large interest in Stations KOIN and KALE, CBS members. In 1935 the Roseburg *News-Review,* one of the leading smaller city daily newspapers, established its own broadcasting station, KRNR.

Aeronautical and marine communication are important in the work of radio stations. Storm warnings, weather reports and medical advice flashed from the State's coastal stations can be picked up by ships hundreds of miles at sea. Broadcasters of this information include KKB, Sherwood; KEK, Hillsboro; KPK, Portland; KCK (Columbia River Lightship) at the mouth of the Columbia, and NPE, Astoria. In addition to these, radio beacons at dangerous points along the coast, at the mouth of the Columbia River and at Cape Blanco, are proving to be invaluable protection against shipwreck.

In the past few years air travel has become more and more dependent on radio. Especially is this true along the west coast, where winter fog adds to the hazard of flying. Stations at Medford, Portland and Pendleton send out regular reports along the airways, and radio beacons have been placed at strategic points throughout the State as aids to aeronautical navigation.

Broadcasting and receiving sets on police cars, enabling officers to converse over long distance, are a recent addition to law enforcement weapons.

Radio has been used on an ever-larger scale by the United States Forest Service, especially in the vast tracts of virgin forest, where travel and communication by the rangers and fire fighters are extremely limited. Small compact sending and receiving sets are now packed by the rangers into forest and mountain regions, in some of which neither telephone lines nor trails exist. These small sets operate on an average radius of ten miles.

The State maintains Station KOAC at Oregon State Agricultural College at Corvallis for the purpose of broadcasting cultural and informative programs of interest to the public. It also has four experimental stations: Salem (W7XBJ), Portland (W7XBD), Benson Polytechnic School, Portland (W7XBHO) and Oregon State College, Corvallis (W7XED). The last-named station transcribes programs released over KOAC, to other Oregon stations.

Architecture

ARCHITECTURAL trends in Oregon have closely paralleled the historical development of the state. In the first forty years of the nineteenth century nearly all of the white men in the state were trappers and fur traders, rough men who, with their Indian wives, contented themselves with little better shelter than that of their aboriginal pre-decessors. The first permanent cabins, blockhouses, trading posts, and missions, were not built until the 40's and 50's. These were simple structures of hand-hewn timbers, with locked and caulked joints, low-pitched roofs, and shuttered windows. A remainder of this early period of settlement is the old Fort Yamhill blockhouse at Dayton.

In 1843 an extensive immigration began. For the most part the newcomers had limited means. With surprising rapidity, however, their economic condition improved and by the close of the decade they were constructing substantial dwellings. This early period of permanent set-tlement in the Willamette Valley, represents an important phase of the state's architecture. Structural design was dominated by the nostalgia of the settlers for their old homes in New England, the Ohio Valley, and the South. At least two-thirds of the homes built during the late 1840's and 1850's show the direct influence of such traditional Colonial and Post-Colonial styles as Georgian, Federal, and Greek Revival. Al-though not distinguished for fineness of detail the houses were archi-tecturally sound. Designs were simple, direct, and well proportioned.

A few of these houses, especially those in isolated sections, retained the solid log construction of the earlier buildings, but most of them were erected with open structural frames covered with lapped siding. The sash, frames, siding and trim were often brought overland or shipped around the Horn. Some seventy structures of this period are still standing, though many of them are in a state of disrepair. A par-ticularly fine example is the Dr. John McLoughlin residence in Mc-Loughlin Park, Oregon City. The design of the Ladd & Reed farm-house at Reedville recalls the colonial architecture of the South Atlantic with its simplicity of line that made it a show place in the 1850's. The central part, with pleasingly proportioned fenestration and a full length gallery porch, is flanked by symmetrical one-story wings. The design of the J. C. Ainsworth house, built in 1852 at Mount Pleasant near Oregon City, shows the influence of the Greek Revival, having a characteristic temple-like two-storied portico with free-hung balcony above the door.

The next three decades were years of great activity marked by the disordered and sprawling growth of cities, the spread of trade, the coming of the railroads and, finally, the rise of a new and wealthy industrial class. Fully a third of the buildings now standing in Oregon were either built during this exuberant Victorian period or show its influence. The majority of these structures have a sentimental rather than an artistic value, being for the most part excessively ornate, and unsuited to their needs. In the northwestern part of Portland, residences of some of the leading families of a former generation display the measure of their unguided taste in the decorative complication of this jag-saw and bracketed era. In the old business section along the waterfront the narrow streets are still lined with mansard-roofed commercial structures erected between 1860 and 1890, with brick, wood, cast-iron, and ornamental plaster facades—all of dubious design. Today these buildings that were formerly important retail business houses are given over to the wholesale trade and to Portland's Chinatown. The only edifice of architectural importance built in this period is the Old Federal Post Office (1875), Portland. Curiously enough, it is not in the Victorian style, but is designed in the Classical Revival of Federal tradition.

With the beginning of the 1890's came the Neo-Classic style—a national trend fostered by a conservative group of academically-trained men. About 1885 Stanford White of the firm of McKim, Mead & White of New York City was commissioned to design the Portland Hotel. To supervise the construction of this building William M. Whidden and Ion Lewis were sent to Oregon. After their work was completed they formed a partnership that exerted a decisive influence on the course of Oregon architecture for a quarter of a century. Many of the state's leading architects of a later period were trained in their office.

Monumental structures began to arise, the designs of which showed a knowledge of and appreciation for the classic idiom. This Neo-Classic architecture is characterized by more formal planning, studied proportions, and carefully rendered detail. The oldest, and perhaps the best, example is the Oregonian Building in Portland, built of steel and faced with red sandstone. It was designed by Reid Brothers of San Francisco in 1892.

After 1905 school-trained and foreign-traveled architects and draftsmen rapidly supplanted the so-called practical builder designers. Various traditional styles were adapted to all classes of buildings. The Reed College buildings, designed in 1912 by Doyle and Patterson of Portland, and the Benson Hotel, built in the same year, are noteworthy examples of the English Tudor style. The University Club, built in 1913 and designed by M. H. Whitehouse, likewise follows the English Collegiate Gothic tradition. Its construction was hailed by press and public as evidence of Portland's growing metropolitan consciousness.

The First National Bank (1916), a white marble structure, and the United States National Bank (1916), both in Portland, are of Neo-Classic design. The former, the work of Coolidge and Shattuck of Boston, is considered one of the finest buildings of its type in America; and the latter, the work of A. E. Doyle of Portland, is notable for its elaborate carvings depicting the history of the pioneer period. Another Neo-Classic structure is the massive Portland Civic Auditorium, by Whitehouse and Doyle.

In 1914 the University of Oregon established a department of architecture under the direction of Dean Ellis F. Lawrence. By 1919 architecture had reached a place of sufficient importance in the public mind for the Oregon Legislature to pass the Architects Registration Law, thereby making Oregon one of the first states west of the Mississippi River to have such an enactment.

Since the World War there has been a definite decline in the classic trend established at the turn of the century by the Chicago Columbian Exposition and by the work of McKim, Mead & White. The contemporary period is marked by the stimulating influence of various theoretical approaches in design—some based upon a strict adherence to the historic styles, others characterized by a free interpretation of the old forms, and finally, those stemming from the radical but solid theory that "form follows function." This latter trend, both scientific and organic, is derived from the teachings of Louis Sullivan and the Chicago School.

Architecture generally has begun to show greater simplicity and refinement. Ornamentation as a decorative element is subordinated to the use of materials with frank consideration of their structural and aesthetic qualities. The design of city, county and state-erected public buildings tends to combine traditional and strictly utilitarian ideas. Outstanding among architects of this period are Louis C. Rosenberg, Frederick A. Fritsch, and Wade Pipes, who is known for his fine residential work throughout the state.

The rising tide of post-war affluence taxed the capacity of Portland office buildings. Two monumental structures designed to remedy this situation deserve special mention: The Pacific Building, erected in 1925, and the sixteen-story Public Service Building, Portland's tallest office building. Both of these substantial structures, designed by A. E. Doyle, are functional in plan and simple in design. They exemplify the modern architectural trend.

Two of Portland's churches show evidence of the cultural influences brought into the state by the tide of westward-flowing immigration. The Church of our Father, Unitarian, is one of the few examples of strictly Georgian Colonial architecture among the city's buildings. It seems a part of New England—birthplace of American Unitarianism—transplanted to a far land. Temple Beth Israel, a large-domed structure of Byzantine design, rich in color, was completed in 1927. Morris H. Whitehouse and Herman Brookman were the architects.

The Multnomah County Library in Portland, designed by Doyle, Patterson and Beach, is a three-storied edifice of modified Italian Renaissance design, surrounded on three sides by a finely carved balustrade with the names of masters of literature and music on its walls. Increasing interest in art motivated the construction in 1932 of Portland's Art Museum by A. E. Doyle and Associates; the building is a simple dignified structure of modified Georgian Colonial design, faced with brick and trimmed with Colorado travertine. Other fine Portland buildings include the Masonic Temple, designed by Frederick Fritsch; the Multnomah Hotel, by Gibson and Cahill of San Francisco; the Public Market, by William G. Holford of the firm of Lawrence, Holford and Allyn, said to be the largest of its kind in America, a utilitarian structure designed along classic lines, and the Finley Mortuary by A. E. Doyle and Associates.

There are few buildings of outstanding architectural design outside of Portland and few architects of more than local importance. Among the more prominent of these are F. C. Clark of Medford, and H. R. Perrin of Klamath Falls, who designed a number of buildings in that city. The most important examples of the work of Mr. Perrin are the Klamath Falls Elks Temple, of modified Greek design, and the Klamath Falls Armory, an imposing modern structure with the statue of a soldier in a niche at one corner and the medallion of a spread eagle above the entrance.

There are many interesting buildings on the campuses of the University of Oregon at Eugene and the Oregon Agricultural College at Corvallis. Most of the recent buildings were designed by the firm of Lawrence, Holford, and Allyn. Among the more interesting are the Art Museum at the University and the Memorial Union Building at the Agricultural College.

Perhaps the most significant modern work in Oregon is the new Capitol group at Salem. The State House, of modified classic design, is constructed of white Vermont marble. The front elevation presents a long low mass broken by two projecting central bays which flank the principal entrance. The monumental portal and the long bay of windows lighting the executive chambers in the flanking wings are filled with decorative metal grille work. Dominating the impressive structure is a cylindrical tower surmounted by a heroic bronze figure representative of the pioneer; the buttressed tower suggests the fluted drum of a classic column. Trowbridge and Livingstone and Frances Keally, Associate Architects, of New York, were the architects. The firm was awarded the commission after winning a national competition for the design. To the left of a sunken garden before the Capitol is the State Library, designed by Whitehouse and Church of Portland, in a style conforming to the other buildings around the plaza. The structure is of Georgia marble, three stories high, with a triple entrance above broad marble steps and adorned with sculptures over each door by Gabriel Lavare of Portland.

In widely scattered sections of the state are examples of minor architectural influences. In Portland some of the buildings carry a subtle suggestion of the Orient. The German colony that settled at Aurora in the fifties and sixties adapted the severe style of their old country homes to their colony houses, many of which are still in use. The Basque emigres in the Jordan Valley region of Malheur County applied adobe and native stone to the architectural elements of their homeland, achieving a distinctive style that is well known for its simplicity and quaintness.

Certain natural building materials and environmental influences have had a major bearing upon the development of architecture in Oregon. An abundance of good lumber at low prices has largely determined the structural methods employed in commercial and public buildings and has greatly increased the extent of individual home building and home ownership. The mild climate west of the Cascade Mountains, particularly in the Willamette Valley and along the coast, and the long rainy season have likewise affected building design and construction. Thus building operations are rarely slowed up at any time of year because of inclement weather; while roofing with flashing to repel moisture has been scientifically developed in Oregon. Deposits of stone suitable for building and clays for brickmaking are available in various sections but, due to the abundance of timber, they have been little exploited.

One individualistic style of residential architecture that developed in Oregon is gradually spreading into other states. Known locally as the "board and batten" style, it consists essentially of a somewhat rambling structure covered with plain vertical boards with battens, or narrow strips, over the cracks. This style grew from the old "box" type house of the pioneers. An outstanding example is the beautiful Connecticut country home of Louis Conrad Rosenberg, who was born in Portland.

The early settlers from New England and the middle states were essentially conservative and their architectural designs reflected this attitude. Even today the modern interpretation is tempered with an innate conservatism. Large office buildings particularly, with their transverse lines, ornamental cornices, and monotonous fenestration, illustrate this trend. Smaller houses are responding to the exigencies of the machine age and becoming more and more standardized.

PART II.

Cities and Towns

Astoria

Railroad Station: 20th St. and Waterfront for Spokane, Portland & Seattle Railway.
Bus Station: 614 Duane St. for Spokane, Portland & Seattle Transportation Co.; 11th St. and Waterfront for Oregon Motor Stages.
Airport: 3 m. SW. on US 101, bus fare 15c, taxi $1.50; no scheduled service.
City Busses: Fare 10c.
Taxis: Basic fare 25c.
Piers: River steamers, foot of 11th St., weekly trips to Portland; ocean steamers, Port Terminals, Portway off Taylor Ave. (consult travel agencies or classified telephone directory for ocean travel).

Accommodations: Five hotels; numerous auto camps.

Information Service: Chamber of Commerce, 14th and Exchange Sts.

Radio Station: KAST (1370 kc.).
Motion Picture Houses: Two.
Athletics: Gyro Field, Exchange St. between 18th and 21st Sts.
Tennis: Y.M.C.A. courts, 12th and Exchange Sts.
Swimming: Ocean beaches: Clatsop Beach (25 miles long), 9 m. SW. on US 101 at Skipanon, 18 m. SW. at Gearhart, 20 m. SW. at Seaside; Cannon Beach, 30 m. SW. on US 101 and unnumbered road. River beaches: Numerous on lower Columbia River, along US 30 and US 101; beaches vary with level of river; inquire locally.
Golf: Astoria Golf and Country Club, 8 m. SW. just off US 101, 18 holes; greens fee $1.

Annual Events: Astoria Regatta, four days prior to Labor Day.

ASTORIA (12 alt., 10,349 pop.), named for John Jacob Astor, is the seat of Clatsop County and the site of the first permanent settlement in the Oregon country. Because of its commerce and industry and its position at the mouth of the Columbia River, Astoria has grown from a palisaded trading post to an important port. Flour mills, sawmills, salmon canneries, and grain elevators line the course of the river, and fishing boats and fleets of ocean-going vessels dock at the long wharves.

Sprawling waterfront warehouses and docks, orderly rows of business blocks along a narrow beach, steep declivities where houses are niched into yellow clay banks, terraced hillsides where substantial residences rise one above the other, and the timbered crests of Coxcomb Hill where the Astor Monument points toward the sky are individual bits of Astoria's pattern but by a whim of nature in fashioning the headland upon which the town is built no general view is possible except from the Columbia River. Yet even this vantage point cannot reveal the caprice that completely eliminated Thirteenth Street from the city plan, yet permitted Bond, the second street in the alphabetical arrangement that originates at the waterfront, to wander through Union town as Taylor Avenue.

Not unlike the Columbia which determined its settlement and growth Astoria displays aspects as enchantingly diverse as its weather, which, according to Finnish residents, may be predicted by reading the fog on the Washington shore of the Columbia. All glitter and brittle air in summer, all hush or foggy mystery in autumn, and all bluster and fury during winter storms, Astoria never lacks the characteristics of the sea that has drawn Finns, Norwegians, and Swedes in such numbers that shop signs in the various languages are commonplace. Finnish is usually spoken in the stores and fraternal orders and churches often conduct their ceremonies in both that language and English. The steam bath, of Finnish heritage, is ritualistically observed both in private homes and in public bath houses.

The site of Astoria was first seen by white men in 1792, when Captain Robert Gray, "on a trading voyage to the N. W. Coast of America, China, etc.," sailed his ship *Columbia Rediviva,* laden with "Blue Cloth, Copper and Iron," into "Columbia's River" for the first time. Captain Gray's journal is lost, but that of his fifth officer, John Boit, reveals how well the area was appraised. "This River in my opinion," Boit wrote, "wou'd be a fine place for to set up a *Factory.* The Indians are very numerous, and appear'd very civil (not even offering to steal)." Gray's men, however, bought "Furs, and Salmon, which last they sold two for a board Nail. The furs we likewise bought cheap, for Copper and Cloth."

The Lewis and Clark expedition, arrival of which in late November, 1805, proved an overland passage practicable from the East, passed a point of land, the future site of Astoria, while "in surch of an eligible place for our winters residence." They wintered seven miles south west of the present city, and turned eastward again in the spring.

Choice of the site of Astoria in April, 1811, was a matter of compromise between the crusty captain of the *Tonquin,* the ship sent out by John Jacob Astor to found a trading post, and two partners of Astor's company. Captain Jonathan Thorn, a Navy man on leave of absence, by insisting on his absolute authority, had antagonized partners and crew on the voyage around the Horn. Duncan McDougal and David Stuart, Astor partners, set out in a small boat from the ship to reconnoiter the lower Columbia. "Not having the captain to contend with," says Washington Irving in his *Astoria,* "they soon pitched upon a spot which appeared to them favorable for the intended establishment. It was on a point of land called Point George, having a very good harbor. . . . These gentlemen, it is true, were not perfectly satisfied with the place, and were desirous of continuing their search; but Captain Thorn was impatient to land his cargo . . . and protested against any more of what he termed 'sporting excursions.' "

Clearings were made, a log residence, a storehouse, and a powder magazine were erected, a vegetable garden was planted, and the post was named Astoria, for "the projector and supporter of the whole enterprise." The Astorians sought immediately to extend their trade and forestall the threat of English expansion into the area from Canada. The *Tonquin,* thanks to the arbitrary methods of Captain Thorn in dealing with the Indians, was lost in an attack farther up the coast. The handful of men remaining at the post, menaced by an Indian uprising, were saved by the stratagem of the factor, McDougal. He threatened to uncork a small bottle, which, he told the Indians, contained the scourge of smallpox; the resulting peace through fear earned for him among the Indians the name of "the Great Smallpox Chief."

The following February an overland party headed by Wilson P. Hunt "swept round an intervening cape, and came in sight of the infant settlement of Astoria . . . with its magazines, habitations, and picketed bulwarks, seated on a high point of land, dominating a beautiful little bay, in which was a trim-built shallop riding quietly at anchor." The united forces then set to work to clinch their trade supremacy in the area and to carry out a commercial agreement with the Russians in Alaska. Parties and cargoes were sent to New York both by land and by sea. A series of reverses, including losses of men and ships, brushes with Indians, and evidences of British encroachment on their area, was capped by the news, received from Canadian traders in January, 1813, that war had been declared between England and the United States.

At this discouraging juncture, when abandonment of the post was considered, the factor McDougal, "a man of a thousand projects, and of great though somewhat irregular ambition," decided to marry a daughter of Concomly, the one-eyed Chinook chieftain who had been loyal to the white men. She was said to have "one of the flattest and most aristocratical heads in the tribe," and the old chief put a high price on her charms. She appeared for the wedding, painted with red clay and anointed with fish oil; "by dint, however, of copious ablutions, she was freed from all adventitious tint and fragrance, and entered into the nuptial state, the cleanest princess that had ever been known, of the somewhat unctious tribe of the Chinooks."

In the face of reports that British men-o'-war were in Pacific waters, the Astoria post was sold out in October, 1813, to the North West Company, a British concern operating in Canada, under circumstances reflecting on the loyalty of McDougal, who later joined the new company. When the British sloop of war *Raccoon* entered Astoria port in late November old Concomly and his warriors came armed and painted to do battle for the post. "McDougal reassured him," says George W. Fuller in *The Inland Empire,* "and exacted his promise not to go aboard the British ship; but Concomly visited the *Raccoon,* and to the Captain he expressed his admiration for British ships and spoke contemptuously of the Americans. [Captain] Black gave him an old flag, a laced coat, cocked hat and sword. On the following day, Concomly came sailing across to Astoria in full uniform and flying the Union Jack." Thereafter he was entirely loyal to the British.

The British took formal command of Astoria and held it under the name of Fort George until 1818, when it was returned to the United States. However, it was still under English domination, and in 1821, when the North West Company consolidated with the Hudson's Bay Company, the post was placed under the charge of Dr. John McLoughlin. The factor felt that Astoria had less commercial and agricultural possibilities than a situation farther up the river. He moved his headquarters to Vancouver, Washington, in 1824 and Astoria became a lookout station and trading post of minor importance. By 1841 all trace of the fort was gone except for a cabin, a shed, and a bare space among the trees.

The first overland immigrants arrived in 1844-45, settling in Clatsop Plains. Ships entered the river in increasing numbers, and on March 9, 1847, the Astoria post office was opened, the first west of the Rockies. By 1850, with a population of 250, the town had established itself as the trading center of the lower Columbia country. The first salmon cannery was built on the river in 1866. Others followed, and soon salmon was shipped to all parts of the world. From this modest start the salmon-canning industry grew to be Astoria's chief asset; the annual pack is valued at from $3,500,000 to $7,000,000.

Beginning with 1880, when it had a population of 2,803 persons, the city experienced a brisk growth. By 1911, at the time of the centennial celebration, its fisheries, sawmills, canneries, flouring mills, and numerous other enterprises made it the second largest city in the state. In 1920 it had 14,027 inhabitants, and held second rank among Oregon cities. At two o'clock on the morning of December 9, 1922, fire broke out along the waterfront. Before the flames were checked at one o'clock the following afternoon, they had reduced thirty-two city blocks—forty acres of buildings—to ashes, and had wiped out the entire business district. Citizens launched a reconstruction program, which made Astoria a fireproof city. The loss of more than three thousand in population in the decade may be attributed to the decline of industry caused by the fire.

Astoria's industry and commerce consist chiefly of fishing, lumbering, dairying, general agriculture, and a rapidly increasing tourist business. Dairying is on the way to becoming a $2,000,000-a-year industry, and specialized as well as general agriculture has been developed. Some of the first cranberry bogs on the Pacific Coast were planted near by and the growing and canning of peas is proving increasingly profitable. The principal manufacturing output includes lumber and box shooks, salmon products, flour, fertilizer, cheese, powdered milk, and medicinal oils and other fish by-products.

POINTS OF INTEREST

1. The SITE OF OLD FORT ASTORIA, 15th and Exchange Sts., is heavily outlined in paint on streets and sidewalks. A square laid out diagonally to the present city streets, the area comprises approximately two city blocks. A marker at the northwest corner of the inter-

section bears a diagram of the fort, showing its construction and plan.

2. The SITE OF ORIGINAL SETTLEMENT AT AS-TORIA, 16th and Exchange Sts., occupied by the city hall, is marked by a granite boulder and bronze plaque, placed by the D. A. R. in 1924. Here the thirty-three members of the Astor party settled temporarily after disembarking from the *Tonquin,* while they were building Fort Astoria.

At the southeast corner of the city hall a stone slab marks the GRAVE OF D. McTAVISH, fur trader, who was drowned in 1814 while crossing the Columbia River. Alexander Henry, who lost his life on the same trip, is buried nearby, but no marker indicates his grave. The two men were rival lovers of Jane Barnes, barmaid and adventuress, and the first white woman in Oregon.

3. The SITE OF THE FIRST POST OFFICE west of the Rocky Mountains, 15th St. between Franklin Ave. and Exchange St., is occupied by a florist's garden. John M. Shively was the first postmaster in the Oregon country, appointed March 9, 1847.

4. The INTERSTATE FERRY SLIP, N. end of 14th St., is the center of a picturesque waterfront life. Each hour of the day and late into the night ferries arrive and depart. Tugs, fishing smacks, deep-sea trollers, pilchard boats, and ocean liners sail in and out or sway quietly to the dirty tide lapping at the green-slimed piling. Machine shops and boat yards along the dock have an atmosphere of purposeful activity, but without an appearance of hurry. Motion seems deliberate and directed, and, whether a dock be crumbling or standing with orderly piles of rope and cargo, there lingers about it an air of permanency associated with the sea.

5. The FLAVEL MANSION (*open 9-5 weekdays*), Duane St. between 7th and 8th Sts., is a striking example of pioneer architecture. Built of lumber freighted around the horn, it is a two-story frame dwelling with turret chimneys, and a three-story tower at the northeast corner accentuates its height. It was erected in the early 1880's by a family prominent in Astoria's civic and cultural life. The estate deeded the house to Clatsop County in 1936 with the stipulation that it be used for philanthropic purposes. It is occupied by the Clatsop County Relief Association, the Red Cross, and other civic agencies.

UNIONTOWN, Astoria's foreign quarter, along the western section of Bond Street, has Chinese restaurants, Finnish steam bathhouses, river union offices, and Japanese and Scandinavian shops.

6. The UNION FISHERMEN'S COOPERATIVE CANNERY (*open 8-5 weekdays*), waterfront behind office at 325 Taylor Ave., is operated by the Union Fishermen's Cooperative Packing Company. The organization is composed of fishermen of the Columbia River area, who process and sell their own catches of salmon. The main fishing season begins the first of May and ends late in August. The secondary season opens September 10 and closes March 1 of the following year.

7. The PORT OF ASTORIA TERMINALS, Portway off Tay-

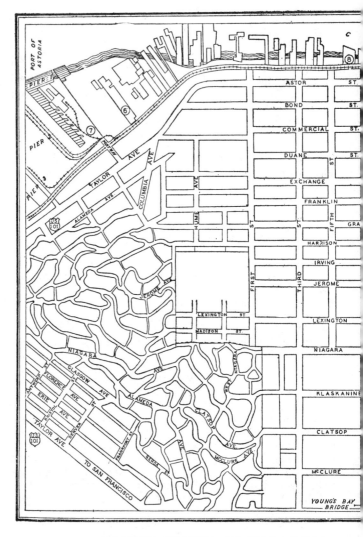

ASTORIA POINTS OF INTEREST

1. The Site of Old Fort Astoria
2. The Site of Original Settlement at Astoria
3. The Site of the First Post Office
4. The Interstate Ferry Sl

The Flavel Mansion
The Union Fishermen's Co-
    operative Cannery
The Port of Astoria Termi-
    nals

8. The Columbia River Packer's
    Association Plant
9. Shark Rock
10. Shively Public Park
11. The Astor Column

lor Ave., is on the Astoria waterfront. Since 1909 the Port of Astoria corporation has gradually acquired properties until the investment is in excess of $5,000,000. The port district extends to all the river towns of Clatsop County and includes Wauna, Warrenton, Westport, and Bradwood. At Pier No. 1 are the port administrative offices, a flouring mill, and large grain elevators. At Pier No. 2, which is equipped with two large locomotive cranes, electric overhead cargo cranes, tractors, trailers, conveyors, and pilers, cargoes of lumber, logging equipment, and fish products are assembled and shipped. Pier No. 3 has a warehouse 1,550 feet long, affording storage facilities for general cargo. Ships from all over the world load and discharge from the terminal and from the many smaller wharves and docks along the waterfront.

The PILLSBURY-ASTORIA FLOUR MILL (*open 9-4 Mon.-Fri.; 9-12 Sat.*), on Pier No. 1, is the largest in the state. Adjacent to the mill are concrete grain elevators of 1,250,000 bushels capacity, with cleaning, washing, and drying equipment. At the end of a long water grade from the Inland Empire grain belt, the mill has many distributional advantages. Its annual production has an estimated value of $5,000,000.

8. The COLUMBIA RIVER PACKER'S ASSOCIATION PLANT (*open during season by arrangement*), N. end of 6th St., is the largest of the lower Columbia River salmon canneries. In season the cannery processes shiploads of salmon brought from distant points, and boatloads of the fish caught by local fishermen. The association maintains fishing fleets in Alaskan waters and other points in the North Pacific.

9. SHARK ROCK, in Niagara Park at 8th St. and Niagara Ave., bears a message left by the survivors of the United States sloop-of-war, *Shark,* which was wrecked at the mouth of the Columbia River. Carved in the rock is the statement: "The *Shark* was lost Sept. 16, 1846." Beneath this is the record of the loss of the *Industry,* which reads: "The *Industry* was lost March 16, 1865. Lives lost 17. Saved 7." More than fifty years after the *Industry* sank the rock was recovered from the sand near 13th and Exchange Sts. The Astoria Kiwanis Club placed it on the ornamental concrete base, as a memorial to the many who have lost their lives by shipwreck at the mouth of the Columbia.

10. SHIVELY PUBLIC PARK, S. of reservoir at S. end of 16th St., on an eminence commanding a view of Young's Bay, Saddle Mountain, and the Coast Range, is centered by a natural amphitheater used for public gatherings. To the southwest beyond Young's Bay is the Lewis and Clark River, which flows past the site of Old Fort Clatsop, the explorers' winter camp. In the park are the Portals of the Past, decorative columns saved from the ruins of the Weinhard Hotel, destroyed in the fire of 1922.

11. The ASTOR COLUMN, summit of Coxcomb Hill (700 alt.), is a cylindrical monument 125 feet high, on which is a spiral frieze 535 feet in length. Executed by A. Pusterla, the frieze depicts the exploration of the Columbia River and the founding of Astoria. Within the

column is a circular staircase leading to an OBSERVATION PLAT-
FORM (*open* 9-5 *daily; adm.* 25c) near the top, from which is a
magnificent view of the Pacific Ocean, the Columbia River, and the
mountainous wooded region about the city. Vincent Astor of New
York, great-grandson of the founder of Astoria, and the Great Northern Railway Company supplied the funds for construction of the tower.

POINTS OF INTEREST IN ENVIRONS

Tongue Point, **2.5** *m.* (*see TOUR* 1). Old Fort Clatsop, Lewis and Clark encampment, **7.7** *m.*; Camp Clatsop, National Guard Camp, **11** *m.*; Fort Stevens,
10 *m.*; Radio Naval Base, **6.4** *m.* (*see TOUR* 3).

Corvallis

Railroad Station: 6th & Madison Sts., for Southern Pacific Lines (branch). Southern Pacific busses from this station connect with main line at Albany Depot, 10th and Lyon Sts.
Bus Station: 353 Monroe St., for Greyhound Lines and Oregon Motor Stages.
City Busses: Fare, 6c.
Taxis: Basic fare 25c.

Accommodations: Three hotels; auto camps.

Information Service: Chamber of Commerce, 306 S. 3rd St.

Radio Station: KOAC (550 kc.).
Motion Picture Houses: Three.
Swimming: Men's Gymnasium, Women's Building, both on Oregon State campus open only to students; Marys River.
Golf: Corvallis Country Club, 3 m. W. on State 26, half-mile from highway, 9 holes, greens fee 25c, Sat. and Sun. 50c.
Riding: Corvallis Riding Academy, 20th and Railroad Sts.; fees 75c first hour, 50c each subsequent hour.

Annual Events: Farmers' Day, Oct.; 4-H Club, June; Benton County Fair, last of Aug.; State High School Band Contest, Apr. or May.

CORVALLIS (227 alt., 7,585 pop.), seat of Oregon State Agricultural College and of Benton County, is on the west bank of the Willamette River just below its confluence with Marys River. The city derives its name from the Latin phrase meaning "heart of the valley," and is in truth, culturally and economically, the heart of a large fertile region. Few Oregon municipalities are more beautiful. Westward the green hills rise gently into the lower slopes of the Coast Range, and to the east beyond the valley, are the sharper crests of the Cascade Mountains.

The first white men to settle in the vicinity of present Corvallis were James L. Mulkey, Johnson Mulkey, and William F. Dixon, who arrived in 1845, and Joseph C. Avery, who came in 1846; they settled on lands purchased from the Calapooya Indians. Avery operated a free canoe ferry to encourage settlement here, sold the first town lots, and in 1849, after returning with others from the California gold fields, established a store.

The town was officially platted and designated the seat of the newly created county of Benton in February, 1851. Known originally as Marysville, Corvallis was given its present name in 1853, to differentiate it from Marysville, California. The town somehow escaped the raw, rough period undergone by most frontier settlements, though there was an occasional case of "justifiable homicide"—mob hanging of a half-breed or an Indian who had made trouble for white people. In 1852 the Baptists erected the first church, and a school was started. Out of this school in 1858 grew Corvallis College. Steamboats began to ply the Willamette and wharves were heaped with freight brought up from Portland at forty dollars a ton.

In January, 1855, the legislature voted to remove the territorial seat to Corvallis. Legislators' baggage and office equipment were moved up the Willamette River on the steamer *Canemah,* which was received in Corvallis with a great demonstration. Asahel Bush, who had been publishing the *Oregon Statesman* at Salem, brought along his presses and issued the paper here. He said of Corvallis at the time: "A first-class court house is nearly completed. There is but one better in the Territory—the one at Salem. . . . The work on the Methodist Episcopal Church here is well advanced; a couple of stores and quite a number of dwellings have also been erected here this summer." The legislators felt that Salem had other advantages than its courthouse, for scarcely had they convened than a resolution was introduced to move back to better accommodations at Salem. In June of the same year the capital was returned to Salem, and Asahel Bush took his *Oregon Statesman* along with it.

Stagecoaches rumbled over the crude roads, and in 1856 workmen strung the city's first telegraph line to the state metropolis. The following year the city was divided into wards, and an ordinance was passed prohibiting people from riding horses on the sidewalks. The second newspaper, the *Union,* began publication in 1859 and continued until 1862, when it was suppressed for disloyal utterances. It was almost immediately succeeded by the *Gazette* (now the *Daily Gazette-Times*), which for a time in the early 1870's was owned and edited by Sam Simpson, the poet.

Wallis Nash, in his *Oregon: There and Back in 1877,* provides a glimpse of the town in that year: "We fitted out our expedition at Corvallis, and there engaged probably the best horsekeeper and the worst cook in the State. Horses were hired from the 'Livery and Feed Stables' in the main street, and half the loafers and idlers in the town clustered round us to watch the selection of six horses out of about twenty standing there, presenting a series of groggy hind-legs and rough coats and tails down to their heels. . . ."

The coming of the railroad in 1878 inaugurated an era of expansion for Corvallis, as the distributing point of Benton County's rich dairying and fruit-producing areas. In succeeding decades the town has developed into a modern city with numerous industries based upon the extensive agricultural and timber resources of the region. Among the commercial enterprises are fruit and vegetable canneries, creameries, hatcheries, flouring mills, and a sawmill with a daily capacity of 100,000 board feet of finished lumber. However, Corvallis remains essentially a college city.

POINTS OF INTEREST

OREGON STATE AGRICULTURAL COLLEGE, 9th, 30th, Monroe, and Washington Sts., occupies a campus of 189 acres, exclusive of farm and forest lands, divided into East Campus, and East, West, Men's, and Women's Quadrangles, with several groupings of buildings not designated by quadrangles. Each section is landscaped with trees and shrubs that beautify the campus and serve as a living laboratory for horticultural study. Among the thirty-six buildings of the institution are the schools of agriculture, commerce, engineering, home economics, forestry, pharmacy, and education. With the exception of five of the older structures the principal buildings have been erected since 1908 and are of harmonious design. Brick and terra cotta are the materials most used, and the Neo-Classic style of architecture predominates.

Corvallis College, an outgrowth of a community school started in 1852, was co-educational and included primary and secondary grades. The school passed into the control of the Methodist Church, South, in 1865. Three years later Congress authorized a land grant to colleges offering instruction in agricultural and mechanical arts and military tactics, and in the same year the state legislature designated Corvallis College for the purpose. The first class under this arrangement was graduated in 1870. In 1885 the state assumed control of the institution, and in 1887, the first unit was built on the present campus.

CAMPUS TOUR

(Unless otherwise stated, all buildings on the campus are open during school hours.)

1. The ADMINISTRATION BUILDING, oldest edifice on the campus, a three-story brick structure, built in 1889, contains offices of the registrar, business manager, comptroller, the workshop theater, and the music department. On the second floor is a memorial tablet erected in 1894 to Benjamin Lee Arnold, president 1871-92.

2. SCIENCE HALL, four stories high, erected in 1902, of gray granite and sandstone, houses the chemistry department, the Rockefeller Research Institute, and chemistry laboratories of the agricultural experiment station.

3. The PHARMACY BUILDING, a three-story brick structure constructed in 1924, has classrooms, laboratories, a model drugstore, a motion-picture amphitheater, and the drug laboratory of the state board of pharmacy. The stock and fixtures of the model drugstore, donated by interested firms, are used for instruction in salesmanship, store management, prescription taking, keeping of poison and narcotics records, inventory, and showcase and window trimming. The state drug laboratory is maintained for the purpose of determining the purity of medicinal substances sold in the state.

4. MUSEUM BUILDING (*open 8-12, 2-5 weekdays; 2-5 Sun.*), built in 1899 as the men's gymnasium, is now headquarters for the

R.O.T.C. band and the Oregon State Symphony Orchestra. Occupying the lower level is the Horner Museum of pioneer relics, Indian weapons, beadwork, baskets, and artifacts from burial mounds. The museum, formally opened February 20, 1925, owes its name and beginning to the late Dr. J. B. Horner, Professor of History and Director of Oregon Historical Research. Specimens from many collections are on display and those not displayed are catalogued and accessible for study. Exhibits of the museum include the J. G. Crawford collection of artifacts from prehistoric burial mounds: the E. E. Boord collection of mounted animals native to the Northwest and Far North; the Wiggins, Lisle, Hopkins, and Rice collections of historic American weapons; the Mrs. J. E. Barrett collection of Indian basketry; the Maggie Avery Stevenson collection of Rocky Mountain relics; paintings and sculptures from the State Committee of Public Works of Art Projects; and a collection of minerals gathered by Andrew M. Sherwood, economic geologist of the Smithsonian Institution and the Carnegie Museum.

5. The ARMORY, a vast enclosed stadium of steel and concrete built in 1910-11, is used for the activities of the R.O.T.C. and of the polo teams. At the northwest corner is a tablet memorializing Major General Ulysses Grant McAlexander, commandant at Oregon State from 1907 to 1911. General McAlexander served in the Spanish-American War in Cuba and the Philippines, and was cited for gallantry at Santiago. In France he first commanded the 18th Infantry, and later, during the second Battle of the Marne, July 15, 1918, the 38th U. S. Infantry. He was awarded the D.S.M., the D.S.C., and a number of foreign decorations.

6. The MEN'S GYMNASIUM, built in 1915 and enlarged in 1921, includes a swimming pool and gymnasium hall, where Pacific Coast Conference basketball games are played. Adjoining the gymnasium is BELL FIELD, the stadium, seating 20,000 spectators.

7. The FORESTRY BUILDING, constructed in 1917, contains classrooms and laboratories for the school of forestry, a collection of manufactured wood products, and a MUSEUM (*open 8-5 weekdays*) of commercial woods from all sections of the United States.

8. The MEN'S DORMITORY (1928) includes five residence halls, and is three stories above a basement, with a five-story central tower. An open arch under the tower affords a view of the hills and mountains. Behind the building is a recreational area with cinder track, tennis courts, and practice fields.

9. KIDDER HALL, built in 1892 as a dormitory and known as Cauthorn Hall, houses the Farm Security Administration and the departments of art and architecture, history, and modern language. The lobby of the building provides a spacious and attractive exhibition hall for loan collections and other works of art. The building was named for Ida Angeline Kidder, librarian, 1908-20.

10. The MEMORIAL UNION BUILDING (1928) at the south end of the West Quadrangle, was erected in 1928 to the memory of college men and women killed in the Spanish-American and World

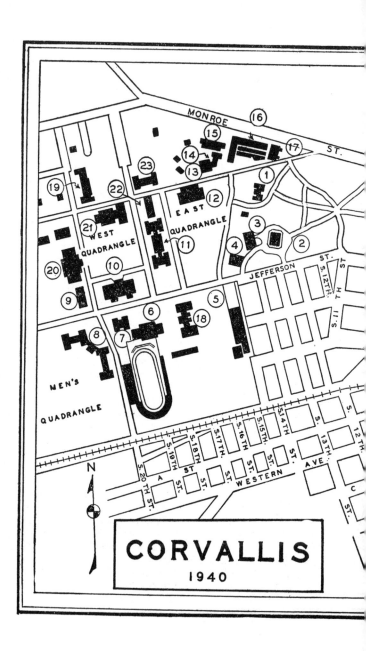

CORVALLIS

1940

Wars. Student social events are held here, and here also are the department of journalism and the offices of student publications. In the COLLEGE HERBARIUM (*open* 8-12, 2-5 *weekdays;* 2-5 *Sun.*), in the basement, are 40,000 sheets of plant specimens. Oregon and the Northwest are especially well represented. The collection is augmented each year by about four thousand specimens.

11. AGRICULTURE HALL, between the East and West Quadrangles, is the dominant building on the campus. Its first unit was started in 1909 and added to in 1913. In the central section are the school of agriculture, the agricultural experiment station, the agricultural extension service, the office of the state leader of 4-H Clubs, and offices, classrooms, and laboratories of the departments of botany, zoology, entomology, and bacteriology. The wings are occupied by the departments of agronomy and horticulture.

Special research in agriculture is carried on at the agricultural experiment station, which consists of the central station at Corvallis and nine branch stations in the state. The stations correlate investigations with pressing farm problems. The improvement of strains through better breeding of poultry and livestock has resulted in the rapid development of these industries. The first hen in the world to lay 300 eggs in a year was bred at the station. Control of plant and animal diseases, introduction of new cash crops, and general improvement of farming methods have been stressed. An agricultural agent is maintained in each county of the state, working directly under supervision from the college.

12. The LIBRARY (*open* 7:50 *A.M.*-10 *P.M. weekdays;* 2-5 *Sun.*), built in 1918, is the only building on the East Quadrangle. The three stories and basement of the structure house 130,000 volumes, in-

---

CORVALLIS POINTS OF INTEREST

Oregon State Agricultural College

1. The Administration Building
2. Science Hall
3. The Pharmacy Building
4. Museum Building
5. The Armory
6. The Men's Gymnasium
7. The Forestry Building
8. The Men's Dormitory
9. Kidder Hall
10. The Memorial Union Building
11. Agriculture Hall
12. The Library
13. The Mines Building
14. The Physics Building

15. The Engineering Laboratory
16. The Mechanic Arts Building
17. Apperson Hall
18. Waldo Hall
19. Margaret Snell Hall
20. Women's Building
21. Home Economics Building
22. Dairy Building
23. Commerce Building

Other Points of Interest

24. The Haman Lewis House
25. Benton County Courthouse
26. The Site Of the Territorial Capitol
27. The Corvallis City Park

cluding an excellent collection on the history of horticulture, and about 1,400 periodicals. Of interest to bibliophiles is the Mary J. L. McDonald collection of more than three thousand volumes in fine bindings, and rare editions. Among its treasures are a page from the *Polychronicon,* Ranulph Higden, reprinted by William Caxton in 1482; a folio bible, printed in 1769 on the press of John Baskerville, and a pearl bible of 1853; a book of poems in Latin by George Buchanan (1506-82) from the Elzevir Press in 1628; and a fifteenth-century antiphonal, composed of Gregorian chants in Flemish, hand-printed and illuminated on parchment, bound in brown calf over the original board covers. Among the more valuable items is an illustrated set of the Gettysburg edition of the *Complete Works of Abraham Lincoln,* edited by Nicolay and Hay. Volume 24 contains autographs of Lincoln and other prominent men of his time. The set is valued at $4,800.

13. The MINES BUILDING, a four-story brick building erected in 1913, is similar to the newer buildings on the campus. It houses the chemical engineering, mining engineering, geology, paleontology, and allied departments. On the second floor are the college GEOLOGICAL COLLECTIONS *(open 8-5 weekdays)*, including 700 minerals arranged according to the Dana classification, a large collection of ore specimens arranged according to the Lindgren classifications, and 150 samples arranged according to Harker's book on igneous rocks.

14. The PHYSICS BUILDING (1928) forms the east wing of the Mines Building. Here are the department of physics, the graduate division, and offices of the dean of the graduate school. On the third floor are the studios of KOAC, the state-owned broadcasting station. A radio extension service is carried on through the station, which operates with 1,000 watts' power on a frequency of 550 kilocycles, and is on the air daily except Sunday from 9 A.M. to 9:15 P.M. The material broadcast is educational and recreational, and the programs are entirely free from commercialism.

15. The ENGINEERING LABORATORY is north of the Physics Building. The main laboratory is 40 by 220 feet and contains three divisions—a materials laboratory, a hydraulics laboratory and a steam and gas engine laboratory—all served by a five-ton electric traveling crane.

16. The MECHANIC ARTS BUILDING (1908), its central part fifty-two feet square and two stories high, is flanked by one-story ells. It houses offices of the department of mechanical engineering, and offices, classrooms, and shops for the department of industrial arts.

17. APPERSON HALL, erected in 1908 and rebuilt in 1920, adjoins the Mechanical Arts Building. It is named for a regent of the college and is devoted to the department of civil and electrical engineering.

Other buildings on the campus are WALDO HALL (18) and MARGARET SNELL HALL (19), women's dormitories, the WOMEN'S BUILDING (20), the HOME ECONOMICS BUILDING (21), the DAIRY BUILDING (22), and the COMMERCE BUILDING (23).

OTHER POINTS OF INTEREST

24. The HAMAN LEWIS HOUSE (*private*), 218 N. 3rd St., an important social center in pioneer days, was built about 1852. Wainscoted and plastered in all rooms, it remains unchanged except for minor repairs. Unevenly fitted floor boards and whittled door pins reveal the hand work that went into the building.

25. BENTON COUNTY COURTHOUSE, Jackson St. extending to Monroe, between N. 4th and N. 5th Aves., was erected in 1888-89. It is a three-story cement-covered brick building surmounted with a clock tower, its white walls gleaming brilliantly through the dense foliage of parklike grounds.

26. The SITE OF THE TERRITORIAL CAPITOL, S. E. corner S. 2nd and Adams Sts., is now occupied by a business block. On the front of the corner building is a bronze plaque commemorating the short period in 1855 when Corvallis was the capital of Oregon.

27. The CORVALLIS CITY PARK, S. end of 4th St. extending from 3rd to 6th Sts., is in a shaded bend of the Marys River just west of US 99W. In the park are a pair of old millstones, quarried in France and shipped around the Horn. In 1856 they were hauled by ox-team from Portland and set up in Chambers' Mill, on the Luckiamute River northwest of Corvallis, where they were in constant use for more than sixty years. The park has recreational facilities and an auto camp.

POINTS OF INTEREST IN ENVIRONS

Hanson's Poultry Farm, **1** *m.;* Prehistoric Burial Grounds, **10** *m.;* Marys Peak, **17.3** *m.* (*see TOUR 2D*). State Fish Hatchery, **29.6** *m.* (*see TOUR 2E*). Peavy Arboretum, **9** *m.* (*see TOUR 10*).

Eugene

Railroad Stations: Southern Pacific Station, 400 Willamette St., for Southern Pacific lines; Oregon Electric Station, 5th and Oak Sts., for Oregon Electric Ry.
Bus Stations: Oregon Hotel, 541 Willamette St., for Pacific Greyhound Line and Oregon Motor Stages; E. Broadway and Willamette St., for Independent Motor Stages; Broadway Cash Store, E. Broadway near Willamette, for the Dollar Line; 92 W. 8th Ave., for the Benjamin Franklin Line.
Airport: 18th and Chambers Sts.; no scheduled service.
Taxis: 25c and upwards according to distance and number of passengers.
City Busses: Fare 7c, four-ride card for 25c.

Accommodations: Six hotels; numerous rooming houses, tourist camps.

Information Service: Chamber of Commerce and A.A.A., 230 E. Broadway.

Radio Station: KORE (1420 kc.).
Motion Picture Houses: Five.
Swimming: Women's Pool in the Gerlinger Hall and Men's Pool in Men's Building—both on U. of O. campus, restricted to college students; Y.M.C.A. building; Willamette River.
Golf: Laurelwood Golf Course, 2700 Columbia St., 18 holes, greens fee, 25c for each 9 holes; Oakway Golf Course, S. Willamette St. near Wood Ave., 9 holes, greens fee 25c.
Riding: Eugene Hunt Club Academy, West Fair Grounds, 13th and Van Buren Sts. Fee $1 an hour.

Annual Events: Oregon Trail Pageant (every three years) in July.

EUGENE (423 alt., 18,901 pop.), cultural and industrial center of the upper Willamette Valley, is the site of the University of Oregon and of Northwest Christian college. It is the seat of Lane County, and the fourth largest city of the commonwealth. By fields and wooded hills, through leaning groves of cottonwood and balm, the Willamette River curves around the northwest quarter of the city. Eastward rise the swelling foothills of the Cascades, and westward the misty summits of the Coast Range.

Essentially a city of homes, Eugene has the appearance of a landscaped park, with comfortable houses and long lines of shade trees bordering its streets. The business thoroughfares are lined with fine brick and concrete structures, while in the neighborhood of the university many large fraternity and sorority houses add to the charm of the residential districts. Economic and cultural interests are well balanced. Varied industrial plants—creameries, canneries, and flour and lumber mills—close to the university, indicate the dual character of the community.

Arriving in the upper valley in 1846, Eugene F. Skinner built a crude log cabin at the foot of a small peak, and there his young wife gave birth to the first white child born in Lane County. Known to the Calapooya Indians as Ya-po-ah, the peak was called by the early settlers Skinner's Butte, and the small settlement that grew up at its base was known as Skinner's. Here the first post office in the region was established in 1853. Skinner's was outside the later corporate limits of Eugene. Judge D. M. Risdon erected the first dwelling within the present limits of the town in 1851. Lane County was created the same year, and several other dwellings and a schoolhouse were erected. James Huddleston opened a store and arriving immigrants cut a millrace and built a sawmill on the river bank. Skinner operated a ferry near the present Ferry Street Bridge, dealt in real estate and, with Judge Risdon, platted a townsite in 1852. Heavy winter rains, however, turned part of the site into a quagmire that earned for it the title of "Skinner's Mudhole." Two fat hogs, trying to root in the mud, are said to have been lost completely. The trend of building then swung toward higher ground. When the town was designated the seat of Lane County in 1853, Skinner and a settler named Charnal Milligan each donated forty acres for county purposes. In recognition of the first settler it was named Eugene City. The first term of the United States district court was held in March, 1852, in a bunkhouse originally built for loggers. Incorporation of the city, "to banish hogs and grog-shops," as one editor put it, was authorized in 1864.

Eugene claimed to be the popular choice for territorial capital in 1856, but there was a dispute over the majority of votes cast. The activity of the settlement, however, induced the Cumberland Presbyterians to build Columbia College in that year. The college building was destroyed by fire of incendiary origin during the first term. It was immediately rebuilt, only to be burned a second time in 1858. Efforts to rebuild it again were abandoned before the third structure was completed. Among the students of this school was Cincinnatus Hiner (Joaquin) Miller, whose father had settled near Eugene. Of this period Miller later wrote: "I have never since found such determined students and omnivorous readers. We had all the books and none of the follies of great centers." He was an outstanding student of Latin and Greek and delivered the valedictory poem (his first in print) at commencement exercises in 1859. One stanza of this early effort survives:

> We are parting, schoolmates, parting,
> And this evening sun will set
> On gay hearts with sorrow starting,
> On bright eyes with weeping wet.

The town had no regularly issued newspaper until New Year's Day, 1862, when the *State-Republican* began publication. In opposition, secessionist sympathizers founded the *Democratic-Register,* which Miller purchased and renamed the *Eugene City Review.* While here he studied law on the side, wrote contributions for his own paper under the name Giles Gaston, sought out another contributor, "Minnie Myrtle," found she was the daughter of Judge Dyer of Port Orford, and, in less than a week married her. Miller was forbidden the use of the mails for his paper on the ground that he was a Southern sympathizer, sold out, bought fruit trees and cattle, and went to Canyon City. Later, while residing in California, he achieved international note as a poet of the Far West.

Early industry of the county centered in agriculture and milling, and the transportation of these products to tidewater markets. The first steamer to ascend the Willamette River to Eugene was the *James Clinton,* in March, 1857. Although the city was considered the head of navigation, an occasional boat ventured farther upstream. The *Relief,* according to the first issue of the *State-Republican,* came up the river from Portland on December 28, 1861, with a cargo of beans and whisky, and other staple commodities, and tied up at the Eugene wharf. For a few years boats plied between the city and Portland, but water transportation was abandoned after construction, in 1871, of the Oregon & California Railroad.

Shortly after the Civil War Eugene's population increased to 1,200, and the industrial life of the region began to develop rapidly. The University of Oregon was established in 1872 and the first class matriculated in 1876. From the first, wheat had been the chief crop in the county, but fruit growing, dairying, lumber, and mining began to be important elements of the domestic economy. Lumbering, with its sawmills, shingle mills, planing mills, and box factories, has constituted one of the chief sources of income for Eugene citizens. Excelsior is made from the cottonwood and balm trees that flourish along the banks of the Willamette and other valley streams. Mining in the Bonanza and Blue River districts for a time added a romantic element to the industrial life.

THE UNIVERSITY OF OREGON

The campus of the university occupies a tract of 100 acres between 11th and 18th Sts. and Alder and Agate Sts. University Street, north and south, and 13th Street, east and west, divide the campus into unequal quadrangles. The old campus between 11th and 13th Streets is planted with trees and shrubbery and well-clipped lawns, while the new campus is more open, interspersed with gardens. From north to south the story of the institution's development is seen in its architecture. On the old campus the buildings are without architectural uniformity, but to the south are more harmonious groupings.

The University of Oregon had its official beginning in 1876. The federal government in 1859 set aside a grant of seventy-two sections of land to establish a state university. No advantage was taken of the act until 1872, when the legislature fixed the site of the institution at Eugene on guaranty of the Lane County delegation that the city would provide a building and campus to cost not less than $50,000. The amount was soon raised; pledges ranged from fifty cents to fifty dollars. Farmers without cash donated wheat; one gave a fat hog. Construction of the first building, Deady Hall, began in 1873, but that year panic struck the country and there followed a struggle to keep the enterprise alive. Finally, however, in 1876, the doors opened and classes began. At first only classical and literary courses were offered. As the state developed, the college of arts and letters, the schools of architecture and allied arts, of education, of law, of journalism, of music, and of physical education, and the college of social science were established. The medical school is at Portland, the extension division is co-existent with the Oregon State System of Higher Education, and the graduate school offers courses both at the university and at Oregon State College.

CAMPUS TOUR

(Buildings are listed according to geographical location from main entrance at 9th and Madison Sts., and are numbered to correspond with numbers on accompanying map. Unless otherwise stated, all buildings are open during school hours.)

1. VILLARD HALL, facing 11th St. at Franklin Blvd., is a two-story brick building with a mansard roof; it is French Second Empire in style. Villard Hall was erected in 1885 and named for the railroad builder, Henry Villard, who gave the university $7,000 in cash in 1881 and $50,000 in Northern Pacific Railway bonds in 1883. In the building are offices and classrooms of the English department.

2. DEADY HALL, built in 1876 of native stone, was for a number of years the entire university plant. It stands on a slight eminence in the center of the old campus, and is of the same architectural style as Villard Hall. It was named for Judge Matthew P. Deady, president of the board of regents from 1873 until his death in 1893. The building is occupied by the classrooms and laboratories of the departments of physics, zoology, botany, and mathematics. It also contains a ZOOLOGICAL COLLECTION (*open by arrangement*) of 5,000 specimens of mammals, birds, and eggs, mostly Oregon fauna.

3. The OLD LIBRARY (*open 8-5 weekdays*), S. of Deady Hall facing 13th St., a three-story brick building, built in 1907 and remodeled in 1914, houses the school of law and the law library. An adjoining fireproof annex contains book stacks.

4. CONDON HALL, SE corner 13th and Kincaid St., designed and built in 1924 as the first wing of a larger structure, perpetuates the name of Dr. Thomas Condon, pioneer geologist and discoverer of many rare fossils, who was a member of the faculty from the founding of the institution until his death in 1907. It houses laboratories and classrooms for geology, geography, anthropology and phychology, as well as the collections of the MUSEUM OF NATURAL HISTORY (*open 8-5 weekdays*). The herbarium contains specimens from Oregon and the Northwest, the eastern United States, and the Philippine Islands. The geological specimens include Miocene and Pleistocene invertebrate fossils from the Coos Bay vicinity, and mammal fauna from

the John Day region fossil beds, in which Dr. Condon made his most noteworthy discoveries.

5. The ART MUSEUM (*open by permission*), centered in the SW. quad facing W. toward Kincaid St., a gift of alumni and friends, built in 1930, is an imposing brick building that shelters the rare and extensive Murray Warner Collection of Oriental Art, given to the university by Gertrude Bass Warner as a memorial to her husband. The collection was started by Major and Mrs. Warner while living in Shanghai, China. In the Chinese group are many paintings by the old masters of China, tapestries and embroideries, cinnabar, jades, porcelains, and ancient bronzes. Among the Japanese rarities are old prints, brocades, temple hangings and altar cloths, embroideries, lacquer, a great palanquin two centuries old, and delicate works in silver, bronze, copper, pewter, and wood. The Korean collection contains ornamental screens, old bronzes, and a chest inlaid with mother-of-pearl. The Murray Warner Museum Library of 3,500 volumes, dealing with the history, literature, art, and life of Oriental countries, fills a room in the museum, and current magazines on art and life in the Far East are in the reading room.

6. The NEW LIBRARY (*open 8-5 weekdays*), built with a view to future expansion, was erected with the aid of a Federal grant and loan in 1936. It has desk and table space for a thousand readers, and stack room for 400,000 books. Among the 275,000 volumes are several collections. The Edward S. Burgess Rare Book Collection contains 500 volumes of manuscripts and incunabula purchased by friends of the university. Dr. and Mrs. Burt Brown Barker presented 1,000 volumes, including works by Shelley, Byron, Browning, Stevenson and others. The Pauline Potter Homer Collection of Beautiful Books comprises 800 volumes noteworthy for their fine bindings and illustrations, and as examples of the work of famous presses. There is also a collection of pamphlets and books about Oregon and by Oregon writers, another comprising 2,000 school and college textbooks, the F. S. Dunn collection of historical fiction, the Overmeyer collection of published works on the Civil War, the Camilla Leach collection of art books, a collection of League of Nations documents (1,050 volumes), and a collection of works by Balzac.

7. The MUSIC BUILDING, erected in 1920, contains studios, classrooms, and an auditorium for recitals and concerts. In the auditorium is a four-manual Reuter organ.

8. McARTHUR COURT, a large concrete basketball pavilion seating 7,000 was erected in 1926. Offices of the Associated Students and of athletic coaches are in the building. It was named for C. N. McArthur, former Congressman from Oregon and graduate of the class of 1901. The Physical Education Building (1936) is an addition to McArthur Court.

9. HAYWARD STADIUM, SW. corner of 15th and Agate Sts., was built with Associated Students' funds. Started in 1919, and finished in its present form in 1931, the stadium has a seating capacity of

EUGENE POINTS OF INTEREST

The University of Oregon

1. Villard Hall
2. Deady Hall
3. The Old Library
4. Condon Hall
5. The Art Museum
6. The New Library

7. The Music Building
8. McArthur Court
9. Hayward Stadium
10. Gerlinger Hall
11. The Pioneer Mother
12. Johnson Hall
13. The Pioneer Monument

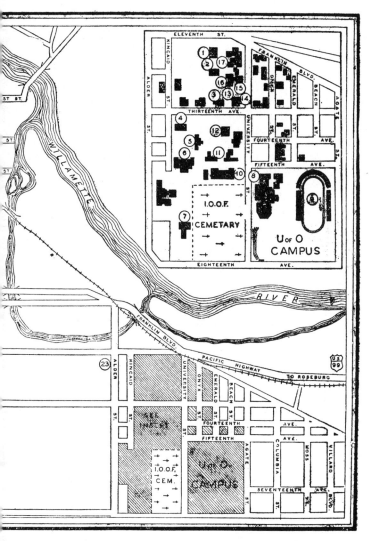

4. Friendly Hall
5. The Journalism Building
6. McClure Hall
7. Arts and Architecture Building

    Other Points of Interest

8. Site of the First Cabin in Eugene

19. The Lane County Pioneer Association Museum
20. The Site of the First Schoolhouse
21. The Spanish-American War Memorial Fountain
22. Skinner's Butte
23. Northwest Christian College

eighteen thousand and was named for William L. (Bill) Hayward, track coach and trainer since 1903.

10. GERLINGER HALL, W. side University St., houses a gymnasium and swimming pool for women, and Alumni Hall, the university social center ANTHROPOLOGICAL COLLECTIONS (*open by arrangement*) are (1939) temporarily housed in the building. The display includes the Condon Collection of archaeological material, the Ada Bradley Millican Collection of basketry, woodwork, and textiles of aboriginal craftsmanship, the Mrs. Vincent Cook Collection of Indian basketry, and the Gold Hill Site Collection of obsidian ceremonial blades, stone implements, and Indian skeletal remains.

11. The PIONEER MOTHER, a heroic bronze statue by A. Phimister Proctor stands in the court between Susan Campbell and Hendricks Halls, women's dormitories. The statue was presented in 1932 by Burt Brown Barker, vice president of the university, in memory of his mother.

12. JOHNSON HALL, facing N. on 13th St., the administration building, contains the central offices of the university, and of the Oregon State System of Higher Education. It also contains Guild Hall, in which dramatic productions are presented. The structure, of brick and ornamental stone, was erected in 1915, and perpetuates the name of John Wesley Johnson, the university's first president, who was a great Latin teacher during the school week and a great duck hunter on Saturday.

13. The PIONEER MONUMENT, in the court between the Old Library and Friendly Hall, is a heroic figure holding a bull-whip and carrying a long rifle slung over the shoulder. Sculptured by A. Phimister Proctor, it was given to the university in 1919 by Joseph N. Teal.

14. FRIENDLY HALL, NE. corner 13th and University Sts., erected in 1893 as the first men's dormitory and remodeled in 1914, houses the department of sociology, the bureau of municipal research, and offices of faculty members. It is named for S. H. Friendly, regent from 1895 to 1915.

15. The JOURNALISM BUILDING, an annex of McClure Hall, contains the school of journalism and the editorial offices of the *Oregon Daily Emerald,* campus newspaper.

16. McCLURE HALL, adjoining the Journalism Building and facing on the old campus, houses classrooms and laboratories of the department of chemistry. The building was named for Professor Edgar McClure, member of the faculty and brilliant scientist, who died in 1897.

17. The three units of the ARTS AND ARCHITECTURE BUILDING, NE. grouped about a central court at the corner of the old campus facing Villard Hall, are of brick and stucco. The first unit was erected in 1901, others added in 1914 and 1922. Here are classrooms, studios, drafting rooms, a gallery for display of student work

and loan exhibitors, and the Architecture and Allied Arts Library. Exhibits are held at intervals throughout the year.

Other buildings on the campus are COMMERCE BUILDING (1921), OREGON BUILDING (1916), EDUCATION BUILDING (1921), JOHN STRAUB BUILDING (1929), and EXTENSION AND HOME ECONOMICS BUILDING.

OTHER POINTS OF INTEREST

18. A stone monument marks the SITE OF THE FIRST CABIN IN EUGENE, 364 2nd St., which was built in 1846 by Eugene F. Skinner, for whom the city was named.

19. The LANE COUNTY PIONEER ASSOCIATION MUSEUM (*open 8-5 weekdays*). NW. corner 6th and Willamette Sts., houses a large collection of pioneer relics gathered by Cal Young and others. Included in the collection are Concord coaches, Conestoga wagons, early types of threshers, plows, mills, logging carts with ten-foot wooden disc wheels, Indian dugout canoes, war clubs, and mortars and pestles.

20. A bronze plaque at 11th St. between Willamette and Olive Sts. marks the SITE OF THE FIRST SCHOOLHOUSE which was attended by Leonora Skinner, first white child born in Lane County. The large frame structure on the site, used by the Knights of Pythias Lodge, was the second public school building in Eugene.

21. The SPANISH-AMERICAN WAR MEMORIAL FOUNTAIN, E. 8th and Oak Sts., on the corner of the courthouse grounds, was erected in 1901, in memory of Lane County volunteers who lost their lives in the Philippines in 1898-1899. The memorial consists of two square stone pillars inscribed with a dedication and the names of the volunteers; an oblong connecting slab bears two drinking fountains.

22. SKINNER'S BUTTE (681 alt.), reached from 1st and N. Lincoln Sts. by a spiral drive, is a city park and recreation ground between the main business section and the Williamette River. From its summit can be seen a panorama of Eugene, the upper Willamette Valley, and the surrounding mountains.

23. NORTHWEST CHRISTIAN COLLEGE, 11th and Alder Sts., was founded in 1895 as Eugene Divinity School. Since then it has been reorganized three times under different names—Eugene Bible University, Eugene Bible College, and Northwest Christian College. Courses are so arranged that students may take some studies in the adjoining University of Oregon.

The ADMINISTRATION BUILDING, built in 1908, the BUSHNELL LIBRARY (*open 8-5 weekdays*), with 100 rare copies of the Bible. One of them, printed in Latin, dates from 1479.

The FINE ARTS BUILDING was erected in 1921. The LOUIS H. TURNER MUSEUM (*open 8-5 weekdays*), in this building, contains many articles sent by missionaries from foreign lands and Indian relics contributed by former students. Also in this building is the GRADUATE

LIBRARY (*open* 9-5 *weekdays*), containing special books for divinity students, including many rare volumes on theology.

Other buildings on the campus are RHEM HALL (1897), the PRESIDENT'S RESIDENCE (1901), and KLINGER GYMNASIUM (1912).

POINTS OF INTEREST IN ENVIRONS

Spencer's Butte, **5** *m.*; Goshen Area of fossilized plant life, **9.2** *m.*; Washburne State Park, **17** *m.* (*see TOUR* 2). Alderwood State Park, **25** *m.*; Triangle Lake, **41** *m.* (*see TOUR* 2F). Willamette National Forest, **28** *m.* (*see TOUR* 4B).

Hood River

Railroad Station: Union Pacific Station, 1st and Cascade Sts., for Union Pacific R.R.
Bus Station: 111 Oak St., for Union Pacific Stages, Washington Motor Coaches.
Taxis: Fare 10c and 25c

Accommodations: Three hotels; auto camps.

Information Service: Chamber of Commerce, 102½ Oak St.

Motion Picture Houses: Two.
Tennis: High school courts open to public in summer.
Swimming: Koberg's Beach, 1 mi. E., near end of Hood River-White Salmon Bridge; entrance fee 10c.
Golf: Hood River Golf Club, 6 m. SW. on Mountain View and Sunset Rds., 9 holes, greens fee 35c.

Annual Events: Mt. Hood Climb, mid-July, sponsored by city and American Legion.

HOOD RIVER (154 alt., 2,757 pop.), seat of Hood River County and business center for a noted fruit-growing region, rises on the steep terraces of the Columbia River between the narrow and precipitous Hood River and Indian Creek gorges. The business district occupies the lower levels, and long flights of weather-beaten stairs climb the cliffs on First and Eugene Streets, connecting the market places with homes clinging to the sheer wall and resting on the heights above. At almost every point the broad river below and Mount Adams, with its flanking ranges on the Washington side, are visible.

From the lower part of town, Mount Hood, 26 miles south, is not visible, but from the heights it is seen in full grandeur, its massive bulk seeming almost at the door. Between the city and the mountain, the orchards of the Hood River Valley stretch almost unbroken, a mass of pinkish-white blossoms in spring, a sea of ruddy fruit in late summer and fall. The panorama is best viewed from the top of the Washington hills across the Columbia River—first the wide stream, then the compact group of business houses on the south shore, then the residences atop the cliff, and, finally, the orchards blending into the base of Mount Hood.

Throngs of visitors come to the city and its environs, especially in summer, and make it their headquarters while exploring the clear streams, green hills, and clean orchard land. When the harvest opens in late August there is an influx of fruit pickers; and trucks, filled with fresh fruit travel to warehouse and cannery, leaving behind the fragrant odor of ripened apples and pears.

Itinerant workers pour into Hood River at the opening of the fruit gathering season. Boys seeking adventure or the chance to earn a few dollars to help them through school, young women trying to get away from the humdrum of home, drift in and soon find a place in the busy crew of harvesters. Roaming families packed in old jalopies trundle up the steep streets toward the upper valley, following the fruit from crop to crop. Pinched little faces showing the lack of food peer from the torn curtains of cars; young bodies covered with ragged clothing huddle among tubs, washboards, and camping plunder. Groups of Hawaiian and Filipino boys, eager to please and learn American ways, labor industriously and make their evening camp a scene of pleasure with the ukeleles and lilting native songs.

When the strawberries ripen in June many Indians come into the valley from the Warm Springs Reservation to gather the fruit, and remain through the loganberry and raspberry season. For generations, Indian women have been adept at gathering *olallies*. While the men idle and smoke, the women and children toil in the sun, deftly harvesting the red berries. It is a common occurrence to see the Indian women with papooses strapped to their backs stooping along the rows. However, the Indians are not attracted to picking fruit that grows on trees; they leave the gathering of apples and pears to white people.

Indian tepees of the village of Waucoma (Place of the Cottonwoods) dotted the ground near the confluence of the Columbia and Hood Rivers when Lewis and Clark arrived in October, 1805, on their way to the Columbia's mouth. It was not until 1852 that W. C. Laughlin and Dr. Farnsworth discovered the abundant grass of the Hood River Valley and moved in with their herds. Winter storms of 1852-53 destroyed their stock and so discouraged the men that they soon left. Nathanial Coe was the first permanent settler, arriving with his family in 1854. The spot then bore the unromantic name of Dog River, because the people of an early emigrant train, being delayed, were forced to subsist on dog meat. Mrs. Coe soon forced a change of nomenclature, refusing to accept mail for the community unless it bore the address of Hood River.

The Hood River Valley developed slowly before the Oregon Railroad and Navigation Company's line reached it in the early 1880's. Heavy timber and deep snow in the valley offered little inducement to homesteaders. Settlers were scattered and money was scarce. Income from cordwood peddled at The Dalles and accepted as legal tender, provided the principal income. But with the coming of transportation conditions changed. Sawmills were built in the heavily timbered valley, beginning an industry that is still important in the area.

Virgil Winchell, an old settler familiarly known as "Doc," often told of the hardships of his childhood. Roads to the "outside" did not exist. Provisions were sometimes brought in on pack ponies, but for the most part they were brought down the Columbia River from The Dalles by boat. One winter, storms began early, cutting off the valley from the outside world, and the settlers were caught without food staples. Larders ran low, and the snow was so deep that it was impossible to go into the woods for game. One day Mr. Winchell, then a small boy, discovered in his father's barn a great many native birds, mostly blue jays and owls that had taken refuge from the cold. He called his father, who immediately chinked all exits and began catching birds. The Winchell family still had a small quantity of flour, and that night at supper they feasted on blue jays and owl pie.

Arrival of the rail line, however, put an end to isolation and many hardships. Attracted by the region's recreational resources, Portland citizens built summer cabins, and in 1889 a group of Portland's capitalists constructed Cloud Cap Inn on the north snow line of Mount Hood and built a toll road to it. The Inn was the first mountain hostelry in the Pacific Northwest.

In the last decade of the nineteenth century, Hood River residents discovered the suitability of local conditions for fruit-raising on a large scale. The first cash crop was strawberries. Professor T. R. Coon, pioneer Oregon teacher, migrated to the Hood River Valley in the eighties, bringing with him a supply of Clark Seedling strawberry plants, which had been developed in the Mount Tabor district of Portland. In a few years the valley was producing Clark Seedling strawberries in car lots. Ranchers, who had been living in comfort but without cash surpluses, soon found themselves in comparative luxury. For years annual shipments have exceeded 300 carloads.

The first apple trees in Hood River were planted by the Coe family, and other pioneer families soon had productive home orchards, but natural barriers stood in the way of commercial development. The valley floor was so densely covered with giant conifers and oaks that clearing land was a slow and expensive process. To help in preparing the ground, land-owners brought in Japanese laborers. The industrious Orientals stayed by the job. They dug out stumps, cut slashing, burned debris, tilled the soil, and transformed cut-over waste into a vast garden.

The first carload of Hood River apples was shipped to New York City in 1900, and from this carload the apple industry in the Pacific Northwest had its real beginning. Rumors of the new industry spread rapidly, and soon there was an influx of settlers bent on becoming gentlemen farmers. Retired business men, navy and army officers, and young college graduates, created a sort of golden era of business and refinement unusual for so small a city. For years Hood River had a University Club with several hundred members, probably the smallest city in the United States to have such an organization.

The region's orchards approximate 10,000 acres, and while apples are still predominant, the acreage of pears has so increased that pear production bids fair to equal the apple output. Cherry culture has also been found profitable and hundreds of tons of Royal Annes, Bings, and Lamberts are produced annually. Anjou pears are shipped to the Sudan district of North Africa.

For several years Hood River was the home of Frederic Homer Balch, missionary preacher and Oregon's most important novelist. Here he wrote *Genevieve, A Tale of Oregon,* and most of *The Bridge of the*

Gods, his best-known work. A resident in the city at various periods after 1913 was George W. Cronyn, who married a native of the valley, and has written, among other books, *The Fool of Venus* (1934), a historical novel of the troubadours, and *Mermaid Tavern* (1937), a fictionized life of Christopher Marlowe, the Elizabethan dramatist. Anthony Euwer, poet, lecturer, and essayist, lived here for a number of years and Percy Manser, the landscape artist, makes his home nearby.

The principal public event in the city is the annual Mount Hood climb sponsored by the city and the American Legion. In July of each year several hundred people from Hood River and other points in the Northwest gather at the legion camp at the foot of Cooper Spur on the east flank of the mountain and begin the steep ascent at dawn.

POINTS OF INTEREST

1. The CITY HALL, 2nd St. between State and Oak Sts., is a one-story brick business block of utilitarian design that houses city offices, including the fire department and jail. In a glass case attached to the north wall of the council chamber is the flag raised at the community's first Fourth of July celebration in 1861.

2. The OLD ADAMS HOUSE (*private*), 13th and State Sts., for decades one of the city's show places, but for many years deserted and fallen into disrepair, has been recently remodeled into a modified Cape Cod style cottage. Formerly in the yard was a large fountain patterned after one of the fountains in the garden of the Palace of Versailles, France. In its pool once swam a gigantic sturgeon captured in the Columbia River. Dr. Adams was in early life a minister, then a lawyer, and in his late years a physician. He was a personal friend of Abraham Lincoln and at one time editor of the Oregon City *Argus.*

3. The APPLEGROWERS' ASSOCIATION CANNERY (*open on application at office, 3rd St. between Railroad and Cascade Aves.*), 6th and Columbia Sts., is adjacent to the Columbia Street warehouse. From late August, when canning starts on Bartlett pears, until late December, when the season ends with the canning of low-grade apples, it is filled with uniformed women workers. After going through mechanical washing and grading processes, the fruit passes on belts through automatic paring and cutting machines to cans and cookers and finally to storerooms.

4. HOOD RIVER DISTILLERIES (*open on application at office*), 1st and Oak Sts., manufactures cull fruits into brandy. The company has the only Federal-bonded warehouse on the Pacific coast outside California.

5. OBSERVATION PROMONTORY, N. end of May St., a scenic vantage point on a high headland at the junction of Hood River and Columbia gorges, provides a panoramic view of mountains, valleys, and rivers. Southward, Mount Hood towers above the formal patterns of orchards, while to the north, beyond the reaches of the Columbia, rise Mount Adams and the Washington hills.

6. ELIOT PARK, occupying Indian Creek gorge from 12th St. to the turbulent Hood River, is a primitive spot where native flowers, shrubs, and trees grow in profusion. The park is the gift of Dr. Thomas Lamb Eliot, for a half-century pastor of the Church of Our Father, Unitarian, in Portland, and one of the first to recognize Hood River as a vacation center.

POINTS OF INTEREST IN ENVIRONS

Wau-Guin-Guin Falls, 1 *m.*; Crag Rats Club House, 1 *m.*; Early Indian Burial Ground, 1 *m.*; Starvation Creek State Park, 9.4 *m.* (*see TOUR* 1). Hood River Experiment Station, 2 *m.*; Panorama Viewpoint, 3 *m.*; Frederic Homer Balch House, 3.5 *m.*; Rev. W. A. (Billy) Sunday House, 6 *m.*; Cloud Cap Inn, 33.1 *m.* (*see TOUR* 1*E*).

Klamath Falls

Railroad Stations: Oak and Spring Sts., for Southern Pacific Lines; 1340 S. 6th St., for Great Northern Ry.
Bus Station: Union Stage Depot, 830 Klamath St., for Pacific Greyhound Lines, Mount Hood Stages, Red Ball Stages, and Oregon, California and Nevada Stages.
Airport: 4-5 m. SE. on State 66.
City Busses: Fare 10c.
Taxis: 50c in city limits.
Docks for Pleasure Boats: Front St. on Upper Klamath Lake.

Accommodations: Four hotels; tourist camps.

Information Service: Chamber of Commerce, and Oregon State Motor Association, 323 Main St.

Radio Station: KFGI (1210 kc.).
Motion Picture Houses: Four.
Tennis: Mills Addition, Home and Stukel Sts.; Moore Park, Rock Creek Highway.
Swimming: Hot Springs Natatorium, 530 Spring St.; New Klamath Natatorium, 1719 Main St.; fees, adults 35c, children 25c.
Golf: Reames Golf and Country Club, 3.5 m. W. on State 236; 9 holes; greens fee, 50c Mon.-Fri., 75c Sat., Sun. and holidays.
Riding: Klamath Riding Academy, S. Sixth St. (The Dalles-California Highway); fees, riding horses 75c first hour, 50c for each subsequent hour; riding lessons 50c an hour.

Annual Events: Upper Klamath Lake Regatta, June; Buckaroo Days, week-end nearest July 4th.

KLAMATH FALLS (4,105 alt., 16,093 pop.), industrial center and seat of Klamath County, is on the eastern slope of the Cascade Range and commands a panoramic vista of snow peaks, evergreen forests, and thriving valley farms. The business section stretches along the banks of Link River and the shores of Lake Ewauna (Ind., elbow), while the residential district occupies rising grounds to the east and north. The city has a clean modern appearance; its growth has taken place almost entirely since 1915, and its buildings and residences are of latter-day architectural styles. Upper Klamath Lake touches the northern city limits. Entirely within the city is Link River—less than a mile in length and said to be the shortest river in the world—which flows through the western edge of town, connecting Upper Klamath Lake with Lake Ewauna. The grayish-blue Klamath River flows from Lake Ewauna across northern California to the Pacific.

Thousands of white pelicans make their summer homes on Lake Ewauna, Link River, and Upper Klamath Lake. From late March to September they can be seen everywhere in and about the city, soaring in flocks against the sun or floating on the waters of lake or river. They nest in the reeds along the shores of Upper Klamath Lake. So intimately is the bird associated with the city that social and athletic organizations, business houses, a hotel and a theatre are named for it.

The old West rubs elbows with the new in Klamath Falls. Typical survivors of the city's most colorful period, men and women who were a part of the pioneering and homesteading eras, linger here. Grizzled ranchers still sit at friendly poker games under the brighter lights of the new town. Sheepherders in from tending flocks on the lonely hills, Indians from the Klamath Reservation, and loggers from the deep woods, mingle freely, lending color to the modern business activity. Because of the many industrial establishments "pay nights" (Saturday nights nearest the first and fifteenth of the month) are carnival-like periods. Great crowds of visitors, mill employees and townspeople, surge in and out of the stores spending the earnings of the previous fortnight. Stores and banks stay open until 10:30, and the moving-picture houses, dance halls and other recreation centers reap a large portion of the million-dollar pay roll before the night ends.

Key city of south-central Oregon, Klamath Falls is the distributing and marketing point for rich lumbering, agricultural, cattle and sheepraising areas. The Klamath Basin contains over 300,000 acres of irrigable land; with more than a million acre-feet of water available in a normal run-off during the irrigation season. The principal crops are alfalfa, grains and potatoes. Shipments of potatoes have, in recent years, averaged well over five thousand carloads annually, and in 1938-39 the potato acreage was more than 20,000, with a crop value in excess of four million dollars. Sheep and cattle are summered on the surrounding ranges in the mountains and remote areas, and wintered in the irrigated section where feed is plentiful. The Klamath Irrigation Project contains almost 200,000 acres under irrigation.

Lumbering and its affiliated activities form the city's chief industry. Within the town and the surrounding region are twenty-eight sawmills and manufacturing plants employing 3,000 men and cutting 350,000,000 feet of lumber annually. It is said that Klamath Falls is the largest box-shook manufacturing district in the United States. Tributary to the city are approximately 30,000,000,000 feet of pine timber.

Settlement of the Klamath Lake country was retarded by the hostility of the Klamath Indians, and the village from which the modern city grew was not established until 1867. Before that time the development of the valley had been sanguinary. Lieutenant John C. Fremont's camp was attacked in 1846, and three of his men were killed. An immigrant train was ambushed in 1850 and almost wiped out. A year later a second train was attacked at Bloody Point on Tule Lake and a mere handful of its hundred members escaped massacre. These and other raids caused the area to become known as the "dark and bloody ground of the Pacific," and it was not until 1864 that Federal troops sufficiently subdued the tribesmen to enable pioneers to settle along Link River with any degree of safety.

The Applegate brothers, Jesse and Lindsey, explored in this region in 1846 and in 1848 organized the Klamath Commonwealth to settle the area; discovery of gold in California, however, led the settlers to another destination. Wendolen Nus, first permanent settler in the Klamath country, built a cabin and established a claim on the west shore of Klamath Lake in 1858. Others settled in the Basin in the early sixties. In 1863 a United States military post, known as Fort Klamath, was established to the north of the lake. In 1864 a treaty was negotiated with the Indians and the Klamath Reservation (see *TOUR* 4) was established.

Linkville, as Klamath Falls was first called, was founded by George Nurse, a sutler from Fort Klamath, who built a cabin on the east bank of Link River at its junction with Lake Ewauna in 1866. Approximately a hundred emigrants had taken up homes in the district by 1867. A log trading post, established by Nurse at the landing of the ferry across Link River, supplied the wants of the scattered settlers. With the Indians confined to the Klamath Reservation and the fear of attack allayed, Linkville became a thriving town, possessing the raw color of most frontier communities. In those early days the Klamath Basin was essentially cattle country; a wild country of rough men. Old time residents still recall many cases of murder and sudden death in gambling and land claim disputes. One big family in the Basin carried on a wholesale business in cattle rustling and other banditry. It was said of them that they were tough and gloried in the fact. In time the entire family was wiped out, most of its members going to their final rest with their boots on.

Security from Indian outbreak was short lived. In 1872 the region was again plunged into conflict. The Modocs refused to remain on the Klamath Reservation and made persistent efforts to return to their former home near Tule Lake. A small band under Chief Keintpoos, better known as Captain Jack, clashed with a body of United States cavalry, routing it and precipitating the bloody Modoc War. Inhabitants of Klamath Falls knew months of terror as the Modoc bands parried thrust after thrust of the Federal troops. However, the soldiers finally overcame the Indians, and Captain Jack and three of his followers were executed.

After the creation of Klamath County in 1882 the city maintained a slow but steady growth. Platted in 1878 in a plan covering forty blocks, it was incorporated in 1889 as Linkville; but this name was changed to the Town of Klamath Falls in 1893. Impetus was given to development when, in 1900, the Klamath Basin Irrigation Project was started by the Federal Government. A few years later a new stimulus came with the building of the first railroad. A branch line was opened by the Southern Pacific from Weed, California, in 1909, as a lumber carrier, and in the mid-1920's the Natron cut-off extension was completed between Klamath Falls and Eugene. From the construction of the first railroad the growth of the city was phenomenal, the population increasing more than six-fold between 1915 and 1930.

The principal recreational events of Klamath Falls are the Klamath

Lake Regatta in June and the Buckaroo Days celebration on the weekend nearest the Fourth of July. The First event features yacht, outboard, rowboat, surfboard, and swimming races, and log-cutting and log-bucking contests. The Buckaroo Days festival, commemorating the period when the Klamath Basin was cattle country, presents the usual rodeo events, riding, roping, bulldogging, wild horse racing, and others of frontier significance.

Klamath Falls has a series of hot mineral springs, one of which discharges 800,000 gallons of water daily at a temperature of 200 degrees. These waters, containing soda, lime, magnesia, iron, and sulphuric, muriatic, and silicic acids are effective in diseases arising from impurities of the blood and for various other complaints. Public and private buildings are heated from these natural hot water springs, and two swimming pools are filled with the waters.

POINTS OF INTEREST

1. The KLAMATH COUNTY COURTHOUSE (*open* 8-5 *Mon.-Fri.,* 8-1 *Sat.*), Main St. between 3rd and 4th Sts., erected in 1918, is a modern two-story building faced with buff brick and trimmed in terra cotta. The entrance pavilion is of the Greek style with Ionic columns. The interior has a six-foot wainscot of Alaskan marble in matched patterns. The architect was E. E. McClaren.

2. The CITY LIBRARY (*open* 9-9 *weekdays*), SE. corner of 5th St. and Klamath Ave., a red brick two-story structure, was built in 1926 on property donated by Mrs. Fred Schallock and C. H. Daggett in memory of Henrietta F. Melhasse. The building is ell-shaped, with a classic portico inside the bend of the ell facing the intersection of Fifth Street and Klamath Avenue. The library has 13,000 volumes.

3. The FEDERAL BUILDING, 7th St. between Walnut and Oak Aves., is a three-story reinforced concrete building, with tile hip roof, first story faced with sandstone, and the upper stories with red brick and sandstone trim. The foundation is of native Oregon granite. The building of modified Italian Renaissance architecture was designed by government architects under the direction of James A. Wetmore.

4. LINK RIVER BRIDGE, SW. end of Main St. at the head of Lake Ewauna, is of ornamental concrete construction, single span without superstructure, and is one of two that span Link River. It is at the site of the old Nurse ferry and bridge, which for many years accommodated all traffic between the Rogue River Valley and the south-central Oregon range country. In spring and summer it offers a view of great numbers of snow-white pelicans, some floating silently on lake or river, others soaring in flocks overhead.

5. The EWAUNA BOX MILL (*open* 8-5 *weekdays on application at office*), 6th & Spring Sts., with a daily capacity of 150,000 feet of finished lumber, is one of the larger mills of the district. Operations can be watched from the time a log is hauled up out of the water until it has been put through the mill. With the log in position on the car-

riage, the big saw screams its way through from end to end, lopping off great slices. At times these cuts are four or more feet in thickness. The thick slices are canted onto rollers that carry them to the edger, which squares the timbers, and then on to the trimmer, where the poorer parts are cut out. This process continues until the log has been transformed into lumber.

6. FREMONT BRIDGE, W. end of Nevada Ave., is a memorial to Lieutenant John C. Fremont, the pathfinder, who, under the guidance of Kit Carson, slashed his way through the Oregon wilderness in 1843 and 1846. In and about Klamath Falls many campgrounds, burial places, and battle sites are marked in his honor. From Fremont Bridge is a fine view of Upper Klamath Lake, made nationally famous by E. H. Harriman, who built an elaborate lodge on Pelican Bay at the northern end of the lake because, it is said, he considered it the most beautiful spot in the west. The bridge is of concrete, single-arched with ornamental railing.

7. MOORE PARK, on Rock Creek Highway W. of Link River, a large area mostly in its natural state, was donated to the city by Rufus C. Moore, a pioneer. In the park is a small Zoo and AVIARY (*open 8-8 daily*), a tennis court, a toboggan slide, and a well-equipped picnic ground.

POINTS OF INTEREST IN ENVIRONS

Klamath Wild Life Reservation, **11** *m*. (*see TOUR* 4). Algoma Point, **12** *m.*; Klamath Indian Reservation, **32** *m.*; Crater Lake National Park, **60** *m.* (*see TOUR* 4D). Lava Beds National Monument, **36** *m.* S. in California (*see TOUR 8A, CALIFORNIA STATE GUIDE*).

Medford

Railroad Station: N. 5th and Front Sts., for Southern Pacific Lines.
Bus Station: Jackson Hotel, 614 S. Central St., for Pacific Greyhound and Inde-
-pendent Motor Stages.
Airport: Municipal Airport, 3 m. NE. on State 62 for United Airlines; Taxi
$1.25.
Taxis: Fare, 25c minimum.

Accommodations: Five hotels; six tourist camps.

Information Service: Chamber of Commerce, 1 E. Main St., near depot; Oregon
State Motor Assn., 34 S. Riverside St.

Radio Station: KMED (1310 kc.).
Motion Picture Houses: Four.
Swimming: Merrick Natatorium, N. Riverside St., fee 25c.
Golf: Rogue River Valley Golf Association, Hillcrest Road, 18 holes, greens fees
$1 weekdays, $1.50 Sundays.

MEDFORD (1,377 alt., 11,007 pop.), summer resort town and fruit
and lumber center, lies in the heart of the Rogue River Valley, which
presents a picture of endless orchards, irrigated by clear mountain
streams and hemmed in, for the most part, by the steep walls of the
Cascade and Siskiyou Ranges, and the broken escarpment of Table
Rock. From the floor of the valley sloping benches and rounded foothills rise to the surrounding mountains, which are heavily timbered with
yellow pine, sugar pine, fir, cedar, oak, madrona and other varieties of
trees. In the spring the valley is filled with coral-tinted blossoms; in
the autumn pears, apples, peaches, plums, almonds, and grapes are harvested.

The city is built on both sides of Bear Creek ten miles from its confluence with Rogue River. Several bridges connect the east and west
sides of the town. Orchards extend on all sides of the city, and numerous fruit trees abound within the city itself. Poor indeed is the home
that has neither apple nor pear trees in its yard. In the last two decades
Medford has made rapid growth, more than doubling in population;
but in spite of this it is a well-planned city. Native trees have been permitted to grow and, supplemented by imported growths, give a park-
like effect to the town. An extensive park system and civic center with
architectural harmony adds to the attractiveness of the city plan. Along
the railroad tracks is an almost unbroken row of fruit-packing and shipping warehouses, fragrant with fruit in late summer and early fall.

Many easterners maintain summer residences in the surrounding foothills and mountains, and Medford's hotels and restaurants are crowded
with visitors. The city is in the heart of an extensive recreational area

and its roads give access to Crater Lake, Rogue River Gorge, the Oregon Caves, Table Rock, a natural bridge near Prospect, many varieties of mineral springs, and numerous scenic and recreational attractions. There is good fishing in near-by Rogue River, and it is said that Jackson County has more deer than cattle.

With the approach of fall the exodus of summer residents is followed by the arrival of a small army of fruit pickers and packers of both sexes and all ages. Throngs jam the sidewalks and automobiles crowd the curb. Among the throngs are youngsters who have trekked across the continent in ancient flivvers to see the long dreamed-of West, roaming families who follow the fruit, flitting from one crop to another, Hawaiian and Filipino boys from their island homes, organizers and knights of the soap-box airing their views on government and economics. Here today and gone tomorrow, they come when the fruit calls them, and, their tasks finished, they vanish until another season beckons them back.

Visitors to Medford in the fall and winter months may note the stacks of wood that stand unprotected from the elements, bearing "wood for sale" signs. Winters are so mild in the Rogue River Valley that householders need not store up wood for winter, but content themselves with buying an occasional load for use on chilly evenings.

The site of Medford, unapproached by a navigable river, was settled late. The well-grassed valley and the surrounding forested mountains abounded in game, and this was a favorite hunting ground for the Indians, who resented white encroachment. When gold was discovered at near-by Jacksonville in 1851 a great many people came from the Willamette Valley to go into mining. As the richness of the gold field diminished, many of them, seeing the fertility of the valley, settled here. The Indians of Rogue River Valley were placed on a reservation under the terms of a treaty of 1856, and the area was thrown open for settlement.

Medford was an "opposition" town, established in 1883 by the Oregon and California Railroad Company (now the Southern Pacific), when Central Point, four miles north, refused to lend financial aid toward completion of the road through the southern part of the state. "Though poor in purse" the people of Jackson County contributed generously to the building of the railroad. Many farmers subscribed quantities of wheat or other grain, a few made direct payments in cash, others filled out their quotas with beaver skins, and sawmill owners gave cross ties to be used in laying the track. Unable to punish Central Point by leaving it off the main line, the railroad for a number of years refused to stop at the town or to sell tickets to that destination. The new town was named Middleford because it was situated at the middle of three fords on Bear Creek, but David Loring, a railroad engineer who had lived in Medford, Massachusetts, suggested the change to the present name.

With wide streets and "a reserved space for public buildings," Medford began as a well-planned town. Saloons were permitted to operate here, though they were barred in some other Jackson County settlements, and an occasional "roughian" disturbed the peace and quiet of the little community, which otherwise got most of its amusement from attending church meetings and dances sponsored by the literary society or the temperance union. Medford was incorporated as a town in 1884, and reincorporated as a city in 1905.

With the support of the railroad, Medford became the distributing point of the sparsely settled valley, but not until the turn of the century, when its fruit began to attract attention, did the town begin a consistent growth. In the first decade of the twentieth century the city grew from 1,790 to almost 9,000 population, the greatest growth taking place about 1908. During these boom days every train was crowded with landseekers from California and the eastern states, bringing capital and scientific knowledge to the fruit industry in the valley. Thousands of acres nearby were planted to pears and other fruits; Medford expanded its borders to four square miles and started public works that are still (1939) an expense to local taxpayers.

As Medford prospered, the old mining town of Jacksonville, the original county seat, dwindled. In 1927 Medford was made the county seat. The previous year the county received a refund from the Federal Government on taxes owing on railroad "grant lands." This land, known as the Oregon and California Grant, was given to the railroads in the eighties as a subsidy, on condition that the railroad dispose of it at $2.50 an acre. The railroad ignored the condition and the Government took back the land in 1915. The "grant counties" then persuaded the Government to compensate them, in the amount of a million dollars, for lost taxes. Jackson county utilized its share of the fund in building a new courthouse, which was completed in 1932.

The commercial life of Medford revolves around the fruit and lumber industries. Orchards planted during the boom have now reached full bearing and the annual pear pack of the district averages about four thousand carloads, which move out in two streams, one to the eastern states and to foreign countries as fresh fruit, and one to the canneries of the Willamette Valley. Six cold-storage plants handle truck and rail shipments and more than $12,000,000 worth of products are annually dispatched to the markets of the world. Jackson County's vast timber wealth is reflected in local industries, which include planing mills, cabinet factories, and a sawmill with a capacity of 250,000 board feet daily. Here great power-driven saws drone and whine, ripping to exact thickness and length great trees logged in the hills and mountains that encompass the valley, and stacks of yellow pine lumber shed on the air a pungency that not even the sharp fragrance of fruit blossoms can dispel. The city also has a modern candy factory, a plate glass works, a flouring mill, three stone-tile and cement-block plants, an iron foundry, a catsup plant, twenty-one fruit-packing plants, a vegetable and meat canning plant, and a large ice plant.

Numerous Federal offices are located in Medford. A branch office of the U. S. Department of Agriculture is fitted with a library-labora-

tory in charge of a pathologist whose duty it is to attend to the horticultural interests of the Rogue River Valley.

POINTS OF INTEREST

1.   JACKSON COUNTY COURTHOUSE, S. Oakdale St. be-
tween W. Main and W. 8th Sts., the most imposing edifice in the city,
is a modern four-story building faced with Indiana limestone and
trimmed in Ashland granite. The entrance pavilion, five bays in width,
is flanked by heavy pylons, while the fourth story is in the form of a
low set-back. The interior trim is of Alaska marble. Designed by John
G. Link, it was completed in 1932.

2.   MEDFORD PUBLIC LIBRARY (*open* 9-9 *weekdays;* 2-9
Sun.) 413 W. Main St., a brick and stone structure of Neo-Classic
design containing more than thirty thousand volumes, some of them rare
and valuable editions, is opposite the courthouse in a park-like block.
One of the acquisitions is a collection of books on animal life, travel,
and history, presented by Edison Marshall, author and big game hunter,
formerly a resident of the city. The library maintains branches in several
smaller towns of the county. In the grounds of the library, as in many
other parts of the city, are huge native oak trees covered with great
clumps of mistletoe, in some instances so abundant that it almost hides
the branches.

3.   MEDFORD CITY PARK, W. Main St. between S. Ivy and
S. Holly Sts., has a central fountain surmounted by a Carrara marble
statue of a youth seated with two dogs upon his knees. The fountain,
which provides drinking water for birds and dogs, was given to the
city in 1929 by C. W. and Callie Palm. The sculptor and designer are
unknown.

4.   NEWBY & SONS FRUIT PACKING PLANT (*open week-
days by arrangement*), First St. and Southern Pacific Ry., is one of the
larger packing, shipping and cold storage plants of the city where fruits
are sorted, graded and packed, as they come from the orchards. After
a special bath in acid or alkaline solutions the fruit is run through
rinses of fresh water and dried by currents of air. Washing machines
deliver the fruit to grading machines, which automatically deliver the
sized fruit to the correct bin. Men and women pack the apples from
the bins into the boxes in which they are to be shipped. Pickers, graders,
and packers all wear gloves and the fruit is not touched by the bare
hand. After packing the fruit is stored in refrigerated rooms or shipped
in refrigerated cars.

POINTS OF INTEREST IN ENVIRONS

Jacksonville, scene of first gold discovery in Oregon, 1851, 6 *m.*; Jackson Hot
Springs, 8 *m.*; Lithia Springs, Ashland, 10 *m.*; Site of Old Fort Lane, 10 *m.*;
Gold Ray Dam in the Rogue River, 12 *m.*; Table Rock, 15 *m.* (*see TOUR* 2).
Rogue River Canyon, 46 *m.*; Natural Bridge, 56 *m.*; Crater Lake, 80 *m.* (*see
TOUR* 4C). Oregon Caves, 94 *m.* (*see TOUR* 2D).

Oregon City

Railroad Station: 7th St. and Railroad Ave., for Southern Pacific Lines.
Bus Stations: 7th St. between Main and Railroad Ave., for Greyhound Stages; Railroad Ave. between 6th and 7th Sts., for Dollar Lines; 5th and Main Sts., for Peden & Rankin.
City Busses: Fare 5c.
Taxis: 10c a mile.

Accommodations: Hotel at West Linn, across river.

Information Service: Chamber of Commerce, Hogg Bldg., 8th and Main Sts.; A.A.A., Ed May Garage, 5th and Water Sts.

Motion Picture Houses: Three.
Tennis: High school courts, 12th and J. Q. Adams Sts.
Swimming: Municipal Swimming Pool, 10th and Madison Sts.; Library Park Wading Pool, 6th and John Adams Sts.
Golf: Mt. Pleasant Golf Club, 9 holes, greens fee 25c; Oregon City Golf Club, 9 holes, greens fee $1.

Annual Events: Territorial Days, usually during last two weeks of Aug.; Mid-Spring Chinook Salmon Run; Lamprey Eel Migration, May-July.

OREGON CITY (72 alt., 5,761 pop.) is a city of first things in Oregon. It was the first provisional and territorial capital, the first town incorporated west of the Missouri River, scene of the first use of water power in Oregon, the first Masonic lodge west of the Missouri was organized here, and a pioneer library and temperance and debating societies were first in the region.

Oregon City is the seat of Clackamas County, situated at the point where the broad, navigable Willamette River drops forty-two feet from a basaltic ledge with a crest more than three thousand feet long. The city owes its importance as a manufacturing center chiefly to utilization of abundant water power furnished by the falls.

The city is best viewed from the west end of the graceful, single-span Willamette River bridge. As the prehistoric inland sea that filled the Willamette Valley gradually drained into the Pacific Ocean, it left three distinct terraces or shore lines, locally called benches, on the precipitous bluff along the east shore of the Willamette River. Occupying the first of these benches, between the river and the cliff, is the business section of the city. A hundred feet above, on the second terrace, is the residential district. Two hundred feet above this is the third bench, stretching eastward toward the green foothills of the Cascade Range and the rigidly symmetrical slopes of Mount Hood. Streets so steep that they seem to stand on end connect these three levels. Many houses edge the cliff, facing the wide expanse of river and forested hills beyond. Almost hidden in trees and shrubbery, they peer down like sentinels from a parapet.

The chinook salmon run in mid-spring, and the flocks of fishermen drawn to it, can be seen from the bridge. Above the span, in the pool below the falls, is a choice spot for more venturesome sportsmen; it is difficult to keep boats in place here, but the salmon rest in the pool before attempting the fish ladder over the falls. The great majority, however, fish below the bridge at a safe distance from the white torrent, their boats anchored in rows at right angles with the current. From the bridge, too, is a birdseye view of Willamette Falls and the industrial plants huddled close on both sides of the river.

White occupancy of Oregon City, in an area that the Hudson's Bay Company did not originally want settled, was forced upon the company because of the pending boundary settlement between the United States and England. "It becomes an important object to acquire as ample an occupation of the Country and Trade as possible," company officials wrote in 1828, "on the South as well as on the North side of the Columbia River, looking always to the Northern side falling to our Share on a division, and to secure this, it may be as well to have something to give up on the South when the final arrangement comes to be made." Dr. John McLoughlin of Vancouver, chief factor of the Columbia department, was ordered to set up a sawmill at "the falls of the Wilhamet (south of the Columbia) where the same Establishment of people can attend to the Mill, watch the Fur & Salmon Trade, and take care of a Stock of Cattle."

Three log houses were built on the site of Oregon City in the winter of 1829-30, and potatoes were planted in the spring. The Indians, resenting this infringement of their territory, burned the houses. A flour mill and sawmill constructed in 1832 made use of the first water power in Oregon. Feeling quickly developed between American settlers and the Hudson's Bay Company, and in 1841 a group of Methodist missionaries organized a milling company, occupying an island below the falls, opposite the property claimed by Dr. McLoughlin; later they built on the shore, directly on his claim. In order to forestall this preemption, Dr. McLoughlin the following year named the town and had it platted by Sidney Walter Moss, who came with the first big group of settlers in 1842 and owned a pocket compass.

The Oregon Temperance Society, founded in 1838, was the first of its kind in the region; prohibition, much agitated at the time, had a safety factor, for no house was safe from Indian entry if it was known to contain liquor. The Multnomah Circulating Library was organized in 1842, with three hundred books and a capital of $500. The Oregon Lyceum and the Falls Debating Society were formed the following year. The latter probably gave impetus to the beginning of civil government in the Northwest; its members frequently debated such questions as "Resolved, That it is expedient for the settlers on this coast to establish an independent government."

The immigration of 1844 added about eight hundred people to the

MBERLINE LODGE, MOUNT HOOD

PUNCH BOWL FALLS, EAGLE CREEK

PLAQUE "THE BEAVER"

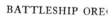

COMING OF THE WHITE MAN, PORTLAND

ELIOT GLACIER,
MOUNT HOOD

ROGUE RIVE
NATIONAL FORE

VERED BRIDGE NEAR DILLARD

OLD BOONES FERRY, WILSONVILLE

BATTLESHIP SEARCHLIGHTS, FLEET WEEK, PORTLAND

PORTLAND AND MOUNT HOO[D]

OHN DAY COUNTRY

BASALT BLUFFS ALONG JOHN DAY RIVER

HIGHWAY SIGN NEAR MADRAS

ONTARI

COYOTE

WILD CAT

PROOF OF A TALL TALE

SEA LIONS, OREGON C[

LK AT WALLOWA LAKE

ON JUMPING WILLAMETTE FALLS   DEER TRACKS IN SNOW

OREGON BEAVER

BLACK BEAR, FREMONT NATIONAL FOR

ONNEVILLE DAM AND MOUNT HOOD

SHEEP MOUNTAIN

MULTNOMAH FALLS

PHANTOM SHIP
CRATER LAKE

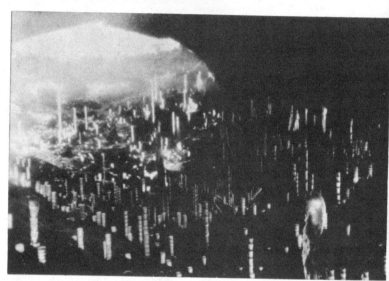

ICE STALAGMITES IN MALHEUR CAVE

BUNCHGRASS,
CENTRAL OREGON

LLOWA MOUNTAINS

HOLLAND GRASS PLANTINGS, OREGON COAST

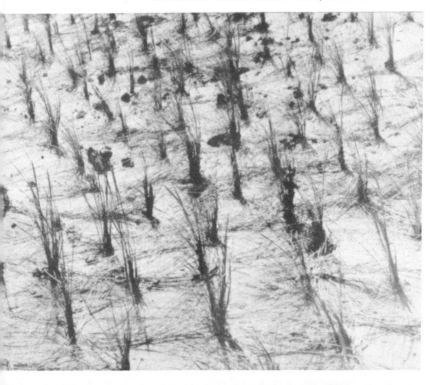

MITCHELL POINT TUNNEL, COLUMBIA RIVER

SNAKE RIVER CAN

population of Oregon City. The provisional government, formed the year before at Champoeg, chose the city as its seat, and the first provisional legislature assembled here in June, 1844. Jesse Applegate was given authority to replat the city, making it larger than the original Moss survey. He used a rope four rods long instead of the usual surveyor's chain, and the variation in the rope's length due to moisture conditions and stretching accounts for the irregular size of the lots. The legislature granted the town a charter, making it the first to be incorporated west of the Missouri River. George Abernethy, who one year later became provisional governor, erected the first brick store in Oregon. In the same year the first furniture factory in the Pacific Northwest was built here.

By 1846 Oregon City had seventy houses and some five hundred inhabitants. In that year the *Oregon Spectotor* began publication, members of the Masonic fraternity organized the first lodge west of the Missouri River, and the first American flag owned by the provisional government was raised.

Oregon City was profoundly shocked by news of the Whitman massacre at Waiilatpu in 1847; the surviving women and children were brought to the town by Peter Skene Ogden, Hudson's Bay agent. The Oregon capital sent men to fight in the resulting Cayuse War, and the murderers of the Whitman party were subsequently tried in Oregon City, sentenced to death, and hanged. In January, 1848, Joe Meek, a colorful character, left Oregon City to carry the request of the provisional legislature for territorial status to Washington, and returned in March, 1849, with the newly appointed territorial governor, Joseph Lane. The city was made territorial capital and remained so until 1852, when the seat of government was removed to Salem.

Oregon City's modern industrial life dates from 1864, when a woolen mill was established by two brothers named Jacobs. Two years later, the erection of the first paper mill on the Coast initiated development of the city's most important industry. In 1925 Oregon City adopted the commission form of government and appointed a city manager.

Several well-known literary figures are associated with the city at the falls. First in time was the host of the Main Street Hotel, Sidney Walter Moss, who wrote *The Prairie Flower,* a tale of Oregon and the Oregon Trail. Edwin Markham, the poet, was born here in 1852, but removed to California with his mother when he was a small boy. Eva Emery Dye, resident of the city for more than forty years, in *McLoughlin and Old Oregon, The Conquest,* and *The Soul of America,* used the historical background of the state as material for her books. A resident for a time was Ella Higginson, author of stories, novels, and poems with an Oregon and Northwest background (*see LITERATURE*).

POINTS OF INTEREST

1. The SITE OF THE FIRST PROTESTANT CHURCH in the Oregon Country, SE. corner of 7th and Main Sts., is occupied

by a store, on the west front of which is a bronze marker commemorative of the old Methodist church, dedicated in 1844. In the winter of 1847 the provisional legislature met in the building.

2. The SITE OF THE FIRST CAPITOL OF OREGON TERRITORY, SE. corner 6th and Main Sts., now occupied by a grocery store, is indicated by a bronze marker on the west wall. The capitol was a plain two-story building, which served after removal of the capital to Salem as the meeting place of the Masonic lodge, the Sons of Temperance, and the county court.

3. The HAWLEY PULP AND PAPER PLANT (*open on application at office*), S. end of Main St., on E. bank of Willamette River, manufactures print and wrapping paper. Organized in 1908, it affords employment for an average of one thousand workers. The site of the *Oregon Spectator* office, "the first newspaper issued in the American territory west of the Rocky mountains" (*see NEWSPAPERS AND RADIO*), is designated by a bronze marker in the wall of the paper company's office. Printed first on February 5, 1846, the paper was published for less than a decade, but it strongly influenced the political and cultural life of the period. One of its earliest editors was George Law Curry, who later became governor of the territory.

On the grounds of the plant was the old Main Street House, the first hotel of the city, a cabin measuring fourteen by seventeen feet. Later the hotel was established in a two-story building on the southwest corner of 3rd and Main Streets and advertised in rhyme:

> "To all, high or low,
> Please down with your dust,
> For he's no friend of ours
> That would ask us to trust."

The proprietor, Sidney Walter Moss, who platted the town, was one of the most colorful of early Oregon characters. Coming to the Northwest in 1842, he was Oregon's first recognized novelist; built the first jail; paid from his own pocket for a free primary school; was at various times assessor and clerk of the circuit court; and conducted, beside his hotel, a store, a ferryboat, and a livery stable. He was convicted and fined for selling brandy to the Indians, and it is said that he would rather fight than eat. It was his custom to stride up and down the street ringing a cowbell to call his customers to dinner.

4. The SITE OF THE McLOUGHLIN MANSION, Main St. between 2nd and 3rd Sts., is occupied by a paper mill. The old house was built and occupied by the "White-Headed Eagle" after his resignation as factor of the Hudson's Bay Company, and later was moved to McLoughlin Park. Across the street, where a woolen mill now stands, was the stockade where Dr. McLoughlin, while factor, safeguarded company stores.

5. On the riverbank W. of Water St. and S. of 5th St., is the SITE OF THE OLD MINT. Early settlers were handicapped by

coin scarcity, substituting as media of exchange "beaver skins, wheat, bills, drafts and orders, gold dust, and silver coins of Mexico and Peru." After the discovery of gold in California, dust and nuggets were brought into Oregon. Merchants allowed only eleven dollars an ounce whereas eighteen dollars was the current value. The provisional government authorized the striking of coins just before news was received of territorial recognition. The need for a medium of exchange was so great that this "mint" was built and operated by a private company of pioneers from February to September, 1849. The Oregon Exchange Company produced $58,000 worth of $5 and $10 pieces from dies and a press constructed from old wagon irons. These pieces, known as "beaver money," because each was stamped with the likeness of a beaver, disappeared from circulation as federal currency grew plentiful. An original ten-dollar coin, the two dies, and the rollers of the press are in the possession of the Oregon Historical Society at Portland.

6. The SITE OF THE BIRTHPLACE OF EDWIN MARKHAM, Water St. between 5th and 6th Sts., is a vacant lot, near the middle of the block. The house, a small yellow cottage, was destroyed in the flood of 1861. The poet Edwin Markham, best known for "The Man with the Hoe," was born here on April 23, 1852. His father, Samuel Markham, was captain of an emigrant train that came west from Michigan, arriving in Oregon City in 1847; he was later a farmer and hunter, and "a good provider." "I remember vividly the Willamette Falls at our back door and the Indians that paraded into my mother's store," Markham told his biographer, William L. Stidger. "My mother [Elizabeth Winchell Markham] not only kept a store to help make a living but she also planted the apple seeds she had brought from Michigan. . . . She was also the poet laureate of the new settlement, the earliest woman writer recorded in Oregon. Her verse celebrated all the local affairs, such as the arrival of ships, the deaths of pioneers, the flight of strange birds." In his *California the Wonderful* Markham recalls his "first years, picking up pebbles on the shore, watching the white waterfalls, gazing on the high mysterious bluffs that look down upon the young city." He remembered Dr. John McLoughlin, "six-feet-six, handsome and impressive," and wrote in the foreword to Richard Montgomery's *The White-Headed Eagle:* "I was taken into the cathedral in Oregon City when the good man was lying in state . . . some strong man lifted me onto his shoulder that I might look down upon the face of the great dead . . . it was my first encounter with Death." Edwin was five at the time.

7. The MASONIC TEMPLE, Main St. between 7th and 8th Sts., is headquarters of the oldest Masonic Lodge west of the Missouri River. It was organized in 1846 after the preliminary meeting called in the first issue of the *Oregon Spectator*. The charter was brought across the plains by ox-team.

8. The CLACKAMAS COUNTY COURTHOUSE, 8th and Main Sts., of modern design, is constructed of reinforced concrete faced with terra-cotta. In the county clerk's office is the original plat of San

OREGON CITY POINTS OF INTEREST

1. The Site of the First Protestant Church
2. The Site of the First Capitol of Oregon Territory
3. The Hawley Pulp and Paper Plant
4. The Site of the McLoughlin Mansion
5. The Site of the Old Mint
6. The Site of the Birthplace Edwin Markham
7. The Masonic Temple

OREGON CITY

1940

Francisco, filed in 1850, when Oregon City was the only seat of American government on the Pacific Coast.

9. Beneath ST. JOHN'S ROMAN CATHOLIC CHURCH, 10th and Water Sts., are buried Dr. John McLoughlin and his wife, Margaret. The headstones are set in the front wall not far from 10th Street.

10. The MUNICIPAL ELEVATOR *(free)*, 7th St. and Railroad Ave., is the city's oddest structure. It is a slender perpendicular steel framework tower with an enclosed elevator shaft, from the top of which a horizontal steel bridge leads to the first residential terrace above the business section. The elevator lifts pedestrians ninety feet up the steep face of the cliff.

11. In McLOUGHLIN PARK, 7th and Center Sts., facing the cliff overlooking the business district and the River, stands the old McLOUGHLIN MANSION (*open* 9-5 *daily*), a rectangular two-story structure with simple dignified lines, characteristic of early Oregon architecture. Dr. McLoughlin built the house in 1845-46 and occupied it until his death on September 3, 1857. The lumber used in construction was cut locally, but doors and windows were shipped around the Horn from the east. Removed from its original site in 1909, the five-bay, hip roofed, clapboarded house was restored by the Daughters of the American Revolution. The upper sashes of the windows have sixteen small panes, the lower ones twelve—an unusual arrangement. A short flight of wooden steps leads up to a plain porch. About the massive front door are narrow side lights and transoms, providing light for the central hall. A stairway rises in a graceful curve at the rear of the hall, and on both sides of the hall are large living rooms. At each end of the house is a wide fireplace and mantel.

Dr. McLoughlin (1784-1857) was appointed chief factor in the Columbia River department of the Hudson's Bay Company in 1824. From his headquarters in Vancouver the tall, white-haired gentleman with the cane ruled as a kindly despot over the whole Columbia country. He ruthlessly but openly crushed competition in the fur trade, was generous to destitute immigrants, enforced prohibition among the Indian tribes, and preserved peace between the Indians and whites. Under orders from the company he established the first settlement at Oregon City, and moved here when he resigned as factor in 1845. His British citizenship, Catholic faith in a Protestant country, and comparative wealth prevented his election to public office. He became an American citizen in 1851, and spent his embittered latter years operating his store and mills, and attempting to collect from those who had obtained seed and supplies from him while he was chief factor. Although she was part Indian, McLoughlin always treated his wife with great deference. More than once he rebuked a colonist for "your manners, before ladies" when he failed to remove his hat in her presence.

North of the mansion is the BARCLAY HOUSE (*private*), built by Dr. Forbes Barclay in 1846, on the site of the present Masonic Temple. It was moved to the park in 1937. Dr. Barclay was surgeon at Fort Vancouver and a close friend of Dr. McLoughlin. The house of Cape Cod colonial architecture is used as the caretaker's residence.

12. The ALBION POST HOUSE (*private*), 1115 Washington St. (now called the Cochran House), was built in 1852, and is a fine example of the Cape Cod colonial type of architecture. An old elm in the yard was brought as a sapling from New England by a sea captain and given to Rev. George H. Atkinson, pastor of the First Congregational church and first territorial superintendent of education.

13. WILLAMETTE FALLS VISTA, W. end of S. 2nd St. between the Pacific Highway and the river, is a small parking space and observation walk affording an excellent view of the falls. Although most of the water has been impounded to furnish power for the mills, the falls remain one of the most interesting features of the city. The annual migration of lamprey eels attracts much attention. The eels begin coming up the Willamette in April, the main run arriving at Oregon City from May to July. When the mills are closed on Sundays, the water is higher, and large numbers of eels work up among the rocks to get over the ledge. When the mills open on Monday the withdrawal of water kills thousands of the lampreys. To prevent pollution, a campaign of extermination has been waged against the eels. Fires are built below the falls where the dead eels are burned.

14. MOUNTAIN VIEW CEMETERY, E. end of Hilda St., is the burial place of Peter Skene Ogden, early Oregon fur trader and Dr. McLoughlin's successor at Fort Vancouver. Left of the entrance stands a granite monument to his memory. Ogden, who led fur-trading expeditions into all parts of the Oregon country, rescued the women survivors of the Whitman massacre from their Indian captors. Ogden, Utah, is named for him. The oldest headstone in the cemetery marks the grave of Dr. Forbes Barclay. Sidney Walter Moss is also buried there.

POINTS OF INTEREST IN ENVIRONS

Marylhurst School for Girls, 3 *m.*; Oswego Lake and old Iron Smelter, 4 *m.* (*see TOUR* 2). Clackamas River, fishing stream, 2 *m.*

Pendleton

Railroad Station: Main and Railroad Sts., for Union Pacific Railroad, and Northern Pacific Railway.
Bus Station: 500 Main St., for Union Pacific Stages.
Airport: 2 m. W. on US 30, then R. 0.5 m., for United Airlines; taxi, $1.
Taxis: Minimum charge, 25c.

Accommodations: Four hotels; auto camps.

Information Service: Chamber of Commerce, Elks Temple, Court and Garden Sts.

Theaters and Motion Picture Houses: Civic theater in Round-Up Park; two motion picture houses.
Tennis: Municipal Tennis Courts, E. Webb and Clay Sts., free.
Swimming: Natatorium, Round-Up Park, free.
Golf: Pendleton Country Club, W. end Raley St., 9 holes, greens fee, 50c Mon.-Fri., $1 Sat. and Sun.

Annual Events: The Pendleton Round-Up, mid-September.

PENDLETON (1,070 alt., 6,621 pop.), seat of Umatilla County and home of the famous Pendleton Round-Up, is the trading center for an extensive grain, sheep, and cattle area. Curving between folded hills, the Umatilla River flows through the city, dividing it into two unequal sections. Often beaver and muskrats can be seen playing in the stream just below the busy city streets. North of the river the hills rise abruptly from the water's edge, bringing to a quick terminus the well-paved streets that for a short distance climb the precipitous slopes. Residences, shadowed by rows of locust trees, overlook the business district that occupies the flat on the opposite side of the river. The principal industries are concentrated along the eastern and southern edge of town. Wheatfields, invisible from the lower levels, stretch in every direction. Towering flour mills produce 2,000 barrels a day, and woolen mills manufacture the well-known Pendleton blankets.

A few riders from the ranges and Indians from the reservation may be seen on the streets of Pendleton at any time of year, but as Round-Up time approaches the city takes on all the appearance of a typical cow town of the Old West. Then on the streets the familiar figures of an almost lost romance appear in picturesque variety. Here they are again, chapped and booted cowboys, saddles creaking, spur-chains jingling; cowgirls in fringed buckskin riding costumes; Indians from the nearby Umatilla Reservation, blanketed and moccasined, the bright-shawled squaws bearing papooses strapped to their backs. Mingled with them are hawkers of souvenirs and strangers from far and near.

The Round-Up, a civic enterprise first produced in 1910 and an annual event since 1912, attracts thousands of visitors during three days of mid-September. Railroads run special excursion trains, on which celebrants eat and sleep while the Round-Up is in progress, and private homes are thrown open to accommodate visitors when other facilities prove inadequate. Profits from the enterprise are spent upon public improvements.

Charles Wellington Furlong, in *Let 'er Buck,* a book about the Pendleton Round-Up, titled with its slogan, gives a picture of the crowd, including cowboys "outfitting in the high-grade shops of the city, which carry for this occasion particularly gala-colored shirts of sheening silk or rich velvet, and studded on collar, front and forearm with pearl buttons as flat and big as dollars, and kerchiefs which would make any self-respecting rainbow pale with envy. On the corner a big-sombreroed, swarthy Mexican puffs silently on his cigarillo; moccasin-footed Umatilla Indians pigeon-toe along, trailed by heavy-set papoose-bearing squaws and beautiful daughters, pausing before the allurements in the display windows. Among the fancy and useful objects, naturally the beautiful blankets and shawls make the greatest appeal not only to the passing Indian woman, but to the white."

The stadium in which the Round-Up contests are held is in the western edge of Pendleton beside the Old Oregon Trail. The contests include lassoing and trick and fancy rope work; wild-horse, stage-coach, pony relay, and squaw races; steer-throwing and bulldogging; and the grand finale of all events, the bucking contests. Around three sides of the vast arena stretch the grandstands and bleachers. Across the arena knee to knee, sits a long line of cowboys, cowgirls, and Indians, mounted on some of the best stock of the range, awaiting their turn to participate in the stirring contests. To the left rise the Indian bleachers, and beyond, toward the river, are the steer and horse corrals and the white-topped tepees of the Indians.

Contestants from California to Canada take part in the numerous events, re-enacting the daily toil and the infrequent pageantry of the Old West. Stage coaches and prairie schooners parade against the vivid background of brilliantly shirted and kerchiefed cowboys and bright-robed Indians. The barbaric regalia of the 2,000 Indians, cherished for this annual display, is exhibited with a true sense of showmanship by descendants of the tribes that once harried the wagon trains. War-bonnets decked with eagle feathers, costumes and robes of finest buck-skin or woven of brilliant wool and decorated with gorgeous scroll-work of beads and elk teeth—a million dollars' worth of finery—flash in the sun as the warriors go through the intricate maneuvers of the war dance. These Indians come from all parts of the Pacific Northwest, to dance their native dances and recreate the war scenes that were once a grim reality to some members of the tribes still living.

Prizes awarded in the various contests are the gold and silver Roosevelt Trophy, valued at $2,500, and presented by the Hotel Roosevelt in New York City in commemoration of Theodore Roosevelt's interest in cow camp and cattle trail; the Sam Jackson Trophy, which honors the founder of the *Portland* (Oregon) *Journal,* for many years a citizen of Pendleton; a silver-mounted saddle, made by Hamley and Company of Pendleton, one of the oldest saddleries in the West; and the *Police Gazette* belt.

As the pageantry of the stadium brings again to life the ancient activities of the ranch and open range, Happy Canyon revivifies the hectic nights of the cow town. Here in the heart of Pendleton has been constructed a spot where everyone can participate in a period of frontier fun. Along Main Street of Happy Canyon rise the false fronts of saloons, dance halls, a hotel, a millinery shop, a Chinese laundry, and several other emporiums of trade. Indians, pioneers, cowboys, and spectators mingle in a realistic revival of the old days when men were "cow-pokes" and cattle were "ornery beef critters"; they dance, put on Indian battles and frontier horseplay.

On the last day of the celebration is held the Westward Ho! parade, a pageant of the Old West on the march. Led by the mounted cowboy band, officials of the Round-Up, hundreds of kerchiefed cowboys and cowgirls riding four abreast, hunters, prospectors, packers, mules, ox-carts, prairie schooners, stage coaches, floats depicting pioneer and Indian life, and lastly the gorgeously costumed Indians in a kaleidoscopic mingling of color pass in review.

The site of Pendleton was on the Oregon Trail, and emigrant trains rattled over the townsite for twenty years before the Umatilla River country was recognized as good wheat land, in the early sixties. But land was cheap even then, for Moses E. Goodwin traded a team of horses to a squatter for 160 acres just below the mouth of Wild Horse Creek on the Umatilla River. Goodwin operated a ferry and ran an inn at which he entertained "an occasional wayfarer." The only other house on the Goodwin tract was occupied by G. W. Bailey.

Creation of Umatilla County in 1862 gave Goodwin and Bailey an opportunity to exercise their genius toward making the farm into a county seat town. Marshall Station was the first county seat, but the election of 1864 to select a permanent county seat eclipsed the presidential election in local interest. Umatilla County then included almost all of northeastern Oregon, and agricultural interests wanted a central location for the transaction of their legal business. Umatilla City, or Landing, at the junction of the Umatilla and Columbia rivers, won the contest, and the county seat was moved there in 1865. Goodwin erected a toll bridge the following year.

Agitation for a new county seat was not long in coming, and Moses Goodwin and G. W. Bailey were in the thick of it. The state legislature in 1868 provided for a general election in which two choices were possible: "the present location of Umatilla Landing as one candidate and the Upper Umatilla, somewhere between the mouths of Wild Horse and Birch creeks, as the other." In the elections of that year Bailey was chosen county judge, and when public sentiment showed itself in favor of a change in county seats he and Goodwin assumed leadership of a movement to have Goodwin's farm declared the county seat. Goodwin's offer was accepted by the commissioners after a few weeks' "search," and the records were removed to Judge Bailey's house in 1869. On his recommendation the new "town" was named Pendleton, for George Hunt Pendleton, Democratic candidate for President in 1868; Pendleton was popular among agricultural people in the West because they regarded his proposal to pay the principal on government bonds in greenbacks instead of gold as a measure of relief from taxation.

Umatilla City promptly brought suit against Pendleton for removing county records from a safe place to a farmhouse, and the new "county seat" was required to give them up until suitable housing could be arranged. Moses Goodwin and Judge Bailey provided most of the funds for a new courthouse, which was built in record time.

In 1870 Goodwin and Judge Bailey had the farm surveyed into blocks and lots, reserving two and a half acres for public buildings. They offered the lots at reasonable prices to induce quick settlement, but the town grew slowly at first. Pendleton's earliest newspaper, the weekly *East Oregonian,* was started in 1875.

The people of Pendleton had anxious moments during the Nez Perce Indian War of 1877, for Chief Joseph, the Nez Perce leader, had married a Umatilla woman from the reservation adjoining the town, and it was feared that the Umatilla people might take up the cause of their relative. There were several reports that Joseph was coming to raid the town, and the Indian agent for the Umatilla reservation called several councils in Pendleton. He succeeded in convincing the Umatillas that it was best "not to get mixed with Chief Joseph's rebellion." The town felt safer after General O. O. Howard and his troops came into the area. Howard went in pursuit of the Nez Perce chieftain, who executed one of the most brilliant 1,400-mile retreats known in history, ending with his capture by General Nelson A. Miles forty miles south of the Canadian line in Montana. Chief Joseph, who was attempting to protect Nez Perce rights to the Wallowa Valley, promised by a treaty in 1855, was sent to Indian Territory.

The town was incorporated in 1880, and at the end of another four years more room was needed for expansion. By a special act of Congress 640 acres were taken from the Umatilla Reservation adjoining the original plot, and were made into a new subdivision. Pendleton suffered severe floods in 1880 and 1882, after which levees were built along the river.

During the seventies and eighties Pendleton was a center for the eastern Oregon cattle country. Herds were assembled here and driven across the mountains into Idaho, Wyoming, and Montana. The cattle drives were lonely and hazardous ventures, and to the cowboys who followed the weary cattle columns for many arid miles, the friendly town was an oasis in a desert land. They raced their cayuses down the dust-deep streets, clinked their spurs as they strode with swaggering gait on the board walks, or tilted glasses of "red-eye" above the scarred and tarnished bar of the Last Chance saloon.

In 1889, when the railroad reached Pendleton, the surrounding region was still in the process of change from cattle to wheat country. The little town of three thousand had twenty-seven saloons and there was wide open gambling.

Two great fires, in 1893 and 1895, burned many of the original wooden buildings, and by the turn of the century most of the local structures were of brick or stone. Church schools, meantime, provided high school or "academy" education for local youth until after 1900.

At the time of the World War a troop of cowboy cavalry was recruited at Pendleton, under the captaincy of Lee Caldwell, a great rider of bucking horses. Troop D, 3rd Oregon Cavalry, was later transferred to the 148th Field Artillery, and saw service at Chateau Thierry, St. Mihiel, Belleau Wood, and the Argonne. They were cited once by American military officials and twice by the French.

Pendleton as the center of an extensive trading area, has a large business section in comparison to its population. Local industries include flour mills, foundries, machine shops, planing mills and creameries.

POINTS OF INTEREST

1. TIL TAYLOR PARK, E. Court and Alta Sts., is named for Tillman D. Taylor, former sheriff of Umatilla County, killed in 1920 while resisting a jailbreak. The park was laid out and landscaped as a setting for the TILLMAN D. TAYLOR MONUMENT, gift of a host of friends throughout the Pacific Northwest, which was unveiled in 1929. An officer of wide reputation, during the eighteen years of his career Sheriff Taylor captured hundreds of criminals, including desperadoes of the most vicious type, without killing any of them. An unerring marksman, he shot only to disable. Taylor met his death while attempting to prevent the escape of four prisoners. He was killed with his own gun, which fell out of the holster as he grappled with one of the men he surprised in his office where they were searching for weapons. While the sheriff was attempting to subdue one prisoner, another picked up the fallen gun and shot him through the heart. The murderers escaped into the hills but a posse of Indians and white men took up the trail and recaptured them. In a dramatic appeal W. R. "Jinks" Taylor, brother of the slain man, prevented an infuriated mob from lynching the slayers, who were legally hanged thereafter at the state penitentiary. The monument, a bronze equestrian statue of the sheriff, rises from a mirror-pool flanked by lily ponds. It is the work of A. Phimister Proctor.

2. The COUNTY COURTHOUSE, Court St. between College and Vincent Sts., a square, two-story concrete-covered brick building with a central clock tower, was erected in 1889, replacing the original building (moved to a site on Clay Street). A monument on the lawn marks the site of the first school in Pendleton, opened in 1870.

3. HAMLEY AND COMPANY SADDLERY (open 8-5 weekdays), 126-135 E. Court St., is an internationally known manufactory of fine saddles and harness. Starting in 1905 with a force of two workers

the establishment now has a personnel of thirty-four employes. The company presents silver-mounted saddles to winners of various events in the Pendleton Round-Up.

4. The PENDLETON WOOLEN MILLS (*open 8-5 weekdays*), Court and Benefit Sts., manufacturers Pendleton blankets in Indian designs, rugs, and wearing apparel. Although the mill is comparatively, small, a two-story structure covering a half-block, it is one of the most important manufacturing establishments of the town, supplying stores in Portland and other cities of the Northwest. It was started as a scouring mill to save the expense of shipping raw wool in grease to New England manufactories. The firm produces almost a million pounds of woolen goods annually, and employs ninety people.

5. The CIVIC CENTER, between Ann, Aura, Alta and Webb Sts., occupies two blocks. Here are the junior high school and gymnasium and the Vert Memorial Building, all of modern brick construction, completed in 1937. The VERT MEMORIAL BUILDING (*open 9-5 weekdays, catalogue available*), houses a large collection of Indian relics and other western curios. There is also in the building a civic auditorium seating 1,200. Architects of the center were George H. Jones and Harold P. Marsh of Portland.

6. PIONEER PARK, Jackson St. between Bush and Madison Sts., was a cemetery in pioneer days, and many old graves and tombstones remain. However, most of the area is now given over to a children's playground, a wading pool, and a municipal bandstand.

7. ROUND-UP PARK, W. edge of city on W. Court St., has an arena and quarter-mile track surrounded by grandstands and bleachers seating 40,000 spectators. Also in the park are the Municipal Natatorium and an OPEN AIR THEATER, the civic drama center, with a stage of natural basalt upon which community plays and pageants are enacted.

In 1928 the Roosevelt Trophy was won for the third time by Bob Crosby which entitled him to be called the world's champion cowboy. The $5,000 Sam Jackson trophy, a replica of A. Phimister Proctors' *The Buckaroo,* which has replaced the Roosevelt Trophy, won permanently by Crosby, has been won twice by Everett Bowman. Other cowboys who have won fame at the Round-Up are Jackson Sundown, nephew of the Indian Chief Joseph, champion all-around cowboy for 1916, and Lee Caldwell, champion for 1915. Caldwell rode three of Pendleton's worst buckers, Two Step, Old Long Tom, and Spitfire, in one day. Hoot Gibson and Art Acord, movie stars, participated in the Round-Up of 1912.

POINTS OF INTEREST IN ENVIRONS

Eastern Oregon State Hospital, 2 *m.*; Umatilla Indian Reservation, 5 *m.*; Emigrant Hill (panoramic view of wheatfields and mountains), 10 *m.*; Bingham Springs, 26 *m.;* Emigrant Springs State Park, 27.5 *m.* (*see TOUR* 1); McKay Dam, 5 *m.* (*see TOUR* 5).

Portland

Railroad Stations: Union Station, NW. 6th Ave. and Johnson Sts., for Southern Pacific Lines, Union Pacific R. R., Northern Pacific Ry., Great Northern Ry. and Spokane, Portland and Seattle Ry. SW. 1st Ave. and Alder St., for Portland to Gresham, and Oregon City Lines (electric interurban).

Bus Stations: Union Stage Terminal, SW. Taylor St. between 5th and 6th Aves., for Greyhound Lines, Interstate Transit Lines, Mt. Hood Stages, North Coast Transportation Co., Oregon Motor Stages, Washington Motor Coach System.

Airports: Swan Island Municipal Airport, 4.5 m. N. of city center, via Broadway Bridge, Interstate Ave., and Greeley Cut-off, for United Airlines; Taxi, 50c, time 10 min. New municipal airport, (ready for use in the summer of 1940) at NE. Columbia Boulevard and 47th St., supersedes Swan Island.

Taxis: Twenty-five cents for first ¼ m., 10c for each ½ m. thereafter; 10c for each extra passenger.

Street Cars and Busses: Basic fare 10c.

Street Numbers: Burnside St. divides the city into N. and S. and the Willamette River into E. and W. districts. Street and Avenue addresses are NE. for the section N. of Burnside and E. of the river except a triangular piece between Williams Ave. and the Willamette River and N. city boundary which is designated as N. SE. numbers are E. of the river and S. of Burnside; NW. and SW. for the regions W. of the river and N. or S. of Burnside St. Streets are numbered N. and S. from Burnside St. and E. and W. from the Willamette River.

Traffic Regulations: Speed limit 25 m. p. h. No U turns permitted in metropolitan area. Downtown streets have parking meters. Only one-way Streets: SW. Park and SW. 9th Ave. S. of Stark to Main St.

Accommodations: One hundred hotels; tourist courts, many with trailer facilities, on main highways leading into the city.

Information Service: Portland Chamber of Commerce, 824 SW. 5th Ave.; Oregon State Motor Association, 1200 SW. Morrison St.; P.C.C.A., 1004 SW. Taylor St.; Motor Club, 139 SW. Broadway; Multnomah Hotel, SW. 4th Ave. and Pine St.; and Benson Hotel, SW. Broadway and Oak St.

Radio Stations: KALE (1300 kc.); KBPS (1420 kc.); KEX (1160 kc.); KGW (620 kc.); KOIN (940 kc.); KXL (1420 kc.); KWJJ (1060 kc.).

Theaters and Motion Picture Houses: Municipal Auditorium, SW. 3rd Ave. and Clay St., concerts and important public addresses; 50 motion picture houses.

Baseball: Portland Ball Park (Pacific Coast League), NW. 24th Ave. and Vaughn St.

Swimming: Mount Scott Tank, SE. 73rd Ave. and 55th St.; Creston Pool, SE. Powell Boulevard and 47th St.; Montavilla Tank, NE. 82nd and Glisan St.; Sellwood Tank, SE. 7th Ave. and Miller St.; U.S. Grant Tank, NE. 33rd and Thompson St.; Peninsula Tank, Albina Ave. and Portland Boulevard; Columbia Tank, Lombard and Woolsey Sts.; Jantzen Beach (commercial), Hayden Island near Interstate Bridge, entrance to park 10c, bathing fee additional 30c.

Golf: Eastmoreland Municipal Links, 2714 SE. Bybee Ave., 18 holes, 30c for nine holes; Rose City Municipal Golf Course, NE. 71st St. near Sandy Boulevard, 18 holes, 30c for nine holes; West Hills Municipal Links, at Canyon Road, 9 holes, 30c for nine holes.

Tennis: U. S. Grant Park, NE. 33rd Ave. and Thompson St.; Washington Park entrance at W. end of SW. Park Place; Mount Tabor Park, SE. 68th St. off Belmont Ave.; Irving Park, 7th Ave. and Fremont St. All free.
Boating: Oregon Yacht Club (*private*), at Oaks Park; Portland Yacht Club (*private*), on Columbia River at Faloma.

Annual Events: Winter Sports Carnival, Skiing Contest, Government Camp, Mount Hood, 4 days in Jan.; Rose Festival, 2nd week in June; Portland Philharmonic Orchestra, summer concerts, Multnomah Civic Stadium, July and Aug.; dog races, Multnomah Civic Stadium, three months in summer; Fleet Week, July or Aug.; International Livestock Show, Sept.

PORTLAND (30 alt., 301,815 pop.), largest city in Oregon, is on both banks of the Willamette River near its confluence with the Columbia. It is a city of varied and extensive industrial output, with more than a thousand manufacturing establishments, employing 25,000 workers at an annual wage of almost $50,000,000. Most of the factories are run by electricity, and the city is largely free of soot and smoke. The principal manufactured products are flour and cereals, lumber and millwork, canned and preserved fruits and vegetables, woolen goods, meats, butter and cheese, foundry ware, and dozens of lesser products. One of the Nation's important fresh-water ports and a port of entry, Portland is terminus for fifty-seven steamship lines, and is the wholesale and retail distribution point for a wide agricultural and lumbering region.

From Council Crest or from the heights behind Washington Park, the city is a vista of green hillsides, with gardens and terraced courts, and dwellings framed in foliage. Beyond lies the business district, while in the middle distance gleams the Willamette, crossed by bridges, and busy with shipping. East of the river long residential avenues reach away to Mount Scott, Mount Tabor and Rocky Butte, and the snowy peaks of Mount St. Helens, Mount Adams, and Mount Hood rise on the northern and eastern horizons.

The older part of the city, west of the Willamette River, occupies a comparatively narrow strip of bench land along the water's edge, backed by hills that extend toward the Coast Range, cutting the metropolis off from the fertile Tualatin Valley. These hills are segmented by the numerous winding drives and streets of Westover, King's Heights, and Portland Heights, culminating in Council Crest at an altitude of nearly 1,100 feet above the business section. The business area is the oldest section of the city, and unsuited to the demands of modern business. The founders of the town provided no alleys, and trucks must load and unload at sidewalk gratings. The streets are short and narrow, many buildings occupy a block or half-black, and the effect is one of congestion.

Four-fifths of the city—a spacious area of recent development—lies east and north of the Willamette. Of the five divisions of the city, only the northwest is relatively undeveloped. However, industrial and manufacturing establishments are being built in this section between Vaughn Street and the Linnton district. Just as old Portland is confined by the Willamette and the neighboring heights, the north section—

St. Johns—is restricted by the Willamette and the sloughs of the Columbia. Many residences, however, are being built in the eastern and southeastern sections of the city and along the western slopes of the hills back of the city. The principal residential districts lie east of the Willamette River, and eight bridges connect them with the business section.

The source of Portland's water supply is an isolated section on the northwest flank of Mount Hood, where a network of small streams flows into Bull Run Lake and Reservoir, and through huge pipe lines to the city. The water is so chemically pure that it need not be distilled for use in electric batteries and medical prescriptions, and is especially suited to the manufacture and dyeing of textiles. On many of the busiest corners are four-bracketed bronze drinking fountains presented to the city by the late Simon Benson, noted lumberman, because he believed that if plenty of good water were available his loggers would not consume so much alcoholic liquor while visiting the metropolis. Whatever the cause, business in Portland saloons fell off about thirty per cent immediately following installation of the fountains.

Although there are several ethnic groups represented in Portland only the Chinese, living principally in a section on SW. 2nd and SW. 4th Avenues, extending from SW. Washington to W. Burnside Streets, have kept their national customs. Scandinavians, Germans, Russians, Italians, Japanese, Jews and English-speaking people from Great Britain, the Dominions, and Ireland, are fairly well scattered over the various sections of the city. Portland negroes, comprising the bulk of the negro population of the state, live mostly on the east bank of the Willamette River, where they have their churches and their own social and civic life.

Chinook Indians were the first to use the site of Portland as a port. They found it a good place to tie up their canoes on trading trips between the Columbia and Willamette rivers, and cleared about an acre of ground gathering wood for their campfires. Captain William Clark of the Lewis and Clark expedition is known to have reached the site of Portland in 1806. The possibilities here were noted by Captain John H. Couch in 1840, when he came from New England to investigate the prospects for a salmon fishery. "To this point," he told a fellow traveler, "I can bring any ship that can get into the mouth of the Great Columbia River."

The first person who actually settled within the present corporate limits of Portland was Etienne Lucier, a French-Canadian, whose term of service had expired with the Hudson's Bay Company. In 1829 he built a small cabin on the east side of the river near the site of the present Doernbecher Furniture Company; he soon removed to French Prairie. In 1842 William Johnson, a British subject, settled in what is now known as South Portland, and built a cabin. In addition to small farming he manufactured and sold a liquid decoction known as "blue ruin" for which he was arrested and fined by the provisional court. He died in 1848 and his possessory rights passed with him.

A 640-acre tract on the west bank of the Willamette, part of the present business district, was claimed in 1844 by William Overton, a lanky Tennesseean who rowed ashore in an Indian canoe. The entire claim, except for the "cleared patch" around the landing, was covered with dense forest. Lacking the trifling sum of twenty-five cents required for filing his claim with the provisional government, he offered Amos L. Lovejoy, who had come to Oregon from Boston, a half interest in the claim if he would pay the filing fee. Lovejoy, considering the site ideal for a harbor town, paid the fee. They made a "tomahawk claim" by blazing trees, a method recognized on the frontier.

Placing little faith in Lovejoy's town-building plan, Overton, who had intended to establish a homestead, traded his half-interest to Francis W. Pettygrove, a merchant from Portland, Maine, for $100 in goods and provisions. Lovejoy convinced Pettygrove of the soundness of his plans. By 1845, four streets and sixteen blocks had been cleared and platted, but the founders were unable to agree on a name for the new town. Lovejoy wanted "Boston"; Pettygrove, "Portland." They tossed a coin, Pettygrove won, and the cluster of log cabins among the stumps was named Portland. Pettygrove erected a log store at the southeast corner of Front and Washington Streets in 1845, on the site where Overton had built his claim shack the year before, and built a wagon road westward to the hills.

Two British officers, Captains Warre and Vavasour, visited Portland in the winter of 1845-46 and reported: "Portland had only then received a name and its inhabitants were felling the trees from which their first homes were to be constructed and their primitive furniture was to be made. With such tools only as saw, augar, pole-ax, broad-ax, and adze, those men labored with zeal that atoned for want of better implements."

James Terwilliger came with the emigrants of 1845, established a claim south of the Overton tract, and the following year built a blacksmith shop. In this same year Daniel H. Lownsdale established the first tannery in the far Northwest. He tanned on a large scale, and turned out excellent leather, which he exchanged for raw hides, furs, wheat, or cash. Captain John H. Couch returned to Portland in 1845 and selected a tract north of the Lovejoy-Pettygrove claim.

In the winter of 1845-46, Lovejoy sold his share of the claim to Benjamin Stark, and in 1848 Pettygrove sold his interest to Daniel Lownsdale for $5,000 worth of hides and leather. The new proprietors added two partners, Stephen Coffin and W. W. Chapman, and formed the Townsite Promotion Company. Coffin established a canoe ferry in 1848. When traffic was heavy he used a raft of canoes. An excerpt from a diary of that year says, "Portland now has two white houses and one brick and three wood-colored frame houses and a few cabins."

John Waymire, a man of boundless energy and versatility, established Portland's first sawmill. His equipment consisted of an old whipsaw brought across the plains from Missouri, and two men to operate it. One stood on top of a log, raised on blocks, and pulled the saw upward; the other, in a pit beneath, pulled the saw downward and was showered with sawdust at each stroke. Great labor was required to cut a few pieces of lumber, but Waymire's "sawmill" encouraged building activity. He also erected the first hotel, a double log cabin of Paul Bunyanesque proportions, where he "furnished meals and a hospitable place to spread blankets for the night." His team of Missouri oxen hitched to a lumbering wagon served as the first local transportation system.

By 1850, the town had a population of 800. Churches and a school had been built; stores, boarding houses, and nearly 200 dwellings lined the streets. A steam sawmill was erected by W. P. Abrams and Cyrus A. Reed, and in December, 1850, the first copy of the *Weekly Oregonian* came from the Washington hand press owned and operated by Thomas Dryer. Portland replaced Oregon City as the largest city of the Northwest. The California gold rush was then at its height, and Portland carried on a heavy trade with that state. Lumber and flour were shipped to California, and local merchants outfitted men joining the frenzied quest for California gold.

First news of the gold discovery brought about an exodus of more than half the able-bodied men in Oregon—merchants deserted their stores, workers left their shops; business was almost at a standstill. However, within a few months, there was a demand for all sorts of goods and food-stuffs at unbelievable prices. Those left at home often made more money than the gold seekers. The continued inflow of money in exchange for Oregon goods created a boom in Portland and the population rapidly increased.

The city was incorporated and the first election held in 1851. Hugh D. O'Bryant, a native of Georgia, was elected mayor. A few days later the city council met and levied a tax of one-quarter of one per cent for municipal purposes. The voters at a special election authorized a tax to purchase a fire engine. At that time the forest came down to the river's edge except that the trees were cut from Front Avenue between Jefferson and Burnside Streets. The stumps remained in the streets and were whitewashed so that pedestrians would not collide with them at night.

In 1851, also, a free school was opened with twenty pupils. That the citizens were not all peaceful and law-abiding is attested by the fact that the first ordinance passed created the office of city marshal and that within two months the town council had requested the committee on public buildings to furnish estimates on the cost of a log jail. A one-story building of hewn timber, 16 by 25 feet, was soon built. One of the first arrests after the city's incorporation was of one O. Travaillott for riding "at a furious rate through the Streets of the City of Portland to endanger life and property." The Portland-Tualatin Plains road was planked, making a comparatively rich agricultural district accessible to Portland. There were almost daily arrivals of sailing vessels from San Francisco, besides a semi-monthly steamer service, between Portland and California points. By the spring of 1852 there were fourteen river steamers docking at the wharves of the city.

The first brick building in Portland was erected in 1853 by W. S. Ladd, a young man from Vermont, who was twice elected mayor of Portland. The building, in a good state of preservation and now occupied by wholesale meat and produce merchants, still stands at 412 SW. Front Avenue.

Trade was stimulated by the Indian wars of the 1850's, for Portland outfitted most of the military forces. In February the town had one hundred stores and shops, and in October, 1858, the *Oregonian* declared with orotund gravity that the "Rubicon has been passed" and that Portland was entered on an era of expansion that could not be halted. The population, estimated in 1858 as 1,750, in 1860 had grown to 2,874.

The original town had been extended to the south, covering present-day Multnomah Stadium area, which was known in 1862 as "Goose Hollow." Most of the women in this suburban settlement raised geese while their husbands hunted for gold or farmed. The flocks of geese became mixed and the "women not only pulled goose feathers, but pulled hair." The matter got into court, and Police Judge J. F. McCoy, unable to sort out the geese, made a Solomonic decision. He sent a deputy out to Goose Hollow to round up all the flocks and divide the geese equally among the complainants. He then closed the matter by threatening to incarcerate the "first woman to start another ruckus over geese."

The discovery of gold in eastern Oregon and Idaho in the early 1860's resulted in heavy trading with inland camps and settlements. These were lively years in Portland. Tin-horn gamblers swarmed in Front Street shacks or operated their roulette and faro layouts in tents set up on vacant lots. The gold rush, however, soon ebbed, and during the Civil War years money was scarce. The city went into debt in 1866, floating a $20,000 bond issue at 12 per cent interest.

The salmon industry began to make headway in 1864. From boatloads of fish at the wharf big ones were sold to hotel keepers at "two bits each, and smaller ones to family men at ten cents each." About 1865 an Irishman named John Quinn started to cut up fish and sell it in more usable amounts, by the pound. Soon he inaugurated Portland's first food delivery service—delivering fish from a basket. His wife, meantime, stayed behind the meat block, cutting and selling fish. A customer once asked Mrs. Quinn if she didn't get tired of her job. She replied, "Oh yes, it is not the most beautiful job, to be sure, but I am going to stay right here at this block until I make twenty thousand dollars, and then I'll quit and get myself the finest silk dress ever bought in this city." One day in 1868 Mrs. Quinn appeared in Vincent Cook's store and bought twenty yards of the finest goods he had. Cook, impressed with the Quinns' success, sold his store, went into the fish business and later into salmon canning, and made millions.

A fire in 1872 destroyed three important city blocks with a loss estimated at half a million dollars. Inadequate fire-fighting equipment was blamed, and agitation began for an improved fire department. A second and greater fire in 1873 began at First and Salmon Streets and devastated twenty-two city blocks. Fire-fighting equipment was brought from Vancouver, Oregon City, Salem and Albany, to aid the local companies. Police rounded up all the Chinese available to relieve white citizens at the hand pumps. It was reported that the Chinese were held to their tasks by tying their queues to the pump handles. Domestic pigeons circled above the flames until, exhausted, they fell.

Wallis Nash describes Portland in *Oregon: There and Back in 1877*: "Portland seemed to us to be nearly as great a place as San Francisco. The approach to it is of the same kind, in so far as that the railway lands us on the eastern side of the Willamette, and that a big ferry-boat transfers us across the river to the city. The city rises from the water's edge, and covers what used to be pine-clad hills. The depth of water allows the grain-ships to lie alongside the wharves to load, and there is a busy scene with the river steamboats and tugs and ferry-boats passing and repassing. The original wooden shanties are being rapidly replaced with great structures of stone and brick. Warehouses are full of grain, wool, skins, canned salmon, and meat; logs and planks of pine and cedar are stacked in high piles. . . ."

In 1883 the final railroad line was completed between Portland and the eastern states. The city, playing host to Henry Villard and his party, celebrated the event with a parade and a general illumination of the town with tallow candles. Following completion of the railroad business increased, money was more plentiful, and manufacturing was stimulated. Spluttering gas and oil lamps were replaced by electric arc and incandescent lamps. Late in the 1880's franchises were granted for street-railway lines, the lines to be run by "horse, mule, cable, or electric." The death knell of the ferry boat was sounded in 1887, when the Morrison Street bridge was built across the Willamette.

In 1891, Portland annexed the towns of East Portland and Albina, the merger adding 20,000 to the city's population. In the first decade of the twentieth century the population increased from 90,426 to 207,314; home building was at its height; land prices soared. This tremendous growth was due in part to the Alaska gold rush, and in part to the Lewis and Clark Centennial Exposition, held in Portland in 1905, which brought the city three million visitors and many new residents. The Federal government brought its huge exhibit from St. Louis, where the year before it had been a part of the Louisiana Purchase Exposition. Foreign countries as well as the states of the Union were well represented.

With its ebullient, untamed and sometimes giddy youth outgrown, Portland found the time and the desire to improve itself. Almost coincident with the first schools and churches, the Multnomah County Library Association was organized. Since 1915 many writers have appeared in Portland. Among them are A. R. Wetjen, Anne Shannon Monroe, Claire Warner Churchill, Mary Jane Carr, James Stevens, Stewart H. Holbrook, Sheba Hargreaves, Philip H. Parrish, Richard G. Montgomery, Hazel Hall, Ethel Romig Fuller, Ada Hastings Hedges, Eleanor Allen, Mable Holmes Parsons, Howard McKinley

Corning, Richard L. Neuberger, Ernest Haycox, Robert Ormond Case, John Reed, and Laurence Pratt (*see LITERATURE*).

Outstanding yearly events in Portland are the Rose Festival, Fleet Week, and the Pacific International Livestock Exposition. The festival grew out of the Portland Rose Society's exhibit of 1889, and in 1904 the society sponsored the first floral parade in which four decorated automobiles were the attraction. The first official Rose Festival was held in 1907. The principal features of the celebration are the crowning of the queen, a rose show at the Civic Auditorium, programs at the Multnomah Stadium, a Junior Pageant, the floral parade, and the "merrykana" carnival parade on the closing night. Chinatown gets out its massive man-carried dragons and sets off myriads of firecrackers. Roses bloom in Portland even at Christmas time; in June the city is filled with all varieties of roses. All of the parks and many of the parking strips along the streets are bright with the bloom of Caroline Testout (the official rose), La France, Talisman, Cecil Brunner, and scores of others.

Portland has been visited each summer since 1936 by a fleet of U. S. naval craft ranging from heavy cruisers to light destroyers. During their ten days' sojourn the ships are the foci of innumerable visitors. During the daylight hours the docks and ships are thronged, at night the white beams of searchlights cut through the darkness. Men and officers are entertained at banquet and reception, with a grand street dance on the last night of shorestay.

The Pacific International Livestock Exposition and Horse Show brings together fine blooded stock from all parts of the Pacific coast, from British Columbia to Mexico, and from many parts of the East. In addition to those for livestock, premiums are given for all sorts of farm and industrial products. The show is housed under one roof that covers eleven acres. The horse show arena is 200 feet wide by 332 feet long.

For years Portland has been recognized as the music center of the Pacific Northwest. For a third of a century the Portland Symphony Orchestra was nationally known, rising to prominence under the directorship of Willem Van Hoogstraten. An orchestra of more than sixty pieces playing a yearly program of fifteen concerts, its activities were temporarily discontinued in 1938. More popular in its appeal are the "Starlight Symphonies," a program of six open-air concerts given each summer at Multnomah Stadium. An audience of ten thousand or more persons listens to the concerts of this 45-piece orchestra under the direction of distinguished American and European directors. The Portland Junior Symphony Orchestra, giving four concerts yearly, is nationally recognized. Throughout the winter season the WPA Federal Symphony Orchestra gives bi-weekly concerts.

POINTS OF INTEREST

1. The OLD POST OFFICE BUILDING, SW. Morrison St. between 5th and 6th Aves., a classic stone structure designed by

M. A. R. Mullet, is in the center of a landscaped square; it accommodates the downtown post office and other Federal offices. Erected in 1875, the building for many years housed the post office and the United States District Court, and was the center of the city's activities. In court sessions it was a humming hive of witnesses, litigants, jurors, lawyers and spectators. Many famous trials were held in this building. Important among them were the land fraud trials begun in 1904 and continued for many years. These trials have been recorded at length in S. A. D. Puter's *Looters of the Public Domain,* published in Portland in 1908. Other cases were the opium smuggling trials of the early nineties, the most noted of which was that of the *United States v. William Dunbar* in November, 1893, which was carried into the U. S. Supreme Court.

2. HOTEL PORTLAND, SW. 6th Ave. between SW. Yamhill and SW. Morrison Sts., was begun in the 1870's by Henry Villard, the railroad builder, but its construction was halted when the Villard fortunes crashed. Later, a company was formed to complete the hotel, which was opened in 1889 with great pomp. Many Presidents, governors, business leaders, and people prominent in world affairs have been entertained in this hostelry. Stanford White, New York architect, designed the building.

3. The FIRST NATIONAL BANK BUILDING, SW. 6th Ave. and SW. Stark St., constructed of Colorado Yule marble and of Neo-Classic design, is a splendid example of the adaptation of classic Greek architecture to modern business purposes. The entrance is in the form of a Doric pedimented loggia. The organization is the oldest financial institution in the Pacific Northwest, and the oldest national bank west of the Rocky Mountains.

4. The U. S. NATIONAL BANK is at the NW. corner of SW. 6th Ave. and SW. Stark St., with entrances on 6th Ave. and on Broadway. The largest banking institution in the Pacific Northwest, it is housed in a classic terra cotta structure adorned with Corinthian columns and pilasters.

5. The UNITED STATES CUSTOMHOUSE, NW. Davis St. extending to NW. Everett St. between NW. Broadway and NW. 8th Ave., faces 8th Ave. and the North Park Blocks. Erected in 1901, and designed by the supervising architect's office of the U. S. Treasury Department, the building, of Italian Renaissance design, is of buff-colored brick with sandstone trim and a granite base. Here are housed the U. S. Customs, Internal Revenue, Weather Bureau, and Army Engineers' offices.

6. The UNITED STATES POST OFFICE, NW. Glisan St. extending to NW. Hoyt St. between NW. Broadway and NW. 8th Ave., is a six-story, limestone structure of Italian Renaissance design, erected in 1918, housing the Post Office, Regional Forestry offices, and other Federal departments. It was designed by Lewis P. Hobart of San Francisco.

7. UNION DEPOT, N. end of NW. 6th Ave., is used jointly

by all steam railroad lines entering Portland. The depot was erected in 1890, and is a large, rambling, stucco-finished structure of modified Italian Renaissance design, surmounted by a tall clock tower.

On display in the depot courtyard is the *Oregon Pony,* a small, early type locomotive used in 1862 on the Portage railroad at the Cascades of the Columbia. This engine was presented to Portland by Davis Tewes, of San Francisco, as a souvenir indicative of the part played by the Oregon Steamship Navigation Company—original owners of the engine—in the development of Oregon commerce.

8. BOSS SALOON, E. end of NW. Glisan Street, although its official address is 57 NW. Flanders Street, a "flatiron" building bearing the sign, Boss Lunch, stands virtually as it was built in the seventies —except for the potency of its merchandise. In the days when it was a popular place for sailors and dock workers, it is said that many a crew was shanghaied from its bar. Built in the early 1870's, as part of the Oregon Central railroad's headquarters, the little building was abandoned as a railroad unit after a few years. For a time it was a gentleman's resort, but with improved railroad facilities and removal of the depot to a point farther from the river, it deteriorated into a waterfront "headquarters for sailors, longshoremen, dockhands and riffraff hangers on, until its unsavory existence terminated with the advent of prohibition."

The wide thoroughfare North of Ankeny Street is *"THE SKID-ROAD,"* known as a meeting place for itinerant workers from all over the country. In former days Burnside Street separated the rough North End "bowery" district from the more genteel parts of town, but now it is the southern boundary of a cheap mercantile district of lounging rooms for itinerants and numerous cheap hotels and flop houses. These are gradually being pinched out to make room for factories and wholesale warehouses. In 1905 Mayor Harry Lane, later United States Senator, clamped down on the women denizens, and scattered them to all parts of the city. Since then the city has had no restricted red light district.

9. ERICKSON'S, stretching the full north side of the block on W. Burnside Street between NW. 2nd and NW. 3rd Aves., was once the most widely known saloon in the Pacific Northwest. It is occupied by beer parlors, a restaurant called Erickson's, and a number of other small establishments.

All western states have boasted of places with a "mile long bar" that usually measured a modest hundred feet; but it is a fact that the mahogany in Erickson's saloon ran to 674 feet. Here loggers, seafaring men, dirt movers, and hoboes from everywhere met to drink and talk. When the flood of 1894 swept into the place, proprietor Erickson quickly chartered a scow, anchored it at 2nd and Burnside, stocked it, and business continued more or less as usual.

10. The SKIDMORE FOUNTAIN, in the triangle at SW. 1st Ave., SW. Ankeny and SW. Vine Sts., is the gift of Stephen Skidmore to the city in 1888. Olin L. Warner was the sculptor; H. M. Wells,

the architect. The granite base is carved into a horse trough supplied with water issuing from lions' heads. The central structure consists of a bronze basin supported by classic bronze female figures. This spot was the Rialto of the 1890's, the center of such night life as there was. "Meet you at the fountain" was a popular expression. Men, horses, and dogs once drank here in the shade of the Bank of British North America. A small colony of artists, musicians, and writers maintain studios in the old Skidmore Building at 29 First Avenue, facing the fountain.

11. NEW MARKET BLOCK AND THEATER, 49 SW. 1st Ave., is the building where in the 1870's and 1880's, Thespians and mountebanks, ranging from E. H. Sothern to Anna Eva Fay, entertained Portland. Erected in 1871 the theater did not open until 1875, when James Keene staged what the posters said was a "truly gorgeous presentation of Rip Van Winkle." No less than one hundred gas lights startled the eyes of pit and gallery. Among the noted people who appeared on the New Market stage were Madam Modjeska, Janauschek, Annie Pixley, Fannie Davenport, Billy Emerson, Baird's Colossal Minstrels, Henry Ward Beecher, Robert G. Ingersoll and John L. Sullivan. The building is a two-story brick structure of utilitarian design 200 feet wide and extending from SW. First to SW. Second Avenue.

PORTLAND'S CHINATOWN is on SW. 2nd and SW. 4th Avenues, extending from SW. Washington to W. Burnside St. Chinese gambling establishments operate widely over Portland, but here are the Chinese stores, markets, tong halls, and eating places that cater more to Orientals than to others. The sidewalks are filled with circular mats on which are dried many articles strange to occidental sight and smell. In the show windows, too, are odd looking foods. Bran-like balls in a wooden box are hens' eggs, the shells coated with a mealy substance to preserve their contents. Their age is said to be great—the greater the better, according to Oriental taste. A 50-year-old egg brings the price of vintage wine. Ducks are recognizable, plucked and immersed in oil, but other dried things of various sizes and shapes—shark fins, small devil fish, oysters, shrimp and some species of mussels—are not easily identified.

12. The CHINESE BULLETIN BOARD, between SW. 2nd and SW. 3rd Aves., on SW. Pine St., is a long wall plastered with a variety of notices and messages in bold, black characters on flaming orange paper. These characteristic ideographs are items of local and international interest and are closely scanned by groups of intent Chinese.

13. CHINESE DRUG STORE, 323 SW. 2nd Ave., contains items strange to Occidentals. One of the popular remedies comes in the shape of a pair of dried turtles held flat together by a binding around their tails, and looking not unlike a fan. The turtles are boiled and the soup eaten as specific for rheumatism. The storekeeper computes on his native calculating rack, or abacus.

14. The GREENE BUILDING, 536 SW. 1st Ave., houses an interurban station of the Portland General Electric Railway Co. Its

ornate facade recalls the days when it operated as Emil Weber's drinking and gambling emporium, a hell hole of activity by day and by night. Activities ceased when Weber was murdered in broad daylight by Sandy Olds, a habitue. Following a periodic cleanup of gambling dens, Emil Weber went to a rival, Charlie Sliter, who operated the Crystal Palace Saloon, and notified him that Sandy Olds was running a game and that if Sliter didn't "fire" Olds, he would report Sliter to the police. A few days later, on May 10, 1889, Weber was accosted by Olds on a street corner. An altercation ensued and in the heat of the argument Weber reached for his handkerchief. Misinterpreting the action, Olds drew a revolver, emptying it into Weber's body, killing him instantly. Olds fought conviction to the supreme court, and escaped with two years in the penitentiary.

15. The ESMOND HOTEL, 620 SW. Front Ave., built in 1881, had a plush bellpull in every room, a luxurious convenience for those days. The Esmond flowered in an era when hotel marriages were the thing, and many Portland families of today are the result of unions sanctioned by ceremonies in its green plush parlors. The hotel entertained Rutherford B. Hayes, while he was President of the United States, John L. Sullivan, and many others.

16. ST. CHARLES HOTEL, SW. corner SW. Front and SW. Morrison St., was the finest and busiest hotel in the Northwest before the Esmond opened. In this mansard-roofed building, begun in 1869 and completed in 1871, Henry Villard and other early railroad giants of the Pacific Northwest lived intermittently. Kate Claxton, Emma Abbot, and other actresses of the 1870's and 1880's, stopped here when they visited the city. In its barroom Sam Simpson, early Oregon poet, held communion with the muse. With his pleasing disposition and readiness of conversation he was welcomed by the idlers of the St. Charles, and usually found little difficulty in borrowing "two-bits until tomorrow," which he spent forthwith for liquor, helping himself liberally to the saloon's free lunch. In his last poem pathetically he wrote:

> "The musical fountain has ceased to flow . . .
> In earthly sense we comprehend
> That death, after all, is life's best friend."

17. The PORTLAND PUBLIC MARKET, on SW. Front Ave. between SW. Salmon and SW. Yamhill Sts., is a large three-story building of modern construction containing many stores and about three hundred farm produce stalls. Merchandise ranging from fresh bean sprouts, ham, pumpernickel and carrots, to pink petunias and wild blackberries in season, are displayed on the brightly lighted stands over which Japanese, Chinese, Italians, and Americans urge customers to buy their wares. A ramp leads to car-parking space on the roof. The building has an auditorium seating 500, in which food shows and demonstrations are given.

18. Near the west end of Hawthorne Bridge at the E. end of SW. Jefferson St. is the BATTLESHIP *OREGON (open 9-5 daily, adm.*

10c; schoolchildren and veterans free). Launched in 1895, this relic of the Spanish-American War made its epic 15,000-mile run in 1898 from Bremerton, Washington, through the Straits of Magellan, to Key West, Florida, in forty-seven days. The great run was made under the command of Captain Robley D. "Fighting Bob" Evans, who earned his nickname at Valparaiso in 1891, while relations were strained with Chile; he threatened "to blow the Chilean navy out of the water" unless they stopped torpedo practice while he was there in command of one light cruiser. They stopped. Evans commanded the *Iowa* in the Battle of Santiago; at one time the fire of the entire Spanish navy was concentrated on his ship. In the same battle the *Oregon* engaged and sank the *Maria Teresa,* Spanish flagship, and, after a chase of forty-eight miles, beached the *Colon.* In 1925 the old ship was given to the state of Oregon, which maintains it as a historic memorial. A mooring basin and park are being constructed (1940) as a permanent anchorage.

19. The PORTLAND CIVIC AUDITORIUM, SW. 3rd Ave. between SW. Clay and SW. Market Sts., erected in 1917, was designed by Freedlander & Seymour of New York City. The exterior, of modified Italian Renaissance design, is of buff brick and stone, with terra cotta and green metal trim. The main auditorium seats 3,527, while with side wings thrown open it has a maximum capacity of 6,700. In the building is the OREGON HISTORICAL SOCIETY COLLECTION *(open 9-5 weekdays; 9-12 Sat.),* entrance at SW. 3rd Ave. and SW. Market St. The society was founded in 1898. In its collection, are thousands of rare and valuable volumes, including the *Journal of John Ledyard,* dealing with Captain Cook's first voyage to the northwest coast in 1788, of which only five copies are known to exist. Another item is the *Diary of Jason Lee,* the first Oregon missionary. In the newspaper collection are files of more than three hundred newspapers, including the *Oregon Spectator,* the first newspaper published west of the Rocky Mountains. The collection also contains more than ten thousand manuscripts, many dealing with provisional and territorial stages of the state's development, hundreds of maps, and old photographs and paintings.

Among the historical objects is the sea chest that Captain Robert Gray carried with him in the *Columbia Rediviva* when he discovered the river named for his ship. Here also is the tiny Mission Press, the first printing press west of the Rocky Mountains. It was first used at Lapwai, now in Idaho, in 1839, to print a primer and certain of the gospels in the Nez Perce language. The Indian collection shows graphically every phase of native life; and there are innumerable objects, including a covered wagon, used by the pioneers. Since 1900 the Society has published the *Oregon Historical Quarterly.*

20. CITY HALL, SW. 5th Ave., between SW. Madison and SW. Jefferson Sts., erected in 1895, of Italian Renaissance architecture, was designed by Whidden & Lewis of Portland. The design of the four-story structure suggests that of a stately town house. The outer walls are of yellow gray sandstone, with a circular portico supported by columns of polished black granite. A bronze plaque commemorating

the architects was placed at the entrance in 1932 by the Oregon chapter of the American Institute of Architects.

21. LOWNSDALE SQUARE, SW. 4th Ave., between SW. Salmon and SW. Main Sts., is named for Daniel H. Lownsdale, one of the earliest owners of the Portland townsite and donor of the plot to the city. The park is the orating ground of the city's soap-box evangels. In fair weather its benches are filled with men from all parts of the world, and innumerable tame pigeons strut on the lawn. In this square, said to be an old feeding ground for elk, is the ELK FOUNTAIN, the work of Roland H. Perry, noted animal sculptor, and the SOLDIERS' MONUMENT, by Douglas Tilden, honoring members of the Second Oregon Volunteers who fell in the Spanish-American War.

22. The MULTNOMAH COUNTY COURTHOUSE, SW. Salmon St. between SW. 4th and SW. 5th Aves., occupying the entire block, was also designed by Whidden & Lewis, and erected in 1913. It is of Neo-Classic architecture, with stone trim, tall Ionic colonnades, and a heavy classic cornice. The base is of California granite, the upper part of white Bedford stone. County offices and courts are housed here. The jail occupies part of the top floor.

23. The PUBLIC SERVICE BUILDING, SW. 6th Ave. between SW. Taylor and SW. Salmon St., a sixteen-story structure with an off-set tower, is the tallest commercial building in the state. Constructed of terra cotta and gray brick it is designed in a modified Italian Renaissance style.

24. The MULTNOMAH PUBLIC LIBRARY (*open 9-9 weekdays; reading room 3-9 Sun.*), SW. 10th Ave. between SW. Yamhill and SW. Taylor Sts., erected in 1913 and constructed of red brick with limestone trim, is of Italian Renaissance design. The three-story and basement structure occupies an entire city block, and is considered the finest library in the Northwest. The interior trim is of domestic and imported marbles, with columns of scagliola. The building is surrounded on three sides by a carved limestone balustrade interspersed with benches. These benches, the cornice of the building, and the spandrels under the large windows, are inscribed with the names of famous artists, writers, philosophers, and scientists. The architects were Doyle, Patterson and Beach. The library has large reference and circulating departments, an excellent technical department, and an extensive collection of Oregoniana. The library has a per capita circulation of eight volumes, and 43 per cent of Portland residents are registered borrowers.

25. The UNITARIAN CHURCH, 1011 SW. 12th Ave., is a small church structure of Georgian Colonial design. In a setting of older residences and curb-side trees, it gives an atmosphere of old New England. The exterior is of brick with cast stone trim, surmounted by a cupola and slender spire. The interior is finished in ornamental wood panels. Jamieson Parker was the architect.

The SOUTH PARK BLOCKS are a series of landscaped areas extending southward for thirteen blocks from SW. Salmon St. to SW.

Clifton St., between SW. Park and SW. Ninth Aves. The blocks are landscaped with trees and shrubs transplanted from the eastern United States, and some of them contain fountains and statuary.

26. The LINCOLN STATUE, in the center of the square bounded by SW. Main St., SW. Madison Sts., SW. Park Ave., and SW. Ninth Ave., shows the Great Emancipator with head bowed and shoulders drooping. Many patriotic organizations participated in the unveiling in 1928. The statue is an original, and under the terms of the agreement between the late Dr. Henry Waldo Coe, the donor, and George Fite Waters, the artist, it may never be duplicated.

27. In the SW. Park Ave. block between SW. Madison and Jefferson Sts., is A. Phimister Proctor's ROUGH RIDER STATUE OF THEODORE ROOSEVELT, also a gift of Dr. Coe. The bronze equestrian figure, mounted on a base of California granite, towers twenty-three feet and weighs three tons. It was dedicated on Armistice Day, 1922, and Vice President Calvin Coolidge made the dedicatory address. The figure of Theodore Roosevelt was designed with the advice and aid of the family; Mrs. Roosevelt made available to the artist the actual uniform and accoutrements used by the Colonel at the battle of San Juan Hill.

28. The PORTLAND ART MUSEUM (*open 10-5 weekdays; 12 M.-5 P.M. Mon.; 7-10 P.M. Wed.; 2-5 Sun. and holidays free*), SW. 9th Ave. between SW. Madison and Jefferson Sts., is owned by the Portland Art Association and was a gift from W. B. Ayer. Of modern design with a trend toward crisp functionalism, the broad building is faced with Oregon brick of a rich golden-red color and Colorado travertine. Especially notable are the three entrance portals with their five metal gates. Built in 1932, it was designed by Pietro Belluschi of the firm of A. E. Doyle and Associates. The Solomon and Josephine Hirsch Memorial wing was added in 1939 through the gift of Ella Hirsch. In the south wing is the Lewis collection of Greek and Roman vases, bronzes, and glass. Other objects in this wing are a Chinese terra cotta figurine, given by L. Allen Lewis; three Chinese paintings, a gift from the Freer Collection; and Greek glass and jade given by the children of Mrs. William S. Ladd. The Doyle memorial collection of Egyptian scarabs and seals is in the small south gallery.

In the large room of the north wing are selections from the textile collections, gifts of Mrs. F. B. Pratt, the Misses Failing, and others. The lace collection is in a small gallery beyond.

The permanent exhibit of French and American paintings is in two galleries on the upper floor. In the small south gallery is a loan collection of Chinese potteries, porcelains, and paintings from the L. Allen Lewis collection, and a display of Japanese prints. Among the permanent displays are pieces of Near-Eastern, Chinese, and Persian pottery. Two other items of unusual interest are an Egyptian vase from Fayoum, northern Egypt, belonging to the Ptolemaic period, and a small bronze cat from a cat cemetery of ancient Egypt. A good collection of casts of Greek and Roman sculpture, given by Henry W. Corbett, the first president of the association, is on the ground floor.

The museum has been the recipient of many fine paintings, among them works of Corot, Delacroix, Monticelli, Courbet, Diaz, Renoir, Pissarro, Inness, William Sartain, Childe Hassam, William M. Hunt, George Fuller, Albert Ryder, and A. B. Davies. Besides the permanent collections, there are circulating exhibitions from the American Federation of Art, the College Art Association, and other groups. There are about sixteen of these exhibits annually.

Other facilities of the museum include a library of 2,000 volumes, a collection of illustrated prints and slides for school use, and the Braum collection of 15,000 photographs and color reproductions of the masterpieces of European galleries. The museum conducts an art school and special lectures are frequently given in the auditorium.

29. SIXTH CHURCH OF CHRIST SCIENTIST, 1331 SW. 9th Ave., is of modern design with heavy, set-back, corner pylons. The building is of reinforced concrete construction faced with light brown brick, and with a slate shingle roof of harmonizing red. The interior woodwork is of oak, the walls and ceiling of plaster, and the floor of terrazzo. The dome over the crossing is covered with acoustical material painted in antique mosaic effect. Morris H. Whitehouse and Associates were the architects.

30. The FINLEY MORTUARY, 432 SW. Montgomery St., is a blending of the traditional with the functional style of design. It is reminiscent of the past, yet strictly modern. The fresh, crisp style was achieved chiefly through the elimination of superfluous detail. The exterior walls are of concrete with brick facings. The entrance is of Indiana limestone. The interior has a plastic finish, with the exception of the main chapel, the walls of which are lined with Philippine mahogany, flat panels set on furring strips in concrete. The mortuary, known as the Morninglight Chapel, was awarded honorable mention in the 1938 National Exhibition of the New York Architectural League, and was listed in 1938 by The Association of Federal Architects as one of the hundred best buildings erected in America since 1918. It was designed by Pietro Belluschi, of the firm of A. E. Doyle and Associates.

31. MULTNOMAH CIVIC STADIUM, SW. Morrison St. between SW. 18th and SW. 20th Aves., is a concrete structure designed after the Roman Coliseum, with a seating capacity of 30,000. Whitehouse and Doyle were the architects. Inter-collegiate and interscholastic football games are played here. In June it is the center of activities of Portland's annual Rose Festival. In summer months dog races attract large crowds.

32. TRINITY EPISCOPAL CHURCH, SW. corner NW. 19th Ave. and NW. Everett St. is a vine-clad stone edifice, designed in the manner of an English parish church with steep gable roof and crenelated corner tower. A parish house, erected in 1939, is joined to the church by a connecting unit.

33. TEMPLE BETH ISRAEL, NW. 19th Ave. and NW. Flanders St., is octagonal in plan, with quotations from the Talmud above each door. The building is of reinforced concrete construction faced with golden-yellow sandstone, the upper portion is of salmon-colored brick and glazed terra cotta. A huge dome surmounts the structure, its apex ninety feet above the floor. Built in 1926, Temple Beth Israel was designed by Morris H. Whitehouse and Herman Brookman, architects, associates with Bennes and Herzog.

34. ST. MARK'S CATHEDRAL, NW. 21st Ave. and NW. Northrup St., designed by Jameson Parker in the manner of an Italian Romanesque basilica, is surmounted by a seventy-five-foot tower and is faced entirely with red brick. It was a gift to the parish from Miss Catherine H. Percival. St. Mark's, one of the oldest religious organizations in Portland, was founded as a mission in 1874, and was organized as a parish in 1889, by the late Bishop Morris.

35. In SAM JACKSON PARK, on Marquam Hill, is the VETERANS' HOSPITAL *(open 2-4 daily)*, a Federal institution offering free medical care to veterans of American wars. It consists of a group of red-brick structures of modified Georgian Colonial architecture, designed by government architects of the Veterans' Administration. The principal units were put into service in December, 1928. The official capacity is 385 beds.

36. The PORTLAND MEDICAL CENTER, W. edge of Sam Jackson Park on SW. Marquam Hill Road, crowns the height of Marquam Hill. On a campus of 108 acres, the group comprises the University of Oregon Medical School, the Multnomah County Hospital, and the Doernbecher Hospital for Crippled Children. The first unit of the Medical School, a three-story, reinforced concrete structure, was built in 1919. The second unit, MacKenzie Hall, similar in design to the first but with twice its capacity, was erected in 1922. The Out-patient Clinic, erected in 1931, connects the Doernbecher Memorial Hospital and the Multnomah County Hospital, and affords teaching facilities for the clinical branch of the Medical School. The Multnomah County General Hospital was built in 1923 at a cost of $1,000,000. Providing space for 300 patients, it offers free medical care to the county's indigent. The architects were Sutton and Whitney, with Crandall and Fritsch, associates. The Doernbecher Memorial Hospital for Children, erected in 1925, is a buff brick, fireproof structure with terra cotta trim. Ellis F. Lawrence was the architect. The Doernbecher Hospital, endowed by the pioneer Portland furniture manufacturer whose name it bears, is maintained partly by the state.

A unit of the University of Oregon Medical School is the new University State Tuberculosis Hospital, the third such state institution. Opened in November, 1939, it cares for 80 resident tubercular cases, conducts an out-patient clinic, and is expertly equipped. Its $290,900 cost was shared by the State and the WPA, and by a $50,000 gift from the widow of Oregon's late Governor Julius L. Meier.

37. COUNCIL CREST PARK (1,107 alt.) is directly west o'

Sam Jackson Park and close to the southwest city limits. It is reached by SW. Broadway Drive and Talbot Roads, and other roads encircle it. The highest point within the city, the view from this eminence in clear weather is approximately forty miles to the west, sixty miles to the east, and more than a hundred miles to the north and south, and includes six snow-covered peaks. To the west, beyond the bowl-like Tualatin Valley, is the Coast Range. Eastward the gorge of the Columbia River is visible from Crown Point to Cascade Locks; to the south are Oregon City and the Willamette Valley; and to the north is the city of Vancouver and the orchards of Clark County, Washington. The small tower on the crest is a United States Coast and Geodetic Survey triangulation station.

38. WASHINGTON PARK crowns the hills directly west of the main business section and is one of the most beautiful of Portland's many parks. It comprises one-hundred acres of hillside, partly improved. At the SW. Park Place entrance stands a thirty-four foot shaft of granite brought from the Snake River and erected in honor of Lewis and Clark, the explorers. The first stone was laid for the base by President Theodore Roosevelt in 1903. Along the driveway (R) is the much-photographed STATUE OF SACAJAWEA, the "bird woman" who guided Lewis and Clark through the mountains. Modeled by Alice Cooper, the statue depicts the Indian woman with her baby on her back pointing out the way to the whites. A little farther on is the statue, THE COMING OF THE WHITE MAN, by H. A. McNeil, which shows two Indians astonished by their first sight of a white man.

In the upper part of the park is the Zoo (*open 8-6 daily*), containing lions, tigers, monkeys, and many animals native to the Pacific Northwest. Deer, elk, buffalo roam the pastures at the far south end of the park.

In the center of the park are the INTERNATIONAL ROSE TEST GARDENS, conducted by the Portland Council of the National Rose Society. Cuttings from all parts of the world are received here and cross-grafted to develop new types.

39. The FORESTRY BUILDING (*open 9-5 daily*), NW. 28th Ave., between NW. Vaughn and NW. Upshur Sts., made entirely of fir, is a weather-beaten structure 206 feet long, 102 feet wide, and 72 feet high. In the vast interior, accentuating the great size, are fifty-two log pillars six feet in diameter, that support the roof and a gallery of small logs. On the floor are sections of great logs nine or ten feet in diameter, and polished slabs of various kinds of commercial lumber. Doubtless the largest log cabin in the world, 1,000,000 feet, board measure, of logs went into its construction. It was a feature of the Lewis and Clark exposition of 1905. It is occupied only by a caretaker.

40. ST. JOHNS BRIDGE, foot of N. Philadelphia Street, of suspension type, designed and built by the bridge engineering firm of Robinson & Steinmann, New York, is one of America's most beautiful bridges. From it there is an excellent view of the Willamette River. Upstream are the Oceanic dock, the Eastern and Western Lumber

Mill, Municipal Terminal No. 1, and other docks. Downstream is Municipal Terminal No. 4, where eleven deep-sea craft can berth simultaneously.

41. UNIVERSITY OF PORTLAND, on triangle formed by Willamette Blvd., Portsmouth Ave. and the river bluff, occupies a beautiful site overlooking the Willamette River. The university was founded in 1901 by Archbishop Christie of the Roman Catholic diocese of Oregon, and is operated by the Holy Cross Fathers of Notre Dame, in Indiana. The buildings consist of Administration Hall, of Renaissance design; Christie Hall, of Tudor-Gothic design, and Howard and Science Halls, of modern functional design. Founded as Portland University, the name of the school was changed to Columbia University, but reverted to the present name in 1935.

Below the bluffs upon which the university is situated is Mock's Bottom (R), a mud-flat dotted with stagnant ponds and crossed by the tracks of the Union Pacific Railroad. In the river is Swan Island, Portland's municipal airport, soon to be superseded by a larger municipal airport under construction (1940) at 47th St. and Columbia Blvd.

42. PENINSULA PARK, N. Portland Blvd. between N. Albina and Kerby Aves., and Ainsworth St., occupies a twenty-acre area, equipped with playgrounds, ball grounds, and a swimming pool. In the park is the SUNKEN ROSE GARDEN *(open)*, occupying six acres and containing more than 1,000 varieties of roses. When the plants are in full bloom the gardens are a mass of vivid color. The plantings are in rectangular beds, surrounded by close-cropped boxwood hedges. From four pergola entrances of red brick, one at each side of the garden, wide flights of red brick steps lead downward past terraced plantings to the lowest level, in the center of which is a large fountain.

43. STATUE OF GEORGE WASHINGTON, a bronze heroic figure at NE. 57th Ave., NE. Sandy Boulevard and the Alameda, is the work of Pompeii Coppini. Set near the apex of a tringular plot in front of the Friendship Masonic Home Association, donors of the site, the statue faces Sandy Boulevard and looks eastward down the old Oregon Trail, the route traveled by the pioneers. Formally dedicated in 1927, it was given to the city by Dr. Henry Waldo Coe.

44. The SHRINE HOSPITAL FOR CRIPPLED CHILDREN, NE. Sandy Blvd. between NE. 82nd and NE. 84th Aves., is a large brick and wood structure of English Renaissance design, erected in 1922. Well-staffed and nationally-known, this children's hospital is conducted by the Masonic order, and is celebrated for its success in the treatment of congenital hip diseases.

45. On Sandy Blvd. near NE. 84th Ave. is the entrance (R), to the grounds of the SANCTUARY OF OUR SORROWFUL MOTHER *(free parking space),* the open air grotto and sanctuary of the Servite Fathers. It is the only one of the twenty-one sanctuaries of the Servite Order outside Europe. The lower level is landscaped, with stations for prayer, and, in the side of Rocky Butte, there is a large altar at which daily services are conducted. The upper level of the

sanctuary is separated from the lower by a perpendicular cliff, and is reached by an elevator *(charge 25c)*. The Sanctuary covers eighteen acres on the lower level and forty acres on the higher level. On the upper level are seven shrines containing thirty-four wood-carvings of Italian design and craftsmanship. On the crest, also, are a monastery serving as a home for the Servite Fathers, and a heroic bronze STATUE OF OUR SORROWFUL MOTHER, depicting the Virgin in an attitude of adoration, overlooking the Columbia River and visible for miles. A special mass is held before the statue on Mother's Day.

46. An aircraft beacon and observation platform at the end of the winding road leading from NE. Fremont St. marks the summit of ROCKY BUTTE (612 alt.), one of three cinder cones of volcanic origin on the east side of the city. Its slopes are rough and broken. A grove of quaking aspen, not ordinarily native to the lower altitudes of western Oregon, grows on the northern side. From Rocky Butte there is a view of the city stretching to the hills beyond the Willamette and northwestward to the lowlands of the Columbia River. In the angle between the rivers are North Portland's large meat packing plants and stockyards. Beyond the Columbia are the peaks of St. Helens, Rainier, and Adams. Eastward the Columbia is lost between encroaching foothills of the Cascades, while slightly to the southeast rises Mount Hood.

JOSEPH WOOD HILL PARK covers three acres on the crest of the butte. The site was given to Multnomah County by Joseph A. and B. W. Hill, in 1935, and dedicated to the public in memory of their father, Dr. J. W. Hill, an early educator. The park was improved during 1937-39 as a WPA project, with stone walls, roadways, and a wide parking platform.

47. The northeastern entrance to MOUNT TABOR PARK is at 69th Ave. and SE. Yamhill St., from which point a curving drive of easy grade leads upward to the summit (600 alt.). This is another of the cinder cones lying along the east edge of the city. From its grassy, tree-shaded crest, there is a view of the East Side and the country between Portland and the Sandy River, fourteen miles distant. Mount Hood gleams white in the east. Facing southeast on the crest is Gutzon Borglum's STATUE OF HARVEY W. SCOTT, Oregon's noted newspaper editor. Below the summit on the southwest slope of the butte are the city reservoirs, where the force of the stream piped from the mountains sixty miles away hurls great jets of water a hundred feet into the air.

48. REED COLLEGE, SE. Woodstock Blvd. between SE. 28th and SE. 36th Aves., was founded as Reed Institute by the widow of Simeon Reed, pioneer railroad builder, "for the increase and diffusion of practical knowledge . . . and for the promotion of Literature, Science, and Art." The buildings, on a large and beautiful landscaped campus, are of Tudor Gothic design reminiscent in detail of Compton Wyngates. The construction is of reinforced concrete, faced with red brick and trimmed with limestone. The dormitory and administration buildings were erected in 1912, and the library in 1930. A. E. Doyle of Portland was the architect.

Opened in 1911, Reed College maintains a College of Liberal Arts and Sciences presided over by a faculty representing more than twenty American graduate schools, who are given opportunities for supplementary foreign travel and research. There are no fraternities or sororities, and no intercollegiate athletic teams. Reed operates as a democratic co-educational community, fostering the spirit of inquiry and investigation, and sharing the advantages afforded by its endowments, memorials, and lectureships with the community outside its campus. The annual enrollment is approximately 500.

The LIBRARY (*open 8-8 weekdays*), contains 54,000 volumes, acquires 2,500 volumes every year, receives about 200 periodicals, and is a depository for government documents. The reading rooms are open to the public, as are many lectures in the Chapel or Commons. The Pacific Northwest Institute of International Relations, and many other conferences of educational interest, are held on the Reed campus.

49. LONE FIR CEMETERY, SE. 20th Ave. between SE. Morrison and Stark Sts., was begun in 1854 when Crawford Dobbins and David Fuller, victims of the *Gazelle* river steamer disaster near Oregon City, were buried here. In the cemetery are markers inscribed in English, Hebrew, German, Japanese, Chinese, French, and Spanish. Here lie Catholics, Protestants, Jews, pagans and free thinkers; white, yellow, black, red, and brown men and women; bums and bankers; senators, governors, and mayors. Among the graves in the cemetery are those of Samuel L. Simpson, early Oregon poet; William Hume, father of the salmon-canning industry; George Law Curry, territorial governor; and W. H. Frush, early-day saloon keeper. On the plot of the Frush grave, marked by a pretentious monument, is the large marble urn in which he annually mixed his Tom and Jerry. On several occasions in late years, the urn has been taken away and used for its original purpose, but is always returned.

Two sections of the cemetery were set aside for the graves of firemen, and many of the markers have elaborate carvings of hooks, ladders, trumpets and shields.

In earlier days, when the Oriental population of the city was larger than it is today, scores of Chinese were buried here, but the bones of those whose families could afford it have been disinterred and sent to China.

50. LAURELHURST PARK, SE. 39th Ave. between SE. Ankeny and SE. Stark Sts., is a thirty-acre recreational area and playground. Large firs rise from the knolls, and the shrubbery is profuse. The park contains many varieties of Oregon plants and flowers, an artificial lake, stocked with ducks and swans, a bandstand, picnic facilities, two tennis courts, and a playground.

51. JOAN OF ARC STATUE, NE. 39th Ave. and NE. Glisan St., is a copy of the original statue in the place de Rivoli, Paris, and was given to the city by Dr. Henry Waldo Coe. It was dedicated in 1925 to the American doughboy.

52. The JANTZEN KNITTING MILLS (*open 9-5 Mon.-Fri.,*

9-12 *Sat.; apply at office*), NE. 19th Ave. and NE. Sandy Blvd., manufacture bathing suits. The knitting department has seventy-five machines, each with about 1500 needles. Following the knitting the fabric is shrunk, cut into shape by electric cutting machines, and sewed on power-driven machines. In its Portland mill the company employs 700 workers. The buildings are modern, well lighted and ventilated, and the grounds beautifully landscaped.

53. The BURNSIDE BRIDGE, joining W. and E. Burnside Sts., a double bascule span of reinforced concrete construction, was dedicated in 1926 and cost approximately $3,000,000. So precisely are its bascules balanced that they move practically of their own weight when once set in motion. It was designed by Hendrick & Kremer, consulting engineers, of Portland and Kansas City. East Burnside Street is one of the main approaches to the city from the east.

POINTS OF INTEREST IN ENVIRONS

Sandy River Bridge, 13 *m.*; Crown Point, 18.2 *m.* (*see TOUR* 1); U. S. Army Post, Vancouver, Washington, 9 *m.* (*see WASHINGTON GUIDE*); Oswego Lake, 7 *m.*; Marylhurst College, 8.6 *m.*; Willamette Falls, Oregon City, 14.5 *m.* (*see TOUR* 2); Multnomah County Fairgrounds, Gresham, 13.7 *m.*; Bull Run Lake, 28 *m.* (*see TOUR* 4*A*).

Salem

Railroad Station: 13th and Oak Sts., for Southern Pacific Lines.
Bus Station: 228 High St., for Greyhound and Oregon Motor Stages; 441 State St., for Independent Stages and Dollar Line.
Airport: Municipal, 2.5 m. SE. on Turner Rd. via S. 14th St.; no scheduled service.
City Busses: Fare 7c.

Accommodations: Five hotels; seven tourist camps.

Information Service: Chamber of Commerce, 147 N. Liberty St.; Oregon State Highway Commission, State Office Bldg., 1146 Court St.; Oregon State Motor Association, 515 Court St.

Radio Station: KSLM (1370 kc.).

Motion Picture Houses: Five.
Swimming: Olinger Field, Capital and Parrish Sts.; Leslie Field, Cottage and Howard Sts.
Golf: Salem Golf Club, 2 m. S. on US 99E, 18 holes, fees 50c for 9 holes; Illahee Golf Club, 5 m. S. on US 99E, 18 holes, fees 35c for 9 holes.
Tennis: Olinger Field, Capital and Parrish Sts.; Leslie Field, Cottage and Howard Sts.; both free.

Annual Events: Cherry Blossom Festival, in spring, when fruit trees are in bloom; Oregon State Fair, September.

SALEM (171 alt., 26,266 pop.), capital of Oregon and seat of Marion County, is the second largest city in the state.

The Willamette River, rolling through forest and meadow, passes along the margin of the town. Westward, across a checkerboard pattern of farms and forest, rises the crest of the Eola Mountains. Farms, orchards, and vineyards cover the slopes of the Waldo Hills to the east, and beyond them the snow-capped Cascade Mountains form the horizon.

Salem's streets are unusually broad. Residences of modern design are half hidden behind trees that line the parkways and dot the lawns. There are no unsightly districts or slums. A landscaped area traversing the city serves as a civic center and embraces Willson Park, which is flanked on the west by the federal and county buildings and on the east by state offices. The shopping district, with its dignified structures, new and old, has an air of stability.

The city, county, and state business conducted in Salem tends to overshadow its industrial activities. The city is also the marketing and distributing center of a rich agricultural area on both sides of the Willamette. Approximately one-third of the fruits and vegetables of the Pacific Northwest are processed in Salem's canneries.

The daily bustle of a small city is intensified when the legislative session brings lawmakers, lobbyists, and political writers to town. Salem is then overcrowded and surcharged with an excitement that does not subside until adjournment.

Salem was founded by Jason Lee, who was sent from New England as the Methodist "Missionary to the Flatheads"; he arrived at Fort Vancouver, Hudson's Bay Company post, in the fall of 1834. Dr. John McLoughlin, the factor, whose real purpose was to confine American settlement to the area south of the Columbia River, advised Lee to avoid the more dangerous Flathead country and settle near French Prairie, where he would have protection, and where the land would lend itself to cultivation. Then he could gather the Indians around him, "teach them first to cultivate the ground and live more comfortably than they could do by hunting, and as they do this, teach them religion."

Lee's first mission was not a success because the "great sickness" wiped out about four-fifths of the Indians in this section; he began another, on the more healthful site of Salem, on June 1, 1840. The missionaries erected a house and combined sawmill and gristmill on this property, and continued their efforts toward education and conversion of the Indians. Becoming discouraged in these efforts, and not anticipating much success from another eastern trip to raise funds, the missionaries decided to lay out a town and sell lots to finance the Oregon Institute, a "literary and Religious Institution of learning," which turned its emphasis to schooling of white children following the great emigration of 1845. Oregon Institute was the forerunner of Willamette University, which was chartered in 1853.

The town was laid out the following year, and the first lots sold were purchased with wheat. In choosing a name for the "town," which had one house when it was platted, the Calapooya Indian name Chemeketa, or "place of rest," was proposed, but the missionary brethren preferred a Biblical word, Salem, with a similar meaning.

Growth of Salem was slow in the 1840's, and discovery of gold in California at the end of the decade drew nearly half the population to the Mother Lode country. A few prospered and brought their new wealth back to Salem, where it contributed to the development of the town.

The territorial legislature, meeting at Oregon City in 1851, chose Salem as the territorial capital. Democratic members, supported by the missionary influence, were apparently instrumental in this move. The *Oregon Statesman,* edited by Asahel Bush, strongly supported the move to Salem, and Thomas J. Dryer, editor of the Whig *Oregonian,* took the opposite side. When the time came for the meeting in Salem, in December of that year, the governor, two members of the territorial supreme court, and a minority of the legislature refused to move from Oregon City, stating that the act was unconstitutional because it contained two unrelated items, contrary to the organic law. A writer to the *Statesman* advanced "the probability that party spirit, to sustain the Governor, had something to do with this strange course of proceeding."

Bush was more forthright; he called the dissidents "a squad of federal nullifiers" and "lickspittles and toadies of official whiggery."

Accommodations were none too good for the legislators, their first session being held in the residence of J. W. Nesmith. In 1852 "there were perhaps a half dozen families living in Salem. The store was owned by John D. Boon. . . . The mission building and mill were standing." The following year Asahel Bush, who had been appointed territorial printer, moved his newspaper to Salem. The legislature, dissatisfied with unfinished buildings and cramped quarters, voted to move the capital to Corvallis in 1855. They traveled on the steamer *Canemah,* and Asahel Bush, in his dual guise as territorial printer and newspaper editor, took his much-traveled printing equipment along. However, Congress had appropriated money for erection of a capitol and other public buildings at Salem, and the Comptroller of the U. S. Treasury refused to recognize the bill moving the capital. The legislators then reembarked from Corvallis following one session there, and came back to Salem. Late that year the capitol was burned, supposedly by an incendiary. Thereafter the legislature met in rented buildings until a new one could be constructed. When Oregon was admitted to the union as a state in 1859, Salem continued as state capital.

During the 1850's Salem had connections with other valley points by river steamer, stage line, and telegraph, and seemed well on its way to an era of prosperity. Hopes were shattered, however, by the disastrous flood in December, 1861. The Willamette, swollen by heavy and prolonged rains, surged over the business district, destroying wharves, sawmills, stores, and residences. Not until 1871, with the coming of the railroad, did a new period of rapid development begin.

During the Hayes-Tilden presidential election of 1876, Governor LaFayette Grover (1823-1911) made a daring political move which, says the *Dictionary of American Biography,* "If it had succeeded, would have elected Tilden president." Governor Grover attempted to disqualify a Republican elector, a postmaster, on the grounds that he could not act because he held public office, and to replace him with a democrat, next highest on the list. He prepared an extended brief to support his position, but the electoral commission ruled against him. The Goveror was threatened with mob violence as a result of this action, and when he resigned the governor's chair the following year to enter the U. S. Senate there was an unsuccessful attempt to prevent his being seated. As editor of the *Oregon Archives* and as a public official in several capacities Grover otherwise served with credit; for a number of years he was a prominent woolen manufacturer in Salem, but spent the latter years of his long life in retirement.

Since that time Salem has had a steady industrial and commercial development, and state institutions have been built here until the city and vicinity now (1940) has all but two of them. The city has linen and paper mills, canneries, packing houses, ironworks, sawmills, and sash and door factories.

POINTS OF INTEREST

1. The MARION COUNTY COURTHOUSE (*Open* 8-5 *Mon.-Fri.;* 8-1 *Sat.*), High St. between Court and State Sts., and extending to Church St., was erected in 1872. Constructed of stuccoed brick, it is of French Renaissance design, with a mansard roof. A conventional figure of Justice with scales and a sword surmounts the high front cupola.

2. The FEDERAL BUILDING (*open* 8-6 *Mon.-Fri.;* 8-12 *Sat.*), Court St. between Church and Cottage Sts., is of modern design and is constructed of Vermont marble, with a California granite base. The lower story which houses the post office, is 136 by 124 feet, and the upper story 50 feet square. The grounds are beautifully landscaped.

3. WILLSON PARK, bounded by Court, State, and Cottage Sts., with its towering shade and ornamental trees, many of them cuttings of historic trees, was the gift of Dr. W. H. Willson, early Oregon missionary.

4. The STATE CAPITOL, Court, State, and 12th Sts., stands in its own park, adjoining Willson Park and seemingly a part of it. In the two parks are more than four hundred varieties of trees. Near the east entrance of the capitol is the CIRCUIT RIDER, a bronze equestrian statue of life size, commemorating the pioneer missionary, Rev. Robert Booth. The sculptor was A. Phimister Proctor.

The present Oregon State Capitol replaces the one destroyed by fire in 1935. Francis Kelly, associated with Trowbridge & Livingstone of New York, is the architect. Oregon associates are Whitehouse and Church. The building, modern in design, has a symmetrical facade that is divided into three main sections and dominated by a cylindrical central dome. The main entrance with its triple doors is surmounted by long windows and flanked by wide projecting bays, the latter taking the form of monumental pylons. The severity of the symmetrical wings is relieved by an effective arrangement of windows, which are designed in five bays separated by the vertical lines of narrow buttresses. These windows provide clerestory lighting for the executive chambers within. A row of square windows pierce the wall of the first story.

The most decorative feature of the exterior is the cylindrical dome, resembling the fluted drum of a column. The base is pierced by a row of narrow stone-grilled openings. The dome is surmounted by a heroic figure, *The Pioneer*, by Ulric Ellerhusen. The building is 400 feet in length, 164 feet in width and 166 feet in height.

The focal point of the interior of the Capitol building is the circular rotunda. It is finished in Travertine Rose, marble-like stone from Montana. In the center of the marble floor is the seal of the State of Oregon. Four large murals depicting the history of the state decorate the upper walls of the rotunda. The two by Barry Faulkner, of New York, tell the stories of Captain Gray landing at the mouth of the Columbia River, and Dr. John McLoughlin welcoming settlers at Fort Vancouver. Those of Frank Swartz, also of New York, picture the Lewis and Clark expedition at Celilo Falls, and a wagon train of 1843. Four smaller murals by the same artists represent Oregon's industrial development. Faulkner's represent the wheat and fruit industries, and fishing, and lumbering. Swartz's depict sheep raising and mining, and dairying and cattle raising. The governor's suite, of three spacious rooms, is finished in native myrtlewood.

5. West of the state house plaza stands the STATE LIBRARY (*open* 8-5 *Mon.-Fri.;* 8-1 *Sat.*), NE. corner of N. Winter and Court Sts., a three-story building with basement and penthouse. The design is modern, to conform with that of the capitol. It is constructed of white Georgia marble, and was designed by Whitehouse and Church, Portland architects.

At the top of a flight of broad steps are three entrance doors, above each of which a marble plaque depicts an event in Oregon history; they were carved by the Portland sculptor, Gabriel Lavare. In the main lobby of the building is a decorative medallion, also by Lavare.

The interior is of oak with Montana travertine marble trim, the main office and board room finished in knotty ponderosa pine. The principal features of the library are the stack and reference rooms, and the Oregon and Government rooms. The stack room, planned to accommodate the library's 400,000 volumes, is three stories in height and has a floor area of 42 by 136 feet. The reference room, of two stories, is paneled in oak, with several wood plaques carved by Lavare depicting Oregon historical scenes. The Oregon Room, separated from the main reference room by bronze and wrought-iron gates decorated with the different Oregon seals in bronze, contains a special collection of reference and historical works, books, documents, and pamphlets, concerning the state. The Government Room is for the special use of legislators and state department employees. Here are gathered all state governmental records, books, and other data.

6. The FIRST PRESBYTERIAN CHURCH, NE. corner of N. Winter and Chemeketa Sts., designed by Whitehouse and Church, was built in 1928-29, of Willamette brick with wood trim. The structure is of modified Georgian design, with columned portico and octagonal spire. To the right an extensive wing houses Sunday-school and recreational activities.

7. SEQUOIA PARK, Marion and Summer Sts., only 150 square feet in area, contains a single redwood tree, eighty feet tall, planted by William Waldo in 1872.

8. The STATE OFFICE BUILDING (*open* 8-5 *Mon.-Fri.;* 8-1 *Sat.*), SE. corner of 12th and Court Sts., erected in 1914, houses subordinate state officials. It is a five-story Neo-Classic structure, embellished with Doric pilasters and rusticated stone work.

9. The STATE SUPREME COURT BUILDING (*open* 8-5 *Mon.-Fri.;* 8-1 *Sat.*), NE. corner of 12th and State Sts., is occupied by offices and courtrooms of the state supreme court and the offices of the state superintendent of public instruction. The Neo-Classic structure,

three stories in height, is constructed of marble with engaged Ionic columns on each facade.

10. WILLAMETTE UNIVERSITY, State St. between 12th and Winter Sts., extending to Trade St., occupies an eighteen-acre campus, with seven buildings and an athletic field. Founded as Oregon Institute in 1842, the college is the oldest institution of higher learning in the Pacific Northwest. In 1844 the trustees of the institute purchased the Methodist mission-school property, including the three-story building, then the most imposing structure in the Oregon country. In 1853 a charter was granted by the territorial legislature creating Wallamet University, the institute being retained as a preparatory department. Later the name was changed to its present spelling, and the institute was discontinued.

Oldest of its structures is WALLER HALL, built (1864-67) in the form of a cross, and named for Rev. Alvin Waller, early-day missionary. The chapel and pipe organ are on the first floor. The UNIVERSITY LIBRARY (*open* 7:30-9 *Mon.-Fri.;* 7:30-5 *Sat.*), contains 35,000 volumes and many valuable historical records, is the newest building on the campus. It is of modified Georgian design.

Administration offices and general classrooms are in EATON HALL, a red-brick and gray-sandstone structure finished in Oregon fir, the gift of A. E. Eaton of Union, Oregon.

SCIENCE HALL, built for the use of Willamette Medical School (now discontinued) with funds raised by Salem physicians, houses the chemistry, physics, and home economics departments. MUSIC HALL, occupied by the school of music, originally housed the Kimball School of Theology. LAUSANNE HALL was named for the ship *Lausanne*, in which a party of missionary men and women came around Cape Horn to Oregon in 1839. The building, completed in 1920, is the women's dormitory.

The GYMNASIUM, a modern three-story building with a gallery, is capable of seating 2,800 persons. THE UNIVERSITY MUSEUM (*open* 7:30-9 *Mon.-Fri.;* 7:30-5 *Sat.*), on the second floor of the gymnasium, contains a collection of birds and animals, Indian relics, historical documents, minerals, woods, shells, and plants.

CHRESTO COTTAGE was erected in 1918 by the Chrestomathean and Chrestophilean societies as a student-faculty social center. The ATHLETIC FIELD has a grandstand seating 5,600 persons.

11. SITE OF THE FIRST STORE IN SALEM, NE. corner Ferry and Commercial Sts., is designated by a bronze marker. Here, in 1848, Thomas Cox opened the first commercial establishment in Salem with a small stock of drygoods.

12. FEDERAL ART CENTER (*open* 10-5:30 *Mon.-Fri.;* 10-5:30, 6-9 *Sat.;* 1-5 *Sun.*), 460 N. High St., established in 1937 by a Salem citizens' group in cooperation with the Federal government, is housed in the old Salem high-school building. The program being carried out by the sponsors includes a free art school, public school and library extension work, art library and reading room, lectures, and

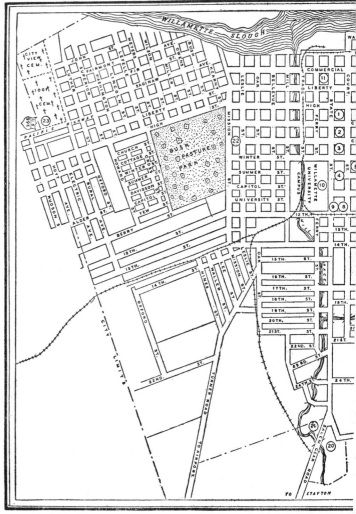

RAY LEDOUX 1939

SALEM POINTS OF INTEREST

1. The Marion County Courthouse
2. The Federal Building
3. Willson Park
4. The State Capitol
5. State Library
6. The First Presbyterian Church

7. Sequoia Park
8. The State Office Building
9. The State Supreme Court
   Building
10. Willamette University
11. Site of the First Store in St
12. Federal Art Center

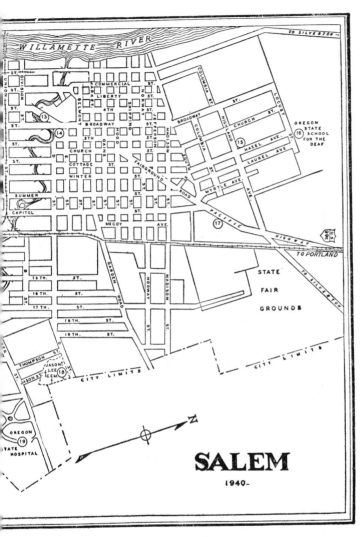

SALEM

1940-

exhibitions of the work of American and foreign artists and of students.

13. The SITE OF THE JASON LEE SAW AND GRIST-MILL, Broadway and Liberty Sts., is noteworthy because the mill that stood here was the first structure in the settlement. The machinery for the mill was brought around the Horn on the *Lausanne,* and was later transported from Fort Vancouver to Salem in Chinook canoes. The preacher-mechanic at first set the millstones incorrectly so that they threw out the wheat instead of grinding it.

On the same site, in 1857, Daniel Waldo established the first woolen mill in Oregon Territory, manufacturing blankets, flannels, and cashmeres. The mill was later burned but was reestablished on South 12th Street as the Thomas Kay Woolen Mills.

14. The HOME OF JASON LEE (*private*), 960 Broadway, was the scene of the first meeting, in 1842, of the founders of Willamette University, and was also the first post office in Salem. The frame residence with its gable roof and bracketed doorway stands as it was built except for an addition by Judge R. P. Boise, Salem's first postmaster and later chief justice of the state supreme court.

15. The BOYHOOD HOME OF HERBERT HOOVER (*private*), stands at the NW. corner of Highland Ave. and Hazel St. After young Hoover was orphaned, he spent several years in Salem with his uncle. It is said that the youth, later President of the United States, drove one of the horsecars on the then new street railway.

16. OREGON STATE SCHOOL FOR THE DEAF (*open 8-12 and 1-4 daily, except Sat., Sun., & holidays*), N. end of Laurel St., established in 1870 and moved to its present site in 1910, educates deaf children between the ages of six and twenty-one.

17. MILES LINEN MILL (*open 9-5 weekdays*), 2150 Fairgrounds Rd., manufactures salmon twine, fish nets, sack twine, shoe thread, and linen yarns from Oregon flax.

18. The JASON LEE CEMETERY, N. end of 25th St., is the last resting place of many of the pioneers who founded Salem. In the Missionary Plot are the graves of Jason Lee and his family. On a large marble headstone is inscribed a record of his work. The inscription on the headstone over the grave of Lee's first wife, Anna Pittman Lee, records that she was the first white woman buried in Oregon. Lee died in 1845, on a visit to his birthplace in Canada, and his body was returned here sixty-one years later.

19. The OREGON STATE HOSPITAL FOR THE INSANE (*open 10-12, 2-4, daily except Sat., Sun. and holidays*), Center and 24th Sts., was established in 1880. Flower-bordered drives lead to the buildings and through the grounds. Twenty-five hundred patients are cared for, many of whom work on the hospital farm a few miles south of the institution.

20. The STATE PENITENTIARY (*open 9-11; 2-4; Mon., Wed. and Fri.*), State and 24th Sts., a buff-colored building erected in 1866, is noted for the development here of the Oregon flax industry, an enterprise started in 1915 to furnish non-competitive labor for prison

inmates. The penitentiary has the largest scutching plant in the United States and the largest single acreage of flax in the world. A lime plant grinds fertilizer that is sold to farmers of the state at cost.

Most notorious of its prisoners was Harry Tracy, the bandit, who escaped in June, 1902, and spread terror throughout the Northwest until his death in a gun fight, two months later, in a Washington wheat field.

21. The STATE FORESTRY BUILDING, State and 24th Sts., is of gray stone veneer and Douglas fir construction. The front is of stone and the sides and back of stone veneer as high as the windows with Douglas fir planking laid horizontally to the eaves. Hand split and shaved cedar shakes cover the roof. The interior of the building is in native woods. The walls of the reception room are of Douglas fir and the floor of broadleaf maple; the walls of the state forester's office are of myrtlewood, the ceiling of tanbark oak and the floor of intermingled white oak, black locust, black oak, and tanbark oak; the deputy forester's office has walls lined with crowfoot hemlock, ceiling of firtex, and floor of white oak. The board of forestry room has a freize of Oregon broadleaf maple burls, each burl "booked" to provide a pleasing design. The ceiling is a patchwork of burl-designs. Other rooms have walls of yew wood, sapstain pine, knotty ponderosa pine, Port Orford cedar, redwood, alder, curly ash, sugar pine, golden chinquapin, juniper, and madrona. The furniture is of native woods in harmony with the interior finish.

22. The STATE SCHOOL FOR THE BLIND (*open* 8-12 *daily;* 1:10-4:30 *except Sat., Sun., and holidays*), Church and Mission Sts., established 1872 in a private residence, has occupied the present quarters since 1892. It is conducted as a free boarding school for blind children, and its courses meet college entrance requirements.

23. In the I.O.O.F. CEMETERY, S. Commercial and Hoyt Sts., are graves of pioneers, state executives, and prominent citizens. Among those buried here are John Pollard Gaines, territorial governor from 1850 to 1853, and Dr. William H. Willson, pioneer missionary, who donated the townsite of Salem.

POINTS OF INTEREST IN ENVIRONS

Indian School at Chemawa, off US 99, 6 *m.* (*see TOUR* 2); Silver Falls State Park, 25 *m.* (*see TOUR* 2*A*).

The Dalles

Railroad Station: Union Pacific Station, N. end of Liberty St., for Union Pacific Railroad.
Bus Station: 311 E. 2nd St., for Union Pacific Stages and Mount Hood Stages.
Airport: Emergency landing field, 2.1 m. N. via Columbia River ferry to Dallesport, Wash.; no scheduled service.
Pier: Port of The Dalles Dock for ocean and river craft, foot of Union St.
Ferry: Connecting with US 830 via Dallesport, Wash.; 50c for car and passengers, 25c for pedestrians.

Accommodations: Two hotels, four tourist camps.

Information Service: Chamber of Commerce, 2nd and Liberty Sts.

Motion Picture Houses: Two.
Tennis: High School courts open to public in summer, free.
Golf: The Dalles Country Club, 3 m. W. on US 30; 9 holes, greens fee 50c weekdays, 75c Sun. and holidays.

Annual Events: Easter Sunrise Services, Pulpit Rock; Pioneer Reunion, early May; Old Fort Dalles Frolic, early September.

THE DALLES (98 alt., 5,883 pop.), seat of Wasco County, is the principal trade center of a large agricultural area in north central Oregon. Navigation development at Bonneville Dam and the dredging of a ship channel from Vancouver, Washington, to the dam will make marine transportation feasible to this point, 189 miles from the mouth of the Columbia River.

The name of the city originated with French *voyageurs* of the Hudson's Bay Company, who found a resemblance between the basaltic walls of the Columbia narrows and the flagstones (*les dalles*) of their native village streets. The city is on the south bank of the river along a great crescent bend. The business district occupies a low bench along the water front, and the residential sections are built on terraces that extend southward, with a maximum elevation of one thousand feet. In The Dalles are numerous upthrusts of basaltic rock, causing many dead-end streets, confusing to visiting motorists and creating peculiar building difficulties. Some residences are perched fifty feet above their nearest neighbors. A flight of stairs, where Laughlin Street climbs from Fifth to Fulton, ascends an almost perpendicular cliff for three blocks.

Old frame buildings shoulder modern masonry structures in the business center, while in the older residential districts are a number of quadrangular houses, with the inevitable ell of pioneer construction. In these the front door generally opens into a central hall, from which rises a stairway with newel and lamp. Modern home design tends toward the rustic. There are, however, a number of stone and pebble houses, such as are found in Italy and on the Dalmation coast; these were built by stone masons, who settled here following their employment at Cascade Locks, the Celilo Canal, and on other public works.

Indians called the site of the city *Winquatt* and *Wascopam*. The former means a hemmed-in bowl; the latter, the place of the wasco, a bowl made from the horn of a mountain goat, now extinct in this section but formerly hunted by the Indians in the surrounding mountains. Both names suggest the bowl-like arrangement of the canyon walls.

Because its narrows and rapids made a break between navigable portions of the Columbia River, the site of The Dalles was geographically fitted to be "the great [Indian] mart of all this country," as Lewis and Clark, first recorded white visitors, found it in the fall of 1805. "Ten different tribes who reside on Taptate [Yakima] and Catteract [Klickitat] River," Clark wrote, "visit those people for the purpose of purchasing their fish, and the Indians on the Columbia and Lewis's [Snake] river quite to the Chopunnish [Nez Perce] Nation visit them for the purpose of tradeing horses buffalow robes for beeds, and such articles as they have not. The Skillutes precure the most of their cloth knivs axes & beeds from the Indians from the North of them who trade with white people who come into the inlets to the North at no great distance from the Tapteet." The Indians also found this a good fishing ground and a strategic point at which to levy tribute on travelers.

Lewis and Clark stopped here on their westward journey "to make Some Selestial observations" and "to treat those people verry friendly & ingratiate our Selves with them, to insure us a kind & friendly reception on our return." They gave the Indians presents, fed them plentifully, and entertained them. Pierre Cruzatte, one of the French voyageurs, played his violin, and York, Captain Clark's giant Negro servant, *"danced for the Inds."* The expedition found seals above and below The Dalles, and "one man giged a *Salmon trout* which . . . I think the finest fish I ever tasted." In spite of their blandishments, however, the party had "ill suckcess" in purchasing horses when they returned here in the spring of 1806. Indians at The Dalles were acquainted with all the nuances of close bargaining; it was only after making purchases at high prices, which were retracted by the Indians to bargain for still higher prices, that Lewis and Clark were able to obtain four horses on which to pack goods eastward.

After the establishment of fur trading stations on the lower Columbia, The Dalles was a rendezvous for traders and Indians. When N. J. Wyeth passed this way in 1832 he found the Wascopam Indians friendly, but "habitual thieves." He "hired the Indians about 50 for a quid of tobacco each to carry our boats about 1 mile round the falls."

The first white settlement was the Methodist mission, established in 1838 by Daniel Lee and H. K. W. Perkins. A Catholic mission was begun three years later, and one source says that the "two missions spent much more time striving against each other instead of striving to save the Indians' souls." By 1847 the Methodist mission had so declined that it was sold to Dr. Marcus Whitman, Presbyterian missionary, for $600. The Whitman Massacre late in that year led to abandonment of the mission and the establishment of Fort Lee in 1849 to subdue the Indians and protect emigrants. The fort was named for its commandant, Major H. A. G. Lee. At this point overland emigrants placed their wagons on rafts and continued down the Columbia by water. The first store was opened the following year, and a rough board hotel was built, which was soon replaced by Umatilla House (razed in 1929), for a half a century internationally known for the excellence of its appointments.

By 1852 a town had grown up around Fort Lee, and shortly after the formation of Wasco County in 1854 the town was laid out and lots were sold. Three years later a charter was granted to Fort Dalles, the name of which was soon changed to Dalles City, the present official designation, but the Post Office Department listed it as The Dalles, which name it retains. Captain Thomas Jordan, commandant at the fort, began publication of the *Journal,* first newspaper between the Missouri River and the Cascade Mountains, early in 1859. Within the year he sold it to W. H. Newell, who changed its name to the *Mountaineer.*

The back-surge of migration, which had streamed into the regions west of the Cascades, came with the gold rush of the sixties. The streets swarmed with the heterogeneous humanity typical in frontier towns, and saloons and gambling houses flourished. The flow of gold was so large that the Federal government erected a mint at The Dalles, but exhaustion of the placer beds was as sudden as the initial rich strikes, and the mint was abandoned.

During the two decades before 1880 the city's population was augmented by an influx of miners, cowmen, and traders. Long lines of freight wagons crawled through the streets and over the trails southward and eastward to the mines and stock ranges. Stages rumbled in from Umatilla, Canyon City, and the high desert regions. Steamboat service on the river was rapidly augmented, but it could not keep pace with the demand for transportation, and livery stables flourished. The Oregon Short Line, a Union Pacific enterprise, was completed in 1884, displacing freight wagons and taking some of the business from steamboat lines.

Following completion in 1896 of the Cascade Locks on the Columbia, about half way between The Dalles and Portland, steamboats could come up the river as far as The Dalles, and the rapids at this point remained the only obstacle to steamer transport as far east as Lewiston, Idaho. Many plans were advanced to overcome the barrier, and a portage railroad was built in 1904. The traffic handled by this road was so great that it led directly to the formation of the Open River steamboat line. Construction of the six-mile Celilo lock canal was begun in 1908 and completed in 1915, but river traffic declined after 1920.

Salmon packing is a major local industry. F. A. Seufert, a resident of The Dalles, designed the fish-wheel (now prohibited by law), which revolutionized salmon fishing. Cooperative associations pack more than thirty thousand barrels of brined cherries annually. The Dalles handles grain worth a million and a quarter dollars each year, livestock worth a million dollars, and wool to the value of a quarter of a million.

With completion of the Bonneville dam project, The Dalles will be at the head of a 200-mile waterway. To accommodate this anticipated traffic the Port of The Dalles has built docks and terminals at a cost of $300,000 to serve ocean and river shipping.

POINTS OF INTEREST

1. The FEDERAL BUILDING, SW. corner of 2nd and Union Sts., is a two-story Neo-Classic structure of gray Tenino sandstone. It houses the post office, the only remaining U. S. land office in eastern Oregon, and the office of the Wasco County agricultural agent. Once one of the busiest centers of activity in The Dalles, the land office has gradually become quiescent following the withdrawal of public lands from homestead entry.

2. The CITY HALL, NW. corner of Court and 3rd Sts., a two-story brick building with native black basalt trim, houses all municipal departments, including the fire department. Set into the east wall is a bronze plaque that marks the site of the first courthouse between the Cascades and the Rocky Mountains. The old building was removed to 320 East 3rd Street when the city hall was built.

3. The WASCO COUNTY COURTHOUSE, NW. corner of Washington and 5th Sts., is a Neo-Classic structure of gray pressed brick and granite, with interior-finish dark gray variegated marble. In addition to all departments of county government, it houses The Dalles chapter of the American Red Cross and the county public health unit. In the county archives is the record of a license for a ferry across Green River, formerly in Oregon Territory but now within the boundaries of Wyoming.

4. The CIVIC AUDITORIUM, NW. corner of 4th and Federal Sts., is a memorial built by the city to World War veterans. Besides an audience hall seating over a thousand persons, there is a ballroom, a community room, a gymnasium, and offices of the National Guard company. The American Legion meets in the community room.

5. The FIRST COURTHOUSE (*private*), 320 E. 3rd St., was built in 1859 on the site of the City Hall and was removed to its present site to make way for that building. At the time of its construction, Wasco County embraced the entire region between the Cascades and the Rocky Mountains, the Columbia River, and the California line. The old building has been given a coat of stucco and is used as a lodging house.

6. The HORN, 205 E. 2nd St., originally a saloon operated by Charles Frank, is a lunchroom with a collection of ancient firearms; the horns of mountain sheep, bison, deer, elk, and other animals adorn its walls.

7. The WILSON HOUSE (*private*), 209 Union St., a small

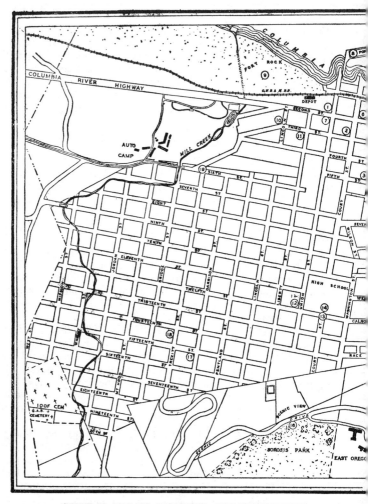

THE DALLES POINTS OF INTEREST

1. The Federal Building
2. The City Hall
3. The Wasco County Courthouse
4. The Civic Auditorium
5. The First Courthouse
6. The Horn
7. The Wilson House
8. The Port of The Dalles Te
   minals
9. Fort Rock
10. St. Mary's Academy

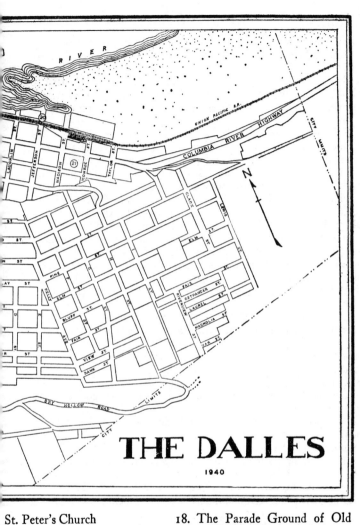

THE DALLES

1940

square frame house, was once the home and post office of the nation's first postmistress, Mrs. Elizabeth Millar Wilson, an appointee of President Grant.

8.   At the N. end of Union St., is the PORT OF THE DALLES TERMINALS, two corrugated iron warehouses on a wharf 1,190 feet in length, equipped with modern marine elevators to serve ocean and river craft.

9.   FORT ROCK, reached by way of a marked trail from the Union Pacific Station, N. end of Liberty St., is on the rocky promontory overlooking the Columbia. This "rockfort camp" was used by the Lewis and Clark expedition in the fall of 1805 and in the spring of 1806. Clark wrote: "we formed our camp on the top of a high point of rocks, which forms a kind of fortification . . . well Calculated for Defence, and convenient to hunt under the foots of the mountain." They had good reason to choose a strong situation; the Indians would probably have killed them for their goods had not their party been a strong one. But they had other troubles: "The *Flees* which the party got on them at the upper & great falls, are very troublesom and dificuelt to get rid of, perticulary as the men have not a Change of Clothes to put on, they strip off their Clothes and kill the flees, dureing which time they remain nakid."

10.   ST. MARY'S ACADEMY, NW. corner of 3rd and Lincoln Sts., has provided high-school instruction for girls since 1863, but until 1930 there was only primary instruction for boys. Among the youths who attended the school was N. J. Sinnott, former Congressman from Oregon and member of the U. S. Court of Claims.

11.   ST. PETER'S CHURCH (Roman Catholic), SW. corner 3rd and Liberty Sts., is a red-brick edifice of Gothic design. Its spire rises 146 feet and is surmounted by a chanticleer weathervane.

12.   In a small city PARK, 12th and Union Sts., opposite the red-brick schoolhouse is an old Oregon Trail marker dedicated by Ezra Meeker, who crossed the plains in 1852, and who in his later years retraced the route by ox-team and covered wagon, and also by airplane.

13.   PULPIT ROCK, 12th and Court Sts., is a natural upthrust of conglomerate in the form of a pulpit, from which early Methodist missionaries preached to the Indians. All religious denominations in the city join in an annual Easter sunrise service at this rock.

14.   Immediately north, below Pulpit Rock, is AMATON SPRING (Place of the Wild Hemp), site of an ancient Indian encampment. The buildings of the Methodist mission, established in 1838, were near this point. Daniel Lee, co-founder of the mission, in his *Ten Years in Oregon* tells of finding "a valuable spring of water, some rich land, and a good supply of timber, oak, and pine, and an elevated and pleasant location for a house almost in their shade; with a fine view of the Columbia River, three miles on either hand. . . . The Indians assisted in cutting the timber, and bringing it upon the spot." The mission was sold to the Presbyterians in 1847 and retransferred to the Methodists the following year; the buildings were damaged during the

occupancy of Federal troops in 1849 and following years, and the Methodist Mission Board was compensated to the amount of $24,000.

15. PIONEER CEMETERY, on winding Scenic Drive, is the burial place of many of the city's pioneer citizens. The cemetery was established in 1859 with the burial of a man named Kelly. The marker has been broken and his first name is unknown. The plot comprises about four acres covered with native oak trees. Wild bunchgrass, sunflowers, lupines, and Oregon grape cover some of the graves. Here are buried Joseph Gardner Wilson (1826-73), first circuit court and supreme court judge from eastern Oregon, and his wife Elizabeth Millar Wilson (1830-1913), the first postmistress whose appointment was confirmed by the United States Senate.

16. SOROSIS PARK, a pine-covered tract at the top of Scenic Drive, is partially improved. Here is a $5,000 marble fountain, the gift in 1911 of Maximilian Vogt, early-day merchant and philanthropist. The bowl of the fountain is ten feet in diameter divided into four sections into which the water flows from bronze lions' heads facing the major points of the campus. Above the bowl rises a square granite shaft surmounted by a bronze decoration with five tines. From the park is an inspiring view of the grain-covered eastern Oregon hills and plateaus, and the snow-capped peaks of the Cascade Range.

17. The OLD FORT DALLES HISTORICAL SOCIETY MUSEUM (*open 9-5 daily*), SW. corner 15th and Garrison Sts., occupies the last remaining building of the Old Fort Dalles group. The museum contains Indian artifacts and American history material, including arrows, stone bowls, baskets, beadwork, and old articles of furniture brought across the plains in covered wagons. Pioneer vehicles owned by the American Legion and stored in sheds near the museum, are exhibited annually at The Old Fort Dalles Frolics. One of them, a stagecoach that once carried President U. S. Grant, bears bullet holes from early-day bandit raids.

18. The PARADE GROUNDS OF OLD FORT DALLES, 14th and Trevitt Sts., is occupied by the Colonel Wright Grade School, named for a fort commandant.

19. THE DALLES INDIAN MISSION MONUMENT, in a triangular plot at 6th and Trevitt Sts., was erected by Willamette University in 1930 to perpetuate the memory of the Methodist mission established here in 1838, by Daniel Lee. The marker was carved from native Oregon granite by Louis Comini, pioneer granite worker.

20. THE DALLES COOPERATIVE GROWERS PLANT (*open by arrangement*), N. end of Jefferson St., processes annually 20,000 barrels of maraschino cherries and employs 250 women seven months of the year. Experiments in collaboration with the Oregon State Agricultural College, beginning in 1927, perfected sulphurous bleaching and acid brines for hardening the cherries. The product is sold in wholesale quantities to eastern confection concerns. The enterprise affords a sure market for the large number of cherry growers in The Dalles area.

21. THE DALLES MINT (*private*), center of block bounded

by E. 2nd, Monroe, Madison, and E. 3rd Sts., is a stone building constructed by the Federal government in 1868. It was built at a cost of $105,000 at a time when gold mining in eastern Oregon and Idaho promised rich returns, but never coined a piece of money. Before the structure could be equipped, the mines so diminished in production that the government sold the building. Today it is the enginehouse of the Columbia Warehouse Company, a grain and storage concern.

POINTS OF INTEREST IN ENVIRONS

Seufert Bros. Cannery, **3** *m.*; Celilo Falls (Indian fisheries), **11** *m.*; Mayer State Park (Rowena Lookout), **10.5** *m.*; Memaloose Lookout, **14.1** *m.* (*see TOUR* **1**).

PART III.

All Over Oregon

Tour 1

(Caldwell, Idaho)—Ontario—Pendleton—The Dalles—Portland—
Astoria; **518.9** *m.* US 30.

Union Pacific Railroad parallels US 30 between Idaho Line and Portland;
Spokane, Portland & Seattle Railroad, between Portland and Astoria. Stage
service throughout.
Paved road, passable except after severe snow and ice storms, when sections
along Columbia River are temporarily blocked.
All types of accommodations; improved camp sites.

US 30 in Oregon closely follows the old Oregon Trail. Lewis and
Clark used boats in the Columbia to reach the coast though later travelers followed the south bank of the river to The Dalles, where they
transferred.

Section a. Idaho State Line to Junction US 730, **221.7** *m.*

US 30 crosses the Oregon line, which is in the SNAKE RIVER,
0 *m.*; the river forms more than 200 miles of the Oregon-Idaho boundary. The river was named Lewis Fork by William Clark in honor of his
fellow explorer Meriwether Lewis. Later the terms Shoshone and Snake
were more often applied, because of Indian tribes that inhabited its
drainage basin. Saptin, or Shahaptin, also frequently applied is derived
from a branch of the Nez Perce.

ONTARIO, **1.4** *m.* (2,153 alt., 1,941 pop.), a townsite in the
1880's, is the principal trade center for the 300,000 acres of the Owyhee
and Malheur irrigation projects (*see TOUR 7a; also TOUR 6a*).
On the irrigated farms, apples and other fruits are produced; and grain
growing, hog raising and dairying are important industries. Ontario is
the shipping point for vast areas of the Owyhee and Malheur Valleys
and is the gateway to the great cattle country of central Oregon, served
by the Oregon Eastern branch of the Union Pacific Railroad extending
127 miles southwestward to Burns (*see TOUR 7a*).

US 30 crosses the Malheur River (*see TOUR 7a*) at **3.7** *m.* In
Fremont's *Journal,* under date of October 11, 1843, he wrote: "about
sunset we reached the *Riviere aux Malheurs* (the unfortunate or un-
lucky river) a considerable stream, with an average breadth of fifty feet
and, at this time, eighteen inches depth of water." From the straight
young shoots of the wild syringa that grow along the river bank, the
Indians fashioned their arrows, which fact gave the bush the local name
of arrow-wood.

Northward from the Malheur the road curves over sage-covered hills, a trail once traversed by Indians, trappers, frontiersmen, missionaries, soldiers, covered wagons, the pony express, the Concord coach.

> "Hickory yoke and oxen red
> And here and there a little tow-head
> Peeping out from the canvas gray
> Of the Oregon Overland on its way
> In Forty-Nine—"

At **8.8** *m.* is a junction with State 90.

Right on State 90 to PAYETTE, Idaho, 3 *m.* (*see TOUR 3, IDAHO GUIDE*).

At **16.8** *m.* US 30 forms a junction with US 30N.

Right on US 30N to WEISER, Idaho, 3 *m.* (*see TOUR 3, IDAHO GUIDE*).

OLDS FERRY at FAREWELL BEND, **30.7** *m.,* established in 1862, was one of the earliest ferries on the Snake River. At Farewell Bend, where the Old Oregon Trail leaves the Snake River and curves northwestward over the ridges to Burnt River (*see below*), the pioneers bade farewell to the river not knowing where they would again reach water. A marker (R) indicates that the expeditions of Wilson Price Hunt, Captain B. E. L. Bonneville, Nathaniel J. Wyeth, and Captain John C. Fremont, camped at this place. Here, on the night of December 22, 1811, the starving Astorians under command of Captain Hunt crossed the ice-filled Snake River. "Mr. Hunt caused a horse to be killed and a canoe to be made out of its skin," wrote Washington Irving in *Astoria*. "The canoe proving too small another horse was killed and the skin of it joined to that of the first. Night came on before the little bark had made two voyages. Being badly made it was taken apart and put together again by the light of the fire. The night was cold; the men were wearied and disheartened with such varied and incessant toil and hardship. . . . At an early hour of the morning, December 23, they began to cross. . . . Much ice had formed during the night, and they were obliged to break it for some distance on each shore. At length they all got over in safety to the west side; and their spirits rose on having achieved this perilous passage."

Hunt, leading his party of 32 white men and Marie and Pierre Dorion, Indian guides, and their two small children, made for the mountains. Five horses had been laden with their luggage, and these horses ultimately served as food.

Fremont wrote in an early report: "Leaving the Snake River, which is said henceforth to pursue its course through canyons, amidst rocky and impracticable mountains where there is no possibility of traveling with animals, we ascended a long and somewhat steep hill; and crossing the dividing ridge, came down into the valley of the Brule' or Burnt River, which here looks like a hole among the hills."

At **35.7** *m. change is made between Rocky Mountain and Pacific Standard Time.*

HUNTINGTON, **36.3** *m.* (2,112 alt., 803 pop.), named for two brothers who platted the townsite, is three miles from the Snake River in the Burnt River Valley. The townsite is a part of the land claim of Henry Miller who settled here in August, 1862, and built the stage tavern known for many years as Miller's Station. The rails of the Oregon Short Line and the Oregon Railway & Navigation Company line were joined here in 1884, and since that time Huntington has been an important railway division point.

Northward from Huntington, US 30 follows the canyon of Burnt River, which it crosses 15 times in 12 miles. As early as 1819 Donald McKenzie spoke of the Brule', saying that Indians had been burning the hills, giving the country a black appearance. Fremont noted: "The common trail, which leads along the mountain-side at places where the river strikes the base, is sometimes bad even for a horseman." All pioneers agreed that the Burnt River canyon was one of the most arduous sections of the old Oregon Trail.

At LIME, **41.6** *m.* (2,223 alt., 18 pop.), a large conveyor crosses over the highway, connecting two units of a cement plant.

At RATTLESNAKE SPRING, **51.9** *m.*, the State Highway Department maintains a drinking fountain and rest rooms.

DURKEE, **57.3** *m.* (2,654 alt., 100 pop.), is the trading post for a quartz and placer mining area and shipping point for cattle. Close by, along Burnt River, are found fire opals of excellent quality.

BAKER, **82.2** *m.* (3,440 alt., 7,858 pop.).

Railroad Station: Union Pacific Depot, W. end of Broadway, for Union Pacific Railroad.
Bus Station: 1st and Court Streets, for Union Pacific Stages.
Taxis: 25c minimum.

Accommodations: Three hotels; six tourist camps.

Information Service: Chamber of Commerce, Baker Hotel, 1701 Main St.

Moving Picture Houses: Three.
Athletic Fields: Baseball Park, Campbell and Grove Street.
Swimming: Natatorium (Adm. 25c), 2450 Grove St.
Golf: Baker Country Club, 9 holes; greens fees, 30c, 0.8 m. SW. on State 7,
Shooting: Baker County Rod and Gun Club, 2.7 m. SW. on State 7.

Annual Events: Baker Mining Jubilee, July.

Baker, on the upper reaches of Powder River, is at the mouth of a shallow canyon, and looks northward over the Powder River Valley. Its wide streets are bordered for many blocks by business houses and the dwellings are shaded in summer by poplar, locust and cottonwood. Rising above the city roofs the ten-story Baker Hotel, one of the tallest buildings in the state, is a conspicuous landmark. The city hall, schools, hospital, and other public buildings, and many other structures, are built of a steel-gray volcanic stone, quarried a few miles south of town. This stone cuts readily when first quarried, and hardens when exposed to the weather.

Although born of the eastern Oregon gold rush, and firmly established as the "gold coast" of Oregon, Baker is a city of numerous interests. Flour mills, grain elevators, and dairies process grain and milk from surrounding farms; packing plants and poultry houses serve cattle and sheep ranches of surrounding ranges, and the valley poultry farms.

Early settlers overlooked the beauty of the Baker site and the utility of its resources. Not until the California gold rush reminded men of the fabled yellow stones, picked up in a blue bucket on the trail, did prospecting begin in the canyons.

The first house in the Baker settlement was built of log, in 1863. Soon a box saloon, a hotel, and a blacksmith shop were opened. In the spring of 1864 Col. J. S. Ruckels built a quartz mill; James W. Virtue erected the first stone structure for his assay office and bank, and the Reverend P. DeRoo opened the Arlington Hotel. The town was laid out in 1865 by Royal A. Pierce and named for Col. E. D. Baker, United States Senator from Oregon and close friend of Abraham Lincoln. Baker was killed at Ball's Bluff, Va., October 21, 1861, while serving in the Federal army.

In 1868 the county seat was changed from Auburn to Baker. Some difficulty arose over the transfer of records and a crowd from Baker went to Auburn with a team and wagon and "very early in the morning everything belonging to the county offices was loaded into the wagon and on the way to their destination before the people of Auburn knew what was going on." In 1874 the town was incorporated as Baker City, but about 1912 "City" was dropped.

In spite of poor transportation facilities Baker did a thriving business in mining supplies and provisions. Merchandise was freighted over the hazardous mountain roads to the mining camps of Rye Valley, Willow Creek, and the Mormon Basin, 75 to 100 miles away. The stage line, carrying the United States mail and Wells, Fargo & Company's express, was transferred from the old immigrant road east of town to Place's toll road through Baker City in 1865. Coaches of the Northwest Stage Company made regular connections with the Union Pacific Railway at Kelton, Nevada, while other lines reached out to Gem City, Sparta, Eldorado, and the Greenhorn Range. Hold-ups by "road-agents" and pillaging of stages and freight wagons by hostile Indians were of frequent occurrence, and swollen rivers and winter storms added peril to many a trip.

Travelers passing through saw more exciting life in Baker City than in any town between Portland and Salt Lake. Miners, gamblers, *filles de joie,* ranchers, cowboys, and sheepherders frequented the dance halls and saloons or mingled on the board walks with the citizenry. Gambling halls, blacksmith shops, livery stables, and feed corrals were the principal industrial establishments. Notwithstanding the two-fisted character of the town, the city commissioners in 1881 passed an ordinance prohibiting small boys from shooting marbles or riding velocipedes on the sidewalks, and required one citizen to remove his potato patch from a lot on a principal street.

In 1880 the Census Bureau found 1,197 people here, including 166 Chinese, males being predominant. According to this census there were only 143 females in the city.

The first train on the new Oregon Short Line arrived here August 19, 1884. The town then boasted a substantial business district with two-story brick or stone structures; and the coming of the railroad further stimulated trade. The Eagle Sawmill Company opened a lumber yard in Baker in 1886; in 1888 the Triangle Planing mill began operation, and in June 1892, the Baker City Iron Works was established. The first newspaper published in Baker County was the *Bedrock Democrat,* on May 11, 1870; soon followed by the *Daily Sage Brush,* the *Reveille,* and the *Tribune.*

The last decade of the century opened with the usual western boom hitting the little "Denver of Oregon," and real estate values sky-rocketed. But the boom soon burst and values settled to their former firm level. Since the turn of the century the city has had a steady grow becoming the trade center of a vast agricultural and stock-producing region and the mining metropolis of the State. Neighboring mines have already produced more than $150,000,000 and Baker County still holds 75 percent of the mineral wealth of the State. A bullion department is maintained at the First National Bank.

The GOLD EXHIBIT (*open 9-3 weekdays*), in the First National Bank at 2001 Main St., contains gold in its various forms: nuggets, dust, and ores. One nugget from the Susanville district weighs 86 ounces and is worth more than $3,000.

The BAKER MUNICIPAL NATATORIUM (*open 9-9 weekdays, adm. 25c*), SE. corner of Campbell and Grove Sts., was built at a cost of $200,000. Springs of considerable mineral content furnish water at 80 degrees, gushing 400 gallons a minute. The main plunge is equipped with shower, steam, needle and tub baths.

The CITY PARK, Grove St., between Madison and Campbell Sts., extending to Resort St. on both banks of the Powder River, has a playground for children, swings, seats, and a bandstand that is used for weekly concerts during the summer. In the park is a monument erected in 1906 to the pioneers of the provisional government period. The monument was built with the contributions of 800 school children.

The CARNEGIE PUBLIC LIBRARY (*open 9-5 weekdays*), SE. corner of 2nd and Auburn Sts., of modified Classical Revival design, is constructed of local stone. On its shelves are 16,000 volumes, several thousand music scores, and a large collection of art prints, many in color, which are used by study clubs.

The BAKER COUNTY COURTHOUSE (*open 9-4 weekdays*), 3rd and Court Sts., is a square, three-story building of local stone, surmounted by a clock tower.

Baker is at the junctions with State 7 (*see TOUR 1A*) and State 86 (*see TOUR 1B*).

North of Baker the route runs through the broad Powder River Valley.

HAINES, **92.9** *m.* (3,334 alt., 431 pop.), is the trading center of a rich farming district. The Elkhorn Range of the Blue Mountains (L) is dominated by five conspicuous peaks; from south to north ELK-HORN PEAK (8,922 alt.), ROCK CREEK BUTTE (9,097 alt.), HUNT MOUNTAIN (8,232 alt.), named for Wilson Price Hunt; RED MOUNTAIN (8,304 alt.), and TWIN MOUNTAIN (8,920 alt.). Fremont wrote of this range: "It is probable that they have received their name of the Blue Mountains from the dark-blue appearance given to them by the pines."

A couple miles north of Haines is the Ford of Powder River called in early days the Lone Tree Crossing. Thomas J. Farnham noted on September 19, 1839: "Cooked dinner at *L'Arbor Seul,* a lonely pine in an extensive plain." Four years later Fremont wrote: "From the heights we looked in vain for a well-known landmark on Powder River, which had been described to me by Mr. Payette as *l'arbre seul* (the lone tree); and, on arriving at the river, we found a fine tall pine stretched on the ground, which had been felled by some inconsiderate emigrant axe. It had been a beacon on the road for many years past." After the cutting of the tree the place became known as Lone Pine Stump.

Crossing the North Powder River, **101** *m.,* US 30 passes a RODEO STADIUM (L) on the edge of NORTH POWDER, **101.3** *m.* (3,256 alt., 553 pop.), founded in the seventies by James DeMoss, father of the famous DeMoss family of concert singers. The city was named for a branch of the Powder River that enters the main stream at this point. The river was so named because of the powdery character of the volcanic soil along its banks.

Left from North Powder on a gravel road that winds along the North Powder River into the WHITMAN NATIONAL FOREST, **12** *m.,* and ascends sharply toward the summit of the Blue Mountains.

At **18** *m.* is a junction with a foot trail. L on this trial **1** *m.* to VAN PATTEN LAKE, one of a closely grouped series of beautiful highland lakes in the heart of the mountainous region known as the ANTHONY LAKES RECREATIONAL AREA. These lakes, headwaters of three major streams—the North Fork of the John Day, the Grande Ronde, and the North Powder—are well stocked with rainbow and eastern brook trout.

On the graveled road is ANTHONY LAKE, **21** *m.* (7,100 alt.), a vacation resort. (*Forest camps, picnic grounds, commercial accommodations; boats and fishing tackle for hire*). The resort is summer headquarters of the district forest ranger. Left from Anthony Lake **0.7** *m.* to BLACK LAKE (*good fishing*); right **0.3** *m.* to MUD LAKE (*camp sites*); and right **1.6** *m.* to GRANDE RONDE LAKE (*boats for hire; camp sites*).

A marker at **104.1** *m.* indicates the camp where Marie Dorion, wife of the half-breed interpreter attached to the Hunt party, gave birth to a child on December 30, 1811. Irving writes: "They . . . suffered much from a continued fall of snow and rain. . . . Early in the morning the squaw of Pierre Dorion . . . was suddenly taken in labor, and enriched her husband with another child. . . . Pierre, . . . treated the matter as an occurence that could soon be arranged and need cause no delay. He remained by his wife in the camp, with his other children and his horse, and promised soon to rejoin the main body, who proceeded on their march. . . . In the course of the following morning the Dorion family made its reappearance. Pierre came trudging in advance, followed by his valued, though skeleton steed, on which was mounted his squaw with the new-born infant in her arms, and her boy of two years old wrapped in a blanket slung at her side."

Crossing a dividing ridge over which the wagons of the pioneers struggled valiantly, the highway drops into the Grande Ronde Valley, called by the French-Canadian trappers *La Grande Vallee'*. "About two in the afternoon," wrote Fremont, "we reached a high point of the dividing ridge, from which we obtained a good view of the *Grand Rond* —a beautiful level basin, or mountain valley, covered with good grass on a rich soil, abundantly watered, and surrounded by high and well-timbered mountains; and its name descriptive of its form—the great circle. It is a place—one of few we have seen in our journey so far— where a farmer would delight to establish himself, if he were content to live in the seclusion it imposes."

Captain Bonneville, saw the valley in 1833 and reported: "Its sheltered situation, embosomed in mountains, renders it good pasturing ground in the winter time; when the elk come down to it in great numbers, driven out of the mountains by the snow. The Indians then resort to it to hunt. They likewise come to it in the summer to dig the camas root, of which it produces immense quantities. When the plant is in blossom, the whole valley is tinted by its blue flowers, and looks like the ocean when overcast by a cloud."

UNION, 116.8 *m.* (2,717 alt., 1,107 pop.), once the seat of Union County, was settled in 1862 by loyal citizens who perpetuated the spirit of their patriotism in the name of the town. Conrad Miller, the first settler, selected land a mile west of the present town in 1860. Union is the center of a rich agricultural and stock-producing area. Catherine Creek, a good fishing stream, runs through the town. The 620-acre EASTERN OREGON STATE EXPERIMENT STATION is at the west city limits; here experiments are made in the growing and improving of grains, grasses, and forage crops. Here also are a dairy unit, a poultry unit, a five-acre orchard, and truck-garden plots.

At HOT LAKE, 122.4 *m.* (2,701 alt., 250 pop.), water gushing from springs has a temperature of 208 degrees, boiling point at this altitude. It is used for both medicinal and heating purposes in a large sanitorium. Irving says, in speaking of the eastbound Astorians under the command of Robert Stuart: "They passed close to . . . a great pool of water three hundred yards in circumference fed by a sulphur spring about ten feet in diameter boiling up in the corner. The vapor from this pool was extremely noisome, and tainted the air for a considerable distance. The place was frequented by elk, which were found in considerable numbers in the adjacent mountains, and their horns, shed in the springtime, were strewed in every direction about the pool."

LA GRANDE, 131.5 *m.* (2,784 alt., 8,050 pop.).

Railroad Station: Jefferson Ave., between Depot and Chestnut Sts., for Union Pacific Railroad.

Bus Station: Terminal, Washington Ave. and 7th St., for Union Pacific Stages and Inland Transit Lines.

Taxis: Rates 25c in city.

Accommodations: Hotels and tourist camps.

Information Service: La Grande Commercial Club and Oregon State Motor Association, Chestnut St. and Adams Ave.

Radio Station: KLBM (1420 kc.).

Motion Picture Houses: Two.

Athletic Fields: La Grande High School (flood-lighted), 4th St., between K and M Sts.

Tennis: Municipal Courts, Walnut St. and Washington Ave.

Golf: La Grande Country Club, 9 holes, $1 weekdays; $1.50 Sun., 3 m. NE. on State 82.

Swimming: Cone Pool (open air), 2 m. W. on US 30; Crystal Pool, N. 2nd St.

Shooting: La Grande Gun Club, 3 m. E. on US 30.

Annual Events: Union County Pioneer Meeting, July; Grange Fair, September.

La Grande (2,784 alt., 8,050 pop.), seat of Union County, lies at the foot of the Blue Mountains near the western edge of the Grande Ronde Valley. Eastward rise the Wallowas, a low wall against the sky, serrated by bristling growths of fir and spruce. The town spreads out across a gently rising slope on the south bank of the Grande Ronde River, its wide streets pleasantly shaded by long rows of deciduous trees. Modern brick and concrete structures lend a metropolitan touch to the little city.

Ignoring the beauty and productivity of its level acres for a quarter of a century settlers passed through the valley toward the Willamette and it was not until 1861 that a few settlers retraced their trail to stake the first claims in this region. They spent the winter about five miles north of the present city and in the following spring Ben Brown moved with his family to the south bank of the Grande Ronde River and built a log house at the foot of the mountains beside the overland trail. He converted his house into a tavern around which arose a small settlement known variously as Brown Town and Brownsville. Upon the establishment of a post office in 1863, the name was changed to La Grande, in recognition of the beauty of the scenery.

The town was incorporated in 1864 and in the same year the legislature created Union County, designating La Grande as temporary county seat. The erection of a two-story frame courthouse started a county-seat fight that lasted 20 years. No vote was taken until 1874 when the town of Union won the contest. Then the citizens of Union descended on La Grande, forcibly appropriated the county records, and carted them home. Ten years later another vote reversed the first plebiscite and La Grande citizens invaded Union and took back the records.

The city was once the home of Blue Mountain University, a Methodist college that ceased to function in 1884. During the Indian uprising of 1878, the alarmed populace took refuge behind the thick brick walls of the old university building. The Indians did not enter the valley, but fear did not fully abate until Gen. O. O. Howard routed the tribes, killed Buffalo Horn, and drove Egan, the Paiute chieftain, from the state.

The Oregon Railway and Navigation line came in 1884, following a tangent across the prairie from the gap at Orodell, two miles to the north, to Pyle Canyon. La Grande, finding itself a mile off the railway, created a "New Town" beside the tracks, though "Old Town," as it is still known locally, remains an integral part of the city. The coming of the railroad opened a wider market for the products of the region and the location of division shops in the city insured a large and permanent payroll. Thereafter the population steadily increased.

Here in her girlhood dwelt Ella Higginson (ca. 1860-), author of three books of poems, a novel, some volumes of short stories, and many songs. Here also lived Mrs. Higginson's sister, Carrie Blake Morgan, poet and magazine writer; Kay Cleaver Strahan, writer of mystery stories; Bert Huffman (1870-), poet and author of *Echoes from the Grande Ronde;* and T. T. Geer (1851-1924), who during his long residence in the town and county, accumulated much of the material for his volume of reminiscences, *Fifty Years in Oregon.*

The industrial life of La Grande centers about the railroad shops and the two large sawmills. Creameries, cold-storage and packing plants, and flouring mills provide additional employment. The principal products of the surrounding country are fruit, livestock, and lumber. La Grande is the chief shipping and distributing point for Union and Wallowa Counties and the starting point for hunting, fishing, and sight-seeing trips into the Wallowa and Blue Mountains.

The city adopted the commission-manager form of government in 1913.

The FIRST UNION COUNTY COURTHOUSE (*private*), SE. corner of 1st St. and B Ave., was erected in 1864 on the site of the former Ben Brown log cabin tavern. During the first year of its existence the lower floor of the courthouse was used as a print shop by the Democratic *Grande Ronde Sentinel* and the Republican *Blue Mountain Times,* the city's first newspapers; county offices were on the second floor. Later the second story was utilized as a schoolroom and sawdust was spread on the floor so that the noise of the children's feet would not disturb the county officials on the floor below. After the removal of the county seat to Union in 1874, the building was used as a church, as a store, and since 1876 as a residence.

The OREGON TRAIL MONUMENT, on a hillside at the west end of B Ave., is a slab of stone three feet high and 15 inches square, with "The Old Oregon Trail, 1843-1853" inscribed on the east face. Scars of the old trail still remain slanting across the rugged slope. From the site is a panoramic view of the Grande Ronde Valley with the city in the foreground surrounded by checkered fields, and in the distance, Mount Emily and Mount Fanny lifting their crests above the Wallowa and Blue Mountains.

The SITE OF BLUE MOUNTAIN UNIVERSITY, W. side of 4th St. between K and M Aves., is now the grounds of the La Grande high school and the Central grade school. In 1875 the university was organized under the auspices of the Columbia Conference of the Methodist Church. For a decade the college flourished, but in 1884 it was discontinued when the conference was divided and the church endowment restricted. The property was then leased for public school purposes and was purchased in 1889. The old La Grande high school, now the Central school, erected in 1899, was constructed partly of bricks from the old university hall, and the material from the old cornerstone was taken out and placed in the cornerstone of the new building.

UNION COUNTY COURTHOUSE, L Ave. between 5th and 6th Sts., constructed in 1904, is a two-story red brick building, surrounded by a landscaped park. Here are the court records since 1864, which have suffered little loss or damage, despite the two forcible removals.

EASTERN OREGON COLLEGE OF EDUCATION, S. of L Ave. between 8th St. and Hill Ave., has a 30 acre campus on an eminence overlooking the city. It was established in 1929 and is the only Oregon institution of higher learning east of the Cascade Mountains. The central, or administrative building, a concrete structure of Italian Renaissance design, erected in 1929, provides offices, classrooms, a library, and an auditorium seating 600. Leading upward to the building, which is 42 feet above the street level, is a wide stairway of buff-colored concrete with ornamental balustrades. The J. H. Ackerman Training School, of similar architecture to the administration building, a laboratory school, sponsored jointly by School District No. 1 of Union County and the State of Oregon, was erected with Public Works Administration funds. One of Oregon's three teachers' training institutions, it serves an average of 350 students.

La Grande is at a junction with State 82 (*see TOUR 1c*).

West of La Grande US 30 winds up the gorge of the Grande Ronde River into the Blue Mountains, Oregon's oldest land, known to geologists as the Island of Shoshone. The Blue Mountains were one of the most formidable barriers in the path of the pioneer. In 1839 Thomas Farnham wrote about "The trail. . . . over a series of mountains swelling one above the other in long and gentle ascents covered with noble forests of yellow pine, fir and hemlock." In the evening "the mountains hid the lower sky, and walled out the lower world. We looked upon the beautiful heights of the Blue Mountains, and ate among its spring blossoms, its singing pines, and holy battlements."

KAMELA, 151.3 *m.* (4,206 alt., 27 pop.), highest railroad pass in the Blue Mountains, is a starting point for camping and fishing trips.

MEACHAM, 156.9 *m.* (3,681 alt., 70 pop.), was named for Col. A. B. Meacham, a member of the Modoc Peace Commission, who established the Blue Mountain Tavern at this point in 1863, just outside the borders of the Umatilla Indian Reservation. In the early 1890's the site of Meacham was platted and given the Biblical appelation of

Jerusalem with a pretentious plaza in the center known as Solomon Square. But the dreams of the new Jerusalem soon abated and the little mountain village reverted to the old name of Meacham.

EMIGRANT SPRINGS STATE PARK (*facilities for picnicking*), **160.2** *m.,* is at a spring said to have been discovered in 1834 by Jason Lee. Right of the highway, opposite the entrance to the park, is a large stone marker, erected in honor of the members of the first wagon train over the trail. It was dedicated in 1923 by President Warren G. Harding.

The UMATILLA INDIAN RESERVATION, entered at **162.6** *m.,* was named for a tribe of Indians that once inhabited the lands adjacent to the Umatilla River. It was established in 1855, and is now occupied by about 1,200 members of the Cayuse, Umatilla, and Walla Walla tribes, who engage in wheat-growing and ranching (*see IN-DIANS AND ARCHEOLOGY*). The reservation has no government school, but missions are maintained by the Roman Catholic and Presbyterian Churches.

The summit of EMIGRANT HILL, **167.8** *m.,* (3,800 alt.), discloses a panorama of the Columbia Basin wheatlands. Fields of waving grain alternate with summer-fallow in a vast checker board of gold and gray, and the wild war cry of the painted savage is replaced by the hum of the combine harvester. On clear days Mount Hood and Mount Adams, more than 100 miles distant, can be seen against the western horizon.

MISSION, **181.2** *m.,* is headquarters for the Umatilla Indian Agency. At the STATE PHEASANT FARM, **181.9** *m.,* grouse, quail, pheasants, and other game birds are bred for release on the uplands of eastern Oregon.

At **185.7** *m.* US 30 forms a junction with State 11, the Walla Walla Highway.

Right on State 11 through wheatfields that stretch in a broad panorama up the slopes of the Blue Mountains (R), crossing the UMATILLA (Ind., water rippling over stones) RIVER, to ADAMS, 12.5 *m.* (1,520 alt., 178 pop.), named for an early wheat rancher. A school, a church, grain elevators, and dwellings are all that remain of a once thriving settlement.

Right from Adams, on a gravel road 10 *m.* to THORN HOLLOW (1,450 alt.), a small Indian settlement on the Umatilla Reservation. Left here to GIBBON, 16.1 *m.* (1,751 alt.), also on the Reservation, which has a school for Indian and white children. At 23.3 *m.,* near the Umatilla River, is BINGHAM SPRINGS, a summer resort centering about the warm sulphur springs. (*Hotel and cabin accommodations*).

The old town of ATHENA, 17.7 *m.* (1,713 alt., 504 pop.), on State 11 by Wild Horse Creek, was a stage station on the road from Walla Walla to Pendleton. It was long the scene of an annual camp meeting with horse racing as an added diversion. A cannery, absorbing the pea yields of former wheatlands, gives the town an increasing economic importance.

Before the Civil War WESTON, 21.3 *m.* (1,686 alt., 384 pop.), did brickmaking and milling and was the first home of the Eastern Oregon Normal School. Until a fire destroyed all but two business houses in the 1880's, Weston was a formidable rival of Pendleton. Pendleton editors complained that Weston was ahead of their town because Weston supported a street sprinkling system, consisting of two Chinese who spent the entire day passing up and down sprinkling the main street from their five-gallon cans of water. The old SALING HOUSE (*private*), on Main St., is a two-story structure of locally-made bricks and has a cupola that was used as a look-out during Indian raids.

The town is the background for *Oregon Detour,* by Nard Jones, a popular novel of recent years.

The summit of WESTON HILL, **30.3** *m.,* commands a splendid panoramic view of the Blue Mountains and the Walla Walla Valley. To the right, is the deep Storm Canyon of the South Fork of the Walla Walla River, with Table Mountain upthrust between it and the North Fork Canyon, on the left. In the foreground, is the deeply etched canyon of the Walla Walla River, with its sun-lit orchard valley, bordered by golden terraces of wheat-covered foothills.

MILTON, **31.4** *m.* (1,010 alt., 1,576 pop.), is on the old stage line between Wallula, Wash., and La Grande. The town was first settled by a few families who prohibited the sale of alcoholic beverages. In the 1880's the opposition led by the miller, who owned water rights on a nearby stream, moved outside of Milton's corporate limits. Buyers of lots in the new townsite received as a bonus free water privileges. Thus was established the town of FREEWATER **32.3** *m.* (1,010 alt., 732 pop.), which sold its liquor at "Gallon Houses," because Federal permits allowed them to sell liquor only in gallon lots. The two towns, which now overlap, are usually referred to as Milton-Freewater. They support a union high school, one of the best in the state.

Milton is the canning and shipping center for a large pea-raising area, the altitude, from 1,000 to 3,500 feet, making several harvesting periods. Formerly wheat was the major crop, but from one-third to one-half of the land was idle under the summer-fallow plan. Now, with the rotation of peas and wheat, all of the land is used. Early in the year farmers lease the land not planted with wheat to pea canneries for cultivation. A mechanical drill, powered by a tractor, does the seeding, and while the plants are growing they are sprayed with pea-weevil poisons by a machine developed by the Agricultural Department of the Oregon State College. The crop is harvested by tractor-drawn swathers that cut the vines close to the ground. An automatic loader lifts the vines and deposits them in dump trucks that carry them to huge stationary viners, where the peas are taken from the pods. They are then placed in boxes, which are loaded into water-cooled trucks and rushed to the canneries, whose season extends from mid-June into August.

After the vines have been stripped, they are stacked and sold to farmers as feed for stock. In 1938 pea-vine ensilage ranked second to alfalfa as roughage for cattle in this area, with an average yield of three and a half tons per acre. The vines are also dried and used as hay.

When harvesting comes to an end discs are attached to tractors and the remaining vegetation is turned into the ground. This increases the fertility of the soil and aids in the control of pea pests.

At **36.7** *m.* is a junction with a gravel road, L. here **12.5** *m.* to an old HUDSON'S BAY FARM, on which one of the original buildings of the company's settlement still stands. Refugees from Waiilatpu, the Whitman Mission, were said to have been sheltered in this house in 1847.

At **36.7** *m.* State 11 crosses the Washington Line and at **38.7** *m.* meets a county road leading northwestward down the Walla Walla River valley.

Left on this road 5 *m.* to the WHITMAN MONUMENT. The old Whitman Mission of Waiilatpu was on the right bank of the Walla Walla River near its confluence with Mill Creek. Near the mission site is a shaft of granite commemorating the Whitman tragedy of November 29, 1847, when thirteen inmates of the mission were slain by Indians. To the left of the grave is the site of the log house built in the fall of 1836 by Dr. Whitman and W. H. Gray, mission blacksmith. A short distance from this cabin stood the main building of the mission a T-shaped structure. At the mouth of Mill Creek was the mission mill. All these buildings were destroyed at the time of the Indian uprising.

Dr. Marcus Whitman, a physician belonging to the Presbyterian church, established the mission in 1836, on the site selected the year before by the Reverend Samuel Parker, commissioned by the American Board of Foreign Missions.

Dr. Whitman was prominent in early Oregon history. In 1843 he induced migration into Oregon so as to force it into the hands of the United States. He turned his mission into a sort of relay station, catering to the needs of the emigrants and tending them in illness. The slaying of the mission inmates hastened Congress in declaring Oregon a Territory.

PENDLETON, 187 *m.*, (1,070 alt., 6,620 pop.) (*see PENDLE-TON*).

Points of Interest: Round-Up Park, Pendleton Woolen Mills, Pioneer Park, Til Taylor Park, County Courthouse.

At Pendleton US 30 forms a junction with US 395 (*see TOUR 5a*), with which it unites westward to a junction at 188.2 *m.*

The EASTERN OREGON STATE HOSPITAL, (L) at 188.5 *m.*, a modern institution, with buildings adequate for 1,325 patients.

West of Pendleton is a section of the vast wheat region of the Inland Empire. In this area two million acres of wheatlands are under cultivation, and one might walk from Pendleton to The Dalles through growing grain. Early spring, tractors, drag plows, harrows, and drills cross rich brown fields; late summer and early fall, combines, drawn by tractors, mules, or horses, harvest the grain. Occasionally 32 horses are handled with one pair of reins as a combine travels around the golden foothills, cutting, threshing and sacking, exemplifying modern efficiency at its peak, in marked contrast with a scythe and cradle used by pioneers. These large-scale operations directed by bronzed harvest crews, are as picturesque as the cattle drives of old. As in other semi-arid portions of Oregon where wheat growing is a major industry, the practice of summer fallow is almost universal. Half the acreage is planted each year and the remaining fields are either allowed to lie idle until weeds are plowed under, or the acreage is plowed and harrowed at frequent intervals during summer to preserve moisture and to keep down weed growth. Tawny squares of ripened grain, alternating with dull blues, purples and blacks of the fallow fields, is the picture just before harvest.

At 188.6 *m.* is a junction with a side road.

Left on this road, former route of US 30, to REITH, 2.7 *m.* (979 alt., 44 pop.), Pendleton Railroad division point. At 8.3 *m.* is HAPPY CANYON, an early-day settlement whose dance halls and gambling dens have been reproduced as a feature of the Pendleton Round-Up. ECHO, 23 *m.* (636 alt., 311 pop.), is a wool and wheat shipping point, near the site of old Fort Henrietta, an early-day army post. At 24.4 *m.* is the junction with US 30 near Stanfield.

At 189.2 *m.* on US 30 is a junction with a gravel road.

Right here to the PENDLETON AIRPORT, 1.1 *m.* (1,500 alt.), the first regular stop of the eastbound United Airline planes from Portland to Salt Lake, Chicago, and New York. A branch route to Spokane makes connections here.

At 194.5 *m.* is the approximate point where the Oregon Trail left the general course of what is now US 30, and crossed high plains to Willow Creek, Alkali Flats, went down Rock Creek Canyon, and crossed the John Day River to The Dalles.

STANFIELD, 210 *m.* (204 pop.), center of a great sheep raising country, was named for the Stanfield family, owners of a nearby ranch.

HERMISTON, 215.5 *m.* (459 alt., 608 pop.), a tree-shaded oasis, with irrigation canals running through its streets is in the Umatilla Irrigation Project. Artificial waterways have reclaimed from the desert the surrounding fields that produce crops of grain, vegetables and fruit and that stand out in startling contrast to the sagebrush. The town is the home of the Eastern Oregon Turkey Association, which ships thousands of birds annually, and it is well known for its desert honey. It was named for the *Weir of Hermiston,* written by Robert Louis Stevenson.

Left from Hermiston on State 207 to BUTTER CREEK, 18.4 *m.,* so named it is said, when volunteer soldiers during the Cayuse Indian War of 1848 appropriated some butter intended for the officers' mess. Another version of the story is that the soldiers on breaking camp left crocks of butter cooling in the stream. The creek courses through a broken country, hideout for a gang of cattle and horse thieves in the 1880's. They carried on their depredations until the stockmen organized vigilante committees. The first victim was hanged on a scaffold made of fence rails. To discourage cattle thieving, as well as to prevent ownership confusion, raisers of stock filed with the county clerks small portions of leather on which were burned their identifying brands. Many of these leather brands are in the courthouses at Pendleton, Heppner, and Condon.

LEXINGTON, 38.1 *m.* (1,418 alt., 180 pop.), is an important wheat-shipping point, named for the Massachusetts town. It began as a "wide place in the road" in 1885 and became a competitor with Heppner for the county seat of Morrow County. The townsite is on the homestead of William Penland for whom Penland Buttes to the north were named. At Lexington State 207 unites with State 74 and turns L. to CLARK RANCH, 46 *m.,* where are the remains of an ancient stone sepulcher, one of several in this region. Found nearby are pictographs and artifacts. Anthropologists have surmised that these graves contain remains of a Mayan people, antedating the American Indians, who left a trail from the Columbia River to Central America.

HEPPNER, 47.4 *m.* (1,905 alt., 1,190 pop.), the seat and commercial center of Morrow County, is situated at the confluence of Hinton and Willow Creeks, on a level valley floor, sheltered between high dome-like foothills. About 1858 cattlemen drove their herds into the region to forage. Finding an abundance of rye grass along the creek bottoms, they established cattle camps and from them grew the first settlements. Sheepmen followed, but their first experiments were unsuccessful and lent encouragement to the cattlemen's hope that the sheep business would fail. Today, however, sheep raising is a leading enterprise.

Heppner, the first permanent settlement in the region, was originally called Standsbury Flat, for George W. Standsbury, whose log cabin was for several years the only white man's dwelling within many miles. Heppner and Morrow established a store in 1872. When the need for a school was recognized in 1873, Henry Heppner, jumping on a cayuse, solicited the scattered settlers for funds. Later, at the suggestion of Standsbury, the town's name was changed. Heppner was completely razed by a flood, which swept down the Balm Fork into Willow Creek, following a cloudburst on Sunday afternoon, June 14, 1903. The wall of water, five feet high, drowned more than 200 persons, and damaged property to the amount of nearly $1,000,000.

Southwest of Heppner State 207 winds up SPRINGLE CANYON to SPRINGLE MILL SUMMIT, 51.9 *m.,* from which are extended views of the Blue Mountains.

HARDMAN, 67.5 *m.* (3,590 alt., 120 pop.), once a center of commercial activity, is a village in a round depression of wheatlands that gives the illusion of great isolation. In the days of stage coaches, there were two villages in this vicinity. Yellow Dog stood on the Adams ranch, about a mile west of the town of Rawdog. There was great rivalry between the two for the stage depot and the post office, and when Rawdog finally won by strength of numbers, it was known for some time as Dogtown. Still later it was called Dairyville, but the name was finally changed to Hardman for Dan Hardman, who had homesteaded the site.

Hardman is one of the few towns in Oregon where the old-fashioned hand-worked pumps and town pump are in use.

South of Hardman the country levels into a wide plateau before dipping sharply into the Rock Creek Canyon, which marks the end of the wheat-growing region and the beginning of the cattle and sheep ranges.

At 79.4 m. is a junction with a dirt road.

Left on this road 0.9 m. to the HARRY FRENCH RANCH, where fire-opals of excellent quality have been found. The opal geodes lie in outcroppings from the surface to two feet in depth. In 1880 there was an "opal rush" to the district.

A boundary of the UMATILLA NATIONAL FOREST is crossed at 83.1 m.; the forest is noted for its magnificent stand of western yellow pine. Limited lumbering and the summer grazing of stock is permitted under Forest Service supervision.

At 89.3 m. is a junction with the Tamarack Mountain road; R. on this rough road 10 m. to TAMARACK MOUNTAIN, a splendid hunting ground where deer abound.

At FAIRVIEW FOREST CAMP, 91.5 m., named for the fine view of the Blue Mountains to the southeast, are the usual camping facilities. South of the camp the highway descends over a sharply winding road into the gorge of the John Day River (see TOUR 6a), which cuts a great gash through the towering mountain ranges of eastern Oregon, to a junction with State 19, 100.3 m. (see TOUR 1D), at a point 3.1 miles east of SPRAY.

At 219 m. on US 30 are the UMATILLA COUNTY STATE GAME REFUGE, which shelters wild birds, especially migratory geese and ducks, and a GOVERNMENT IRRIGATION DAM. Below the dam, the Umatilla River's bed shows a curious rock formation similar to that at Celilo Falls (see below).

At 221.7 m. is a junction with US 730 (see TOUR 5a).

Section b. Junction with US 730 to Portland, 192.7 m.

West of the junction with US 730, 0 m., US 30 is called the Upper Columbia River Highway. It follows the south side of the river's magnificent gorge most of the way across the state.

UMATILLA, 0.9 m. (294 alt., 345 pop.), at the confluence of the Umatilla and Columbia Rivers, was founded in 1863 under the name of Umatilla Landing as a shipping point for the Powder River and Idaho mines during the rush to the gold fields. In June, 1863, its buildings numbered 53, thirteen of which had been erected in four days. The *Oregonian* for June 24, 1863, reported: "Very little regard is paid to the pretended title of the proprietor, Mr. Lurchin, as any one who wishes a lot just naturally jumps it." As a result the town boasted over 100 substantial buildings within six months after its founding. Twenty-five stores supplied the needs of citizens, packers, and stampeders, and two large hotels accommodated the traveling public. Wild-eyed mule skinners and gents with gold in their pokes and a hankering for whiskey roared through the streets, and freight wagons, stage-coaches, and pack trains clattered in from the dusty trails.

When Umatilla County was formed in 1862 Marshall Station, forty miles up the Umatilla River, was designated the county seat, but the seat was moved to Umatilla Landing in 1865, where it remained until 1868 when it was removed to Pendleton. In the years that followed Umatilla became the shipping point for large cargoes of grain from the eastern Oregon fields, but the Oregon Railway and Navigation line, constructed in the early eighties, diverted traffic and the town declined in importance as a port.

IRRIGON, 8 *m.* (297 alt., 65 pop.), on the site of old Grande Ronde Landing, a former stopping place for travelers, derives its name and sustenance from the irrigation district of which it is the center. An experiment farm nearby demonstrates the agricultural possibilities of the rich soil.

At **11.2** *m.* is a junction with a side road.

Right on this road to PATTERSON FERRY, 1 *m.* (*toll for cars and five persons*, $1; *round trip*, $1.50) connecting with US 410 at Prosser, Washington.

On a slight knoll (R) at **19.7** *m.* is a mounted specimen of Indian picture writing. The engraved boulder was found on the bank of the Columbia River a few miles east of its present location.

BOARDMAN, **19.8** *m.* (250 alt., 100 pop.), lies in an area that holds the fossilized remains of many prehistoric animals. Specimens include part of a mastodon tooth, bones of fishes, of the three-toed horse, of the rhinoceros, and bits of turtle shell.

Left from Boardman on the Boardman Cut-off across a barren stretch of sage-brush plains to an unimproved road at 15 *m.*
Left 1 *m.* on the dirt road, dusty and deeply rutted as it was in the days of the wagon trains, to WELLS SPRINGS and the WELLS SPRINGS CEME-TERY. The cemetery (L) is identified by its high, rabbit-tight fence. Here were buried several pioneers, also Colonel Cornelius Gilliam who on March 24, 1849, was killed by the accidental discharge of his gun.

West of Boardman US 30 follows the river, a green band separating bleak and barren shores.

CASTLE ROCK, **25.6** *m.* (241 alt., 10 pop.), once a busy community, now is a station on the railroad edging an empty plain. The magazine *West Shore* for October, 1883, records: "Castle Rock. . . . now contains an express office, post office, saloons, dwellings, schools, etc. . . . The growth of western towns is wonderful."

HEPPNER JUNCTION, **35.1** *m.* (241 alt.), distinguished by an airplane beacon on the cliff (L), is the junction of the Union Pacific Railroad main line with its Heppner branch, as well as the junction of US 30 with State 74.

Left from Heppner Junction on State 74 through a narrow rimrock-walled cleft up Willow Creek. Rust-colored, basaltic cliffs are in vivid contrast with emerald green alfalfa fields, sub-irrigated by gravity flow of water from Willow and its tributary creeks, and from underground springs. As the route continues into the gradually rising country, wheat fields roll away to the benchlands on either side of the highway.

During gold rush days, miners traveling from lower Columbia River points to the Idaho and John Day mining districts, passed through Willow Creek Valley, hastening south by way of Dixie Creek and the forks of the John Day River. Processions of Columbia River Indians followed this road, to hunt deer, pick berries, and camp in the Blue Mountains, returning down the creek for the salmon fishing at Celilo.

At 15.1 *m.* is a junction with a gravel road; L. here 0.5 *m.* to CECIL, (618 alt., 15 pop.), by the Oregon Trail crossing of Willow Creek. The settlement was an important stage station. The WELL, where travelers obtained drinking water for themselves and their teams, remains at the center of the village street.

On State 74 is MORGAN, 20.4 *m.* (10 pop.), in early days called Saddle. The stage station of the name was situated, until 1888, on a side road about 2 *m.* northwest of the present site. SADDLE BUTTE is right.

IONE, 29 *m.* (1,090 alt., 283 pop.), is strategically situated near the mouth of Rhea Creek, and is also at the junction of the Boardman Cut-off Highway (L). During the late nineteenth and early twentieth centuries, Ione was considered an ideal picnic site for conventions, celebrations and pioneer gatherings.

At 32.7 *m.* is a gravel road; R. here 6 *m.* to the OREGON CREAM-O-LINE RANCH, the only palomino horse ranch in the Pacific Northwest. Palominos are golden and cream, or ivory-colored horses, a gentle and tractable product of fine breeding, that are used for show purposes and for racing.

LEXINGTON, 37.7 *m.* (1,418 alt., 180 pop.), a shipping center for wheat, is at a junction with State 207 (*see above.*)

West of Heppner Junction, US 30 crowds close upon the river, in places climbing along the basaltic cliffs, affording views of the gorge and the piling mountains to the north in Washington.

ARLINGTON, 46.5 *m.* (224 alt., 601 pop), first known as Alkali, was given its present name by N. A. Cornish in commemoration of the home of Robert E. Lee. The first dwelling was erected on the site in 1880 by Elijah Ray, and the town of Alkali was platted two years later by J. W. Smith. The town was incorporated in 1887. Ducks and geese are plentiful in the vicinity; the open season is from October 21 to November 19, inclusive. Hunting rights are often rented from the ranchers at $8 to $10 a day. The Arlington Ferry (*cars*, $1; *round trip*, $1.50) makes connections with Roosevelt, Wash. At Arlington is a junction with State 19 (*see TOUR 1D*).

Passing through BLALOCK, 55.4 *m.* (216 alt., 16 pop.), US 30 threads the narrow gorge through which the Columbia has cut its channel. From SQUALLY HOOK at 70.1 *m.*, Mount Hood is seen to the southwest, rising above the waters of the Columbia River.

The JOHN DAY RIVER, 70.5 *m.*, called LePage's River by Lewis and Clark for a member of their party, honors a member of the Astorians. Washington Irving describes John Day as "a hunter from the backwoods of Virginia. . . . about forty years of age, six feet two inches high, straight as an Indian; with an elastic step as if he trod on springs, and a handsome, open, manly countenance. He was strong of hand, bold of heart, a prime woodsman, and an almost unerring shot." Day, with Crooks and several French-Canadians, fell behind on the Snake River, while Hunt forged ahead with the main party in the winter of 1811-12 (*see above*). The following spring when, after many hardships, the two Americans reached the mouth of the John Day River "they met with some of the 'chivalry' of that noted pass, who received them in a friendly way, and set food before them; but, while they were satisfying their hunger, perfidiously seized their rifles. They then stripped them naked and drove them off, refusing the entreaties of Mr. Crooks for a flint and steel of which they had robbed him; and threatening his life if he did not instantly depart." In this forlorn plight they were found months later by a searching party and taken to Astoria. Day decided to return to the States with Robert Stuart's party, but before reaching the Willamette he became violently insane and was sent back to Astoria where he died within the year.

In the striated gorges carved by the swift waters of the John Day River are written the successive chapters of Oregon's geological evolution.

Across the river from RUFUS, 75.5 *m.* (180 alt., 70 pop.), stands the STONEHENGE MEMORIAL to the World War dead, a reproduction of the ruin in England. It was built by Samuel Hill.

At 78.1 *m.* is a junction with US 97.

Right on US 97 to the Maryhill ferry, 0.4 *m.* (*fare* $1; *service as needed*). From the north bank ferry landing in Washington, US 97 continues to the junction with US 830, 1.2 *m.*; L. here 2.9 *m.* on US 830 to MARYHILL CASTLE, also built by Samuel Hill. It is a three-story rectangular structure of concrete, set on a bluff 800 feet above the river. Though the building was dedicated by Queen Marie of Roumania in 1926, it was not opened to visitors until 1937. Queen Marie gave to the museum a life-size portrait of her daughter, a desk, chairs, and other pieces of furniture. Hill lavished a fortune on the estate but never made it his home. However, he left a bequest of $1,200,000 for completing and maintaining it as a museum. In a crypt repose the owner's ashes, commemorated by a tablet bearing the inscription: "Samuel Hill—amid Nature's unrest, he sought rest."

At BIGGS, 80.4 *m.,* is a junction (L) with US 97 (*see TOUR 4a*).

MILLER, 84.4 *m.* (168 alt., 11 pop.), is a grain-shipping station. US 30 crosses the Deschutes River, 85.3 *m.,* on the CHIEF DUC-SAC-HI BRIDGE, an arched concrete structure named for a chief of the Wasco tribe, who operated the first ferry across the river. The Deschutes, often designated on old maps as Falls River, has been an important fishing stream for both Indians and whites. Lewis and Clark found that the river, "which is called by the Indians Towahnahiooks," was "divided by numbers of large rocks, and Small Islands covered by a low growth of timber."

CELILO, 88.2 *m.* (158 alt., 47 pop.), at Celilo Falls, is a canoe portage as old as the fishing stations still held by the Indians under a treaty granting exclusive and perpetual fishing rights to them. Long before Lewis and Clark passed here, fishing stands on these rocks were handed down by the Indians from father to son. Robert Stuart of the Astorians writes in his journal: "Here is one of the first rate Salmon fisheries on the river. . . . the fish come this far by the middle of May, but the two following months are the prime of the season—during this time the operator hardly ever dips his net without taking one and sometimes two Salmon, so that I call it speaking within bounds when I say that an experienced hand would by assuidity catch at least 500 daily—"

When Lewis and Clark visited the falls they found ". . . great numbers of Stacks of pounded Salmon neetly preserved in the following manner, i.e. after suffi(ci)ently Dried it is pounded between two Stones fine, and put into a speces of basket neetly made of grass and rushes better than two feet long and one foot Diamiter, which basket is lined with the Skin of Salmon Stretched and dried for the purpose, in this it is pressed down as hard as possible, when full they Secure the open part with the fish Skins across which they fasten th(r)o. the loops of the basket that part very securely, and then on a Dry Situation they Set those baskets . . . thus preserved those fish may be kept Sound and sweet Several years." Here at Celilo the Indians still spear or net the fish in the traditional manner, protected by treaty from infringement on their ancient rights. Near the north end of the falls is the old village of WISHRAM, described by Lewis and Clark in their *Journals* and by Washington Irving in *Astoria*. This village furnished many fine studies of Indian life to Edward Curtis in preparing his *North American Indians*.

Lewis and Clark, finding seventeen Indian lodges along here, "landed and walked down accompanied by an old man to view the falls. . . . we arrived at 5 Large Lod(g)es of natives drying and prepareing fish for market, they gave us Philburts, and berries to eate." A portage railroad, 14 miles long, was opened in 1863. The canals and locks here were constructed by the Federal Government in 1905 to accommodate wheat shipments. Below the falls the OREGON TRUNK RAILROAD BRIDGE spans the river, its piers resting on solid rock above the water.

SEUFERT, 97.4 *m.* (138 alt., 10 pop.), was named for the Seufert family, who established a large salmon and fruit-packing plant at this point. Many Indian petroglyphs and pictographs are on the bluffs facing the Columbia; prehistoric as well as historic aborigines of the region came here to fish for salmon, and while some of the pictures of fishes, beavers, elks, water dogs, and men were doubtless made as primitive art expression, others were carved and painted to carry messages.

At **97.8** *m.* is a junction with State 23.

Left on State 23 along gorge-enclosed watercourses to the plateau ran the Barlow road, first road over the Cascades from The Dalles region to the Willamette Valley. The route crosses Wasco County, once an empire in itself. With boundaries that reached from the Columbia River to the California-Nevada Line, and from the Cascades to the Rockies, it was the parent of 17 Oregon counties, the greater part of Idaho, and portions of Wyoming and Montana. The name, meaning a *cup,* or *small bowl of horn,* was derived from a local Indian tribe, known for its art of carving small bowls from the horns of wild sheep.

In 1905 a very large apple orchard was planted on the plateau but it is now an expanse of wheat fields with but an occasional scraggy apple tree. The promoters proposed to sell individual investors separate lots on the basis of perpetual care, the owners to reap continuous dividends after the mature trees began pro-

ducing. The soil was ideal for grain, but the moisture, though sufficient to produce large crops of wheat by dry-farming methods, was inadequate for fruit.
After the owners had lost the opportunity of making large profits, during the
World War, when high wheat prices were enriching their neighbors, they be-
latedly grubbed up thousands of trees to return the land to grain.

On the edge of DUFUR, 17 *m.* (1,319 alt., 382 pop.), is the BARLOW
DISTRICT RANGER STATION of the Mount Hood National Forest. (*Camp
fire permits for restricted areas and information.*) One of the earliest settlements
in this region, Dufur overlooks undulating wheat fields and diversified farmlands, with the rugged contours of Mount Hood on the western horizon (R).

Right from Dufur on a gravel road that runs southwest to meet various forest
roads entering recreational areas in the eastern sections of MOUNT HOOD
NATIONAL FOREST.

From TYGH RIDGE on State 23, 26.9 *m.* (2,697 alt.), the former long Tygh
grade, for many years notoriously steep and difficult, the highway skirts a canyon
(L) hundreds of feet in depth. Paralleling the present highway, are three other
gashes on the hillside, made by early road builders, the winding trail-like thoroughfares of the Indians and emigrant wagon trains, the stage road, and a rutty
passage for horse-drawn vehicles and early Model-T's that hazardously ventured
into this part of Oregon 20 years ago.

At 34.3 *m.* is a junction with State 216.

Left on State 216, 7.9 *m.* to SHERAR'S BRIDGE, at the falls of the Deschutes River. It was here, in 1826, that Peter Skene Ogden, chief fur trader
for the Hudson's Bay Company, found a camp of 20 native families. An Indian
trail, later used by the fur traders, crossed the river at this point by a slender
wooden bridge. During the salmon runs, descendants of these early tribesmen, who
held fishing privileges under a Federal treaty, still gather annually to spear
salmon or catch them with dipnets below the falls.

Joseph Sherar collected exhorbitant tolls from travelers and stockmen for use
of his bridge, near which he established a stage station and pretentious inn.
Stephen Meek's exhausted wagon train of 1845 camped at this place, and the old
ruts made by the 200 wagons are still visible on the ranch of E. L. Webb north
of the bridge.

TYGH VALLEY, 34.7 *m.* (1,111 alt., 60 pop.), is in the valley of Tygh Creek,
which took its name from the Tyigh Indian tribe. Fremont called the place
Taih Prairie. North of the town are the race track and the exhibit buildings of
the Wasco County Fair Association, which holds its annual fairs in early
September.

Right from Tygh Valley, 6 *m.* on a dirt road to WAMIC (1,664 alt., 106
pop.), in a stock raising country. This road is along the route of the old Barlow
Trail that led westward parallel to White River and crossed the Cascade divide
at Barlow Pass. Above Smock Prairie, southwest of Wamic, the ruts of ox-drawn
wagons remain on the hillsides.

WHITE RIVER, 35.8 *m.,* a tributary of the Deschutes, is noted for excellent
fishing.

At 39.3 *m.* is a junction with a county road; (L.) here 2 *m.* to the OAK
SPRINGS STATE TROUT HATCHERY, in the Deschutes River Canyon.
Millions of rainbow trout are propagated annually for restocking the Deschutes
and other popular fishing streams of the region. The young fish, held in feeding pools until almost a legal size, are distributed in tank trucks, equipped with
compressor machines to keep the water aerated. Former methods of distribution,
when no provision was made for supplying oxygen, resulted in considerable loss
of fingerlings. A chemical quality of the Oak Springs water keeps the young
trout from fungus growths that destroy the fish in many hatcheries.

State 23 joins State 50 at 42.3 *m.*

THE DALLES, (Fr. *Flagstones*) 100.8 *m.* (95 alt., 5,885 pop.)
(*see THE DALLES*).

Points of Interest: Federal Building, City Hall, Wasco County Court House, The Horn, Fort Rock, St. Mary's Academy, and others.

West of The Dalles US 30 follows the gorge of the Columbia River as it threads its way through the Cascade Range. Southwest towers Mount Hood, and northward across the Columbia Mount Adams. On some early maps these mountains are labeled the Presidents' Range, an attempt having been made in 1839 to use the names of chief executives to denominate the most prominent peaks.

West of ROWENA, 109.2 *m*. (148 alt., 60 pop.), the highway climbs the face of a steep cliff by a series of sharp curves and switchbacks known as the Rowena Loops.

Opposite Rowena, near LYLE, Wash., is the grave of Frederic Homer Balch (1861-1891), near that of his sweetheart, Genevra Whitcomb, whom he commemorated in his posthumously published novel, *Genevieve: A Tale of Oregon.*

ROWENA CREST, 111.8 *m*. (706 alt.), is in MAYER STATE PARK; parking place. From the crest one has a panoramic view of cliff and winding river.

ROWENA DELL, 112.6 *m.,* a sheer-walled canyon (R) was infested by rattlesnakes until pioneers fenced the lower end and turned in a drove of hogs. Then for a time the dell was called Hog Canyon.

Memaloose View Point, 115.5 *m.,* overlooks MEMALOOSE ISLAND, the "Island of the Dead," for hundreds of years an Indian burial place. Many of the bleached bones of generations of Indians have now been moved to other cemeteries along the Columbia, taken away from burial houses where they had been placed. A white marble shaft marks the grave of Victor Trevitt, an Oregon settler who asked that he be buried among his friends, the Indians.

MOSIER, 118.1 *m*. (95 alt., 192 pop.), at the confluence of Mosier Creek and the Columbia River, is in a small fruit-growing section well known for its apple cider. The MOSIER TUNNELS, 119.5 *m.,* one 261 feet and the other 60 feet long, often referred to as the Twin Tunnels, penetrate a promontory more than 250 feet above the river. West of this point the contrast between the barren, semi-desert contours of eastern Oregon and the lushness of the Pacific Slope becomes apparent.

At 124.6 *m*. is a junction with State 35 (*see TOUR 1E*).

US 30 crosses HOOD RIVER, 124.8 *m.,* a glacier-fed stream known in pioneer days as Dog River, a name said to have resulted from the adventure of an exploring party in early days who were compelled to eat dog meat to avert starvation. Lewis and Clark named the stream Labiche River for one of their followers.

HOOD RIVER, 125.6 *m*. (154 alt., 2,757 pop.) (*see HOOD RIVER*).

Points of Interest: Historic Flag, Old Adams House, Applegrowers' Association Warehouse, Applegrowers' Association Cannery, Hood River Distilleries, Observation Promontory, Eliot Park, etc.

The COLUMBIA GORGE HOTEL (R), **127.2** *m.*, a large structure of striking lines, was built in 1921-22 by Simon Benson, pioneer lumberman. Just behind the hotel the picturesque WAW-GUIN-GUIN FALLS drop over a sheer cliff to the river below. Nearby is the Crag Rats Clubhouse, owned by a mountain climbing organization having a membership limited to those who have climbed at least three major snow peaks; members must climb at least one major snow peak annually to remain in good standing.

MITCHELL POINT TUNNEL (*watch for traffic signals*) **130.3** *m.*, was bored through a cliff overhanging the river. In its 385-foot length are hewn five large arched windows overlooking the Columbia. The great projecting rock through which the bore was made was known among the Indians as the Little Storm King, while the sky-sweeping mountain above was called the Great Storm King.

The village of VIENTO (Sp., *wind*), **133.3** *m.* (103 alt., 14 pop.), is fittingly named, for the wind blows constantly and often violently through the gorge.

VIENTO STATE PARK (R), **133.4** *m.*, is a wooded area that is popular as a picnic ground; through it runs scenic Viento Creek.

Starvation Creek empties into the Columbia at **134.5** *m.* Here is STARVATION CREEK STATE PARK, so named because at this point in 1884 an Oregon-Washington Railroad & Navigation train was marooned for two weeks in thirty-foot snowdrifts, and food was with difficulty carried to the starving passengers. Newspapers of that day gave columns of space to this story, telling how car seats were burned in addition to all coal in the locomotive tender, that passengers might be kept from freezing.

Near LINDSAY CREEK, **135.7** *m.*, is a bronze plaque commemorating the commencement in 1912 the building of the first section of the Columbia River Highway. SHELL ROCK MOUNTAIN, **136.9** *m.* (2,068 alt.), is opposite WIND MOUNTAIN, which is in Washington. The Indians believed that the Great Spirit set the whirlwinds blowing in constant fury about Wind Mountain as a punishment to those who, breaking the taboo, had taught the white men how to snare salmon.

The Dalles and Sandy Wagon Road was authorized by the Oregon Legislature in 1867 and appropriation made for its construction. The road was built to a point 15 miles west of Hood River. Portions of the old dry masonry retaining wall may still be seen a hundred feet or so above the Columbia Highway, especially at Shell Rock Mountain.

COLUMBIA GORGE RANGER STATION, **142.8** *m.*, is the headquarters of the MOUNT HOOD NATIONAL FOREST.

Left from the Columbia Gorge Ranger Station along the east fork of Herman Creek on Pacific Crest Trail through the heavy underbrush and pine growth of the Mount Hood National Forest. The trail mounts along the stream that pours its gleaming water in continuous cataracts, to CASEY CREEK (*improved camp*), 4 *m.* South of this point the route climbs the swelling base of MOUNT HOOD (*see MOUNT HOOD*) to GREEN POINT MOUNTAIN (*improved campsites*), **7** *m.* WAHTUM LAKE (*improved camp*), **12.5** *m.* (3,700 alt.), reflects the jagged crest-line of dense pine forests.

Continuing southward the trail winds around the sharply rising shoulder of BUCK PEAK (4,768 alt.), to jewel-like LOST LAKE, **22.5** *m.* (3,140 alt.), (*see TOUR 1E*). Mount Hood's white slopes seemingly lift from the yellow sands of the lake shore and the calm waters reflect the image. Although Lost Lake was viewed by the Indians with superstitious dread, its shores have long been a popular recreational area for white men. (*Forest Guard Station; resort; bathing; boating; trout fishing.*)

CASCADE LOCKS, **145.8** *m.* (120 alt., 1,000 pop.), Here in 1896 the Federal Government built a series of locks around the treacherous Cascades rapids. It is said by geologists that these rapids were caused by avalanches that slipped from the heights of Table Mountain impeding the free flow of the river. From earliest times the Indians of the region were noted for their ugly and thievish natures. Lewis and Clark, on their return from the mouth of the Columbia, noted that "the Wahclellahs we discovered to be great thieves. . . . so arrogant and intrusive have they become that nothing but our numbers saves us from attack. . . . We were told by an Indian who spoke Clatsop that the Wahclellahs had carried off Captain Lewis's dog to their village below. Three men, well armed, were instantly dispatched in pursuit of them, with orders to fire if there were the slightest resistance or hesitation. At the distance of two miles they came within sight of the thieves, who, finding themselves pursued, left the dog and made off. We now ordered all the Indians out of our camp, and explained to them that whoever stole any of our baggage, or insulted our men, should be instantly shot."

Washington Irving, in writing of Robert Stuart's passage of the rapids in 1812, calls the Cascades "the piratical pass of the river," and that "before the commencement of the portage, the greatest precautions were taken to guard against lurking treachery or open attack." However, in 1824, Sir George Simpson wrote in his *Journal*: "Left our Encampment at 2 A. M. and got to Cascade portage. . . . Here we found about 80 to 100 Indians who were more peaceable and quiet than I ever saw an equal number on the other side of the mountain; it was not so many years ago as on this very spot they attempted to pillage a Brigade under charge of Messrs. A. Stewart and Ja Keith when the former was severely wounded and two of the Natives killed; but since that time they have given little trouble and this favorable change in their disposition I think may be ascribed in the first place to the prompt and decisive conduct of the Whites in never allowing an insult pass without retaliation & punishment, and in the second to the judicious firm and concilitary measures pursued by Chief Factor McKenzie who has had more intercourse with them than any other Gentleman in the Country."

Skilled Indian paddlers or French-Canadian boatmen were sometimes able to shoot the Cascade rapids successfully, particularly during spring freshets, but customarily even the most daring disembarked and portaged their cargoes. Prior to the building of the Barlow road (*see TOUR*

4A) in 1846 all travelers seeking passage to the lower Columbia or Willamette Valleys halted at The Dalles, dismembered their wagons, loaded them upon rafts, and steering the rude barges down the Columbia to the Cascades, docked at the Cascades and portaged wagons and goods around the dangerous white water. Ropes, used as shore lines, guided the rafts to safety.

The Columbia River water route continued popular both for passengers and for freight, and a portage road was constructed in 1856 to accommodate traffic. Rather than following the water level, later used by the railroad portage, the original wagon road around the Cascades, climbed 425 feet, a steep ascent for the plodding oxen used to draw cumbersome wagons. Toll roads later permitted the passage of cattle and pack trains, but it was not until 1872 that the Oregon legislature made an appropriation to construct a road through the gorge. The present highway has been developed from the narrow, crooked road built with that appropriation. A serious barrier to quantity freight transportation during the era when mining booms in Idaho and eastern Oregon made steamboat transportation on the Columbia a huge business, the Cascades were again mastered, this time at water level by a wooden-railed portage tramway over which mule-drawn cars, laden with merchandise, rattled from one waiting steamer to another. This proved so profitable a venture that steel rails replaced the wooden ones, and the *Oregon Pony,* first steel locomotive to operate in Oregon and now on exhibition at the Union Station grounds in Portland, was imported to draw the cars. The importance of the Columbia River as a traffic artery being established, the locks were later built by the Federal Government being established, the locks were later built by the Federal Government. Nard Jones' novel, *Swift Flows the River,* is based on the steamboat era of the Columbia centering about the Cascades.

The entrance (R) to the BRIDGE OF THE GODS is at **146** *m.;* this is a cantilever toll bridge (*cars,* 50c; *good for return within three hours*) spanning the river just west of Cascade Locks, and occupies a place where, according to Indian legend, a natural bridge at one time arched the river. This bridge, they say, was cast into the river when Tyhee Sahale, the Supreme Being, became angry with his two sons, who had quarreled over the beautiful Loo-wit, guardian of a sacred flame on the bridge. The two sons and the girl, crushed in the destruction of the bridge, whose debris created the Cascades, were resurrected as Mount Hood, Mount Adams, and Mount St. Helens. This legend is used by Frederic Homer Balch in his romance, *The Bridge of the Gods.*

EAGLE CREEK PARK (L), **148.7** *m.,* one of Oregon's finest recreational areas and picnic grounds, was constructed and is maintained by the United States Forest Service. On the banks of plunging Eagle Creek are rustic kitchens, tables and extensive parking facilities.

1. Left here on the Eagle Creek Trail, that winds up the mountain side to WAHTUM LAKE, 13.5 *m.* Construction of the trail presented many difficulties; parts of it are cut through solid rock, and in one place it passes behind a waterfall. Along the trail are GHOST FALLS and the DEVIL'S PUNCH

BOWL. The latter, a fresh-water cauldron hemmed in by pillars of basalt, abounds with steelhead trout.

2. Right across Eagle Creek from Eagle Creek Campground on the WAUNA POINT TRAIL, which leads 5.5 m. through Eagle Creek and Columbia Gorge canyons to WAUNA POINT (2,500 alt.).

BONNEVILLE, 150 m. (50 alt., 800 pop.), is at Bonneville Dam, begun by the Federal Government in 1933 and finished in 1938. The dam, designed by United States Army engineers, raised the level of water to a point four miles above The Dalles. Many of the river's beauty spots and historic sites were submerged by this impounding of water. The Cascades and much of the shore line disappeared beneath the rising waters of the great reservoir. The dam spans the Columbia River from Oregon to Washington, a distance of 1,100 feet. Bradford Island, an old Indian burial ground separating the river's two channels, is at the center of the mammoth barrier. There is a single-lift lock, 75 feet wide and 500 feet long, near the Oregon shore; a power plant with two completed units, each of 43,000 kilowatts capacity, and with foundation for four additional units; a gate-control spillway dam creating a head of 67 feet at low water; and fishways designed to permit salmon to ascend the Columbia to their spawning grounds on its upper tributaries. The slack-water lake formed above the dam creates a 30-foot channel between Bonneville and The Dalles, a distance of 44 miles. With the deepening of the Columbia between Vancouver, Washington and the dam, to a depth of 27 feet, the river will be navigable to sea-going craft for 176 miles inland. The final cost of the project, including its ten hydroelectric units with a capacity of more than a half million horsepower, will be more than $70,000,000.

Bonneville was named for Captain Benjamin de Bonneville, whose exploits were set forth in *The Adventures of Captain Bonneville* by Washington Irving.

At MOFFET CREEK, 151.4 m., the highway crosses a large flat-arch cement bridge. The span, 170 feet long, is 70 feet above the stream.

The JOHN B. YEON STATE PARK, 152 m., was named in honor of an early highway builder.

At the eastern end of the McCord Creek Bridge, 152.6 m., is a petrified stump that is believed to have matured long before the Cascade Range was thrust up.

Left from the eastern end of the bridge on a trail along the creek to ELOWAH FALLS.

At 153.2 m. BEACON ROCK, across the Columbia (R), is seen. Alexander Ross, the fur trader, called it Inshoach Castle. A landmark for river voyagers for more than a hundred years, it is now surmounted by a beacon to guide airplanes. A stirring chapter of *Genevieve: A Tale of Oregon* relates dramatic events that took place on its summit. A foot trail has been carved in its side from base to crest.

HORSETAIL FALLS, 156.6 m., forming the design that gives it name, shoot downward across the face of the sheer rock wall into an excellent fishing pool. Spray from the pool continually drifts across the highway. East of the falls towers ST. PETERS DOME, a 2,000-foot basalt pinnacle.

ONEONTA GORGE, 156.9 *m.*, is a deep, narrow cleft in the basalt bluff through which flows a foaming creek. Fossilized trees caught by a lava flow, are entombed in its perpendicular walls.

Left from the highway on a trail to ONEONTA FALLS, 800 ft., hidden in the depths of the gorge. The water, falling into the narrow ravine, stirs the air into strong currents giving it a delightful coolness even when temperatures nearby are high.

MULTNOMAH FALLS, 159 *m.*, inspired Samuel Lancaster, builder of the Columbia River Highway, to write: "There are higher waterfalls and falls of greater volume, but there are none more beautiful than Multnomah," a sentiment approved by many observers. The source is near the summit of Larch Mountain 4,000 feet above the highway. After a series of cascades the waters drop 680 feet into a tree-fringed basin.

Left from Multnomah Falls on a foot trail, across a bridge above the short stretch of creek between the upper and lower falls, to LARCH MOUNTAIN, 6.5 *m.*, (4,095 *alt.*).

WAHKEENA (Ind. *most beautiful*) FALLS, 159.6 *m.*, named for the daughter of a Yakima Indian chief, are considered by some the most beautiful of the many falls in the gorge. There is no sheer drop, but the waters hurl themselves in a series of fantastic cascades down the steep declivity. Wahkeena Creek has its source in Wahkeena Springs only a mile and a half above the cliff over which the waters plunge.

MIST FALLS, 159.8 *m.*, where the water drops from a 1,200-foot escarpment were thus mentioned by Lewis and Clark: "Down from these heights frequently descend the most beautiful cascades, one of which [now Multnomah Falls] throws itself over a perpendicular rock. . . . while other smaller streams precipitate themselves from a still greater elevation, and evaporating in mist, again collect and form a second cascade before they reach the bottom of the rocks."

COOPEY FALLS, 161.9 *m.*, according to Indian legend is at the site of a battle of giants.

BRIDAL VEIL, 162.7 *m.* (40 alt., 204 pop.), is a lumber-mill town in a small valley below the highway. Formerly Bridal Veil Falls was noted for its beauty but the waters now are confined in a lumber-flume.

Two sharp rocks between which pass the tracks of the Union Pacific and known as the PILLARS OF HERCULES or SPEELYEI'S CHILDREN, the latter name commemorating the feats of the Indian coyote god, rise (R) beyond FOREST HILL.

In the shadowy grotto of SHEPPERD'S DELL, 163.7 *m.*, a sparkling waterfall leaps from a cliff. A white concrete arch bridges a chasm 150 feet wide and 140 feet deep. Near the bridge the highway curves round a domed rock known as BISHOP'S CAP or MUSHROOM ROCK.

LATOURELLE FALLS, 164.9 *m.*, take a sheer drop of 224 feet into a pool at the base of an overhanging cliff. LATOURELLE BRIDGE was so placed as to give the best view of the falling waters.

The GUY W. TALBOT PARK, 165.1 *m.*, is a 125-acre wooded tract overlooking the Columbia.

Winding along the forested mountainside the highway reaches CROWN POINT, 167.3 *m.*, 725 feet above the river on an overhanging rocky promontory. The highway makes a wide curve, in the center of which is the VISTA HOUSE. This impressive stone structure, a modern adaptation of the English Tudor style of architecture, modified to conform to the character and topography of the landscape, was built at a cost of $100,000. The foundation about the base of the Vista House is laid in Italian-style dry masonry, no mortar having been used. Men were imported from Italy to work here and elsewhere along the highway. The windswept height, once known as THOR'S CROWN, commands a view of the river east and west for many miles.

Inside the Vista House is a bronze tablet recording the explorations of Lieut. William Broughton of Vancouver's expedition, who came up the Columbia River in 1792.

The SAMUEL HILL MONUMENT, 168.5 *m.*, is a 50-ton granite boulder dedicated to the man who was chiefly responsible for building the Columbia River Highway.

CORBETT, 169.9 *m.* (665 alt., 90 pop.), set in rolling hills, is at the eastern end of a cultivated area. The road cuts between the cliffs and the waters at the SANDY RIVER, 174.5 *m.* This stream, flowing from the glaciers on the south slope of Mount Hood, was discovered by Lieut. William Broughton on October 30, 1792, and named Barings River for an English family. The bluffs near the river mouth now bear the name of the discoverer. Lewis and Clark passed this point on November 3, 1805, and in their *Journals* records the immense quantities of sand thrown out. They wrote: "We reached the mouth of a river on the left, which seemed to lose its waters in a sandbar opposite, the stream itself being only a few inches in depth. But on attempting to wade across we discovered that the bed was a very bad quicksand, too deep to be passed on foot. . . . Its character resembles very much that of the river Platte. It drives its quicksand over the low grounds with great impetuosity and . . . has formed a large sandbar or island, three miles long and a mile and a half wide, which divides the waters of the Quicksand river into two channels." The river is noted locally for its annual run of smelt (*eulachan*), which ascend in millions each spring to spawn. When they appear the word goes out that "the smelt are running Sandy." Cars soon crowd the highways, while hundreds of people snare the fish with sieves, nets, buckets, sacks or birdcages. (*Special license required,* 50c.)

TROUTDALE, 177.7 *m.* (50 alt., 227 pop.), is a trade center for a fruit and vegetable producing area specializing in celery growing. Between truck gardens and dairy farms, US 30 crosses the bottom lands of the widening Columbia Valley to FAIRVIEW, **180.3** *m.* (114 alt., 266 pop.), and past orchards, bulb farms, and suburban homes to PARKROSE, **185.2** *m.*

PORTLAND, **192.7** *m.* (32 alt., 301,815 pop.) (*see PORT-LAND*).

Points of Interest: Skidmore Fountain, Oregon Historical Society Museum, Art Museum, Portland Public Market, Sanctuary of our Sorrowful Mother, and many others.

Portland is at junction with US 99 (*see TOUR 2a*), State 8 (*see TOUR 8*), State 50 (*see TOUR 4A, US 99W* (*see TOUR 10*).

Section c. Portland to Astoria, 104.5 m.

US 30 leaves PORTLAND, **0** *m.*, on NW. Vaughn St. and St. Helens Road, a part of the Lower Columbia Highway, and passes through a busy industrial district along Portland's lower harbor. Wharves line the Willamette River bank (R) and factories and warehouses occupy the river flats.

The highway passes under the west approach to the ST. JOHNS BRIDGE, **6.5** *m.*, an attractive suspension bridge high above the river.

LINNTON, **7.9** *m.*, a part of Portland since 1915, was founded in the 1840's by Peter H. Burnett, later, first governor of California. He visioned the tiny town as the future metropolis of the Columbia Valley but Portland drew most of the shipping trade and Linnton languished. At present it is an important industrial district of the city; large lumber shipments leave from its wharves.

At **12.7** *m.* is a junction with the Burlington Ferry approach, a plank viaduct leading to a ferry (*free*) crossing Willamette Slough.

Right on this viaduct to the ferry landing, **0.5** *m.*, off which is SAUVIE ISLAND (850 pop.), which retains much of its pastoral charm. Numerous fishermen and duck hunters frequent the lakes and swales of this popular recreational area. Land of island is quite fertile; bulb culture and truck gardening have become increasingly important in recent years.

Frederic Homer Balch wrote in his Indian romance, *The Bridge of the Gods*: "The chief of the Willamettes gathered on Wappatto Island, from time immemorial the council-ground of the tribes. The white man has changed its name to 'Sauvie' island; but its wonderful beauty is unchangeable. Lying at the mouth of the Willamette River and extending many miles down the Columbia, rich in wide meadows and crystal lakes, its interior dotted with majestic oaks and its shores fringed with cottonwoods, around it the blue and sweeping rivers, the wooded hills, and the far white snow peaks,—it is the most picturesque spot in Oregon."

In spite of the fact that the island has a comparatively small population with neither stores nor shops and with but one small sawmill to represent the industrial interests, it is by no means isolated. Many people go there, so many that the small ferry is crowded to capacity. Because of its numerous lakes, ponds and bayous, the island is a popular haunt for duck hunters, and many club houses dot its length. Fishermen seek the shores of the Gilbert River for the crappies, catfish, black and yellow bass, sunfish and perch, that lurk in these sluggish waters. Men grown weary of the turbulence of mountain streams and the elusive antics of the fighting trout, find peace and relaxation in the lazy swirl of the waters and the bobbing of the cork-float when a channel-cat or crappie takes the bait.

The first white men to visit the island as far as known were the Lewis and Clark expedition on November 4, 1805. "We landed on the left bank of the river, at a village of twenty-five houses; all of these were thatched with straw and built of bark, except one which was about fifty feet long, built of boards. . . . this village contains about two hundred men of the Skilloot nation, who seemed well provided with canoes, of which there were at least fifty-two, and some of them very large, drawn up in front of the village. . . ." The exploring party stopped a short distance below the village for dinner. "Soon after," Clark recorded, "Several canoes of Indians from the village above came down, dressed for the purpose as I supposed of Paying us a friendly visit, they had scarlet & blue blankets Salor Jackets, overalls, Shirts and hats independent of their usial dress; the most of them had either Muskets or pistols and tin flasks to hold their powder, Those fellows we found assumeing and disagreeable, however we Smoked with them and treated them with every attention & friendship.

"dureing the time we were at dinner those fellows Stold my pipe Tomahawk which they were Smoking with, I immediately serched every man and the canoes, but could find nothing of my Tomahawk, while Serching for the Tomahawk one of those Scoundals Stole a cappoe (*coat*) of one of our interperters, which was found Stuffed under the root of a tree, near the place they Sat, we became much displeased with those fellows, which they discovered and moved off on their return home to their village."

In 1832 an epidemic decimated the native population, and Dr. McLoughlin removed the survivors to the mainland and burned many of the straw and board huts of the settlements.

In 1834 Captain Nathanial J. Wyeth built a trading post on the island and named it Fort William. "This Wappato island which I have selected for our establishment," he wrote, "consists of woodland and prairie and on it there is considerable deer and those who could spare time to hunt might live well but mortality has carried off to a man its inhabitants and there is nothing to attest that they ever existed except their decaying houses, their graves and their unburied bones of which there are heaps." Wyeth set his coopers to making barrels to carry salted salmon to Boston. However, his trading activities met with such persistent opposition from the Hudson's Bay Company that in 1836 he was forced to abandon the enterprise.

In 1841 McLoughlin established a dairy here, placing Jean Baptiste Sauvie, a superannuated trapper, in charge. The place has since borne the name of the old dairyman.

The hills (L) recede and the highway enters the Scappoose Plains, a fertile district devoted to potato culture, truck gardening, and dairying. SCAPPOOSE (Ind. *gravelly plain*), **20.9** *m.* (56 alt., 248 pop.), is on the site of an old trading post and farm of the Hudson's Bay Company, under the charge of Thomas McKay. Chief Kazeno, mentioned in the annals of the Astorians and of many other later writers, had his village close by. It was here that the great Indian highway, later the Hudson's Bay trail between the Columbia River and the upper Willamette Valley, had its beginning. When Lieut. W. R. Broughton of the Royal Navy, visited the Columbia River in H. M. S. *Chatham* of Captain Vancouver's squadron in 1792, he found at Warrior Rock, on Wappato (Sauvie) Island opposite Scappoose, Indians with copper swords and iron battle axes. These Indians said that they had obtained these axes from the other Indians many moons to the eastward. Scappoose appears to have been a great trading center for the Indians on the lower Columbia during many centuries. The virulent disease which almost wiped out the Indians of the Sauvie Island region began among the Indians at Scappoose Bay and was attributed to "bad medicine" administered by Captain Dominis of the brig *Owyhee,* which had been trading in the river.

The first white man to settle on Scappoose Plain was James Bates, an American sailor, who probably deserted from the *Owyhee* in 1829. The town of Scappoose had a slow growth and was not incorporated until July 13, 1921. In 1934 fire destroyed several buildings. Today it is a trading center for a prosperous farming community with large potato warehouses and a pickle factory.

MILTON CREEK, 28.5 *m.,* was named for the old town of Milton founded in the late forties at its confluence with Willamette Slough. The Oregon *Spectator,* in its issue of May 16, 1850, carried the following advertisement: "TOWN OF MILTON—Is situated on the lower branch of the Willamette River, just above its junction with the Columbia. The advantages of its location speak for themselves. All we ask is for our friends to call and see the place. For particulars apply to Crosby & Smith, Portland and Milton." A few months later the editor of the *Spectator* wrote: "The town of Milton one mile and a half above St. Helen's is fast improving and may look forward to its future importance. . . . We are told that the flats or bottom lands which occasionally overflow, are of great extent and produce abundant grass for the grazing of immense flocks and herds, besides offering the opportunity to cut large quantities of hay." A few years later, waters flooded the town and its business was gradually absorbed by near-by St. Helens.

ST. HELENS, 28.6 *m.* (98 alt., 3,944 pop.), a river port, is also a market and court town. Its manufacturing plants produce insulating board, pulp and paper, lumber, and dairy products.

The site of St. Helens was first known as Wyeth's Rock for the early trader, Nathaniel Wyeth, who had built a temporary post here in 1834. Captain H. M. Knighton took up the site as a donation land claim and in 1847 laid out the town as a competitor of the newly established Portland, which he contemptuously referred to as "Little Stump Town." It is said that Knighton named the town both to honor his native city of St. Helens, England, and for the beautiful mountain that rises a few miles to the northeast. According to some early records the vicinity was also referred to as Plymouth Rock or Plymouth and the earliest election district established here was named the Plymouth precinct. The earliest school was established in 1853 by the Reverend Thomas Condon, a noted scientist, who later became professor of geology at the University of Oregon. He added to his small salary as pastor of the St. Helens Congregational church by his teaching. The KNIGHTON HOUSE, 155 S. 4th St., was built in 1847 with lumber shipped around Cape Horn from Bath, Maine. Many of the town's buildings, including the COLUMBIA COUNTY COURT HOUSE, at First St. on the river bank, are built of stone from local quarries.

DEER ISLAND, 34.2 *m.* (48 alt., 75 pop.), is a small community opposite the island of the same name visited in 1805 and again in 1806 by Lewis and Clark. The naming of Deer Island is thus accounted for in the report of Lewis and Clark: "We left camp at an early hour, and by nine o'clock reached an old Indian village. . . . Here we found a party of our men whom we had sent on yesterday to hunt, and who now returned after killing seven deer in the course of the morning out of upwards of a hundred which they had seen."

GOBLE, 40.6 *m.* (25 alt., 91 pop.), is at the former landing of the Northern Pacific Railway Ferry at Kalama, Washington, before the building of the railroad bridge between Vancouver and Portland.

LITTLE JACK FALLS, 43.9 *m.* (125 alt.), tumbles over a precipice beside the highway.

RAINIER, 47.5 *m.* (23 alt., 1,353 pop.), named for Mount Rainier, which is often visible to the northeast, was an important stop in the days of river commerce. The town was founded by Charles E. Fox in 1851. First called Eminence, its name was later changed to Fox's Landing and finally to Rainier. In 1854 F. M. Warren erected a large steam sawmill and began producing lumber for the homes and other buildings of the settlers. Rainier was incorporated in 1885. At Rainier is a toll-bridge connecting with Longview, Washington (*car and driver,* 80c; *maximum,* $1).

From the winding curves of RAINIER HILL (671 alt.) there is a fine view of Longview, Washington, and the narrow roadway of the bridge spanning the river, hundreds of feet below. The summit is reached at 50.6 *m.*

Descending, the highway crosses ubiquitous BEAVER CREEK, 51.4 *m.* Within the next 15 miles westward the road spans the stream a dozen times. The country now presents wide expanses of logged-off land.

At 61.7 *m.* is a junction with a gravel road.

Right on this road to QUINCY, 1 *m.* (18 alt., 303 pop.), center of a drained and diked area of the Columbia River lowlands; L. here 3 *m.* on a dirt road to OAK POINT. The Winship brothers of Boston attempted to establish a trading post and settlement at this place which is known as Fanny's Bottom. On May 26, 1810, while Astor was still maturing his plans for the Pacific Fur Company, Captain Nathan Winship arrived in the Columbia River with the ship *Albatross*. He began construction of a two-story log fort and planted a garden. However, the attempt was abortive. Robert Stuart, of the Astorians, wrote in his diary under date of July 1, 1812: "About 2 hours before sunset we reached the establishment made by Captain Winship of Boston in the spring of 1810—It is situate on a beautiful high bank on the South side & enchantingly diversified with white oaks, Ash and Cottonwood and Alder but of rather a diminutive size—here he intended leaving a Mr. Washington with a party of men, but whether with the view of making a permanent settlement or merely for trading with the Indians until his return from the coast, the natives were unable to tell, the water however rose so high as to inundate a house he had already constructed, when a dispute arose between him and the Hellwits, by his putting several of them in Irons on the supposition that they were of the Chee-hee-lash nation, who had some time previous cut off a Schooner belonging to the Russian establishment at New Archangel, by the Governor of which place he was employed to secure any of the Banditti who perpetrated this horrid act—The Hellwits made formidable preparations by eng-ging auxiliaries &c. for the release of their relations by force, which coming to the Captain's knowledge, as well as the error he had committed, the Captives were released, every person embarked, and left the Columbia without loss of time—"

CLATSKANIE (cor. Ind., *Tlatskanie*), **64.8** *m.* (16 alt., 739 pop.), bears the name of a small tribe of Indians that formerly inhabited the region. The town is on the Clatskanie River near its confluence with the Columbia and is surrounded by rich bottom lands devoted to dairying and raising vegetables for canning. In 1852 E. G. Bryant took up the land upon which a settlement grew up with the name of Bryantsville. In 1870 the name of the town was changed to Clatskanie and it was incorporated as a city in 1891. State Fisheries Station No. 5, for restocking the river with fingerling salmon, is at this point.

At **65.2** *m.* is the junction with State 47.

Left on State 47 over a mountainous grade into the Nehalem Valley and across a second ridge into the Tualatin Valley to FOREST GROVE and a junction with State 8 (*see TOUR* 8) at 56.1 *m.*

WESTPORT, **74.5** *m.* (32 alt., 450 pop.), is one of the many lumbering and fishing towns scattered along the waters of the Columbia.

The highway ascends the Coast Range in a series of hairpin turns to CLATSOP CREST, **79.7** *m.,* overlooking the Columbia River and the country beyond. In the immediate foreground is long, flat PUGET ISLAND, where grain fields and fallow lands weave patterns of green and gray, and sluggish streams form silvery canals. Although the island is close to the Oregon shore, it lies within the State of Washington. It was discovered in 1792 by Lieut. Broughton of the British Navy, who named it for Lieut. Peter Puget.

US 30 twists down to HUNT CREEK, **80.7** *m.,* then climbs a spur from which a desolate waste of logged-over land extends in all directions. A high, sharply etched mountain (L), with sides bare of vegetation, shows the results of unrestricted timber cutting.

At **92.5** *m.* is a junction with an improved road.

Right here to SVENSON, **0.7** *m.* (10 alt., 100 pop.), less a town than a series of fishing wharves, extending into the Columbia River, which broadens to a width of five miles. Tied up at these docks are many fishing crafts. These small boats, their engines hooded for protection from spray and weather, ride restlessly in the tide's movement. Net-drying racks stretch at length over the salt-soaked planking, where fishermen mend their linen nets between catches.

It is from these docks, and the many that closely line the river's south shore from this point to Astoria, a distance of eight miles, that a large portion of the salmon fishing fleet puts out.

The principal method of taking fish in the Columbia is by gill-netting. The gill-netter works with a power boat and a net from 1,200 to 1,500 feet long. On one edge of the net are floats to hold it up and on the other edge weights to hold it down and vertical in the water. Fish swarming upstream strike the net and become entangled in the meshes, held by their gills. The gill net fishermen usually operate at night; at such times the river presents a fascinating spectacle, dotted with lights as the boats drift with the current.

Seining operations are employed on sand shoals, some of them far out in the wide Columbia estuary. One end of the seine is held on shore while the other end is taken out into the river by a power boat, swung around on a circular course and brought back to shore. As the loaded net comes in, teams of horses haul it into the shallows, where the catch is gaffed into boats. Seining crews and horses live in houses and barns on the seining grounds. Fishing crews often work in water to their shoulders.

Trolling boats are larger than gill-netters and cross the Columbia bar to ply the ocean waters in their search for schools of salmon, and for sturgeon, which are taken by hook and line. They carry ice to preserve their cargo, as they are sometimes out for several days.

Mysterious are the life and habits of the salmon which provide the lower Columbia with perhaps its main industry. Spawned in the upper reaches of the river and its tributaries, the young fish go to sea and disappear, returning four years later to reproduce and die where they were spawned. Each May large runs of salmon come into the river and fight their way against the current; each autumn the young horde descends. Full-grown King Chinook salmon weigh as much as 75 pounds each.

Until 1866, the salmon were sold fresh or pickled whole in barrels for shipping. In that year the tin container came into use. By 1874, the packing industry had become an extensive commercial enterprise. Artificial propagation, to prevent fishing out of the stream, began in 1887. Today, about 3,500 fishermen are engaged in various methods of taking fish in the Columbia River district, and about 1,800 boats of various sizes and types are used. It has been estimated that as many as 20,000 persons now depend upon the industry for a living. The value of the annual production, most of which is canned at the processing plants at Astoria and elsewhere on either side of the river, is estimated at ten million dollars.

US 30 crosses the little JOHN DAY RIVER, 97.9 *m.,* another stream named for the unfortunate Astorian of whom Robert Stuart says as he camped a few miles up the Columbia: "evident symptoms of mental derangement made their appearance in John Day one of my Hunters who for a day or two previous seemed as if restless and unwell but now uttered the most incoherent absurd and unconnected sentences. . . . it was the opinion of all the Gentlemen that it would be highly imprudent to suffer him to proceed any farther for in a moment when not sufficiently watched he might embroil us with the natives, who on all occasions he reviled by the appellations Rascal, Robber &c &c &c—"

Nearing the western sea that they had been sent to find, Lewis and Clark recorded enthusiastically, on November 7, 1805, "Ocian in view. O the Joy." On the following day he wrote: "Some rain all day at intervals, we are all wet and disagreeable, as we have been for several days past, and our present Situation a verry disagreeable one in as much, as we have not leavel land Sufficient for an encampment and for our baggage to lie cleare of the tide, the High hills jutting in so close and steep that we cannot retreat back, and the water too salt to be used, added to this the waves are increasing to Such a hight that we cannot move from this place, in this Situation we are compelled to form our camp between the Hits of the Ebb and flood tides, and rase our baggage on logs." On the 9th he wrote: "our camp entirely under water dureing the hight of the tide, every man as wet as water could make them all the last night and to day all day as the rain continued all the day, at 4 oClock P M the wind shifted about to the S.W. and blew with great violence immediately from the Ocean for about two hours, notwithstanding the disagreeable Situation of our party all wet and cold (and one which they have experienced for Several days past) they are chearfull and anxious to See further into the Ocian, The water of the river being too Salt to use we are obliged to make use of rain water. Some of the party not accustomed to Salt water has made too free use of it on them it acts as a pergitive. At this dismal point we must Spend another night as the wind & waves are too high to preceed."

At **100.7** is TONGUE POINT STATE PARK; here is a junction with a gravel road.

Right on this road to TONGUE POINT LIGHTHOUSE SERVICE BASE, **0.7** *m*. Built on a projection extending into the wide mouth of the Columbia River, this base is the repair depot for the buoys that guide navigators along the watercourses of the two states. Tongue Point was so named by Broughton in 1792. A proposal to establish a naval air base at this point, agitated for many years, has been at last approved by Congress (1939) and funds appropriated for beginning construction.

On November 10 the Lewis and Clark party, unable to go far because of the wind, camped on the northern shore nearly opposite this point. The camp was made on drift logs that floated at high tide. "nothing to eate but Pounded fish," Clark noted. "that night it Rained verry hard. . . . and continues this morning, the wind has luled and the waves are not high." The party moved on but after they had gone ten miles the wind rose and they had to camp again on drift logs. Neighboring Indians appeared with fish. The camp was moved on the 12th to a slightly less dangerous place and Clark attempted to explore the nearby land on the 13th: "rained all day moderately. I am wet &C.&C." On the 14th: "The rain &c. which has continued without a longer intermition than 2 hours at a time for ten days past has destroy'd the robes and rotted nearly one half the fiew clothes the party has particularly the leather clothes." Clark was losing his patience by the 15th; even the pounded fish brought from the falls was becoming mouldy. This was the eleventh day of rain and "the most disagreeable time I have experienced confined on the tempiest coast wet, where I can neither git out to hunt, return to a better situation, or proceed on." But they did manage to move to a somewhat better camp that day and the men, salvaging boards from a deserted Indian camp, made rude shelters. The Indians began to give them too much attention, however, "I told those people. . . . that if any one of their nation stole any thing that the Senten'l whome they Saw near our baggage with his gun would most certainly Shute them, they all promised not to tuch a thing, and if any of their womin or bad boys took any thing to return it imediately and chastise them for it. I treated those people with great distance."

The party moved on to a place on the northern shore of Baker Bay, where they remained for about ten days. From this point Clark went overland to explore, inviting those who wanted to see more of the "Ocian" to accompany him. Nine men, including York, the negro, still had enough energy to go.

On the 21st: "An old woman & Wife to a Cheif of the Chunnooks came and made a Camp near ours. She brought with her 6 young Squars (*her daughters & nieces*) I believe for the purpose of Gratifying the passions of the men of our party and receiving for those indulgience Such Small (presents) as She (the old woman) though proper to accept of.

"These people appear to View Sensuality as a Necessary evel, and do not appear to abhor it as a Crime in the unmarried State. The young females are fond of the attention of our men and appear to meet the sincere approbation of their friends and connections, for thus obtaining their favours."

Here the explorers had further evidence that English and American sailors had previously visited the Columbia. The tattooed name, "J. B. Bowman," was seen on the arm of a Chinook squaw. "Their legs are also picked with defferent figures," wrote Clark. "all those are considered by the natives of this quarter as handsom deckerations, and a woman without those deckorations is Considered as among the lower Class."

Three days later Lewis and Clark held a meeting to decide whether the party should go back to the falls, remain on the north shore or cross to the south side of the river for the winter. The members with one exception voted to move to the south shore, where they set up a temporary camp on Tongue Point. From this place they hunted a suitable site for the permanent camp (*see TOUR 3a*).

ASTORIA, **104.5** *m.* (12 alt., 10,349 pop.) (*see ASTORIA*).

Points of Interest: Fort Astoria, City Hall, Grave of D. McTavish, Flavel Mansion, Union Fishermen's Cooperative Packing Plant, Port of Astoria Terminal, and others.

In Astoria US 30 meets US 101 (*see TOUR 3a*).

Tour 1A

Baker—Salisbury—Hereford—Junction with US 28; 46.1 *m.*, State 7.

Gravel road.
Local stages between Baker and Unity; Baker and Bourne.
Hotels in towns and camps.

State 7 penetrates one of the richest mining regions of early Oregon. Tucked away in canyons or stark against mountainsides are the few crumbling buildings of old camps and abandoned towns. The discovery of gold in Griffin's Gulch in the fall of 1861 brought thousands east from the Willamette Valley and up from California to pan the streams and pluck nuggets from pockets in decaying ledges. In the 1890's came a second period of activity, a hardrock boom no less intense than the earlier placer fever. After the early white miners had left for fields with richer strikes hundreds of Chinese poured into the region to pan the tailings. Farmers came into the Powder River bottoms as the gold played out and the mining camps disappeared.

The western part of the route crosses a semi-arid range country along the headwaters of Burnt River.

State 7 branches south from US 30 (*see TOUR 1a*) at Baker, **0** *m.* and crosses the tracks of the Sumpter Valley Railroad, the state's last narrow-gauge line. Constructed in the 1890's to develop the timber holdings of several Mormons, it was an important factor in the growth of the district. A two-car train with a wood-burning locomotive called the "Stump Dodger" made the run for many years between Baker and

Prairie City. Passenger service has been discontinued and only logs and freight are hauled over the line as far as Austin.

In GRIFFIN CREEK, 2.3 *m.* Oregon gold was first discovered on October 23, 1861. Henry Griffin of Portland had come into the Malheur River region with a party of gold-seekers searching for the fabled Blue Bucket Mine (*see TALL TALES & LEGENDS*). Though most of the members had become discouraged and turned homeward, Griffin and three companions had continued northward toward the headwaters of the Powder River. While his companions were making a noon camp here Griffin shoveled gravel into his pan and washed out the handful of coarse gold that started the stampede.

At **7** *m.* is the junction with a dirt road.

Right on this road along Blue Canyon Creek into the heart of the old mining region. At 2.6 *m.* (L) many spearheads and arrow-heads have been found. The SITE OF AUBURN (R), 3.3 *m.,* is marked by a grove of weeping willows, a few plum trees, and a single apple tree. After gold was discovered here in 1861 log cabins were built and a blockhouse was erected as a protection against Indians. The town, named for Auburn, Maine, began to mushroom in 1862 when droves of prospectors rushed in. It was the metropolis of the mining region, with 1,270 claims having been recorded within a year for the surrounding hilly, stream-gouged area, so rich that two Frenchmen panned about $100,000 worth of gold dust in the fall of 1862. When Baker County was created in the autumn of that year Auburn became its seat.

At its zenith, in 1863-64, Auburn had a population of 5,000 and was the second largest town in the state. It was wide open and became a magnet for gamblers, bunco men and their ilk. But the town had this code—a wanton killing would not be tolerated. Therefore French Pete, a miner, was hanged on Gallows Hill (L) for putting strychnine in his partner's flour, and Spanish Tom died the same way for wielding a Bowie knife. In later years many Chinese came in, to operate laundries, restaurants, and gambling houses, and also to garner any gold that had been overlooked by the careless white man.

An account book kept by a merchant from June 29 to October 7, 1868 listed these prices: four pounds of sugar, $1.00; one pound of tea, $1.25; one sack of flour, $2.25; five pounds of beans, $.80. Liquor prices were: whiskey $1.50 a quart; brandy and gin, $1.25. The only toothbrush was sold for $.50. The Chinese were heavy buyers of rice, ginger, beanstick, tea, and all kinds of dried or preserved fish.

After the discovery of gold in Idaho in 1867, Auburn began to decline. The next year the county seat was moved to Baker, and one by one the buildings were deserted; later they were torn down by ranchers and carted away for firewood. Nearby were three cemeteries, one for whites and two for Chinese. One of the latter was washed away in a "second washing" for gold.

The site of the LITTLEFIELD HOMESTEAD, 3.8 *m.,* the first taken up in Baker County, is marked by a grove of cottonwood trees. David S. Littlefield was a member of the first gold-discovery party.

At **9** *m.* State 7 forms a junction with a gravel road.

Right on this road along the north bank of Powder River to SUMPTER, **19.6** *m.* (4,424 alt.), an almost deserted town of the "hard-rock" mining era. In 1902 an editorial in the local paper asked: "Sumpter, golden Sumpter, what glorious future awaits thee?" The answer today is a U. S. Forest station, one store with a pool hall, and the crumbled remnants of a business section that once stretched seven blocks up the steep hill. The town was so named because three North Carolinians, who chose a farmsite at this point in 1862, called their log cabin Fort Sumpter—a misspelling of "Sumter." For many years the camp existed by grace of the few white miners who explored the district and hundreds of Chinese who followed them. With the coming of the railroad in 1896 and the opening of ore veins on the Blue Mountains, Sumpter became a city of 3,000 inhabitants. The total yield of the Sumpter quadrangle from both placer and deep mines has been nearly sixteen million dollars. Names of the most productive mines were Mammoth, Goldbug-Grizzly, Bald Mountain, Golden Eagle, May Queen, Ibex, Baby McKee, Belle of Baker, Quebec, White Star, Gold Ridge, and Bonanza. Twelve miles of mine tunnels were in operation at one time. The town even had an opera house where fancy dress balls were held, but the sheep-men of the region were not welcome at them. The vigilante committee warned sheepmen away from the gold country on the threat of fixing them up "until the Angels could pan lead out of their souls."

The story of Sumpter after 1916 is almost a blank. The few people who remained became accustomed to the sound of crumbling walls and to using doors and window frames for firewood. The smelter erected during the last days of the boom still stands. Pack rats live in the vaults of two former banks.

Right from Sumpter, 6.7 *m.* along Cracker Creek to the town of BOURNE, (5,397 alt., 1 pop.), the smallest incorporated town of the state. It came into existence as the lively gold camp of Cracker in the 1870's, and in its latter days, as Bourne, was notorious for the number of wild-cat ventures. Many persons in the East were inveigled into disastrous investment by gilt-edged prospectuses from the town. Two weekly newspapers were published here by the same firm, one giving factual information for home consumption; the other, contained glowing accounts of rich strikes and fabulous mining activities. The exodus from the camp occurred about 1906, when most of the producing mines were closed. A cloudburst in 1937 washed down many buildings and changed the course of Cracker Creek.

A dazzling white house on the hillside is a monument to one of Oregon's most flagrant mining swindles. Surrounded by terraced grounds, with crushed-quartz pathways leading up to it the house still presents a striking appearance. Piles of quartz tailings from the mines rise in rose-colored pyramids in the formerly landscaped lawns. In the living room is a massive fireplace of rose and white gold-bearing quartz. A stairway of peeled and stained logs leads up six feet from the living rooms to a dining floor. The glass has long since disappeared from the huge windows, the doors have been removed, and only shreds of the expensive floor coverings remain. Wall-paper brought from England has been torn from the walls, though here and there ragged and faded remnants flutter in the breeze.

Designed and built by J. Wallace White, the mansion was erected in 1906 from proceeds of the Sampson Company, Ltd., of New York, London and Bourne, a wildcat mining organization that fleeced hundreds of their savings. White continued his operations for many years, amassing a large fortune, though he was eventually arrested in the East for using the mails to defraud.

West of Sumpter is GRANITE, 35.6 *m.* (4,688 alt.), where a Grand Hotel, an ornate three-story building with thirty rooms, still stands—empty and dilapi-dated. Granite was first called Independence because the first settlers, prospectors from California, arrived on July 4, 1862. When application was made for a post office at Independence it was found that there was already a post office of this name in the state and the governor chose the present name. Unlike many of the mining camps of eastern Oregon, Granite relied more on trade and on its distributing and shipping business than on the pay-day sprees of miners. But when the many mines were worked out the town dwindled and disappeared. Deserted tunnels, jagged heaps of tailings, dilapidated cabins, occasional graves, remind the few inhabitants of the days that they still hope may come again. Only tourists and fishing and hunting parties serve to keep the place alive. In 1938 Granite's one general store still had in stock 24 derby hats, a number of black corsets with beaded tops, and a few dozen gaily-colored women's garters with spangles.

South of SALISBURY, 9.2 *m.* (3,675 alt., 4 pop.), a railroad station. State 7 winds through the yellow jackpines of the WHITMAN NATIONAL FOREST to DOOLEY MOUNTAIN SUMMIT, 17 *m.* (5,392 alt.), which commands wide vistas of the Blue Mountains. The Dooley Mountain Toll Road, joins State 7 at **17.5** *m.* (L). It was named for John Dooley, an emigrant who purchased the road from B. F. Koontz, of Baker.

Reaching Burnt River the road swerves westward through the BURNT RIVER GAME REFUGE, **26.1** *m.,* to HEREFORD, **35.6** *m.* (3,658 alt., 32 pop.), named for a Hereford bull of renown in the extensive range country the hamlet serves. In 1885 the Oregon Horse & Land Company, operating in the district, imported 109 Percheron horses from France for breeding purposes—47 males and 62 females. The outfit was the largest operating in Oregon at the time; in 1885 it branded about 11,000 horses.

Left from Hereford to the DIAMOND-AND-A-HALF DUDE RANCH, **4.5** *m.,* at the southern edge of the Whitman National Forest. This ranch, established by the Whites shortly after their arrival in 1869, is still in the hands of the family. Visitors are regaled with tall tales by the wranglers, ride herd with the cowhands, and go on hunting and fishing trips into the Blue Mountains.

At **46.1** is the junction with US 28 (*see TOUR 6a*), at a point **1.7** miles northwest of Unity.

Tour 1B

Baker—Richland—Robinette — Copperfield — Homestead (Cuprum, Idaho); **84.3** *m.* State 86 and unnamed road.

Gravel road in lower sections, elsewhere dirt.
Limited accommodations, in towns.

East of the broad uplands of the upper Powder River and the fertile Baker Valley, State 86 crosses the broken terrain to the river's confluence with the Snake; paralleling that stream for thirty miles, to a terminus at the interstate bridge into Idaho at the opening of the Grand Canyon of the Snake (*see TOUR 1C*).

Tucked in numerous gulches along the tributaries of Powder River are sites and ruins of towns and camps of the gold rush days of the 1860's. Here gold was at a premium, human life and morals at a discount. Such law as existed was administered by officials subservient to the proprietors of saloons and dives, and although recorded killings were few, "accidental" deaths and "suicides" were not infrequent. For a brief period before 1914 the boom town of Copperfield, never a mining town as its name might imply, revived a shoddy counterpart of those early towns. In former days when millions in gold were mined the area was populous, but with the exhaustion of the rich sands, it became for a time practically deserted. Although only a few of the mines are now being worked, some of these are large producers. In the region are also considerable deposits of silver and copper.

State 86 branches east from the junction with US 30, (*see TOUR 1a*) in Baker, 0 *m.* and passes through a district of small truck farms and alfalfa ranches in the Powder River Valley.

At **2.2** *m.* is a junction with State 203, a graveled road.

Left on State 203 to the BAKER AIRPORT (R), **2.1** *m.,* used by transcontinental planes, although not a regular stop.

PONDOSA, **20.9** *m.* (3,200 alt., 300 pop.), is a lumber town, and MEDICAL SPRINGS, **22.3** *m.* (3,388 alt., 40 pop.), is a commercial resort on the edge of the WHITMAN NATIONAL FOREST. State 203 continues to a junction with US 30 in UNION **42.7** *m.* (*see TOUR 1a*).

East of Baker Valley State 86 passes over a low saddle formerly traversed by the Old Oregon Trail.

At **9.6** *m.* is the junction with a dirt road.

Right on this road to the VIRTUE MINE, **3** *m.,* first of the gold bearing quartz mines in the Powder River district, and one of the richest. The first ore was carried by horseback several hundred miles to The Dalles and other water transportation points. James W. Virtue, pioneer mine operator and banker, was its owner for many years. Between its discovery in 1862 and its final shutdown in 1924 the mine produced $2,200,000. The shaft house on a small hill is a conspicuous landmark. Scattered over Virtue flats a level stretch of arid sagebrush land between the mine and the highway are tumbled-down farm buildings, that recall the shattered hopes of homesteaders who profitably dry-farmed the land during the period of high prices just after the World War but were forced to abandon their claims when prices fell. It is planned to reclaim these flats by irrigation.

At **17.6** *m.* on State 86 is the junction with a dirt road.

Left here to KEATING, **3** *m.* (2,650 alt., 68 pop.), at the confluence of Ruckles Creek with the Powder River, headquarters of the Thief Valley Irrigation District, a Federal project supplying a small section of the lower Powder River Valley. Thief Valley was so named because a horse thief was hanged there in 1864.

At **20.7** *m* on State 86 is the junction with the Middle Bridge Road.

Left on this road, crossing the Powder River, to SPARTA, **12** *m.* (4,120 alt., 25 pop.), remnant of a mining town founded in the 1860's. The Sparta mines once had an annual output of several million dollars, but when the richest pannings had been taken miners pulled up stakes and sought other fields. Following close on their heels, came bands of Chinese, who had been released from construction work with the completion of the first transcontinental railroad. They scoured the gulches and gullies gleaning the tailings, but were continually harassed, robbed and even murdered by those who objected to the presence of the Orientals. This bad feeling culminated in their forcible ejection from the diggings by a band of "stalwarts," who were dissatisfied with the mild provisions of the Chinese Exclusion Act. Only a few weathered skeletons of shacks and false-front shops stand on Main Street. The hillsides and gulches are scarred with prospect holes and piles of tailings. The shaggy lynching pine remains, and the "arrow tree" still points the way to Sparta.

A ROADSIDE FOUNTAIN (R) is at 30.4 *m.* From the center of a large flat-surfaced granite boulder spouts a 12-foot, geyser-like stream of water that falls into a basin chiseled in the rock. The water is always fresh and cold, and never freezes.

At 45.8 *m.* is the junction with a dirt road.

Left here up Eagle Creek to NEW BRIDGE, 2.5 *m.* (2,400 alt., 38 pop.), named by Joseph Gale, (*see TOUR* 8), who spent his last years here, and was the first postmaster. He was buried on his old homesite, conspicuous because of the profusion of lilac bushes that he planted. His home has been moved and rebuilt.

RICHLAND, 46.1 *m.* (2,213 alt., 212 pop.), named for the fertility of the surrounding soil, is the trade center of the farmers and dairymen of Eagle Valley.

At 52.6 *m.* the route diverges from State 86.

Left on State 86 over winding grades to HALFWAY, 11.1 *m.* (2,653 alt., 351 pop.), in Pine Valley, an isolated upland farming country hemmed in by barren hills. The town has its own water system, electric light and power plant, cooperative creamery, and is the home of the annual Baker County Fair.
Left from Halfway, 5.5 *m.* on a dirt road to CARSON, (3,355 alt., 90 pop.), and CORNUCOPIA, 11.5 *m.* (4,800 alt., 10 pop.), a town described in the September, 1885, issue of *West Shore* as having "one nice frame house," and many "tents and log cabins, built rather hastily to accommodate the first rush. The town can boast of *five saloons, one store,* two restaurants, blacksmith shop, barber shop, butcher shop and livery stable; also a lodging house, which, while neatly kept for a young town, is hardly patronized enough, as the traveling class in such camps objects seriously to too close confinement and prefers camp life. . . ." The Cornucopia Mine has a 6,300 foot shaft and from its 30 miles of underground workings comes one-half of Oregon's gold output. Opened in the early 1880's the mine has produced many millions of dollars worth of gold and silver.

Diverging (R) from State 86, at 52.5 *m.,* the route continues down the widening canyon of the lower Powder River to its confluence with the Snake, 55 *m.* (1,935 alt.), then swings along the west bank of that stream to ROBINETTE, 56.5 *m.* (1,900 alt., 46 pop.), the northern terminus of a branch line of the Union Pacific Railroad, formerly extending about 25 miles farther along the Snake. The abandoned roadbed has been converted into a highway.

The OXBOW POWER PLANT, 77.3 *m.* (R), in a large bend of the Snake, supplies power and light for a wide area. The once flourishing town of COPPERFIELD, 77.9 *m.* (1,725 alt., 8 pop.), is near the lower curve of the Oxbow in the Snake River. This town was laid out in 1908 by four Baker speculators because of the presence of large crews of men engaged in building the power plant to the south and a railroad tunnel. These promoters bought a quarter section between the railroad and the power plant, cleared large sums in the first six months by selling lots and retired from the scene. The boom town soon had every conceivable type of business, both legal and illegal, with the latter in the ascendency. The inhabitants aped the wickedness of the mining towns of the 1860's and boasted of it. The railroad construction gangs often clashed in "free-for-alls." It is said that one conflict that lasted more than an hour was accompanied by the tinny tunes from the mechanical piano in Barney Goldberg's saloon. Rocks and beer bottles, and other missiles, as well as fists, were used, but when truce was finally called from sheer exhaustion, enemies drank from the same bottle, bound up each others wounds, and set the date for the next encounter.

The leading citizens of Copperfield including the mayor and the members of the council either ran saloons or were financially interested in them. A few peaceful citizens finally tired of the disorder and appealed to the governor for help. He ordered the Baker County authorities to clean up Copperfield by Christmas; but they refused to act. On New Year's Day, 1914, Governor West dramatically sent his small secretary in with a declaration of martial law, accompanied by an "army of invasion" consisting of five national guardsmen, and two penitentiary guards commanded by a colonel of the National Guard— who was also warden of the state penitentiary. Notified of the approach of the "army" with a female representative of the governor the mayor ordered the town decorated for a glorious welcome. Flags and bunting hung in the streets, and all bars were embellished with pink and white ribbons and such flowers as were available. The entire town was lined up to greet the train. Accompanied by her "army," "war" correspondents, photographers, and almost the entire populace, the secretary marched at once to the town hall, mounted a platform, gave the governor's orders for the resignation of all officials connected with the saloon business; said that if they refused she would hand over the governor's declaration of martial law, disarm everyone in town, close all saloons, burn all gambling equipment, and ship all liquors and bar fixtures out of town. The officials turned down her demands, and the secretary immediately commenced to carry out her threats. The audience was silent throughout the proceedings, and there was little protest when the expeditionary force collected all six-shooters present and piled them on the platform. Just 80 minutes after her arrival the secretary boarded the train for her return journey. The men remained to mop up. A few months after the departure of the guardsmen, fire, of suspected incendiary origin, left the town in ruins, and it was never rebuilt.

North of Copperfield, State 86 leads to HOMESTEAD, 82.1 m. (1,675 alt., 150 pop.), by the Snake River at the eastern edge of the copper belt. During the World War the town was the scene of extensive mining operations, but operations ceased in 1922.

State 86 crosses the Snake River and becomes Idaho 45 at the Idaho Line, 84.3 m. in the river.

⫿⫿⫿⫿⫿⫿▣⫿⫿⫿⫿⫿▣⫿⫿⫿⫿⫿▣⫿⫿⫿⫿⫿▣⫿⫿⫿⫿⫿▣⫿⫿⫿⫿⫿▣⫿⫿⫿⫿⫿▣⫿⫿⫿⫿⫿▣⫿⫿⫿⫿⫿▣⫿⫿⫿⫿⫿

Tour 1C

La Grande—Elgin—Enterprise—Joseph—Wallowa Lake Resort; **78.8** *m.*, State 82.

Oiled gravel road; occasionally closed by snow. Union Pacific Railroad branch roughly parallels route between La Grande and Enterprise. Daily stages between La Grande and Joseph, and between Enterprise and Paradise. Good accommodations in towns.

This route runs through the beautiful Grande Ronde Valley and gives access to the rugged wilderness of the Wallowa Mountains. Here forests are protected from despoilation and streams are closed to commercial fishing. Rising sharply from a basaltic plain in tiers of magnificent peaks, the short Wallowa Mountain range thrusts up a mass of marble and granite. Ten peaks rise more than 9,000 feet in an area covering less than 350 square miles, and almost an equal additional number rise more than 8,000 feet. In appearance the Wallowas are more rugged than the Blue Mountains, and, in their isolation, form an imposing sight. From their slopes flow a number of streams that have cut deep, rock-walled canyons, and plunge over ledges in long ribbons. Glacial meadows are tapestried with brightly colored wild flowers. In the forests are many lakes set in beautiful frames. East of the mountains is the Grand Canyon of the Snake River—also called Hell's Canyon, 6,748 feet in depth at one point, and separating Oregon and Idaho.

State 82 branches northeast from US 30, **0** *m.* (*see TOUR 1a*) on Hemlock St. in LA GRANDE.

ISLAND CITY, **2.4** *m.* (2,743 alt., 116 pop.), grew up around a store opened by Charles Goodenough in 1874. It is on an island formed by a slough and the Grande Ronde River, which drains into the Snake in Washington. Peter Skene Ogden, the Hudson's Bay trapper, referred to this stream in his *Journal* as the Clay River, and also as *Riviere de Grande Ronde.*

Right from Island City on a gravel road to Cove, 14 *m.* (2,892 alt., 307 pop.), on the eastern side of the valley in a pocket formed by Mill Creek near the foothills of Mount Fanny (7,132 alt.), four miles to the east. It is the market center of a diversified farming, dairying, and fruit area, and provides transportation and guides for trips in the region. A dirt road follows Mill Creek, 7 *m.*, to MOSS SPRING GUARD STATION, where a pack trail begins. BIG MINAM HORSE RANCH, 15 *m.* (*open May to Nov.*), a dude outfit with a landing field, is on a mountain prairie (3,600 alt.), surrounded by rimrock. It is situated by the river from which it takes its name, a fine fishing stream whose course is accessible by trail. Little Minam River flows into the larger stream about six miles from the ranch.

ALICEL, **8.3** *m.* (2,754 alt., 300 pop.), in the heart of a wheat-growing district, has several large grain elevators cooperatively owned.

IMBLER, **12.2** *m.* (2,711 alt., 204 pop.), is a grain-shipping point in a thickly settled farming region.

ELGIN, **20.3** *m.* (2,666 alt., 728 pop.), draws the trade of fruit-growers and lumbermen. After 1890, when the Oregon Railway & Navigation Co.'s branch line was completed to this place, the town was the shipping and distributing point for an extensive territory. Horse-drawn stages brought travelers long distances over bad roads to this railhead.

Left from Elgin on graveled State 204 over the summit of the Blue Mountains, **17.3** *m.* (5,158 alt.), to TOLLGATE, **21** *m.* Covering the Tollgate meadow is 40-acre Langdon Lake (*public camp and kitchen*), formed by damming the waters of Looking-glass Creek. In winter this area offers excellent skiing, skating, and other sports. At this point is the TOLLGATE RANGER STATION of the Umatilla National Forest. State 204 continues to a junction with State 11 (*see TOUR 1*) in WESTON, **41.4** *m.*

The summit of MINAM HILL, **29.5** *m.* (3,638 alt.), is reached by gradual ascent through rolling farmland between the Grande Ronde and Wallowa rivers. At CAPE HORN promontory, **32** *m.*, is a striking vista (R) of the rugged canyon of the Minam River and the forested Wallowa Mountains.

East of MINAM, **35** *m.* (2,535 alt., 60 pop.), at the confluence of the Minam and Wallowa Rivers, State 82 runs through the canyon of the Wallowa beside rushing waters and below towering cliffs.

THE FOUNTAIN, **41** *m.*, is a camping place by a cold mountain spring.

WALLOWA, **48.5** *m.* (2,940 alt., 749 pop.), has a large sawmill and a flour mill. It is an old "cow town" and still retains some of its frontier character. The farmers who trade here do general farming, fruit growing, and sheep and cattle raising.

1. Right from Wallowa to BEAR CREEK CANYON, **10** *m.* (*picnic and camp grounds; good fishing after high water.*)

2. Left from Wallowa on a dirt road, following the Powwatka Ridge, which affords views of impressive MUD CREEK CANYON, to TROY, **34** *m.* (2,950 alt., 200 pop.), which selected its classical name in 1902 after several others had been rejected by the Post Office Department.

LOSTINE, **56.2** *m.* (3,362 alt., 176 pop.), by a river of the same name, is sometimes called "the lost town of Lostine," because it is in a valley 30 miles from the officially platted site, which is on top of a mountain. A surveyor's blunder accounts for the discrepancy.

1. Left from Lostine **4** *m.* to the FIRST BURIAL PLACE OF CHIEF JOSEPH, Nez Perce chieftain, who died in 1872. His body was later removed to Wallowa Lake (*see below*). His son was the Chief Joseph whose military leadership was outstanding (*see HISTORY*).

2. Right from Lostine along the Lostine River into the heart of the Wallowa Mountains and the EAGLE CAP PRIMITIVE AREA of 223,000 acres within the Wallowa National Forest. The road follows the canyon to the LOSTINE

FORKS (*guides and horses available*), 19 *m.*, from which point all travel is by trail.

The rugged Eagle Cap Area is the most impressive in the region. Among the peaks are Eagle Cap (9,695 alt.), Sacajawea (10,033 alt.), honoring the interpreter of the Lewis and Clark expedition, and Matterhorn (10,004 alt.) Also here are Aneroid, Sentinel, Peat's Point, and Glacier Mountain, all of them nearly 10,000 feet high. The southwest face of the Matterhorn, which resembles the mountain in Switzerland for which it was named, has a sheer face of white marble. On the sides of Eagle Cap are two residual glaciers, one of which, the Benson, is notable for its peculiar shape and rainbow colors. In abundance and variety of wild life, this region is outstanding. Streams and lakes furnish excellent fishing (*trout, steelhead, land-locked salmon*). The salmon are locally called blue-backs, or "yanks" because of the manner in which they are caught by fishermen who use deep, weighted lines and yank the fish out violently. The area was formerly a haunt of the fierce silvertip or grizzly bear. The small band of bighorn sheep for whom a reserve (*see below*) has been established frequently wanders into this area, roaming the remote fastnesses, and it is estimated that there are 3,000 elk and 10,000 mule deer in the district.

ENTERPRISE, 66.4 *m.* (3,755 alt., 1,379 pop.), living up to its name, is the bustling trade center for ranchers in the Wallowa Valley. It is also the county seat, and headquarters of the Wallowa National Forest (*information from forest supervisor*).

1. Left from Enterprise on a gravel road to the STATE FISH HATCHERY, 1 *m.* on the Wallowa River, now mainly devoted to the propagation of trout.

2. Right from Enterprise on an unimproved dirt road to MARBLE FINISHING PLANT, 0.2 *m.*, where an unusual black marble is cut and polished. The marble is taken from the quarry at 0.4 *m.*

3. Left from Enterprise on State 3, graveled, through a logged-off region that parallels rugged JOSEPH CREEK CANYON and at intervals offers views of the deep gorge with the creek a silver line two thousand feet below.

At 34.6 *m.* is the junction with a dirt road; L. here 1 *m.* to FLORA (4,000 alt., 60 pop.), formerly an outfitting point for summer sheep camps and now the trading point for a dry-farming section, producing diversified crops.

At 35 *m.* is a junction with a dirt road; right here to PARADISE, 2 *m.* (3,500 alt., 60 pop.), a stock-raising and general farming area, and a former sheepmen's outfitting point. Community life centers about the church, the school, and the grange. In winter, this region is isolated by heavy snows that frequently pack to fence levels. At such times, all travel is on foot, horseback, bobsleds, or in homemade, horse-drawn sleighs.

State 3 crosses the Washington State line, 44 m.

Southeast of Enterprise State 82 continues up the valley of the Wallowa River.

At 69.8 *m.* is the junction with a dirt road.

Left on this road through hilly farming and stock-raising country of MIDWAY, 13 *m.* at the junction with the Zumwalt Road. Left 11 *m.* from Midway to ZUMWALT (80 pop.); the road continues to BUCKHORN SPRINGS, 25 *m.* (*camping and picnicking facilities.*)

Right from Buckhorn Springs 1 *m.* to BUCKHORN POINT on the Snake River rim. This point commands an impressive view of a canyon deeper than that of the Colorado and quite as awe-inspiring though less dramatic in color. More than a mile below the rim, the Snake River winds through the gorge toward the Columbia. Seen from the rim, the river is deceptively calm and gives no hint of its dangerous rapids and whirlpools.

JOSEPH, 72.8 *m.* (4,400 alt., 504 pop.), an outfitting point, bears the name of two great Nez Perce chieftains, father and son. Both Chief Josephs ruled this Valley-of-the-Winding Waters, the hereditary home of their people until 1872. The younger Chief Joseph (*see HISTORY*), led his people in a long and losing struggle against white invasion and fought their banishment from their ancestral home.

1. Right from Joseph on a dirt road to its end, 2 *m.* to HURRICANE CREEK CANYON, 5 *m.* For grandeur of scene—with high waterfalls, stark canyon walls, and immense marble peaks intermingled with stretches of meadows and streams—this trail is perhaps the best in the forest.

2. Left from Joseph on the Little Sheep Creek Road and abruptly down through the Imnaha River Canyon to IMNAHA, 30.6 *m.* (1,850 alt., 45 pop.), district headquarters for the Wallowa National Forest.

Right from Imnaha on a single-track forest service road, with occasional turnouts, which climbs steadily from the canyon floor. At 5 *m.* is a broad turnout affording an impressive view. To the west are seen five ridges of the Wallowas, with intervening canyons and, nearer, the depths of the canyon from which the road has just emerged, with the river a narrow band of tree-lined water. The road reaches the plateau of GRIZZLY RIDGE, 10 *m.*, and follows the main Imnaha-Snake River Ridge, to the MEMALOOSE GUARD STATION, 22 *m.*

On HAT POINT, 23 *m.* (7,000 alt.), is a 70-foot Forest Service lookout tower. Eastward, the point commands a fine view of the Grand Canyon of the Snake and the lofty, snow-capped peaks of the Seven Devils Range; westward and southward is the broken Imnaha River basin, with the vast snow-tipped bulk of the Wallowas beyond. This remarkable gorge is deeper than the Grand Canyon of Colorado: it averages 5,500 feet in depth for a distance of forty miles and is both the narrowest and deepest gash in the continent. From Huntington, Oregon, to Lewiston, Idaho, the Snake descends on an average of nine feet a mile.

State 82 continues along the east shore of WALLOWA LAKE, a beautiful body of water at the base of steep, forested mountains. The GRAVE OF OLD CHIEF JOSEPH, marked by a stone shaft, is on a knoll (R) between the highway and the northern end of the lake.

WALLOWA LAKE LODGE, 78.8 *m.*, is at the southern end of the lake. (*Hotel and housekeeping cabins, moderate rates; club house and nine-hole golf course; excellent fishing; boats, pack and saddle horses and outing equipment for hire; guides. The M. J. G. Dude Ranch nearby has usual attractions*). South of the lake is the WALLOWA MOUNTAIN SHEEP REFUGE, set aside for Oregon's surviving band of bighorn sheep, estimated 30 in number. The sheep do not always recognize the boundaries of the area and may not be at home to greet visitors.

Tour 1D

Arlington—Condon—Fossil—Servicecreek—Spray—Kimberly—Junction US 28; 123.6 m. State 19.

Graveled road. Union Pacific Railroad branch line roughly parallels route between Arlington and Condon.
Hotels in towns; tourist camps.

State 19, a section of the John Day Highway, crosses part of the great wheat belt of central Oregon and of the arid range country, where the only conspicuous vegetation for many miles is sagebrush and juniper. The highway penetrates the region of the important John Day Sedimentary Deposits, with its remarkable fossils. The region, with its succession of startling contours, jagged skylines, sharp pinnacles rising from mountains of solid rock, and gashes through volcanic formation, often brilliantly colored, has great fascination. The barren splendor of the canyon of the John Day River, which the highway follows for many miles, is not duplicated in Oregon.

State 19 branches southward from US 30 at ARLINGTON, 0 m., (*see TOUR* 1b) and follows a narrow, winding canyon to a plateau called SHUTLER FLATS, 7.1 m. (710 alt.), named for a type of wagon popular with the early emigrants, one of which was found abandoned here along the Oregon Trail, that crosses State 19 at this place. At one time Shutler Flats was ranched by a man who owned 20,000 acres of wheat land. Later it was subdivided into smaller holdings.

CONDON, 37.7 m. (2,844 alt., 940 pop.), seat of Gilliam County, was formerly called Summit City, then Summit Springs. The latter name was applied because of the sweet-water springs at which stage drivers, freighters, and other travelers paused. The present name was given for Harvey C. Condon, nephew of Dr. Thomas Condon, the geologist who brought the near-by fossil region to the attention of the scientific world. The high plateau on which the city lies was once an Indian ceremonial ground. Later it was used for cattle roundups. From the elevated site on clear days are visible the Ochoco Mountains, the Blue mountains, and the Cascade Range. Condon is in the heart of vast rolling wheat fields for which it is the distributing center, with extensive warehouses and elevators.

South of Condon the road dips down the Condon Canyon to DYER STATE PARK (*picnicking facilities*), 47.4 m., named for J. W. Dyer. The narrow rim-rock walled area is shaded by cottonwoods, red osier willows, and elderberry bushes.

FOSSIL, 58.5 m. (2,654 alt., 538 pop.), the seat of Wheeler County, at the confluence of Butte and Cottonwood creeks, was so named because of the fossils found on the ranch where the townsite was platted in 1876. Highway construction often uncovers interesting fossils, such as those of the saber-toothed tiger, found in a cut just north of town.

Right from Fossil on State 218, over a winding mountain grade offering an excellent view of forest-covered mountains, to CLARNO, 20.5 *m.* (1,304 alt., 45 pop.), on the John Day River. It was named for Andrew Clarno, one of the earliest white settlers on the river and an Indian fighter, who settled on Pine Creek in 1866. This town lies at the western edge of the great fossil deposits. Those nearest the town (*not accessible by automobile*), the CLARNO SECTION OF THE JOHN DAY FOSSIL BEDS, have yielded many specimens of Eocene tropical fruits, nuts, and leaves, and are particularly rich in specimens of the two-toed, three-toed, and four-toed horse. These animals, which lived many millions of years ago, and were no larger than a fox, is believed to have been the ancestor of the modern horse.

West of Clarno the road leads up a narrow winding canyon, exceedingly steep for the first half mile. The remaining climb is over a graveled road with easy grades and curves. At every turn are views of the majestic John Day Gorge, with Craggy Rock lifting its jagged peak almost due east. At the top of the grade, 30.8 *m.*, is a view-point offering a magnificent panorama of the John Day region.

West of the summit the highway descends to ANTELOPE, 35.8 *m.* (2,631 alt., 136 pop.), named for the herds of the horned animals that formerly ranged this region. It is one of the few remaining typical stock towns of central Oregon. Except for a modern school its buildings look as they did in stagecoach days. Bullet scars in them are evidence of the times when scores were settled according to the law of the six-gun. H. L. Davis, editor of the Antelope newspaper in 1928, made the town the setting for scenes in his novel *Honey in the Horn*, winner of the Harper (1935) and Pulitzer (1936) awards.

The roads to the rock formations and agate beds in the vicinity are not well defined (*obtain local directions or guide*). John Silvertooth, authority on the town's history and local minerals, has a fine collection of rock specimens. State 18 continues to SHANIKO, 43.7 *m.* (*see TOUR 4a*).

South of Fossil on State 19 is a junction with an improved road at **67.2** *m.*

Left on this road to KINZUA, 5.8 *m.* (450 pop.), in a yellow pine lumbering area. Here is one of the largest pine mills in eastern Oregon, owned by a company that has timber holdings adequate for 50 years of continuous operation.

SHELTON STATE PARK (R), **69.4** *m.* (3,362 alt.), (*camping facilities*) on State 19 was given to the state by the Kinzua Lumber Company, who stipulated that the park should be named for Lewis D. Shelton, pioneer of 1847 and surveyor who cruised all the company's holdings in the vicinity. The park is the annual summer meeting place for the Eastern Oregon Pioneer Association. At **70.1** *m.* is (R) a stone arch erected in 1924 to the memory of the Eastern Oregon Pioneers.

SERVICECREEK, **79.2** *m.* (1,719 alt., 6 pop.), in the center of a timber belt, was settled about 1885. It was named so because of the great number of service-berry bushes in the vicinity.

SPRAY, **92** *m.* (1,772 alt., 110 pop.), early a ferrying point on the John Day River, was settled in the sixties and named for J. F. Spray, one of the first residents.

At 95 *m.* is the junction with State 207 (*see TOUR 1a*).

In KIMBERLY, 105 *m.,* are a service station and other tourist facilities.

Left from Kimberly on a gravel road to MONUMENT, 14.6 *m.* (1,983 alt., 97 pop.), a ranching community on the edge of the PAINTED HILLS, a region sculptured into fantastic shapes and stained a hundred shades, from mauve to brilliant red. The road winds between rugged buttes to HAMILTON, 25 *m.* (3,738 alt., 25 pop.), a small ranching settlement named for J. H. Hamilton, stockman and lover of fine horses, who settled here in 1874.

South of Kimberly the John Day River has carved a deep canyon. Throughout this section, volcanic ridges, bluffs, and isolated mountains are laid open from bedrock to rim, as if by a giant chisel, exposing a geologic record of Oregon's physical history. Embedded in these eroded pinnacles and resembling glacial ice in texture, are fossils of prehistoric flora, in particular treefern leaves, reeds, and grasses.

JOHNNY KIRK SPRINGS (*picnicking facilities*), 116.1 *m.,* named for a pioneer of Grant County, is surrounded by one of the most important fossil regions of the United States. It yields relics of the Oligocene Epoch, particularly rich in specimens of the three-toed horse and other Tertiary fauna.

At 117.7 *m.* through a ranch yard and up Waterspout Gulch, the the JOHN DAY FOSSIL BEDS in a ridge where a layer of pale green calcareous deposit a thousand feet thick is exposed. The ridge is so spectacularly eroded in its upper reaches that it is called the New Jerusalem. In these deposits are fossilized relics of the period when this high region of badlands, sagebrush plain, and wheatfields was low tropical jungle inhabited by rhinoceroses, saber-toothed tigers, giant sloths, oreodonts, miniature horses, and other ancestors of present-day animals, as well as curious and extinct species. As shown by great numbers of specimens, including agatized roots and leaves, palm, redwood, magnolia, fig, and ginko trees grew in profusion in this place where the hardy sagebrush now survives with difficulty. After the gigantic upheaval that resulted in formation of the Coast Range, volcanic eruptions covered the land with lava and ash. Then came the great ice-cap over the lands to the north and, yet later, the slow melting period during which some of Oregon's chief rivers were formed. As these, including the John Day, cut down through the crust accumulated through the ages, they revealed the deposits that tell the story of the land's prehistoric life.

Among the Oregon emigrants of 1852 was a clergyman, Thomas Condon, who was particularly interested in geology. A cavalry officer, member of a punitive expedition against the natives of central Oregon in the 1860's, brought the first specimens from this area to The Dalles and to Mr. Condon's attention. Soon Mr. Condon had visited the beds himself in the company of other Indian fighters. In 1870 he sent a small collection of teeth from the beds to Yale University, bringing the natural museum to the attention of scientists. In 1889 a Princeton University expedition removed two tons of specimens from the beds and many other groups have also worked here. Only a small part of the region has been explored.

At 118.2 *m.* the exposed strata of a lofty cliff (L), bared by erosion, tells the geologic history of the region for millions of years.

At 123.6 *m.* is the junction with US 28 (*see TOUR 6a*).

||||||||||||⚬||||||||||||⚬||||||||||||⚬||||||||||||⚬||||||||||||⚬||||||||||||⚬||||||||||||⚬||||||||||||⚬||||||||||||⚬||||||||||||⚬||||||||||||⚬||||||||||||

Tour 1E

Hood River—Mount Hood P. O.—Bennett Pass—Barlow Pass— Junction with State 50; 44.8 *m.*   State 35.

Asphalt paved roadbed; closed between Cooper Spur Road and Junction with State 50 during heavy snows.
All types of accommodations; also public forest camps.

This route, one of the chief approaches to the Mount Hood recreational area, threads its way through the narrow Hood River Gorge, crosses the Hood River Valley orchards, pierces deep canyons close to the eastern base of Mount Hood and scales the Cascade divide.

State 35 branches south from US 30, 0 *m.,* at the eastern edge of the city of HOOD RIVER (*see TOUR 1b*). The huge hydro-electric plant, 0.5 *m.,* in the canyon of the Hood River, serves the fruit-packing plants and the homes of the Hood River Valley, which is intensely electrified.

Also in the gorge are the tracks of the Mount Hood Railroad, which carries the valley's fruit to packing and processing plants, and lumber from a large sawmill at Dee to the mainline railroad.

At 1 *m.* is the junction with a graveled road.

Right on this road to PANORAMA POINT, 2 *m.* (582 alt.), overlooking the entire lower valley. Miles of orchards are broken by alfalfa fields and berry ranches, all sharply outlined by the mesh of irrigation canals bringing water from Mount Hood. Here and there on little hills are clumps of forest trees, survivors of the fir and pine that once covered the secluded valley. In May white blossoms transform the valley into a huge flower bowl. In early autumn the fruit trees glow with ripe apples and pears, and the oaks and maples flame with color. In winter the trees and earth mingle in a gray monotone, dominated by the gleaming white peaks of Mount Hood and Mount Adams.

South of the Junction State 35 emerges into the widening valley, passing neat apple and pear orchards, where orchard crews work during spring, summer and fall, and occasionally in winter. Irrigation began in the valley about 1900 and through constant vigilance and scientific application has reached a high state of efficiency. Land must have enough but not too much moisture, and to maintain the quality of the soil orchard floors should be planted with a cover crop that is eventually plowed under. Once during the winter and several times during other periods of the year the orchards must be sprayed with chemicals to destroy insect pests, particularly the codling moth. Care must be taken that the chemical does not destroy the bees that are needed for pollenization. Danger not only lurks in the trees where the bees garner the nectar from the blossoms but also in the ground cover with its wild flowers. If the rancher succeeds in spraying without killing the bees he is still at times faced with a problem of fertilization. Some trees may have too few blossoms to provide the necessary pollen and flowering branches must be grafted from sections where blooms are more numerous. However, the result of this expensive work is worthwhile because Hood River fruit commands top prices.

The harvesting—picking, sorting, and packing—is done by itinerant workers but labor conditions in the valley are better than in other parts of the West because the people who have developed the land are for the most part well educated and face their problems squarely. In the early years the harvesting crews lived along the irrigation ditches, but the pollution of water led to the establishment of camps similar to camps in recreational areas. Because of this the orchardists draw the cream of the pickers and have less turnover during the rush season. Hard as the work is the camps have a holiday air about them at the end of the day.

Because of the type of settler in this valley the section is noted for the high standard of its schools and for the comfort of its ranch homes

At **6.2** *m.* is the junction with a graveled road.

Left on this road to the BILLY SUNDAY RANCH, **0.2** *m.*, purchased by the evangelist in 1909. Sunday grew grain and bred cattle.

At **6.7** *m.* on State 35 is the junction with a paved road.

Right on this road to ODELL **1.5** *m.* (710 alt., 25 pop.), a fruit-packing center, named for William Odell who settled here in 1861.
WINANS, **9.2** *m.* (863 alt.), is named for Ross Winans, who in the 1880's erected a hotel for hunters. The structure, no longer standing, was noted for its square observation tower.
Right from Winans **2.4** *m.* to DEAD POINT TROUT HATCHERY, which produces annually about 3,000,000 rainbow and Eastern brook trout fingerlings, and a smaller number of steelheads for local lakes and streams. At this point is a forest camp (*camping and picnicking facilities*).
DEE, **10.7** *m.* (950 alt., 100 pop.), is built about a large sawmill.
The West Fork of the Hood River is crossed at its confluence with the Lake Branch, **17.2** *m.* The West Fork, fed by melting glaciers, is usually milky, while the Lake Branch, fed by springs, is always crystal clear. Both streams offer excellent trout fishing.
The route climbs to LOST LAKE, **24.2** *m.* (3,140 alt.), which mirrors the image of snowy Mount Hood. No other view of the mountain is as beautiful as this one. (*Forest camp with picnicking facilities; swimming; rowboats and fishing tackle for hire.*)
The shores of Lost Lake, according to legend, were long favorite summer and autumn camp grounds of the Indians. It is told that in days when the oldest

grandfathers were mere papooses, a tribe gathered here for a potlatch. One evening, after the squaws had returned from the berry patches with well filled baskets, the men had brought in tender venison, and a feast of roast meat had been prepared, a snow-white doe pursued by wolves suddenly broke from a thicket, plunged into the lake, swam to the middle, dived beneath the surface and disappeared. A medicine man pronounced the event an omen of very bad luck. The Indians broke camp and never returned to the lake.

In 1912 a young Indian couple who had been educated in an eastern college and did not share the beliefs of their elders came here to camp. During a storm a bolt of lightning struck the tree under which they were standing and killed the bride. Today no Indian can be persuaded to visit Lost Lake.

At **10.6** *m.* on State 25 is a FOREST RANGER STATION (*information and fire permits*).

At MOUNT HOOD (P. O.), **13.5** *m.* (1,467 alt., 65 pop.), Mount Hood is visible in clear weather—a gigantic, snow-covered pyramid looming against the blue sky.

DIMMICK STATE PARK (1,550 alt.) (*camp sites and tables*), **15** *m.,* is a small wooded area.

At **15.7** *m.* is the junction with an improved road.

Right on this road to PARKDALE, 0.3 *m.* (1,743 alt., 125 pop.), center of commercial and packing activities in the upper valley. Strawberry raising is locally important and in early June a Strawberry Festival is held.

From the LAVA BEDS, 1.6 *m.,* flow a number of the finest springs in the valley.

The northern boundary of the MOUNT HOOD NATIONAL FOREST is crossed at **23** *m.* The forest encloses Mount Hood and extends across the Cascade Range. The road climbs rapidly through heavy timber.

The junction (3,415 alt.) with the Cooper Spur Road is at **23.8** *m.*

Right on this road to a LOOKOUT POINT, 7.1 *m.* (4,995 alt.), affording a superb view of the Hood River Valley orchards, groves, meadows and the surrounding mountains.

At 9 *m.* is the junction with a gravel road; L. here 1.5 *m.* to TILLY JANE FOREST CAMP (5,600 alt.) (*picnicking facilities; guide service obtainable usually in July*). Just across the canyon is the base camp of the American Legion, which annually sponsors a climb to the summit of Mount Hood (*see MOUNT HOOD RECREATION AREA*).

CLOUD CAP INN (5,985 alt.), is at 10.5 *m.* (*see MOUNT HOOD RECREATION AREA*).

South of Cooper Spur Road State 35 dips into the canyon of the East Fork of Hood River where it crosses and recrosses the stream.

SHERWOOD FOREST CAMP, **28.1** *m.* (3,100 alt.), is maintained by the U. S. Forest Service.

HORSE THIEF MEADOWS (R), **31.5** *m.* (3,400 alt.), was so named because a band of outlaws once had a hide-out here. In 1884 a man named Phillips appeared in Hood River Valley and engaged Dave Cooper, for whom Cooper Spur was named, to assist him in a search for the cabin of the men who, he said, four years before had taken $25,000 in gold from a stage coach near Walla Walla, Washington. He believed that the gold had been cached near the cabin. Although the cabin was found—deserted—no gold was discovered so far as is known.

The ROBIN HOOD FOREST CAMP (3,560 alt.), is at **32.1** *m.* (*information at nearby Double Three Forest Service Station*).

At **35.9** *m.* is MEADOWS CREEK (*summer home sites here rented by government at reasonable annual rates*).

HOOD RIVER MEADOWS FOREST CAMP, **36.1** *m.* (4,480 alt.), is a large open space covered with coarse grass and mountain flowers. It affords a close-up view of Mount Hood. The lupine, which blooms at lower levels in June and July, is in flower here in late August.

SAHALE FALLS, **36.5** *m.* (4,575 alt.), is an ethereal cascade (R) of the East Fork of Hood River. There is a fountain (L) at the roadside. The road now swerves in long loops to cross the divide.

From BENNETT PASS, **37.3** *m.* (4,670 alt.), is an impressive view of Mount Hood. Its scarred, bleak walls here seem to bar further progress.

The road descends to WHITE RIVER, **39.5** *m.*, a tributary of the Deschutes noted for summer floods caused by the melting of White River Glacier on the southeastern slope of Mount Hood. The bridge (4,280 alt.) is dangerous when the river is a torrent.

BARLOW PASS, **41.9** *m.* (4,158 alt.), was used by the first wagon train and the first road into the Willamette Valley. It was developed to enable emigrants to avoid the hazardous raft trip down the Columbia River. The pass is named for its discoverer, Samuel Kimsbrough Barlow, a pioneer of 1845 (*see TOUR 4A*).

A cross at **43.9** *m.* is dedicated to a woman member of the 1845 emigrant train who died at this point. Her husband made a coffin from a wagon box and buried her here.

At **44.8** *m.* (3,648 alt.), is a junction with State 50 (*see TOUR 4A*) at a point three miles east of Government Camp.

Tour 2

Vancouver, Wash.—Portland—Salem—Albany—Junction City—Eugene—Roseburg—Grants Pass—Medford—Ashland—(Weed, Calif.); 345.3 m. US 99, US 99E.

Paved road, sometimes temporarily blocked in the Siskiyou Mtns., by ice or snow. Southern Pacific Railroad parallels route between Portland and California line; Portland Electric Power Company Interurban, between Portland and Oregon City. Excellent hotels; improved tourist camps at reasonable rates.

US 99 traverses Oregon, north to south, through its most densely populated area. It threads the streets of Portland, passes through suburban towns and hamlets, bisects the beautiful Willamette Valley, climbs a range of canyon-gashed mountains, and descends into the Umpqua. Farther south it scales another mountain and dips into the Rogue River Valley before crossing the lofty Siskiyous.

This was the first paved road of any considerable length in Oregon, and it still carries a heavy traffic; because of the great number of trucks and busses on it it is less of a pleasure route than US 101. Along its general course the early Concord stages, with their six-horse teams, careened over corduroy roads on the six-day run between Portland and Sacramento. In the narrow defile of Canyon Creek, south of Roseburg, and on the slopes of the Siskiyous the old road is visible from the highway. First pushed southward from Portland to Salem in 1857, and to Eugene in 1859, the line gave through coach service by 1861. In 1872 the railroad from the north reached Roseburg, but for several years thereafter stages continued to cover the gap across the Umpqua and Siskiyous into the upper Sacramento Valley.

Section a. Vancouver, Wash., to Junction City; 114.3 m. US 99E

The south city limits of VANCOUVER, 0 *m.* (115 alt., 15,786 pop.), coincides with the Oregon-Washington state line. On the north bank of the Columbia River, and linked with Portland by the Interstate bridge, Vancouver (*see WASHINGTON STATE GUIDE*) was one of the first permanent settlements made by white men in the Pacific Northwest. The present city, reflecting both modern and early architectural influences, is the shipping and marketing center for a diversified farming and lumbering area. In the city is located one of the largest grain elevators in the Pacific Northwest.

Although Captain George Vancouver's lieutenant, William Broughton, touched the site of the present city in 1792, the settlement was not founded until 1824, when John McLoughlin removed the Hudson's Bay Company's Pacific Northwest headquarters to Belle Vue Point from Fort George. Within two years McLoughlin and his employes had constructed a stockade of fir posts, 40 log buildings and a powder magazine made of stone, cleared a considerable area, established a sawmill, a forge, and were grazing 700 head of cattle on the adjacent lands. As Chief Factor of the company, McLoughlin had extraordinary powers, governing a vast territory, and extending the scope of the Hudson's Bay Company's influence to Alaska, Hawaii and California. While he fought encroachment upon the territory north of the river, it is evident that he believed the United States would eventually acquire the lands south of the water-course through settlement of the territorial dispute then raging between this nation and Great Britain.

Great Britain's hegemony in the Oregon country was ended by the treaty of 1846, the United States acquiring what is now Washington, in addition to Oregon, and McLoughlin's feudal domain slipped from his grasp. The factor removed to Oregon City, but Fort Vancouver continued to be an important settlement. Without the presence of Mc-Loughlin's armed retainers, who had exerted control over unruly Indians, American settlers were in greater peril, but the government established a military post in 1848, and settlement continued under the protection of Federal troops. From Fort Vancouver military expeditions set forth to subdue hostile tribes throughout the two territories. Young Phil Sheridan and Ulysses S. Grant were stationed here for short periods. Grant, in his *Memoirs,* tells of his efforts to add to his scant army pay by raising potatoes upon lands adjacent to the fort. The vegetables sold at that time at the fabulous price of $45 per hundred pounds. Grant described the incident: "Luckily for us, the Columbia River rose to a great height from the melting of the snow in the mountains in June, and overflowed and killed most of our crop. This saved digging it up, for everybody on the Pacific Coast seemed to have come to the conclusion at the same time that agriculture would be profitable. In 1853 more than three-quarters of the potatoes raised were permitted o rot in the ground or were thrown away . . ."

With the establishment of the military post, a townsite was platted nd named Vancouver City, by Henry Williamson, who had arrived from Indiana in 1845. The town thrived, there being 95 houses in the newly organized Clark County, according to a census taken in 1850. An acrimonious dispute over land holdings arose between the Hudson's Bay Company (which still functioned as a commercial enterprise), missionaries, the War Department, and private citizens. When all disputes and suits were settled the claims of the War Department and immigrant Amos Short were upheld by the courts.

Fort Vancouver had a strong influence upon the cultural life of early Oregon. The first theatrical performance ever held in this region was on the British gunboat, *Modeste,* while moored at Vancouver in February, 1846. Such fashion as the country boasted was displayed at the fort, under British occupancy, and later, at parties given by American officers. In the fifties, residents of Oregon City and the struggling village of Portland were ferried across the river to participate in gay affairs at the home of Richard Covington, who seems to have been the social arbiter of the town, or in the quarters of Lieutenant-Colonel Benjamin de Bonneville. Settlers and officers amused themselves with amateur theatricals and dances. In 1867 a company of actors on tour presented the melodrama *Robert Macaire* and the comedy *Tootles.* Social activities reached their acme when tickets to a St. Patrick's Day ball and supper at the Alta House were sold for $5 each.

VANCOUVER BARRACKS, bounded by 5th Street (Evergreen Highway), Fourth Plain Avenue, and East and West Reserve Streets, has 300 buildings. Among the oldest of these is NUMBER TWO BARRACKS, in Officers' Row. The log walls of the crude original building have been sheathed with boards, but the harsh outline of the structure remains unchanged since the days when Sheridan, Grant, and others who won fame in the Civil War were quartered at the fort.

There are few modern buildings on the reservation, with the exception of several two-apartment houses, made of brick, in colonial design, which were constructed recently for the use of married non-commissioned officers.

The COVINGTON HOUSE (*open 11-4, 2nd and 4th Tues. each month*), at southwest corner 39th and Main Streets, built about 1845 is a reconstruction of what is believed to have been the oldest private dwelling in the state. Its architecture is similar to that of Hudson's Bay Company buildings, a sloping roof surmounting hewn logs and weathered clapboard sidings. Here Richard Covington entertained officers, Hudson's Bay officials, and such few women as were on the frontier during the middle century.

PEARSON ARMY AIRPORT, 5th and E. Reserve Sts., with its hangars, shops, and administration buildings, was the terminus of the first Soviet flight across the North Pole. The three Russian aviators who took off from Moscow on June 18, 1937, grounded their plane at the field after a 63-hour dash over unmapped arctic wastes, fog forcing the birdmen down short of San Francisco, their destination. The Soviet flyers were greeted upon their arrival by Brigadier General George Marshall, since appointed chief of staff of the United States Army. The then Soviet Ambassador Troyanovsky came to Portland and accompanied the flyers to San Francisco after they had been entertained in Portland by civic leaders and officials of city, county and state government.

The PIONEER MOTHER in Esther Short Park, 8th St., between Columbia and Esther Sts., a heroic size bronze statue, depicts an immigrant woman clutching a rifle. Three small children cling to the pioneer woman's skirt. The park in which the statue stands commemorates Esther Short, who with her husband, Amos, were among the first United States citizens to arrive in the city of Fort Vancouver, having been preceded by but one man, Henry Williamson of Indiana. Esther Short bore a child during the long overland journey and she and her husband were refused aid by the British authorities when they arrived destitute at the fort. A remarkable woman, Mrs. Short is said to have knocked down a Hudson's Bay Company employe who attempted to drive the family away from Vancouver.

The FIRST APPLE TREE, E. 7th and T Sts., was planted in 1826 by Chief Factor McLoughlin, who it is said nurtured seeds brought from London by one Captain Acmilius Simpson.

US 99 crosses the Columbia River, the Washington State Line, on the INTERSTATE BRIDGE (*free*), opened in 1917. The total length of the structure, rising in the center 175 feet above low water, is 3,531 feet. The bridge commands a superb view of the great river which has played so important a part in the settlement and development of Oregon. The bateaux of the French-Canadian voyageurs, laden with bales of furs, shot its rapids and paddled its smooth waters, and the rafts of the home-seekers ventured its hazardous gorge (*see TOUR 1a*). Long before the whites arrived the river had been closely interwoven with the life of the Indian race. Pictographs and petroglyphs carved on the basaltic walls of the Cascade Gorge record the older culture.

Discovered and first entered by the Yankee skipper, Robert Gray, in the *Columbia,* on May 11, 1792 (*see HISTORY*), and explored in that year by the English Lieutenant, Broughton, the river was soon visited by ships of many nations. After 1811, when Astor's fur traders established Astoria (*see ASTORIA*), the river was the scene of heavy traffic as traders brought furs down it to Vancouver, and British ships loaded them for distribution all over the world.

At the southern end of the bridge, US 99 crosses Hayden Island upon which is JANTZEN BEACH (R), a commercial amusement park (*open early May to mid-Sept.; adm.* 10c).

PORTLAND, 7.5 *m.* (30 alt., 301,815 pop.) (*see PORTLAND*).

Points of Interest: Skidmore Fountain, Chinese Drug Store, U.S.S. *Oregon,* Oregon Historical Society Museum, Portland Museum of Art, Multnomah Public Library, Sunken Gardens, and others.

In Portland are junctions with US 30 (*see TOUR* 1), US 99W (*see TOUR* 10), State 8 (*see TOUR* 8), and State 50 (*see TOUR* 4A).

At 8.6 *m.* US 99E passes under the eastern approach to Ross Island bridge, carrying State 50.

Right across Ross Island bridge into SW. Kelly Ave.; L. on SW. Gibbs to SW. Macadam Ave., an alternate route to Oregon City along the west bank of the Willamette River.

SW. Macadam Road follows the river bank past the west end of the SELL-WOOD BRIDGE, 3.3 *m.,* the southernmost of Portland's eight Willamette River bridges. RIVERVIEW CEMETERY (R), 3.4 *m.,* is a beautiful memorial park.

Just south of the Sellwood bridge, and extending for more than a mile is POWERS PARK, a narrow strip between the highway and the river. Through a fringe of firs are views of the river, of squatty house-boats along the far shore, and of the sleek, green turf of WAVERLY GOLF COURSE.

OSWEGO, 5.8 *m.* (98 alt., 1,285 pop.), is a suburban town by Oswego Lake, a long, narrow body of water, with wooded shores holding country estates and country clubs. Through the hills and along the lake front are miles of bridle trails constructed for the MULTNOMAH HUNT CLUB, which is near the western end of the lake.

Left from the eastern end of the lake 0.2 *m.* to the ruins of the old Willamette Iron Company BLAST FURNACE. A chimney 20 feet high is the only trace of a plant that reduced ore mined in the hills behind Oswego.

WEST LINN, 11.3 *m.* (1,966 pop.), took its name from Linn City, an ambitious waterfront settlement on the Willamette River, on the site where a large power plant and paper mills now stand. Linn City was established as Robin's Nest by Robert Moore, an immigrant of 1840, who was a leader in establishing the provisional government. In 1844 he began to operate a ferry between Oregon City and Robin's Nest. In time the community was named Linn City, to honor U. S. Senator Linn of Missouri, an ardent advocate for the seizure of Oregon. The town was washed away by the great flood of 1861 and never rebuilt.

From West Linn the highway crosses the Willamette River. Upstream (R) are the Willamette Falls and the paper mills. At the eastern end of the bridge is OREGON CITY, 12.2 *m.* (*see OREGON CITY*), at a junction with 99E (*see below*).

Just south of Ross Island bridge the route veers into McLoughlin Boulevard. Ross Island is (R) covered by a dense growth of cottonwoods and willows. Beyond the river rise the smokestacks of the South Portland factories and above them, the dwellings of Terwilliger Heights under the shadow of Council Crest (*see PORTLAND*).

The JOHNSON CREEK MEMORIAL BRIDGE, **12.8** *m.,* is just above the site of the sawmill constructed in 1847 by the Reverend William Johnson. This mill supplied lumber for many years for homes in Milwaukie and Portland. The creek is a unit of an extensive flood control project of the WPA.

MILWAUKIE, **12.9** *m.* (96 alt., 1,767 pop.), is a quiet suburban town spread over low hills. Founded in 1848 by Lot Whitcomb (1806-1857), it soon became the rival of Portland and other river towns for the commercial supremacy of the Oregon country. Here, on the banks of the Willamette, Whitcomb and his associates constructed the *Lot Whitcomb,* in its day the finest steamboat plying the river. Milwaukie failed to become the important commercial port that its founder had hoped.

The LUELLING HOUSE (L), close to the street and shaded by a huge weeping willow, is at the corner of Jackson St. The simplicity of the two-story structure, with its low wing and small balustraded entrance portico, is hidden by vines and shrubs. In 1847 Henderson Luelling (1809-1878) brought his traveling nursery of 700 fruit trees across the plains from Iowa, and established Oregon's first nursery in Milwaukie. He planted the first Royal Anne cherry tree in the state and in the 1860's originated the Black Republican and Bing cherries. The Royal Anne is canned and shipped from the valley in large quantities as a fruit and is also used to make the decorative maraschino cherries. The Black Republican was so named for political groups of the day, and the Bing for Luelling's Manchurian gardener.

JENNINGS LODGE, **16.9** *m.,* a suburban community, was named for Berryman Jennings, a pioneer of 1847 and receiver for the Oregon City Land Office under President Buchanan. It is the home of W. L. Finley, the naturalist. The STARKER GARDENS here display many rare Oriental plants and ship many species of rock plants. Here grow nearly 75 kinds of heather.

At **18** *m.* is the street (L) to the city center of GLADSTONE (1,384 pop.). The town lies along the north bank of the Clackamas River, the river-front drive curving gracefully with the bank of the stream. Because of the nearness of Oregon City and Portland, the business district is small, but a preponderance of residences line tree-shaded streets. At the eastern edge of town is the old CHAUTAUQUA PARK, for long the center of popular lyceums in Oregon.

The JOHN McLOUGHLIN BRIDGE, **18.3** *m.,* spanning the Clackamas River, is a memorial to the "father of Oregon" (*see HISTORY*). That the Clackamas River is an excellent fishing stream was attested by Rudyard Kipling, who wrote in his *American Notes.* "I have lived! The American Continent may now sink under the sea, for I have taken the best that it yields, and the best was neither dollars, love, nor real estate." With an eight-ounce rod he had spent 37 minutes landing a twelve-pound fighting salmon. "That hour," he wrote, "I sat among crowned heads greater than all. . . . How shall I tell the glories of that day."

OREGON CITY, 19.7 *m.* (102 alt., 5,761 pop.) (*see OREGON CITY*).

Points of Interest: McLoughlin Mansion, Edwin Markham Birthplace, Crown-Willamette Paper Mills, Hawley Pulp and Paper Mill, and others.

At Oregon City is a junction with State 215 (*see TOUR 2A*).

NEW ERA, 24.9 *m.* (102 alt., 48 pop.), consisting of two or three buildings, one of which is an abandoned grist mill on Parrot Creek, is the scene of the annual summer camp-meetings of the Spiritualist Society of the Pacific Northwest. The commodious and pleasant camp grounds lie a short distance up the creek. The community was founded by Joseph Parrott, who named it for a visionary publication of the day.

CANBY, 29.1 *m.* (154 alt., 744 pop.), is a trade center in a bulb and flax growing region consisting of some of the most fertile land of the valley. In the spring and early summer, brilliant fields of daffodils and tulips border the highway. In the vicinity is grown a great deal of fiber flax which is prepared for market by a scutching and retting plant here. Canby was named for Gen. E. R. S. Canby, commander of the Department of the Columbia, who was slain at the peace council in the Lava Beds during the Modoc uprising of 1873 (*see TOUR 4b, also HISTORY*).

BARLOW, 30 *m.* (101 alt., 40 pop.), once a trading center for a rich agricultural region was named for Samuel K. Barlow, who took up a donation land claim here. He was the explorer and builder of the Barlow Trail (*see TOUR 1E*), historic pioneer road across the Cascade Mountains. His grave is in a local cemetery.

The old BARLOW HOUSE (L), a hundred yards from the highway at the end of a long avenue of black walnut trees that were set out by William Barlow, son of Samuel K. Barlow, in the sixties. William Barlow sent East for a bushel of black walnuts; the transportation charges amounted to $65. However, Barlow sold the young trees that he grew from the nuts at a profit of almost $500. The avenue of trees is from this shipment.

PUDDING RIVER, crossed at 31.8 *m.*, was named by Joseph Gervais (*see TOUR 2B*), and Etienne Lucier, Hudson's Bay Company trappers, after they had enjoyed a sumptuous repast of elk-blood pudding at its confluence with the Willamette.

AURORA, 32.1 *m.* (120 alt., 215 pop.), was settled about the middle of the nineteenth century by a colony of old-country Germans and "Pennsylvania Dutch," united under the precepts of their teacher and leader, Dr. William Keil (1812-1877). "Every man and woman must be a brother or sister to every other man and woman in our family under the fatherhood of God," said Dr. Keil. "No man owns anything individually but every man owns everything as a full partner and with an equal voice in its use and its increase and the profits accruing from it.

But in no other way do we differ from our neighbors. As a community we are one family. 'From every man according to his capacity, to every man according to his needs' is the rule that runs through our law of love. As between ourselves we are many with one purpose. In contact with outsiders we are one dealing with many, but with justice and honesty and neighborliness, withholding no solicitude or needed act of charity or mercy, and giving it without money and without price where there is any call for it, to the limit of our ability in money or food or clothing or service in sickness or in health."

For a dozen years Dr. Keil and his followers had been at Bethel, Missouri, where, on six thousand acres in Shelby County, they had developed a prosperous community of homes, mills, and shops, supporting several hundred families. This satisfied them for a long time but, in order to develop a fuller community life, Dr. Keil determined to seek a new location in the Oregon country.

The new community in Oregon was named Aurora Mills, in honor of Dr. Keil's favorite daughter. The first houses were of logs but it was not long before these were either weatherboarded or replaced by frame structures. The favorite dwelling was a two or three-story building with a large brick chimney at either end. Huge fireplaces provided warmth and cooking facilities. The first to rise was "the big house," the home of Dr. Keil, a large, three-story building with a two-deck porch across the east front. A store, bachelor-hall, and a church, were erected, and family homes began to appear here and there over the countryside. Many of these buildings are still standing: the WILL, the KRAUS, the KEIL HOUSES, and the GEISEY STORE in Aurora, and numerous farm homes in the surrounding country, some of them remarkably well preserved. Numbers of these old homesteads are still occupied by descendants of old colony families.

One of the earliest buildings to rise in Aurora was its famed hotel. Here meals were served to the general public and to stage passengers before the coming of the railroad and to train passengers afterwards. Epicures have waxed eloquent in praise of the delectable viands served at Aurora. "Aurora fried potatoes surpass all other fried potatoes. Aurora home-baked bread is without peer in the broad land. Aurora pig sausage has a secret, if captured, that would make a fortune for an enterprising packer." So declared one, while another glowed with memories of the old days: "And they liked to eat good meals; indeed they did. Aurora cooking was famous all over Oregon. . . . Why did trains stop for meals at Aurora when the Portland terminal was only twenty-nine miles away? Because the trainmen wanted the better meals they could get at Aurora—better meats, better vegetables, better pies and puddings."

The original village of Aurora was not located as at present. The old colony community was situated largely on the west bank of Mill Creek a little above its junction with the Pudding River, and across the creek from the modern town. Here the first farms and garden plots were cleared and the first houses built beside the old stage road. Near

the road are several ancient, dilapidated, and curious appearing structures, and a few rows of old and gnarled fruit trees, reminiscent of the
time when Aurora was one of the principal fruit-growing sections of
the Northwest. Henry Theophilus Finck, noted music critic and boyhood resident of Aurora, dwells enthusiastically on the quality of Oregon
apples: "By rare good luck, my father was able to buy a house with a
fine apple orchard on the hill only a half mile from the village. It was
one of the very first and best of the many commercial orchards for which
Oregon soon became famous. I find from my diary that we harvested
up to 2,000 bushels in one year. . . ."

Just behind the Keil house, at the edge of a little ravine, is the family
cemetery of the Keils, in what was formerly Keil Park, the graves
marked by simple stones inscribed in German. At the brow of the hill,
near where the public school is now, was the old community park, known
throughout the lower Willamette region for its picnics and gala gatherings. Many of the moss-hung maples which lent welcome shade to
stranger and colonist alike, are still standing, while an old gooseberry
hedge is almost lost in the dense undergrowth.

From its first plantation the colony prospered, due largely to strict
economy of living and unflagging industry. Thousands of acres were
brought under cultivation, vineyards were planted, and orchards were
set out. One who visited the colony remarked: "All this valley was like
a province in Germany. Farming was carried on in the thrifty German
way, and everywhere was heard the German tongue."

During the winter when there was little farm activity the people
worked in the mills and shops. The Aurora commune produced some
very fine articles of furniture, clothes, basketry, chests, and implements.
Today the spool-beds, chests, chairs, tables, and other articles manufactured there are sought eagerly by collectors and discriminating householders, who prize highly these simple and artistic pieces of the German
craftsmen.

Social life in the community was somewhat restricted. Church services,
band and orchestra concerts, "butcher frolics," and the various festivals,
provided relaxation. Tables were spread with the sumptuous products
of the German kitchen and cellar, and everybody was welcome to share
in the feast without cost, the stranger as well as the members of the
commune. The band played during the feasting. The evening was spent
in dancing. "At Christmas time the church was decorated with two huge
Christmas trees. The celebration, which was rather unique, took place
at the early hour of four on Christmas Day. For this occasion, also,
hosts of strangers arrived. The program consisted of a talk by the
preacher, congregational singing, and music by the band. Then huge
baskets of cakes, apples, and quantities of candy were distributed. Colonists and strangers shared these absolutely alike. The trees were allowed
to remain standing until New Year's Day, and then the gifts were distributed among the children of the colony."

School at Aurora was kept open the year round but little was taught
except reading, writing, and arithmetic. Professional training was en-

couraged, but for a classical education there was little place. Music was the one cultural subject permitted and encouraged by Dr. Keil, and Aurora became the musical center of the State. The Aurora band was in demand for fairs, picnics, and political meetings. In April, 1869, Ben Holladay paid the commune $500 for the services of the band on the voyage of the Portland party to Puget Sound. Harvey Scott called it "the best musical organization of its time."

The Aurora experiment endured about 25 years, then reaction against the autocratic rule of Dr. Keil began to manifest itself. As Jacob Miller remarked: "Such an enterprise can succeed in but one of two ways: either through a natural-born leader, who is deeply impressed that he is serving God, or else by a military power." As long as Dr. Keil was able to make his people accept him as the former, they obeyed him as if he were a father. In time the spell he held over the older folk began to weaken and younger generations came on, with different ideals and different purposes. Necessarily there was a reorganization and final abandonment of the theory of "equal service, equal obligations, and equal reward." However, the complete disintegration was delayed until the death of Dr. Keil in 1877. Upon that event, no one being willing or able to assume the leadership thus left vacant, the property was divided among the members, each according to his original contribution and length of service in the colony.

With the division of property accomplished, the Aurora colony ceased to function as a communal organization. Thenceforward the members faced the world as individuals. After more than half a century few of the old colony people remain, but many of their descendants still maintain farms round about and a few of the business enterprises of Aurora perpetuate colony names. However, as the years pass and the old houses are torn down, Aurora more and more loses its unique old-world appearance, and gradually assumes the undistinguished air of an Oregon country village of the twentieth century.

South of Aurora are numerous hop fields or "yards." A hop field is easily recognizable because of its spider-web of wire, strung on posts 10 to 12 feet high, to support the vines which form a canopy of green over weedless earth. The luxurious vines form impenetrable walls from one end of the field to the other, with the laterals about 10 feet apart. Many of the hop farms have vines that are 30 years old. In the early fall, when the hops are ready for the harvest, the trellis of vines is lowered to the earth, and armies of men, women, and children gather the blooms. Between 25,000 and 30,000 pickers are required to harvest the crop, and at picking time, a tent city springs up about every hop field of any size. Hop festivals, similar to the European harvest festivals are often held.

HUBBARD (R) **36.5** *m.* (210 alt., 330 pop.) (R), is a trading center in an area growing and canning strawberries, raspberries, loganberries, youngberries and blackberries. The high school (R) stands on the approximate site of Charles Hubbard's cabin, built in 1849. Hubbard gave land for a townsite when the Southern Pacific Railway was built.

At **38.4** *m.* is the 273-acre OREGON STATE TRAINING SCHOOL (L), whose inmates tend highly developed tracts producing small fruits and diversified farm products. Four hours are spent in school each day and four hours in work. In addition to agricultural training, the school provides training in various trades. The institution, established in 1891, cares for delinquent boys between 10 and 18 years of age.

WOODBURN, **40** *m.* (183 alt., 1,675 pop.), in a berry-raising district has a large cannery (L). Bulb culture is also carried on in the environs and in spring the fields of bright flowers make the countryside a huge garden.

At **42.9** *m.* facing the highway (L) is the SAMUEL BROWN HOUSE, built in the early 1850's by a man who had made a small fortune mining gold in California. For many years it was a station on the Oregon-California stage line. This house, constructed as a long, low story-and-a-half salt-box, and still exhibiting the New England characteristics, has been remodeled by the addition of a second floor over the central third with a gabled roof that has been extended forward to form the pediment of a two-story porch. The second floor has a latticed balustrade. It is now occupied by Sam H. Brown, grandson of the builder.

At **43.3** *m.* is a junction with Champoeg State Park road (*see TOUR 2B*).

The land of the LAKE LABISH district, **51.3** *m.*, has been acquired by Japanese gardeners who raise much celery and market it through cooperative organizations. The soil is beaverdam, rich and mellow, the bottoms of lakes formed in pre-settlement days by dams constructed by beavers.

At **51.6** *m.* is a junction with a graveled road.

Right here to CHEMAWA INDIAN SCHOOL, **1.3** *m.*, with 450 students from various northwestern states. The school operates a large farm and has dormitories, school-rooms, and shops representing an investment of more than $1,000,000.

SALEM, **57.5** *m.* (191 alt., 26,266 pop.) (*see SALEM*).

Points of Interest: State Capitol; Willamette University; Jason Lee House; Miles Linen Mill; State Penitentiary; Sequoia Park, and others.

South of Salem the highway winds through low rolling hills, where cultivation exposes the typical red shot soil in marked contrast with the green of pear, cherry, and prune orchards which cover the slopes.

LOONEY BUTTE (R), **72.7** *m.* (630 alt.), was named for Jesse Looney, an early settler. The hills gradually diminish in height as the road nears the valley of the SANTIAM RIVER, named for a tribe of Calapooyan Indians.

JEFFERSON, **74.3** *m.* (241 alt., 391 pop.), is on the north bank of the Santiam River. Once it was the head of navigation on the Santiam, though travel on any part of the river was difficult except during high water. Jefferson was formerly the seat of a pioneer school known as Jefferson Institute. The Scottish botanist, David Douglas, discovered many interesting plants in this vicinity, among them the native tobacco. On November 15, 1826, he swam the cold, swollen stream and thought nothing of danger, though mourning because his precious collection of plants had become soaked in the crossing.

Left from Jefferson on a graveled road, to MARION, 1.5 *m.* (315 pop.), where on the outskirts is the VIVA LA FRANCE MONUMENT honoring a Jersey that at one time held three world championships for milk and butter-fat production.

The JACOB CONSER MEMORIAL BRIDGE, crossed at the southern edge of Jefferson, was named for a pioneer of 1848.

Right from the southern end of the bridge on an unimproved road to a neglected cemetery, marking the SITE OF SYRACUSE, 1 *m.*, founded in 1848 by Milton Hale. In the autumn of 1845 Hale staked his claim on the south side of the river. Returning with his family, in the spring of 1846, he found the river impassable, and with an ax, an adze, and an augur, he constructed a ferry-boat to convey his possessions across. Other travelers arriving before the barge was completed waited to use it in crossing. Thus encouraged, Hale continued to operate the ferry for many years. Nearly all of the emigrant travel to the upper valley on the east side of the Willamette passed this point. The town of Syracuse, on the south side of the river, soon had a rival on the north in Santiam City, which became an important trading point. Both towns prospered for some years, then disappeared, until no trace of them except the cemetery remains.

At 81.4 *m.* is the ALBANY CIVIC AIRPORT, used frequently for United States Army transport air maneuvers.

ALBANY, 83.1 *m.* (214 alt., 5,325 pop.), seat of Linn County, is on the curving east bank of the Willamette River at its junction with the Calapooya. The level plain that stretches eastward from the river to the foothills of the Cascade Range affords no point of vantage for a view of the city. However, owing to this flatness of terrain, the streets and squares exhibit a regularity unusual among Oregon towns. Though industrially and commercially progressive, Albany has a quiet and restful conservatism apparent in its architecture as well as social life. Broad well-shaded streets pass substantial houses and business blocks built several decades ago. The city is a trading center for farmers of Linn, Benton, and Polk counties, ships wool, grain, rye-grass and vetch seed, and cascara bark, a medicinal product collected from the nearby upland forests; it has a chair and box factory, a meat-packing plant, a tannery, a saddlery, a foundry and machine shop, several creameries, and a flour-ing mill.

The city was established in 1848 by Walter and Thomas Monteith, who named it for their native town in New York. The Calapooyas had called the district Takenah (deep and placid pool) because of the clear basin at the junction of the two rivers. Early settlers jeered at the Indian name, asserting that the word should rightly be translated as "hole in the ground." The Indian title is perpetuated in the civic park.

The early history of Albany parallels that of other Oregon towns.

A period of activity was followed by a temporary stagnation, caused by the exodus, in 1849, of most able-bodied men to the California gold fields.

The *Oregon Spectator* was forced to suspend publication because, as its editor wrote: "the printer, with 3,000 officers, lawyers, physicians, farmers and mechanics" was leaving for the gold fields. For a time, buildings in Albany as elsewhere stood in a state of semi-completion, farms were abandoned, and business was at a standstill. The return of the gold-seekers however, stimulated expansion and established a new era of prosperity. Some of the argonauts who left during the early days of the stampede returned during the winter months; Joseph Lane wrote on March 8, 1849, "that of those who had come back from the mines to winter, most were going back, and that most of those who had not been were going." Lane estimated that one million dollars in gold dust had been brought into the Oregon territory by returning miners; the historian, Bancroft, declares that some returned $30,000 to $40,000 richer after a year's absence, and states that "most of those who did not lose their lives were successful." Such settlers, either shrewd or timid, who remained in Oregon, reaped enormous profits from the sale of food-stuff and lumber.

Significant events in the history of the town were the building of a grist mill in 1851, the arrival, in 1852, of the *Multnomah,* the first steamboat from down-river, the building of the first courthouse in 1853, the first schoolhouse in 1855, the first church in 1857, the publication in November 1859, of the *Oregon Democrat,* the city's first newspaper, and the incorporation of the city in 1865.

Early Albany was the scene of many hard-fought political battles and was noted as the birthplace of the Republican Party in Oregon. On August 20, 1856, Free State men held a meeting and adopted a platform that included the bold declaration: "Resolved, that we fling our banner to the breeze, inscribed, free speech, free labor, a free press, and Fremont." February 11, 1857, delegates from eight counties assembled in Albany at a territorial convention and selected a committee to prepare an address on the slavery question which placed the issue squarely before the people for the first time. In the sixties Southern sympathizers were numerous in the city and made themselves known vocally, and fistically, if occasion presented. During the stormy period of 1861, a cannon, mounted on the bank of the Willamette and used during local celebrations, was stolen and sunk in the river by "Joe Lane Democrats" to prevent the victorious "Cayuse Republicans" from firing it as a triumphal gesture. The old howitzer lay in the river for almost 70 years, when it was dredged from the bottom and placed on exhibition by a local sand and gravel company.

In 1870 the Oregon and California Railroad (now the Southern Pacific) reached Albany, and a few years later the Corvallis and Eastern connected the city with tidewater at Yaquina City and stretched east-ward toward the summit of the Cascades. Later short spurs were extended into the rich surrounding areas, and products of farm and forest poured into the city where processing plants were built to receive them.

Writers who have been identified with Albany are Sam L. Simpson, author of many poems collected after his death into the volume, *Gold Gated West,* Charles Alexander, author of *Fang in the Forest, Bobbie, a Great Collie,* and winner in 1922 of the O. Henry memorial prize with his story, *As a Dog Should,* and Fred Pike Nutting, who conducted the oldest newspaper column in Oregon under the name of "Misfits" in the Albany *Democrat-Herald.*

The MONTEITH HOUSE (*private*), 518 W. 2nd St., is the first house erected in Albany. Although remodeled about 1918 it retains the original architectural lines. The first unit of the structure was built as a claim cabin in 1848 by Walter and Thomas Monteith, founders of Albany. It stood facing Washington Street at Second, and the dividing line of the two claims ran through the house so that the brothers could occupy the cabin in common but each could live on his own claim. The cabin, enlarged in 1849 and finished in 1850, became the civic and social center of the new settlement, sheltering the first religious service in Albany, and serving as the first store.

TAKENAH PARK, 4th at Ellsworth St., is named for the old Indian designation of the district at the mouth of the Calapooya River. The Weatherford Tablet in the park commemorated J. K. Weatherford (1850-1935), who for fifty years was a director of the Albany schools. The marker stands beneath a young Douglas fir tree, planted by Mr. Weatherford, which, during the Christmas season, is illuminated with colored lights. Another memorial tablet in the park marks the old Oregon-California Wagon Road, over which the great trek to the gold fields took place.

OLD STEAMBOAT INN (*private*), Water St. near Ellsworth St., E. of the southern approach to the Ellsworth St. Bridge, was built in the early fifties. Standing on the brink of the Willamette River near the old boat landing it was an important stopping place for steamboat travelers, before the coming of the railroad, and served as a stage station for the lines up and down the valley and eastward across the Cascades into Central Oregon. The house, as originally constructed, has two stories with a double-decked porch across the entire front and a large chimney at each end.

SITE OF FIRST BRIDGE, foot of Calapooya St., marks the point where the Willamette River was first spanned at Albany. Built in 1892, the bridge was abandoned in 1925, but the cement piers are still in use as supports for the steel towers of the Mountain States Power Company's high voltage lines. Near this spot the early Oregon poet, Sam L. Simpson, is said to have composed his well-known poem, "Ad Willametum," better known as "The Beautiful Willamette," published in the Albany *States Rights Democrat* April 18, 1868.

BRYANT PARK, on the peninsula between the Willamette and Calapooya Rivers, known as Bryant Island, is reached by a covered bridge across the Calapooya at the W. end of 3rd St. Near the entrance to the park a rough boulder monument bears a bronze plaque inscribed to Hubbard ("Hub") Bryant, donor of the land to the city. There are about 80 acres of natural hardwood forest, a baseball diamond with bleachers, a children's playground, a municipal swimming pool, and horseshoe courts. Part of the park is set aside as a camp accommodating several hundred auto tourists. Takenah, or the "deep placid pool," is in Bryant Park. A short distance above the pool is a point made memorable by David Douglas, the botanist, who camped there in November 1826.

South of Albany the valley widens into prairie-like expanses, with many scattered groves. Fields are larger and grain farming and seed-growing dominate. Canadian or field peas, alsike clover, Hungarian, hairy, and common vetch, and Italian rye grass, a forage crop much in demand in the East and Southwest, are grown.

TANGENT, 90.2 *m.* (248 alt., 127 pop.), was named because of the long straight stretch of Southern Pacific track that passes through the town.

1. Right from Tangent on a gravel road to the Calapooya River, 2 *m.*, along which is a scattered chain of PREHISTORIC MOUNDS, that extends from Albany to Brownsville (*see TOUR 2A*). A number of the most important are near the point where the road crosses the river. Stone mortars and pestles, arrow points, shell, stone, and copper beads are sometimes found, together with skeletons. The road continues west following a winding course to OAKVILLE, 6 *m.*, with the first church housing the Willamette Congregation, organized in 1850, the oldest United Presbyterian Church Society still existing in the western half of America. The building is sheltered by wide-spreading oaks.

2. Left from Tangent on a gravel road to the junction with a dirt road, 8 *m.*, L. here 0.5 *m.* to the DENNY PHEASANT FARM. On this farm, the first ring-necked, or Chinese pheasants, brought to Oregon were liberated in 1882. They were sent by a brother of the farm owner who was in the consular service at Shanghai. Now there are thousands of the magnificent birds in the Willamette Valley.

South of Tangent the prairie-like expanses are dotted at intervals by dome-like buttes. Formed by volcanic upthrusts, it is believed that at one time they formed islands in the waters that formerly filled this valley. Their upper strata abound with marine fossils, and about their bases are found ancient mammalean remains, including the tusks and teeth of mammoths and mastodons. In the surrounding foothills petrified wood is frequently exposed by the weathering of crumbling volcanic tufa (*see GEOLOGY AND PALEONTOLOGY*).

At 92.8 *m.* the highway crosses the Calapooya River, a small winding stream named for the Calapooya tribe of Indians that formerly roamed the valley. Across wide vistas the high Cascade Range is visible (L), with Mount Jefferson and the Three Sisters prominent on the skyline.

At 95.2 *m.* is a junction with a gravel road.

Left, here to BOSTON, 2 *m.*, where only the THOMPSON FLOURING MILL, built in 1856 and still in operation, remains to mark the town, that was platted in 1863. Richard Finley and his associates constructed the mill and laid plans for a flourishing community. As its trade territory increased, other businesses were established. People from all parts of the Willamette Valley and as far south as Yreka, California, came to settle in the village.

Boston was famous for its county fair, which, though primitive when compared with present-day events, was the great annual celebration of the settlers.

Local and community rivalry developed over the horse races and the agricultural exhibits, because the virgin soil produced vegetables of extraordinary size.

Boston flourished until the railroad built in the early 1870's, missed it by two miles. After Shedd (*see below*) was established about a railroad station it quickly won business away from its older neighbor and people drifted away to other places.

SHEDD, 95.9 *m.* (263 alt., 125 pop.), was named for Captain Frank Shedd, on whose donation land claim it grew up after the coming of the railroad in 1871. Rising prominently from the flat terrain are (L) Wards Butte (858 alt.) and Saddle Butte (646 alt.).

South of Shedd the swales are blue in springtime with the hyacinth-like blooms of the camas, Indian food-root. The carrot-like white-flowered Indian *Yampah,* the *carum* of the botanists, also abound; the slender plants spring from crisp, nutlike bulbs that were also relished as food by the natives.

HALSEY, 101.1 *m.* (282 alt., 300 pop.), named for William L. Halsey, vice-president of the Willamette Valley Railroad at the time of construction, ships grain, wool, and seed crops.

HARRISBURG, 110 *m.* (309 alt., 575 pop.), is a typical river town, with old buildings and traditions of the steamboat era. Here, in 1848, was established a primitive ferry—merely two boats lashed together with a platform for carrying one wagon; while the horses or oxen were forced to swim behind it. Later a scow was built to carry both wagon and team. The ferry was operated until 1925 when a bridge was built.

At 113.8 *m.* is the junction with US 99W (*see TOUR* 10); southward the route is US 99.

JUNCTION CITY, 114.3 *m.* (324 alt., 922 pop.), was named in 1871 in anticipation of becoming the meeting place of two railroads. Junction City is a prosperous trading point for people of the adjacent valleys.

Section b. Junction City to California State Line, 231 m. US 99

South of JUNCTION CITY, 0 *m.,* the highway runs through a flat section, with deep alluvial soil. Orchards of prunes, pears, cherries, peaches, walnuts, and filberts line the highway, interspersed with plantings of small fruits and commercial gardens. Peppermint growing and distillation of the oil has proved commercially practicable on the moister bottom lands.

At 1.9 *m.* is a junction with US 28 (*see TOUR* 2E).

EUGENE, 14.5 *m.* (423 alt., 18,901 pop.) (*see EUGENE*).

Points of Interest: University of Oregon, Skinner's Butte, Pioneer Museum, and others.

South of Eugene for several miles the route closely parallels the Willamette River (L).

At 17.5 *m.* is a junction (L) with US 28 (*see TOUR* 6a). Near this point, the forks of the Willamette River converge, joined by the

McKenzie River, which flows from the high Cascades. The open valley continues southward but the encircling hills slowly close in. Farms become smaller and stock raising and lumbering are important.

CORYELL PASS, 18.9 *m.,* overlooks a stretch of the Willamette River.

GOSHEN, 21.1 *m.* (500 alt., 93 pop.), yet another trade town, was named by Elijah Bristow, an early settler who believed the valley to be the Land of Promise. Goshen is at a junction with State 58 (*see TOUR 4C*).

South of Goshen the highway traverses the Goshen Floral Area, so called because of the fossils of tropical and sub-tropical flora unearthed from the underlying rocky strata. Many specimens have been found in a rocky cut at 22.9 *m.,* close to the highway. When the Southern Pacific Railway, which runs beside the highway at this point, was being constructed large numbers of finely preserved leaf casts were obtained, among them those of the fig, smilax, magnolia, laurel, ebony, oak, chestnut, and viburnum (*see GEOLOGY AND PALEONTOLOGY*).

CRESWELL, 26.7 *m.* (531 alt., 345 pop.), was founded in 1872 by Ben Holladay and named for the Postmaster General at that time. Creswell Butte (892 alt.) rises just south of the town.

COTTAGE GROVE, 35.6 *m.* (640 alt., 2,475 pop.), is in the heart of a lumbering region, though stock raising, dairying, and fruit culture are also carried on. Here in 1920 lived Opal Whitely, 22 years old, who caused a furore in the world of letters and of psychology when the *Atlantic Monthly* published serially *The Story of Opal: The Journal of an Understanding Heart,* purported to have been written by Opal Whitely when she was five or six years old. In the "diary" she appeared as a child in a logging camp, a changeling of royal parentage, whose friends were a fir tree named Michael Angelo Sanzio Raphael; a crow named Lars Porsena of Clusium; a most dear wood rat called Thomas Chatterton Jupiter Zeus; a pet pig named Brave Horatius; and a shepherd dog, Peter Paul Rubens. Opal disappeared from public notice after various curious adventures.

The Coast Fork of the Willamette River divides the town into an eastern and western section. In 1894 the west-siders sent a representative to Salem who persuaded the legislature to designate the west side as Cottage Grove and the other as East Cottage Grove. The east-siders resented this and incorporated their section of the town under the name of Lemati, thus leaving Cottage Grove off the railroad. The latter, however, had the post office and it became the duty of the Cottage Grove marshal to go to Lemati to meet the mail trains. When he neglected to remove his badge of office on crossing into alien territory the Lemati marshal immediately arrested him and clapped him into jail, there to languish until Cottage Grove paid his fine. After two years a reconciliation was effected, whereby the towns were united and incorporated under one name.

Left from Cottage Grove on an improved road up Row River to DORENA, 7 *m.,* a village in the foothills of the Calapooya Mountains. Row River was so named because of a "row" or disagreement between two pioneer families living on its banks.

DISSTON, 19 *m.*, a small lumber town at the confluence of Layng and Frank Brice Creeks, was named for a well-known brand of saws.

BOHEMIA, 30 *m.,* lies almost at the summit of the ridge between the Willamette and the Umpqua rivers, the center of the historical Bohemia Mining District, about 225 square miles of mountainous country heavily timbered with old fir, spruce and hemlock. Turbulent mountain streams fighting their way through gorges, wooded scarps, and jagged peaks, make this a region of great natural beauty. Deer, elk, cougars, bears and other game are found here in abundance.

The district was named for "Bohemia" Johnson, the man who discovered gold-bearing quartz in 1863. Johnson, an emigrant from Bohemia, is said to have killed an Indian and with another man hidden in the mountains to prevent capture. When later he brought gold out of the mountains great excitement ensued. But when it was discovered that the "dust" was not found in stream beds but must be extracted from the quartz ledges by machinery the excitement soon died out and, until 1891, only intermittent attempts were made to mine the region. However, in that year, Dr. W. W. Oglesby located and opened the Champion and Noonday mills at Music Ledge. The height of activity in the district came in 1900 after assays had demonstrated the richness of the strike. It is estimated that up to 1910 the district yielded between five hundred thousand and a million dollars. When the free milling ledges were exhausted and the cost of working the lower grade ores became prohibitive the region was gradually abandoned. From time to time attempts have been made to re-open the district and some mines are again beginning activity, but all the operations are in low grade ores.

DIVIDE, 40.3 *m.* (751 alt.), is on the crest of the watershed between the Willamette and Umpqua Valleys. This inconspicuous pass was important to the pioneer adventurers, for it was here that they left the placid valley country and plunged into a region inhabited by Indians alert for plunder.

At 47.1 *m.* is the junction (R) with an old Territorial Road, an important artery of commerce in the early 1850's, extending across the Coast Range to Scottsburg, on the lower waters of the Umpqua, thus providing the interior with transportation to the ocean.

DRAIN, 53.8 *m.* (304 alt., 497 pop.), the shipping point for a fruit, vegetable, and turkey growing area, was named for Charles Drain, last president of the Oregon Territorial Council. It was the site of one of Oregon's first normal schools. The old building stands on the hillside (L). Drain is at the junction with State 38 (*see TOUR 2G*).

YONCALLA, 59.1 *m.* (336 alt., 252 pop.), another rural trade town, was the home of Jesse Applegate, explorer, road builder, and Indian fighter of southern Oregon, captain of the famous "Cow Column," one of the first wagon trains to reach Oregon in 1843. He adopted the Indian name for the tall hill near the town; the hill in turn was named for a powerful chief of the early days.

Roselle Applegate Putnam, daughter of Jesse Applegate, in a letter dated January 25, 1852, wrote: "I have only one more question to answer which is one that really should have been answered long ago, that is what is Yoncalla—now it is not a town nor a place of man's creation nor of a white man's naming—but it is a hill round and high and beautiful; a splendid representative of hills in general—it is ten miles in circumference and one and a half in height. The north side of it is covered with fir timber, oak, hazel and various kinds of underwood—this thicety forest has been from time immemorial a harbor for deer, bear, wolves and many other kinds of wild animals. . . .

"The hill is called after a chief who with a numerous tribe once inhabited these valleys—among the few remaining survivors of this tribe that occasionally came to beg a crust of bread or an old garment that is getting worse for the wear—there are some old ones who remember the chief, say that he was a great physician and skilled in witchcraft— which is a belief still prevalent among them—his men hunted bear and deer on this hill and caught salmon in the streams around it and the women dug roots in the valleys and gathered nuts and berries on the hills—they were a numerous and happy nation—but now the busy multitudes are low and still—the dense forest whose echoes were then only wakened by the war song and the wolf's howl are now half demolished by their enterprising successors—the game is frightened away by the sound of the axe and the crack of the whip—the acorns, nuts and roots are yearly harvested by their hogs so that if these ancient owners were still living they would be deprived of their means of sustenance.

"At this time there are four men living around the foot of Yoncalla who have between four and five hundred of cattle whose chief pasturage is on this hill—besides fifty head of horses and an unnumbered stock of hogs . . . my father's claim lies at the foot of it—he keeps the post-office and called it after this hill—he is very fond of hunting and this is his hunting ground he has killed two bear and upwards of forty deer on it since he has been living there."

RICE HILL, **64.6** *m.* (710 alt.), the divide between the valley of Elk Creek and the Umpqua Valley, before the era of modern roads was a most difficult one and many an emigrant train was long delayed before reaching its summit.

The Umpqua Valley is made up of many adjoining valleys, with the farmlands usually restricted to the level portions closely bordering the stream. In the sheltered, almost windless Umpqua drainage area fruits ripen early and may be marketed with unusual profit. Prunes, cherries, pears, and apples are abundant; small fruits, blackberries, loganberries, youngberries, raspberries, and strawberries provide occupation for many, both in their culture and in their preservation. Broccoli, or winter cauliflower, is an important commercial crop. Maturing in late winter or early spring, it is in great demand in more northern and eastern markets, and is shipped in large quantities. The Umpqua Valley has also large stands of sugar pine, Douglas and white fir, hemlock, spruce, and cedar.

A granite monument (L) at **72.1** *m.* commemorates the Reverend J. A. Cornwall and family, who built the first immigrant cabin in what is now Douglas County near this site in 1846. On the trip to the West the Cornwalls traveled part of the way with the ill-fated Donner Party, which attempted to take a short cut into California, with fatal results.

OAKLAND, 73.3 *m.* (427 alt., 321 pop.), on Calapooya Creek was named for the groves of Oregon white, or Garry oak that dot the valley, bearing great clumps of the broad-leaved mistletoe. The first town of Oakland, three miles north of the present site, was a stopping point for the old California Stage Company's coaches and the center of four diverging mail routes leading to the bustling mining region of Jacksonville, to Eugene, to Marysville (Corvallis), and to Scottsburg, on the lower Umpqua.

The region about Oakland is supported by farming, stock raising, dairying, fruit growing, and lumbering, but the town's principal revenue comes from the shipment of turkeys. In late autumn and early winter, long lines of trucks loaded with dressed birds draw up at weighing platforms. Early in December a turkey show is held here, where local turkeys, both live and dressed, compete with those brought from many parts of the United States.

South of Oakland the character of the country shows a marked change in vegetation. Hills are more rugged, firs are fewer, and mingled with the oak groves are many red-barked, evergreen madronas.

SUTHERLIN, 76.1 *m.* (519 alt., 457 pop.), named for a pioneer family, is the cradle of the great turkey raising business of the Northwest. It was here, in 1851, that Mr. Sutherlin (1824-85) established the first turkey farm in Oregon. Shortly thereafter he brought fruit trees from Oregon City and planted the first orchard in southern Oregon. Sutherlin's wife, Lucy Richardson, rode Kentucky Belle, a bluegrass thoroughbred, across the plains; this horse became the ancestor of many famous race horses of the Willamette Valley. Sutherlin Valley was first called Camas Swale, because in the spring the floor of the valley was so thickly covered with the deep blue blossoms of this plant that it appeared to be a peaceful blue lake surrounded by forested hills.

South of Sutherlin, is (L), the OREGON WOODS CAMP, 78 *m.* (*adm.* 25c), a roadside museum entered through a high and unusual crib-work arch of logs, the plans for which, the owner declares, were conceived in a dream.

At WILBUR, 81.3 *m.* (464 alt., 146 pop.), the Umpqua, later called Wilbur Academy, was established in 1854 by the Rev. James H. Wilbur, (1811-87), a Methodist clergyman; it was closed in 1900. The first building was a rough log structure with a few rough pine desks. Like other Oregon pioneer places of learning, the "Rules" of the academy prohibited: "Profane, obscene or vulgar language or unchaste yarns or narratives, or immoral gestures or hints; any degree of tippling anywhere; any sort of night reveling." The pupils for the academy came "from southern Oregon, from about Jacksonville, Leland, Canyonville, Cow Creek, Lookingglass and from the northerly parts of the county, from Yoncalla, Elk Creek, Green Valley and the classic precincts of Duck Egg, Tin Pot and Shoestring."

The NORTH UMPQUA RIVER crossed at 84 *m.*, was named for the country through which it flows. Formed by tributaries in the Cascade and Calapooya ranges, the North and South Umpqua unite a few miles west of this point to form the main stream which cuts through the Coast Mountains, the lower reaches forming a wide estuary. The river affords excellent fishing for trout in the upper reaches and great silver salmon and fighting steelheads in the middle and lower channels. WINCHESTER POOL, at the crossing of the river, is a favorite lurking place for that king of all western fish, the Royal Chinook salmon.

At the southern end of the bridge are the remnants of WIN-CHESTER, 84.2 m. (459 alt.), founded by the Umpqua Exploring Expedition of 1850, and named for Herman Winchester, its captain. The town was the seat of Douglas County until 1854, when Roseburg (*see below*) was chosen in its stead. The people of Winchester not only yielded to that decision but actually moved a large part of their town to augment the successful contestant. Between Winchester, and Roseburg is the WHITE TAIL DEER REFUGE (L), a reserve of about twenty thousand acres. At 89.7 m. is the junction with a paved road.

At 89.7 m. on this road to the NORTHWEST NATIONAL SOLDIERS' HOME, 0.9 m. established as the Oregon State Soldiers' Home. This became federal in 1933, and now has modern buildings and equipment to care for 360 veterans.

ROSEBURG, 89.6 m. (478 alt., 4,362 pop.), seat of Douglas County is built along a gentle curve of the Umpqua River at its confluence with Deer Creek. In spite of round houses and car shops, fruit and vegetable canning factories, sawmills and wood-working plants, the little city maintains a domestic, settled air among the steep green hills that surround it on all sides. Homes stand on broad tree-shaded lawns and the citizens are prouder of their gardens than they are of the businesses on which their prosperity depends. Roses are the topic dearest to the householders' hearts. Having established an annual Rose Festival (May), the citizens lavish much labor and thought on their gardens, each trying to outdo the other in profusion and variety of blooms. But the town, first called Deer Creek, was not named for the popular flower; the title honors Aaron Rose (1813-89) a settler of 1851 in this then remote valley. The practical nature of the Roseburger is shown in the fact that the annual festival also celebrates the strawberry, an important crop of the environs. The fruit matures so early in this sheltered valley that the combination is practical.

Roseburg city fathers in 1882 were concerned over the laundry problem and decreed that: "Any woman who had been lawfully married and had a legitimate child or children to support may operate a hand laundry upon recommendation of the committee on health, and police."

On January 14, 1889 an ordinance was passed to prevent the use of bells on cows and other domestic animals between the hours of 8 P. M. and 6 A. M. Previous to the ordinance one citizen frequently detached the bells from cows and threw them in the gutter when on his way home in the evening, thus hoping to get a good night's sleep.

Roseburg was the home of Oregon's first Territorial Governor, Joseph Lane, who became a candidate for the Vice Presidency of the United States in 1860. His grave is in the MASONIC CEMETERY.

MOUNT HOOD AND INTERSTATE BRIDGE

INDIAN TEEPEES MOLALLA BUCKAROO

WARM SPRINGS INDIAN

BASQUE GIRLS, MALHEUR COUNTY

COLUMBIA RIVER INDIANS

INDIAN BURIAL GROUND, MEMALOOSE ISL.

LY DAY VEHICLES, THE DALLES

INDIAN TEEPEES UMATILLA RESERVATION

ASTOR COLUMN, ASTORIA

MOUNT HOOD FROM LOST LAKE

BONNEVILLE DAM

OREGON COAST, CURRY COUNTY

OUNT HOOD IN WINTER

WHEAT FIELDS, GRANDE RONDE VALLEY

ROSEBURG

LA GRAN

GAME STUDIES SURVEY

INDIANS FISHING AT CELILO FALLS

SURF FISHING, OREGON CO.

RCHERS' CAMP WITH DEER

ONE MONTH'S CATCH

FISHING IN DESCHUTES NATIONAL FOREST

From the business center (R) is a fine view of MOUNT NEBO (1,100 alt.), across the Umpqua. This angular mountain was the place, according to local tradition, where the logger's giant mythical hero, Paul Bunyan, paused on his busy way with Babe the Blue Ox. It now holds an airways beacon.

It was on Sugar Pine Mountain, west of Roseburg, that David Douglas, the Scotch botanist, discovered the sugar pine, so named for its sweet resin. He first learned of these trees when he saw its seeds in the pouch of an Indian at the falls of the Willamette near the present Oregon City. In October, 1828, while traveling southward with Hudson's Bay traders, he found his long-sought tree, magnificent in size, and with extremely long pendant cones. "These cones," wrote Douglas in his *Journals,* "are only seen on the loftiest trees, and the putting myself in possession of three of these . . . nearly brought my life to a close. As it was impossible either to climb the tree or hew it down, I endeavored to knock off the cones by firing at them with ball, when the report of my gun brought eight Indians, all of them painted with red earth, armed with bows, arrows, bone-tipped spears and flint knives. They appeared anything but friendly. I endeavored to explain to them what I wanted, and they seemed satisfied, and sat down to smoke, but presently I perceived one of them string his bow, and another sharpen his flint knife with a pair of wooden pincers, and suspend it on the wrist of his right hand. Further testimony of their intentions were unnecessary. To save myself by flight was impossible, so without hesitation I stepped back about five paces, cocked my gun, drew one of the pistols out of my belt, and holding it in my left hand and the gun in my right, showed myself determined to fight for my life. As much as possible I endeavored to preserve my coolness, and thus we stood looking at one another without making any movement or uttering a word for perhaps ten minutes, when one, at last, who seemed the leader, gave a sign that they wished for some tobacco: this I signified that they should have if they fetched me a quantity of cones. They went off immediately in search of them, and no sooner were they all out of sight, than I picked up my three cones and some twigs of the trees, and made the quickest possible retreat, hurrying back to camp, which I reached before dusk."

At 96.8 *m.* is the junction with State 42 (*see TOUR 2H.*)

DILLARD, 98.6 *m.* (540 alt., 11 pop.), on the South Umpqua, was named, as were so many Oregon towns, for the owner of the donation land claim on which it was built. Fine cantaloupes are grown hereabouts. Along the South Umpqua is seen rare Oregon myrtle, also discovered by David Douglas. The tree, easily recognized by its symmetrical, closely branched crown, has foliage that is glossy and ever green, with an odor very much like that of the bay. Indians ate the seeds of the tree and made tea from the bark. Its attractive mottled wood, now becoming very rare, takes on a high polish and is much used in cabinet work, and for bowls, vases and other small articles. Large pieces of furniture made from it have high market value.

MYRTLE CREEK, 109.7 *m.* (639 alt., 401 pop.), on a stream of the same name, serves an area where lumbering, fruit growing, dairying, and poultry raising is carried on. This region was once the range of great prehistoric mammals, as is indicated by a fossil tusk ten inches in diameter at the butt and six feet long, discovered in 1927.

At **113.9** *m.* is the junction with an improved road.

Right on this road to RIDDLE, **3** *m.* (705 alt., 195 pop.), a distributing point for lumbering and mining camps, and farms growing pears, prunes, and broccoli. Water for irrigation and power is furnished by Cow Creek, so named because in its canyon an emigrant once recovered cattle from thieving Indians.

CANYONVILLE, **119.7** *m.* (767 alt., 167 pop.), at the northern end of Canyon Creek Gorge, is also a trade town that developed as a station on the California-Oregon Stage route. In 1851 Canyonville, or Kenyonville as it was then called, had only two cabins, those of Joseph Knott and of Joel Perkins, who operated a ferry across the South Umpqua. The streams of the vicinity were the scenes of great activity when rich ledges of gold-bearing quartz were discovered.

The highway follows Canyon Creek along a route traversed in 1846 by the South Road Expedition, hunting a passage to the east. For various reasons settlers in Oregon were seeking another route across the Cascades. The Barlow Road, developed to avoid the trying and expensive passage down the Columbia, was considered too difficult to induce much travel; moreover, settlers further up the Willamette Valley were anxious to divert new arrivals to the areas in which they had taken up land and immigrants were prone to settle near the point where they reached the valley. Further, persons who were living in the upper valley were anxious to gain supporters in the struggle with the members of the Methodist missionary parties who had early seized control of valley government. Both factions were anxious to have a road across the mountains that could be used by troops they hoped would be sent to protect them if the argument with Britain over control of Oregon culminated in war.

In 1846 the colonists of the south organized an expedition to discover a southern pass and blaze a trail. Levi Scott, the leader, soon turned back to enlist more men. Among the fifteen who made the second start were Jesse and Lindsay Applegate. Near this point a party coming up from California had been attacked by Indians and one man had been severely wounded. Proceeding cautiously they crossed the mountains, swung down into northern California, turned eastward to follow the Humboldt of Nevada and then cut up to Fort Hall on the Oregon Trail. There Jesse Applegate was able to induce some members of the 1846 migration to follow his lead over the new trail; the rest of the party went ahead to clear the road.

Lindsay Applegate later wrote of the road-makers' experiences: "No circumstance worthy of mention occurred on the monotonous march from Black Rock to the timbered regions of the Cascade chain; then our labors became quite arduous. Every day we kept guard over the horses while we worked the road, and at night we dared not cease our vigilance, for the Indians continually hovered about us, seeking for advantage. By the time we had worked our way through the mountains to the Rogue River valley, and then through the Grave Creek Hills and Umpqua chain, we were pretty thoroughly worn out. Our stock of provisions had grown very short, and we had to depend to a great extent, for sustenance, on game. Road working, hunting, and guard duty had taxed our strength greatly, and on our arrival in the Umpqua valley, knowing that the greatest difficulties in the way of immigrants, had been removed, we decided to proceed at once to our homes in the Willamette." But the journey was not so easily accomplished by the immigrants as the road makers had hoped. Tabitha Brown (*see TOUR 8*), a 63-year-old member of the train, wrote of the journey from the standpoint of the party led by Jesse Applegate: "We had sixty miles of desert without grass or water, mountains to climb, cattle giving out, wagons breaking, emigrants sick and dying, hostile Indians to guard against by night and day, if we would save ourselves and our horses and cattle from being arrowed and stole.

"We were carried hundreds of miles south of Oregon into Utah Territory and California; fell in with the Clamotte and Rogue River Indians, lost nearly all our cattle, passed the Umpqua Mountains, 12 miles through. I rode through in three days at the risk of my life, on horseback, having lost my wagon and all that I had but the horse I was on. Our families were the first that started through the canyon, so that we got through the mud and rocks much better than those that followed. Out of hundreds of wagons, only one came through without breaking. The canyon was strewn with dead cattle, broken wagons, beds, clothing, and everything but provisions, of which latter we were nearly all destitute. Some people were in the canyon two or three weeks before they could get through. Some died without any warning, from fatigue and starvation. Others ate the flesh of cattle that were lying dead by the wayside."

Canyon Creek flows through a part of the UMPQUA NATIONAL FOREST.

COW CREEK GAME RESERVE (R), a mountainous and timbered area is surrounded on three sides by Cow Creek.

The summit of the CANYON CREEK PASS (2,302 alt.) is at **128.6** *m.*

AZALEA, **130.6** *m.* (80 pop.), in a little open valley surrounded by forests of fir, yellow pine, oak, and alder, was so-named because of abundance of this plant with its beautiful tinted blossom in the vicinity.

At **138** *m.* is the junction with an improved road.

Right on this road to GLENDALE, 4 *m.* (1,425 alt., 800 pop.), supposedly named for Glendale, Scotland, in the heart of a mining and lumbering region.

The SITE OF THE SIX-BIT-RANCH, **138.6** *m.* was a station on the Oregon and California State route in the early fifties and was so named because of an interruption made by the owner when soldiers were about to hang an Indian near the ranch; the owner demanded that the hanging be delayed until the Indian paid six bits that he owed him.

STAGE ROAD PASS, (1,916 alt.) is crossed at **140.5** *m.*

WOLFCREEK, **144.2** *m.* (1,276 alt., 130 pop.), has two names; the railway station is Wolf Creek, but the postoffice department makes the name one word. WOLF CREEK TAVERN, opened in 1857 and still in use, is a long neat two-story building, with a two-story wing. The roof of the two-story veranda, which runs across the front of the main building, is formed by an extension of the roof of the house. Panelled doors with transoms and side lights open onto the porch from the central halls on each floor. The structure, little changed through the years, stands behind a white picket fence. Many travelers of note have stopped here, among them President Hayes, Jack London, and Sinclair Lewis.

South of Wolfcreek, US 99 sinuously ascends to the summit of Wolf Creek Hill, **147** *m.,* and to GRAVE CREEK, **150.4** *m.* Grave Creek was so named because Josephine Crowley, daughter of Leland Crowley, died and was buried here in 1846. October 30, 1855, occurred the Battle of Grave Creek—sometimes called the Battle of Hungry Hill, or the Battle of Bloody Springs—in which six Oregon volunteers and three regulars were slain by Indians.

SEXTON MOUNTAIN (3,855 alt.), above SEXTON MOUN- TAIN PASS, **154** *m.,* (2,046 alt.), is surmounted by a forest lookout and an airway radio station and beacon.

As the highway descends, manzanita, with roundish, evergreen leaves and red-barked branches, is seen. In this area it often covers immense tracts with its dense, elfin-like forests. The fruit of the manzanita is like a small plump apple, dry and tasteless, which the Indians ground into a fine meal that was leached with water, to produce a rich and delicious cider.

On the side of Sexton Mountain, at **160.9** *m.,* is a roadside monument (L), erected to Burrell M. Baucom, a state policeman and World War veteran, who was killed at this point in the performance of his duties, July 1, 1933. Baucom was slain when he stopped Harry Bowles, 21, and John Barrier, 17—two youths he had stopped to question about an auto they were driving. Barrier admitted firing the three shots that killed the state trooper. The monument, made of southern Oregon granite, bears a bronze plaque inscribed: "In memory of Burell M. Baucom an officer and soldier brave of heart, sincere of purpose, and faithful to trust, who fell here July 1, 1933, in performance of his duty, this tablet in inscribed by his fellow members of the Oregon State Police and Oregon National Guard. Dedicated February 25, 1934."

At **163.4** *m.* is a junction with a market road.

Right on this road, to MERLIN, 3 *m.,* site of early gold mining activity. The laboratories of a former mining and milling company are still standing. The ruins of prehistoric pit houses near Merlin are among the earliest anthropological remains found in Oregon.

At GALICE, 17 *m.,* also a pioneer gold mining town, are the ruins of a Rogue River Indian War powder house and arsenal, built about 1854.

"Galice Creek" has its origin in an episode that took place in early times between the "pack train" men and an old Indian who lived there. Old John would watch for a mule train to strike camp, and then he would draw up his blanket until only his eyebrows and face were visible, seat himself on the ground near the camp fire, and every turn in the culinary operations of getting supper would cause him to say, NIKA TIKA MUCKA MUCKE, which was an appeal for something to eat. Packers were liberal men and the appeals of even a savage never went unheeded, but patience sometimes when overtaxed will call out other qualities in the man, and these rude pioneers, when they had filled their old beggar almost to bursting, on the evening of their arrival were not in good humor when he took up his station for breakfast and commenced his same plaintive wail demanding 'gleece' which meant bacon. They concluded to fill him up for good, and taking a side of fat bacon, they cut slices and handed to him, which he greedily devoured for a while. At last he signified a sufficiency by shaking his head and saying, WAKE TIKA GLEECE. But you may judge of his surprise when the packer drew a six shooter and cocking the weapon drew a bead on old John and handed him another slice and ordered him to eat it, and another, and another, each time enforced by coercive demonstrations with the pistol until the old Indian's outraged stomach could stand no more. He lost his appetite for gleece and the creek has always borne the name of Galice Creek since that event.

ALAMEDA, 21 m., another mining town whose glory has departed, now contains the RAND UNITED STATES FOREST RANGER STATION. At the mouth of Grave Creek, a few miles north of town but inaccessible by automobile, lie LITTLE MEADOWS and BIG MEADOWS, which were rallying points for Oregon volunteers in the Rogue River Indian wars. These points were the scenes of several skirmishes.

The whole country in the "Gorge of the Roaring Rogue" is highly mineralized with deposits of gold, silver, and copper. The gorge is one of the wildest regions of all Oregon. It is almost inaccessible except where new and improved roads lead into it from a number of points. It is a mecca for hunters and fishermen who come from many parts of the world, but only experienced boatmen should venture upon its waters, for its bars and rapids, and its Hell Gate Canyon are hazardous. Many well-known people have summer lodges in the deeper wilderness; hunters, explorers, and writers, come here for rest and recreation. Peter B. Kyne and ex-President Herbert Hoover fish the river regularly, as formerly did Zane Grey.

GRAVE CREEK BRIDGE, 25 m., is at the end of the auto road down the Rogue. Pack trains of horses or mules furnish the only regular transportation between Grave Creek Bridge and Agness, on the lower river. Horses and packers are available for trail trips at Galice, Illahee, and Agness. From Grave Creek Bridge a pack trail leads down the Rogue River to RAINIE FALLS, 27 m., WHISKEY CREEK, 28 m., and the HORSESHOE BEND GUARD STATION, 38 m.

MULE CREEK GUARD STATION and the post office of MARIAL, 49 m., are at the mouth of Mule Creek. This creek was originally John Mule Creek and the name appears as such in mining records from 1864 to as late as 1904 when the present name filters in. John Mule was an Indian who for many years made his home on the meadow at the mouth of the stream. In the sixties two miners on John Mule Creek had a falling out and one of them, called Dutch Henry, shot the other with a rifle, but his opponent, known as Big George Jack, struck Dutch Henry with an axe. The two men were found two days later, still alive but too badly wounded to be moved; whereupon miners built a cabin over them and sent more than eighty miles for a doctor. Both men recovered.

ILLAHEE, 55 m. (see TOUR 2H), is a village and commercial resort (horses and packers available). Many years ago John Fitzhugh was mining near Illahee. His provisions running low he went in search of game. His shoes were worn out so he went barefoot. He had gone but a short way when he noticed what he took to be a bear track and he followed the spoor for the best part of the day. Finally he scrutinized the tracks more closely and came to the conclusion that he had been tracking himself all the time. In relating the story he ended: "I don't know what would have happened if I had caught up with myself as I am a pretty good shot."

AGNESS, 63 m., is another packing center and commercial resort for hunters and fishermen on the north bank of the Rogue. From Agness to Gold Beach the trip must be made by motor boat. Points touched are LOWERY'S, 75 m., LOBSTER CREEK, 83 m., BAGNELL FERRY, 89 m., WEDDERBURN, 94 m., and GOLD BEACH. 95 m. on US 101 (see TOUR 3b).

GRANTS PASS, 168 m. (948 alt., 4,666 pop.), the seat of Josephine County, lies at the southern end of a narrow valley on the bank of the Rogue River. With long streets bordered with tree-shaded houses diverging from the compact business district toward the enclosing hills, the city presents an aspect of modernity. The Southern Pacific bisects the town and store buildings press upon the tracks from either side. Modern structures have replaced the old false-front wooden buildings and filling stations and ice-cream parlors have taken the place of the hitching racks and dim-lighted saloons of other days. However, Saturday night is still a time of unusual activity when ranchers, miners, and lumberjacks, mingle with townsmen and tourists along the brightly lighted streets.

The town, which came into existence as a stopping place on the California Stage route, was named by enthusiastic builders of the road over the pass when a messenger told them of General Grant's capture of Vicksburg. It is the trading, banking, and shopping center of the Grants Pass Irrigation District, which produces pears, prunes, apples, grapes, and cherries, and is an active dairying region. In the environs gladiolus culture is carried on and during the blossoming months, June to August, the flower fields present a gorgeous sight. An annual gladiolus show is held during the fourth week in July.

There is considerable logging nearby and sawmills and wood-working plants are numerous. The city draws much wealth from the mines in the surrounding mountains. Gold, copper, platinum, silver, and chromium are among the more important minerals. Miners still come in from the back country with their dust, which is bought by local banks. The mineral resources of the region, together with the proximity of the Oregon Caves (see TOUR 2I), have drawn the attention of many citizens to the collection of minerals. Some excellent exhibits are those in the lobby of the Hotel Del Rogue, 6th and K Sts., the Caves Grotto at the Redwood Hotel, 6th and E Sts., and the semi-precious stones collected by Eclus Pollock.

The CITY PARK on the south bank of the Rogue provides facilities for swimming, boating, tennis, and other sports. The Oregon Cavemen, a social and service club, hold annual festivities and carnivals, in which the members impersonate their primal forbears. The Cavemen claim the marble halls of the Oregon Caves as their ancestral home. Symbolically their food and drink consists of the meat of the dinosaur and the blood of the saber-tooth tiger. The officers of the organization are Chief Big Horn, Rising Buck, keeper of the wampum, Clubfist, Wingfeather, and Flamecatcher.

Rogue River is one of the best fishing streams of the nation. Fishing riffles are within a mile of the city, and up and down the river are more than 200 miles of fine fishing waters. In the city is the HEADQUARTERS OF THE SISKIYOU NATIONAL FOREST, 6th and F Sts.

US 99 crosses the Rogue River, 169 *m.,* on the graceful CAVEMEN'S BRIDGE to a junction with US 199 at 169.3 *m.* (*see TOUR 2I*).

US 99 curves sharply left and at 169.4 *m.* is a junction with State 238.

Right on State 238 to MURPHY, 4.1 *m.* (1,600 alt.), and PROVOLT, 13.9 *m.,* small mountain hamlets. Right from Provolt on a gravel road, 6 *m.* along Williams Creek to WILLIAMS, which came into existence as Williamsburg in 1857, when gold was discovered on Williams Creek. Miners flocked in until there were a thousand residents, but the camp soon passed into oblivion.

At 12 *m.* the graveled road ends at a camp (*over-night facilities*). From this point a trail leads over the mountains to the OREGON CAVES, 22.3 *m.* (*see TOUR 2I*).

On State 238 is APPLEGATE, 18.4 *m.* (30 pop.), in a mining, fruit-growing, and lumbering region. It was named for Jesse and Lindsay Applegate (*see above*). In early days all streams of this region were worked for gold and some small fortunes were taken from the gravel. Local legend perpetuates the tale that a Chinaman, "Chiny Linn," removed more than two million dollars in gold from his claim but this is probably erroneous as the district was never one of the great producers.

In Jackson Creek at JACKSONVILLE, 34.9 *m.* (1,600 alt., 806 pop.) in January, 1852, James Cluggage and J. R. Poole discovered gold. Now untrimmed trees, dropping low over moss-grown houses and crumbling brick buildings, line streets once noisy with the tramp of miners' feet, or shrill with the chatter of pig-tailed Orientals. Cornices of old brick structures threaten to fall and demolish sagging corrugated awnings, beneath which miners, harlots, and merchants once paraded. Bearded men now drowse on benches outside dusty shops where dozens of empty whiskey bottles displayed in windows are reminders of a lively past. Following the decline of gold production, Jacksonville lost its population, and in 1927 the county seat was moved to Medford. Small back-yard mines take the place of family gardens in a place where men washed as much as a pint cup of gold in a day. William Hanley (1861-1935), the eastern Oregon cattle baron, was born here.

In the window of the J. A. BRUNNER BUILDING, erected in 1855 and on occasion used as a refuge from Indians, are gold scales on which hundreds of thousands of dollars worth of gold dust were weighed. In the building is a museum of pioneer relics. In the UNITED STATES HOTEL where President Hayes and General William T. Sherman spent a night, are displayed leg irons, ox shoes, a cradle for grain, gold coins and scales, and many other articles. According to legend, the METHODIST CHURCH was built in 1854 with one night's take at the gaming tables. In this small building gamblers, roughly-dressed proprietors, and sedate bankers, dropped their nuggets into the collection plate. The melodeon was brought around Cape Horn, up the coast to Crescent City, and over the mountains on the backs of mules. The church, a simple white clapboarded structure, has a small bell tower and steeple in one gabled end. The OLD BARN was used for the relay horses of the California-Oregon Stage Line. The BEEKMAN BANK, built in 1862, made express shipments of gold to Crescent City, the California port. East of Jacksonville, State 238 passes through an attractive suburban area of small houses and orchards to MEDFORD, 39.9 *m.* (*see MEDFORD*), at the junction with US 99.

At SAVAGE RAPIDS DAM, 175 *m.* on the Rogue, salmon and steelhead flash in the sunlight as they leap the falls.

ROGUE RIVER, 178.3 *m.* (1,025 alt., 286 pop.), is on the north bank of the Rogue River and is connected with the highway by a bridge (L).

Established as Woodville, it was known in pioneer times by the expressively significant moniker of "Tailhold." It has borne the present name since 1912. The town, situated at one of the early ferries of the Rogue River, clusters on the rocky north bank of the river among ragged growths of pine.

Directly across the river from the town is a "rattlesnake farm" or "garden" where 8,000 rattlesnakes are being fed and "fattened" to provide rattlesnake meat (an expensive delicacy), and venom, which is used medicinally. A Los Angeles packing company purchases the meat and a drug company the poison, which is often prescribed in epileptic cases and in the preparation of anti-toxins. The public is invited to visit the rattler farm, and if any person will bring a live native rattler with him the standing price is one dollar each. To keep the serpents at home there is an inner wall of masonry four feet high and three feet below the surface of the ground, and an outer wall eight feet high and three feet below the surface.

A monument here marks the SITE OF THE DAVID BIRDSEYE HOUSE built of square hewn timbers in 1855. It was used as a fortress and called Fort Birdseye in the Rogue River Indian wars.

ROCKY POINT HOUSE (L), 184.3 *m.,* about 200 yards from the highway, was built by L. J. White in 1864. From the time of its erection until the coming of the railroad in 1883, it was a tavern on the stage line between Redding, California and Roseburg. Once the scene of colorful activity when stages swept up to its broad porches and dislodged the motley cargo of adventurers, bad men, miners, and immigrants, the building is now the property of a large pear orchard and packing plant.

The tavern was built of hand-hewn timbers. Of southern Colonial style, it is of rectangular shape, two stories high, with low pitched roof and a double decked porch the full width of the house. A large chimney for fireplaces dominates the west end of the house. It is perhaps the only complete surviving example of the old stage coach taverns still having its horse stalls and carriage house attached in a long wing at the rear. The building is of heavy box-type construction, built of undressed boards placed on end with no studding and covered with dressed siding which is painted white.

GOLD HILL, 186.6 *m.* (1,108 alt., 502 pop.), like many of the places in this region, owes its name to a discovery of gold in the surrounding uplands. Here, in 1860 was established the first quartz mill in Jackson County. Limestone and marl are abundant, and large Portland cement manufacturing plants utilize this material.

Left from Gold Hill on State 234 to SAMS VALLEY, 7 *m.,* formerly the home of Chief Sam of the Rogue River tribe. At 9 *m.* is the junction with a graveled road; R. here 2.6 *m.* to the marked TABLE ROCK TREATY SITE, where on September 10, 1853, Gen. Joseph Lane, concluded peace negotiations with the Rogue River Indians, who had taken arms against the whites who had plowed up their ground, depriving the Indians of food plants and driving away their game. The surrounding country was the scene of the battles of 1851.

Southeast of Gold Hill US 99 crosses the Rogue River, and at **186.8** *m.* diverges from the old Jacksonville stage road (*see above*).

At **191.6** *m.* is the junction with a gravel road.

Left on this road to the monument marking the SITE OF FORT LANE, 0.5 *m.* Built in 1853 by Capt. Andrew J. Smith, the fort was military headquarters in that region for several years and it was here that the treaty was signed after the Indian wars. The property of the fort was relinquished to the Department of the Interior in 1871. At 2 *m.* are TOLO and the GOLD RAY DAMS, which impound the Rogue River for use in irrigation and for power development.

CENTRAL POINT, **195.8** *m.* (1,290 alt., 821 pop.), is a shipping point for farm products, fruits and vegetables. Central Point was so named because it was near the center of the valley where two stage routes crossed.

MEDFORD, **200** *m.* (1,377 alt., 11,007 pop.), (*see MEDFORD*).

Points of Interest: Jackson County Court House, City Park, Medford Public Library, fruit packing plants.

South of Medford US 99 passes through orchard tracts, with large pear packing plants at intervals.

PHOENIX, **204.7** *m.* (1,566 alt., 430 pop.), settled in 1850 by Samuel Colver, is said to have received its name after a disasterous fire. In 1855 a blockhouse called Camp Baker was erected here; manned by fifteen men it withstood a siege by the Rogue River Indians. Originally known as Gastown, Phoenix was platted in 1854, before which it was a stage stop where meals were served by a very loquacious woman. The SAMUEL COLVER HOUSE, built in 1855 of logs and later sheathed with sawed lumber, served as a refuge from the Indians. The logs beneath the sheathing are pierced by loopholes for rifle fire. Directly west of the house is the smaller house of Hiram Colver, a brother.

TALENT, **207** *m.* (1,586 alt., 421 pop.), first called Wagner, was renamed to honor A. P. Talent, who platted the townsite in the early 1880's.

South of Talent US 99 follows up Bear Creek, crossing it many times.

JACKSON HOT SPRINGS (R), **210** *m.*, a favorite swimming pool for pioneer boys, have been commercially exploited.

At **211.9** *m.* is the junction with a gravel road.

Right here to ASHLAND MINE, 3 *m.*, still in operation. This is a region of small widely scattered gold deposits, where a spring freshet, ditching in the fields, or even a spadeful of turned-up garden earth may reveal a nugget.

ASHLAND, **212.5** *m.* (1,900 alt., 4,544 pop.), lies at the southern extremity of the Rogue River Valley on the banks of Bear Creek which winds through the town. Southward the towering Siskiyous cut the horizon. Northward the broad reaches of the valley, checkered with pear and apple orchards, stretch away to the fretful waters of the Rogue River. The town was named in 1852 by Abel D. Hillman either for Ashland, Ohio, or for the birthplace of Henry Clay at Ashland, Virginia. The post office was first called Ashland Mills because of a grist mill here. The trade of farmers and orchardists and the handling of their products is the principal source of community revenue, though lumbering, mining, and the shipment of gray granite and white marble from nearby quarries add to the city's assets. The first marble works here were established in 1865.

In August Ashland holds a Shakespearean Festival at the Elizabethan Theater, which in the early 1900's housed the annual Chautauqua series. The building had been condemned and after the dome was removed, Angus Bowman, who later became director of the Shakespearean theater, noticed the resemblance to the Globe Theater of Shakespeare's time. A sixteenth century stage was built and costumes made from discarded clothing found in the Ashland attics for the first festival in 1935. In addition to several Shakespearean plays there are archery contests, bowling on the green, and folk dances. A prize is awarded to the man who grows the most handsome spade beard, and the male citizen who cannot, or will not raise a beard is sentenced to spend an hour in the stocks in the city square. Some of the actors are home talent but most of them are out-siders who are not paid from the festival; many of the latter support themselves by odd jobs—bell-hopping, gardening, dishwashing, farm work—during their stay at Ashland.

Ashland is in a region of mineral springs; at the civic center is LITHIA PLAZA, in which are two fountains with copious flows of lithia water. One fountain, of bronze, has been dedicated to H. B. and H. H. Carter, early settlers, and is ornamented with the heroic-sized figure of a scout; the other fountain is of gray granite, quarried and polished nearby.

Adjoining the plaza is LITHIA PARK (*playgrounds, tennis and horseshoe courts; tourist camp*), a large tract of hardwood and fir, attractively landscaped. In this park is a zoo containing wild animals of the region.

North of the park on a sloping hillside is a marble STATUE OF ABRAHAM LINCOLN.

At the southern limits of Ashland, US 99 passes the campus of the SOUTHERN OREGON COLLEGE OF EDUCATION, one of three in the state. This institution was established (1869) as Ashland College by the Methodist Episcopal Conference.

At 213.6 m. is the junction with State 66 (*see TOUR 5E*). Here US 99 begins to rise rapidly towards the main range of the SISKIYOUS (Ind., bob-tailed horse). In 1828 Alexander McLeod, a Hudson's Bay trapper, was heading a party in the mountains; they were lost in a snow-storm, suffered severe privations, and lost several horses, among them the bob-tailed race-horse belonging to the leader. This mountain pass was thereafter called "the pass of the Siskiyou," a name that was later given to the whole range.

The forests of the Siskiyous appear green and fresh, with yellow pine, Douglas fir, hemlock, cedar, and sugar pine, mingled with many oaks and madronas. In the higher regions grow the Brewer spruce and Sadler oak. Undergrowth consists of manzanita, blue and white flowered *ceanothus* (wild lilac), and the red-berried kinnikinnick, whose leaves were formerly used as a substitute for tobacco. Beneath the taller growths are many flowers, while in places the whole forest floor is carpeted with an aromatic mint-like vine, the *yerba buena* of the Spanish-California missionaries, the Oregon tea of the more northern settlements.

A few miles to the west of the open, sunny summit of SISKIYOU PASS, 225.3 *m.* (4,522 alt.), occurred a most notorious train holdup. On October 11, 1923, the three D'Autremont brothers, Hugh, 19 years of age, and Roy and Ray, 23-year-old twins, swung onto the tender of the southbound Shasta Limited No. 13 just outside of the small station of Siskiyou and ordered the engineer to stop the train, which he did at the southern end of Tunnel Number 13. Under the leadership of Hugh the amateurs at crime shot and killed the engineer, the fireman, and a brakeman. When the mail clerk opened the mail-car door in answer to the order to come out, they shot at him, but he managed to close the door in time. Unable to enter the car the bandits dynamited it, but the gases and flames from the explosion further thwarted them and they fled into the rough Siskiyou wilderness without a penny for their efforts. In their haste, they left some supplies and other articles behind them. The most important to detectives was a pair of overalls, in a pocket of which was the receipt for a registered letter signed by Hugh.

Immediately the railroad's telegraph wires sizzled with the news. The U. S. Post Office Department threw out the largest net it had ever cast for fugitives. The Southern Pacific and the American Railway joined the state of Oregon and the Federal government in offering dead-or-alive rewards that totaled $5,300 for each culprit. Bulletins and posters bearing pictures of the brothers appeared conspicuously in every railway station and post office in the country. Canada and Mexico also posted "wanted" notices. The search spread to all parts of the world and descriptions of the men were issued in seven languages.

Many fake clues were followed before a soldier early in 1927, landing in San Francisco after serving in the Philippines, noticed the resemblance between the picture of Hugh D'Autremont on a post office circular and a soldier in the 31st Infantry in the Islands. The authorities were notified and Hugh was captured on February 12 and was brought to Oregon, where he was indicted for murder.

The trial opened on May 3 at Jacksonville, becoming the town's most important event since the gold stampedes of the 1850's. A mistrial resulted when one of the jurors died, and a second trial began on June 6 and ended on June 21, when Hugh was sentenced to life imprisonment.

Meanwhile, the search for the twins continued and on June 8 they were arrested in Steubenville, Ohio, where they had been living and working as the Winston brothers. Ray had married and had one child. They had heard of Hugh's capture and after first denying their identity, waived extradition and were returned to Oregon, where they confessed to the crime. Hugh then admitted his guilt. The twins were also given life sentences.

At **231** *m.* US 99 crosses the California Line, 54 miles north of Weed, California. *(Plant inspection at line.)*

Tour 2A

Oregon City—Mulino—Silverton—Stayton—Lebanon—Brownsville— Eugene; 115.5 m.   State 215, State 211, unnumbered roads.

Road partly paved, partly graveled.
Southern Pacific Railroad branch line parallels route.
Usual accommodations.

The delightful back-country route winds southward through a fertile farming country facing the evergreen foothills of the Cascade Range. Closely following an early road opened by the Hudson's Bay Company brigades, and later developed as the California-Oregon Territorial Road, it penetrates many isolated villages that bear new hallmarks of the present. Split-rail worm fences divide fields and covered bridges span many of the streams. Farm houses with moss-covered shake roofs silvered by the sun and rains of a hundred years stand beside the highways that run between busy modern towns and dying villages.

State 215 branches southeastward from US 99E (*see TOUR 2a*) in OREGON CITY, 0 *m.*, and passes through meadows and orchards to the Molalla Valley, once a hunting ground of the Klamath, Molalla, and Calapooya. The Klamath made yearly visits to their allies and kinsmen of the district by way of the old Klamath Trail, which crossed the Cascades near Mount Jefferson. The first white men to come to this territory were led by Donald McKenzie of Astor's Pacific Fur Company, who explored and trapped in the region in 1812.

MULINO (Sp. *molino,* mill), **10.6** *m.* (236 alt., 106 pop.), was first called Howard's Mill after the nucleus of the grist mill (R) had been erected in 1851.

The highway crosses the Molalla River to LIBERAL, **12.8** *m.* (256 alt., 22 pop.), the trading center of a farming and dairying district.

At **13.4** *m.* is a junction with State 211.

Left on State 211 to MOLALLA, 1.6 m. (371 alt., 655 pop.), in an area where farming, lumbering and fruit-growing are carried on. The first white man to settle in the vicinity was William Russel, who took up a claim in 1840. The Molalla Buckaroo, the largest rodeo in western Oregon, is held here annually about July Fourth.

The main route, now the southern sector of State 211, cuts across the flat lands between the Molalla and Pudding rivers. The valley Indians used to burn the tall grass in the area to round up the game.

MARQUAM, 22.7 m. (291 alt., 150 pop.), named for Alfred Marquam, a settler, is in a region supported by the culture of hops and prunes.

At 24.7 m. is the junction with a paved road.

Right here to MOUNT ANGEL, 6 m. (167 alt., 979 pop.), where in 1883 a monastery was established by the Order of St. Benedict. In 1904 Mt. Angel's College and Seminary was built on Mount Angel Butte (485 alt.) just east of the town. It is reached by a winding drive that commands a far-reaching view of the valley. The long three-story building of light-colored brick has at each end short ells extending forward with gabled ends. In the center is a chapel, forming a third wing which consists of a two-story gabled structure entered through a small enclosed portico; above it and somewhat to the rear rises a much gabled section, which with lower extensions at the side produces the effect of a clerestory. Nearby is a large cooperative creamery operated by the order. The aborigines called the butte Topalamhoh (place of communion with the Great Spirit).

In the center of Mount Angel, is SAINT MARY'S PARISH CHURCH, its spire visible for many miles, of a modified Gothic structure and elaborately decorated.

The town is a trading point for hops, prunes, and flax. In a FLAX SCUTCHING PLANT (*visited on application*) the fibres of the flax are beaten free. It is one of three establishments of its kind built by the state with federal aid in the Willamette Valley.

SILVERTON, 29.6 m. (249 alt., 2,462 pop.), takes its name from Silver Creek, which flows through the town at the edge of the Waldo Hills. The nucleus of the settlement, called Milford, grew up around a sawmill built in 1846, at a point two miles east.

The parents of Edwin Markham, the poet, settled on a donation land claim a short distance north of Silverton, but later moved to Oregon City where their son was born.

Silverton Bobbie, a dog of the town, was taken east in 1926 and disappeared from the car in Indiana. He turned up again at this place, having found his way home alone. His wanderings were described imaginatively in *Bobbie, a Great Collie,* by Charles Alexander.

Left from Silverton on State 214 to SILVER CREEK FALLS STATE PARK (*picnicking facilities*), 15.5 m., an area including nine attractive waterfalls, several of which are almost 200 feet high. The falls are all within a radius of three miles and are easily reached by forest trails.

State 214 circles R. to a junction with the main route, 25.4 m.

South of Silverton the route follows an unnumbered road and climbs over the Waldo Hills, where Samuel L. Simpson (1845-1909), author of the volume of poems *Gold Gated West,* spent several years of his youth. T. T. Geer, governor of Oregon from 1899 to 1903, was born near Silverton in these hills in 1851. He went to school at Salem but when he was fourteen came back here to work at his cousin's farm. In 1877 he came again to the farm and made his living on it for twenty years. On the farm he wrote his book *Fifty Years in Oregon* (1912). Frank Bowers, the cartoonist, Margaret Mayo, the playwright, and Margarita Fischer, screen actress were also from this neighborhood.

The earliest white settlement in the Waldo Hills was made in 1843 by Daniel Waldo. Years later he wrote: "Oregon was just like all other new countries. For a long time we had to pack our own blankets and no place to sleep. There was only a little town at Oregon City. I always kept people without charging them a cent. I accommodated quite a number of people in my house out here on the road. We had not very many beds; they would sleep on the floor anyhow. I would give them their supper and breakfast. It was pretty hard on the women but they were healthy. . . . There was no sickness. More of the people got drowned in ten years than died . . . We had parties here in the early times and once in a while a dance. They [the settlers] would go fifteen or twenty miles and think nothing of it. They would ride at a pretty good jog, men and women both. There were about as many women as men, young and old and married and all kinds. . . . There was plenty to eat then; plenty of pork, beef and wheat. We had a fiddle of course . . . "

The BIRTHPLACE OF HOMER DAVENPORT (*private*) is (L) at **34.2** *m*. The cartoonist whose most notable creation was the suit covered with dollar marks on Mark Hanna was born here on his father's donation claim in 1851. On the back porch of the tree-shaded farm dwelling is a drawing by Davenport which he made while a boy. He was continually drawing cartoons and likenesses of local people and of farm animals on the walls and smooth boards of the barn, on the woodshed and house, or any surface available. Davenport never lost his love for the Waldo Hills, and once said: "From this old porch I see my favorite view of all the earth affords. . . It's where my happiest hours have been spent."

SUBLIMITY, **43.6** *m*. (538 alt., 214 pop.), (*see TOUR 7A*), is at a junction with State 222, with which the route is united to STAYTON, **45.9** *m*. (447 alt., 797 pop.), (*see TOUR 7A*). Here State 222 turns L.

Southward, the unnumbered route crosses the North Santiam River and winds crookedly southwestward along the river, then southward to SCIO, **55.7** *m*. (300 alt., 258 pop.), which was named for a town in Ohio, named in turn for the island of Chios in the Mediterranean. It was near here that Joab Powell, the circuit rider, organized the Providence Baptist Church in 1853. Powell ranged over the Willamette Valley preaching salvation by immersion. "Uncle Joab" wore home-made jean trousers "four feet across the seat," and as a preliminary to preaching would place a chew of tobacco in his mouth. He invariably commenced his sermons by saying, "I am Alpha and Omegay," and, when his appeals failed to obtain a response, would remark, "There is not much rejoicing in Heaven tonight." Powell was a great eater and preferred cabbage to potato for breakfast.

The unnumbered road continues southward; below a junction with State 226 it is paved.

LEBANON, 69.5 *m.* (341 alt., 1,851 pop.), (*see TOUR 7b*), is at the junction with State 54.

Right from Lebanon on a country road to the old settlement of TALLMAN, 4.5 *m.* (306 alt.), birthplace of Frederic Homer Balch, novelist (*see HOOD RIVER*).

South of Lebanon the route is united briefly with State 54, turns R. from State 54, then L. winds between hills and cultivated fields, over unnumbered roads to BROWNSVILLE, 83.7 *m.* (358 alt., 746 pop.), at the entrance to the Calapooya Valley. First called Kirk's Ferry, it was later named for Hugh L. Brown, a settler of 1846, who with his nephew, Capt. James Blakely, laid out the townsite in 1853. The community grew up about woolen mills, established by local citizens as a cooperative venture, with machinery and a textile expert brought from the East.

George A. Waggoner, pioneer of 1852, one of the first railroad commissioners of Oregon, and author of *Stories of Old Oregon,* and Z. F. Moody, governor of Oregon, 1882-1887, lived here. The Reverend H. H. Spalding, who crossed the Rockies with Marcus Whitman and their wives, also lived here for a time.

Many of the pioneer structures are decaying, but the town has the atmosphere of a bygone day in spite of its granite monument to the memory of James Blakely. There is an extensive park on the banks of the Calapooya River.

Here are two PREHISTORIC MOUNDS, one on East Penn Street in North Brownsville and the other across the river in South Brownsville. While no excavations have been made, it is believed that these mounds are part of a chain of 89 along the Calapooya River between Albany and Brownsville (*see INDIANS*).

South of Brownsville the route closely follows the Springfield Branch of the Southern Pacific Railroad, crossing it numerous times. The region is uniformly level, with extensive plantings of rye grass for seed and hay. Dairying, sheep-raising, turkey culture, and general farming are carried on.

At 85.3 *m.* is a right angle turn at a junction with an unimproved road.

Left on this road to the SITE OF UNION POINT, 1.7 *m.,* scene of the meeting of February 10, 1852, at which was consummated a union of the various branches of the Presbyterian churches in Oregon. Union Point was on the Old Territorial Road, which, south of the settlement, entered a defile in the hills long called the Big Gap. This road, now neglected and almost impassable, was the course taken by early travelers to and from the Upper Valley and by gold-seekers of 1849 and 1854.

At 88 *m.* is TWIN BUTTES, (508 alt.), near the railroad (L). After crossing the railroad the road swings south past BOND BUTTE,

(500 alt.), distinguished by an airway beacon on its summit. East of Bond Butte are the prominent INDIAN HEAD BUTTES (1,294 alt.). Behind them rise foothills of the Cascades, tier upon tier. This region was once inhabited by the fierce grizzly, now almost extinct.

ROWLAND, 94.2 m., is only a railroad station but in the early 1860's it was a trading point.

At 104.1 m. is the junction with a narrow lane.

Left on the lane (*muddy and impassable in rainy weather*) to the marked HULINS MILLER HOMESTEAD, 1.7 m., where after crossing the plains with his father, Cincinnatus Heiner (Joaquin) Miller, the poet (*see TOUR 5a*), lived from 1854 until 1856, when he was fifteen years old. The present farmhouse rests on the foundations of the Miller house. Sunny Ridge, on which the house stands, offers a magnificent view of the surrounding region. The entire Miller family were highly appreciative of the primitive beauty of the Willamette Valley. The great mountains in the rear, young Miller wrote, were "topped with wonderful fir trees that gloried in the morning sun, the swift, sweet river, glistening under the great big cedars, and balm trees in the boundless dooryard."

COBURG, 107.7 m. (399 alt., 263 pop.), at the foot of the Coburg Hills (L), is a trading center of farmers. In early days this was a stopping place for travelers on the Territorial Road.

The McKenzie River, 110 m., was first explored by Donald McKenzie of the Pacific Fur Company, who built a trading camp on the bank in 1812. The route continues southward with devious windings and crosses the Willamette River to meet US 99 (*see TOUR 2b*) in EUGENE, 115.5 m. (*see EUGENE*).

Tour 2B

Junction US 99E—Gervais—St. Louis—St. Paul—Champoeg State Park; 19.6 m. State 219 and unnumbered roads.

Macadamized road.
Few accommodations.

The route traverses French Prairie, the region where settlement and government began. In this section Oregon's earliest farmers, retired trappers of the Hudson's Bay Company, established farms; here came the early Methodist missionaries and Catholic fathers. Wagon train immigrants settled on donation land claims. In this area arose the first low mutterings of discontent that presaged the establishment of the Provisional Government at Champoeg on May 2, 1843.

The route branches north from US 99E, **0** *m.* (*see TOUR* 2*a*), at a point 3.4 miles south of Woodburn, and runs across a flat prairie, past well kept farmsteads with old time houses, orchards of prunes and peaches, and acres of high-trellised hop vines to GERVAIS, **0.4** *m.* (183 alt., 254 pop.), named for Joseph Gervais, a French-Canadian member of the Astor overland party that reached Oregon in 1811 (*see TOUR* 1*a*). Gervais remained at the Astoria post after the Pacific Fur Company had sold it to the North West Company—later amalgamated in the Hudson's Bay Company.

About 1828 he retired from the service and McLoughlin permitted him to settle in this valley—though such settlements in fur country had not been permitted by the company. His claim was by the Willamette River, several miles from this town. A number of his countrymen, all former employees of the Hudson's Bay Company, were settling in the same area, which in time was called French Prairie. Dr. McLoughlin gave out seed-wheat to the settlers on the promise that they would return the same amount to him after the harvest. In his house was held the "Wolf Meeting," the assembly that led to the formation of an American local government.

The town of Gervais was established when the Oregon & California Railroad, now the Southern Pacific, was built through the valley in 1868-72. The French-Canadian origin of the settlers is apparent in the business signs bearing French names on many of the old stores. Two fires and a shift of trade to larger centers has kept the village small.

ST. LOUIS STATION, **2.5** *m.,* is the Oregon Electric Railway stop for ST. LOUIS, **3.** *m.* (180 alt., 50 pop.), which grew up about the Roman Catholic church established by Father Vercruisse in 1846. The settlement consists of a church, a parish house, a parish school, and a handful of scattered houses. In the old cemetery is the GRAVE OF MARIE DORION, who accompanied the Astor overland party of 1811 (*see TOUR* 1*a*). According to an early description, she was a tall, dignified, and strikingly handsome woman of much character.

At **4.2** *m.* the route turns R. on State 219.

ST. PAUL, **12.3** *m.* (168 alt., 148 pop.), was settled by retired Hudson's Bay trappers and their Indian wives in the late 1830's. In 1839 the Reverend Francis Norbett Blanchet established a Roman Catholic church here which he served until 1845, when he became bishop of the Archdiocese with headquarters in Oregon City. The settlers had built a chapel here in 1836; a remnant of this structure remains, as does a grapevine early planted by the Jesuits. The ST. PAUL ROMAN CATHOLIC CHURCH built in 1846 was enlarged on Victorian Gothic lines in 1898. Some of the bricks used in the building were made by the Blanchet party from clay taken from a pit still visible to the rear of the church.

In the ROMAN CATHOLIC CEMETERY, on the outskirts of the town were buried Archbishop Blanchet, Dr. William J. Bailey, an early physician, and Etienne Lucier, first settler on French Prairie.

At **16.3** *m.* R. on a paved road to the Champoeg Park lane, **18.5** *m.*;

L. here to the entrance to CHAMPOEG MEMORIAL STATE
PARK, 18.8 *m.*, covering the site of the first settlement in the Wil-
lamette Valley. A little log museum not far from the entrance holds
Indian and pioneer relics.

Here when the whites arrived in Oregon was an Indian village at a
place called Cham-poo-ick because of an edible plant growing in
abundance. The village was headquarters of the local chieftain and the
point where the scattered tribesmen gathered several times a year before
setting off on expeditions to spear salmon and hunt. For this reason
William Wallace and J. C. Halsey came down from Astoria in 1811
and established a crude trading post for the Pacific Fur Company. It
was named Fort Wallace. After the North West Company bought out
the Astor holdings in Oregon it continued to maintain this post, and in
1813 Alexander Henry came here to visit his nephew, William Henry,
who was then in charge. After the North West Company was absorbed
into the Hudson's Bay Company and Dr. John McLoughlin was made
Chief Factor of the Department of the Columbia, the post was somewhat expanded. McLoughlin had been ordered to make his posts more or
less self-sufficient, so he started some grain growing in the neighborhood and continued to ignore the rule against permitting settlement in
the fur territory by retiring trappers. These trappers wanted to remain
because they had made contract marriages with local Indian women.
Gradually the number of half-breed children in the valley increased but
McLoughlin asked his company in vain for teachers and clergymen.
When Jason Lee arrived in the Columbia Valley in 1834 with the announcement that he was going to establish a mission on the upper
Columbia among the Flatheads, McLoughlin deflected him southward,
partly in an attempt to keep Americans as far south of the Columbia
as possible and partly from a sincere desire to give his charges some
spiritual leadership. But since the French-Canadians were Roman Catholics and Methodism did not appeal to them, Lee turned his attention
to valley Indians. It was several years before a priest arrived to establish a mission here.

In the meantime the number of buildings at Champoeg along what
was gaily called Boulevard Napoleon continued to increase and this
became one of the chief settlements of the valley. The post had been
rechristened Fort Champooick—a name later corrupted.

Though the number of Indian converts was very small the number
of Methodist missionaries in the valley continued to increase. In time
Dr. McLoughlin became aware that the Americans were taking considerably more interest in laying claims to land than in saving souls.
One non-missionary in the valley was Ewing Young, who had arrived
in 1834 and had later helped bring cattle to the valley from California,
part of them for himself and part for the Hudson's Bay Company.
Such government as existed in the territory was company laws; the
Hudson's Bay Company had held complete feudal rights in the lands
where it first operated and had worked out a series of rules under
which its employees lived. Each chief factor served as both judge and

jury in his district and only those accused of serious crimes were sent east across Canada for trial and judgment. The difficulty in the Oregon country was that no nation held title to it; treaties several times renewed between the United States and Great Britain and the renunciation of claims by other countries had left the region open to "joint occupation" by the United States and Great Britain. The American missionaries refused to accept the rulings of the Hudson's Bay Company, which was in actual occupation of the country for Britain and acting as Britain's legal agent. Hudson's Bay employees, and former employees who had settled in the valley far outnumbered the Americans, of whom there were less than 250 in all Oregon. Nonetheless, the Americans were increasing their demands that their government "seize" the territory and that an American government be set up.

This was the situation in 1841 when Ewing Young died leaving considerable cattle and some other property but no heirs. Various people looked with envy on the valuable cattle but were not sure how they could acquire them.

A meeting was finally called by the Americans and an executor to the Young estate was appointed. Meanwhile Young's stock ran wild in the Chehalem Valley and wolves and panthers were soon attracted by the easy prey. The marauding beasts gradually grew bolder in approaching the central Willamette settlements; cows, calves, and colts were killed. The settlers finally called what came to be known as the first "Wolf Meeting." It met at the Oregon Institute on February 2, 1843; it was agreed that each person present should be assessed $5 to pay bounties on all wolves, lynxes, bears, and panthers killed. French-Canadians as well as citizens of the United States attended. At a second "Wolf Meeting," held at the home of Joseph Gervais on March 6, the real intent of many was revealed, a resolution being unanimously adopted for the appointment of a committee of twelve to "take into consideration the propriety of taking measures for civil and military protection of this colony."

That meeting took place on May 2, in the office corner of the local Hudson's Bay Company warehouse. Many of the British subjects had attended with the idea that this was merely another "Wolf Meeting" to further organize protection. As soon as they became aware of the true purpose the resolution was voted down and most of the French-Canadians withdrew. Employees of the company were indignant over the use of the warehouse for what they considered seditious purposes and the Americans withdrew to a nearby field. There was much talk of inalienable rights, of loyalty to the Hudson's Bay Company whose factor had made numerous grants of credit to the Americans. Then big Joe Meek, the trapper, shouted enthusiastically, "Who's for a divide? All in favor of the report and an organization follow me." Legend records that when the milling had ceased 50 men were on Meek's side of the field, 50 on the other, with two men undecided. These were Etienne Lucier and his friend, F. X. Matthieu, both French-Canadians. Lucier hesitated because someone had told him that should the United States

Government come into control here it would tax the windows in his house. Matthieu, who then lived with Lucier, argued convincingly otherwise, and in the end the pair took their position with those favoring organization. Though many had already refused to participate and had withdrawn, it was concluded "a majority" had decided for local government. The report of the committee was then disposed of article by article and a number of officers chosen. Nine Americans were named to act as a committee that would draw up a program of government.

When the legislative committee made its first report at a mass meeting at Willamette Falls (Oregon City) on July 5, it created four "legislative" districts, Champooick, one of them, had Champoeg settlement as its judicial center. On the east the district ran to the Rocky Mountains, and included much of what later became Idaho, and parts of Montana and Wyoming.

The commercial importance of this settlement, through its three decades of existence, was large. According to a report to the Hudson's Bay Company made by Peter Skene Ogden and James Douglas, the physical investment in 1847, amounted to £ 1700 sterling. But property values were booming. When the company withdrew from American territory in 1852 it demanded twice that amount for loss of the property.

There were two fires in the community in the 1850's. A store occupied by two Germans but owned by Ed. Dupuis, was burned in September, 1851, and about $7,000 worth of goods were ruined. In 1853, again in September, fire demolished the new dwelling of Dr. Bailey. Only the doctor's stock of medicines was saved from the house, and that only briefly because soon afterwards a runaway horse trampled them in the yard where they had been deposited.

A glorious Fourth of July celebration was held here in 1854. In the forenoon a procession formed in the town's center and marched to the house of Ed. Dupuis, where Dr. Edward Shiel read the Declaration of Independence. Later, the Salem *Statesman* said, "the celebrants enjoyed a sumptuous dinner . . . given beneath the roof where the first celebration took place in Oregon, and where the first laws . . . were enacted. After dinner the guests proceeded on a pleasure excursion, three miles up the river, on board the steamer *Fenix.*" Back at Champoeg, toasts, loudly cheered by voice and the shooting of firearms, concluded the program, and the *Fenix* drew six rousing cheers as it departed for Canemah and Oregon City.

During November 1861, the whole Willamette Valley experienced heavy rains and in December the river flooded the lowlands here and elsewhere. The waters rose so fast that many of the residents were trapped in their homes and stores and had to be rescued by men in rowboats. Gradually even the heavy hewn timbers of the warehouse loosened and were swept away. Two saloons on the high south side of town were the only buildings that remained. The town was never rebuilt.

In 1900 the Governor of Oregon and the secretary of the Oregon Historical Society, with the aid of the last survivor of the Champoeg meeting, Francois Xavier Matthieu, made a trip to determine the site and the state legislature in 1901 designated 107 acres here as a state park. The names of the men who were believed, on best authority, to have been among the 52 who voted for the establishment of a provisional government, are engraved on a granite shaft marking the alleged site of the meeting.

‖‖‖‖‖▣‖‖‖‖‖‖▣‖‖‖‖‖▣‖‖‖‖‖▣‖‖‖‖‖▣‖‖‖‖‖▣‖‖‖‖‖▣‖‖‖‖‖▣‖‖‖‖‖▣‖‖‖‖‖▣‖‖‖‖‖▣‖‖‖‖

Tour 2C

Salem—Rickreall—Dallas—Junction with State 18; 29.7 m. State 22.

Paved road.
Tourist camps at convenient points; hotels in Salem and Dallas.

State 22 crosses the farms and orchards of the Willamette and Rickreall valley and passes over hills between the tributaries of the Yamhill River, to meet State 18, the Salmon River cut-off a mile south of Willamina.

Branching west from US 99E at SALEM (*see TOUR 2a*) **0** *m.* State 22 crosses the Willamette River, **0.4** *m.*, on an arched span that affords an excellent view of the river. Occasionally a river boat, survivor of the fleet that once plied the Willamette, approaches or leaves the wharf (L) near the Salem end of the bridge. On summer days the river is dotted with canoes and small boats (*available near wharf*, 25c *an hour*).

WEST SALEM, **0.8** *m.* (140 alt., 974 pop.), does lumbering and prepares maraschino cherries. (*Tourist camp for trailers*). West Salem is at the junction with State 221 (*see TOUR 10*).

West of the Willamette, State 22 passes through orchards, hopfields, and berry farms, and curves between the river and (R) the encroaching Eola Hills.

HOLMAN STATE PARK (R), **4** *m.*, is a tract of woods on a hillside, with spring water piped to the roadside.

EOLA, **4.5** *m.*, was first called Cincinnati because of a fancied resemblance of the site to that of Cincinnati, Ohio. In early days it lost a bid to be made the state capital by two votes. With its chance for expansion checked the town in 1856 changed its name to Eola, derived from Aeolus, Greek god of the winds. The once prosperous community waned in importance with the growth of Salem, its successful rival.

The HOUSE OF I. J. PATTERSON, governor of Oregon from 1927 to 1929, is (R) at **4.9** *m.*

OAK KNOLL GOLF COURSE (R), **6.6** *m.*, is a nine-hole public course (*greens fee* 50c).

The La Creole River is visible (L) at **7** *m.* Many insist that the river should be called Rickreall, that it was so called by the Indians in the days when they dug camas bulbs along its banks. Others insist that La Creole was the name used by French-Canadians in memory of an Indian girl who was drowned in it. As a compromise, the stream is called La Creole River below Dallas and La Creole Creek at Dallas and Rickreall above it.

The NESMITH HOUSE, *(private),* **8.8** *m.,* was the early home of Col. James W. Nesmith, who served in the U. S. Senate during the Civil War. The structure, built in the 1850's, has been altered many times and has probably lost much of its original appearance.

At RICKREALL, **10.2** *m.* (210 alt., 127 pop.), is a junction with US 99W *(see TOUR* 10).

DALLAS, **14.4** *m.* (340 alt., 2,975 pop.), on the banks of La Creole Creek, was settled in the 1840's and was at first named Cynthia Ann, for Mrs. Jesse Applegate, wife of the trail-maker *(see TOUR 2b),* but this was later shortened to Cynthian. The present name honors George Mifflin Dallas, Vice President of United States during Polk's administration. The first building in the settlement was La Creole Academic Institute, later called La Creole Academy.

The earliest business center was on the north bank of the creek, but after a successful contest with Independence for the court house of Polk County, during which the citizens raised $17,000 to build a narrow gauge railroad to the town as an inducement, the center of affairs shifted to the south bank. The court house was built on the flat land there and the town was platted around the court house plaza.

One of the earliest woolen mills of the state was established here in 1856, and a short time later an iron foundry was built. Since early days, however, lumbering has been the industrial mainstay of the surrounding region and the town sawmills yearly prepare great quantities of lumber for shipment. There are also prune-drying and packing plants here, providing seasonal work for hundreds.

1. Left from Dallas, 0.4 *m.,* on the Ellendale Road to (L) the JOHN E. LYLE HOUSE, an excellent example of pioneer Oregon architecture. Built in 1858, the house is in good condition in its grove of tall trees. It is a story and a half frame structure with an unusually high gabled roof. An equally high gable, with even steeper slope, breaks the front of the roof and forms the usual pediment of a one-story portico with four square columns.

ELLENDALE, 2.5 *m.,* a deserted town, developed around a grist mill built here in 1844 by James A. O'Neal *(see below).* It was first called O'Neal's Mills and later Nesmith's Mills. Near his mill O'Neal erected a store and living quarters, and before long a postoffice was opened. But in 1849 the mill was sold to James W. Nesmith and Henry Owen, who in turn, four years later sold it to Hudsons & Company. In announcing the purchase of "the flouring mills and contents . . ." in the *Oregon Statesman* for July 19, 1853, the new firm assured its prospective customers that it was prepared to "furnish flour of the first quality to miners and the country trade"; that it had completed "arrangements whereby fresh stocks of merchandise would be received by boat from San Francisco twice monthly"; and that it was the intention of the firm to have its "upright and circular sawmill" in operation by October.

To keep the latter pledge, Ezra Hallock and Luther Tuthill in 1854 built a dam a mile above the grist mill and there built the sawmill. It was the only mill of the kind for miles around and people flocked to see it. Part of the equipment was the only planer in that section of Oregon, all lumber having previously been dressed by hand; its installation proved a master stroke of enterprise on the part of the mill, which furnished much of the lumber for many of the buildings still in the neighborhood.

In the early 1860's, Judge Reuben P. Boise, one of the outstanding members of the Oregon bar, and several others bought the mill and incorporated themselves as the Ellendale Woolen Mill Company, rebuilt the building, installed new machinery, and constructed a boarding house and other dwellings for mill employes. Ellendale, rechristened in honor of Mrs. Ellen Lyon Boise, rapidly grew into a busy village.

The small white building (R) was used as SLAVE QUARTERS for negroes belonging to one of the mill owners before the Civil War. The long, low house (L), was the old store and boarding house.

2. Left from Dallas, 11.7 m., on State 223 to LEWISVILLE; in the HART CEMETERY nearby is the GRAVE OF JAMES A. O'NEAL (see above), who came to Oregon with the Wyeth party in 1834, and who served as chairman of the second "wolf meeting," held on March 6, 1843 (see TOUR 2B), and as member of the legislative committee appointed by the meeting.

At 12.3 m. on State 223 is a junction with a graveled road; on this road 3 m. to AIRLIE (40 pop.), named for the Earl of Airlie, president of the syndicate of Scotch business men who bought the narrow gauge railroad built by the people of Yamhill County and in 1881 extended it to this point.

KING'S VALLEY, 22 m. (325 alt., 129 pop.), was named for Nahum King who settled here in 1847. The town developed about a flouring mill established in 1853 and still in use. The KING HOUSE, built in 1852, is one of the best preserved houses in the state.

At 22.3 m. on State 223 is a junction with a graveled road; R. here 2 m. to the CHAMBERS GRIST MILL, built by Rowland Chambers in 1853. The original wheel and several of the feed-grinders are still in use. The power for the mill is furnished by the Luckiamute River, named for the Lakmiut, a subdivision of the Calapooya Indians, who made their homes on its banks.

On State 223 at 24.3 m. is the junction with a graveled road; R. here 1.5 m., to HOSKINS, a crossroads with a store, near which is the SITE OF FORT HOSKINS (R), named for Lieutenant Hoskins, who was killed in the battle of Monterey during the Mexican War. It was established in 1856 and built under the supervision of Lieut. Phil Sheridan to protect the settlers and to prevent the Indians penned up in the Coast Reservation from invading the valley. About 150 men were stationed here. The site commands a wide view of the valley.

In Hoskins is the JAMES WATSON HOUSE built in the early fifties. It is said to have been the first plastered house in the state.

State 22 turns north at Dallas and passes through prune and cherry orchards and over low hills covered with scrub oak. It was in this vicinity that the Applegates (see TOUR 2b)—Charles, Lindsay, and Jesse—settled in 1844 and laid out their mile-square claims. The GERMAN BAPTIST CHURCH, (R), 19.7 m., is near the SITE OF JESSE APPLEGATE'S CABIN, where the first articles of the Oregon unofficial government were revised.

In an old INDIAN BURIAL GROUND (R), 20.7 m.—now a pasture—many Indian relics have been found.

At MILL CREEK, 24.6 m., is the junction with the graveled Mill Creek road.

Left here to the CRUIKSHANK FARM (*private*), **0.2** *m.* where Madame Ernestine Schumann-Heink came to live for a time to rest after a strenuous concert tour abroad.

At BUELL, **25.2** *m.* (379 alt., 83 pop.), is a chapel erected in 1860. WALLACE BRIDGE, **29.4** *m.*, over the South Yamhill River, is at the junction with State 18 (*see TOUR 10A*).

Tour 2D

Albany—Corvallis—Philomath—Toledo—Newport; 67.8 m. State 26.

Yaquina Branch of Southern Pacific Railroad roughly parallels route.
Paved road.
Hotels and tourist camps.

This route follows the west bank of the Willamette River through a fertile farming district between Albany and Corvallis. West of Corvallis it enters the foothills of the Coast Range, passes to the north of Marys Peak, and over the range to the coast. The route is an important link between US 99E and US 99W and between mid-Willamette Valley towns and Pacific Ocean beaches. The first road over this route was built along an old Indian trail, and a stage route established between Corvallis and Yaquina Bay in 1866.

State 26 branches westward from US 99E in ALBANY (*see TOUR 2a*), **0** *m.*, and crosses a modern bridge over the Willamette River. Near the west end of the bridge is the nine-hole BRIDGEWAY GOLF COURSE (*greens fee 50 cents*), **0.3** *m.*

The W. C. T. U. CHILDREN'S FARM HOME (L), **6.8** *m.*, consists of 285 acres of land with numerous cottages and other buildings. A modern school building has been constructed.

CORVALLIS, **10.5** *m.* (230 alt., 7,585 pop.), (*see CORVALLIS*). *Points of Interest*: Benton County Court House, site of territorial capitol, City Park, Old Mill Stones, Haman Lewis House, Oregon State Agricultural College.

Corvallis is at the junction with US 99W (*see TOUR 10*).

HANSON'S POULTRY FARM (R), **12.5** *m.*, is noted for individual, pen, and flock production records. Hanson's White Leghorns have set many world's records for egg production. The poultry farm cooperates with Oregon State College in experimentation with poultry housing and feeding.

At **13.6** *m.* is the junction with a gravel road.

Left on this road 0.4 *m.* to PLYMOUTH CHURCH and COMMUNITY CENTER, an essay in neighborly cooperation. Church and social gatherings, in which the entire neighborhood takes part, are held periodically at the community center. The same spirit of cooperative effort extends to the planting and harvesting of crops so that there is no need of hired help to accomplish needed work.

PHILOMATH (gr. *lover of learning*), **16.3** *m.* (279 alt., 694 pop.), received its name from Philomath College, chartered in 1865 by the United Brethren Church as a coeducational institution devoted to the liberal arts and ministerial training. The college held an important place in the educational economy of the state for two generations. The influence of the school was not at all lessened by the positive character of its moral and religious instruction. Professor Henry Sheak, who was connected with the college for most of its existence, was noted as the "Father of Local Option" in Oregon. Competition with state-endowed institutions and inadequate financial support forced the abolition of the college in June, 1929. The buildings and campus are (R) at the western edge of town.

Sponsors of Philomath College discouraged the establishment of factories, as it was feared that the moral tone of the community would be lowered by the influx of an industrial population. The town grew up about the college and drew its support from the agricultural and lumbering activities of the adjacent district. Recent attempts to establish processing plants for fruits, vegetables and milk have not been successful. The *Benton County Review,* the only newspaper in the county outside Corvallis, was established in 1904 and is still published weekly. A resident of Philomath for a number of years was Dennis H. Stovall, author of numerous children's stories.

PHILOMATH JUNCTION, **17.3** *m.,* is the site of a small sawmill, tourist camp, and service station. Here is the junction with State 34 (*see TOUR 2E*).

West of Philomath Junction the route closely parallels the Newport Branch of the Southern Pacific Railroad. This line was built in the early 1880's under the name of the Oregon Pacific Railroad and was originally intended to extend from deep water at Yaquina Bay (*see TOUR 3a*) eastward across the Coast Range, the Cascade Range, and the high desert to a junction with the Oregon Short Line on the Snake River near Ontario (*see TOUR 1a*). In 1859 according to Dennis Stovall, Jerry Henkle led a party to the coast near Newport (*see below*) and "on their return to the valley the Henkle party blazed the trail that later became the main traveled highway into the Yaquina Bay Country. In the early sixties Congress granted lands to the "Corvallis and Acquinna Bay Military Wagon Road Company" incorporated in 1863 with a capital stock of $5,000. Eight years later the stock was increased to $300,000. It was operated as a toll road. In 1872, Col. T. Egenton Hogg incorporated the Corvallis and Yaquina Railroad Company. The first train over the new road, rechristened the Oregon Pacific, was in March, 1885; and connections with steamers from Yaquina Bay to San Francisco began on September 14 of the same year. The line now is used only as a freight feeder for the Southern Pacific.

At **18.2** *m.* is a crossing of Marys River, said to have been named in 1846 for Mary Lloyd, the first white woman to ford the stream. West of this point the highway follows this stream to the summit of the Coast Range, crossing it numerous times.

At **19.1** *m.* is the junction with the gravel Wood Creek Road.

Left on this road along Wood Creek to a trail at 8.6 *m.,* leading (L) to the top of MARYS PEAK, 11.6 *m.* (4,097 alt.), the highest point in the Coast Range. The peak is in the Siuslaw National Forest; the area around the mountain was recently increased by purchase of 8,000 acres. Corvallis owns several hundred acres on the east slope, as protection for water supply. From the crest the Pacific Ocean is visible beyond the seaward foothills. The Indians called the mountain *Chintimini;* it received its present name from the same source as Marys River.

At **21** *m.* is the junction with graveled Kings Valley Road (*see TOUR 2C*).

BLODGETT, **27** *m.* (633 alt., 12 pop.), a sawmill hamlet on the banks of the Marys River, was first named Emerick when established in 1888, but shortly thereafter the name was changed to honor William Blodgett, a pioneer settler. West of the SUMMIT, **35.7** *m.* (804 alt.), the highway follows Little Elk Creek through narrow canyons to the Yaquina River.

EDDYVILLE, **43.4** *m.* (92 alt., 41 pop.), is at the confluence of the Little Elk Creek and the Yaquina River. These streams afford excellent angling.

At **51.4** *m.* is the junction with a gravel road.

Left on this road to ELK CITY, 5.1 *m.* (16 alt., 43 pop.), a point of departure for hunting and fishing parties. It was platted in 1868 by A. Newton, the first town in the present confines of Lincoln County, and was named for the herds of elk roaming the region. The first settlement at Elk City was made by the Corvallis and Yaquina Bay Wagon Road Company, who erected a warehouse here in 1866. This is ordinarily the head of small-boat navigation on the Yaquina River. Here was the overland terminus of the stage and mail route, the rest of the distance to the bay being by water. During the major active period of the Oregon Pacific Railroad, Elk City flourished as an important point on the route, but as the railroad declined so did the town.

PIONEER MOUNTAIN, **54.3** *m.* (423 alt.), commands a wide view of the Pacific Ocean. From the summit the highway descends through a heavily wooded canyon into a widening tide-land valley.

TOLEDO, **60** *m.* (64 alt., 2,137 pop.), seat of Lincoln County, was named by Joseph D. Graham, son of an early pioneer, for Toledo, Ohio. The first post office was established in 1868 and the town grew slowly until 1917, when the Federal government established a gigantic spruce production plant here to supply lumber for airplane building for the World War. During this period, 1,500 men of the famous "Spruce Division" were stationed in Toledo, engaged in cutting spruce. At the end of the war, the plant was sold to private interests. It is the largest spruce mill in the world, with a capacity of 400,000 board feet every eight hours, employing in normal times an average of 400 men. Other Toledo mills also manufacture lumber and its by-products.

At **60.7 m.** the road crosses the tide flats, winding between low hills covered with dense forests of spruce, fir, and hemlock.

At **65.7 m.** from an elevated point, Yaquina Bay, an arm of the Pacific Ocean, is visible in the distance.

At NEWPORT, **67.8 m.** (134 alt., 1,530 pop.), State 26 forms a junction with US 101 (*see TOUR 3a*).

Tour 2E

Philomath Junction—Alsea—Waldport; 59.1 m. State 34.

Asphalt or rock-surfaced road.
Hotels at Alsea and Waldport; some tourist camps along route.

State 34 is a link between the Willamette Valley and the rugged central Oregon coast. It climbs the heights of the Coast Range and after crossing the summit, follows the Alsea River to Waldport. The highway borders tributaries of Marys River and Crooked Creek into the Alsea Valley, where it swings around the base of Digger Mountain and passes through narrow defiles to the sea. The territory traversed was originally hunting and fishing grounds of the Alsea Indians, who were removed to the Siletz Reservation. Apparently, they had camped within the area for many years, for excavators of Alsea Indian fishing camps have found as many as 20 tiers of their shell mounds. The old Alsea wagon road ended at the head of the Alsea Valley, from which trails led over the mountains into the Tidewater district.

State 34 branches southeastward from State 26 at PHILOMATH JUNCTION, **0 m.** (*see TOUR 2D*) and crosses Marys River on one of the covered bridges frequently found spanning Oregon streams.

West of ROCK CREEK, **4 m.,** the highway begins the ascent of Alsea Mountain. Sparse growths of yew, cedar, and mountain laurel appear among the stands of pines, alders and maples. The Oregon yew found on these slopes is considered by archers as an excellent wood for bow making. On the side of the mountain (L) are the ruts of the old wagon road over which the teams of pioneers toiled on their arduous journeys to Alsea Valley (*see below*).

The summit of ALSEA MOUNTAIN, **9.7 m.** (1,403 alt.), overlooks a splendid panorama of peaks and canyons. West of the summit

State 34 winds down the mountain through fire-scarred forests to YEW CREEK CAMP, **13.4** *m.* (*trout fishing; cabins*).

The ALSEA STATE TROUT HATCHERY (L), **15.6** *m.,* one of the largest on the coast, propagates cutthroat trout, chiefly for the replenishment of mountain streams.

Westward the valley widens and small farms border the roads. Mountain balm trees, peculiar to this section, appear on the hillsides among the firs and pines. The mountains around the Alsea Valley are frequented by numerous game animals. The blacktailed Columbian deer is often encountered; formerly there were also many white-tailed deer and elk, or wapiti. Other animals in the region are the black or cinnamon bear, and less often the cougar, the lynx, and the bob-cat.

One of the first white settlers of the Alsea Valley was Edward Winkle. An early writer has pictured him as he appeared "with moccasins on his feet, his ever-present trusty rifle on his shoulder and butcher-knife in belt. Whither his inclination led him there he went, through mountain passes without regard to road or trail, always depending upon his weapon for food." It is related that upon one occasion, in order to attack a bear bayed by his faithful dog, it became necessary to crawl under the brush for some distance and finally to pass under a log. As he straightened from his prone position he found himself face to face with Bruin, who struck him on the breast, tore off his clothing and lacerated his flesh. His dog came to the rescue and the bear, turning upon him was about to end his career when Winkle closed in with his knife and fought the bear hand to hand to the death. Man and dog were barely able to creep to their cabin, where they both lay for several days before help came to them.

ALSEA, **18.7** *m.* (244 alt., 100 pop.), is in a broadened section of the Alsea Valley, at the confluence of the North and South Forks of the Alsea River. The first settlers arrived in the valley in 1852 and late that year the Ryecraft brothers opened the first farm. The town is the only commercial center in the valley whose important industry is lumbering. It is a rendezvous for fishermen seeking steelhead and trout in the Alsea and its tributaries, and for deer hunters in the fall.

The highway crosses the eastern boundary of the SIUSLAW PROTECTIVE AREA at **19.7** *m.* Although this heavily wooded area is not in a national forest it is under the administration of the forest service. ALSEA GUARD STATION, on Mill Creek, is at **20** *m.* Mill Creek was named for the Lone Star Flouring Mills, formerly situated at the confluence of the creek and the Alsea River.

At **25** *m.* the highway crowds between the river and DIGGER MOUNTAIN, for many years a barrier to travel. Digger Creek is crossed at **30.5** *m.* MISSOURI BEND, **31.5** *m.,* was so named for the Missouri settlers who first farmed this section of the Alsea Valley.

The eastern boundary of the SIUSLAW NATIONAL FOREST is crossed at **32.4** *m.*

BEAR CREEK LODGE, **33.7** *m.,* a mountain inn, is near Bear

Creek Bridge. At the STATE FISH HATCHERY, 46.8 *m.,* are propagated steelhead and cutthroat trout.

At TIDEWATER, 48.5 *m.,* the river widens into an estuary, salt waters mingling with the fresh. In season there is much trolling for salmon at this point. In this region the Alsea River formerly comprised the northern boundary of the Alsea Indian Reservation, with head-quarters at Agency Farm near Yachats (*see TOUR 3b*). David D. Fagan's *History of Benton County* records: "When the white men began to settle in the Alsea district they found there the remnants of three tribes: the 'Alseas' by the bay and on the coast, a people of fishers; the 'Klickitats' who hunted in the woods and over the mountains to the south; and the 'Drift Creek Indians' whose homes were scattered through the heavy timber round Table Mountain and on the streams heading thereabouts, to the east and northeast of Alsea. Though gener-ally at enmity with each other yet there were times when, feuds laid aside, the hunting tribes visited their neighbors by the ocean in peace, bringing with them the spoils of the chase to exchange for the sea fish and shell fish of the Alseas. Then fires were lighted and feasting and jollity went on day after day together." The Alsea tribe was called "salt water" or "salt chuck" Indians.

The first settler in the lower Alsea was G. W. Collins who came in 1860 as Indian agent for the sub-agency of the Alsea Indian Reservation.

WALDPORT, 59.1 *m.* (20 alt., 367 pop.), on the south shore of Alsea Bay is at the junction with US 101 (*see TOUR 3b*).

‖‖‖‖‖‖‖❏‖‖‖‖‖‖‖❏‖‖‖‖‖‖‖❏‖‖‖‖‖‖‖❏‖‖‖‖‖‖‖❏‖‖‖‖‖‖‖❏‖‖‖‖‖‖‖❏‖‖‖‖‖‖‖❏‖‖‖‖‖‖‖❏‖‖‖‖‖‖‖❏‖‖‖‖‖‖‖❏‖‖‖‖‖‖‖

Tour 2F

Junction with US 99—Cheshire—Blachly—Swisshome—Mapleton—Cushman—Florence; 67.5 m. State 36.

Southern Pacific Railroad branch parallels State 36 between Swisshome and Cushman.
Paved road.
Accommodations scant; tourist camps.

State 36 is one of the ten highways that link the interior valleys to the Pacific Ocean beaches. Fur traders and emigrants blazed the old trail now followed by the highway in its winding course from the Wil-lamette Valley over the Coast Range to tidewater.

State 36 branches westward from the junction with US 99 (*see TOUR 2a*), 0 *m.,* at a point 1.8 miles south of Junction City and follows the shallow valley of Bear Creek between vineyards, orchards, hopyards and berry fields into the foothills.

CHESHIRE, 3.9 *m.* (323 alt., 33 pop.), on the Corvallis-Eugene spur of the Southern Pacific Railroad, is a shipping point for the fertile Bear Creek Valley. West of Cheshire beyond a low divide is a branch of the Long Tom River. In his *Journal* of a trip from Fort Vancouver to the Umpqua in 1834, Hudson's Bay factor, John Work, spoke of the river both as the Sam Tomleaf River and as the Lamitambuff. Douglas in his *Journals* called it the "Longtabuff River" and Wilkes' *Narrative* has "Lumtumbuff." At the head of the branch is the LOW PASS (1,173 alt.), 19.4 *m.*, and a descent into the Lake Creek Valley.

BLACHLY, 22.4 *m.* (690 alt., 12 pop.), is a small cross-roads village with a grange, church and Union High school serving the agricultural population of the mountain-hemmed valley. There is excellent angling for cutthroat, rainbow, and Eastern brook trout in the streams of the vicinity. The encroaching mountains give covert to deer and other game.

TRIANGLE LAKE, 25.5 *m.*, is about a square mile in area formed by a fault across Lake Creek. The outlet is a waterfall over the precipitous ledge. Along the western shore of this small wedge-shaped lake are recreational resorts for dwellers of the upper Willamette Valley region.

The eastern boundary of the SIUSLAW NATIONAL FOREST is crossed at 39.4 *m.*, an area of green forest growth, the interstices crowded with underbrush characteristic of the coast region.

SWISSHOME, 44.8 *m.* (118 alt., 50 pop.), so named because its early settlers came from Switzerland, is a small agricultural settlement at the confluence of Lake Creek and the Siuslaw River. "Yangawa" is the name that John Work gave this river when he crossed it in 1834.

Cascara trees grow abundantly in the Siuslaw Valley. The peeling and drying of the bark has become a small industry in western Oregon. The bark is stripped from the trees in the spring when there is an abundant flow of sap; after it has been dried in the sun it is hauled to urban centers for sale.

West of Swisshome the Siuslaw River threads a devious course through the Coast Mountains, widens as it nears the sea, and flows between rich alluvial fields, dairy pastures, and goat ranches.

MAPLETON, 53 *m.* (17 alt., 130 pop.), head of deep-water navigation on the Siuslaw River, is a shipping and marketing center for a prosperous region. The town is a mecca for anglers who troll for Chinook and silversides salmon or cast for steelheads and cutthroats. The U. S. Forest Service maintains a ranger station at this point.

On December 22, 1888, Captain W. W. Young made a preliminary examination of the Siuslaw according to the river and harbor act of August 11, 1888, stating that the river and harbor were worthy of improvement. The timber is "so extensive that even at $1.00 per thousand feet the saving would amount to a sum greater than the cost of improving the entrance."

Continued recognition of the Siuslaw was given by the introduction of bills by Senator Mitchell and Congressman Hermann to provide $80,000 for the construction of a lighthouse at Heceta Head, eight miles north of Florence.

In the fall of 1889 Mr. Hermann visited Eugene and promised to exert his influence towards obtaining a life-saving station at the mouth of the Siuslaw and the establishment of regular mail service between Eugene and Florence.

Finally, on May 31, 1890, a dispatch from Hermann stated that Congress had appropriated $50,000 for beginning a jetty at the mouth of the river. Eleven months later the Representative announced that the Siuslaw project was being prepared by the chief engineers.

Great indignation was aroused in Eugene in June 1891, when the engineers' report stated that the Siuslaw was not worthy of improvement at the time. Eugene citizens sent protests to Washington. In August, Representative Hermann announced that the engineer had overestimated the cost. Shortly afterwards the work was ordered to commence. This so thrilled George Melvin Miller, brother of the poet Joaquin Miller, that he rode to Florence on horseback to deliver the good news before the mail could bring it.

In the meantime, feeling was so intense against the engineer that the citizens of Florence had him hung in effigy. Miller's arrival directed their resentment to enthusiasm, but the remnants of the stuffed image still swayed in the breeze.

CUSHMAN, **64.8** *m.* (23 alt., 145 pop.), maintains a complete port organization, which controls its deep-sea commerce. Ocean boats are often at its docks. The hills above the rich adjacent farm lands produce much valuable Port Orford cedar, a conifer noted for its beauty and size, that grows naturally only in a narrow belt along the coast of southern Oregon and northern California (*see TOUR 3b*).

FLORENCE, **67.5** *m.* (11 alt., 339 pop.) (*see TOUR 3b*), is at the junction with US 101 (*see TOUR 3b*).

Tour 2G

Drain—Elkton—Scottsburg—Reedsport; 50.1 m. State 38.

Paved road.
Hotel at Elkton, auto camps at other convenient points.

State 38, a link between US 99 and US 101, follows Elk Creek to the Umpqua River and closely parallels that stream westward. The name Umpqua, of Indian origin, has also been applied to the country along the river, to the mountains, to forts, to towns, and to a forest reserve. The Spanish navigator, Bartolome Ferrelo, is said to have reached the mouth of the Umpqua in 1543 and some romanticists like to believe, Sir Francis Drake sailed the *Golden Hynde* into the river and there set ashore in the wilderness his Spanish pilot, Morera. This, however, probably took place farther south. Spanish archives record that in 1732 a ship disabled by severe weather entered the Umpqua, and ascended it as far as the site of Scottsburg, where repairs were made. Many trees were cut down and, the decayed stumps were seen by the first white settlers, who were told by the Indians about the vessel that had arrived there many years before, manned by white men with beards. The Hudson's Bay Company sent expeditions to the river early in the century and in 1828 the trapper and explorer, Jedediah Strong Smith, followed the river with a party of fur hunters that were almost annihilated by the natives, three men only escaping (*see TOUR 3b.*)

Differing from other links between the interior and the sea coast, State 38 passes through the Coast Range at an almost even water grade.

State 38 branches west from US 99 (*see TOUR 2b*) at DRAIN, **0** *m.,* and traverses an open valley with farms and dairies and then enters a region in which groves of scrub oak cover abrupt hills in a narrowing valley.

A tunnel at **10.3** *m.* passes through a high headland in a loop of Elk Creek. Directly above the tunnel is ELKTON TUNNEL STATE PARK, as yet (1940) unimproved.

The site of ELKTON, **14** *m.* (140 alt., 90 pop.), early attracted attention from white men. On the bank of the Umpqua in 1832 the Hudson's Bay Company established a post perhaps as a result of Jedediah Smith's rich harvest of furs in this area. Having successfully recovered Smith's furs, Chief Factor McLoughlin had little fear that the natives would repeat the attacks they had made on Smith's party. Like other Hudson's Bay posts, this one had a substantial warehouse of hewn slabs, a barn, and some small dwellings inside a large stockaded area. As this was one of the smaller posts the traders made little attempt to cultivate fields; beyond the raising of sufficient cattle and vegetables for post needs, they busied themselves almost exclusively with furs. The post was eventually abandoned, probably soon after 1850, when the United States had control of the territory. In that year the Winchester and Payne Company sent a boat, the *Samuel Roberts,* from San Francisco to the Umpqua to find a site for a town and also to prospect for gold. An exploring expedition came up the river to this place, which was considered but rejected. Then in 1854 the townsite was surveyed for the establishment of the seat of Umpqua County. The first session of the court was held in a woodshed and was presided over by young Matthew P. Deady, who was later to become one of the leading jurists of the state and notable for his promotion of education. In time the town became the midway station of the Drain-Scottsburg stage route and the appearance of the six-horse team was the leading event in local life.

Gradually the place dwindled in importance and at present is a small trading village in the midst of the mountains.

West of Elkton the river is a succession of rapids, where in autumn fishermen from many parts of the state gather for the salmon and steelhead runs. In 1871 the steamer *Enterprise* made a trip as far as SAWYER'S RAPIDS, 23.7 *m.*, but the channel was too shallow except at flood time to make navigation inland possible.

Long Prairie is a narrow strip of bottom land eight or nine miles long by the winding stream. It is hemmed in by partly timbered mountains. Old orchards, trees draped with moss, mark it as the scene of early settlement.

The valley abruptly narrows at **29.8** *m.* and winds through the Coast Range between ridges timbered from water's edge to crest. The river makes a long curve to the north, past the WELL CREEK GUARD STATION, **31.5** *m.* A decided change in the character of vegetation is noticed as the flora of the interior valleys gives way to that of the coast regions. Instead of oak and Douglas fir, myrtle and round-topped chinquapin is seen, with its deep furrowed bark, leaves yellow and green, and spiny nuts. Also seen are the smaller chittem (*cascara sagrada*) and the lodge-pole pine sometimes straight as a lance, sometimes twisted and stunted by wind.

SCOTTSBURG, 33.3 *m.* (46 alt., 105 pop.), at the head of navigation, was once the metropolis of southern Oregon. Founded in 1850 by Levi Scott, who with the Applegates, opened the South Road across the Cascades in 1846, it soon became a center of business activity. The discovery of gold along the creeks and rivers of the Siskiyous in 1852 attracted throngs and Scottsburg immediately became an important outfitting point. Ships laden with food and other supplies for the miners arrived from San Francisco and dwelling and business houses rose quickly between the river and the hills. Long lines of pack-mules pawed the dust of the street as they waited to start off on wilderness trails to the camps. At the height of its prosperity, the town had 15 mercantile establishments, a grist mill, and many saloons and gambling houses. The *Umpqua Gazette,* first newspaper published in southern Oregon, made its appearance here. The leading hotel was owned by the blind Kentuckian, Daniel Lyon, who had wandered like a troubadour through the gold camps, singing and playing a guitar, until he had accumulated enough gold to purchase it. Every one with money stayed at Lyons' Hotel, including "Fighting Joe" Hooker, then supervising construction of a military road from Scottsburg into California, but later commander of a Union army division. Lyons was assisted by a wife whom he had met at the home of Henry Clay. She survived him, to see the end of Scottsburg in 1861 after the mining excitement had subsided, when Umpqua flood waters created great havoc.

This LOWER TOWN, which was washed away, is now a dreary stretch of brush and weed-covered sand.

West of Scottsburg the receding hills are covered with heavy stands of Douglas fir, hemlock, and Sitka or tideland spruce. Near the coast are excellent stands of Port Orford cedar (*see TOUR 3b*). Groves of Oregon myrtle or California laurel grace hills and valleys.

State 38 crosses the eastern boundary of the ELLIOTT STATE FOREST, **35.1** *m.*, a small tract, largely composed of second growth Douglas fir. It is used as a forestry laboratory by the Oregon State Agricultural College.

BRANDY BAR (R), **35.3** *m.*, an island in the river, received its name when the schooner *Samuel Roberts* grounded here in the summer of 1850. The crew, waiting for the tide, started to while away the time with a cask of brandy. The incensed captain heaved the casks overboard. (*Boating, fishing, and swimming*).

MILL CREEK, **36.9** *m.*, is at the junction with a dirt road.

Left here to LOON LAKE, 6 *m.* (*fishing and boating*), covering about 1,200 acres. This lake, discovered in 1852 and so named for the bird found here in abundance, was formed by a huge landslide that blocked Mill Creek Valley. Other small lakes within this area are accessible by foot or on horseback over well marked trails.

West of Mill Creek is a region of tidal flows, farm lands, and low green pastures belonging to dairymen.

West of CHARLOTTE CREEK, **39.5** *m.*, for several miles the road is cut into a rocky cliff. Canyons are lush with the broad-leaved, shrubby salal, and streamsides grow thick with red and amber salmonberry.

DEAN CREEK, **44.4** *m.*, was named for two brothers who settled at its mouth in 1851. West of KOEPKE SLOUGH, **46** *m.*, State 38 follows a dike across lowlands. Into the wide flowing Umpqua, once came many ships to load lumber, but fishing boats are now more numerous. The waters teem with runs of salmon. Great blue herons live along the shallows and on the waters are wide floating log booms upon which cormorants perch at attention.

REEDSPORT, **50.1** *m.* (28 alt., 1,179 pop.) (*see TOUR 3a*), is the junction with US 101 (*see TOUR 3a*).

Tour 2H

Coos Junction—Ten Mile—Camas Valley—Myrtle Point—Coquille: 61.8 m. State 42.

Paved road. Pacific Greyhound stages.
Standard accommodations.

State 42, an important link between US 99 and US 101, swings southwestward in a great arc from the upper Umpqua Valley across the Coast Range. It passes through the farming region of the foothills, the forested hills around Camas Mountain Pass, and the green pastures of the Coquille River Valley.

Branching southwestward from US 99 at COOS JUNCTION, 0 *m.* (534 alt.), State 42 leads across Lookingglass Valley, the greater part of which is excellent farm land. Hoy B. Flournoy, who settled here in 1850, was a member of a party of settlers who organized in Polk County for the purpose of exploring southern Oregon. They went as far south as Rogue River and the members were greatly impressed by the beauty of the little valley, which was so named because Flournoy thought the green grass appeared to reflect light like a mirror.

Lookingglass Valley is the setting for several chapters of *Honey in the Horn,* the 1936 Pulitzer Prize Novel, by H. L. Davis, although for fictional purposes he placed it in eastern Oregon.

The first white settler in Lookingglass Valley was Daniel Huntley, who came in the fall of 1851. For a time he and H. B. Flournoy were the only settlers in a wide area of country. Milton and Joseph Huntley, Robert Yates, and J. and E. Sheffield, settled in the valley in 1852. By the fall of 1853, the whole valley was covered by donation land claims, nine sections of plow land being quickly taken.

The country west of the South Umpqua, embracing Lookingglass, Olalla, Ten Mile, and Camas, suffered considerably during the Indian wars. In 1855 a band of 64 Umpqua Indians lived on Lookingglass Creek, three miles below the present town of that name, supposedly under the care of J. M. Arrington. They grew restless when hostilities began further south, and fearing an attack, the white settlers organized and struck the first blow on October 28, 1855; eight Indians were killed and the others driven to the mountains. The fugitives joined the hostile tribes on Rogue River, obtained reinforcements, and returned in December, 1855, to wreak vengeance upon the settlers. Houses were burned and property destroyed from the South Umpqua to South Ten Mile. The whites had united and were augmented by volunteers from various localities, and met the Indians in the Battle of Olalla, in which James Castleman was wounded, the only casualty suffered by the whites. "Cow Creek Tom," one of the Indian chiefs, was killed and eight others mortally wounded. The Indians were completely routed and the white settlers recovered most of their stolen cattle.

In April, 1856, the settlers provided further protection for themselves, when, under authority of a proclamation issued by Gov. George Law Curry, a company of 30 "Minute Men" was organized at the schoolhouse in Lookingglass. David Williams was chosen captain, William H. Stark, first lieutenant, and William Cochran, first sergeant.

Outcroppings of coal were discovered in the early 1850's in the vicinity of Lookingglass Prairie. James Turner, owner of the first sawmill on Lookingglass Creek, and R. M. Gurney, made the first discoveries.

BROCKWAY, 1.9 *m.* (524 alt., 62 pop.), is in a farming, fruit-growing and stock-raising district. A post office here was formerly called

Civil Bend, but was discontinued for a time, and, when re-established, named in honor of B. B. Brockway, an early resident.

At **9.3** *m.* is a junction with a dirt road.

Left on this road to OLALLA (Ind., *O-lil-y,* berries), **1.7** *m.,* a country settlement, devoted to general farming. It is probable that the purple-flowered, native salmonberry, a red or amber fruit resembling raspberries, was the reason that the Indian word was applied to the town. The present name was given by the Post Office Department.

TEN MILE, **9.4** *m.* (681 alt., 9 pop.), probably so named because it was ten miles from Flournoy, is a former pioneer settlement in the Lookingglass Valley. Ten Mile Valley, drained by Ten Mile and the Olalla Creeks, was first settled about 1852 by John Byron.

The principal industries of Ten Mile Valley are farming and stock-raising, though a gold mine was operated on Olalla Creek about five miles south of Ten Mile. Wells & Ireland formerly operated a grist mill in the valley.

West of Ten Mile the ascent is rapid through a heavily forested region of Douglas fir, sugar and yellow pine, spruce, cedar, hemlock and yew, to the summit of the Coast Range at CAMAS MOUNTAIN PASS, **14.9** *m.* (1,468 alt.). Each fall, in pioneer times, wagons heavily loaded with wheat, creaked from the isolated mountain valleys over these densely timbered slopes to the new settlement of Roseburg, then a long day's journey.

CAMAS MOUNTAIN STATE PARK (R), is a scenic tract of 160 acres.

From Camas Mountain Pass, State 42 descends through an area of straight, slender trees, and enters the mountainlocked CAMAS VALLEY, **15.9** *m.,* a fertile area, about seven miles long and three miles wide. The name of the valley is derived from a blue-flowered plant (Ind., *La'Kamas*), which grew here in such profusion in the early days that Solomon Fitzhugh, William Day, and A. R. Flint, discoverers of the valley in 1848, looking down upon the blossoms for the first time, mistook the pale blue fields for a lake. The bulbs of this plant are starchy and edible, one of the most important of primitive food plants. The Indians cooked them in earth-covered pits over red-hot stones, and pressed them into cheese-like cakes to dry and store for winter use. White pioneers also mashed these roots into a pulp and cooked them in the same manner as the pumpkin, making excellent pies (*see FLORA AND FAUNA*).

CAMAS VALLEY (P. O.), **17.4** *m.* (1,133 alt., 302 pop), is the center of a fertile area drained by the Coquille (fr. shell) River which flows to the Pacific Ocean. The name of this river is thought to have been applied by French traders of the Hudson's Bay Company because of the many shells of clams and mussels found at the river's mouth.

Camas Valley was formerly known as Eighteen-Mile Valley, being approximately that distance from the settlement of Flournoy (*see above*). The first permanent settlement was made on March 8, 1853, by William Day, Abraham Patterson, and Alston Martindale. Other settlers soon followed. In 1856 there were only three women in the valley, the wives of William Day and Martindale and the daughter of Adam Day. Mrs. Martindale before her marriage was Nancy Fitzhugh, daughter of the patriarch, Solomon Fitzhugh, who helped draft Oregon's constitution.

One of the first sawmills in Camas Valley was operated by Prior, Ferguson & Devitt, upon the headwaters of the Coquille River. It cut 3,000 feet a day and was surrounded by excellent timber, including fir, cedar, sugar pine, and oak.

Descending from Camas Valley, the highway crosses the Middle Fork of the Coquille at 19.8 *m.*, at which point the valley is left behind and the highway again enters the timbered hills of the coastal lumbering region. Here one can see almost every operation of the industry, from the lone shake-splitter who falls his own trees and rives out hand-made boards with froe and mallet, to the great modern camps powered by electric donkey engines. At certain locations are towering spar-trees from which "high lead" lines swing huge logs across hills and canyons for miles, and drop them beside the road, where they are loaded on trucks and trundled to tide-water sawmills. Other logs are left in the river bed to be carried down to the bay by winter floods.

As the road drops from Camas Valley, it narrows, with many sheer rocky cuts through the cliffs. Though the country is yet rough and mountainous, the seacoast influence is soon felt in the increasing number of round-topped myrtle trees which appear, and by occasional glimpses of ducks, gulls, cormorants, and other water fowl. Yew trees, which once supplied the Indians with their strong bows, grow on craggy cliffs.

This is the country of the Coos Indians, whose recorded myths add interest to many features of the route. Perhaps the blue-flowered camas marks the spot where the Coos heroine, Night Rainbow, and her young grandson defied the great Grizzly Bear, their persecutor, and slew him. Another tells of the Great Fire-wind, which drove the Indians into the sea to escape its consuming heat.

REMOTE, 34.2 *m.* (238 alt., 15 pop.), surrounded by mossy old orchards, is a pioneer settlement, whose name was likely suggested by its distance from other communities.

BRIDGE, 41.5 *m.* (145 alt., 39 pop.), a small rural settlement, was named for a bridge across the Coquille. The post office was established on July 6, 1894.

At 49.7 *m.* is the junction with a macadam road.

Left on this road up the valley of the South Coquille River through the villages of BROADBENT, 2.7 *m.* and GAYLORD, 10.7 *m.* to POWERS, 18.7 *m.* (500 pop.), the terminus of the Coos Bay branch of the Southern Pacific Railroad and the outfitting point for the Johnson Creek and Salmon Creek gold mining area.

South of Powers the route enters the SISKIYOU NATIONAL FOREST, 23.2 *m.*, passes COQUILLE FOREST CAMP, 23.3 *m.*, and COAL CREEK FOREST CAMP, 24.3 *m.*, traversing a magnificent stand of Port Orford cedar. Climbing to the summit just west of BALD KNOB, 42.7 *m.* (3,614 alt.), the highway descends to BIG BEND RANCH, 47.5 *m.*, on the north bank of Rogue River. The ranch pasture is an emergency airplane landing field.

Down the Rogue River is ILLAHEE, 48.6 *m.* (173 alt., 25 pop.), starting point for several trails into the back country. Chiseled from the sides of the forested mountains, the highway skirts the turbulent Rogue to AGNESS, 54.7 *m.* (113 alt., 10 pop.), where there is a Forest Service ranger station. A heavy-duty suspension bridge spans the Rogue and leads to primitive regions spotted with deposits of chromite, gold, and other ores.

MYRTLE POINT, 52.5 *m.* (90 alt., 1,362 pop.), is named for the abundance of the shrub around here, the wood of which is beautifully mottled, and is manufactured into fine cabinet work. On the (R), at the eastern edge of the town is an avenue of these trees. The pioneer Hotel Myrtle stands on Spruce Street. At the confluence of the three forks of the Coquille River, Myrtle Point is the trade center of a rich agricultural and dairying region. Within its environs are eight cream-eries with a combined annual output of hundreds of thousands of pounds of butter, and more than a million pounds of cheese.

Because of the cool, moist climate, specialized forms of agriculture are carried on here. Summer and autumn crops of green peas command a premium. The soil and climate are also especially adaptable to the growth of Reed canary grass, one of the heaviest producing pasture grasses in the world. Another prized grass is the Carrier's or Coast bent grass, used extensively for lawns and golf greens.

West of Myrtle Point the valley widens and hills and pastures appear. The mild climate, with frequent rainfall and the absence of heavy frosts, assures abundant crops of cranberries in these fertile flood lands. In late June pale, rose-colored blossoms cover the marshes. Harvesting of the berries in late September and early October furnishes seasonal employment for many workers. Better grades of the berries are hand picked, while others are gathered by use of especially constructed boxes, equipped with forklike prongs, called scoopers.

COQUILLE, 61.8 *m.* (40 alt., 2,732 pop.) (*see TOUR 3b*), is at the junction with US 101 (*see TOUR 3b*).

Tour 21

Grants Pass Junction — Wilderville — Wonder — Kerby — (Crescent City, Calif.) ; 42.4 m. US 199.

Paved road, open all year except during severe snow or sleet when it may be temporarily blocked.
Southern Pacific Railroad spur parallels US 199 between Grants Pass and Wilderville.
Accommodations few, but improved campsites available.

US 199, the Redwood Highway, follows the old trail over which the Argonauts of the early 1850's rushed north from California's waning gold fields to the new diggings on southwestern Oregon creeks. As the direct route between the miners' base of supplies at the ocean port of Crescent City, California, and the placer camps of the northern territory, it was traveled by a motley horde of fortune-seekers who might have stepped straight from Poker Flat.

The old highway was a military road when volunteers in homespun and blue-jacketed regulars fought federated Indian tribes in a series of wars that lasted more than a decade. The old road was a route of hazard and necessity; the new one is safe and connects vast scenic and playground areas in Oregon with California's redwood empire. The road, slashed through a virgin wilderness of jagged mountains, deep ravines, and swift water courses traced the beginning of southwestern Oregon's commercial growth. From the Rogue River and its two chief tributaries, the Illinois and the Applegate, a mesh of smaller streams, spreads out across the lower valley, and from them irrigation canals carry water across fruitful bottomlands. Many residents of the valley work small mining claims along with their farms.

US 199 branches west from US 99 at GRANTS PASS JUNCTION, 0 m. (see TOUR 2b), and passes into the southern extremity of the Rogue River Valley.

The APPLEGATE RIVER, 6.8 m., named for the pioneer family (see TOUR 2b), swarmed with miners during the gold rush of the 1850's. At one time the banks of the stream were honeycombed with miners' excavations. On every gravel bar the sunlight flashed upon pans and picks. Fortunes in gold dust were washed out and a considerable amount of placer mining is still evident.

WILDERVILLE, 8.5 m. (936 alt., 12 pop.), is a hamlet on the threshold of a narrow valley that extends to the California Line. It was first called Slate Creek but was given its present name August 12, 1878, when Joseph L. Wilder was appointed postmaster. Cultivated fields yield to tumbled hills that rise into forested mountains.

South of WONDER, 11.6 m. (1,078 alt.), the region grows more rugged. The village was ironically named by settlers who "wondered" how a merchant who established a store at this point might hope to make a livelihood.

West of the summit of HAYES HILL, 16.7 m. (1,658 alt.), a corner of the Siskiyou National Forest is crossed. In Deer Creek Valley forests crowd close to the road. Against the dense growth of pine, madrona trees stand out in bright relief. The graceful madrona, with dark-green leaves, smooth bark, waxy white blossoms, and scarlet, edible fruit, is beautiful to look upon.

The ANDERSON STAGE STATION, 18.6 m. (R), on the banks of Clear Creek, was known also as Fort Hays for the Hay family that lived here. It stands on what is now the Smith Ranch and was built in 1852 as a tavern and stage station. During the Rogue River Indian Wars of 1855-56 it was a refuge. One of the bloodiest battles of the wars was fought there on March 24, 1856. A group of volunteer soldiers and miners beseiged by Indians succeeded in repelling them

after an all-night battle. There were several casualties, out the numb<
is not of record.

The window frames of the old building, which quiver as motor car;
roar down the modern highway, shook once with the passing of earlier
traffic—mule trains from Crescent City with flour, bacon, and beans
for the northern diggings, and rumbling stagecoaches with mail and
passengers, strong-boxes crammed with Oregon gold, and armed guards
riding the boots of the cumbersome vehicles. Weathered clapboards cover
the original logs of the building.

Near the second crossing of Clear Creek, **20** *m.,* is (R) a PIONEER
CEMETERY.

SELMA, **20.9** *m.* (1,324 alt., 37 pop.), a post office and store serves
the miners who work chrome ore claims in a part of the Illinois Valley.
Ore produced in the district is freighted to the railroad by way of this
tiny settlement, an outlet in the precipitous hills that hem in the valley.

Southwest of Selma the route spans half a dozen creeks and winds'
over the sharply lifting hills that form the divide between the Deer
Creek and the Illinois River Valleys. In the Illinois Valley volunteers
and tribesmen fought many pitched battles. Many early gold strikes
were made in this vicinity.

KERBY, **27.2** *m.* (1,262 alt., 40 pop.), was an important trading
center and placer mining camp of the early Oregon gold rush (*bear
hunting in November; dogs and guides available*). In 1858, when it
supplanted Waldo as the seat of Josephine County, Kerby was a mushroom town of tents and rude shacks and was known as Kerbyville. Once
a settlement of 500 or more inhabitants, it faded into oblivion when the
rich placer claims in the vicinity were worked out. Of its many saloons,
brothels, and stores only a few sagging buildings remain. An OLD
HOUSE (L) with a balcony and columns was a stagecoach station;
the OLD BARN in which relay horses were stabled is (R) at **27.3** *m.*

Mining operations in the vicinity of Kerby were continued after
prospectors deserted the creeks from which surface gold had been
panned. Quartz mining, introduced but recently, has also produced a
considerable amount of ore. The Kerby district also yields gold, iron,
quicksilver, cobalt, ilmenite, an ingredient for paint-making, and in-
fusorial earth, used in the manufacture of furnace linings.

CAVES JUNCTION, **29.7** *m.,* (1,348 alt., 250 pop.), so named because it is upon the threshold of the route leading to the Oregon Caves
National Monument (*see below*),is a rapidly growing village with many
new buildings and stores.

Left on State 46 from Caves Junction to CHAPMAN CREEK, 2.5 *m.*

1. Right **2.5** *m.* from Chapman Creek on a dirt road through a region of
active and abandoned mining camps to the ghost town of ALTHOUSE. A few
crumbling stone chimneys and fireplace heaps are all that remain of this once
prosperous mining community.

Near Althouse is the SITE OF BROWNTON, scene of a placer strike that
yielded much gold including one nugget valued at $1,200. The forest has re-
claimed the old camp.

Beyond Chapman Creek State 46 parallels the East Fork of the Illinois River, then Tycer Creek, and at about **7** *m.* reaches Sucker Creek, which it follows through wooded hills and broken-crested mountains to the OREGON CAVES NATIONAL MONUMENT, 19.7 *m.* (*open May 15-October 15; two-hour tour; warm clothing advisable; special winter guide service; lodge open during entire year; tourist cottages; United States Forest Camp*).

The Oregon Caves, known as "The Marble Halls of Oregon," are a series of spectacular caverns in ELIJAH MOUNTAIN (7,000 alt.), a towering limestone and marble formation in the Siskiyou Range. The mountain was named for Elijah Bristow, a pioneer who discovered the caves in 1874, while pursuing a bear that disappeared into the mountainside. The mountain is a labyrinth of chambers, corridors, and passageways of incredible beauty, carved by the relentless flow and drip of water in subterranean darkness.

In earliest time this region was twisted by volcanic movements which made great rents in the rocks. Melting glaciers formed streams, one of which found its way through the fissures and left deposits of gravel. The stream enlarged the fissures and fashioned them into grottos. Slow deposits of limestone formed the white incrustations that give the caves their name. At present, a stream, probably much smaller than the glacial river, gushes from the grotto and tumbles down a canyon between forested hills.

The entrance to the caves is a narrow interstice, almost hidden by overhanging ferns and beetling crags of rock. The descent is through a low-roofed tunnel into a broad, starkly white, chill chamber, where last preparations and examinations of clothing are made.

Carved through unreckoned ages are wierdly beautiful caverns in which clusters of intricately sculptured marble hang from frescoed ceilings like frozen lotus flowers. Stalagmite and stalactite join together, forming columns like vast organ pipes; they emit sweet thin music when struck by metal. Out-thrust from the walls are shelves adorned with bric-a-brac fashioned by nature, some of it grotesque, but all of it arresting in its cold brilliance. Fluted columns and pillars rise along the passages, shimmering like pearl when the search-lights play upon them. Colored lights, at intervals through arched vaults, give the marble walls a blue and crimson translucence. A spoken word echoes and reverberates in the stillness.

The route leads over chasms spanned by steel bridges, down corridors that twist back upon themselves, and through narrow apertures and broad chambers. More than fifty points of interest are featured and others are constantly being discovered as further explorations are made. There is NIAGARA FALLS, a waterfall frozen eternally into marble. JOAQUIN MILLER'S chapel is a vast cathedral-like room, named for the poet, who visited the caves in 1907. The crystal tubes of the QUEEN'S ORGAN in this room give forth musical sounds. Deeper within the mountain is PARADISE LOST, a high-vaulted chamber from which hang the pendants of crystal chandeliers. In the GHOST stalactites and stalagmites suggest supernatural, white-robed figures. DANTE'S INFERNO is a yawning chasm in which marble, under crimson lights, resembles the contents of a boiling cauldron. Along the passages and corridors and in all the chambers are fantastic formations named for their resemblance to figures of fact or fiction. The exit from the caves is through a long tunnel, cut for 550 feet through solid rock, that opens upon a wooded hillside, bright with alpine flowers. The western Tofieldia and the rare bog asphodel are found in this region. The yellow monkey flower and the wild hellebore also grow in profusion. In the spring crimson rhododendrons paint great splashes of color against the green hillsides.

President Taft proclaimed the caves and 480 acres of adjacent land a national monument in 1909. The Grants Pass Cavemen, formed to publicize the natural wonder, have done much to bring it to the attention of the world. The surrounding area offers a superb scenery and the usual recreational features found in a mountainous region. A system of forest trails leads around Elijah Mountain, a distance of about four miles.

The OREGON CAVES GAME REFUGE surrounds the caves, and the district teems with wild life, bear and deer frequently becoming quite tame under the protection of the refuge officials.

Among the unusual fauna in the area is the lemming, a small rodent resembling the common mouse in color. It ranges widely from the Alaskan coast across the continent to Arkansas and Tennessee. The animal is a distant relative of the lemmings that make a periodical migration across the tundras of northern Europe.

The OREGON CAVES CHATEAU is encircled by a scenic drive that winds under terraces of limestone, tapestried with velvet moss, with the mountain rising almost sheer behind it. It is entered by way of the fourth floor level into a spacious lounge. Beneath it is the dining room into which a mountain waterfall plunges, forming a stream that flows across the building and out through another wall.

South of the junction with State 46, US 199 follows the valley of the West Fork of the Illinois River over a graveled flat, boulderstrewn, and surrounded by forest and pasture land.

At **36.6** m. is the junction with a dirt road.

Left from the junction across a plank bridge over the West Fork of the Illinois River, **0.9** m., and through a region of manzanita and scrub-pine. At **3.7** m. is WALDO (1,583 alt.), the site of the old mining town called Sailor's Diggings because the settlement was founded by a ship's crew who deserted their vessel at Crescent City in the 1850's and established placer claims from which a large amount of gold was mined. Waldo reached its zenith in the 1860's as thousands of Chinese miners worked claims in its vicinity, but declined as the placer diggings waned. Abandoned hydraulic mining operations are in evidence throughout the valley.

TAKILMA, **4.2** m. (1,567 alt.), another ghost town of gold-rush years, is the center of extensive copper-mining activities.

South of the junction LONE MOUNTAIN (1,598 alt.) rises as if to block the highway, but the road sweeps around in a long curve, zigzagging through lush forests and along the brinks of almost sheer precipices.

Tall pines are dwarfed at intervals by redwood trees, the advance guard of the mighty redwood forests of California. Imposing because of their great diameter and their soaring height, these beautiful trees increase in number as the California Line is approached. Once indigenous to all Oregon, the redwood, after the convulsion that created the Cascade Range, withdrew to the mild and moist coastal area of extreme southern Oregon and northern California. The tree reaches a not unusual height for pinaceous growths, 200 to 300 feet, but its diameter ranges to 30 feet or more.

US 199 crosses the California Line, **42.4** m. at a point 43.9 miles northeast of Crescent City, California (see *CALIFORNIA GUIDE. TOUR 2a*).

Tour 3

(Aberdeen, Wash.) — Astoria — Seaside — Tillamook — Newport —
Marshfield—Gold Beach—(Crescent City, Calif.); US 101.
Washington Line to California Line, 394.4 *m.*

Paved road.
Spokane, Portland, and Seattle Railroad parallels route between Astoria and
Seaside; Southern Pacific Railroad between Mohler and Tillamook and between
Reedsport and Coquille.

US 101, which closely parallels the rocky Oregon Coast and affords
striking views of sea and shore, follows in part an Indian trail over
which, according to legend, passed Talapus, the Indian coyote god,
when he was fashioning the headlands and bays and setting a limit to
the tide. Traders early followed the stretches of beach below the present
route before covered wagons had flattened the underbrush on higher
land. But most travel along the coast in early days was by water, though
boatmen had to be exceedingly careful in the treacherous coastal tides.
From 1853, when Ferrelo, under orders from the Spanish viceroy in
Mexico City, pushed up the coast in search of the mythical Straits of
Anian—which were supposed to provide a passage across the continent
—until long after 1792 when Robert Gray entered the mouth of the
Columbia River and Lieutenant Broughton explored it, the shore waters
were the scenes of perilous adventure.

South of the tidal estuary of the Columbia, the salt marshes and low
sand-spits of the northwestern rim of the state, cliffs crowd close to
the ocean. Construction of a motor road along the coast, to be called
the Roosevelt Military Highway, was begun in 1921 after long urging
by Benjamin F. Jones of Newport and in the face of derision because
of the difficulties of the project. The highway was completed in 1932.

It was only then that along the coast real development began. Their
long isolation has given the sea-board towns a certain individuality
though they share the characteristics of villages on any coast subject
to violent storms. Summer cottages here and there are trim and brightly
painted but the majority of the houses have a haphazard look; each has
been placed where its owner thought he could gain the most protection
from wind and waves. Most of the weatherboarding, locally called
shiplap, and shingles are a uniform silver gray. Formerly shingle "sec-
onds" could be had at the mills without cost, or for very little, and
many coast homes were covered with them. Shingles over shiplap were
considered the best walling though discouraged coasters insist that a
weatherproof house simply cannot be built—the wind will whip rain
through the most cleverly joined and mortised walls. The same wind

tears loose both clapboards and shingles, so every house more than a few years old is bound to show the marks of repeated repairs, unless the owner has given up the struggle. Another characteristic of the coast is the number of buildings standing on piling over inlets. While some of the villages ramble over flats, quite as many are huddled in the lea of a steep hill or cliff. There are even occasional houseboat colonies.

In spite of the summer fogs and winter rains the stream of visitors to the region is growing steadily; the physical grandeur of the terrain, and the smell of evergreen forests tanged with salt air and heightened by mist form an exhilerating combination.

Section a. Washington Line to Newport, 154 m.

This section of the route, which is one of the most spectacular in the United States, is never long out of sight of the sea. It crosses inlets and marshes on beautiful modern bridges; passes through villages reeking with the smell of salmon oil and decaying flotsom softened by the tantalizing odor of brine-soaked pilings, and proceeds over sand-reaches where many bits of bone and shell from the refuse pits of an earlier civilization are exposed by the wind.

US 101 crosses the Washington Line, in the middle of the Columbia River at a point 87 miles south of Aberdeen, Wash. Travelers cross the river on the Point Ellice-Astoria ferry. (*Car and driver* $1; *passengers* $.25 *each*).

At ASTORIA, **0** *m.* (*see ASTORIA*), is the junction with US 30 (*see TOUR* 1c).

Here US 101 swings R. then L. around SMITH'S POINT, **2** *m.*, at the entrance to Young's Bay, an arm of the Columbia. In the water lie the decaying hulls of half-completed merchant ships, abandoned at the close of the World War. The headland, on the opposite side of Young's Bay, about three miles away, is POINT ADAMS (*see below*), near which in 1792 Lieut. William Broughton, an English officer, anchored his brig *Chatham* and set out with small boats to explore the bay and river, naming them in honor of Sir George Young of the royal navy.

US 101 crosses Young's River, **3.4** *m.*, and at **4.8** *m.* meets Miles Crossing Road.

Left here up Young's River to (L) the UNITED STATES NAVAL RADIO STATION, 0.5 *m.*, which broadcasts weather observations and storm warnings for the Oregon and Washington coast and reports conditions on the bar at the mouth of the Columbia River. At 10 m. the road loops around Young's River Falls.

At 13 *m.* is the junction with a dirt road; R for 12 *m.* to SADDLE MOUNTAIN STATE PARK, the Swal-la-lachast, (home of the Thunder Bird) in Clatsop legend. Here she laid the eggs that rolled down the mountainside and hatched into tribes of men. On the mountain (3,266 alt.) are trails, shelters, and picnic grounds. Much hunting for deer—and occasionally for elk, and fishing for trout is done in this area.

US 101 crosses the Lewis and Clark River, **5.7** *m.*, named for the leaders of the overland expedition sent by President Jefferson in 1804 to find a route "to the Western Ocean" (*see HISTORY*). William Clark and Meriwether Lewis led the expedition across the Rocky Mountains and down the Columbia River, reaching this coast late in 1805. The Shoshone squaw, Sacajawea, and her husband, a French-Canadian, acted as interpreters for the party.

At **6.5** *m.* is the junction with a gravel road.

Left here to the SITE OF FORT CLATSOP, 1.5 *m.*, the winter encampment of the Lewis and Clark party in 1805-06.

Now overgrown with evergreens, the site is designated by a flagpole and is marked by a plaque. On December 7, 1805, Clark recorded: ". . . after breakfast I delayed about half an hour before York Came up, then proceeded around this Bay which I call (have taken the liberty of calling) Meriwethers Bay the Christian name of Capt. Lewis who no doubt was the 1st white man who ever Surveyed this Bay. [Clark was in error on this]. . . . This is certainly the most eligable Situation for our purposes of any in its neighbourhood."

On December 8 the rest of the party arrived and within a short time trees had been felled and rude huts erected around an open square. Some of the men were sent to the Pacific shore to make salt from sea waters, others to hunt, and the remainder, working against time and weather, completed the shelters sufficiently to enable the party to move in by Christmas.

The first American Christmas in the Northwest was a meager affair. Clark wrote: "at day light this morning we were awoke by the discharge of the fire arms of all our party a Selute, Shouts and a Song which the whole party joined in under our windows, after which they retired to their rooms were chearfull all the morning. after breakfast we divided our Tobacco which amounted to 12 carrots one half of which we gave to the men of the party who used tobacco, and to those who doe not use it we make a present of a handkerchief, The Indians leave us in the evening all the party Snugly fixed in their huts. I recved a present of Capt. L. of a fleece hosrie [hosiery] Shirt Draws and Socks, a pr. Mockersons of white weazils tails of the Indian woman, & some black root of the Indians before their departure. . . . The day proved Showerey wet and disagreeable. . . . our Dinner concisted of pore Elk, so much Spoiled that we eate it thro' mear necessity." They were without salt to season even that.

On the 26th Clark wrote: "we dry our wet articles and have the blankets fleed, The flees are so troublesom that I have slept but little for 2 night past and we have regularly to kill them out of our blankets every day for several past." The fleas were contributed by the Indians on their daily visits. On the 27th he added, "Musquetors troublesom."

Clark noted also: "With the party of *Clatsops* who visited us last was a man much lighter Coloured than the nativs are generaly, he was freckled with long duskey red hair, about 25 years of age, and must Certainly be half white at least, this man appeared to understand more of the English language than the others of his party, but did not Speak a word of English, he possessed all the habits of the Indians." In *Adventures on the Columbia* (1832) Ross Cox also described such a man and said he was the son of a sailor who had deserted from an English ship. He was said to have had the words "Jack Ramsey" tattoed on his arm. "Poor Jack was fond of his father's countrymen," Ross says, "and had the decenty to wear trousers whenever he came to the fort [Astoria]. We therefore made a collection of old clothes for his use; sufficient to last him many years." The Indians told them of several parties of white men who had landed on the Oregon coast in the eighteenth century and of a red-haired sailor who had been washed ashore about 1760—indicating the presence of European traders on the Oregon Coast long before Gray saw the mouth of the Columbia.

The Clatsops became such frequent and troublesome visitors at the fort that, ". . . at Sun set we let the nativs know that our Custom will be in future, to Shut the gates at Sun Set at which time all Indians must go out of the fort and not return into it untill next morning after Sunrise at which time the gates will be opened, those of the *Warciacum* Nation who are very forward left the house with reluctiance." In view of the Indians' conceptions of property rights, this seems to have been an expedient ruling.

By March the leaders believed that the mountain snows would be melting, and the return to the East could be made. On March 23 Clark reported: "loaded our canoes & at 1 P. M. left Fort Clatsop on our homeward journey. at this place we had wintered and remained from the 7th of Decr. 1805 to this day and have lived as we had any right to expect, and we can say that we were never one day without 3 meals of some kind a day either pore Elk meat or roots. . . ."

By the junction with the Fort Clatsop Road is the ASTORIA MUNICIPAL AIRPORT, 6.6 *m.,* terminus of the Portland-Astoria airway. Because of its strategic importance as a sea-plane base, the federal government contributed to its development in 1936.

At 7.9 *m.* is the junction with a paved road.

Right here to WARRENTON, 2 *m.* (8 alt., 683 pop.), one of several places where the chief business is razor-clam canning. The road continues through the undulating dunes, marshes, and fertile lowlands—a strip about 4 miles wide and 24 miles long—of Clatsop Plains, composed of sediment deposited by the Columbia River, and now worn into ridges by wind and tide.

POINT ADAMS COAST GUARD STATION, 5 *m.,* was named for Vice President John Adams in 1792 by Capt. Robert Gray. In 1775 Capt. Bruno Heceta (*see below*) named it Cabo Frendoso (Leafy Cape.) Though Heceta had reached the river, he did not realize the fact and lost for his sovereign the chance to claim the Oregon country. Before the coming of the railroad, Point Adams was the point of debarkation from Portland passenger steamers for summer vacationists bound for Seaside (*see below*). Transfer was made to creaking democrat wagons which covered the 20 miles to the old Seaside House.

FORT STEVENS, 6 *m.,* the only coastal fortification in Oregon, has a small garrison. Each summer the encampment of the coast artillery of the Oregon National Guard is held here.

At 11.1 *m.* is the junction with a gravel road.

Right here to CAMP CLATSOP, 0.5 *m.,* used in summer by the infantry and field artillery units of the Oregon National Guard. Maneuvers are usually held in July.

The road turns southward, passing the GRAY MEMORIAL CHAPEL, (R) 11.2 *m.,* on the site of a Presbyterian church dedicated in 1851 by a congregation organized in 1846 by the Reverend Lewis Thompson. W. H. Gray, one of the founders, wrote the first local history of Oregon (1869). The chapel erected by his daughter is a square brick structure with a very long and somewhat lower brick wing. The roof of the main unit rises to a square bell tower topped by a steeple. The pedimented entrance portico has walled sides and a recessed entrance between tall columns.

DELMOOR, 15.7 *m.,* was named by J. S. Dillinger, who established a cranberry bog here in 1912. In spring this section of the route is banked with Scotch broom. In earlier days this plant was imported from Scotland for use in broom making and was later used to bind the drifting sands on Clatsop Plains. Sometimes 15 feet high and bearing long sprays of golden pea-like flowers, it is constantly spreading farther south along the coast. An annual May Festival celebrates the seasonal bloom.

At **18** *m.* is the junction with a paved road.

Right here to GEARHART, **1** *m.* (16 alt., 125 pop.), a beach resort with an excellent 18-hole golf course on which the Oregon golf championship matches are played in late summer. Many conventions are held in the town.

SEASIDE, **20.4** *m.* (16 alt., 1,565 pop.), (*hotels, tourist cottages; sea-water natatorium*), Oregon's largest seaside resort, spreads across the narrow Necanicum River—which parallels the coast—and up and down a long narrow sandy bar. On the ocean side of this bar is a sea-wall that also forms a "boardwalk" above the beach. At the southern end of town the ground rises abruptly into a wooded ridge that bulges westward and forms a high, bold promontory.

Seaside gained its first prominence during the 1870's when Ben Holladay, who came into prominence in the days of the Overland Stage and was later a railroad promoter and builder (*see TRANSPORTA-TION*), built the sumptuous Holladay House, a place to entertain his illustrious friends. It became noted; guests were brought here at times from San Francisco by chartered steamers to be lavishly entertained.

On the promenade at the foot of Main Street is the END OF THE TRAIL MONUMENT, commemorating the Lewis and Clark journey. Near the southern end of the promenade on Q St. are the ruins of the SALT CAIRN, a heap of brine-crusted rocks protected by an iron railing. It was built by the men Lewis and Clark sent to get salt by boiling down sea water. Clark wrote that he: "directed . . . Jos. Fields, Bratton Gibson to proceed to the Ocean at some convenient place form a Camp and Commence making Salt with five of the largest Kittles, and Willard and Wiser to assist them in carrying the Kittles to the Sea Coast." Messengers reported that "the men had at length established themselves on the coast about 15 miles S. W. from this, near the lodge of some Killamuck families; that the Indians were very friendly and had given them a considerable quantity of the blubber of a whale which perished on the Coast some distance S. E. of them; part of this blubber they brought with them, it was white and not unlike the fat of Poark, tho' the texture was more spongey and somewhat courser. . . ." Lewis had some of the blubber cooked and liked it. Lewis continued: "they commenced making salt and found that they could obtain from 3 quarts to a gallon a day; they brought with them a specimine of the salt of about a gallon; this was a great treat to myself and most of the party, having not had any since the 20th Ult. mo.; I say most of the party, for my friend Cap't Clark, declares it to be a mere matter of indiffer-ence with him whether he uses it or not; for myself I must confess I felt a considerable inconvenience from the want of it; the want of bread I consider trivial provided, I get fat meat, for as to the species of meat I am not very particular, the flesh of the dog the horse and the wolf, having from habit become equally familiar [as] with any other, and I have learned to think that if the chord be sufficiently strong, which binds the soul and body together, it does not so much matter about the materials which compose it."

Right (*straight ahead*) from the southern end of First St. on a trail (*rocky for about a mile*) that swings south following an old logging road and climbs up the ridge that terminates near TILLAMOOK HEAD (1,260 alt.), 4 *m.* Along the ridge are sweeping views of the territory northward. From the Head, TILLAMOOK LIGHTHOUSE is seen offshore, rising 41 feet on an isolated rock so sheer that people visiting the lighthouse frequently have to be landed in a breeches buoy. The base of the lighthouse is 91 feet above the water. Winter gales sweep this rock with hurricane force and the lighthouse keeper is frequently isolated for long periods. This lighthouse is described in John Fleming Wilson's sea stories (*see below*). Far below the crest of Tillamook Head, gulls wheel above the waves that swirl in DEATH TRAP COVE that has caused the death of adventurous visitors.

South of Seaside US 101 follows the NECANICUM RIVER, 23.3 *m.*, through green lowlands, bordered with alders and willows and yellow-patched in spring with huge skunk cabbages, whose leaves were used by the Coast Indians to wrap their food in the cooking pits. Lettuce and peas are the principal crops grown on farms in this district.

At CANNON BEACH JUNCTION, 24.1 *m.,* is the junction with a road paved with asphalt.

Right on this road, winding through groves of gigantic hemlock to CANNON BEACH, 5 *m.* (25 alt., 125 pop.), an ocean resort so named because a cannon was washed ashore here from the American sloop *Shark*, wrecked in 1846 at the mouth of the Columbia River. She had been sent up the coast during the turbulent discussions that ended with the annexation of the Oregon Country by the United States. The cannon stands beside the foot trail that leads southward along the coast. Just offshore is HAYSTACK ROCK (300 alt.).
The road continues southward tunneling ARCH CAPE, 11.4 *m.* It has been carved into a bluff at Neah-kah-nie Mountain, 500 feet above the sea. Neah-kah-nie, one of the many places along the coast south of this point with names beginning with the Indian prefix *ne* (place), was known to the Tillamooks as "the place of the Fire Spirit." Neah-kah-nie Mountain (1,638 alt.), has been the setting for several books, among them being *Beeswax and Gold* by Thomas Rogers; *Ward of the Redskins* by Sheba Hargreaves, and *Slave Wives of Nehalem* by Claire Warner Churchill.
At 18.8 *m.* is the junction with an improved road; R. here 0.3 *m.* to MANZANITA (150 pop.), both a beach and mountain resort. A collection of relics here is associated with the Neah-kah-nie treasure story. It was on the beach near this point that the whale reported by Lieutenant Clark was washed ashore (*see above*). The town is in a cove protected by the rugged headlands to the north.
The main road turns inland to NEHALEM (Ind., place of peace), 21.1 *m.* (16 alt., 245 pop.), and crosses the Nehalem River to a junction with US 101, 22.2 *m.,* near Wheeler (*see below*).

From Cannon Beach Junction US 101 veers inland several miles into the Necanicum (Ind., place of lodge) Valley, where herds of elk, protected by law, have been placed. The NECANICUM STATE FISH HATCHERY, 31.3 *m.,* annually releases millions of trout fingerlings in coast streams.

In its loop inland the highway skirts the rugged area over which Captain Clark struggled with a small party that was eager to see the whale that had been cast ashore (*see above*). By her only request of a personal nature Sacajawea was with the men on this journey, papoose on her back. Reports many years later said that her sight of the "big fish" was the only thing on the journey that Sacajawea never tired of talking about after her return to her people.

NECANICUM JUNCTION, 33.5 *m.*, is a junction with State 2; the super-highway between Portland and the sea (*see TOUR 9*).

US 101 crosses the North Fork of the Nehalem River, 41.3 *m.*, which it follows downstream.

Sharp declivities, now denuded of spruce, cedar, and hemlock, indicate the site of former high-line logging which is characterized by the network of cables, blocks, and guy lines strung from spars (trees denuded of limbs), along which logs are pulled by donkey engines from one ridge to the other. High-climbers—whose insurance rates indicate the great risks of their calling—trim and top 200-foot trees, up which they climb with the aid of spurs and a rope loop attached to a belt. Out in the timber a chokerman places a heavy wire slip-loop, or choker, around a log and a rigging-slinger attaches this loop to the main cable, when the hooker yells "Hi", then the whistle-punk presses an electric grip and the donkey 1,500 feet away, whistles a short, sharp blast. The donkey-puncher, or engine operator, "opens her up" and the log rises above stumps and brush as he yards it to the landing. As soon as the chaser has unhooked the log, a haulback returns the choker to the woods.

US 101 crosses the Nehalem River to MOHLER, 51.6 *m.* (27 alt., 50 pop.), which has a cooperative cheese factory (L) that, like others in the region, is identified by its yellow paint. Many people of Swiss birth or descent operate dairies in the vicinity. They are particularly fond of playing the accordion and yodeling during their leisure hours.

At 52.6 *m.* is the junction with the Cannon Beach Road (*see above*).

At WHEELER, 53.5 *m.* (48 alt., 280 pop.), by Nehalem Bay, the shrill scream of shingle-mill saws and the odor of fresh cedar-wood is as characteristic of the town as is the cry of the gulls that soar above the three fish-packing houses along the waterfront.

Immediately west of Wheeler is HOEVET, 54.3 *m.*, (200 pop.) remnant of a once prosperous mill town. The Hoevet post office functions within a few blocks of the Wheeler post office, the offices serving probably less than 300 persons.

LAKE LYTLE (L), 60.5 *m.* (15 alt.), a brackish, shallow body of water, is a state bird refuge. Many species of aquatic birds nest and feed along its reedy shores. Occasionally a man is seen behind a blind snaring ducks and geese for a state game farm, where they are used for study and propagation.

ROCKAWAY, 61.1 *m.* (15 alt., 300 pop.), is another attractive resort *(sea water natatorium),* with a wide beach. Off-shore are the arched TWIN ROCKS.

From the north BARVIEW, 64.4 *m.* (16 alt., 60 pop.), overlooks the narrow entrance to Tillamook Bay, named for the Indians who lived in the district. In 1788 Capt. Robert Gray crossed the bar, anchored his ship *Lady Washington* (*see HISTORY*), inside the bay, and sent men ashore to find fresh fruits and game for his scurvy-weakened men, and hay for his cattle. Robert Haswell, the mate, named the place Murderer's Harbor because a "Black Boy", a member of the crew, when endeavoring to recover a cutlass that had been stolen by Indians, had been killed. They endeavored to rescue the boy, but as Haswell wrote in his report: "the first thing which presented itself to our view was a very large group of the natives among the midst of which was the poor black with the thief by the colour loudly calling for assistance saying he had cought the thief, when we were observed by the main boddy of the Natives to haistily approach them they instantly drenched their knives and spears with savage fuery in the boddy of the unfortunate youth. He quieted his hold and stumbled but rose again and stagered towards us but having a flight of arrows thrown into his back and he fell within fifteen yards of me and instantly expiered while they mangled his lifeless course." Captain Gray hurriedly put to sea.

South of the bay is CAPE MEARES (700 alt.), with its lighthouses; the view of the cape is sometimes obscured by mist or spray. The headland was named for Capt. John Meares, English explorer, who a month before Gray's visit, had declared the bay closed by a sand barrier. He called it Quicksand Bay.

The route swings inland to skirt the shores of the bay and passes the TILLAMOOK BAY COAST GUARD STATION, 64.2 m.

GARIBALDI, 66 m. (10 alt., 213 pop.), facing the bay, was formerly an important mill town. The dikes along the Miami River, 67.4 m., as well as those along other rivers in cheese-making Tillamook County, have earned the district the name of Little Holland. Grazing in meadows yellow with buttercups are the cows that produce milk for the cheese kitchens, where cream cheese is made and placed in long rows of shelves in the cooling rooms to mellow.

On HOBSONVILLE POINT (R), 68.4 m., overgrown with alders, once stood the lively lumber town of Hobsonville. An empty hotel and several bleached frame dwellings remain; the mill ruins were recently washed into the bay. This rocky point was called Talapus Cradle by the Tillamooks because they thought it resembled a gigantic cradle board, shaped like those used to flatten the heads of all free-born infants.

BAY CITY, 70.5 m. (17 alt., 427 pop.), named for Bay City, Michigan, a fishing town. During a salmon run in Tillamook Bay the catches of the night fishing fleets are dressed and stored in local canneries (admittance by arrangement at offices).

The 18-hole public ALDERBROOK GOLF COURSE (small fee), 72.6 m., has an excellent club house.

A section of the highway just west of the Kilchis River Bridge, 74 m., is frequently inundated during winter rains. It is said that during these floods some motorists find salmon on their running boards.

TILLAMOOK, 76.9 m. (23 alt., 2,549 pop.), seat of Tillamook County, is the prosperous trade center of the dairying region. Early in the morning the dairy ranchers—never called farmers—begin to arrive at the factory weighing-in platforms, where an attendant checks the quantity of milk delivered and takes samples for the butter-fat test that determines the rate of payment. After the ranchers have delivered their milk they drive to the whey tank to load empty milk cans with the liquid that is left after removal of the milk curd. This whey is valuable as hog feed.

By eight in the morning, after all the milk has been received, the cheese-makers empty the fresh milk into huge stainless steel vats and add rennet, salt, and coloring matter to it before turning steam into the jackets around the vats. As soon as coagulation starts long rakes of wire begin a steady movement through the curd to cut and break it. When the curd has been completely separated from the liquid it is pressed into molds of various shapes that have been lined with cloth. Finally, the containers of the new cheeses are stamped with the trade name and coated with paraffine. The round disks are placed in long rows in curing rooms where cool air of constant temperature is circulated.

Butter-making is now being carried on in connection with cheese-making in various places, the cheese being made from the skim milk.

Most cheese-masters are quite willing to permit visitors to sample the pleasant-tasting fresh curd. Even visitors who do not care for its taste usually like to eat a small amount because of the peculiar squeaks produced when it is chewed. Here are cooperative cheese factories that are well worth a visit. Here also are lumber mills and box factories.

Loggers, fishermen, and dairymen are seen on Tillamook streets, particularly on Saturday. The notice "No caulked boots allowed" is seen in the places where woodsmen congregate. These caulks, sharp spikes attached to the soles of shoes, are a necessity in the woods where life depends on swift and sure balance. Some of the establishments provide shingles or pieces of tire casing for the convenience of their customers; the logger steps on these, which adhere to his shoes and walks or slides along without damaging the floors. Loggers, not permitted to smoke while at work, are identified by their chewing tobacco and "snoose" (snuff), by their boots and "tin pants" (water-proofed canvas trousers cut short or "stagged"). Knee boots are commonly worn by dairymen who wade through marshes to herd their cows. Hip-boots, and sou'wester, and sometimes a beach slicker, identify the fishermen.

Tillamook is the western terminus of the Wilson River Highway (*see TOUR 8*).

Right from Tillamook to NETARTS (*boats for deep-sea fishing*), 7.6 *m.* (46 pop.), a beach resort by Netarts Bay, where waters have been planted with Japanese oysters. Several varieties of clams are dug here.

The road continues to OCEANSIDE, 10.1 *m.* (24 pop.), another resort. Offshore are THREE ARCH ROCKS, massive wave-worn monoliths, mentioned in many of the early ships' logs, that have been made a bird refuge. The rocks are crowded with bird and sea life. At their base during low tide are sea lions (*see below*). This is the locale of an essay in Dallas Lore Sharp's book, *Where Rolls the Oregon.*

At SOUTH PRAIRIE, 80.9 *m.*, is a large CHEESE FACTORY (*visitors 8-12*), one of the many in the lower valleys of the Trask and Tillamook rivers.

At 94.5 *m.* the route crosses a narrow strip connecting two sections of the SIUSLAW NATIONAL FOREST. The route traverses this forest at intervals for 150 miles.

The NESTUCCA RIVER (*steelhead trout, late fall and early winter*), **96.5** *m.*, was named for a local tribe called by Lewis and Clark, Neustuckles—Nestuckles, and Nestuccas. Commercial fishing in this stream is prohibited.

HEBO, **97.3** *m.* (54 alt., 275 pop.), at the junction with State 14 (*see TOUR 10A*), was named for Mount Hebo (L).

South of Hebo for a distance of 30 miles the highway skirts a unit of a large area of burned-over land developed as a forest conservation and recreational project carried on by the Farm Security Administration. Holland grass has been planted to halt the advance of sand dunes on the forests.

South of CLOVERDALE, **99.9** *m.* (26 alt., 189 pop.), a dairymen's trading center, the highway follows a dike separating tideland pastures along the Little Nestucca River. The small sharpened shovels used to dig blue clams, along the river are called "clam guns".

NESKOWIN (Ind., plenty of fish), **110.2** *m.* (17 alt., 65 pop.), has a wide view of the ocean and an excellent beach. Numerous varieties of fish, including cutthroat and steelhead trout, Chinook and silverside salmon, bass, halibut, flounders, and perch inhabit the waters.

Between the Neskowin drainage basin and that of the Salmon River, evergreens grow so thickly along the highway that there is scarcely any undergrowth except huckleberry. When this section of highway was constructed, the hemlocks and firs were cut in short lengths and corded along the right-of-way. Since there was no way to burn them without endangering forest and no demand for the wood, the huge piles have remained along the roadside.

OTIS, **121** *m.* (37 alt., 23 pop.), was the western terminus of the Salmon River Toll Road. At OTIS JUNCTION, **121.4** *m.*, US 101 meets State 18 (*see TOUR 10A*).

NEOTSU (*golf course and club house; summer regatta*), **124.6** *m.*, is at the northern end of DEVIL'S LAKE. The Indians believed that in these waters lived a monster that occasionally rose to the surface to attack men.

OCEAN LAKE, **126.6** *m.* (115 alt., 400 pop.), is a coast town supported by sportsmen and vacationists. DELAKE (*hotel and camps*), **127.5** *m.* (62 alt.), at the southern end of Devil's Lake, received its name from the pronunciation given Devil's Lake by Finnish people, who settled in the area as fishermen.

On the beach at NELSCOTT, **129.2** *m.* (35 alt., 150 pop.), as elsewhere along the Oregon coast, Japanese floats—colored glass balls, are frequently found. These floats—used as net supports by oriental fishermen—are carried across the ocean by the Japanese current. They are prized by vacationists for decorative purposes. A line of substantial cottages face the ocean here.

TAFT, **130.4** *m.* (11 alt., 23 pop.), is the scene of the annual Red-Head Round Up (*first week in August*), which brings together the region's titian-crowned beauties to compete for prizes. This small town with a hotel and cottages, has a greatly augmented population in summer. Taft is at the southern end of the conservation unit. US 101 rounds Siletz Bay, named for the Siletz, most southerly Salishan tribe. At KERNVILLE, **132.7** *m.* (26 alt., 150 pop.), at the southern end of Siletz Bay, the highway crosses the Siletz River.

Left from Kernville on State 229 to the FORMER AGENCY OF THE SILETZ INDIAN RESERVATION, 23.8 *m.* As established in 1855 the Siletz Reservation covered more than one and one-third million acres but as the white population of Oregon increased the newcomers decided that there was too much valuable land in the hands of the natives. Though there were more than 2,000 Indians on the reservation in 1867, war, famine and disease had reduced the number to about 550 in 1887. By 1892 the allotments to the Siletz group covered only 47,000 acres. In 1925, though the number of Indians had increased the Siletz Agency was closed. The agency caring for all Indian affairs west of the Cascades is now at Salem; members of various tribes—Coos, Umpqua, Siuslaw, Rogue River, and Tututni—live on individual allotments and the rest are largely squatters on public domain. John Fleming Wilson's novel, *The Land-Claimers* (1911), tells the story of those who rushed into the Siletz lands when they were thrown open to white settlement. Many of those who came in hopefully to establish homestead claims and build their cabins in this last frontier have left; deserted cabins and clearings now covered with brush are relics of their brief stay. Because many antagonistic tribes had been placed on the reservation, it was the scene of numerous affrays. Indian braves were sometimes buried with a $20 gold piece in one fist and a knife in the other—prepared to pay or fight their way through to the happy hunting ground. Lieut. Phil Sheridan was stationed here during a part of his Oregon sojourn.
State 229 continues to a junction with State 26 at 31.9 *m.* (*see TOUR 2D*).

BOILER BAY, **138.5** *m.,* was so named because a steamship boiler was lodged between the rocks near the north shore many years ago. BOILER BAY STATE PARK, **138.7** *m.,* borders a wild sweep of rugged shore traversed by an excellent road.

Just south of the park, on a sloping hillside (L), are half-covered SHELL HEAPS, some of them an acre or more in extent, remains of Indian feasts. The refuse, mixed with sand, provides material for good beach roads.

At DEPOE BAY, **104.1** *m.,* (57 alt., 75 pop.), just east of DEPOE BAY STATE PARK, the shore line is rugged. The resort is on a secluded cove where tall-masted, deep-sea trollers anchor. The name is said by some to be derived from the cove, a haven or "depot" for boats, and by others to commemorate Charley Depoe, a local Indian. Close to the highway is the SPOUTING HORN (R), aperture in the rocks through which the tide rushes upward in a geyser of spray.

The DEPOE BAY AQUARIUM (*small fee*) contains many specimen of marine life, both beautiful and grotesque, among them red snappers, dogfish, and octopuses. The collection of sea anemones is very attractive. A MUSEUM (*small fee*) contains 500 mounted birds, 3,000 birds' eggs, a fine collection of butterflies, Indian relics, and mounted animals.

Fish races are held annually here. In 1936 about 15,000 people placed wagers under the pari-mutuel system. Any deep-sea fish is eligible and in 1935 the first entry was an octopus. The races are held in a painted trough having a lane 50 feet long for each "contestant." The starting point is painted white and the finish line is the entrance to a dark recess. The fish on being released seek the hiding hole, flashing to the far end of the lane and shaking a numbered balloon that gives the key to the order of their finish.

At WHALE COVE, 141.6 *m.*, are many caves cut in sandstone cliffs. ROCKY CREEK STATE PARK (*picnicking facilities*), 141.9 *m.*, overlooks a rocky shore.

ROCKY CREEK BRIDGE, 142.5 *m.*, dedicated in 1927, a memorial to Benjamin F. Jones, "Father of the Oregon Coast Highway", connects a section of the highway formerly called "Ben's own wagon road." This high concrete single-arch bridge spans a deep narrow rocky ravine at a point close to the ocean.

OTTER CREST STATE PARK, 144.2 *m.* (454 alt.), on a high promontory, overlooks one of the most impressive seascapes between Astoria and Newport. Its rugged shore kept Meares, Vancouver, and other explorers at a distance. Iron Mountain, a cone-shaped peak, is directly south.

Sea otters, long prized for their glossy fur, formerly abounded in these waters. The Indians made robes of the skins before they learned their value to the whites for trade in oriental markets. The story of the sea otter's place in Oregon history is told in *The Quest of the Sea Otter* by Sabra Conner.

At 145.5 *m.* is the junction with an improved road.

Right here to DEVIL'S PUNCH BOWL STATE PARK, (*tables and fireplaces*), 0.5 *m.* Immediately below a sandstone bluff is the DEVIL'S PUNCHBOWL where the incoming tidal waters rush through two openings in a deep, round cauldron to boil up, then recede. Offshore is OTTER ROCK, a sea-bird rookery, formerly the haunt of thousands of sea otters.

South of the entrance to the park, are the vestiges of trestles that carried the Pacific Spruce Corporation's wartime railroad, built to reach immense forests of spruce, whose wood was used in making airplane frames and propellers.

OCEAN PARK, 146.7 *m.* (25 pop.), facing rocky reefs, overlooks a rookery offshore where gulls, cormorants, and other waterfowl nest.

AGATE BEACH, 151.3 *m.* (124 alt., 150 pop.), is noted for its abundance of agates. The Oregon coast between Tillamook and Coos bays has exceptionally fine and extensive beach deposits of jasper, water agates, moss agates, "Oregon jade," and fossilized wood.

Right from Agate Beach to YAQUINA HEAD LIGHTHOUSE, 1 *m.* Built in 1873, it was to have been placed on Otter Crest but construction materials were delivered here by mistake. The rugged promontory, YAQUINA HEAD, was erroneously called Cape Foulweather by some early mariners, a designation given to Otter Crest by Captain Cook in 1778. The ocean dashes at the base of the cliffs and screaming sea birds dart and circle above the rocks. South of the head, is an extensive MARINE GARDEN, that can be visited at low tide. Starfish, soldiers of the sea, and sea anemones abound here.

NEWPORT, 154 *m.* (134 alt., 1,530 pop.), (*hotels, tourist camps, natatorium; boats for clamming, crabbing, and deep-sea fishing*), spreads across a blunt ridged peninsula between the ocean and Yaquina Bay. Though the first settler arrived in 1855 it was several years before there was a village here. Traders and fishermen were the first arrivals. Then the people of the Willamette Valley discovered it to be a delightful resort area and the Ocean House, built in 1866, and the Abbey House and Fountain House, opened in 1871—all facing the bay—began to draw visitors who would take the five-day coastal voyage to San Francisco as a diversion. Others engaged in the clam-digging and crabbing that still attract many. This section remains the commercial center of town, which flourished in the 1890's when Yaquina Bay ships carried away the products brought across the range from the Willamette Valley on the old Oregon Pacific Railroad.

Newport is now primarily a resort with a somewhat Victorian appearance in the older areas. Shell-fishing gives it some commercial importance. Crabs, clams, and oysters—the latter artificially planted to renew the supply—are shipped inland. Oystering is done in flat-bottomed boats with the aid of long-handled tongs.

The view of the bay at sunset, when the fishing fleet rides at anchor, is particularly attractive. This bay is also the anchorage for the deep-sea fishing boats that carry visitors across the bar to fish and to watch for the porpoises, sea lions, and whales occasionally seen offshore.

Visitors also hope that careful search may one day discover four valuable diamonds that were thrown into the waters in 1915. A Portland resident who died in that year stipulated in his will that these stones, which had belonged to his mother, should be thrown into the water to keep them forever from others.

John Fleming Wilson (1877-1922), the author of numerous books (*see LITERATURE*), lived here for about three years after his marriage in 1907. Mariner, school teacher, and newspaper reporter, he was able to leave $90,000 earned by writing stories and novels, some of which were based on material gathered in the Yaquina Bay district.

OLSONVILLE, part of Newport, on the shore of the bay, was the site of a blockhouse established by Lieut. Phil Sheridan in 1856. Sheridan selected the only suitable spot for the little fort but found the site covered with hundreds of burial canoes. After mediation the Indians suddenly agreed to the removal of the canoes, but refused to take them away themselves. At high tide, Sheridan's soldiers launched the strange flotilla and the canoes, each bearing its dead, drifted slowly out toward the sunset with the receding waters.

Newport is at the junction with State 26 (*see TOUR 2D*).

Near the northern end of NYE BEACH, which is the ocean side of Newport, is JUMP-OFF JOE, the rock from which, legend says, the usual Indian maiden and her lover flung themselves. The monolith is the remains of a rocky cape that formerly extended from the mainland. On the beach English coins have been found dated 1788, the year Gray and Meares first explored the coast. Like other maritime towns, Newport has a HAUNTED LIGHTHOUSE, which stands on the narrow promontory north of the entrance to Yaquina Bay.

Section b. Newport to the California Line, 240.4 m.

This section of US 101 even more closely hugs the sea than does the section to the north. Villages are fewer because the Coast Range here presses closer to the sea.

At the southern edge of NEWPORT, 0 *m.*, the highway passes through a landscaped park, then crosses the YAQUINA BAY BRIDGE, 1 *m.*, a graceful cantilever structure, completed in 1936. The bridge deck, rising to 138 feet above the channel water, is high enough to permit the passage of ocean-going craft. Yaquina Bay cupped by green hills is L., and the bar and jetties, long fingers extending seaward from the promontories, are R. The north shore rises sheer 150 feet, but the south shore is low, with partly wooded dunes.

It was hoped in the 1880's to make SEAL ROCKS, 10.5 *m.*, a summer resort. A large hotel was built but the place was then too inaccessible to visitors. Today the village consists of a store, a post office, and several cabin camps. Sea lions still bask on the rocks offshore.

Salal, huckleberry, and rhododendron grow luxuriantly in this region. Fir, pine, cedar, spruce, and hemlock trees appear brilliantly green in winter against dead fern, bare-limbed deciduous trees, and burned-over areas. The flowers of the rhododendron are reflected in small, brackish lakes in the hollows. The massed rhododendron blossoms are so striking that less showy blooms, such as heather, blue lupine, and scarlet paint brush, are often overlooked. Sand grasses and the trailing yellow verbena, whose root the Indians prized as food, carpet the ground.

ALSEA BAY BRIDGE, 14.9 *m.*, is another long cantilever structure, with three spans giving a clearance of 70 feet.

WALDPORT, 15.5 *m.* (20 alt., 367 pop.), (*trips with fishing fleet arranged*), on the south shore of the bay, was settled in 1880, and its inhabitants still make a living by clam and crab fishing and packing, though summer visitors are an increasingly important source of income. Here are manufactured the brightly colored cedar floats that mark the crab-fishermen's nets, which resemble huge butterfly nets, with steel rings at the top and sinkers at the lower end, where bait is fastened. These nets are used near the ocean shore and in the bays, while copper or iron crab pots are employed farther out on the "banks." An annual Crab Festival is held here.

Waldport is at the junction with State 34 (*see TOUR 2E*).

US 101 now parallels the beach, which was for many years the only road between Newport and Yachats. Incautious drivers often mired wagons and automobiles in wet sand, and then struggling to save their vehicles, some were caught by the in-tide. (*Cars should not be driven on beach just before or during return of tide*).

On the wild beach meadow (R), is an extensive, grass-covered kitchen midden, or shell heap, where Yakonan, seated about their fires tossed aside the emptied shells of clams, oysters, and crabs as well as stripped animal bones. As the mass of refuse grew in size through the years it was at times covered lightly with sand and earth to lessen the noisome odor of decomposition. Tribes from as far north as Tillamook Bay and as far south as Coos Bay, joined in these "skookum chuck" feasts. Similar shell mounds, considerably overgrown, are found elsewhere along the Oregon coast.

YACHATS (Ind., at the foot of the mountains), 24 m. (15 alt., 320 pop.), at the mouth of the Yachats River, is a popular resort with an excellent beach. Yachats Bay gravels yield agates, flowered jasper, blood stones, and petrified woods.

For many years "Dunk" Dunkelberger was a blacksmith at Yachats for several gyppo logging outfits. One day a hobo entered the shop and asked for a job. Business was slack and Dunk wanted to get rid of the "bo" as quickly as possible so he told him that the job was his if he could make a three-way weld, a task that was considered impossible. Then Dunk went out to lunch chuckling to himself and expecting the tramp to be gone when he got back. The hobo was gone when he returned, but he left behind Dunk's duckbilled tongs neatly welded together about the horn of the anvil in a perfect three-way weld. It took Dunk almost two days to saw and file the tongs from the anvil and re-temper its horn.

The highway, here on a shelf of rock, widens in the seaward face of CAPE PERPETUA, to a masonry-guarded viewpoint at 26.2 m. For some miles south of Yachats the Siuslaw National Forest extends to the rockbound coast, and trails and other recreational facilities have been developed. Near the cape a trail leads (R) down to the DEVIL'S CHURN, a cavern that spouts water at intervals.

At 26.7 m. is the junction with an improved road.

1. Left here to the top of CAPE PERPETUA, 2 m. (800 alt.), discovered by Captain Cook on March 7, 1778, on a trading voyage and so-named by him for St. Perpetua, the martyr who was put to death on that day in the year 203. On the promontory are an observation cabin and covered picnic cabins.

2. Left from US 101 on a second dirt road to the CAPE PERPETUA FOREST CAMP, 0.1 m.

SAND DUNE GARDENS, 35.6 m., sharply elevated on the eastern side, are exceptionally beautiful. The sand-laden wind has trimmed the shrubs into remarkably similar patterns. Racks of brush along the highway protect it from the encroachment of the sands. In the early days Chinamen mined for gold between China Creek and the top of Heceta Head. Two dilapidated structures of their camp remain.

Rugged HECETA HEAD (520 alt.), 37.6 m., named for Bruno Heceta, the Spanish explorer who saw it in 1775, rises sheer above the ocean. HECETA HEAD LIGHTHOUSE has flashed its powerful beams for the benefit of mariners since 1894.

DEVIL'S ELBOW TUNNEL, 38.1 m., at the southern end of CAPE CREEK BRIDGE, is a 680-foot bore through a jutting headland. It is in the 35-acre DEVIL'S ELBOW STATE PARK. The highway swings around a cliff, high above the ocean, affording a startling land and sea view.

The SEA LION CAVES (*accessible by trail and stairway from highway; guide service included in adm. fee*), 38.8 *m.*, are ocean caverns inhabited during the winter by a herd of about 300 sea lions. The caves are at the base of a cliff just around the curve below the tunnel. The herd is ruled by an old chieftain whose throne is the center rock in the main cavern, a chamber 1,500 feet long and colored green, pink and pale yellow.

The huge Stellar's sea lions, found along the Oregon coast, are chestnut when young, tawny when old. These aquatic mammalian carnivora, which average 12 feet in length, were named by Dr. Stellar, a German scientist with the Russian expedition headed by the explorer Bering in 1741. Because of their color and lion-like roar he called them "Lions of the Sea." During the summer they live on the rocky islands off the coast of Alaska; they leave for the Oregon shore about September 1. When the herd reaches this place the members mate and breed. Old and skillful males will gather about them so numerous a "harem" that young bulls sometimes go for years without mates. Strangely, the pups protest vigorously against entering the water. The full-grown sea lion if cornered will attack a person and can cover the ground faster than a man can run. In May or early June the herd leaves again for Alaska.

The Pigeon Guillemont, a migratory bird that spends most of its life on the open sea, also comes here. The perpendicular cliffs at the entrance to the cove are the habitat of the tufted puffin, or sea parrot.

SUTTON LAKE (R), 44.2 *m.*, MERCER LAKE (L), 44.8 *m.* and MUNSELL LAKE (R), 47.4 *m.*, are small duneland bodies of water among gray-trunked lodgepole pines. In June the pastel tints of rhododendrons brighten the dark recesses beneath the conifers.

At 49.9 *m.* is a junction with State 36 (*see TOUR 2F*).

FLORENCE, 50 *m.* (11 alt., 339 pop.), by the Siuslaw River, is a fishing town and the trading point for farmers of the small Siuslaw Valley. Formerly row boats and "one-lungers," boats powered by one-cylinder marine engines, were used for valley transportation. Errands were run, children taken to school, and parents went to churches and sociables in boats, frequently powered by the winds or the tides. George Melvin Miller, brother of Joaquin Miller, the poet, helped develop the town. Florence holds an annual Rhododendron Festival. The SIUSLAW RIVER BRIDGE is another in the series carrying the highway over a difficult route.

South of Florence the wild azalea replaces the rhododendrons on the hills. This brightly flowered shrub thrives best in open spaces, and reaches the height of its beauty and fragrance in May and June.

The JESSIE M. HONEYMAN MEMORIAL PARK, 52.7 *m.*, was named for a woman who was untiring in her efforts to enhance the beauty of the state.

The highway now passes an area with some commercial and private summer camps.

By CLEAWOX LAKE (Ind., clear water), **53.1** *m.* (82 alt), is (R) the Eugene Area Girl Scouts' Summer Camp. WOAHINK LAKE, **54.2** *m.,* is one in a series of dune-locked lakes extending southward. (*Watch for deer crossing highway; signs indicate their usual crossings.*)

At **56.3** *m.* is the junction with a dirt road.

Left here to large SILTCOOS LAKE, **0.5** *m.,* named for a local Indian chief.

The SILTCOOS RIVER, outlet of Siltcoos Lake, is crossed at 56.5 *m.* South of the river is a region of marching dunes where windblown sands are constantly sweeping inland. The slopes of cuts have been planted with grass and shrubs to hold them in place.

At CARTER LAKE (R), **58.8** *m.,* is a Forest Service campground. TAHKENITCH LAKE (Ind., many arms), **62.6** *m.,* is famous for its bass fishing. ELBOW LAKE, **63.9** *m.,* provides excellent fishing.

Descending rapidly, the route reaches GARDINER, **69.6** *m.* (18 alt., 300 pop.), established in 1850 by shipwrecked men from the *Bostonian.* Its snug houses, built against the hillside, almost all of them painted white, are monuments to the ideals of W. F. Jewett, who as a young man was manager of the local lumber mill. He insisted that everything under his supervision, from the rows of merchandise on the company store shelves, to the front yards of his employees' homes be neatly cared for, and he urged that all houses be painted white, as in his native Maine. The popularity of white paint spread, until churches, schools, stores, and residences matched the gleaming sails of the lumber schooners that at that time, docked here. Jewett's hand is also seen in the long avenue of poplars along the single street, where neat white picket fences in spring protect lilacs' fragrant blossoms. Gardiner was probably the scene of Dr. Alan Hart's novel, *Doctor Mallory* (1935); it was here that he practiced medicine for a short time in 1918.

The UMPQUA RIVER BRIDGE, **71.3** *m.,* spans the stream at a point not far west of the junction with the Smith River, named for Jedediah Smith. In July, 1828, Smith's party of nineteen trappers camped on the Umpqua, possibly on Bolon Island. While Smith and two others were scouting for a suitable crossing, the rest of the party was attacked by natives and $20,000 worth of furs were taken. Only one man survived and he made his way to Vancouver where he met Smith and his two companions. Dr. McLoughlin, chief factor of the Hudson's Bay Company, regained the furs for Smith and bought them from him. Smith showed his gratitude by insisting that the fur company of which he was a partner retire from the region claimed by the English. Near this island the highway crosses a many arched steel bridge with a cantilever span over the main channel of the Umpqua River.

REEDSPORT, **71.6** *m.* (28 alt., 1,178 pop.), is built on marshy tide land. Its best known citizen is Robin Reed, editor of the *Port Umpqua Courier,* former national amateur wrestler and Olympic champion. Much of Reedsport was filled in from earth cut from the sandy clay banks of the hills behind the town. Most of the population lives in the dozen or so two-story rooming houses and hotels, and is composed of transient laborers. There is little residential section, the majority of the dwellings being scattered over the town's edges.

Reedsport is at the junction with State 38 (*see TOUR 2G*).

South of Reedsport US 101 climbs through denuded hills where stumps and blackened snags are evidences of the death of the local lumber industry.

WINCHESTER BAY, **76.2** *m.* (16 alt., 50 pop.), first a trading point called West Umpqua, is now primarily a summer resort and fishing village by the Umpqua River, about three miles from its mouth. Across the Umpqua (R) is the SITE OF FORT UMPQUA, established in 1856 by Captain Steward at the close of the Rogue River Indian War. In the summer of 1862 the paymaster arrived and found everyone stationed at the fort out on a hunting trip. His report of this incident, and the fact that there were no Indians here caused the fort to be abandoned. An effort was made to re-establish it, and Capt. J. B. Leeds was on the point of leaving San Francisco with troops when the order was countermanded. The old blockhouse and soldiers' quarters were moved to Gardiner.

At **77.3** *m.* is the junction with a dirt road.

Right here to UMPQUA RIVER LIGHTHOUSE, 1 *m.*, erected in 1857.

CLEAR LAKE (L), **78.9** *m.,* is the source of Reedsport's water supply. At **83.8** *m.* is (R) the EEL CREEK RECREATIONAL AREA AND FOREST CAMP.

HAUSER, **91.3** *m.* (27 alt., 126 pop.), named for Eric Hauser, who constructed sections of the Southern Pacific Railroad in this vicinity, is among extensive cranberry bogs (*see TOUR 2H*). Flocks of wild ducks and geese feed nearby. At this point, the highway veers farther inland and passes through a forested tract.

The COOS BAY BRIDGE, **97.8** *m.,* nearly a mile long and the most costly of the bridges that carry US 101 along the Oregon coast, is comprised of a series of concrete arches and, over the busy channel, three of the suspension type with an elevation of 150 feet. At the southern end of the bridge is SIMPSON PARK, named for Capt. A. M. Simpson, founder of North Bend, and long identified with local lumbering and shipping. It is said that he was Peter B. Kyne's inspiration for the character, Cappy Ricks.

NORTH BEND, **99.2** *m.* (41 alt., 4,012 pop.), called Yarrow by settlers of 1853, is on a peninsula jutting into Coos Bay. It has a sawmill, a shipyard, three fishery plants, and a crab-packing plant.

Right from North Bend on a paved road through a suburban area to EMPIRE, **3.5** *m.* (43 alt., 493 pop.), formerly called Empire City. Its first settlers were Jacksonville men who left that place (*see TOUR 2b*), during the height of the local gold fever. The town soon had a lumber mill and did considerable shipping, particularly a low grade coal that was for a time mined south of Marshfield. Local trade declined as North Bend grew in prominence, though Empire people were slow to accept their fate. One mill was kept in good condition; during 40 years of idleness the machinery was greased at intervals and turned over. This faith was justified because the mill resumed operations during the World War and has been operated in a small way since then. Fish canneries and a pulp mill also provide local employment.

In CHARLESTON, 8.7 m. (10 alt., 150 pop.), is a COAST GUARD STATION, by the mouth of Coos Bay.

MARSHFIELD, 102.1 m. (19 alt., 5,287 pop.), is almost continuous with North Bend; together, the towns form the fifth largest city in the state. Marshfield, is near the top of the crooked arm of Coos Bay, which is usually crowded with schooners being loaded with lumber cut in the forests on the slopes of the Coast Range. Of particular importance is the Port Orford cedar, whose straight grain, lightness, and tensile strength creates a demand in world markets.

The first cabin in this district was built by a trapper named Tolman in 1853. In the following year he left and a retired seaman, Capt. George Hamilton, moved in. Hamilton, following the wilderness custom, took an Indian woman for a wife and managed to subsist without neighbors until the arrival of John and George Pershbaker a few years later. George Pershbaker provided stock for a trading post to meet the needs of men arriving to work in the shipyards John Pershbaker had established. Pershbaker's first boat was a tug, the *Escort;* later his plant built the schooners *Staghound, Louise Morrison, Ivanhoe,* and *Annie Stauffer,* and the barkentine *Amelia.* But the population still grew very slowly; in 1884 it still had only about 800 people. In addition to its isolation, one factor that hindered growth was the type of ground on which the town had been founded and from which it had taken its name. In 1908 lumber interests decided to overcome the natural handicaps of the townsite where they were erecting a mill and started dredging operations to deepen the channel through the crooked bay and to use the silt removed from the channel to raise the town land. Still growth was slow. Then came the World War with its enormous demands for spruce to be used in construction of the new fighting craft—the airplanes. The Southern Pacific tracks were hastily extended southward to the Coos Bay towns and on up into the forests. During the war years Marshfield mushroomed into a city whose streets on Saturday were filled with harddrinking, exuberant lumberjacks and roistering ship-loaders. After the war, activity lessened but did not die, and the town settled down to a solider kind of development. A fire of 1922 swept away three blocks of old business buildings and many jerry-built affairs constructed during the boom; though this was considered a disaster at the time it was probably a blessing because the buildings that replaced those that had burned were more modern and of better construction. The new highway has also been a boon, putting the town on the second most important interstate artery of the West Coast and destroying its former isolation. A new local industry of minor importance, is the working of myrtlewood into souvenirs for tourists. Another local industry is the canning of pilchards; this fish is also crushed for its oil and the residue is treated and shipped as fertilizer and poultry food.

The COOS BAY LUMBER COMPANY PLANT (*open to*

visitors), established in 1908 at the northern edge of town, is the mainstay of local prosperity. When it was sold in 1928 it was one of the most valuable lumber-mills of the Northwest.

South of the mill runs the waterfront, a main attraction to imaginative visitors. Schooners from far ports dock here and the waterfront life has the lively characteristics found only in younger ports. With the sailors mingle fishermen, as considerable commercial fishing is carried on in waters nearby.

The CITY PARK, at the northern edge of town, has a large lake, picnicking spots, trails and extensive plantings of the luxuriant shrubs and plants native to the damp coastal area.

On Telegraph Hill, also in the northern end of the city, is a CHINESE CEMETERY, relic of the days when oriental labor was imported to work in the coal mines. According to Chinese custom, many of the bodies have been exhumed and sent back to China.

South of Marshfield the native bent grass is extensively cultivated because of the wide demand for landscaping purposes.

At **107.4** *m.* is the junction with an improved road.

Left here to the COOS COUNTY COUNTRY CLUB (*open to public; small fee*), 1 *m.*, which has a 9-hole golf course and an attractive club house.

US 101 here runs through the soft-coal belt that covers in all about 500 square miles. The first mine was opened in 1855, but the workings were never highly profitable and operations are now carried on only in a small way.

Slow but definite changes in the character of vegetation occur as the route moves southward. White-barked alders and yellow maples yield largely to Oregon myrtle, a glossy-leafed evergreen that here grows singly on open hillsides or in groves along the meadows. When not crowded, the trees grow so symmetrically they look as though they had been trimmed. The wood takes on a brilliant polish and is much used for making novelties sold along the route. Housewives substitute the spicy leaves for bay leaves in seasoning meats.

COQUILLE (Fr., small shell), **120.6** *m.* (60 alt., 2,732 pop.), on the Coquille River, is the seat of Coos County, a region where considerable dairying is carried on. Within the city limits it is possible to fish for several varieties of salmon, steelhead, and trout.

For many years Coquille was the head of navigation for river boats. On their regular runs clumsy old stern-wheelers packed with merchandise and lively with the shouts of laborers, paddled up to the wharves. But construction of the modern highway destroyed the picturesque character of the town, which desires to look as much like other towns as possible.

Coquille is at the junction with State 42 (*see TOUR 2H*).

RIVERTON, **126.7** *m.* (16 alt., 150 pop.), is the trade center of farmers who specialize in pea-raising. The pea-raising farms are recognized by their vine covered trellises.

The remnants of PARKERSBURG (R), **134.8** *m.* (34 alt., 20 pop.), are across a meadow at the mouth of Bear Creek. This place was once a rival of other Coos County ports. Lumber mills were opened here in 1867-68, then shipyards to build schooners to carry timber to market. A salmon cannery, built in 1885, brought added prosperity but was burned some years later. Then lumber traffic was diverted to deeper waters and the town died.

BANDON, 138.5 m. (10 alt., 1,516 pop.), a resort town with a beach at the mouth of the Coquille River, with long cypress hedges, gleaming white lily beds, and gnarled pines, was known as the most beautiful town in southern Oregon, until a disastrous fire swept in from the forests to the east and wiped it out. Reconstruction was begun in 1938 with Federal aid and on plans prepared by the Oregon State Planning Board, which provides for a better arrangement of facilities, wide streets, recreational areas, and better educational facilities. Trees and grasses are being planted on the burned over environs and the design of business structures is being controlled.

The town, which is near the site of an Indian village, was first called The Ferry and then Averill. Lord George Bennet, an Irish peer, who settled here, finally gave the place the name of his native town. He imported the Irish furze, that in early spring yellows the sand hills along the highway southward; a thorny shrub, its pea-like flowers have an odor similar to that of cocoanut oil.

Between the highway and the ocean, lies a series of dune-sheltered lakes. Stunted huckleberry is mingled with rhododendron and azalea. Pitcher plants, with grotesque cobra-like heads, grow in this region, the variety *chrysamphora californica* is found only along the coast.

The valuable white Port Orford cedar (Lawson cypress), is seen frequently. It is now in particular demand for use in the manufacture of Venetian blinds. It also ranks high for use in boats; Sir Thomas Lipton always insisted that his cup challengers be built of this cedar.

LANGLOIS, 152.3 m. (88 alt., 250 pop.), is a dairymen's trade town. In the early days two cooperage plants supplied nearby towns with tubs for preserving fish. Later two sawmills appeared and are still operating.

At 153.4 m. is the junction with a dirt road.

Right here to FLORAS LAKE, 3 m., a small body of fresh water cut off from the sea by low sand dunes, called *Qua-to-ma* by the Indians. On the shore of the lake is the site of Pacific City, first called Lakeport, promoted in 1908 on the supposition that a canal could be built between the sea and the lake, temporarily the largest town in Curry County. Land was cleared, wharves were built, sidewalks laid, a public park platted, dwellings, business blocks, and a three-story hotel erected. Carpenters worked day and night, while long lines of teams hauled lumber from Bandon and Port Orford. A newspaper, the *Floras Lake Banner,* was established and forthwith began to publicize the place. People flocked in from all quarters of the country, all bent on making their fortunes. Six thousand lots were sold, the first for $12.50 apiece but later ones at $300 each.

When the first excitement had abated a few citizens began to ask questions. Where were the industries to spring from? What about raw materials? What was to be shipped out of the port? All the products that the contiguous country could supply wouldn't make one shipload of freight. The final blow fell when, though the War Department had given permission to dig the canal, it was discovered that the town was 40 feet above sea-level and that if the canal were dug the lake would empty itself into the Pacific unless elaborate locks were built. People who could, left at once. Merchants closed their stores and professional men their offices. Guests grew scarcer at the hotel and on Thursday, November 6, 1909, the clerk closed the register with the obituary: "Not a dam sole." Only a few brush-grown walks and the crumbling foundation of the hotel remain.

DENMARK, 154.8 m. (97 alt., 96 pop.), is the trading center of dairymen of Danish birth or descent. A fossil bearing sandstone bed extends from here north to the mouth of the Coquille River.

PORT ORFORD CEDAR STATE PARK, 157.7 m., extends along the highway for half a mile. It holds one of the fine stands of this tree.

SIXES, 160 m. (109 alt., 49 pop.), is on the banks of a small river of the same name noted for its steelhead. The name is probably derived from the Chinook jargon salutation, *Klahowya Sikhs*. Along the upper waters of the Sixes are some gold deposits and in the early days black sands near its mouth yielded considerable dust to diligent panners.

At 161 m. is the junction with a gravel road.

Right on this road through rhododendron and azalea thickets and over lupine-covered hills to the CAPE BLANCO CATHOLIC CHURCH (L), 4.4 m., now in ruins; bats cling to the altar and the glass in the pointed window frames is shattered. By the walk is the flower-matted grave of Patrick Hughes, founder of the parish and builder of the church.

CAPE BLANCO LIGHTHOUSE, 5.5 m., stands on the most westerly point of Oregon. Bricks for the structure were made on the spot in 1870. Captain Martin D'Aguilar saw and named the cape, in 1603, after his ship had become separated in a storm from that of his captain, Sebastian Viscaino. Flores, D'Aguilar's pilot, named the point Blanco (Sp., white) because of its chalky appearance.

ELK RIVER, 161.7 m., is a narrow stream abounding in trout and salmon. Cattle on prosperous dairy farms now feed where elk once roamed. These animals as they traveled along the headlands in single file, left trails that became the roads of frontiersmen.

The region about PORT ORFORD, 165.6 m. (56 alt., 300 pop.), was sighted in 1792 by Capt. George Vancouver, who named it for the Earl of Orford. This rambling village on a bluff has wide view of the Pacific.

Near the village is BATTLE ROCK where nine gold hunters were landed in June 1851 with supplies and a cannon by Capt. William Tichenor of the *Seagull*. Shortly thereafter the Coquilles attacked the invaders who were able to drive them off and flee to the settlements along the Umpqua. Captain Tichenor returned with 69 more men—who established a camp they called Port Ophir.

Here Curry County's government was organized in July, 1856, at the home of Frederick Smith, whose house served as county offices for a time. James Upton soon began to publish a newspaper, which was printed in a woodshed. Lacking a clergyman, the inhabitants adopted the Hudson's Bay Company system of contract marriages.

Though Port Orford was long a shipping point for cedar, it was not incorporated until 1935. In the early days the cedar logs were lowered by high line from the bluff to the decks of the schooners anchored in the bay.

At the southern limits of Port Orford stands (R) the KNAPP HOTEL, a plain white weathered building erected by Louis Knapp about 1867. Until lighthouses were built to warn sailors off the rocky Curry coast, a lamp was placed nightly in the hotel window for this purpose. The Knapp's became notable for their hospitality to ship-wrecked or stranded sailors, who would gather in the men's parlor around a stone fireplace with myrtle wood mantel. Now rooms in the hotel are designated by names of illustrious persons who have slept in them. There is a Sherman Room, an Ellen Tichenor Room, a Joe Meek Room (*see HISTORY*), a W. H. Seward Room, and a Jack London Room. Seward, Secretary of State in Lincoln's cabinet, stopped here on his way to visit Alaska whose purchase he had helped to ne-gotiate. Jack London is said to have written part of *The Valley of the Moon* while staying here.

Port Orford was the home of Minnie Myrtle Dyer, poet of the 1860's, when she married Joaquin Miller (*see TOUR 5a*), who had admired her printed verse and started a correspondence that led to Miller's visit here, where after only three days they were married and started off on horseback through the wilds to the Willamette Valley. The marriage lasted only eight years and Mrs. Miller later took revenge by lecturing caustically on her former husband.

Oregon's "lost meteorite," locally proclaimed as one of the largest to come to earth but never found, is said to have fallen about 40 miles east of the town in 1864.

South of Port Orford the mountains press close to the sea and the highway curves along a shelf high above the waves. HUMBUG MOUNTAIN STATE PARK, **169.9** *m.,* includes HUMBUG MOUNTAIN (1,748 alt.), a massive promontory, formerly called Tichenor's Humbug because Captain Tichenor (*see above*) and party became lost and mistook the mountain for another landmark.

Green-walled BRUSH CREEK CANYON, **173.1** *m.,* is the deepest gorge crossed on this section of the coast highway.

ARIZONA INN (R) **180.1** *m.,* on Myrtle Creek, is a tavern of stagecoach days.

At **182** *m.* is the SITE OF FRANKFORT, a former village with a shipping dock on SISTERS ROCKS, just offshore, reached from the mainland by a bridge and wooden railway.

The name of EUCHRE CREEK, **185** *m.,* is probably a corruption of the Tututni word Ykichetunne (people at the mouth of a river). South of the creek are sandy hills bright in season with yellow verbena and vivid lupine.

At **190** *m.* is the junction with an improved dirt road.

Right here to GEISEL MONUMENT STATE PARK, 0.5 *m.*, a memorial to the family of John Geisel who with his three sons was slain by Indians during the Rogue River War of 1856. The mother and daughter were captured but later released.

WEDDERBURN, 196 *m.* (24 alt., 100 pop.), on the north bank of the Rogue River, is a vacation resort with a small myrtle wood factory and a small hotel. For years it had a salmon cannery but was shut down because of the closing of the Rogue to commercial fishermen. The Rogue is famous for steelhead and salmon fishing; small boats are able to ascend the river about 32 miles. The route crosses the Rogue River on the long, arched concrete ISAAC L. PATTERSON BRIDGE, named for a former Oregon governor.

GOLD BEACH, 197.1 *m.* (71 alt., 500 pop.), seat of Curry County, was first called Ellensburg, then Sebastapol. Seat of the most primitive county in Oregon and long isolated by lack of roads, Gold Beach has only begun to shed its pioneer appearance. Orientals, Indians, and white men made up the population in early days when gold was passed freely across the counter of the log-cabin saloon that was also the county's first courthouse. The town was so named because of the placering done in the 1850's at the mouth of the Rogue. Floods of 1861 swept these beach deposits into the ocean, but small operations for gold and platinum are still carried on up stream and mining sometimes muddies the current to such an extent that its brown waters are seen far offshore.

At 204.6 *m.* is the junction with an improved road.

Right here to high CAPE SEBASTIAN, 1 *m.*, which juts into the ocean to form one of the striking landmarks of the southern coast, rising 700 feet sheer above the water. Good roads and trails lead to view points commanding splendid views of the Pacific. The cape was named by Captain Viscaino, in 1603.

From this point is visible (R) CAPE FERRELO (*not accessible from the highway*), named for Bartolome Ferrelo, first white explorer known to have sailed along the Oregon coast (1543).

Making sweeping curves, sometimes along ledges of gold-bearing quartz and sometimes through heavy timber, the route passes a huge KITCHEN MIDDEN (R) 208.7 *m.*, and descends to PISTOL RIVER, 210.7 *m.* The name of both post office and river commemorate James Mace's loss of a firearm in the stream, in 1853. Previously it was known as Chetl-Essentan for the Indian village near its mouth. On June 17, 1856, during the Indian wars, about 80 volunteers at Pistol River, killed and captured enough members of the Chetco tribe to force their surrender. One of the claims filed with the United States Government for damages during this time was for the loss of a wagon load of apples worth $500.

CARPENTERVILLE, 218.5 *m.*, (1,715 alt., 35 pop.), is the highest point on the highway. Mount Shasta is seen (L) on clear days. Ghost forests, where fires have blackened the trees, mark the approach to HARRIS STATE PARK, 232.3 *m.*, which overlooks a narrow beach and bird rookeries offshore.

BROOKINGS, 234.2 *m.* (129 alt., 250 pop.), by Chetco Cove, grew up around a large sawmill.

US 101 crosses Winchuck River (Ind., Windy River), **239.9** *m.,* and at **240.4** *m.* crosses the California Line, at a point 21 miles north of Crescent City, Calif.

|||||||||||▣||||||||||||▣||||||||||||▣||||||||||||▣||||||||||||▣||||||||||||▣||||||||||||▣||||||||||||▣||||||||||||▣||||||||||||▣||||||||||||▣||||||||||||

Tour 4

(Maryhill, Wash.)—Biggs Junction—Grass Valley—Cow Canyon Junction—Redmond—Bend—Klamath Falls—(Weed, Calif.) ; 305 m. US 97.

Paved road.
Union Pacific Railroad parallels route between Biggs Junction and Bend; Great Northern Railroad between Cow Canyon Junction and Klamath Falls; Southern Pacific Railroad between Chemult and California Line.
Hotel and camp accommodation.

US 97, the Sherman Highway and The Dalles-California Highway, crosses a section of wheat country where large-scale operations are carried on. Farther south the green, and ripening grain fields yield to the grazing lands of great sheep ranches. Though a few large cattle ranches remain, sheep dominate the vast range monopolized by the cattlemen up to the beginning of the present century.

A chain of rugged snow-capped mountains, great pine forests, recent lava fields and cinder buttes, the rimrock desert country, arid plains extending to great distances and offering scanty forage to cattle and sheep, rolling wheat fields, upland farms and stock ranches of central Oregon, and such easily accessible natural attractions as Crater Lake and Newberry Crater give to this route an unusual diversity of interests.

The history of the road is implicit in the men and beasts that made it: the moccasined Indians, explorers and trappers; the hard-hoofed covered-wagon oxen; the milling cattle, driven by picturesque cowboys; the jerk-line teams of the freighter; the horses of the stagecoach, four and six; the cavalcades of Indian fighters; the booted loggers, miners, and all the host of adventurers of Old Oregon.

It was approximately over this route that Capt. John C. Fremont traveled in 1843, exploring the region and mapping geographical features. But long before the first white men had made their way into central Oregon, a network of trails had been worn by nomadic Indians.

Section a. Washington Line to Bend; 144.2 m. US 97

US 97 crosses the Columbia River, **0** *m.,* the Oregon-Washington Line, one-half mile south of Maryhill, Washington, on the Maryhill Ferry (24-*hour service; fare* $1.00 *per car of five persons*). On the river bank (L), are the remaining buildings of GRANT, the shipping point for wheat from Sherman County in the old river transportation days, until swept away by floods in 1894.

At **0.4** *m.* US 97 unites with US 30, (*see TOUR 1b*) *to* BIGGS JUNCTION, **2.7** *m.* (173 alt.), where it diverges (L) into a sheer-walled canyon known as SPANISH HOLLOW, and begins a gradual climb out of the Columbia Gorge. Some of the early migrants over the Oregon Trail descended this passageway to get to the Columbia River from the upland route they had been following. Until the coming of the railroad, in 1897, the canyon was the tortuous course for jerk-line outfits bearing heavy loads of wheat from the plateau top to the boat landing at Grant. The term "jerk-line" comes from the single rein that extended to the lead horse from the driver who usually rode the nigh wheel horse and signaled a turn to the right or left by a single or double jerk on the rein.

In commemoration of these old days, a jerk-line outfit made a final trip from Shaniko to The Dalles in 1926. The train, three wagons piled high with baled wool, was drawn by a team of wheel horses, ahead of which were strung ten other horses. As it passed through the principal towns of Sherman County and through Biggs to The Dalles it attracted more attention than a circus parade.

The walls of the canyon flatten out into an undulating upland at THORNBERRY, **7.4** *m.* (898 alt., 50 pop.), a small railway station. On the first major bench of the plateau is WASCO, **12.1** *m.* (1,271 alt., 400 pop.), largest town in Sherman County, so named because of its location within the previous borders of Wasco County. It was at this point that the Oregon Trail crossed a pioneer road leading southeasterly from the Columbia River into the interior.

DE MOSS SPRINGS, **17.7** *m.* (1,573 alt.), named for a family of roving musicians, once widely known as a health resort, is now almost abandoned. Beginning with entertainment for cowboys and settlers, the De Mosses purchased and utilized stagecoaches of the mining days for travel from town to town, and by 1893 had gained such prominence that they were made official song writers for the Chicago World's Fair. The elder De Mosses made a gift of the old townsite, whose streets they had named for musicians and the avenues for poets, to the county for park purposes.

MORO, **21** *m.* (1,857 alt., 352 pop.), **seat** of Sherman County, is also the center of wide expanses of wheat and pastures.

At the eastern edge of Moro, on a portion of the original Henry Barnum homestead, is the MORO BRANCH AGRICULTURE EXPERIMENT STATION, supported by state and federal funds and devoted to cereal grains and experimentation in dry land problems.

One of its nurseries contains more than 700 varieties of wheats, barleys, and oats. Barnum's son was Sherman County's first breeder of thoroughbred Hereford cattle, which have taken many prizes.

The Cascade Range, crowned by Mount Hood and Mount Jefferson, dominates the western horizon. At many points are magnificent views of these snow-capped peaks. In every direction the landscape is softened by the purple haze of great distances.

GRASS VALLEY, 31.1 m. (2,269 alt., 208 pop.), a trading center and grain-shipping point, derived its name from the luxuriant bunch grass which grows in the valley now occupied by the town. It was a division point on the pioneer stage line between The Dalles and Canyon City, whose chief enterprise was devoted to assuaging the thirst of weary travelers through a desert land.

KENT, 43.9 m. (2,709 alt., 94 pop.), surrounded by a far-stretching area of grain ranches, is said locally to have been the setting for Zane Gray's novel, *The Desert of Wheat*.

Characteristic of this region are the alternate stretches of growing wheat and fallow land which in early summer resembles a vast checkerboard of tawny grain and dark, harrowed earth. To conserve the scanty moisture wheat is planted in alternate years, and where the soil is not being cropped it is harrowed repeatedly until the surface is a fine mulch that rises in slow-moving pillars of dust enveloping tractor-drawn harrows as they crawl across the long undulations of the land. From any eminence on the highway a far-flung panorama of gold and umber gives a sense of space, distance. The wind blows much of the time, and to escape it ranch houses are built in depressions, a circumstance that makes the rolling country seem uninhabited save for ranch crews and their machines, diminished by distance to the size of insects, at work in some immense, unfenced field. At harvest time the whole countryside is suddenly alive with the business of getting in the grain. Tractor-combines, with their crews of itinerant laborers, set out across the golden slopes where a single swath may take a half day or a day to cut. The wheat towns, quiescent during the rest of the year, spring to life as wheat-laden trucks swing toward the elevators. On Saturday nights harvest hands congregate in the nearest towns where cafes, small movie houses, and general stores keep open late. The atmosphere is predominantly male, for harvest hands, unlike the fruit pickers, do not bring women folks with them. At this time, in the small towns, waitresses and female clerks attract more than customary attention.

At 46.6 m. US 97 crosses the old Bakeoven-Wilcox stage road, whose deep ruts are still conspicuous. Huge sheep ranches predominate in this region, with an occasional return to fields of grain.

SHANIKO, 59.6 m. (3,342 alt., 100 pop.), as the terminus of the Biggs-Shaniko branch of the Union Pacific Railroad is an important wheat, wool, and stock-shipping point, with extensive grain warehouses, corrals, and loading chutes. The town was named for August Scherneckau (called Shaniko by the Indians) whose ranch house was a station on the old stage route from The Dalles to central Oregon. When

Harriman and Hill raced to build a railroad up the Deschutes River in 1909 Shaniko became construction headquarters because of its accessibility and so experienced a boom. Its two-story brick hotel, still an important landmark and the chief building in town, was then the center of intense activity, not only because of the presence of large numbers of railroad men, but also because Shaniko was then the transportation frontier between the freight wagons from the interior and the railroad.

It was in the neighborhood of Shaniko that the last of the battles in the war between the cattlemen and sheepmen occurred. For about twenty-five years after the middle eighties, the cattle barons stubbornly resisted the invasion of the sheepmen. Having ruled the public domain for a generation, the cattlemen had come to believe they had an inalienable right to its exclusive use and sheep were slaughtered by the thousands before the cattlemen gave up the vain struggle. Sheep now dominate the range, as is evidenced each spring and fall, when the flocks are moved to and from the mountain pastures. During these moves motorists are sometimes compelled to wait considerable time for flocks to cross the highway.

This is a country of space and almost continuous wind. Its people, until quite lately off the beaten track, reflect the hardihood of existence in a semi-arid region where neighbors, being few and far between, are therefore cherished. To turn off the main highway onto unmarked roads across the high prairies is to find stark ranch houses, buried in the windy silence of the treeless wastes, their owners devoted to a routine as solitary as it is monotonous. The automobile is still their greatest luxury for it brings them close to neighbors and towns and even tempts them to visit the populous country west of the Cascades.

Right from Shaniko on State 218 to the dilapidated BAKEOVEN STAGE STATION, 12 *m.* It was so named because a German baker, stranded with his flour and other supplies after the Indians had stolen his horses, set up a rough clay and stone bakeoven and made bread which he sold to miners and prospectors on their way to the Baker district (*see TOUR 1A*). For a time, it is said, he developed a flourishing business and the old oven stood for many years.

Southwest of Shaniko, the highway continues over a rolling upland of wheat and range lands to COW CANYON JUNCTION, 71.6 *m.*, at the junction with State 50 (*see TOUR 4A*).

To the southwest, above the violet haze, loom Broken Top and the Three Sisters, and flanking them are Mount Washington, Three-Fingered Jack, Mount Jefferson, Mount Wilson, and Mount Hood. To the north, in Washington, Mount Adams emerges dream-like from the distance.

South of WILLOWDALE, 80.3 *m.* (1,764 alt., 52 pop.), in the Poney and Hay Creek bottomlands, the owners of big sheep and cattle ranches raise hay for winter feeding. The Rambouillet breed, introduced in this district, is a wool and meat-producing animal. The sheep feed slowly over the highland meadows, often within the national forests, in the summer months, and when threat of snow appears are slowly driven down into the valleys to the home ranches.

MADRAS, 100.3 *m.* (2,242 alt., 291 pop.), is the seat of Jefferson County. The surrounding country is rich in minerals and semi-precious stones and there are petrified forests. In this area are many of the colorful agate and opal-filled nodules, commonly termed "thunder eggs." An old legend of the Warm Springs Indians relates that they were cast out of the craters of Mount Jefferson and Mount Hood by the Spirits of Thunder who inhabited the mountains. Many thousands of these specimens, found lying loose over the rolling, sage-covered hills, have been gathered from the region about Madras. When cut and polished they make excellent and often valuable exhibits for museums and private collections. The interior agate filling is also utilized for gem stone cutting.

Left from Madras on an unimproved road to the old HAY CREEK RANCH, 11 *m.,* one of the old sheep ranches, where purebred Rambouillet sheep are raised. Its 200,000 acres encompass mountain and forest ranges, valleys for the growing of hay, wild meadows, and expanses of bunch grass and sagebrush.

In the country south of Madras are the sites of several formerly populous towns, established in the days of the Harriman-Hill railroad rivalry. The spectacular race of these railroad tycoons to penetrate the extensive forested and farm lands forms one of the most dramatic episodes in the history of central Oregon. When the plan of Hill to build up the east side of the Deschutes River reached the ears of Harriman, the latter at once launched plans to build a competing line up the opposite side of the Deschutes Canyon. Separated only by the few hundred feet of river bed, the rival construction gangs worked furiously day and night. Twenty-five hundred workers on both sides of the stream toiled incessantly and used every form of obstructionist tactics that ingenuity could devise. Men were killed by "accident" and officers of the law were helpless to prevent disorder. In the wild race, the giants bought farms, closed public roads, and fought in the courts. They vied with each other until the roads reached Metolius, when an agreement was made and a single line built the rest of the way to Bend.

METOLIUS, 104.6 *m.* (2,537 alt., 38 pop.), deriving its name from the Metolius River (*see TOUR 7*), is in a leading fishing and recreational area of the state.

CULVER, 109.2 *m.* (2,636 alt., 50 pop.), was formerly the seat of Jefferson County, and 20 years ago was the scene of a contest with Madras for possession of the county seat.

Right from Culver on a gravel road to the resort region of the Cascade Mountains. THE COVE, 5 *m.,* is at the junction of the Deschutes and Crooked rivers. In the canyon, 1,000 feet below the plateau level, are exposed ancient Deschutes sands, containing fossils of prehistoric ages.

At 114.9 *m.* is the junction with an improved road.

Right on this road, to OPAL CITY, 1 *m.,* named for OPAL SPRINGS (*reached by a steep foot trail*), in the Crooked River Canyon 800 feet below the Canyon's rim. Few of the stones brought to the surface show "fire" but they make interesting specimens.

At Opal City, is the J. B. MENDENHALL RANCH (*visitors welcome*), in whose house and yard is a collection of geological specimens, including some rare fossil flowers, leaves and animal remains gathered in the vicinity.

CROOKED RIVER BRIDGE, 118.8 *m.,* is 330 feet long and 304 feet above the water. The deep chasm it spans is all the more striking as the surrounding country is fairly level. The PETER SKENE OGDEN STATE PARK, embracing 103 acres at either end of the bridge, honors the explorer of central Oregon who became chief factor of the Columbia region in the Hudson's Bay Company.

At **123** *m.* is the junction with an improved road.

Right on this road to LOWER BRIDGE, 6 *m.,* where there is a plant for the manufacture of various articles utilizing diatomaceous earth. Face powders, paints, and plasters are made from this deposit, as well as insulating materials.

Right from Lower Bridge to STEELHEAD FALLS, 11 *m.,* where the Deschutes pours over a lava barrier in the Deschutes National Forest.

REDMOND, 127.8 *m.* (2,996 alt., 994 pop.), is the hub of the central Oregon recreational area, and the center of an intensely cultivated district devoted to potato culture, dairying and turkey raising. Netted Gem potatoes have won attention in far markets, and alfalfa grown under irrigation, often in four crops, is in demand.

Redmond is at the junction with US 28 (*see TOUR 6*).

Much of this area is characterized by juniper trees, with distorted trunks and heavy evergreen foliage, and silvery-toned purple berries every other year. The juniper of Oregon has been used in a limited way for pencil making, and, because of its beautiful grain, by novelty manufacturers for candlesticks, bowls, nutcrackers, and small chests.

BEND, 144.2 *m.* (3,629 alt., 8,848 pop.), in a varied region of snow peaks, desert, and evergreen forest, is the seat of Deschutes County and the chief industrial city of central Oregon. The swift current of the Deschutes River sweeps in a graceful curve through the heart of the city. To the west looms the Cascade Range, the Three Sisters towering white-crested above the lower peaks that thrust upward in a jagged line like the blade of a huge, broken-toothed saw. Eastward, Pilot Butte lifts its symmetrical cone at the very boundary of the city, while beyond spread the lava-rocks and junipers of the inter-mountain desert. Early travelers, resting from their dreary trip across the wind-driven wastes, reluctantly bade the spot good-bye as they again took up their trek toward the Willamette Valley, and named the curve in the river "Farewell Bend," the latter part of which has persisted through the years.

The city owes its economic importance chiefly to the lumber industry, although agriculture has been no small factor in development. More than 16 billion feet of timber, after a generation of ruthless cutting, still stand in the Bend area, and two sawmills annually produce a third of a billion feet of finished lumber. Yet the city has none of the stark ugliness of some mill towns. It conserves the natural charm of its environment by well-planned streets skillfully laid out through a naturally wooded park. Modernization characterizes the business area, and schools, hospitals, parks, clubs, and libraries add to the material comforts of the residents, 90 percent of whom own their homes.

Bend was not a pioneer settlement in the sense of early establishment. Farewell Bend was the only place for many miles where the Deschutes River could be easily forded, and the high butte there was an excellent landmark. For a time, however, better routes diverted travel from the bend and it was forgotten, except by the few cattlemen who ranged their stock thereabouts. Then in 1900, A. M. Drake, an easterner who had come west in search of health, heard of its high altitude and dry climate. Accompanied by his wife he visited it, and Mrs. Drake became so enamored of its beauty they decided to remain.

Three or four years later, the Deschutes Irrigation and Power Co. secured rights to 200,000 acres, which it put under irrigation. In 1904 the Pilot Butte Development Company platted the town and after 1909 growth became steady, when 300,000 acres of agricultural land were thrown open to entry under the homestead law. During the passing years timbermen filed on the great stand of pine on the nearby mountains, and wheat and lumber so attracted transportation interests that in 1911 the Oregon Trunk, subsidiary of the Great Northern, and the Deschutes Railroad, subsidiary of the Union Pacific, started a frenzied race to push their lines up the Deschutes River and on down into the Klamath Lake country.

Then timber became the source of fabulous wealth, as the flat cars began to roll along the newly-laid rails. Men whose names were prominent in the country's financial circles invested in Bend property. Tom Shevlin, noted Yale football player, came out in 1915 and built the Shevlin-Hixon sawmill, and the same year a start was made on the Brooks-Scanlon mill. With the coming of these industries, the original population of 21 persons (1900) increased to 536 by 1910, and ten years later, to 5,415. This was an increase of 910 percent, a record in the United States for the decade.

Bend is the center of an extensive recreational territory. More than 100 lakes and 300 miles of fishing streams lie within 50 miles of the city. There are swimming and boating on clear mountain lakes, horseback rides along forest trails, camping in primitive areas, golf on a mile-high course; there are lava cones, lava tunnels, lava forests; ice-caves and subterranean rivers; canyon depths and mountain heights.

DRAKE PARK, Riverside Blvd. at Deschutes River, is a 10-acre park in a setting of virgin pine.

HARMON PARK, Harmon Blvd. and Milwaukie Ave., across the river from Drake Park, is a well-equipped children's playground, endowed by the Harmon Foundation of New York.

The HOME OF KLONDIKE KATE (*private*), 231 Franklin Ave., among the pines 20 feet above street level, is finished in raked shakes, with a large porch extending across the entire front supported by natural timber pillars. The foundation is of rugged lava rock. Situated on an eminence, its site affords an excellent view of the Cascades to the west, set in a frame of pine trees. Klondike Kate, colorful character of Alaska gold rush days, came to Bend after seeing a motion picture that depicted the city's scenic charms. A beautiful girl, convent-bred and educated, she was the toast of Dawson; a singer and dancer upon whom the sourdoughs and "chechakos" showered their gold dust. Dressed in Parisian gowns and wearing a fortune in diamonds, she entertained the lonesome miners, listened to their hopes and sympathized with their sorrows and disappointments. With earnings that frequently ran as high as $750 a night, she made and gave away two fortunes. A few years ago she was married to John Matson, former Alaska sour-dough and a life-long admirer.

The SHEVLIN-HIXON LUMBER MILL (*open weekday working hours*), W. side of the river at foot of Riverside Ave., operates five great bandsaws. The mill equipment is operated by electric motors powered by steam-driven generators and has a daily capacity of 66,000 feet of lumber.

The BROOKS-SCANLON LUMBER MILL (*open weekday working hours*), at S. city limits, is Bend's other large mill. Its machinery and output is practically a duplication of the Shevlin-Hixon plant.

Points of Interest in Environs are: Lava Butte, 12 *m.*; Lava River Cave, 13 *m.*; Lava Cast Forest, 21 *m.* (*see TOUR* 4); Elk Lake, 36 *m.* (*see TOUR* 4B); Terrance H. Foley State Park (4,139 alt.), E. *edge of city*; Arnold Ice Cave, 18 *m.* (*see TOUR* 7).

Bend holds a water pageant on July 4th, and a flower show the second week in August. The city has 13 hotels and 11 tourist camps. Recreational centers are: O'Donnell Field, First and Kearney Sts.; High School Field, Third and Clay Sts.; Harmon Playground, Harmon and Nashville Sts.; Bend Swimming Pool, Bend Auto Park; Deschutes River; Bend Golf Course, 2.5 m. S. on US 97, 9 holes, fees 35c; Baxter's Riding Academy, 3 m. E. on State 54.

Section b. Bend to California Line, 160.8 m. US 97

South of BEND, 0 *m.*, the country changes sharply. The volcanic base of the soil is everywhere apparent. Unlike the forests west of the Cascades, these in a dryer climate are practically devoid of underbrush. Rank upon rank, the straight pines stand like an army on parade, the open spaces affording endless vistas of unvarying level sameness. The dry air is fragrant with a piney scent; logging crews are passed on the road; loggers and their equipment are visible in the clearings, hardy men with an air of the big woods about them. Logging railroads extend far into the interior and huge trains bring the logs to the mills. The lumber camps are mobile villages of bunkhouses, cookhouses, and administrative quarters, built on the chasses of box cars. Almost any unmarked road leading westward from the highway strikes toward the high Cascades and the innumerable lakes, lying among snow peaks, where old snow lingers close to still, cold water teeming with trout. Streams that cross and recross the roads going in are a delight; they flow quietly, icy and translucent, through almost silent forests and little mountain meadows lush with water grasses. Here the note of a bird or the rustle of the wind in the pine tops is an event.

At 11 *m.* is the junction with a dirt road.

Right on this road to LAVA BUTTE, 0.5 *m.* (5,026 alt.), one of the few world craters that can be visited by automobile. This comparatively recent cinder cone, of the type found in central Oregon, has a crater 150 feet deep. Lava from the south side flowed to the west and north, damming the Deschutes River and forming a lake that overflowed to the north and created a number of waterfalls. A ski hill on the north side provides an excellent jump.

LAVA RIVER CAVES STATE PARK (L), 12.9 *m.*, was so named for the geologic wonder that occurred during a volcanic upheaval, known as the Paulina uplift (*see below*), when a river of molten lava flowed out of cooling lava, and left a 5,462 foot tunnel (*open in summer; guides*).

At 14.3 *m.* is the junction with a dirt road.

Left on the road to LAVA CAST FOREST, 8.9 *m.*, on the northwestern slope of Newberry Crater (*see below*), within the Deschutes National Forest. This phenomenon was caused by a flow of lava that engulfed a forest of green trees to a depth of 20 feet. The lava cooled sufficiently to mold before the wood burned out, leaving innumerable casts as perfect as though made from plaster. The flow covers several square miles and is spread over previous flows of much greater age. "Sunken gardens" on these older flows are surrounded by vertical lava walls. A MUSEUM is reached by walking a quarter-mile over broken lava *(wear old shoes).*

At 24.1 *m.* is the junction with a dirt road.

Left on this road to PAULINA FALLS, 11.5 *m.*, tumbling over high cliffs into a rocky cauldron of Paulina Creek. At 11.6 *m.* is PAULINA LAKE (6,331 alt.) *(lodge, cabins; boats and outboard motor-boats for rent)*, a beautiful, irregularly-shaped body of forest-surrounded water, in the bowl of NEW-BERRY CRATER. Among the attractions are lakes trapped in the summit of a volcanic peak, boiling and ice-cold mineral springs, and rocks that float.

Some scientists contend that the mountain was a great pyramid towering to a height of 20,000 feet until an internal explosion blew away its crest. Others believe that it was built up by lava eruptions to a point considerably higher than its present elevation of 8,000 feet. More than 150 cones, often 300 feet in depth, are around the slopes of the dead volcano. The flow that created the Lava Cast Forest came from one of these. The activity of this crater belongs probably to the Pliocene Age, but its chief development came in the Pleistocene Age, and the volcano continued to erupt spasmodically until a few hundred years ago. It contains many caldera features similar to Mauna Loa, on Hawaii Island, including broad shields of lava, a summit crater, and numerous cones.

There are three separate and vast flows of obsidian, one stained by iron to beautiful shades of yellow and red. Pumice, ejected in the molten state but filled with gas that later escaped and left water-tight cells, is plentiful. It is used for polishing and for sound-proof and fire-proof tiles. Commercially it equals the best grade imported from Italy.

The original crater may or may not have been filled with water, but secondary volcanic activity forced up northern and southern ridges of cones across the center, dividing it into two parts, Paulina Lake filling the western half and East Lake, the eastern half. Also in the area is Lost Lake, a smaller body of water. Soda springs and both hot and cold sulphur springs, utilized as curative agents, are on the northern and southern sides of the crater.

Newberry Crater was discovered November 16, 1826, by Peter Skene Ogden on his way from Harney and Malheur lakes to the Deschutes River. It was named for Dr. John Strong Newberry, physician and noted geologist, who accompanied the Williamson Expedition that explored central Oregon in 1855.

Rearing its jagged ramparts above the crests of the Paulina Mountains, is (R) the tall pinnacle of PAULINA PEAK (8,000 alt.), named for Chief

Paulina, the implacable foe of the white men, who had his retreat in the crater. The peak commands views into four states. The panorama of the entire Cascade Range from Mount Shasta in California to Mount Adams and Mount St. Helens in Washington is visible.

At 13.8 *m.* is the junction with a dirt road; R. on this road 0.3 *m.,* to OBSIDIAN CLIFF, 100 feet high, extending a mile or more eastward. This vast deposit of black and striated volcanic glass lies upon the foundation of pumice over which it was originally poured.

At 14.4 *m.* is LOST LAKE (R), a diminutive crater lake, not visible from the road.

EAST LAKE (6,731 alt.), 16.4 *m.* (L), with neither an inlet nor an outlet (*lodge; cabins; boats; hot and cold mineral springs; baths*), is heavily stocked with eastern brook trout and silversides which feed on the abundant fresh-water shrimp. At the southern rampart is a lake of black obsidian, which for ages was much sought by the primitives of central Oregon to be used as heads for spears and arrows.

At 23.4 *m.* the road turns left and at 36.4 *m.* is the junction with the road to ARNOLD CAVES (*see TOUR 7A*).

On US 97 at 27.5 *m.* is a junction with the Century Drive (*see TOUR 4B*).

LAPINE, 30.2 *m.* (4,234 alt., 111 pop.), is named for an abundance of pine in the vicinity.

At 32 *m.* is the junction with State 31 (*see TOUR 5C*).

CRESCENT, 47.9 *m.* (4,452 alt., 60 pop.), is an important trading point, headquarters for the District Ranger of the Deschutes National Forest, and the site of an old stage station. A party of 100 men led by Lieut. R. L. Williamson, with Lieut. Phil Sheridan, later famous in the Indian and Civil wars, and Dr. John S. Newberry, physician and scientist, explored this region in 1855 to determine the feasibility of a rail route from California to the Columbia River.

At 52.4 *m.* US 97 crosses the northern boundary of a section of the Deschutes National Forest. It was through this region that Capt. John C. Fremont passed with his party of twenty-five in 1843, "always within sound of falling waters." He was impressed by the beauty of the country and the nobility of the pine forests. A wheeled howitzer was occasionally discharged to frighten hostile Indians, always to the delight of the Indian guides. The party crossed the Deschutes several times and journeyed southward, exploring and naming geographic features (*see TOUR 5C*).

At 57.7 *m.* is the junction with State 58 (*see TOUR 4C*).

CHEMULT, 65.4 *m.* (4,762 alt., 55 pop.), was named for an Indian chief, one of the signers of the treaty of 1864 (*see below*). WALKER MOUNTAIN (L), (7,000 alt.), was named for W. T. Walker, who with a party authorized by the legislature to establish a military road from the Willamette Valley to Fort Boise, explored the country in 1852. A marker indicates that the section of the Oregon Central Military Road between Crescent Lake and Klamath Marsh crossed the route at this point. The first emigrant party over this route entered the Willamette Valley in 1853 (*see TOUR 4C*). With a ski course west of town, Chemult is headquarters for winter sports.

BEAVER MARSH, 71.9 *m.* (4,640 alt.), is noted for extensive commercial deposits of pumice, a volcanic substance used for polishing purposes and for sound and fire-proof tiles. A marker indicates that the Fremont party passed this point December 9, 1843, and another states that the north-bound Williamson party passed here on August 24, 1855.

The KLAMATH INDIAN RESERVATION, the northern boundary of which is crossed at 75.7 m., was set aside by the treaty signed at Council Grove, October 14, 1864, for the Klamath, Modoc, and Yahooskin Snake Indians, though 35 different tribes are represented. The largest of the three Indian reservations in Oregon, it contains more than a million acres, of which only about one-fourth has been allotted, the remainder being reserved for timber and some of the finest grazing lands on the Pacific Coast. Two hundred thousand head of cattle from the middle western dust-bowl areas were brought here for distribution. The census of 1935, shows 1,420 Indians on the roll, descendants of formidable tribes whose resistance to white colonization once caused this entire region to be known as the "dark and bloody ground of the Pacific." The Indians are numerous in the Modoc Point and Chiloquin district (see below), but also inhabit the vicinity of Beatty (see TOUR 5D). Many own farms and ranches along the Sprague, Sycan, and Williamson rivers; others are employed in lumber mills and logging camps. Very few of the women now engage in the tribal art of weaving sweet-grass baskets and making beadwork.

David Douglas probably visited the Klamath country in 1826, during his travels as a botanist under protection of the Hudson's Bay Company. He is described as wandering through the forests, a pack upon his back and a gun across his shoulder, with a shaggy terrier at his heels. His skill at shooting birds on the wing, and calling down fire from heaven (with a lens) for his pipe, kept the natives at an admiring distance.

In the early 1870's the region was the scene of an intermittent and stubborn struggle between whites and Modoc Indians, whose descendants live on the Klamath Reservation. The conflict lasted until the Modocs agreed to return to the Klamath Reservation, after they had made their final stand at the Lava Beds, near the southern boundary of the state (see TOUR 5D).

At 75.7 m. also is the junction with State 230, a paved road.

Right on State 230 to DIAMOND LAKE, 20 m. (5,182 alt.), one of the most beautiful of the Cascade Lakes (see CRATER LAKE).

SAND CREEK, 91.6 m., rises in Crater Lake Park and flows eastward into Klamath Marsh. Crossed by an old Indian Trail, and later a stage road, it was named for its treacherous quicksand in which teams and saddle horses often became mired.

A boundary of the ROGUE RIVER NATIONAL FOREST is crossed at 94.1 m.

At 94.6 m. is the junction with paved State 232.

Right on State 232 to the PINNACLES OF SAND CANYON, 3 m., where spires and columns appear as if carved out of soft volcanic material (see

CRATER LAKE). State 232 intersects the Crater Rim Drive at **6** *m.* (*see* *CRATER LAKE*), a short distance from Rim Village.

SUN PASS, **98.1** *m.* (5,403 alt.), at the summit of SAND MOUN-TAIN, is densely wooded with yellow pines. At **99.7** *m.,* is a sweeping view of the mountain-encircled Klamath Basin. Green meadows alternate with dark forests, and through them winds the placid Wood River. Union Peak (7,698 alt.), rises (R) above the Cascade skyline.

At **105.6** *m.* is the junction with State 62, the Crater Lake Highway (*see TOUR 4D*).

The SITE OF OLD FORT KLAMATH (R) is at **105.7** *m.*; from 1863 to 1890 this was an army post from which the government carried on Indian campaigns. It was here that the notorious Captain Jack, leader in the Modoc War (*see below*), Schonchin Jack, Black Jim, and Boston Charley were hanged for the treacherous killing of General E. R. S. Canby and the Reverend E. Thomas, Superintendent of Indian Affairs, and the wounding of A. B. Meacham, the three peace commissioners who were advancing under a flag of truce, April 11, 1873, in an effort to reach peaceful settlement of the bloody and costly war. Other lives were saved by the intervention of Winema, the Indian interpreter and the heroine of the Modoc Wars. Their graves on the parade grounds of the old fort are marked.

CROOKED CREEK, **109.6** *m.,* is at the junction with a dirt road.

Left on this road to the KLAMATH STATE FISH HATCHERY (*picnic facilities*), **0.5** *m.,* for eastern brook and rainbow trout.

KLAMATH AGENCY, **111.6** *m.* (4,176 alt., 150 pop.), head-quarters for the Klamath Indian Reservation, which lies mainly east of the highway.

At **112.8** *m.* is the junction with a graveled highway.

Left on this road to CHILOQUIN, **5** *m.* (4,189 alt., 491 pop.), a typical Indian settlement of the Klamath Reservation, with the English version of an Indian family name.

At AGENCY LAKE, **114.6** *m.,* is the northern inlet of Upper Klamath Lake. On the night of May 5, 1846, Capt. John C. Fremont and his party encamped on the western shore of the Upper Klamath, and for the second time as an explorer he did not post a guard. Early in the morning fifteen Klamaths attacked the camp and two Delawares and an Iroquois half-breed of the Fremont party were killed. The remaining Delawares wanted revenge and were satisfied when Fremont agreed to attack the big Indian village at the head of the lake. After rounding the northern extremity of the lake, a reconnoitering body under Kit Carson was sent ahead. On May 12 they came upon the Indian village at the mouth of the Wood River and a battle ensued. When Fremont and the main body arrived the Indians were driven from their village and fourteen of them killed. Their huts, made of long rushes and willows, were burned, as was the scaffolding on which salmon were being dried.

After the fight, while riding through the forest with Carson and

Segundai, the Delaware chief, Fremont saw an Indian aiming an arrow at Carson. He fired and missed, but charged his horse, Sacramento, at the Indian, knocking him to the ground where he was clubbed to death by Segundai. Fremont's explorations in Oregon were ended when he was ordered to California.

Historians believe that this battle was the cause of the Klamaths' hatred for the whites and for a quarter of a century this region saw the most serious Indian trouble in the history of Oregon.

At **118.9** *m.* is the Williamson River, named for Lieut. R. S. Williamson, which drains a large part of the Klamath Reservation.

MODOC POINT, **124.3** *m.* (4,146 alt., 200 pop.), on the eastern shore of Upper Klamath Lake, was the home of the Modocs under Captain Jack, before their return to Lost River, which precipitated the Modoc War. Here is the LAMM LUMBER COMPANY PLANT (R), one of the large sawmills of the district.

South of Modoc Point the highway borders the UPPER KLAMATH LAKE, about eight miles wide, and 40 miles long, the largest body of fresh water west of the Rockies, and the remnant of an ancient inland sea. It separates the pine-clad eastern slope of the mountains from the gray, rim-rocked hills of the central Oregon plateau. Crater Mountain rises to the north, Mount McLoughlin to the west, and the white slopes of Mount Shasta break the horizon to the south.

Nearly every water-fowl known in North America can be found on these waters. Hordes of geese and ducks linger about the lakes in their annual migration each autumn, remaining until mid-winter before continuing south. One of the most interesting of the water birds is the majestic, snow-white pelican, protected by law. The federal government, taking advantage of natural nesting grounds in this vicinity to preserve America's bird life, has set aside several sections as bird refuges. The lake also provides water for the Klamath Lake irrigation district of 60,000 acres, only about one-fifth of the area potentially within reach of the lake.

At **129.8** *m.* US 97 crosses the southern boundary of the Klamath Indian Reservation.

At **132.7** *m.* is the junction with a paved road.

Right on this road to ALGOMA, **0.2** *m.* (4,151 alt., 250 pop.), named for a lumber company, a name derived from an Indian word meaning "Algonquin waters."

KLAMATH FALLS, **143.5** *m.* (4,106 alt., 16,093 pop.) (*see KLAMATH FALLS*).

Points of Interest: Court House; Veterans' Memorial Building; Link River Bridge; the Ewauna Box Co. Mill; Lumber Mills; Fremont Bridge; Moore Park; Hot Springs Natatorium; Reames Golf and Country Club.

Klamath Falls is at the junction with State 66 (*see TOUR 5D*).

Right from Klamath Falls on State 236 across the Fremont Bridge, spanning the Link River, around the southern and western shores of Upper Klamath Lake to the beautiful Lake of the Woods summer Recreation Area. The route crosses Wocus Marsh and enters one of the great yellow pine forests.

At HOWARD BAY, 17.4 *m.* (4,169 alt.), on the banks of Denny Creek, is a marker commemorating the Indian attack on Captain John C. Fremont near this point on May 5, 1846.

At 25.7 *m.* is the junction with a gravel road. R. here 2 *m.* to PELICAN BAY, a recreation area. At 2.4 *m.* is the SITE OF HARRIMAN LODGE, built by E. H. Harriman of railroad fame in the last years of his life. It was burned in 1929.

ROCKY POINT, 2.9 *m.* (4,153 alt.), is a scenic promontory and lake resort (*cabins; boats; fishing tackle for rent; supplies*).

West of the junction, State 236 continues to a forest service trail and Dead Indian Road, 33.8 *m.*, at the entrance to the LAKE OF THE WOODS RECREATION AREA.

1. Left on the forest service trail 12 *m.*, to the MOUNTAIN LAKES PRIMITIVE AREA. Within its borders are Mount Harriman (7,950 alt.), Crater Mountain (7,800 alt.), Mount Carmine (6,250 alt.), Greylock Mountain (7,850 alt.), High Knob (6,500 alt.), and Aspen Butte (8,209 alt.). Hiking or horseback trails lead to Harriette and Como Lakes (*camps and roadside shelters*) and up the sides of Mount Harriman and Aspen Butte.

2. Left on Dead Indian Road 1.5 *m.* to LAKE OF THE WOODS (4,960 alt.), one of the most beautiful lakes in the Northwest, in a setting of pines, with Mount McLoughlin in white silhouette across the wooded shores, (*lodge; cabins; fishing tackle and boats for rent; saddle horses*).

Continuing west State 236 reaches the LAKE OF THE WOODS GOLF COURSE, 35 *m.*, and the FOREST GUARD SUMMER HEADQUARTERS, 36.1 *m.* FISH LAKE, 42 *m.* (4,687 alt.), is known for its trout fishing (*cabins; boats and fishing tackle for rent; supplies*).

MIDLAND, 151.2 *m.* (4,092 alt., 46 pop.), probably received its name because it is on land partly surrounded by marshes.

WORDEN, 157.7 *m.* (4,014 alt., 46 pop.), was named for a pioneer, William S. Worden. To the (L) of the highway, at the southern end of the dry bed of Lower Klamath Lake is the KLAMATH LAKE BIRD RESERVE. This reservation in Klamath County, Oregon, and Siskiyou County, California, was set aside as a refuge in 1908, subject to the primary use of the lands by the Bureau of Reclamation. It contains 81,619 acres, 61,139 of which are in Oregon.

Lower Klamath Lake, once a singularly beautiful expanse of water bounded by tules, and the home of myriads of breeding waterfowl, has been almost completely dry for many years as a result of an attempt to convert it into agricultural land. The conditions that obtained before its drainage were described by Mr. William L. Finley: "Here are numerous ducks, including mallards, canvasbacks, pintails, gadwalls, mergansers, cinnamon teal, and ruddy ducks. The marshes are also the homes of Canada geese, sandhill cranes, bitterns, coots, and rails. Along the mud flats are avocets, stilts, phalaropes, snipe, killdeers, and other waders. On the lakes are colonies of numberless gulls, night herons and great blue herons, cormorants, grebes, terns, and pelicans. I have seen the marshes white with the nesting multitudes."

After 1917, when control gates were closed and the waters of the Klamath River prevented from entering into the lake, its destruction was rapid. Water remaining was soon lost through evaporation, and tule and peat fires continued the destruction until there remained only a desert. A large portion of the land thus uncovered was useful for no other purpose than a bird refuge and the remainder was burdened with mandatory reservations that discouraged any attempts at agriculture.

Since this drainage, sportsmen and conservationists have agitated for the restoration of Lower Klamath, and government engineers have recently reported a plan and it is expected that the work of returning Lower Klamath Lake to its one-time ideal condition for birds will be begun soon.

In its present condition, a few birds still use the Lower Klamath Refuge, but in nothing like their former numbers. Killdeers still nest around the few lakes remaining on the refuge, and small numbers of ducks and geese still stop in migration.

US 97 crosses the California Line at **160.8** *m.* (*see CALIFORNIA GUIDE, TOUR 3A*).

Tour 4A

Cow Canyon Junction—Maupin—Government Camp—Sandy—Gresham—Portland; 123.2 m. State 50.

Asphalt-paved; closed during severe winter storms.
Motor stage service.
Improved forest camps, hotel resorts, auto camps, at short intervals.

This highway, the chief road between Portland and the Mount Hood recreational area, more or less follows the wagon trail developed in 1846 to take emigrants into the Willamette Valley without passage down the dangerous Columbia River. In 1846 the road was opened as the Barlow Toll Road and for nearly 20 years long caravans climbed over it on their way to the promising land of the west. During the next decade miners followed the road to the gold fields of eastern Oregon.

Crossing a shoulder of Mount Hood, the highway passes through a region notable for its beauty. For miles the highway winds through lanes of virgin forest made more beautiful during the late spring and summer by masses of blooming rhododendron. Glacial streams, born of the perpetual snows on Mount Hood's cloud-swept summit, tumble down rocky channels close to the motorist. West of the Cascade Divide the country is being intensively developed as a recreational area. Many forest roads and trails lead from State 50 to wilderness spots or climb to alpine heights (*see MOUNT HOOD*). Below the forests the route flattens out among the farms of the Willamette Valley and suburbs of Oregon's chief city.

State 50 branches northwest from US 97 (*see TOUR* 4), **0** *m.,* at COW CANYON JUNCTION, a point 12 miles southwest of Shaniko, and parallels the gorge of the Deschutes, mounting gradually to CRITERION SUMMIT, **4.9** *m.* (3,559 alt.), overlooking spectacular boulder-strewn slopes and tumbled ridges. The highway twists northward over gray, stony hills where only tough bunch grass, juniper, and sagebrush find footing and crosses the Deschutes River, which has cut a gorge through the central plateau. The river is unnavigable; its falls and rapids give it its name—*Riviere des Chutes* (river of the falls). When Lewis and Clark passed its mouth in 1805 they referred to it in their Journals by its Indian name, Towahnahiooks, and renamed it for Captain Clark. But the name bestowed later by Canadian employees of the Hudson's Bay Company prevailed. The gorge of the Deschutes was a serious problem to men who attempted to shorten the early overland routes to the Willamette Valley.

MAUPIN, **22** *m.* (902 alt., 249 pop.), in the Deschutes River canyon, was named for Howard Maupin, reputed slayer (1867) of Paulina, the chief of a marauding band of Snakes and outlaw whites, who for years terrorized the scattered settlers. Maupin was the operator of a ferry. The town is a favorite resort of Portland amateur fishermen and supports several establishments catering to anglers.

State 50 continues westward across a high sagebrush region with scattered junipers.

At **32.2** *m.* is the junction with a dirt road.

Left on this road to WAPINITIA, 1 *m.* (2,023 alt., 35 pop.), and into the WARM SPRINGS INDIAN RESERVATION, 4 *m.,* which covers 300,000 barren acres set apart for the natives in 1855. By treaties negotiated by Gen. Joel Palmer (*see TOUR* 10), members of the Tenino, Wasco, Paiute, and Klickitat tribes were herded here. Today about 725 Indians live here on government rations since crops are too poor to support even this number of people.

Winding through the broad reaches of the semi-arid lands, the road continues to SIMNASHO (Ind. cor. *Simnassa, thorn bush*), **12.7** *m.* (2,357 alt., 25 pop.), the center of many Indian activities and festivals, including a Harvest Festival held after the huckleberry crop is gathered. WARM SPRINGS, **32.8** *m.* (1,535 alt., 50 pop.), is administrative headquarters for the reservation. There is a boarding school for children, providing primary education. Students desiring advanced courses may attend high school at Chemawa, near Salem (*see TOUR 2b*). (*No public accommodations, though meals are available at Government Employees Club. No liquor permitted on reservation.*)

State 50 climbs from the sagebrush into the open stands of pine, characteristic of the eastern slope of the Cascades. Toward the summit, dense fir and hemlock growths appear. At **42.7** *m.* the MOUNT HOOD NATIONAL FOREST is entered (*see NATIONAL FORESTS*). At BEAR SPRINGS, **46.5** *m.* (3,219 alt.), is an improved Forest Service camp.

Left from Bear Springs on a dirt road through the Warm Springs Reservation to (R) HE HE BUTTE (3,128 alt.), 12.5 *m.,* where is an agency sawmill.

At BLUE BOX JUNCTION, **57.1** *m.* (3,825 alt.), State 50 meets the Olallie Lakes Road.

Left on this road (*open Aug.-Sept.*), which leads southward through forests in proximity to the Pacific Crest Trail. It passes CLEAR LAKE BUTTE (4,440 alt.) and winds to NORTH GATE, 3.8 *m.* (*cabins*). BIG MEADOWS (3,330 alt.), 6 *m.*, are open uplands surrounded by blue-green pine forests on the western slope of the Cascades. South of CLACKAMAS LAKE (L) and the CLACKAMAS LAKE RANGER STATION (3,337 alt.), 8.3 *m.*, the road recrosses the rugged summit (4,172 alt.), 14 *m.*, to the eastern side of the range. From WARM SPRINGS MEADOWS (3,703 alt.), 20.2 *m.* (*shelters*), it lifts through alternate stretches of forest and meadow to recross the wooded buttes westward. PEAVINE MOUNTAIN (4,893 alt.) rises ahead at 23 *m.* as the road turns south. PINHEAD BUTTE (L), 24.2 *m.* (5,585 alt.), overlooks the road.

The route at 27.7 *m.* passes between (L) LEMITI BUTTE (5,450 alt.) and (R) SISI BUTTE (5,614 alt.) high on the western skyline. In this region deer walk boldly from forest coverts, beaver splash in the creeks that wind through harsh grasses, and bear amble into the meadowland. OLALLIE MEADOWS (*camp grounds*) extend southward at 31.4 *m.* The route climbs to OLALLIE LAKE, 35.5 *m.*, in the center of the OLALLIE LAKES RECREATIONAL AREA (*tourist cabins; campers' supplies; saddle horses; boats*). Olallie, the largest (175 acres) of several lakes here, affords excellent fishing, and is warm enough in mid-summer for bathing. Left at the northern extremity of the lake on a trail that leads 4 *m.* to the crest of OLALLIE BUTTE (7,210 alt.), where a fire tower commands a magnificent panorama. Fifty lakes are visible without field glasses; more than 100 with them.

MONON LAKE (*camp grounds*), 37.5 *m.*, only a little smaller than Olallie, and BREITENBUSH LAKE (*forest guard station; improved campsite; shelter*), 40.7 *m.* (5,600 alt.), with more than 20 acres of water, below towering peaks, have a blue satin sheen when the sky is cloudless. Sandy beaches afford opportunity for bathing. Left from Breitenbush 8 *m.* on a trail through Jefferson Park to MOUNT JEFFERSON.

The main forest road again crosses the divide, continuing in a northwesterly direction, with forested slopes rising on either hand and turbulent streams plunging under bridges. At 49 *m.* BALD MOUNTAIN looms (R). Here the road leaves the Mount Hood National Forest and enters the Willamette National Forest. BREITENBUSH MOUNTAIN (4,805 alt.) rises to the south at 52 *m.* in a region of dense evergreen forests. BREITENBUSH SPRINGS (*bath houses, hotel, public camp sites*), 53.7 *m.*, is a resort in an area with more than 50 mineral hot springs (170°F). The road, here graveled, continues to DETROIT, 65.7 *m.*, on State 222 (*see TOUR 7a*).

BLUE BOX SUMMIT, 58.6 *m.* (4,024 alt.), is the highest point on the route. FROG LAKE (*improved camp sites*), 59.3 *m.* (3,872 alt.), is a small body of water. Passing through a heavily forested area, State 50 crosses the EAST FORK OF THE SALMON RIVER, 64.1 *m.*, and the WEST FORK, 64.4 *m.*, to a junction (3,648 alt.), with State 35 (*see TOUR 1E*), 64.6 *m.* West of this junction State 50 skirts the southern base of Mount Hood.

At 65.5 *m.* is the junction with the eastern Timberline Lodge Road (*route one-way at lower end*).

Right on this road, which climbs the south shoulder of the mountain in a series of loops rising about 350 feet in the mile. At 2.4 *m.* is a panorama of a vast expanse of timbered foothills (R) below snow-crested Mount Jefferson and the tips of the Three Sisters.

At 5.6 *m.* is the junction with the descending one-way section of the route; L. here 5 *m.* to State 50. At the end of the uproad stands TIMBERLINE LODGE (6,000 alt.) at 6 *m.* (*see MOUNT HOOD*).

At 66.6 *m.* on State 50 is a junction with a graveled road.

Left here to SWIM (*tourist cabins; baths*), **0.3** *m.* (3,600 alt.), a resort built around warm mineral springs. Beyond STILL CREEK FOREST CAMP, **0.4** *m.* (3,700 alt.), the road reaches an upland meadow that in pioneer days was named SUMMIT MEADOWS, and affords a view of the lofty pinnacles of Mount Hood. All that remains of the old VICKERS SUMMIT HOUSE, **1** *m.*, a relay station on the Barlow Stage Road, are two corral gate posts (L). Perry Vickers, said to have been the first Mount Hood guide, was proprietor of the hotel until he was killed in 1882 by a fugitive thief. He is buried in a picketed enclosure (R), **1.2** *m.*, along the roadway. An EMERGENCY AIRPLANE LANDING FIELD (L) is at **1.4** *m.*

At **67** *m.* is a junction with the west Timberline Lodge Road (*see above*).

At the OREGON TRAIL FOREST CAMP (R), **67.2** *m.* (3,900 alt.), is a roadside fountain. From the camp is an impressive view of the mountain.

BARLOW MONUMENT (R), **67.4** *m.*, is a park containing only 25 square feet, and was established to honor Samuel K. Barlow and his wife (*see TOUR 1E*). Declaring that God never made a mountain without some place to go over it, Barlow set out from The Dalles, in October 1845, to find a short route into the Willamette Valley, that would supplant the laborious and dangerous boat route down the Columbia River. Mountain men and Hudson's Bay trappers had insisted that the attempt was futile. Led by Barlow and Joel Palmer, a party with 13 wagons made the trip. After wallowing through huckleberry swamps, prying their wagons out of mire, fording torrents, and fighting their way through virgin forests, they abandoned the wagons near this place and reached the settlement at Oregon City in December, the final members arriving on Christmas Day. In the following July they came back and continued their road-blazing with the wagons. Barlow applied to the legislative committee of the Provisional Government for permission to build and operate a toll-road over the route he had cut. With the aid of Philip Foster, who furnished the capital, he began construction, and the work was so far along by August 1846, that the road was used thereafter. It spanned a distance of about 85 miles between toll-gates near Wamic (*see TOUR 1b*) and Oregon City.

But the early road was far from perfect. One traveler later recalled: "Some men's hearts died within them and some of our women sat down by the roadside—and cried, saying they had abandoned all hope of ever reaching the promised land. I saw women with babies but a week old, toiling up the mountains in the burning sun, on foot, because our jaded teams were not able to haul them. We went down mountains so steep that we had to let our wagons down with ropes. My wife and I carried our children up muddy mountains in the Cascades, half a mile high and then carried the loading of our wagons upon our backs by piecemeal, as our cattle were so reduced that they were hardly able to haul up our empty wagon."

GOVERNMENT CAMP (*service stations; hotels; tourist cabins; food*), **67.5** *m.* (3,870 alt.), is a resort settlement on private land within the Mount Hood Recreational Area. The place was so named because it was the camp of a detachment of soldiers sent overland in 1849 to man the newly acquired territory. They were forced to abandon some of their wagons here and on them left a warning sign: "Government Property—Do Not Touch."

At the camp is a junction with the Pioneer Bridle Trail (*see below*).

Left from Government Camp on a trail to MULTORPOR MOUNTAIN SKI JUMP (4,500 alt.), 1 *m.* To the west is the SKI BOWL, terminus of the fast Ski Racing Trail, or Slalom course, which descends the northeast slope of TOM-DICK-HARRY MOUNTAIN.

West of Government Camp, the highway spirals down the steep slope of LAUREL HILL, so named by the pioneers because of the profuse growths of rhododendron, which they called laurel, as in the East. Laurel Hill was the scene of hardships that taxed the fortitude of the Barlow party. They found it a hazardous descent of two miles, with only three benches, or levels, where oxen could rest. Trees still bear marks that reveal the tedious progress of the trail-blazers as they lowered their wagons by ropes down the precipitous slopes. "We went down Laurel Hill like shot off of a shovel," William Barlow, a son, recorded.

In a diary kept while traveling the road in 1853, E. W. Conyers observed: "The road on this hill is something terrible. It is worn down into the soil from five to seven feet, leaving steep banks on both sides, and so narrow that it is almost impossible to walk alongside of the cattle for any distance without leaning against the oxen. The emigrants cut down a small tree about ten inches in diameter and about forty feet long, and the more limbs it has on the better. This tree they fastened to the rear axle with chains or ropes, top end foremost, making an excellent brake."

YOCUM FALLS (L), 70.3 *m.,* was named for Oliver C. Yocum, who spent 22 years on Mount Hood as guide and in 1900 built the first Government Camp Hotel, since destroyed by fire.

Left from Yocum Falls on a foot trail to MIRROR LAKE, 1.3 *m.,* an exceptionally beautiful body of water mirroring Mount Hood.

Near the foot of Laurel Hill is an underpass, 70.8 *m.,* of the Pioneer Bridle Path (*see below*). Zigzag River, named for its crooked channel and fed by one of Mount Hood's 11 glaciers, is crossed at 71.9 *m.,* near (R) the TWIN BRIDGES FOREST CAMP (2,907 alt.).

Right from this camp on an easy foot trail around ZIGZAG MOUNTAIN to PARADISE PARK (6,000-6,500 alt.) 6 *m.* on the West Branch of the Pacific Crest Trail (*see MOUNT HOOD TOUR* 2). Close under the glaciers of the southwestern expanse of the mountain in this isolated area is a profusion of sub-alpine flowers. Mount Hood lilies, blue lupine, yellow squaw grass, and scarlet Indian paint brush color the slopes.

The OREGON TRAIL TAVERN, 72.7 *m.,* is a commercial resort. Hanging on its walls is a picture of the former building at the lower Barlow Road Tollgate. At 76 *m.* is ONE-MILE BRIDGE over the Zigzag, near the point at which covered wagons crossed. The ford is discernible (L) from the highway.

At **76.8** *m.* (L) is the site of the LOWER TOLLGATE on the Barlow Road, where successive proprietors levied toll on all immigrants. The rates were $2.50 for each wagon, and $1.00 for each head of stock. Many a settler arrived at the gates unable to pay, but Mr. Barlow would accept a note. He always permitted widows to pass without payment.

At **77** *m.* is a junction with the Pioneer Bridle Trail.

Left on this well-improved trail following the course of the old Barlow Road, roughly parallel to the highway; it leads up the mountainside to GOVERN-MENT CAMP, **11** *m.* (*see above*).

RHODODENDRON, **77.7** *m.* (1,600 alt., 50 pop.), so named because of the profusion of this vivid-flowered shrub, is the trade center of a summer colony. (*Hotel, cabins, service station, tourist supplies, swimming pool, saddle horses*).

Bordering the highway below Rhododendron, and adjacent to it, are a number of commercial camps and resorts. The ZIGZAG RANGER STATION, **80** *m.* (1,400 alt.), is Forest Service headquarters for the district (*camp-fire permits and information*), on the west boundary of the Mount Hood National Forest. The Zigzag River flows into the Sandy River (*see TOUR 1b*) a short distance north of the station in an area formerly called Elk Flat.

At **80.7** *m.* is a junction with an improved road.

Left on this road to WELCHES, **1** *m.* (*accommodations; golf course*), from which the Salmon River Trail winds through a rugged country with excellent hunting and fishing; lower 9.5 miles is in good condition but the remainder to SALMON RIVER MEADOWS, **25** *m.*, should not be followed without a guide.

WEMME, **81.3** *m.* (1,300 alt.), was named for E. Henry Wemme, a Portland manufacturer and philanthropist who willed to the state of Oregon his interest in the old Barlow Road.

Near BRIGHTWOOD (*tourist facilities*), **84** *m.*, is the site of the ROCK CORRAL, frequently mentioned in pioneer annals. In the center of a pole enclosure where the immigrants' stock was kept at night was a great rock, now hidden by undergrowth and young trees. For a time the Barlow tollgate was here.

SANDY, **97.4** *m.* (1,012 alt., 234 pop.), is the business center of eastern Clackamas County.

1. Right from the eastern entrance to Sandy over a gravel road to BULL RUN, **4.5** *m.* (300 alt., 35 pop.), on the Bull Run River, so named because runaway cattle from wagon trains ran wild in the woods. Bull Run is at the entrance to BULL RUN RESERVE, an area of 102 square miles protecting the watershed that is the source of Portland's water supply. It is closed to the public by act of Congress.

a. Right from Bull Run **9.5** *m.* up the river to BEAR CREEK DAM, which holds in reserve enough water to supply Portland for more than a year. BULL RUN LAKE, about 15 miles farther east on the northwest slope of Mount Hood (*inaccessible except by trail*) fed by underground springs, is the source of Bull Run River.

b. Left from Bull Run **3** *m.* on a gravel road to DODGE PARK, an area of 26 acres, at the confluence of the Sandy and Bull Run Rivers, that is a part of Portland's municipal park system (*picnic tables; dressing room for swimmers, camp stoves, bathing beach*). Trails lead from the Park to vantage points with wide beautiful views.

2. Right from the western limits of Sandy on paved Bluff Road, which runs north along the rim of the Sandy River Canyon. At 0.9 *m.* is a point above the river from which the heavily timbered and rugged area of the Bull Run Reserve (R) is seen.

At 3.5 *m.* is a junction with a gravel road; R. here 2 *m.* to DODGE PARK (*see above*). Veering west, the Bluff Road continues to an intersection with State 50, 7.6 *m.*, at a point 6.6 miles west of its point of departure (*see below*).

3. Left from the western limits of Sandy over State 211 to EAGLE CREEK, 7.1 *m.* (340 alt., 82 pop.), named for a nearby stream. In this village is the site of the FOSTER HOME. After the long hard trip across the mountain, the early emigrants welcomed the hospitable farmstead of the Philip Fosters, whose pasture became a regular camping ground, and whose corrals were utilized for the weary stock. Continuing southward State 211 crosses EAGLE CREEK 8.1 *m.* to ESTACADA, 12.3 *m.* (465 alt., 524 pop.), on the Clackamas River. The canyon-like walls of the river in the heavily timbered country, which is interspersed with farm clearings, give the town and vicinity an appearance of isolation. In the vicinity are several large plantings of ginseng, a medicinal herb whose culture requires special conditions of soil and climate.

At **97.8** *m.* is the junction with Bluff Road (*see above*).

Northwest of Sandy, State 50 continues through a rolling region of farms and berry fields with intervening groves of firs. At **104.5** *m.* is the junction with the western end of the Bluff Road (*see above*).

On clear days there is an unusually fine view of Mounts St. Helens, Adams, and Hood at **107.7** *m.*

GRESHAM, **109.1** *m.* (295 alt., 1,635 pop.), business center of an extensive berrying area, is the scene of the Multnomah County Fair.

West of Gresham, State 50 follows Powell Boulevard through suburban Portland, crossing the Ross Island Bridge over the Willamette, **121** *m.* to the center of PORTLAND, **123.2** *m.* (*see PORTLAND*).

Tour 4B

Bend—Todd Lake—Sparks Lake—Elk Lake—Lava Lakes—Fall River —Pringle Falls—Junction US 97; 68 m. The Century Drive.

Graveled and dirt road.
Limited accommodations.

The Century Drive, winding through a region of primitive beauty, penetrates to the foot of a group of imposing peaks, and leads into the crater of a prehistoric volcano, encounters crystal-clear creeks and rivers, forest-fringed lakes, fine stands of ponderosa pine, glacial meadows, barren lava buttes, cinder cones, obsidian cliffs, and pumice deserts. The streams and lakes, well-stocked with trout, are fed by perpetual mountain snows. Wild game in abundance, including mule deer, elk and antelope, roam the forests.

The route branches westward from Greenwood Avenue on Wall Street in BEND, **0** *m.,* on US 97 (*see TOUR* 4), and crosses the Deschutes River. At **2.6** *m.* is the beginning of Century Drive which the route now follows.

West of Bend's two large sawmills (L), **2.8** *m.,* the route parallels the Deschutes through a reforested sector of cut-over land. BACHE-LOR BUTTE, **4.5** *m.* (9,060 alt.), a symmetrical cone, looms prominently on the Cascade skyline. At **6.5** *m.* the SOUTH SISTER (10,354 alt.), one of the highest peaks in Oregon, and the jagged peaks (R) of BROKEN TOP (9,165 alt.), dominate the horizon (*see below*).

Through the DESCHUTES NATIONAL FOREST, **12.5** *m.,* the route follows a oneway road with occasional turn-outs and heavy grades.

At **13.6** *m.* is the junction with a dirt road.

Left on this road to EDISON ICE CAVE, **7.5** *m.,* where prehistoric relics have been found beneath the ice.

At **18.9** *m.* is an unusual view of Bachelor Butte rising above the forest. Through a narrow pass, at **22.3** *m.,* not more than 100 yards wide, the drive runs between Bachelor Butte (L) and Tumalo Mountain (1,772 alt.). Here is the junction with a forest trail.

Left on the trail up the northeast slope of Bachelor Butte to the FOREST LOOKOUT on its summit, **3** *m.,* commanding a wide view of the Cascades, particularly of the Three Sisters and Broken Top, and to the east, the Paulina Mountains.

DUTCHMAN'S FLAT, **23** *m.,* is a pumice field with ghost-like trees. The seven major glaciers on the sides of the South Sister, Broken Top, and the tip of the North Sister (R), gleaming in the sunlight loom to the west.

At **25.3** *m.* is the junction with a dirt road.

Right on this road to TODD LAKE, **0.5** *m.* (6,100 alt.), one of the most beautiful lakes on the Century Drive. It is not large but the setting is superb, with Broken Top high above the tree-fringed shores. (*Unimproved forest camp*).
Right from Todd Lake to BROKEN TOP CRATER (*drive carefully into crater*), **3.5** *m.,* the most rugged feature of the region. It was once a part of the ancient volcano of "Mount Multnomah," which was a mile or more higher than the still majestic remnants.

North of the Todd Lake junction the drive passes through a lava flow (L), and after crossing another pumice field, reaches the northern end of SPARKS LAKE, **28.6** *m.,* a camping and mountain climbing outfitting point, from which trips are made to Green Lakes at the foot of South Sister.

West of Sparks Lake is the DEVIL'S GARDEN (*forest camp*), **29.7** *m.,* a mountain meadow near Satan's Creek.

The DEVIL'S CHAIR, 29.9 *m.,* is a clump of immense rocks forming a narrow pass on which are (R) undeciphered Indian pictographs. An Indian legend relates that a Warm Springs brave induced a Klamath maiden to return north with him, and that later, he and a band of his warriors were ambushed at this pass by Klamaths led by a rival lover. Every Warm Springs Indian was killed and the Klamaths inscribed these pictographs as a warning for all Warm Springs people to stay on their own side of the pass.

South of DEVIL'S LAKE *(forest camp)*, 30 *m.* (4,389 alt.), are the gray spectres of a dead forest on the banks of Hell's Creek, 30.7 *m.,* and WICKIUP PLAIN, 32.7 *m.,* a plateau of pumice dunes. The South Sister rises bleak and austere nearly a mile from the plain. In the immediate foreground is one of the great obsidian cliffs of the McKenzie Lava Field *(see TOUR 6b)*, with lava flows in all directions. Where the cliff terminates it has broken into countless fragments, some no larger than small boulders and others as large as a house, and most of them in a variety of grotesque shapes suggesting with their polished surfaces ultra-modern sculpture. It is said that the Indians of this locality held a monopoly on the working of this rich obsidian treasure and that arrow heads from this quarry have been found as far east as the Mississippi. It is presumed that these early industrialists profited considerably from their trade in obsidian. This is the climbing base for the mountain.

ELK LAKE, 36 *m.* (4,893 alt.), two miles long and a half a mile wide, is the best developed recreational area in the district. This lake, fringed with somber green forests, with the towering crest of South Sister reflected in its waters, is a picture of primitive charm *(lodge; boats, saddle horses)*. Eastward across the lake Bachelor Butte, a perfect volcanic cone over 9,000 feet in height, gives the illusion of imminent eruption from its extinct crater. Its steep, boulder- and rubble-strewn slopes are almost impossible to climb.

At 38 *m.* is the junction with a forest road.

Left on this road to MUD LAKE, 2 *m.* (4,893 alt.), noted for its big eastern brook trout.

BIG LAVA LAKE (L), 40.1 *m.* (4,738 alt.), with Little Lava Lake, is the source of the Deschutes River.

At 41.6 *m.* is the junction with a side road.

Right on this road is LITTLE LAVA LAKE (4,737 alt.), and FOREST CAMP, 1.2 *m.* Both this lake and Big Lava Lake afford good fishing.

At 41.9 *m.* is the Cultus Lake Trail (R).

The road crosses at 44.2 *m.,* the headwaters of the Deschutes River. *(Forest guard and forest camp.)*

Left on a dirt road to CRANE PRAIRIE RESERVOIR, 1.5 *m.*

At 45.3 *m.* is the junction with a side road.

Right on this road to CULTUS LAKE, 8 *m.,* an attractive small lake in a forest setting of white, lodgepole and ponderosa pine. It takes its name from *kaltas,* Chinook jargon, "bad" because the waters of Cultus Creek could not be used. Above its shore rise the peaks of Pack Saddle Mountain. Except for a forest camp, it is as yet undeveloped as a recreational area.

At 9.7 *m.* is a junction with a forest road. R. on this road 1.5 *m.* to LITTLE CULTUS LAKE and FOREST CAMP. From the lake a foot trail leads 1.6 *m.* to a Lookout Station on the summit of CULTUS MOUNTAIN (6,756 alt.).

At FALL RIVER, 57.3 *m.,* are a State Fish Hatchery and a Forest Guard Station. The latter is built on a narrow point of land between two large springs, the sources of Fall River.

At 59.8 *m.* is the boundary of the PRINGLE FALLS EXPERIMENTAL FOREST STATION, maintained by the U. S. Forest Service. It is one of five forest laboratories in the state devoted to the study of tree growth, insect control, and other forest problems.

At 60.2 *m.* is the junction with a side road.

Right on this road to PRINGLE FALLS FOREST GUARD STATION, 0.5 *m.*

DESCHUTES RIVER BRIDGE, 60.3 *m.,* spans the stream just above PRINGLE FALLS, site of an early sawmill and mill town by the same name. In the river at the head of the falls are remnants of the mill and mill dam, while on the right bank of the river is a log rollway on which is a huge pile of decaying logs. The falls and town were named for O. M. Pringle, who came to central Oregon from Salem about 1874, and started a sawmill.

Crossing the Little Deschutes River, 66.8 *m.,* the road joins US 97 at 68 *m.,* a point three miles north of Lapine.

Tour 4C

Junction with US 97—Crescent Lake—Odell Lake—Oakridge—Goshen; 87 m. State 58.

Southern Pacific Railroad parallels route.
Gravel road; closed in winter.
Accommodations restricted to resorts and forest camps.

State 58 is the shortest route between US 97 and US 99, linking eastern Oregon and the Willamette Valley. One of the oldest of roads, it is among the last to become a modern highway. It is the high-speed trans-Cascade route from Portland to San Francisco. Its scenery ranges from the mile-high Cascades to pastoral lowlands. In passing through the Deschutes and Willamette National Forests, it traverses a popular recreational region. On the route are a number of Oregon's most beautiful lakes and peaks, innumerable streams, waterfalls, and alpine meadows. Frequent trails lead to hidden wilderness spots, or up mountains.

For more than 60 miles, the route roughly parallels the old Willamette Military Road, over which migrants toiled on the last lap of their journey into the upper Willamette Valley. Ruts worn into the earth, and scars left on trees by wheel hubs are still visible from the highway.

State 58 branches northwest from US 97, *0 m.*, at a point 7.7 miles north of Chemult and cuts through the Deschutes National Forest. In this area are many large and beautiful specimens of ponderosa pine, their coral-barked trunks rising straight from a needle-carpeted floor free of undergrowth.

At *4.3 m.* is a junction with a dirt road.

Left on this road 2 *m.* to EMIGRANT CROSSING over the Little Deschutes River, where in the 1850's seekers after homes crossed the stream on rafts improvised from their wagons. The WILLAMETTE MILITARY ROAD, little improved and now almost abandoned, follows the course hewn from the wilderness by these migrants on their way to the Willamette Valley.

When pioneers came into Oregon they found the Cascade Mountains the worst obstacle in their journey. The most eventful crossing of the Cascades by the Middle Fork of the Willamette was that made in October, 1853, by a train of 1,500 men, women and children, with nearly 300 wagons and much livestock, who attempted the pass on the verge of winter. Owing to previous delays, this party, a detachment of the great migration of 1853, did not reach the Cascade Divide until October.

Snow was flying, provisions were extremely low, animals were dying, and the travelers, worn out from their hardships after months of overland travel, were in despair. Another Donner tragedy was narrowly averted by the timely arrival of settlers from the Willamette Valley.

The settlers from Linn and Lane counties, desiring a direct road from Fort Boise, had earlier in the year begun to open the route, the first link of which was from the valley up the middle fork of the Willamette River to the summit. It was this road that made it possible to succor the stranded pioneers at Willamette Pass and enable them to complete their journey to the valley.

In 1864, the Oregon Central Military Road was organized as a commercial route from Eugene to the Owyhee River. It followed in the main the old trail.

CRESCENT CREEK, *12.9 m.*, has its source in Crescent Lake and is a tributary of the Little Deschutes River.

At *15.5 m.* is a junction with a dirt road.

Left on this road to CRESCENT LAKE RESORT, 2.5 *m.* (4,839 alt.), and CRESCENT LAKE, on the main line of the Southern Pacific. (*Lodge and cottages; Forest Guard station; free telephone; camp-fire permits and general information; motor craft, row boats, fishing tackle, and saddle horses for hire*). Shadowed by Diamond Peak, Crescent Lake, in the heart of the Cascades, is a beautiful scene. It is well stocked with trout, including rainbow, eastern brook, Mackinaw, Dolly Varden, and Loch Leven, affording excellent fly and troll fishing. Crescent Lake, with its fine sandy beach, its many wilderness trails, including the Skyline or Pacific Crest Trail, an improved Forest Camp with outdoor grills and camp tables, is one of the most popular of all the resorts in the Cascades. A scenic road through virgin timber encircles the lake.

At **18.6** *m.* is a junction with a side road.

Right on this road to DAVIS LAKE, 6 *m.* (4,390 alt.), another charming Cascade lake. (*Forest Guard station provides free telephone, and camp-fire permits are issued; information given*).

At **18.7** *m.* is a junction with a side road.

Left on this road to ODELL LAKE RESORT, 0.5 *m.* (4,792 alt.), (*lodge and cottages; improved Forest Camp; Forest Guard station; free telephone; camp-fire permits; information; hunting and fishing licenses*). ODELL LAKE, a vividly blue body of water about six miles long and three miles wide, with sounded depths to 2,000 feet, occupies a depression cut by an ancient glacier. MAIDEN PEAK (7,811 alt.), is mirrored in its waters, and four other peaks, MAKLAKS MOUNTAIN (6,990 alt.), MOUNT YORAN (7,132 alt.), LAKE-VIEW MOUNTAIN (7,063 alt.), and ROYCE MOUNTAIN (6,186 alt.), are silhouetted against the skyline. Odell Lake is noted for angling and is well stocked with rainbow and eastern brook trout for fly casting, and Dolly Varden and Mackinaw trout for trolling. It was named for William H. Odell, Surveyor-General for Oregon, who was connected with the building of the Willamette Military Road. From Odell Lake scenic trips can be made by the Pacific Crest Trail and other trails to Waldo Lake, Gold Lake, Salt Creek Falls, and other beauty spots.

At the west end of Odell Lake, **23.7** *m.*, is a junction with the Pacific Crest Trail.

Left on the trail on foot or horseback along the summit of the Cascades to CRESCENT LAKE, **10** *m.*, and NIP AND TUCK LAKES, **15.5** *m.*, small bodies of water lying close together, and to the UMPQUA NATIONAL FOREST, **17.6** *m.* The far, eastern slopes of the Cascades are visible from a point along the Trail at **18.4** *m.*
From MAIDU LAKE, **27.8** *m.*, the route rises to an eminence disclosing a view, in broad panorama, of the plume-like forests, sharply uplifted buttes, ravines, and plains. The Umpqua Valley (R) is visible from another rise at 30 *m.*, a broad landscape framed by green pine boughs and mountain peaks.
The Pacific Crest Trail winds southward to the Thielsen Creek Trail and the junction with the Clearwater Automobile Road at 33 *m.*, roughly paralleling the Trail from the junction to DIAMOND LAKE, **37.9** *m.* (5,182 alt.), (*see CRATER LAKE*). Among the scenic southern Oregon lakes is Diamond Lake, encircled by wooded hills that rise in undulating stretches of forest green to the snow-clad peaks of MOUNT THIELSEN (9,178 alt.) and MOUNT BAILEY (8,356 alt.), (*lodge; cabins; fishing; boating; swimming; supplies; post office*).

At **23.9** *m.* is a junction with an improved dirt road.

Left on this road to SUMMIT LODGE, **1.5** *m.* (4,792 alt.), a picturesque inn built of lodgepole pines. (*Modern cabins; motor and rowboats for hire; excellent fishing*). This resort is a center for winter sports and offers fine skiing and snow-shoeing.

East boundary of the WILLAMETTE NATIONAL FOREST is at PENGRA PASS, **24.2** *m.* (5,128 alt.), named for B. J. Pengra, pioneer of 1853, one time Surveyor-General for Oregon, in charge of building the old Willamette Military Road (*see above*).

McCREDIE SPRINGS, **41** *m.* (2,079 alt., 19 pop.), on Salt Creek, is one of Oregon's older pleasure and health resorts centering about mineral springs. (*Cabins; hotel and post office; hot mineral baths; store; on Southern Pacific Railroad; June to September*).

At **50.7** *m.* is a junction with an improved road.

Right on this road to OAKRIDGE, **1.2** *m.* (1,208 alt., 400 pop.), (*tourist accommodations*). This town, named for the oak trees nearby, is the distributing point for a large area.

1. Right from Oakridge on the Salmon Creek Road to FLAT CREEK RANGER STATION, **1** *m.*, headquarters for Forest Service operations in this part of the Willamette National Forest. At SALMON CREEK FALLS, **4** *m.*, is an improved Forest Camp and a series of fishing pools. At **5.5** *m.* is BARK SHACK CAMP, from which the road continues to the Salmon Creek Trail leading to WALDO LAKE, **25.5** *m.*, near the summit of the Cascades.

2. Right from Oakridge on the Box Canyon Loop, open only in summer, to a junction with US 28, near Belknap Springs, **60** *m.* (*see TOUR 6b*).

FERRIN FOREST CAMP (*camping facilities*), **52.9** *m.*, is (L) near a picturesque bend in the Willamette River.

HELL GATE BRIDGE, **54.2** *m.*, spans the Middle Fork of the Willamette River, (*tourist accommodations*).

DECEPTION CREEK BRIDGE, **55.2** *m.*, is near a beautiful cascade in the river shadowed by balm trees growing on the gravel bars which contrast strangely with the somber evergreens on the mountainside. Balm buds, which are fragrant in the spring, were used by pioneers, who boiled them in tallow or lard to make a healing, fragrant salve.

MOSSY MAPLE FOREST CAMP, **65.1** *m.*, is situated in a sylvan spot on a gravel bar just below the highway, among old mosscovered maples from which it gets its name.

Willamette National Forest boundary is at **67** *m.*, and at **69.4** *m.* is a good view (L) of EAGLE'S REST, a high, rocky promontory on a forest-clad mountainside. Eagles once found it a safe nesting place.

DEXTER, **75.4** *m.*, is the center of an old community once known as Butte Disappointment (R), thus named because Elijah Bristow and five other men from the Pleasant Hill neighborhood, while pursuing a band of marauding Indians in 1848, were prevented by the swollen waters of the Willamette River from reaching the butte, where they expected to pick up the trail.

The PLEASANT HILL CEMETERY (R), **81.5** *m.*, is one of Oregon's oldest burial plots. Here lie many of the first settlers of Lane County, including Elijah Bristow, who founded and named the community of Pleasant Hill.

At **82** *m.* is a junction with a side road.

Left here to the SITE OF THE ELIJAH BRISTOW HOUSE, **0.5** *m.*, the first house in Lane County, built by Elijah Bristow, Oregon pioneer of 1846. He was a Virginian, a veteran of the War of 1812 and of the Creek Indian War. The site is now occupied by a farmhouse. The original Bristow home stood to the rear of this dwelling, at a point now occupied by a water tank mounted on a wooden tower.

PLEASANT HILL CHURCH, **82.1** *m.* (L), is the oldest church of the First Christian denomination in Oregon, organized by Elijah Bristow in August 1850 with 23 charter members. It was the center of early social and religious life and the Pleasant Hill Picnic, an annual event in June, owes its origin to the religious community life. An annual evangelistic meeting was early an important function. Converts of this denomination were taken to the nearby Coast Fork of the Willamette River for baptism. The ceremony was usually preceded by a dinner attended by settlers.

BRISTOW MEMORIAL FOUNTAIN, (L) **82.3** *m.,* constructed of stones and the mantelpiece taken from the original Bristow home fireplace, perpetuates the name of Pleasant Hill's founder. The drinking trough, a part of this memorial, which once provided thirsty animals with water, has long since dried up and is overgrown with ivy.

State 58 crosses the Coast Fork of the Willamette River on a bridge at **84.2** *m.,* the point where in early times converts from the Pleasant Hill Christian Church were baptized.

State 58 now enters the widening valley of the Coast Fork, or the Land O' Goshen, as it was originally called. From certain points of vantage on the highway, a vast bare spot, the exact shape of the continent of South America, is conspicuous on the side of distant WINBERRY MOUNTAIN (2,828 alt.), one of the peaks of the high Cascades. When snow whitened this area, Klamath Indians in the Willamette Valley picking hops and performing other labor, knew that it was time to start for their distant homes if they would reach them before the mountain passes were blocked. Thus, the mountain became known as The Barometer.

GOSHEN, 87 *m.,* is on US 99 (*see TOUR 2b*).

Tour 4D

Klamath Junction—Fort Klamath—Annie Spring Camp—Crater Lake —Prospect—Medford; 92.5 m.   State 62, the Crater Lake Highway.

Paved road; after severe snow storms road often temporarily closed.
Motor stages connect with the Great Northern and Southern Pacific Railroad at Klamath Falls and the Southern Pacific Railroad at Medford, during the Crater Lake Park season, July 1 to October 1.
Hotel at Fort Klamath and at resorts on the Rogue River; tourist cabins, forest camps.

The Crater Lake Highway is a main thoroughfare between eastern and western Oregon. On the route is Crater Lake National Park, which contains one of the most beautiful bodies of water in America. Through pine forests, that form an almost continuous aisle, the route crosses the crest of the Cascade Mountains, and descends the Rogue River, one of the famed fishing streams of the Northwest, to the valleys and orchard-covered hills of southern Oregon.

By the general course of an old military road, the highway traverses a section closely associated with the Rogue River and Modoc Indian wars. At Fort Klamath, near the eastern end of the route, the curtain was rung down on southern Oregon Indian disturbances; near the western end, the Indians began the warfare that was to last many years. Early settlers, miners, and travelers, from the first, met with vicious antagonism which was combatted, often with a severity that bordered on savagery.

State 62 diverges west from US 97 (see TOUR 4b) at KLAMATH JUNCTION, 0 m., and crossing WOOD RIVER, 1 m. (4,174 alt.), reaches FORT KLAMATH, 1.5 m. (4,184 alt., 100 pop.), trade center of a cattle raising district, and a depot for large quantities of raw furs taken from animals trapped in the adjacent marshes. (Hotel and service station; winter sports headquarters) The village is surrounded by quaking aspens with an evergreen background interspersed by fields of red clover.

FORT KLAMATH PICNIC GROUNDS (R), 5.8 m., has a spacious public swimming pool. At 6.7 m. a boundary of the ROGUE RIVER NATIONAL FOREST is crossed, and at 7.2 m. is ANNIE CREEK FOREST CAMP (R).

The SKI JUMP, 7.3 m. (R), is the center of the Crater Lake winter sports festivals, which include ski jumping and snowshoe contests and the finish of Alaska dog-team races started at Klamath Falls. The events take place in February on two days which include the Sunday nearest Washington's birthday.

The southern entrance to CRATER LAKE NATIONAL PARK is at 7.7 m. (see CRATER LAKE). State 62 swings into the park grounds to COLD SPRINGS CAMP, 15.2 m., and ANNIE SPRING CAMP, 17.9 m. (6,016 alt.). Annie Creek and Spring were named in 1865, for Annie Gaines, one of the two white women first to descend to the edge of Crater Lake. (All incoming automobiles are registered here.)

Right from the camp on State 209 to the Crater Lake Lodge, 6 m., (see CRATER LAKE).

At CASCADE DIVIDE, 18.1 m. (6,201 alt.), summit of the range, is WHITE HORSE CAMPGROUND (L).

State 62 descends rapidly through forests of young pine and, near the west boundary of the Park, 24.7 m., passes through growths of fir, hemlock, and spruce.

WHISKEY CREEK, 27.9 m., a tributary of the Rogue River, was the scene of a skirmish, in 1855, between volunteer troops and a band of Indians. The creek is said to have been named after a bootlegger, who in 1865 planned to take a load of whiskey from Jacksonville over the mountains to Fort Klamath. Snow impeded his progress and he buried his load for the winter. When he returned in the spring he found that his cache had been discovered by soldiers from Fort Klamath. At 34 m. is a junction with State 230.

Right on State 230 to DIAMOND LAKE, 27 m. (see *CRATER LAKE*).

At 34.3 m. is FAREWELL BEND FOREST CAMP (R).

The ROGUE RIVER GORGE is seen (R) at 35 m. Here the Rogue River, circling a rocky headland, plunges through an extremely narrow gorge from ledge to ledge in foaming cataracts. The fishing for rainbow, cutthroat and eastern brook trout is excellent from June to September.

UNION CREEK, 35.2 m., named from a nearby creek, is the point of departure for hiking and saddle trips to points of interest in the upper Rogue River area. (*Pack and saddle horses for hire.*) A ski run with shelter and fireplace is at this point.

At 35.3 m. is the UNION CREEK DISTRICT RANGER STATION (*information*).

At 35.5 m. is a junction with a forest road.

Right on this road to a NATURAL BRIDGE, 3.5 m.

Dominating the forest at 40.7 m. (R) is a MAMMOTH SUGAR PINE (*Pinus lambertiana*). A marker on the trunk states that the tree is 500 years old; the height 250 feet, the diameter 8 feet 7 inches, and the lumber content 29,400 board feet.

At 45.7 m. is a border of the Rogue River National Forest.

PROSPECT, 46.7 m. (2,598 alt., 125 pop.) (*accommodations*), was formerly called Deskins. The town was named for the operator of a pioneer sawmill built in the early 1870's. The machinery was packed in by mule from Red Bluff, California. Doors and window casings for old Fort Klamath were sawed by Deskin, also lumber for many houses in Jacksonville, at that time the metropolis of southern Oregon.

At 47.7 m. across the ravine (L), MILL CREEK FALLS drop over a high cliff as a finale to a succession of cascades.

SKOOKUM CREEK, at 48.7 m., is the location of the hydro-electric plant of the California-Oregon Power Company, which serves much of southern Oregon.

WILDWOOD CAMP is at 50.7 m., and CASCADE GORGE RESORT, with cabins and accommodations, is just east of the CASCADE GORGE BRIDGE, 53 m. McLEOD'S, 61.7 m. (1,538 alt.), is a wayside store.

At 62 m. a road leads left over Rogue River near the mouth of BIG BUTTE CREEK. At the headwaters of Little and Big Butte Creeks occurred a number of important engagements during the Indian wars of 1853-56. The encounters with troops occurred December 24, 1855, and it is said that only the squaws remained alive.

CASEY'S CAMP, 62.4 m., is a resort with cabins and accommodations for fishermen. At 65.7 m. is ROGUE ELK, another fishing resort (*hotel, service station and supplies*).

TRAIL, 68.8 m. (1,426 alt., 26 pop.), was named for the devious

Indian trail that wound along Trail Creek from the Rogue to the Umpqua River. It formed a short cut between an early military road and Roseburg. Trail Creek was the scene of an important engagement in the Indian wars of 1853-56. After a short fierce battle between Trail and Evans creeks, the Indians were forced back to Table Rock, at which place finally was made an important treaty, September 10, 1853, that was expected to end the Indian troubles (*see TOUR 2b*).

MEDFORD, 92.5 *m.* (1,374 alt., 11,007 pop.) (*see MEDFORD*), is at a junction with US 99 (*see TOUR 2b*).

||||||||||▷||||||||||▷||||||||||▷||||||||||▷||||||||||▷||||||||||▷||||||||||▷||||||||||▷||||||||||▷||||||||||▷||||||||||▷|||||||

Tour 5

(Pasco, Wash.)—Cold Springs Junction—Pendleton—Mount Vernon —Burns—Lakeview—(Alturas, Calif.) ; 393.6 m.   US 395.

Paved and gravel roads. Part of highway closed during heavy snows.
Union Pacific Railroad parallels route between Pendleton and Pilot Rock and between Seneca and Burns.
Hotel and tourist accommodations.

Section a.   Washington Line to Junction State 54; 236.8 *m.*   US 395

US 395, the Three Flags Route, is a section of a great highway system that crosses Canada, the United States, and Mexico. In Oregon it goes through the central part of the eastern section of the state, traversing great wheat-lands in the northern section, the forested slopes of the Blue Mountains and a high arid plateau, and penetrates one of the last cattle domains. With these mountains and the desert as background, the miner, the cattle king, the lumber baron, and the wheat rancher have played their adventurous roles and reaped the wealth of Oregon.

US 395 crosses the Washington Line, 0 *m.*, six miles south of Wallula, Wash. (*see WASHINGTON GUIDE*), and follows the south bank of the Columbia River between walls of columnar basalt that show many superimposed flows of lava marking the geologic ages, to COLD SPRINGS JUNCTION, 9.8 *m.* (363 alt.).

1. Right from Cold Springs Junction on US 730, which follows the Columbia River, to UMATILLA JUNCTION, 9.9 *m.*, at the junction with US 30 (*see TOUR 1a*).
2. Right from Cold Springs Junction, on the Cold Springs Landing Road, passing a railroad section house, a farmers' warehouse, and a school in the sagebrush, the only evidences of human activity, to COLD SPRINGS LANDING, 0.7 *m.*, on the banks of the Columbia. This road was built in the 1880's to

connect the developing wheat empire with a proposed boat landing for grain shipment from the surrounding country. The coming of the railroad made the landing unnecessary.

It was near this point that Astor's overland expedition, under Wilson Price Hunt, saw the Columbia River in January, 1812 (*see TOUR 1a*).

Southeast of Cold Springs Junction US 395 crosses a plateau that has reverted from a wheat-growing area to a typical Oregon desert, and descends into COLD SPRINGS CANYON.

HOLDMAN, 22.3 *m.* (1,000 alt., 30 pop.), under its canopy of locust trees, is a small agricultural settlement named for a pioneer family. South of Holdman is an extensive wheat-growing region.

From the crest of a hill at 33.8 *m.* is an extended view of a vast plateau, with its ocean-like fields of grain waving in the wind. The ranch houses stand back from the highway, each in a clump of trees with windmills rising above the tree-tops.

PENDLETON, 40.1 *m.* (1,070 alt., 6,621 pop.) *(see PENDLETON)*.

Points of Interest: Round-Up Park, Woolen Mills, Pioneer Park, Til Taylor Park, Umatilla County Courthouse, and others.

Pendleton is at the junction with US 30 (*see TOUR 1a*), which unites briefly in the town with US 395.

South of Pendleton US 395 climbs a low divide and drops down into the McKay Creek Valley. McKAY RESERVOIR (L), 46.3 *m.,* was built to provide additional irrigation water during the summer when the Umatilla River supplies insufficient water for the Furnish, Stanfield, and West Umatilla Irrigation Projects. The dam forms a lake three miles long, on which ducks and geese are protected by game laws.

PILOT ROCK, 55.1 *m.* (1,659 alt., 275 pop.), in Birch Creek Valley, is a grain-shipping town. It is named for a large basaltic bluff in the vicinity. The fields mark the southern boundary of the wheat region.

NYE, 63.2 *m.* (2,303 alt.), is at the junction with State 74 (*see TOUR 1b*).

BATTLE MOUNTAIN STATE PARK, 78.1 *m.* (4,167 alt.), covering 370 acres, near the top of the divide between the Umatilla and John Day rivers, commemorates the battle of Willow Springs, the last engagement with Indians in Oregon. Early in 1878 the Paiutes and Bannocks, who had attempted to form a confederacy of all the tribes of the Northwest to overthrow the whites, crossed from Idaho into Oregon, gathering renegades along the way, and created a reign of terror throughout the northeastern part of the state. On July 6, Gen. O. O. Howard, in command of the United States Army post at Vancouver, Washington, defeated Chief Egan, Paiute leader, and pursued his band down the Malheur River and out of Oregon.

At 89 *m.* is the junction with an improved gravel road.

Left on this road to UKIAH, 1.4 *m.* (3,347 alt., 100 pop.), the scene of an annual rodeo, which gives a realistic portrayal of the Old West. A district RANGER STATION of the Umatilla National Forest is here.

LEHMAN SPRINGS, 18 *m.* (*hotel and cabins; camping facilities; swimming*), is centered about hot sulphur springs. The springs are on the upper ridges of the Blue Mountains, which offer magnificent panoramas of the surrounding slopes, forested with yellow, mountain, and lodgepole pine.

South of Ukiah Junction US 395 follows tortuous Camas Creek to its confluence with the North Fork of the John Day River.

A boundary of the WHITMAN NATIONAL FOREST is crossed at 103.3 *m.,* at the North Fork of the John Day River. High mountain lakes and streams (*excellent campsites*) abound with fish. Elk, mule deer, and black and brown bear roam within its boundaries. Among the smaller creatures are beaver, marten, badger, ermine, and racoon.

DALE RANGER STATION, 103.6 *m.,* is the entry point for an extensive recreational area.

South of DALE (*service station and limited camping facilities*), 104.3 *m.* (2,918 alt.), the highway climbs a winding grade through a fine stand of yellow pine, and at 110.9 *m.* reaches the summit of the divide (4,127 alt.), between the drainage of the Middle and the North Fork of the John Day River. In the northern part of Grant County range several hundred elk, one of the largest herds in the state, preserved by rigid protection.

The Middle Fork of the John Day River, crossed on a concrete bridge at 116.7 *m.,* flows through a deep gorge, which opens into a forest growth wherever a piece of level ground will support a tree.

LONG CREEK, 129.6 *m.* (3,757 alt., 139 pop.), lies in a beautiful saucer-shaped valley, with the northern ramparts of the John Day River gorge towering along the southern horizon. It is surrounded by one of the last cattle raising areas. During the 1880's and 1890's Long Creek was a typical western cow town with one to three shootings a week.

Left from Long Creek to GALENA, 12 *m.,* in the center of a region rich in Galena ore. In the 1860's the mines were worked extensively, and are now active.
At 21.5 *m.* is the junction with an unimproved road. L. on this road 3 *m.,* to SUSANVILLE, former mining center, named in 1862 by a group of miners, who came into the country during the gold rush from Susanville, California.

From the summit of the divide (4,711 alt.), between Long and Smith creeks, 134.7 *m.,* is a view of the bowl of Long Creek Valley, with mesas and rimrocks lifting until they merge into the Blue Mountains. To the south the Aldrich and Strawberry ranges form a jagged line across the horizon with the tree-lined Fox Valley in the foreground.

FOX, 137.6 *m.* (4,390 alt., 20 pop.), in a stock-raising area, was named for Fox Creek, tributary of the North Fork of the John Day River. Fox was the center of mining activity in the 1880's, when Black Butte and other territory surrounding Fox Valley were prospected during a two-year gold rush.

BEECH CREEK, 139.7 *m.* (4,450 alt., 42 pop.), near the headwaters of Beech Creek, named for a pioneer who lived near its mouth, is a small trading center for a sparsely settled cattle country.

MOUNT VERNON, 159.9 m. (2,896 alt., 75 pop.), trading center of a farming and cattle country, is at the junction with US 28 (*see TOUR 6a*). Between Mount Vernon and JOHN DAY, 168.3 m. (3,083 alt., 432 pop.) (*see TOUR 6a*), US 395 and US 28 are united (*see TOUR 6a*).

South of John Day US 395 winds up Canyon Creek, which proved to be so rich in gold dust and nuggets, that $8,000,000 was taken from its muddy waters in one decade. Now the diggings are scars on the canyon walls. Huge water-smoothed boulders, left when the soil was removed by hydraulic mining operations, lie along the creek and desolate the once beautiful valley.

CANYON CITY, 170.5 m. (3,194 alt., 268 pop.), seat of Grant County, was born in 1862 of the camp that sprang up on Canyon Creek following the discovery of gold on Whiskey Flat, a half-mile north of the present town, by a party of miners searching for the fabled "Blue Bucket Mine" (*see TALL TALES AND LEGENDS*). At the height of the gold rush about 10,000 miners and their camp followers trooped up and down the one street of Whiskey Gulch.

The street was choked with pack trains bringing in supplies. The Pony Express galloped into camp three times a week from The Dalles, 225 miles away, after having crossed swollen rivers, parched desert stretches, and mountain defiles that concealed lurking Indians. Later a freight service was inaugurated to carry supplies to the miners and gold dust from the diggings three times a week between the two cities over the old Dalles Military Road (*see TOUR 6a*).

Clashes between unionist Oregon miners and the confederate California element, added to the white heat of the gold excitement. When the California miners raised the Confederate flag on REBEL HILL (L) above the camp, on July 4, 1863, the Oregon men stormed up it and tore the flag down.

Although a fire in 1937 destroyed many of the old landmarks, weathered buildings still stand on the high banks of Canyon Creek. Above them in the rimrock is a CEMETERY, set aside for the "bad men."

In June, Canyon City is the scene of the Whiskey Gulch Celebration, and meeting place of the Grant County Pioneer Association. On the courthouse lawn the oldest woman resident is honored and the oldest man resident decorated with a gold badge.

The JOAQUIN MILLER CABIN (*apply at courthouse for admittance*), hidden (L) from the highway on a hill, is a four-room structure restored to appear much as it was when occupied by the poet. Within the cabin are a bellows organ, photographs of the Miller family, an old flag with thirty-eight stars, crude furniture, and other pioneer relics. Cincinnatus Heiner (Joaquin) Miller (*see LITERATURE and TOUR 2A*) came to the Willamette Valley from Indiana in 1854. In 1864 he bought a band of cattle and with his wife and baby crossed the Cascades and settled in the new mining camp at Canyon City. The first orchard in the settlement consisted of trees brought on pack animals by Miller and planted at the rear of the cabin. They still bear fruit.

In 1907 Joaquin Miller after many years' absence returned to Canyon City where he wrote *A Royal Highway of the World,* a letter written to the judges and commissioners of Grant and Harney counties, protesting against the muddy "six-foot Indian trail" between Canyon City and Burns that served as a road. It was so smothered in brush that the stage drivers were compelled to carry axes to lop off the undergrowth. South of Canyon City US 395 follows this route, now called the Joaquin Miller Highway.

At the CHARLES BROWN SERVICE STATION, near the upper end of Main Street, is a collection of old freighter bells and other mementoes of the mining days.

At **174.4** *m.* is (L) the CANYON CREEK GAME REFUGE (*hunting by bow and arrow only permitted*), an area of about '130 square miles and one of the few archers' preserves in the United States.

The MALHEUR NATIONAL FOREST, **176.8** *m.,* embraces a great part of the Strawberry Range of the Blue Mountains.

At **178.5** *m.* is the JOAQUIN MILLER RESORT (*tourist cabins and campsites; pack horses and guides*), a small recreational camp.

Left from the resort to the WICKIUP CAMP, 8 *m.,* which the forest service is developing at the mouth of Wickiup Creek for hunters and fishermen.

On a plateau that is more than 5,000 feet in elevation is one of the largest stands of ponderosa pine that remain in the West. Their straight orange or sepia trunks rise to lofty heights. Tags indicate the mature or decadent trees which may be felled for lumber. This method of cutting in cycles based on an estimate that 60 years will elapse before seedlings are timber size should provide a continuous yield.

STARR FOREST CAMP, **184.6** *m.* (5,159 alt.), is at the summit of the divide between the John Day and the Silvies rivers. Driveways for stock are often visible. From 100 yards to a quarter of a mile in width, they usually follow the high ridges. The forest service posts the center line of the driveway and sometimes the side-lines within which stockmen are required to keep their animals and to cover a certain mileage each day.

BEAR VALLEY, **193.4** *m.* (L), was the setting for a range war between cowmen and sheepmen that flared a quarter of a century ago, when a sheep herder taking his flock to graze across a line laid in the dust by cattlemen was murdered and his band of 1,500 sheep slaughtered. It is also the scene of several cowboy stories by Ernest Haycox, Oregon author.

SENECA, **194.3** *m.* (4,668 alt., 275 pop.), near the mouth of Bear Creek, is a logging and milling center for a yellow-pine lumbering region. Some of the timber is shipped to Bend for sawing. A temporary camp (R) shelters the Indians hired by the logging company. The untidy tents, with stovepipes through their tops, are pitched on the banks of the willow-bordered creek.

South of Seneca, the Silvies Valley is dotted with ranches that are the winter feeding grounds for great herds of cattle. Often as early as October, cattle ranchers begin to feed their stock. Wagons are loaded at stacks of wild or cultivated hay and then driven to the corrals or fields. When it snows runners are used and another team or two of horses added. After a heavy snow, or during a blizzard, the cow hands struggle from early daylight until dark through drifts sometimes as high as the horses' backs to make the rounds and help the hungry and nearly frozen cattle.

The Silvies River, a stream that drains Grant and Harney counties, was named for Antonine Sylvailles, who with a party of trappers, was sent into central Oregon by Peter Skene Ogden in 1826 and reported finding the river rich in beavers.

SILVIES, 204.5 m. (4,587 alt., 50 pop.), is a supply point for the valley. At 216.9 m. a boundary of the Malheur National Forest is crossed. A superb growth of yellow pine free of underbrush makes this region an upland park.

The route climbs to an elevation of 5,000 feet, passes CROWFLAT RANGER STATION, 218.4 m., and traverses a burned-over area, in which the scorched trees with orange trunks stand like giant paint brushes. The JOAQUIN MILLER FOREST CAMP is at 220.4 m., and at the summit is IDLEWILD FOREST CAMP, 222.6 m. (5,342 alt.),

At the head of Devine Canyon is the JOHN DEVINE MONU-MENT 223.7 m., erected in 1928 of cobblestone, with a bronze plaque and a fountain. One of the cattle barons of the 1870's and 1880's, Devine was a familiar figure of Harney County as he jolted over dusty or muddy roads in a high rocker-spring buggy. In 1871 he rode into Oregon from California on a prancing white horse with silver-mounted trappings, his attire that of a Spanish don—a wide-brimmed black hat, tight trousers, and a bolero jacket. Backed by a Sacramento capitalist he bought large tracts of swamp land which the state of Oregon was selling for $1.25 an acre, only ten per cent of which was needed to obtain possession. Ranchers at the foot of Steens Mountain were bought out and additional land accumulated until Devine and his partner held about 150,000 acres.

A popular method of acquiring land during the homesteading period was the "dummy" entry, whereby a person would live on a piece of land for the length of time required by law to gain possession of it and then move his house on wheels to another location. Devine followed another course. He applied for a purchase in the name of some person in the region and then certified it as a notary public. The state land office mailed the grant to Devine who immediately transferred it to the name of his partner. The persons whose names had been used never suspected that they had applied for land and Devine's partner never knew he had so much land in his name. Other parts of his holding were properly acquired by buying out smaller ranchers.

But Devine's empire did not last long. The state legislature declared illegal the patent to the swamp land which he had bought and opened it for sale. Speculators grabbed it and Devine had to buy them out. In 1888 and 1889 the rivers dried up and the ranges became arid. Cattle died by the thousands. It was then that the partnership became bankrupt. Henry Miller bought the property and employed the former owner to manage it. When Miller saw that the man he had hired could not take orders from anyone else, he gave back to Devine the 6,000 acre Alvord Ranch (*see TOUR 5A*), at the base of Steens Mountain and there Devine passed his last years.

Emerging from the forest at 225.4 *m.*, the highway drops down Devine Canyon, above which pinnacled rocks rise like chimneys. In Harney Valley scattered juniper takes the place of the luxuriant forest growths. South of the confluence of Devine Canyon and Poison Creek, 231.4 *m.*, the highway parallels a logging railroad.

At 233.5 *m.*, is a panorama of the Harney Valley, an apparently boundless reach of space and sunshine. This great valley has been the scene of much colorful drama of the Oregon cattle kings, whose traditions remain in a number of historic ranches scattered over the valley. This area of 2,500 square miles, a former lake bottom of arid and semi-arid land reaching to the dim horizon of hazy desert hills, lies in the northern end of Harney County (*see TOUR 7a*). Against the southeastern horizon looms snow-crested Steens Mountain.

At 236.8 *m.* is the junction with State 54 (*see TOUR 7a*), with which US 395 is united for 29.5 miles (*see TOUR 7a*).

*Section b. Western junction with State 54 to California Line,
127.3 m. US 395*

This section of US 395 passes through the heart of the old range country. It was here that the cattle frontier made its last stand. The kingdom of rope and branding iron has fallen, but a number of isolated ranches remain more or less as they were three quarters of a century ago, though the region is now largely given over to the raising of sheep.

California cattlemen were attracted to Oregon by the excellent grazing grasses and in the late 1860's large holdings were acquired in Harney and Malheur counties. The most powerful of the cattle barons was Henry Miller (1827-1916), a German immigrant who started out as a butcher in San Francisco. He became interested in the cattle business and in 1858 formed a partnership with Charles Lux that lasted until Lux's death in 1887. They accumulated a million acres and more than a million head of cattle, mainly because of Miller's grasping, thrifty and indomitable nature and his ability to outwit competitors. It was said that he could travel from the Kern River in California, up through Nevada, to the Malheur River region in Oregon without spending a night off of his land.

One day Miller was riding through very rough country with a large sum of money in his saddle bags and was suddenly confronted by a bandit who took the cash. When Miller explained that he was going on a long journey and would have to buy food, the bandit handed back twenty dollars. Some days later Miller was in a saloon when a group of rough men entered and ordered drinks. As soon as one of them spoke Miller recognized the voice of the robber, and went over and tapped him on the elbow. When the bandit turned around Miller handed him some money and said, "This is the twenty dollars you so kindly loaned me." The cattleman left before the bandit realized what had happened.

The organization he built was closely knit, and besides cattle, included two banks and their branches, reservoirs, and thousands of miles of irrigation canals. Under his guidance grasses and livestock breeds were cultivated and a great industry developed. Small ranchers were benefited by his canals and advice on farming and raising cattle, and towns sprung up on land that had been arid but was reclaimed and made productive through his efforts. After Miller's death his son-in-law, J. Leroy Nickel, became head of the organization.

There were also the dynamic Peter French and William Hanley, the last of the cattle barons, who selected Harney Valley where he could "look a long way out and a long way up." His career spanned a major portion of the period that saw the rise and fall of the cattle barons. At the time of his death (September, 1935), he ranked as the only individual stockman who had retained sizeable holdings. The others had given way to corporations.

This section is dotted with beds of lakes formed by the upthrust of the Cascades. Some lakes evaporated, others found outlets, or were clogged by showers of volcanic ashes. Many contain water during the brief rainy season, while others are always dry. Lakes that do not disappear completely during the summer shrink to small bodies of water surrounded by white alkali shores. Others retain only enough moisture to become meadows.

WAGONTIRE, 28.4 m. (4,725 alt., 7 pop.), was named for WAGONTIRE MOUNTAIN (6,504 alt.), a few miles to the northwest. The mountain was so named because a wagon tire lay for many years beside the road on its slope. Near the summit are bountiful springs. The mountain has been the scene of water-hole feuds between cattlemen and homesteaders who attempted to fence the springs from the public domain. The disputes were settled by the federal government.

ALKALI LAKES (R), 48.5 m., is dry except when winter rains form small pools in the gray-white soil. On the horizon are a number of craggy buttes and small mountains.

ALKALI STATE SECTION STATION (no drinking water between this point and Valley Falls) is at 50.4 m. South of the station is a desolate valley of sagebrush, greasewood, and rabbit brush. Wind blows across the waste incessantly and heaps the sand into dunes. Occasionally a small band of antelope races through the sagebrush. Along the rocky arroyos, lizards and rattlers sun themselves.

ABERT RIM (L), 75 m., a striking formation, extends for 19 miles along the eastern edge of Abert Lake. It rises 2,000 feet above the plateau, with an 800-foot lava cap that ends in a sheer precipice.

The scarp is an almost perfect fault and one of the largest exposed faults in the world. The summit of Abert Rim is a plateau, which slopes gradually to the east, with a fringe of pines and wide areas of grazing land beyond. The forest service maintains a LOOKOUT STATION (*accessible by horseback*) on one of the high points.

At one place at the base of Abert Rim, on huge boulders, are crude pictographs, rock foundations of primitive huts, arrowheads, and occasionally a skeleton. There is a legend that an Indian band drove a party of whites across the level upland of the plateau and, unsuspectingly, over the cliff. Relics of broken wagons, guns, and a few scattered bones that have been found in years past, give credence to the tale. Camel and rhinoceros fossils and many others have been found in the region of Abert Lake.

Lieutenant Fremont and his party discovered Abert Lake and Rim on December 20, 1843 (*see TOUR 5C*), in their search for the mythical Buena Ventura River that was supposed to flow from Klamath Lake into San Francisco Bay. They were named in honor of Colonel J. J. Abert, a U. S. topographical engineer and Fremont's chief. Once upon the summit, the exploring party stood with all of central Oregon before them. To the north and west they gazed across rolling hills, towering rimrock, and deep valleys; to the east over the great chain of lakes in the Warner Valley; and to the south toward California.

When Fremont saw it, Abert Lake was 50 square miles of water, but in years when precipitation has been below normal, it has been completely dry. The lake, like many others in central Oregon, is potentially rich in mineral deposits, vast quantities of soda and borax being found in its sands.

VALLEY FALLS, 89.9 *m.* (4,321 alt., 45 pop.), is named for the falls of the Chewaucan River. The surrounding valley is the scene of a vast cattle round-up each year (*see TOUR 5C*). Valley Falls is at the junction with State 31 (*see TOUR 5C*).

CHANDLER STATE PARK, 95.5 *m.,* was given to the state by Mr. and Mrs. S. B. Chandler in 1929.

West of the park is a low pass called Juniper Crest (4,960 alt.), from which the eastern ramparts of the Cascade range (R) are visible.

At 107.9 *m.* is the junction with the Warner Creek Road.

Left on this road over a divide and down into the Warner Valley to ADEL, 28.5 *m.* (4,542 alt., 100 pop.), the trading center for the South Warner Valley, in the heart of a vast range country.

Left from Adel to PELICAN LAKE, 30 *m.,* and CRUMP LAKE, 35 *m.,* known for the vast numbers of wild swans during the winter months. Near Crump Lake, at the narrows of the valley, is a stone CAUSEWAY built by the soldiers of Gen. George Creel, Indian campaigner, to transport his equipment to a post on the other side of the lake. Broken arrowheads are reminders of Indian battles in this region. PLUSH, 46.6 *m.* (4,515 alt., 25 pop.), is a North Warner Valley trading point and the center of a livestock region.

Right from Plush to FLAGSTAFF LAKE, 58 *m.,* and the HART MOUNTAIN ANTELOPE REFUGE, 67.2 *m.,* a federal reserve for many species of wild animals and birds. It was established in 1930 by the state and taken over in 1936 by the federal government. HART MOUNTAIN (8,020 alt.) is the principal feature of the refuge, but the area is far more extended. The mountain was named for the heart-shaped brand of a former cattle ranch at its base. The cowboys misspelled the word.

The refuge contains about 200,000 acres of mountain and plateau country. The mountain sides and canyons are clothed with groves of aspen and yellow pine. A herd of 10,000 prong-horned antelope, the largest herd in the United States, flourishes under protection of federal and state laws. They graze over the plateau and are sometimes visible in large bands from the highway. Mule deer also inhabit the refuge, and their number has grown to several thousand during the past few years.

The Order of Antelope, organized around a campfire in the reserve in 1932 for the purpose of protection and perpetuation of the fleet-footed animals, holds an annual outing on the rugged slopes of Hart Mountain. Membership and participation in the outing is limited to "kindred souls." The 1938 convention was attended by about 150 men, all with a background of wild-life activities.

Coneys or Pikas, tiny cousins of the rabbit, are among the smaller creatures that inhabit the slide rocks along the canyon rims. They live on grass and weeds, which they gnaw down to dry in the sun and store for their food during the winter. At the approach of rain, they hide their hay under sheltering rocks to keep it dry. Other small animals are rabbits, porcupines, chipmunks, and squirrels. Bobcats and coyotes frequent the range to prey on them, but federal hunters keep their number at a minimum.

Among the species of bird life are sage hens, golden eagles, hawks, falcons, great horned owls, sage sparrows, red-winged blackbirds, meadow-larks, hummingbirds, western tanagers, finches, chickadees, woodpeckers, warblers, fly-catchers, and wrens.

From LYON RANCH, 74 *m.,* several dirt roads and trails diverge into the several corners of the refuge.

East from Lyon Ranch the route crosses high sage plains to a junction with State 205 at BLITZEN, 110 *m.* (*see TOUR 5B*).

HUNTER'S HOT SPRINGS, (R) 110.3 *m., (cabins; fishing and swimming),* containing chlorine, the only GEYSER in Oregon that spouts continuously, is at the northern edge of Lakeview. On windless days the column of water rises 40 feet. In the geyser pool wild ducks and geese find refuge. Here is an attractive HOTEL, the center of a health resort.

LAKEVIEW, 112.8 *m.* (4,800 alt., 1,799 pop.), seat of Lake County, headquarters of the Fremont National Forest, and site of a government land office, was established in 1876 on the site of the old Bullard Cattle Ranch. It was for many years a "cow town," and while still a trading center for a large cattle and sheep industry, it now has a box factory, five sawmills, planing mills, and other wood-working plants. This attractive city, is four miles from the northern end of Goose Lake, on a level plain.

Before any white men were known to have penetrated the Goose Lake country the Hudson's Bay Company had assembled such complete data from unknown sources that Colonel J. J. Abert, U. S. topographical engineer, was able to prepare a reasonably accurate map of the section in 1838, five years before Captain John C. Fremont made his exploring journey.

When the southern migrant route leading from the Oregon Trail, was opened in the middle 1840's, the wagon trains were so ravaged by Indians that in 1849 troops under Colonel William H. Warner were sent to subdue them. The command was ambushed and Colonel Warner killed. In spite of the continued efforts of troops the country was so dangerous that for many years no settler ventured into it.

After the Indians were sent to the reservation, in 1871, the region became a vast cattle range, which joined the equally vast grazing area of central Oregon. Then came the range wars between the cattlemen and sheep raisers. No one will ever know how many men were assassinated and how many sheep were slaughtered before the government ended the strife by establishing the Fremont Forest and opening the disputed grazing lands to homesteaders.

The early government land office was the scene of many stirring episodes connected with the opening of the public domain, such as T. M. Overfelt's sensational horseback ride from the Silvies River to Lakeview, to attend the government land sale of the valuable Agency Ranch (*see TOUR 7a*), of which he and his partner, Henry Miller, did not learn until the last moment. By relaying from ranch to ranch, he covered the distance of nearly 200 miles, in less than 24 hours, arriving in time to outbid his two competitors, only to have his check refused, though it was later honored by the government.

In 1900 Lakeview was destroyed by fire, only the courthouse and the Methodist church surviving the flames. The town was soon rebuilt with brick business blocks, water, and electric systems.

Because of his affection for the town, Dr. Bernard Daly, pioneer physician, who died in 1920, formed a trust fund of his great fortune, which was to be used to educate "all worthy children" of Lake County. For a number of years all children of the county were educated, but the demand on the foundation became so great that since 1928 the trustees have been compelled to limit the number.

Lakeview's annual Rodeo, in September, draws spectators and participants from a wide area.

Lakeview is at the junction with State 66 (*see TOUR 5D*).

US 395 crosses the California Line in the center of NEW PINE CREEK, 127.3 *m.* (4,700 alt., 142 pop.), 39 miles north of Alturas, California *(see CALIFORNIA GUIDE, TOUR 6).*

Tour 5 A

Burns—Lawen—Crane—Follyfarm—Fields—Denio—Nevada Line; 154.3 m. State 78 and unnumbered roads.

A gravel road, frequently closed during heavy snows; south of Crane dirt roads usually impassable after a heavy rain. Water available only at settlements.
The Oregon Short Line Railroad parallels route between Burns and Crane.
Accommodations meager.

State 78 follows the Silvies River and skirts the eastern end of Malheur Lake, crossing the nearly level floor of the Harney Basin. Swinging southward the route crosses a desolate area bordering the eastern scarp of Steens Mountain. For many miles there are few traces of human habitation or animal life, except an occasional jackrabbit scampering across the road, a sandhill crane on a dune, or an eagle soaring over the rimrock. Except for the rare patches of wild hay and alfalfa of the valleys, the only vegetation is bunch grass, sagebrush, rabbit brush, and juniper, with an occasional row of Lombardy poplars. At the southern end, the route penetrates the district of the borax development of the last century.

Branching from US 395 at Burns, **0** *m.*, *(see TOUR 5a)*, State 78 crosses the SILVIES RIVER, **0.9** *m.*, and continues through a partially irrigated area.

LAWEN, **16.7** *m.* (4,101 alt., 50 pop.), was named for Henry Lauen, a settler of 1867. This settlement, with a white schoolhouse, was on the shore of Malheur Lake before it receded. The lake, four miles south, is now part of the Malheur Migratory Bird Refuge, established by executive order, August 18, 1908, when the government set aside 95,155 acres. Since then the "P" Ranch, a 65,000-acre tract formerly owned by Peter French, has been obtained, and with the acquisitions now in progress the total acreage of the refuge will be 169,775. Two C.C.C. camps are maintained and to prevent the lake from overflowing an extensive dike and canal system has been constructed. The dike, 70 feet wide at the base and 20 feet at the top, runs in a north and south direction for ten miles.

Each summer large numbers of redheads, ruddy ducks, mallards, gadwalls, cinnamon teal, pintails, shovelers, and blue-winged teal nest on the refuge. In addition there are sandhill cranes, pelicans, terns, gulls, egrets, herons, ibises, and grebes. About 100 mule deer and many antelope are in the refuge and it is well-stocked with beavers, racoons, minks, and muskrats.

South of Lawen is an arid ranch country, sparsely cultivated. Wind mills rise above the few weathered habitations, and strands of wire divide the desert ranches. The level sage-covered valley extends for miles in every direction.

CRANE, 28.5 *m*. (4,132 alt., 275 pop.), is a shipping point for cattle, sheep, and wool, and for wild horses, used for feed and fertilizer. The town supports the only Union High School in the county outside of Burns. For many years, Crane was the terminus of the Oregon Short Line Railroad, and flourished as trade center for the region. This sun-parched settlement was named for Crane Creek, to the east of the town, a nesting place for sandhill cranes.

South of Crane the route follows dirt roads, traversing desolate stretches of sagebrush and scattered bunch grass.

At 39.5 *m*. is the junction with an unimproved road.

Right on this road to PRINCETON, 1 *m.*, four houses in the dry Virginia Valley. It was named for Princeton, Massachusetts, by a musician who arrived here in 1910.

South of the junction the route climbs through low MALHEUR GAP, 49.3 *m.*, to a junction with a dirt road, 54.2 *m*.

Left on this road across a sage covered flat to the MALHEUR CAVE (R), 2.8 *m.*, on Indian Creek, a tunnel-like passage about one mile long, averaging 50 feet in width, and from 10 to 25 feet high, with a symmetrically arched ceiling. The surface of walls and ceiling resembles glazed pottery, and evidently was subjected to intense heat in ages past. Of quaternary basaltic formation, the walls present a beautifully mottled effect, ranging from ebony through shades of gray and bronze to a brilliant red. From the entrance, the floor of the cavern inclines for the first 200 feet then swerves to the northeast for a half-mile. The other half-mile of the grotto is filled with remarkably clear water; neither inlet nor outlet has been discovered and swimmers feel no current. Malheur Cave presents a rare phenomenon, in that during the winter ice stalagmites are formed without the usual stalactites.

The Paiute Indians formerly used the cave as a fort and refuge. Evidences of Indian entrenchments still remain. The entrance has been walled with stone, and stone breastworks form secondary lines of defense. Spearheads, arrowheads, mortar stones, and other evidences of Indian occupancy have been found near the cave.

South of the junction the road swings eastward around INDIAN CREEK BUTTE, 61.7 *m*. This is a region of rimrock and broken crags (*drive carefully*). At intervals snow fences line the road. South-eastward, over arid reaches of scattering sage and juniper, appear the distant Cedar Mountains.

In the vicinity of FOLLYFARM (*store, service station*), 66.7 *m*. (4,068 alt.), J. N. Neal unsuccessfully attempted to irrigate his land. He humorously called the place Neal's Folly, which soon became Follyfarm.

The route continues along the western side of the low, rolling SHEEPHEAD MOUNTAINS to ALBERSON, 79.7 *m*. (4,185 alt.), on Juniper Lake (R). A wide-spreading plateau country, broken by buttes and barren hills, marks the STEENS MOUNTAIN GAME REFUGE, established for the protection of game animals.

Westward rises the precipitous fault scarp of STEENS MOUN-TAIN (9,354 alt.), whose massive, rugged bulk dominates the landscape for 50 miles, rising nearly a mile above the surrounding plateau. It is really a range, with snow-covered crests, slopes clothed with sparse growths of juniper and sagebrush, and cataracts pouring through small canyons to the lowlands. The eastern scarp rises steeply to the summit and slopes gently westward for 25 miles to the breaks of the Donner und Blitzen River (*see TOUR 5B*). Forty-two flows of lava are visible on the sheer eastern side of the mountain. The western declivity is well-watered by a network of streams that unite and flow into Malheur Lake.

The Basque herders of this region take their sheep to summer pastures far up in the Steens, which also shelter much wild life, deer especially, and, to the westward, herds of antelope.

The range was named for Major Enoch Steen, head of an expedition, which, in 1860, drove a band of Snake Indians to the summit, then annihilated them.

At the base of the long escarpment of Steens Mountain is (L) the ALVORD RANCH, 102.5 *m.* (4,246 alt.), one of the colorful old cattle ranches of Harney County, comprising about 25,000 acres. The jagged snowy crest of Steens Mountain, rising on one side, and the Alvord Desert, melting into the purple haze of the Wild Horse Mountains on the other, give the place isolation. Deer sometimes leap fences into the meadows and graze with the cattle.

In 1864 a troop of the First Oregon Cavalry under Capt. George B. Curry rode along the edge of the desert and entered this oasis, the only green spot of any size in many square miles of arid country. The men found what they were seeking, a winter campsite, with acres of grass, horse-high, undulating in the autumn wind and named it for Maj. Benjamin Alvord, at that time commander of the Department of Oregon. The old ranch house is built on the supposed site of Captain Curry's camp.

In the 1870's John Devine (*see TOUR 5a*) bought up the Alvord region but went bankrupt. He spent his last years here.

ANDREWS, 117.5 *m.* (4,154 alt., 60 pop.), a typical Basque settlement (*see TOUR 6A*), was named for an early cattle man. This remote little sheep station has but two or three stone buildings. Dark-eyed herders, innumerable sheep dogs, and foreign speech give the place an old-world atmosphere. Near the settlement, Wild Horse Creek empties into Alvord Lake (L), which during wet seasons overflows the southern margin of the Alvord Desert.

South of Andrews, the route enters the borax region, in which an interesting and lucrative industry was developed by the Rose Valley Borax Company. Chinese labor was used to gather the crude borax which lay in rich deposits over the dry lake beds. This was shoveled into vats and the refined solution was run off into crystallizing tanks. The crystals were dried and sacked, were shipped as pure borax to the factories. Between 1898 and 1902, 400 tons yearly were sent out of Oregon. In 1911, borax was still being shipped, but later competition with the California deposits caused the Oregon fields to be abandoned.

It is said that $10,000,000 worth of borax and soda remain in the fields.

FIELDS, **132** *m.* (4,244 alt., 30 pop.), at the junction with State 205, was named for Charles Fields, who, in the early 1860's, took up a homestead and established an overland stagecoach and freighting station. In frontier days the place was known as Fields Station. It now consists of a post office and general store. Fields is situated at the eastern end of Broad Valley, which separates Steens Mountain and the Pueblo Mountains. Superb panoramas of the two lofty mountain ranges, lost in desert haze, compensate for the gray sagebrush wastes of the plateau surrounding the town.

At **137** *m.* is a junction with a desert road.

Left on this road to the BORAX HOUSE, **0.3** *m.* on the rim of BORAX LAKE. It was erected in 1900 as living quarters, by Chinese laborers employed in working the deposits. Built of bricks made from residual borax remaining after the refining process, the only lumber materials in its construction, are window casings, doors, and rafters. Borax Lake, fed by a spring within the lake, has a temperature of 130° F., and carries a heavy percentage of borax.

At RED POINT SCHOOL, **146.6** *m.,* is a junction with an unimproved road.

Left on this road to the TROUT CREEK FOSSIL BEDS, **8** *m.* This area abounds in Tertiary floral fossils.

DENIO, **154.3** *m.* (4,245 alt., 50 pop.), on the Oregon-Nevada Line was named for Aaron Denion, who became the first postmaster in 1897. He also built the hotel, an adobe structure still standing. In the early days, Denio was a thriving town with nearly a thousand inhabitants. It was not unusual for 50 head of horses to be quartered in the corrals. Wool from the north was hauled through Denio by six-horse wagons, and borax trains of five wagons drawn by twenty mules, lurched through the dusty streets toward Winnemucca. Since the closing of the borax industry Denio has markedly declined.

Crossing the State Line at Denio, the route continues to Winnemucca, Nevada.

Tour 5 B

Burns—Narrows—Frenchglen—Blitzen—Fields; 119.7 m.   State 78. State 205.

Unimproved roads in the southern section; frequently impassable after heavy rains or snow storms.
Settlements and supply points scattered; water scarce. Accommodations very limited.

This route leads through a remote part of Harney County, between

Malheur and Harney lakes and along the western slopes of Steens Mountain. Much of the glamour of the Old West still lingers about this frontier territory that refuses to yield to civilization. Over a vast territory of sagebrush and scanty vegetation broken by mountain ranges, rimrock, tablelands, and barren hills, large herds of cattle graze, and in the more secluded valleys roam droves of wild horses. In recent years, great bands of sheep, under the industrious ownership of Spanish Basques, have overrun many of the old cattle ranges. The road lies through the large Government-owned Malheur Migratory Bird Refuge, which shelters many beautiful and rare varieties of wild life. The remoteness of the region, the ever-changing color of the desert landscapes, the limitless horizon, and the weird mirages, add fascination to the route.

Branching from US 395 (*see TOUR* 5) at BURNS, **0** *m.,* State 78 passes BURNS AIRPORT, **1.7** *m.;* R. here on State 205 to WRIGHT'S POINT, **12.2** *m.* (4,390 alt.). This gigantic fault across the floor of Harney Valley, extending as a sheer wall for 25 miles from east to west, was named for General Wright, Indian campaigner, who had a military camp in the vicinity (1865). It has a flat top, and, when viewed from Burns, appears somewhat like a huge railroad fill. The summit of the narrow ridge, only 300 feet wide, affords views of the Strawberry and Aldrich ranges, to the north, the Steens Mountain to the southeast, and the intervening bluffs, mesas, and foothills, covered with tawny sage and juniper trees.

Under the Carey Act, enacted by Congress, in 1894, a grant of 1,000,000 acres of arid land was made to Oregon (1901), with the proviso that the necessary irrigation should be developed and the land occupied and reclaimed by actual settlers. Under this provision, seven attempts were made to draw water from Silvies River, from Silver Creek, from Malheur Lake, and from artesian wells. But the desert prevailed, and by 1911, all projects filed on had been declared unfeasible, after which development rights were either cancelled or relinquished.

At **24.9** *m.* is a junction with an unimproved road.

Right on this road to the DOUBLE O RANCH, **17** *m.,* formerly owned by William Hanley (*see TOUR* 5*b*). With its 17,000 acres and its ranch buildings set under tall poplars, the Double O is one of the typical old time cattle ranches of Oregon. Through the front gate, eight miles from the front door, many famous people came to visit the genial frontiersman. His personality, philosophy, and devotion to the public welfare and the cause of wild life had made him a widely known character. Several lakes add interest to the great ranch and offer migratory birds a resting place in their airways from Alaska. Fed by warm springs, the lakes provide a haven during winter months. Wild swans, geese, ducks, herons, pelicans, and the rare and beautiful white egrets, so nearly exterminated by plume hunters, make this spot a favorite habitat.

NARROWS, **26.3** *m.* (4,110 alt., 20 pop.), is on the slender connecting link of land between HARNEY and MALHEUR LAKES, and when the lakes are filled this is the only point in the vicinity where a crossing may be made. A remarkable distinction between the two lakes is the difference in the properties of the waters. While Malheur is fresh and sweet, Harney is distinctly alkaline, due to the fact that the former is supplied with fresh water from the Silvies and Donner und Blitzen Rivers (*see below*), and the latter is fed principally by the overflow from Malheur Lake.

These lakes were discovered by Peter Skene Ogden, in 1826. Early arrivals named them the Bitter Lakes. In 1908, the area was set aside by President Theodore Roosevelt as a bird and game refuge, now known as the MALHEUR MIGRATORY BIRD REFUGE. In 1936, the Federal Government expanded the sanctuary at an expenditure of more than a million dollars. The present area is 159,872 acres. The lakes were always a favorite nesting ground for migratory birds. Mallards, geese, swans, night herons, pelicans, egrets, and many other varieties gather each season in numbers so vast that often their flights cloud the sky. (*Waterfowl hunted only at stated seasons by licensed persons outside the Refuge and never within its boundaries.*)

South of the Malheur lakes, State 205 follows up the DONNER UND BLITZEN RIVER, paralleling the Bird Refuge, which lies on both sides of the stream. In 1864, when a troop of cavalry under Col. George B. Curry, engaged in the Snake Indian War, the river was crossed during a storm, and given the German name for thunder and lightning.

At **45.7** *m.* is a junction with an improved dirt road.

Left on this road to the DIAMOND CRATERS, 6 *m.,* spectacular volcanic formations consisting of 20 craters that occupy an area of five square miles and are surrounded by approximately 30 square miles of lava of a recent flow. At 11.5 *m.* is DIAMOND (12 pop.), named for the cattle brand of the Diamond Ranch.

FRENCHGLEN, **63.7** *m.* (4,195 alt., 34 pop.), was the old headquarters of the P Ranch, one of the most colorful centers of Oregon's old riata kingdom. It was named for Peter French, a prominent and picturesque cattle baron, and his wife's family. The townsite is now included in the Malheur Bird Refuge.

In the early 1870's the youthful Peter French found the Blitzen Valley an amazing expanse of wild meadow. Stretching for 70 miles along the Blitzen River, from the foothills of Steens Mountain, 250 miles in any direction from a railroad, it was a cattlemen's paradise. The Blitzen tumbled down the rocky slopes of Steens Mountain to spread out lazily for many miles, between rimrock barriers, through the green marshlands, and into Malheur Lake. Peter French, who came from California to establish a cattle domain similar to that of the Spanish grandees, and who was the most loved and the most hated cattle king in southeastern Oregon, lived and died a glamorous figure in the days of the bitter cattle wars. For years, undisputed baron of a vast area, until the coming of the settlers, Peter French fought to retain his empire by the high-handed methods of the epoch. His daring and dominant personality made him an unforgettable figure. Stories of the P Ranch in the gun-fighting days of the Old West have become romantic lore of the rimrock. His vaqueros went armed and sometimes they were killed by concealed marksmen. On one occasion Peter French made a spectacular one-man stand against the Indians and put them to rout; on another, not so fortunate, he raced his mustang to the very door of his ranch house, with savages whooping at his heels. The noted trial and the acquittal of the settler who shot him down, in 1897, marked the twilight of the old cattle regime.

At his death, a portion of the ranch of 150,000 acres passed into the hands of a livestock company, and later was acquired by the Federal Government. In 1935, the remaining 65,000 acres were bought to add to the Malheur Bird Refuge, and the marshes have gone back to a state as primitive as in the days when their solitudes were disturbed only by wandering animals and wandering Indians.

South of Frenchglen, at 64.8 m., is a junction with a dirt road.

Right on this road to the RANCH HOUSE OF THE P RANCH, 1.2 m. Sheltered by tall poplars, the typical white frontier house, built by Peter French, is still standing.

CATLOW VALLEY, 66 m., is a vast, upland valley, once the bed of a lake, 75 miles long and 30 miles wide. From this valley and the Steens Mountain region many wild horses are driven out to the various shipping points. These splendid creatures, outlaws of the range, are swift and wary, and can only be captured by driving them into box canyons. The horse round-ups have occasionally been managed by airplane. At 76.4 m. is CATLOW, vestige of a once-prosperous village.

At 83.3 m. is a junction with a desert road.

Right from the junction 15 m. into the HART MOUNTAIN GAME RANGE (see TOUR 5b), a Federal Reserve for the protection of wild life.

BLITZEN, 83.7 m., is a typical old cattle town.

South of Blitzen are the dry GARRISON LAKES (L), 95.1 m., with the wide sweep of the Catlow Valley ending in the Steens Mountain foothills, above which tower the snow-covered peaks (L). Hart Mountain is a jagged silhouette against the western horizon (R).

FIELDS, 119.7 m. (4,244 alt., 30 pop.), called Fields Station when it was a Station-hotel on a frontier stage line, is at the junction with the Denio road (see TOUR 5A).

Tour 5C

Valley Falls—Paisley—Summer Lake—Silver Lake—Junct. with US 97; 120.6 m. State 31.

Paved or graveled road.
Stages daily between Lakeview and Lapine.
Accommodations limited.

The Fremont Highway follows in part the route traveled by Lieut. John C. Fremont on his journey of 1842-43. It crosses part of the great central Oregon plateau, a vast semi-arid upland, threading a course through a bewildering pattern of forests, deserts and sharply scarped peaks, a region old even as geologists reckon time. Lakes bone-dry or quick with shining water, sandy deserts billowing in chalky waves, grassy marshes, and green-wooded plateaus lie in its path.

State 31 diverges from US 395 at VALLEY FALLS (*see TOUR 5b*), **0** *m.*, and leads northwest up the valley of the Chewaucan (Ind., *place of the wild potato*) River, to THE NARROWS, **11.4** *m.*, a slender neck of land between stretches of the CHEWAUCAN MARSH. Many old Indian campsites and relics have been found near-by. The marsh covers a wide area with the rich green of hay fields breaking against black swampy soil. Herds of cattle wade deep in the wild grasses around the waterholes. Clustered about this oasis in the desert are cattle ranches. Brands of the cattlemen painted in tall figures on the roofs of barns and seared into the hides of living stock, indicate that this is still a vital section of the traditional West.

Fremont reported under date of December 19, 1843: "It [the marsh] was covered with high reeds and rushes, and large patches of ground had been turned up by the squaws in digging for roots, as if a farmer had been preparing the land for grain. I could not succeed in finding the plant for which they had been digging. There were frequent trails, and fresh tracks of Indians; and from the abundant signs visible, the black-tailed hare (jackrabbit) appears to be numerous here. It was evident that in other seasons this place was a sheet of water."

The plant to which Fremont referred is the wild camas, a bulbous plant that was used extensively by the Indians, but which has been supplanted in modern times by the potato. The Chewaucan Marshes are now partially drained and are used as pastures and hay lands.

The ZX CATTLE COMPANY RANCH (L), **20.2** *m.,* is one of the ranches of the Chewaucan Land & Cattle Company. Stock grazes over extensive sections of government land as well as over private holdings. A small army of cowboys look after stock of the ZX brand. In late summer the cattle are concentrated in the Sycan Marsh to the west where the steers fatten on the tall grasses. In October and November cattle destined for slaughter houses are driven to the nearest shipping point. Tanned riders, clothes white with powdered alkali dust, and the lumbering "chuck wagons" follow the bellowing herds.

PAISLEY, 22.2 m. (4,369 alt., 259 pop.), is a frontier town on the Chewaucan River. It is said to have been named in 1873 by Charles Ennis after his native city in Scotland. Against a background of radio, electric lights, and gasoline filling stations, the western tradition is still reflected in garb and custom. Cowboys ride through the streets and the watering trough and hitching post still stand. Paisley is headquarters for the Chewaucan Land & Cattle Company, the largest of Oregon's stock-raising enterprises, which has 32 subsidiary ranches.

At 28.6 m. is the southern extremity of SUMMER LAKE, discovered by Fremont in 1843. He wrote: "December 16. We traveled this morning through snow about three feet deep, which, being crusted, very much cut the feet of our animals. . . . Toward noon the forest looked clear ahead, appearing suddenly to terminate; and beyond a certain point we could see no trees. Riding rapidly ahead to this spot, we found ourselves on the verge of a vertical and rocky wall of the mountain. At our feet—more than a thousand feet below—we looked into a green prairie country, in which a beautiful lake, some twenty miles in length, was spread along the foot of the mountains, its shores bordered with green grass. . . . Not a particle of ice was to be seen on the lake, or snow on its borders, and all was like summer or spring. The glow of the sun in the valley below brightened up our hearts with sudden pleasure; and we made the woods ring with joyful shouts to those behind; and gradually, as each came up, he stopped to enjoy the unexpected scene. Shivering on snow three feet deep, and stiffening in a cold north wind, we exclaimed at once that the names of Summer Lake and Winter Ridge should be applied to those two proximate places of such sudden and violent contrast. . . .

"When we had sufficiently admired the scene below, we began to think about descending, which here was impossible, and we turned towards the north, travelling always along the rocky wall. We continued on for four or five miles, making ineffectual attempts at several places; and at length succeeded in getting down at one which was extremely difficult of descent. Night had closed in before the foremost had reached to bottom, and it was dark before we found ourselves together in the valley."

Summer Lake, with an area of about 60 square miles, has no outlet, and the waters are strongly alkaline. The Ana River, a short stream gushing full-bodied from the earth near the northern end of the lake, is the chief source of its vitality. Fremont says that his party traversed an Indian trail between Winter Ridge and Summer Lake. The highway follows closely this Indian Trail to SUMMER LAKE, 51.5 m. (4,242 alt., 20 pop.), a small postal and supply point for the convenience of isolated ranchers.

PICTURE ROCK PASS, 57.6 m. (4,832 alt.), is a low summit

named for Indian petroglyphs on a rock about 20 feet (L) from the highway. Represented on the rock are pictures of men and animals and one or two abstract symbols.

SILVER LAKE, 60.6 *m.*, is a dry lake bed that stretches white sands over an area of about 20 square miles, bordered by drifting sand dunes like a miniature Sahara.

At **63.6** *m.* is a junction with a desert road.

Right on this road to THORNE LAKE, 3 *m.*, in which are crumbling geologic formations that have been named Sunken City. In the area northeast of Thorne Lake archaeologists have found many fossil remains of prehistoric flora and fauna. A dry lake about 20 miles northeast of Thorne Lake is called Fossil Lake.

SILVER LAKE (P.O.), 73 *m.* (4,345 alt., 122 pop.), at the southern edge of Paulina Marsh, is a marketing center for cattlemen and sheepmen whose herds and flocks graze in the nearby Fremont Forest and the Paulina Marshes. Twenty settlers established the nucleus of the town in 1873 and in 1875 a post office was opened. On Christmas day, 1894, occurred a catastrophe still fresh in the memory of the older inhabitants. At a celebration in the town hall an overturned oil lamp set fire to the building and 43 of the 200 occupants perished in the flames and 31 more were seriously burned. The high mortality was due to the clogging of a single exit which opened inward. It is said that the State law requiring all doors of public buildings to open outward was due to the Silver Lake disaster. A stone monument in the Silver Lake cemetery is dedicated to the men, women and children who perished in the fire.

Silver Lake was the center of a brief but sanguinary sheep and cattle war in 1904. Nearly six thousand sheep were slaughtered with "rifles, pistols, knives and clubs."

HORSE RANCH, 91.8 *m.* (4,492 alt.), is an old ranch and trading post at the eastern edge of the Deschutes National Forest.

Right from Horse Ranch on a gravel road to FORT ROCK (P. O.), 6.8 *m.*, a once prosperous village in a dry-farming community, founded in 1908. Now a weather-beaten huddle of crude frame buildings, the town once supported three stores, two saloons, a newspaper with a circulation of 500, creamery and cheese factory, church, and graded school. The town had its being through the attempt to farm the almost waterless Fort Rock Valley, but after a decade of struggle the attempt was abandoned.

Fort Rock was named for a huge basalt column rising like a fortress a mile to the north. The mountain rising abruptly from the desert floor is shaped like an imperfect crescent a third of a mile across the walls a sheer 325 feet in height. It was used as a place of defense by warring Indians, and once aided in the preservation of an immigrant train. The pioneers had wandered from the trail when they discovered a band of hostiles were following them. Reaching Fort Rock ahead of the enemy they blocked the approach with wagons and successfully stood off their assailants.

Crossing boundary of the Deschutes National Forest at **92.4** *m.*, State 31 follows the southern edge of the DESCHUTES GAME REFUGE for several miles.

At **93.8** *m.* is a junction with a dirt road.

Right on this road to THE HOLE IN THE GROUND, **4** *m.,* an almost perfectly round depression more than a half mile in diameter and 300 feet deep. It is conjectured that the cavity was caused by a meteor.

SUMMIT STAGE STATION (R), **103.8** *m.* (4,705 alt.), an old log building, was a stopping place on the old road from Bend to Lakeview, used during the settlement of central Oregon.

At **120.6** *m.* is a junction with US 97 (*see TOUR 4b*), at a point 1.8 miles south of Lapine.

Tour 5D

Lakeview—Beatty—Klamath Falls—Keno—Ashland; 159.1 m. State 66.

Paved or rock-surfaced road; snow storms temporarily block portions of road. Oregon, California and Eastern Railroad parallels route between Bly and Klamath Falls.
Motor stages serve entire route.
Accommodations range from improved camp sites to first-class hotels.

State 66 cuts through the heart of the old Paiute, Klamath, and Modoc Indian territory. After years of depredations and the bloody Modoc War of 1873 the tribes were sent to the reservations where they are now stable agriculturalists. A segment of the Klamath Indian Reservation is crossed. The geographic features of the route vary markedly; a semi-arid sagebrush desert, uplands of yellow pine, open cattle ranges, and heavily timbered mountains. Civilization has left few marks on much of this section, great areas remaining almost as primitive as when the first covered wagons toiled over the dim trails.

The highway branches west from US 395 (*see TOUR 5b*), at LAKEVIEW, **0** *m.* to run through desert made arable in some places by irrigation, and climbs slowly to an elevation that commands magnificent panoramas. A boundary of the Fremont National Forest is crossed at **11.4** *m.* BOOTH STATE PARK (*picnic grounds*), **13.8** *m.,* is a 170-acre wilderness tract.

DREWS CANYON, a defile cut deep into the lava cliffs and bare plains of the high country, leads to DREWS GAP, **15** *m.* (5,306 alt.). DREWS RESERVOIR, **18.9** *m.,* about seven miles long and a mile wide, impounds the water of Drews Creek and distributes it through small canals to irrigate the wide basin adjacent. Wild geese and other migratory birds frequent the gray-blue water, and cormorants nest in the bleached branches of shore pines.

West of the Reservoir the forests are more dense. A boundary of the large MULE DEER GAME REFUGE, covering about 200 square miles, is crossed at 23.9 m. QUARTZ CREEK, 27.8 m., was the scene of early mining operations. The settlement of QUARTZ MOUNTAIN, 30.2 m. (5 pop.), is near the summit of QUARTZ PASS, 30.8 m. (5,508 alt.); the square red posts appearing frequently along the route indicate the right of way when snow-drifts blot out the road.

BLY, 43.7 m. (4,356 alt., 40 pop.), derives its name from the Indian P'lai, used to distinguish the stream that flowed out of the upper country from the Williamson River of the lower region. P'laikini were people who lived high above the plain; the term was also used to denote the Christian God, and in a broader sense, the adjective heavenly. The stream from which the town was named flows through a valley two miles north of the settlement and is now known as the Sprague River, commemorating the activities of Capt. F. B. Sprague, Indian fighter, who commanded Fort Klamath in 1866.

Cattlemen tell of a huge grizzly bear, old "Twisted Foot," that roamed in the vicinity of Sprague River in the early 1880's. "Twisted Foot," whose paw left a track about the size of a Mexican sombrero, is reputed to have killed over $500 worth of cattle for one cattleman alone, in addition to carrying on an extensive butchering business for other stock owners. Eluding hunters for several years the grizzly continued to plunder cattle bands until June, 1885, when he was killed by Indian Dick. According to the Ashland Tidings of that date old "Twisted Foot" was one of the largest animals of his kind ever known in Southern Oregon. He measured three feet between the ears and four feet from the point of the nose to the top of his ears. . . .

Bly was formerly a noted cattle town, but recently it has become a lumbering center. It is also district headquarters for the Fremont National Forest, and a shipping point for sheep and wool.

KLAMATH INDIAN RESERVATION is entered at 48.3 m. (see TOUR 4b). The area is a cattle and sheep-grazing country. Rail fences separate ranchlands from tracts sparsely covered with ponderosa pine.

At 55 m. is a junction with a dirt road.

Left on this road which crosses the Sprague River to the MASEKESKE CEMETERY, 0.5 m. Hundreds of aborigines are buried on a low, bleak hill, beneath closely set white headstones, which, from a distance, resemble a forest of bleached, limbless trees.

BEATTY, 56.7 m. (4,344 alt., 81 pop.), is a cattle and lumbering town and shipping center. Stores and post office serve both red and white residents of the Klamath Reservation. The town was named in honor of a pioneer missionary.

West of Beatty are sagebrush hills on which the black and yellow balsam root blooms in early spring. This plant, similar to small sunflowers, was mentioned by Capt. Lewis who ate an Indian bread made from the seeds mixed with dried service berries.

At **61.7** *m.* is a junction with a gravel road.

Right on this road, 1.5 *m.* to a dirt road; R. here 1.5 *m.* to the SCHONCHIN CEMETERY, an Indian burial ground named for Schonchin Jack, Modoc War chief. It is the final resting place of Winema, heroine of the Modoc War and niece of the formidable Captain Jack, also a Modoc War chief (*see TOUR 4b*). Married at an early age to a white man, Winema mastered the English language and became an interpreter and intermediary in negotiations between her people and their conquerors. During the Modoc uprising, Winema saved the life of Reservation Superintendent A. B. Meacham at the risk of her own. For her devotion to the cause of peace, Congress later voted her a life pension. The D. A. R. has erected over her grave a tablet bearing the inscription, "Winema—the Strong Heart."

Northwest of the junction, the road leads to the village of SPRAGUE RIVER, **9** *m.* (4,220 alt., 150 pop.), center of social and commercial activity for a considerable portion of the Klamath Indian Reservation.

From the summit of BLY MOUNTAIN, **66.7** *m.* (5,087 alt.), the highway makes a serpentine descent into a level valley, in which farms and herds of dairy cattle mark an important phase of southern Oregon's development. DAIRY, **78.6** *m.* (4,120 alt., 294 pop.), is a shipping and distributing center, set among green fields. Agriculture in the vicinity represents the triumph of irrigation over natural aridity, for the lowlands of the dairy ranches were once a treeless waste known as Alkali Valley.

Left from Dairy on a dirt road to BONANZA, 7 *m.* (4,100 alt., 141 pop.), another dairying community, so named because springs in its vicinity promised permanent water for irrigation, and consequent prosperity.

OLENE (Ind., eddy or place of drift), **88.1** *m.* (4,147 alt., 62 pop.), on the banks of LOST RIVER, is virtually a suburb of Klamath Falls, and the center of a prosperous dairy and potato raising district. Low stone root houses, protecting produce from freezing, are frequent. Rows of Lombardy poplars rise along the road. The battle which precipitated the Modoc Indian War was fought upon the banks of Lost River (*see below*). This unique stream, literally a lost river, has its source and outlet about fifteen miles apart in the state of California, while most of its 100-mile length is in Oregon. The river is lost into underground channels in its course through the volcanic terrain of Langell Valley, finally ending in Tule Lake. Now, however, because of almost complete utlization for irrigation, practically no water from Lost River flows into the lake, which is slowly disappearing.

At **92.1** *m.* is a junction with State 39.

Left on State 39 down the valley of Lost River noted for its production of fine potatoes through modern irrigated farms where much alfalfa is raised.

MERRILL, 14 *m.* (4,069 alt., 306 pop.), the Oregon entrance to the LAVA BEDS NATIONAL MONUMENT in California, is an agricultural trading center in the Klamath Irrigation Project. (*Maps and information on the National Monument at local service stations. No motor service, gasoline, oil, or food supplies in the area. An improved free campground is in charge of a National Park ranger during the summer.*)

At **16.6** *m.* is a junction with a dirt road; R. on this road crossing Lost River, **18.3** *m.* Near the bridge is a U. S. Reclamation dam resting directly on a rocky ledge, in Oregon pioneer annals called the STONE BRIDGE. It was crossed by the Southern Pass prospecting party on July 6, 1846 (*see Tour 2b*), which was searching for a route from Fort Hall into the Umpqua and Willamette valleys. Lindsay Applegate wrote: "Before proceeding very far we discovered an Indian crouching under the bank, and surrounding him, made him come out. By signs, we indicated to him that we wanted to cross the river. By marking on his legs and pointing up the river, he gave us to understand that there was a place above where we could easily cross. Motioning to him to advance, he led the way up the river about a mile and pointed out a place where an immense rock crossed the river. The sheet of water running over the rock was about fifteen inches deep, while the principle part of the river seemed to flow under. This was the famous Stone Bridge on Lost River, so often mentioned after this by travelers. . . ." On November 29, 1872, this bridge was the scene of the first clash with the Indians in the last Modoc War.

Following the former west shore of Tule Lake, a comparatively small area of water and marshland used as a migratory bird refuge, and as farm acreage, and named by the Applegate party for its dense growths of cat-tails, the route continues southward crossing the California Line, **19** *m.* At **32** *m.* is the northern boundary of the LAVA BEDS NATIONAL MONUMENT (*see TOUR 7A, CALIFORNIA STATE GUIDE*), whose 45,000-acre lava area is one of the most spectacular in the West.

It was here during the last Modoc War (1872-73) that a band of 71 Modocs, led by Capt. Jack, held at bay a troop of regular soldiers and volunteers. Capt. Jack and the other leaders were captured and hanged at old Fort Klamath (*see TOUR 4b*).

US 66 continues to KLAMATH FALLS, **97.1** *m.* (4,112 alt., 16,093 pop.) (*see KLAMATH FALLS*), where it unites with US 97 (*see TOUR 4b*) to a point at **100.1** *m.*

The route of State 66 in this area was used by early stage and freight lines between the Klamath Basin and settlements along the Rogue River. For twelve miles the Klamath River (L) rushes down a rocky channel among pine-crested hills. The river rises in Lake Ewauna, within the city limits of Klamath Falls, flows southwest 150 miles across northern California and into the Pacific Ocean. It is believed that Lieut. John C. Fremont mistook this water-course for the fabled Buena Ventura River (*see TOUR 4b*).

KENO, **109.2** *m.* (4,093 alt., 150 pop.), is in a logging and farming region on the banks of the Klamath River. Keno was named after a bird dog, which, in turn, had been named after a card game popular during the frontier era. Crossing the summit of HAYDEN MOUNTAIN, **121.4** *m.* (4,696 alt.), US 66 descends into a shallow valley, then climbs to the summit of PARKER MOUNTAIN, **130.4** *m.* (4,362 alt.).

PINEHURST, **135.8** *m.* (3,368 alt., 10 pop.), a hamlet in a yellow pine belt, was once known as Shake, deriving the name from the hand-hewn pine "shakes" or shingles covering the framework of early settlers' homes.

LINCOLN, **138** *m.* (3,684 alt.), is another tiny sawmill village. The fragrance of pine fills the air as the road curves up the slopes to the summit of GREEN SPRINGS MOUNTAIN, **143.4** *m.* (4,551 alt.). At this point the highway crosses a boundary of the Rogue River National Forest.

On the summit of the mountain, is a junction with a foot trail.

Right on this trail through a heavily forested country to LAKE OF THE WOODS, 40 m. (*see TOUR* 4*b*).

WAGNER SODA SPRINGS, 148.2 m., is a resort at the foot of the mountain, one of the many spas of southern Jackson County. (*Tourist accommodations*).

KLAMATH JUNCTION, 153.4 m., is the junction with a former route of US 99.

Left here to the new US 99 (*see TOUR* 2*b*), at SISKIYOU, 7.6 m.

State 66 continues to a junction with US 99 at 159.1 m., on the edge of ASHLAND (1,900 alt., 4,544 pop.) (*see TOUR* 2*b*.)

Tour 6

Ontario — Vale — Mitchell — Prineville — Redmond — Sisters — Springfield; 389.8 m. U.S. 28.

Branch line of Union Pacific Railroad parallels route between Ontario and Brogan. Summer stage service over entire route. No service in winter between Redmond and Springfield.
Roadbed paved at intervals; other sections generally well graded with gravel or rock surface. McKenzie Pass through the Cascades is blocked by snow from early winter to early summer.
Hotels at centers; tourist camps, improved forest camps, and resorts.

This route is one of contrasts. It spans miles of arid plateaus, three forested mountain ranges, and terminates in fertile valleys west of the Cascade Mountains. In the eastern section are wide horizons and the tang of sagebrush and juniper. At the western end, only an hour's travel from sun-drenched highlands, are green hills kept verdant by the moist winds from the sea. Along this route is some of the most spectacular scenery of Oregon, such as the Canyon of the John Day River and the McKenzie Lava Fields.

In its course across Oregon the route passes through many places made significant by the old cattle-ranching days of eastern Oregon, and the gold-rush era; by Indian uprisings, and military activity. The present highway is roughly a portion of the old Dalles Military Wagon Road that crossed the wilderness between The Dalles and Snake River.

Section a. Ontario to Redmond, 278 m. US 28,

West of ONTARIO, 0 m. (2,153 alt., 1,941 pop.) (see TOUR 1a). US 28 crosses an irrigated section of the MALHEUR RIVER VALLEY (see TOUR 7a) at CAIRO, 4.6 m. is a junction with State 201 (see TOUR 6A).VALE, 16.4 m. (2,247 alt., 922 pop.) (see TOUR 7A) is at the junction with State 54.

US 28, following the course of the Dalles Military Wagon Road, winds over gentle grades up Willow Creek to JAMIESON, 34.1 m. (2,504 alt., 35 pop.), and BROGAN, 40.6 m. (2,683 alt., 79 pop.), trade centers of fruit growing, farming and livestock districts.

At 41.1 m. old Dalles Military Wagon Road diverges from the highway.

Right on this road to the SITE OF CAMP COLFAX, 15 m., a post established in 1865 as protection for pioneer wagon trains and miners.

MALHEUR, 20 m. (2,155 alt., 21 pop.), formerly Malheur City, was a gold camp in the 1870's. Gold was discovered in 1863 by miners from nearby Eldorado and many rich placers and veins were worked. Mrs. Mary Collins-Richardson was proprietor of a store and saloon. Her flower beds, the pride of the town, were bordered by empty whiskey bottles, half-buried in the soil. Up the gulch from Malheur City were MARYSVILLE and ELDORADO, other lively mining camps that have completely disappeared. The *Bedrock Democrat* of Baker City for May 13, 1873, reports: "During the day the streets of Eldorado are deserted, all men at work in the tunnels back of town. Great hopes are placed on the benefits to be derived from the 'Big Ditch' (*see below*) under construction by Packwood and Carter; water will be in the ditch in less than ten days. The future of Eldorado looks very bright." One early resident remembers that the miners were good to the children and often gave them small pinches of gold dust to buy stick candy.

West of BROGAN HILL SUMMIT, 48.5 m. (3,983 alt.), the highway crosses an upland plain straight as the path of a bullet. To the left extends the wide, flat sage desert, flanked by bare gray hills and dotted with abandoned shacks of disappointed homesteaders.

IRONSIDE, 63.6 m. (3,774 alt., 75 pop.), center of a dairy and livestock district, is named for Ironside Mountain, nine miles southwest. The mountain was named for the metallic appearance of its rocks.

ELDORADO PASS, 71.7 m. (4,623 alt.), is at the summit of a spur of the Blue Mountains. (*Change made here between Mountain and Pacific Standard Time.*) West of the summit is the old ELDORADO DITCH, 71.9 m., now abandoned. The "Big Ditch," begun for placer miners in the gold-rush period, was completed in 1873. Winding for 120 miles along the main and lateral ridges from Last Chance Creek of the South Fork of the Burnt River, through El Dorado to Malheur City, it was the largest channel of its kind on the west coast and upon it floated rafts of logs destined for building at the mines. It carried 2,500 miners' inches of water and cost $250,000. From this region, in the eventful 1860's, adventurers took millions in gold dust from the new El Dorado. In their wanderings they established and deserted town after town, and camp after camp.

At **75.4** *m.* is the junction with a dirt road.

Left on this road to SOUTH FORK FOREST CAMP, **7** *m.* (4,300 alt.), in the Whitman National Forest.

UNITY, **82.4** *m.* (4,030 alt., 34 pop.), adjacent to the old Powder River mining region of the Blue Mountains, is the heart of a livestock section and is district ranger headquarters for the Whitman Forest.

At **84.1** *m.* is a junction with State 7 (*see TOUR 1A*).

This section of the Burnt River Basin is bisected by the Middle Fork of Burnt River, a stream flowing into the Snake River east of Huntington. US 28 crosses a boundary of the Whitman National Forest at **92.7** *m.* and after a sharp and winding climb reaches OREGON FOREST CAMP, **94.5** *m.* (4,600 alt.).

Below the summit of the range, (5,098 alt.), **95** *m.* is a circuitous descent to the headwaters of the Middle Fork of the John Day River.

At **103.1** *m.* is the Squaw Meadows Trail.

Left on this trail to BALDY MOUNTAIN, **17** *m.* (7,634 alt.), a region of marked geologic interest. Baldy Mountain and a surrounding area of about 20 square miles are said to be the oldest land west of the Rockies and the first to emerge from the waste of waters that enveloped the present Oregon. It is known to scientists as the island of Shoshone, named by Dr. Thomas Condon. A RANGER STATION of the Whitman National Forest is at this point during the fire season.

At **104.3** *m.* is the BLUE MOUNTAIN RANGER STATION.

At **104.7** *m.* is a junction with a gravel road.

Right on this road to AUSTIN, **2.7** *m.* (4,074 alt., 50 pop.), where an aura of the past lingers in an old roadhouse and stage station which has been in continuous operation since stagecoach days. The hotel, established by a Mrs. Newton, was first called Newton's Station. Later, when Minot Austin bought the hotel and ranch the station name was changed and Mrs. Austin became widely known as an excellent cook. Today the old hotel is principally patronized by hunters and fishermen and other vacationists.

BRIDGE CREEK FOREST CAMP, **111.1** *m.,* is at the western edge of the Whitman National Forest and a half mile east of DIXIE PASS, **111.6** *m.* (5,280 alt.). It was named during Civil War days by California miners, Southern in sympathy, and is one of three points on this route at which elevations of a mile or more are reached. On the descent are excellent views of the rugged Strawberry Mountains to the southwest.

PRAIRIE CITY, **121.9** *m.* (3,546 alt., 438 pop.), is a livestock and mining center in the upper John Day Valley. The quiet little town, tucked away among picturesque foothills, still maintains much of the atmosphere of early days. It was named for the flat lowland area of its original site three miles up Dixie Creek. Just north of Prairie City on Dixie Creek is the SITE OF DIXIE, mining center of the 1860's. The old mining camp of Dixie came into existence on the heels of gold discoveries in the Blue Mountains, and being on the road to Auburn (*see TOUR 1A*), almost immediately, it received a heavy influx of miners moving to or from that town. It soon had a population of 300 or 400 miners. No attempt was made to plat the camp, and it grew up in a rambling, haphazard manner. Ten years after gold was discovered, the district was placered out and miners departed, and other inhabitants moved down the creek, establishing Prairie City. Founded in 1871, in a rich agricultural district, the town was supported by farming and livestock rather than by mining, though gold dredges still operate on Dixie Creek. The Prairie City Roller Mills began turning out flour in 1885. Granite beds near Prairie City produce excellent building stone, and quarrying is developing into an important industry. In commemoration of the old mining days, Prairie City stages an annual Round-up and Jamboree.

Left from Prairie City on a dirt road into MALHEUR NATIONAL FOREST, 8 *m.* At 12.5 *m.* is STRAWBERRY CREEK FOREST CAMP (6,000 alt.) and STRAWBERRY LAKE, 14 *m.* (5,403 alt.), a scenic mountain lake on the shore of which is a State fish hatchery.

Right from the lake, 1.5 *m.* on a foot trail to STRAWBERRY MOUNTAIN (9,600 alt.), where the Forest Service maintains a LOOKOUT STATION. From the summit is a panorama of forested mountains, veiled in their perpetual blue haze. The mountain, once known as Logan Butte, derives its present name as does the lake, from the creek along which there is an abundance of wild strawberries. It is at the northwest corner of the CANYON CREEK GAME REFUGE (*hunting by bow and arrow only*).

At **131.8** *m.* is Little Pine Creek (3,319 alt.).

Left on a trail along the creek, to the SITE OF MARYSVILLE, 2 *m.*, thriving mining camp of the 1860's, forlorn huddle of tumbledown shacks. Marysville was established in April 1862 by a group of miners from Marysville, Calif., and soon grew to several hundred population. In 1864 the second school district in Grant County was started at Marysville, the only other district being at Canyon City. Twenty-one pupils attended the first year with Elizabeth Chope as teacher. The total amount of money expended in the district for the first year was $97.34.

JOHN DAY, 135.3 *m.* (3,083 alt., 432 pop.), at the confluence of Canyon Creek and the John Day River, one of the glamorous mining and cattle towns, has preserved the traditions of the gold-rush decade and the cattle-ranching epoch.

John Day was a young Virginian and scout of the Astor overland expedition (1811), led by Wilson Price Hunt (*see TOUR 1a*). When the party was fighting its way through the bleak Snake River region, Day became ill and fell behind. Two companions remained with him, one of whom died that winter from exposure and hardship. Day and his other companion, Ramsay Crooks, struggled through the Blue Mountains and along the valleys and canyons of the John Day, finally reaching the Columbia River in May, 1812, after great suffering. They were discovered on the banks of the Columbia by a group of Astorians. Their clothes were in tatters, and they were so emaciated that they were not at first recognized as white men. Day became insane and died later in Astoria.

During the gold days of 1862-64, the mail was carried on horseback from The Dalles to Canyon City, largely over Indian trails, one of which led along the John Day River and through the place. The mail was strapped to the saddles of daring riders. The postage rate was 50c a letter, and newspapers found a ready sale at a dollar each. With the development of mining, the riders often carried thousands of dollars worth of gold dust. Hostile Indians and bandits imperiled the riders' lives. Narrow escapes and hold-ups, were not uncommon, but the tradition prevailed that "the mail must go through," and the dangers were accepted as a part of the day's work. When the competing H. H. Wheeler Company entered the field and war began, it is reported that the original company, in a race with its competitor, once traveled the 225 miles from Canyon City to The Dalles in 28 hours, with only the necessary changes of horses and riders. Later, supplies were brought into the frontier town by pack trains or freight wagons over the Dalles Military Wagon Road. The first stage line to travel the Wagon Road was established in 1864; the first regular mail contract was let in 1865 to H. H. Wheeler, for whom Wheeler County was named, and who was often at the reins during many of the perilous trips. All supplies are now brought in and produce shipped out by modern trucks.

The present John Day is the trading center for a large range and gold-mining country, headquarters for the Malheur National Forest, and scene of the annual Grant County Fair. Farm produce of all kinds is raised by the descendants of gold miners. At this point US 28 forms a junction with US 395 (*see TOUR* 5.)

On the outskirts of John Day is the LAZY-T RANCH, 135.8 *m.* (R), established in 1862. Not only cattle, but race horses and polo ponies are raised on the ranch. As a dude ranch, it specializes in hunting parties into the wild John Day country.

Right from John Day over an unimproved road to MAGOON LAKE, 12 *m.* (4,500 alt.), at whose lower end is an immense earth slide, in which pine trees are still growing. The trees are tilted at various angles, just as they were carried down by the avalanche. By the lake is MAGOON LAKE FOREST CAMP (*excellent fishing and deer hunting*).

MOUNT VERNON, 143.8 *m.* (2,871 alt., 75 pop.), in a stock-raising country was named for a nearby mountain. At Mount Vernon is a junction with US 395 (*see TOUR* 5).

At 153.6 *m.* is a junction with a dirt road.

Left on this road to the Whitman Forest Boundary, 3.3 *m.,* which is the northern boundary of THE MURDERERS CREEK AND DEER CREEK HUNTING AREA. Both creeks are tributary to the South Fork of the John Day River. At the approach of winter large herds of mule deer gather in the area. It is also the habitat of cougars, black bears, bobcats, and coyotes. Along the creeks are beaver, Oregon's earliest source of wealth.

This section was the scene of many clashes between Indians and white settlers and miners. Murderers Creek received its name from one of the clashes in which a party of prospectors were attacked and almost wiped out. Late in the fall of 1862 five miners camped on the creek were attacked by Indians who were hidden behind rocks. One man was killed outright, one died a short time later after crawling into the bushes, and a third died the next day at a ranch in the John

Day Valley. A fourth man died after reaching Canyon City from the effects of a poisoned arrow; only one survived.

DAYVILLE, 167.1 *m.* (2,345 alt., 106 pop.), a former stage station that now caters to a traveling public of a faster age, is the center of a wide range country. To the south rise the serried contours of the Aldrich Mountains.

BATTLE CREEK, 169.9 *m.,* was named for a battle between two bands of Indians, in 1870.

PICTURE GORGE, 172.6 *m.,* a deep cleft through which the John Day River pours its foaming torrent, is so narrow that even in summer its depths are shadowed and gloomy. Stratified, crumbling basalt cliffs rear to a height of 500 feet.

The PREHISTORIC PICTOGRAPHS (L) that give the gorge its name are at 173 *m.* on a comparatively smooth stretch of lava wall at an angle facing east. Scientists state that the crude markings, painted in red oxide, have been there 50 to 80 centuries. No satisfactory interpretation of their symbolism has ever been advanced. They are about three feet above the ground, but their weathered dullness makes them obscure.

MITCHELL JUNCTION, 173.9 *m.* (2,229 alt.), is at the junction with State 19 (*see TOUR 1D*).

West of Mitchell Junction, US 28 follows Rock Creek, which flows into the John Day River, through a narrow canyon similar to Picture Gorge, and in the next 15 miles climbs 1,500 feet. Between Mitchell Junction and Redmond US 28 is known as the Ochoco Highway, named for an early Indian chief.

At 174.8 *m.* is a trail.

Left on this trail over a low pass to RATTLESNAKE CANYON, 3 *m.,* where prolific yields of fossils have been uncovered. These fossils are from Pliocene formations which have produced relatively large mammalian fauna and are of later date than the Columbia lava epidemic. In contrast the John Day fossil beds (*see TOUR 1F*) are Oligocene or lower Miocene in age and were laid down before the flow of the Columbia lavas.

At 190.7 *m.* is a junction with a dirt road.

Left on this road to a junction with a dirt road, 3 *m.* R. 2 *m.* on this road to the SITE OF OLD CAMP WATSON, another of the military posts established during the early 1860's. The camp was named for Lieut. Steven Watson of the First Oregon Cavalry, who was killed in a skirmish with Chief Paulina's band of Paiutes at a place since known as Watson Springs on the Beaver Creek branch of Crooked River. Camp Watson was established in 1863 by the Oregon Volunteers of the Canyon City road expedition. The camp was occupied from 1863 to 1866 by the First Oregon Cavalry when it was relieved by Troop I, First United States Cavalry. Many were the encounters with Indians. An item from *The Dalles Mountaineer* of August 3, 1867, states: "By the arrival of Buchanan and Company's Express from Canyon City and Camp Watson we are in receipt of the following items. Colonel Baker returned to Camp Watson on the 28th from his scout to Stein's Mountains and the Harney Lake Country. He brought in twenty-two prisoners and two captured horses, and in the different skirmishes with the Snakes he killed twelve. This is decidedly the most successful scout that has ever been made against the Snakes from this side of the Blue

Mountains. The entire road from here to Boise is now entirely free from Indians. This is the first time we have been able to make this statement since the settlement of the country."

A stage station, established in 1863 at **201** *m.* was the first permanent settlement in the district. It was kept by two bachelors, C. A. Myers and "Alkali Frank" Hewot. Said *The Dalles Times-Mountaineer,* Oct. 15, 1896: "Every traveler over the long and wretched road between here and Canyon City made it a point to stop with Myers and Hewot. They lived in an adobe mansion which was a marble palace compared with some of the frontier residences of those days and they had the reputation of furnishing the best meals to be had east of the Cascade Mountains. Both were bachelors and as the years rolled by and household cares increased with increasing travel the hearts of the two bachelors felt an aching void for the touch of a woman's hand and the companionship and ministry that a woman alone can render. But which of them should go wife hunting? That was the question, for each was perfectly satisfied that the other should be the matrimonial victim. At last the controversy was settled by the two bachelors agreeing to play a game of seven-up, the loser to go and hunt a wife. The game was played and Mr. Hewot won and Mr. Myer a short time afterward started for California, where he found the woman that has shared his joys and sorrows for more than thirty years."

The MONUMENT TO H. H. WHEELER, **202.7** *m.,* commemorates a mail carrier on the route between The Dalles and Canyon City who was attacked and wounded by Indians near this spot on September 7, 1866, his mail looted, and his coach burned (*see below*).

MITCHELL, **206** *m.* (2,278 alt., 211 pop.), for many years the trading post for a wide mining and stockraising area, was started in 1867 as a stage station on The Dalles-Canyon City route. The first post office was established in 1887 and named for John H. Mitchell, later United States Senator from Oregon.

Burned out, washed out, beset at times by desperadoes, Mitchell has had an unusually dramatic existence. In 1884 a nine-foot wave rushed over the bluff above the town, filled the streets with boulders some weighing a ton, carried away houses, wagons and implements, and deposited mud and gravel on the floor of Chamberlain and Todd's saloon a foot deep. The town was attacked by fire March 25, 1896, and nine buildings destroyed. Again, in August, 1899, ten buildings were burned.

On July 11, 1904, a cloudburst precipitated a wall of water 30 feet high onto the town. Everything was destroyed save a few buildings high enough to be out of the water's reach. Only two lives were lost owing to the fact that the terrific din of the onrushing flood warned the people who escaped to the nearby hills. Two months later a smaller flood struck the town but as little was left to destroy the damage was slight.

At **206.5** *m.* is a junction with State 207 (*see TOUR 1D*).

At **210** *m.* is a junction with a graveled surface road.

Right on this road, which is a portion of the old Dalles Military Road, to

OVIDENCE BAPTIST CHURCH   WEST UNION BAPTIST CHURCH

. PAUL CATHOLIC CHURCH   TUALATIN PLAINS PRESBYTERIAN CHURCH

OLD FORT DALLES, HISTORICAL MUSEUM

SETH LUELLING HOUSE, MILWAUKI

OE MEEK, MOUNTAIN MAN

INDIAN, PENDLETON ROUND-UP

INDIAN CHIEFS, PENDLETON ROUND-UP

PIONEER HOMESTEAD (from old print)

THE DALLES METHODIST MISSION (old prin

HOP PICKERS, WILLAMETTE VALLEY

ONION HARVEST, ONTARIO

TURKEYS, REDMOND

LINN COUNTY FLOURING MILL

PEA HARVEST

KLAMATH IRRIGATION PROJECT

SETTLERS ON OWYHEE PROJECT

OREST FIRE IN COAST RANGE

PAPER MILL, OREGON CITY

BRIDAL VEIL LUMBER FLUME

PIONEER LOGGING

CUT-OVER LAND, SILTCOOS

EARLY-DAY LOGGERS, TILLAMOOK

SEA-GOING LOG RAFT

ISAAC JACOB HOUSE, PORTLAND

PORTLAND PUBLIC MARKET

AUDITORIUM, PORTLA

N ENTRANCE, TIMBERLINE LODGE

MAIN DOOR, TIMBERLINE LODGE

IN LOUNGE, TIMBERLINE LODGE

NEWEL POST, TIMBERLINE LODGE

ART MUSEUM, PORTLAND

ENTRANCE PUBLIC LIBRARY, PORTLA

BURNT RANCH, 13 *m.* Burnt Ranch was a station on the early The Dalles-Canyon City stage line.

Preceded only by the pony express and the pack trains, the first stage line between The Dalles and the placer mining district at Canyon City, in the John Day Valley of Oregon, was established by the man for whom Wheeler County is named, Henry H. Wheeler. He put stock and equipment on the 180-mile run between the two cities on May 1, 1864, and before he sold the line four years later had survived some of the most thrilling experiences that ever befell any man in Eastern Oregon.

Wheeler started his stage service from The Dalles and on his first trip to Canyon City carried eleven passengers. On the return trip he had a like number, each person paying forty dollars for his passage between the two places. On this first trip, and for a long time afterward, Wheeler drove his own stage, drawn by four horses, and had the reputation of being a skillful driver. The stage made three trips a week between The Dalles and Canyon City and in addition to passengers carried express and mail. The first mail contract was awarded to Wheeler in 1865.

Between the years 1864 and 1868, the Indians were constantly on the warpath and a detailed account of all the various fights that Wheeler had with the savages would in themselves make a thrilling volume. Perhaps his outstanding encounter with the Indians, in which he displayed exceptional courage, occurred September 7, 1866.

On that day, Wheeler, accompanied only by H. C. Page, the agent for the Wells-Fargo Express Company, was driving the route between Dayville and Mitchell. Aboard the stage, in addition to the United States mail, were ten thousand dollars in greenbacks, a number of valuable diamond rings, three hundred dollars in coin, and other valuables. About three miles east of the site of the present town of Mitchell, a band of fifteen or twenty Indians appeared and opened an attack. The first shot struck Mr. Wheeler in the face, the bullet going through both cheeks, carrying away several teeth and a part of the jawbone. Despite his injuries, Wheeler jumped to the ground and, while Page kept the Indians at bay, managed to unhitch the lead team. Upon these two horses, neither of which had been ridden before, the two men escaped to the Meyers Ranch where C. W. Meyers and "Alkali" Frank Hewot kept a roadhouse.

After Wheeler's wounds had been dressed, the indomitable stage owner and his companion returned to the scene of the attack, where they retrieved the mail and such other valuables as were left by the savages when they departed. The Indians had cut all of the top off the stage, had ripped open the mail bags and scattered their contents. Apparently not realizing their value, the attackers had dumped the greenbacks on the ground and the currency, except for a small sum, was recovered.

One of the most noted of the stage stations on the route from The Dalles to Canyon City in those days was on the south bank of the John Day River, at the extreme western edge of Wheeler County. The name Burnt Ranch was given the station in 1862, after an attack by marauding Indians who burned the buildings and menaced the lives of the occupants. The community today still carries the name Burnt Ranch and a post office is located there. The original ranch was owned by James N. Clark, who, in 1866, settled at the mouth of Bridge Creek and established himself on a stock ranch.

Burnt Ranch became widely known to early-day travelers in eastern Oregon. It comprised a low-roofed house with a covered porch extending across its front; a large barn with stock corrals, and huge stacks of hay for feeding the stock of the stage company. In front of the house, between it and the barn, ran the long dusty road with its parallel, winding lines of ruts where wheels had worn deep into the soil, a fringe of willows and cottonwoods revealing the presence of the stream whose waters gave scanty life to the parched herbage. One writer has described the hospitality to be found within the station thus: "Within the hospitable doors of the stage station, a charry fire will be found blazing and crackling in a huge fireplace, bringing joy to the soul and comfort to the cramped and chilled body of the traveler, even as the table nearby, laden with hearty and toothsome fare brings satisfaction to his long neglected and rebellious stomach. There may be higher joys in life than this, but it would be hard to convince the traveler who had ridden all night with a taciturn driver, his feet tucked away under the apron and his hands anon desperately clutching the side-rail as the stage suddenly sank into the trough of one 'ground swell' or rose upon the crest of another, the thermometer meanwhile utterly neglecting its duty of keeping the atmosphere at a comfortable temperature, but such is the case."

The same writer, apparently remembering the taciturnity of the stage driver the night before, yet convinced that he is a sort of superman and lord of all he surveys, continues: "Utter and complete satisfaction with one's present condition must be the highest joy in life, whether it be that of a clam idly floating with the tide, a Napoleon at Austerlitz, or a Christian Science healer who has a successful contest with a case of toothache, and this is the feeling of the stage driver as he sits at his matutinal meal and feels the soothing warmth that steals over him from the flowing fireplace. One by one the stages are being driven out before the on-coming iron horse, and, while we welcome the new and appreciate its advantages, we can but cast a half-regretful sigh at the disappearance of the things that were."

How the noted stage station came to be called Burnt Ranch, is explained as follows by the *Grant County News* in its issue of August 6, 1885: "In 1866, James Clark was occupying the position of a pioneer settler there and had a very comfortable home. Along in the early fall his wife departed to the Willamette Valley to visit her people. One bright September morning, Jim and his brother-in-law, George Masterson, forded the John Day River and were cutting up a lot of driftwood on the opposite bars. Suddenly they discovered a band of Indians rushing down the hill from the Ochoco country. The men had left their rifles at the house and they thought there was a possible show to reach them ahead of the Indians. They unhitched the horses and climbing on bareback, raced for the house. But when they saw the Indians were going to get there first, they swerved to the left and struck up Bridge Creek, with the enemy in hot pursuit.

"It took but a few miles of hard riding to use up Masterson's work horse and he told Clark to keep on and save himself. Masterson then jumped from his horse and struck into the brush. He jumped into the creek and, swimming down stream a little distance, found a deep hole, overhung with thick brush, where he 'camped.' The Indians chased Clark a few miles farther and then returned to finish Masterson. But he confined himself to his covered haunt, and after hunting all around for him, the Indians gave up and returned to the house, where they took everything they considered of value. Clark kept on to the nearest ranch, eight miles distant, where he found a number of packers with whom he returned to the scene of action. They yelled for Masterson, and at last taking chances on their being friends, he came out of his hole of hiding almost chilled to death.

"The party then went on to the house, which was found smouldering in ashes and the Indians gone. The raiders had cut open the featherbeds, taking the ticking and scattering the feathers abroad, and also doing other acts of destruction. What was a happy home a few hours before was now a scene of desolation, but Providence had ordered the safety of the occupants. Another house was constructed, but ever since that time the place has been called Burnt Ranch, and that is the name of the post office there to this day."

Sometime after his house and other buildings had been destroyed, James Clark, owner of the ranch, engaged with C. W. Lockwood in the operation of a stage line between Canyon City and The Dalles. While driving stage, Clark put up one night at Howard Maupin's cabin at Antelope Valley. During the night the Indians tore an opening in the stone corral and drove off a bunch of Maupin's stock. As Clark started to resume his trip next morning, Maupin told him if he saw the Indians, to come back and that the two of them would go in pursuit. This Clark agreed to do.

As the stage topped a rise a short distance from Cross Hollows, another station on the stage line, Clark sighted the Indians. Turning the stage around, Clark, and his lone passenger, returned to Maupin's ranch at Antelope. From there the three men started after the Indians and shortly overtook them. Maupin threw his gun to his shoulder and shot Chief Paulina, breaking his thigh. The other Indians seeing their Chief was down, turned and fled, abandoning the stolen stock. Riding closer to Paulina, Maupin again raised his gun with the intention of finishing him.

At this junction, Clark, who had ridden up and recognized the Indian, yelled: "Don't shoot him, Maupin; don't kill that Indian. Let me finish him! That's the Indian who chased me so far on Bridge Creek and burned my cabin and barn." Maupin is said to have lowered his gun, whereupon Clark emptied his own gun into Paulina.

Between **211** *m.* and **213** *m.* are seen the PAINTED HILLS, stained with brilliant ochres, reds, yellows, and mossy greens.

US 28 winds under the sheer walls of COURT HOUSE ROCK, **219.8** *m.,* and enters the OCHOCO (Ind. Willow) NATIONAL FOREST, **221.1** *m.,* which contains a fine stand of ponderosa pine. At **221.1** *m.* also is MOSSY ROCK FOREST CAMP (4,100 alt.) and at **221.3** *m.* the BEAVER DISTRICT RANGER STATION. At **224.8** *m.* is the WILDWOOD FOREST CAMP (4,500 alt.), and at **226.4** *m.* is OCHOCO PASS (5,289 alt.), the summit of the Ochoco Mountains. These mountains, largely within the National Forest, are the westermost spur of the Blue Mountains. They have an average elevation of 4,500 feet. On several high points lookout stations are maintained. Mule deer and other wild life are abundant. Near the summit of the mountains is the 2,000-acre OCHOCO DIVIDE NATIONAL AREA, in which native timber is preserved for scientific research and future generations.

This route, winding for miles through lanes of stately pines and opening to panoramas of the Blue Mountains, is among the most beautiful of the many forest drives of Oregon.

Mining is still followed in the drainage basin of Ochoco Creek and at the old mining town of HOWARD, **231.5** *m.,* the log houses are occupied and the long-deserted mines again active. Situated as it was at the mouth of Scissors Creek the camp was originally known as Scissorsville.

West of Howard the descent is rapid, as it drops to the confluence of Ochoco and Canyon Creeks, **234.5** *m.,* an area in which are the well-equipped OCHOCO FOREST CAMP and the OCHOCO RANGER STATION, **234.9** *m.* The highway touches the northwest edge of the OCHOCO GAME REFUGE of 170,000 acres, in which has flourished a small band of young elk, released in 1932. Within its boundaries are many fossil remains of both sea and land life and extinct plants.

At **240** *m.* is the junction with a dirt road.

Left on this road up Wolf Creek to SULPHUR SPRINGS (*camp*), **7** *m.,* a resort.

OCHOCO RESERVOIR, **249.1** *m.* (3,144 alt.), impounds the water of Ochoco Creek. Its storage capacity irrigates a district of 22,000 acres.

At **249.8** *m.* is a junction with a dirt road.

Right on this road up Mill Creek and into the Ochoco National Forest, 5 *m.* STEIN'S PILLAR, 8 *m.*, is a solid rock pillar on a natural rock pedestal. It is 350 feet high and 120 feet in diameter and as sraight as though carved by a sculptor.

PRINEVILLE, 259.2 *m.* (2,865 alt., 1,027 pop.), seat of Crook County, was named for Barney Prine, its first settler. He arrived in the Ochoco in 1868, and two years later Monroe Hedges laid out the townsite of Prineville. An early resident tells of the founding of the town: "During the summer of 1868 Barney Prine started Prineville by building a dwelling house, store, blacksmith shop, hotel and saloon. He was all of one day building them. They were constructed of willow logs, 10 by 14 feet in size, one story high, and all under one roof. His first invoice of goods cost $80; his liquor consisted of a case of Hostetter's Bitters, and the iron for the blacksmith shop was obtained from the fragments of an old emigrant wagon left up on Crooked River."

About 1873 a post office was established. At that time Prineville was the only town of consequence south of The Dalles in the Deschutes drainage area. Some of the bloodiest encounters of the "sheep and cattle wars" took place in the Prineville region. The cattlemen were dubbed by the harassed sheepmen "The Crook County Sheep-Shooters' Association."

The chief industries in the surrounding country are dairying, poultry raising, grain and forage crops, the raising of sheep and pure-bred cattle, The annual county fair is held at Prineville in October. The former Oregon Interstate Fairgrounds are now the RACING STABLES of John D. Spreckles, San Francisco capitalist. Not to be without rail transportation, the city owns and operates the Prineville Railway, connecting the city with Prineville Junction, on the Union Pacific about three miles north of Redmond. This railroad, 18 miles in length, is the only one in Crook County. The attractive OCHOCO INN, of Spanish architecture, is the only modern hotel in a wide area.

Left from Prineville on State 27, which leads south up the Crooked River Valley to the Crooked River Highway, 21.4 *m.*, a gravel road; L. here along the canyon of Crooked River. For 15 miles the road follows this narrow cleft, at times clinging to the edge of its precipices and overlooking the thread of silver far below.

At POST, 18 *m.* (3,347 alt.), the canyon broadens out, rounded hills appear, and farms crowd down to the rim of the gorge. The town, the center of a wide rangeland, is the approximate geographical center of Oregon.

At 29 *m.* rare insect fossils are found in the cliffs (*not accessible by automobile*).

West of Prineville US 28 crosses the CROOKED RIVER, 260.4 *m.* The deep canyon is one of the inspiring scenic features of central Oregon. Crooked River flows from its headwaters in the rugged terrain, an Oregon badlands region, in a generally westerly direction between the Ochoco Mountains and the detached "island range," the Maury Mountains, source of many streams feeding into Crooked River. Its flow is uniform because of the seemingly inexhaustible reservoirs that hold excess water and release it when the river drops below storage level. In places Crooked River has eaten its way 650 feet into solid basalt, to form palisaded canyons that create an atmosphere of mystery and desolation.

Except for a wide valley near Prineville, basaltic walls stand along the river's course like the parapets of an abandoned fortress. The majestic palisades were thought by the Indians to be the handiwork of their ancient gods. There are spots where the canyon widens for short distances to accommodate stock ranches, but along much of its course, its cliffs are too steep to permit habitation. In a stretch of 30 miles there is but one place at which even a pack horse can cross the river.

OCHOCO STATE PARK, 260.3 m., is an attractive wooded area of 32 acres in an otherwise treeless section. A high butte in the center of the park offers a beautiful mountain view.

From an eminence at 263.2 m. is an extended view of the long serrated crest of the snowcapped Cascade Range edging the horizon. Bachelor Butte, Broken Top, Three Sisters, Mount Washington, Black Butte, and Mount Jefferson thrust their cold snows heavenward, and a mile farther along, Mount Hood, looming far in the northwest, joins the stately procession. Vista after vista of these splendid mountains are presented in constant panorama as the highway bears westward toward the distant foothills.

POWELL BUTTE, 269.7 m. (3,065 alt., 15 pop.), center of an irrigation district known for its superior potatoes, is about two miles north of the buttes for which it was named. The buttes were named for a member of the family of Joab Powell, pioneer circuit rider of Linn County (see TOUR 1A).

Crossing DRY RIVER, former course of a great prehistoric stream, 271.5 m. (see TOUR 7a), US 28 reaches REDMOND, 278 m. (2,996 alt., 994 pop.), the trade center of an irrigated area of diversified farms and a wide range of cattle country. Redmond is at the junction with US 97 (see TOUR 4a).

Section b. Redmond to junction with US 99W; 111.8 m. US 28

This section of the route, called the McKenzie Highway, receives its name from the McKenzie River which it follows down the west slope of the Cascade Mountains. A part of the route between Prineville and Sisters follows the grade of the old Willamette Valley and Cascades Mountain Wagon Road (see TOUR 7b).

West of REDMOND, 0 m., at CLINE FALLS, 4.4 m. (2,836 alt.), US 28 crosses the Deschutes River (see TOUR 4a), then climbs over a high, partially irrigated plateau to a junction with State 54 at 19.6 m. (see TOUR 7b).

SISTERS, 20.2 m. (3,182 alt., 130 pop.), is district ranger headquarters of the Deschutes National Forest, and an outfitting point for hunting, fishing, and camping parties. This is the last point for 35 miles at which any kind of supplies may be procured. Sisters is so named because of its proximity to the THREE SISTERS, snow-capped peaks to the south.

At **20.5** *m.* is a junction with State 54 (*see TOUR 7b*).

Continuing through forests of ponderosa and lodgepole pine, the road at **28.5** *m.* begins to climb the timbered slopes.

WINDY POINT, **32.2** *m.,* is at the base of Black Crater.

Left **2** *m.* from Windy Point on a foot trail to a Forest Lookout Station on BLACK CRATER (7,260 alt.), which offers a splendid panorama.

At **34.6** *m.* is a junction with a dirt road.

Left **1** *m.* on this road to LAVA LAKE FOREST CAMP, a small lake and camp in the lava beds.

McKENZIE PASS, **35.2** *m.,* (5,325 alt.), is in the McKENZIE LAVA FIELDS, a portion of Oregon's most extensive lava flow. The igneous deluge, which many geologists believe took place within historic time, covered thousands of acres with a jagged sea of lava. Three layers of lava are in the bed. The earliest, the gray andesite of an ancient flow, is scored by glaciers and strewn with volcanic dust, cinders, and debris of the second disturbance, and over it, are heavy sheets of black or burnt umber lava of the most recent flood.

About two miles to the R., along the backbone of the mountain, in the center of the field is BELKNAP CRATER (6,877 alt.), from which scientists believe, these billions of tons of lava cascaded down the mountain in two congealing torrents. The north stream flowed into the upper McKenzie River Valley, and the other poured to the west towards the plateau traversed by US 28. They formed many of the beautiful mountain lakes, numerous falls in the McKenzie River (*see below*), and the large number of cinder cones, ridges, and buttes that fill the area.

The DEE WRIGHT OBSERVATORY, maintained by the Forest Service, is reached by a flight of stone steps (R). Eleven narrow windows are spaced at intervals around the lava walls of the tower-like room. Each of these windows is focused on a particular mountain peak, with its name and distance from the viewpoint carved into the stone. Additional large windows command a wide sweep of the Cascade Range. Immediately visible are Belknap Crater, with a forest lookout on the rim of Little Belknap Crater, Mount Washington, the North and Middle Sister, and Mount Scott. To the north extends the Cascade Range, with the snowcapped tops of the higher peaks rising at intervals over vast areas of timbered mountainsides. Mount Hood and Mount Jefferson, tower above the lesser peaks. To the east is the plateau over which the highway has just passed, with its scattered stands of pine and desolate stretches of semi-arid land. To the south are more lava fields, and the glacier-torn sides of the Three Sisters. Far to the south towers Mount McLoughlin.

McKenzie Pass was named for the McKenzie River, the beautiful rushing stream from the heart of the Cascades. The pass was open to travel in 1862, after gold was discovered in eastern Oregon by Felix Scott and a party of 250 men, who started over the pass from the Willamette Valley with 106 ox teams and wagons and 900 head of cattle and horses. They chopped their way through the forest, building the road as they went, and finally crossed the divide by what is now known as the Old Scott Trail, two or three miles south of the present route. Later a party of Eugene men built a toll road through the lava to the present crossing. Parts of this road, so steep and rough that it was very little used are still visible from the highway. Tolls were abandoned in 1891. In 1910 an automobile chugged over the summit and within recent years the present adequate highway was constructed. Joaquin Miller, with his wife and baby, was ambushed by Indians on this pass in 1864, when Miller was turning his face toward his new home in Canyon City after his newspaper was suppressed by the Government (*see TOUR 5a*).

At McKenzie Pass Summit US 28 intersects the Pacific Crest Trail.

Left from the Dee Wright Observatory on the trail through scattered Jack pines that fringe the tortured lava fields, to the THREE SISTERS GAME REFUGE, 1 *m.*, and BIG MATHIESEN LAKE, 3.4 *m.* South of WHITE BRANCH CREEK, 8 *m.* (*campsite*), the route continues to PROUTY MONUMENT, 11 *m.*, which marks the grave of H. H. Prouty, an early mountaineer. SUNSHINE CAMP (*large shelter; telephone*), just beyond, is the base for climbs to the THREE SISTERS (L). The great triumvirate of mountains rises against a horizon broken by lesser peaks, tumbled foothills, and swelling ridges of the Cascades. Incredibly white and vast, the Three Sisters yield little in magnitude to more lofty Mount Jefferson or Mount Hood. Pitted with glaciers, they are heaped with moraines, and slashed with a thousand small ravines and crevasses. Glacial ice clings to the higher levels of the great battered cones. Crusted snows that melt in summer send torrents down the slopes to water the forests and the broad, flower-grown meadows about the mountain's base. Geologists maintain that the Three Sisters are the splintered remnants of a hypothetical Mount Multnomah, which was blown to fragments by volcanic gases during prehistoric times. The three peaks are formidable and difficult of ascent to all but experienced mountaineers.

This trio of mountains, overshadowing the Trail, wear caps of perpetual snow, and fields of jagged, glistening ice cling to their scarred flanks; below lie flowered meadows and dense forests. North Sister is the most difficult to scale, South Sister the easiest. On the crest of the latter is a small lake, cupped in an ancient volcanic pit, believed to be the highest crater lake in the United States.

South of Sunshine Camp the trail traverses a jagged terrain to the OBSIDIAN FIELDS, 12.6 *m.*, an extensive area of jet-black obsidian, or volcanic glass (*campsites nearby*), to LINTON CREEK, 15.4 *m.* (*improved camp*), and JAMES CREEK, 19.2 *m.* (*campsite; large shelter*), the base from which explorations of nearby SEPARATION CREEK are made, and from which ascents of the South Sister are begun.

West of the dividing line between the Willamette National Forest and Deschutes National Forest, 35.9 *m.*, the highway descends gradually through the volcanic terrain.

At 37.2 *m.* is a junction with a dirt road.

Left on this road to HUCKLEBERRY FOREST CAMP, 0.5 *m.* (5,000 alt.), a gathering place for Indians on their way to mountain berry fields.

At 37.4 *m.* is CRAIG MONUMENT, dedicated to John Templeton Craig, pioneer mail carrier and road builder, who, in 1875, lost his life in a blizzard while making a trip over the road that he had helped to build. The memorial, a rock and cement tomb, was erected by the Oregon Rural Letter Carrier Association and dedicated in 1930.

At **37.8** *m.* is WEST LAVA FOREST CAMP, just beyond which is an excellent view of the lava beds (R).

At **41.2** *m.* is the junction with a dirt road.

Right on this road to SCOTT LAKE FOREST CAMP, 1 *m.* (4,900 alt.), by SCOTT LAKE, one of the most beautiful of the Cascade lakes. It is a favorite fishing, hunting, and hiking area.
Left on this road, called Scott's Trail because it is the route taken by Felix Scott and his party. The Pacific Crest Trail is at 3 *m.* (*see above*).

At **42** *m.* is the junction with a dirt road.

Left on this road to FROG FOREST CAMP, 0.3 *m.;* L. here on a foot trail to the OBSIDIAN CLIFFS, 2 *m.*, on White Branch Creek. They are striking formations of black volcanic glass that cooled so rapidly they did not crystallize (*see above*).

The highway drops rapidly down White Branch Creek, which has its source in Collier Glacier on the North Sister, in a series of sweeping reverse curves as it descends the tortuous Dead Horse Hill (*drive carefully*). White Branch Creek was in the path of the mighty glacier that once extended for 40 miles westward from the Three Sisters, covering what is now the valley of the McKenzie River with ice, in places, 1,200 feet thick.

At **47** *m.* is ALDER SPRINGS FOREST CAMP (3,600 alt.).

Left from the forest camp 1 *m.* on a foot trail to LINTON LAKE (*excellent fishing*), which was formed by a lava stream damming the valley. Two streams of water tumbling down the mountain side and dropping about 1,000 feet in a series of beautiful falls and cascades feed the lake. It has no visible outlet, the water disappearing through an underground channel in the lava rock.

From the bottom of WHITE BRANCH CANYON, **49** *m.,* steep sides (R) rise to lofty heights and show gray outcroppings of andesetic rock through the rich verdure.

In the WHITE BRANCH WINTER SPORTS AREA, **50.4** *m.,* the Forest Service has developed ski runs and provided a spacious log shelter with fireplaces and kitchens.

LOST CREEK RANCH, **53.3** *m.* (1,956 alt.), at the foot of Dead Horse Hill, is the first supply point west of Sisters. The creek received its name from its disappearance and reappearance among the lava beds.

Passing LIMBERLOST FOREST CAMP, **55.7** *m.* (1,750 alt.), the highway reaches YALE'S RANCH, **56.8** *m.* (1,678 alt.), and a junction with a dirt road.

Right on this road up the McKenzie River to BELKNAP HOT SPRINGS, 1 *m.* (*natural mineral baths; warm open-air swimming pool; lodge; cabins*), a popular Oregon rendezvous for health seekers. It continues to a number of forest camps; BOULDER, 2 *m.*, OLALLIE CREEK, 7 *m.*, KIRK CREEK, 10 *m.*, TAMOLITSH FALLS, 12.5 *m.*, KOOSAH FALLS, 15 *m.*, and CLEAR LAKE, 18 *m.* (*No supplies for sale north of Belknap Springs.*) At 21 *m.* is a junction with State 54 (*see TOUR 7b*), an alternate route to Sisters and Bend in early spring if the snows have been heavy on McKenzie Pass and slow in melting.

McKENZIE BRIDGE, 62 *m.,* long an important crossing of McKENZIE RIVER and adjacent to a wide recreational area, is one of Oregon's most attractive mountain playgrounds. This is the supervising center for the Willamette National Forest and the most popular base in the entire area for hiking, hunting, fishing, and pack and saddle trips. (*Detailed information about trips and other matters available at the District Ranger Station; pack and saddle horses, guides and equipment, for hire; stores, hotels, cabins, cottages available.*) The beautiful, rushing McKenzie River adds the final touch of charm. In this region are held the winter sports carnivals given annually by the Eugene Obsidians. The McKenzie River, one of Oregon's famed fishing streams, rises in Clear Lake 16 miles north of McKenzie Bridge. The giant springs that feed the lake give to its water a transparency that reflects the greenery of hilly shores. (*Fishing from boats in upper river prohibited; but fly casting from boats permitted in lower river.*) The highway follows this stream, frequently broken by cascades and rapids, the greater part of the way to Springfield (*see below*). Resorts and summer homes line the river banks for many miles.

Left from McKenzie Bridge on a dirt road up Horse Creek to HORSE CREEK FOREST CAMP, 1 *m.*

Right 1 *m.* from the forest camp on the King Road to Castle Rock Trail, a well-graded foot trail leading to the top of CASTLE ROCK, 6.5 *m.* (3,800 alt.). Continue up the Horse Creek Road to FOLEY HOT SPRINGS, 4 *m.* (1,700 alt.), a commercial resort and recreation center named for Dr. Foley, who homesteaded the site 60 years ago.

At **62.6** *m.* is McKENZIE FOREST CAMP, one of the most highly developed and popular forest camps in the area, with a half-mile frontage on the river.

At **65.3** *m.* is a junction with a dirt road.

Left on this road, not improved and passable in summer only, to a number of forest camps: STRUBE'S, 2 *m.,* EAST FORK, 5 *m.,* DRIFT POINT, 6 *m.,* FRENCH PETE'S, 11 *m.,* DUTCH OVEN, 16 *m.,* HOMESTEAD, 18 *m.,* TWIN SPRINGS, 20 *m.,* FRISSEL CROSSING, 22 *m.,* and ROARING RIVER, 23 *m.* The road surmounts the divide at BOX CANYON FOREST GUARD STATION, 26 *m.* (3,682 alt.), forming a junction with State 58 at OAKRIDGE, 60 *m.* (*see TOUR 4C*). This route, in combination with US 28, State 58, and US 99 form what is known as the BOX CANYON LOOP. It penetrates a country known for superb scenery and fine fishing.

At **66.8** *m.* US 28 leaves the Willamette National Forest.

At **68.7** *m.,* is a junction with a dirt road.

Right on this road to LUCKY BOY SCOUT CAMP, 1 *m.,* on BLUE RIVER. At 2 *m.* the road terminates in a trail leading 11 *m.* to the lookout on CARPENTER MOUNTAIN.

BLUE RIVER, **71.8** *m.* (1,056 alt., 73 pop.), is at the confluence of Blue River and the McKenzie. (*Accommodations limited; horses and guides available.*)

The five-mile stretch from the mouth of Blue River to MIDWAY, **76.6** *m.,* is a popular boat-fishing section. The McKenzie drops more than 60 feet in this distance, with occasional swift rapids, so the sport of boat fishing is not without excitement. Below Midway is swifter water, terminating in MARTINS RAPIDS, 83.6 m. Although passable by boat, these rapids are hazardous and require knowledge of the stream. Below the rapids the river is more placid.

VIDA, 86.4 m. (788 alt., 28 pop.), by Gate Creek, has a STATE SALMON HATCHERY, and on HATCHERY CREEK, 88.4 m., is a STATE TROUT HATCHERY that stocks several Cascade Mountain lakes and portions of the McKenzie River. (*Both hatcheries open to visitors.*)

Near the confluence of Hatchery Creek and the McKenzie is the dam from which water is diverted for the Eugene municipal power plant at LEABURG, 93.7 m., (680 alt., 25 pop.).

SPRINGFIELD, 111.2 m. (459 alt., 2,364 pop.), is an industrial and lumbering center on the east bank of the Willamette River. A FLAX PLANT was built here in 1936 as a WPA project. The BLANK MILL is the first mill in the United States to specialize in production of yarn from the fur of Angora rabbits (1934). The weaving of Angora wool is an infant industry. The rabbit fur is combined with sheep's wool to be spun by the machines as only human fingers can spin the pure Angora, which is "finer than silk and lighter than swansdown." The clip of one rabbit in one year is about 12 ounces. Each rabbit is clipped four times a year and the number one grade sells for five or six dollars a pound. Enthusiasts claim that the yarn from the rabbit fur is many times warmer than wool.

West of Springfield, US 28 crosses the Willamette River, 111.5 m. to a junction with US 99 (*see TOUR 2b*), 111.8 m., 2.4 miles south of Eugene.

Tour 6A

Cairo — Nyssa — Adrian — Jordan Valley — Rome; 115 m. US 30S, State 201.

Branch line of Union Pacific Railroad roughly parallels route between Cairo and Adrian.
Paved road between Cairo and Adrian; between Adrian and Jordan Valley road graveled or rock surfaced; remainder mainly unimproved.
Accommodations limited and area sparsely settled; cars should be well serviced.
Gas, oil, and water should be replenished at every opportunity; extra water should be carried, both for radiator and drinking purposes.

State 201 leads into the country of the Basques. These picturesque people have isolated themselves in this section of southeastern Oregon to follow an ancient occupation brought from their native Pyrenees of Spain. The Basque sheepherders, singing their native songs as they tend their flocks, add color to the gray sagebrush hills. The region is one of volcanic buttes and rimrock, of meager streams and dry lake beds, of deserts and endless horizons. Juniper, sagebrush, rabbit brush, and the native grasses of the uplands, with occasional scattered clumps of willows and poplars that mark the irrigated stretches, make up the scanty vegetation.

In the northern section the route crosses the newly developed area of the Vale-Owyhee Irrigation Projects, which are bringing many thousands of arid acres of Malheur County under cultivation. As it continues toward the interior it penetrates a geologically interesting area, which, because of its isolation, has remained virtually unknown.

US 30S, branching south from US 28 at CAIRO, 0 *m.* (2,170 alt., 20 pop.) (*see TOUR 6a*), parallels the Snake River to NYSSA, 7.8 *m.* (2,179 alt., 821 pop.), the center of a dairy, poultry, and fruit-growing area, and the nearest railroad point of importance to the Owyhee Irrigation Project (*see below*). Many square miles of the best farming lands are tributary to Nyssa, a fertile region dotted with green poplars, locusts, and fruit trees. Fields of sugar beets, potatoes, and alfalfa, gradually give place to wheat and grazing lands.

At Nyssa is a $2,500,000 beet sugar refining plant, the largest and newest plant of the six operated by Amalgamated Sugar Company of Ogden, Utah, whose steel and concrete buildings are spread over 190 acres. Established in 1938, the plant employs 300 persons who work in three eight-hour shifts and provides work for 2,000 seasonal field hands. Trucks and trains bring the beets from 18,000 acres of the Owyhee reclamation area of Malheur County to the yards of the refinery where they are stored in long, high, flat-topped piles with rounded ends and flaring sides. From these piles the beets are flumed into the factory where they are thoroughly washed, after which they go on a roller picking table where jets of water remove loose foreign matter. After being cut into thin strips called *cossettes* (Fr. chips), a conveyor dumps them into battery cells (large vats), where the sugar juice is diffused from the beets with hot water and a fairly dense sugar solution. The juice goes from the battery to the first carbonation where milk or lime is added. Lime coagulates and renders insoluble part of the non-sugars. After a second carbonation the sugar in solution is separated by filtration from lime and non-sugars. Later, this juice is again treated with carbon dioxide gas and once again filtered to remove the remaining lime. The juice is filtered five times before going to the crystallization process.

One of the most highly skilled jobs in the factory is the operation of the vacuum pans where the sugar crystals are formed. Thick juice, together with melted brown sugar, is pumped to these vacuum pans where the syrup is evaporated until the sugar crystallizes from the surrounding syrup into crystals of a size suitable for the market. Centrifugal machines are used to drain the liquor from the crystals, which are then taken to the drier before being sacked. The outer edge of the baskets travel at a speed of three miles a minute.

The sugar is sacked automatically in various sizes ranging up to 100 pounds. The sacks are then sewed and conveyed to a large air-conditioned warehouse, whose capacity is half a million 100 pound bags with the trade mark "White Satin." The factory completes the process of sugar making in nine hours, producing more than a ton and a half a minute throughout the 24 hour day.

South of Nyssa the route follows State 201.

At **16** *m.* is a junction with a dirt road.

Right on this road to the OWYHEE DAM, 22 *m.*, a part of the great Vale-Owyhee Project (*see TOUR 6a*), the largest irrigation development in Oregon. (*Pomona Grange maintains improved picnic grounds. See superintendent at Dam about campsites and fires. Guide service, 25c. Motor-boats for hire, 25c per person for two-hour trip. State licenses required for fishing and hunting.*)

The Owyhee Dam, a magnificent, white concrete monolith wedged between the basaltic cliffs of the narrow gorge of the OWYHEE RIVER, is the second highest dam in the world. Behind it is the Owyhee Reservoir, impounding the flood water from more than 10,000 square miles of the Owyhee drainage basin, and forming a lake 52 miles long and from one mile to six or seven miles wide. The distribution system of siphons, pipe-lines, and tunnels, aided by pumping stations, conveys sufficient water to irrigate an extensive area of land that has been arid waste for untold centuries. Already a portion of the project's 65,000 acres is bearing bountiful crops of alfalfa, fruits, small grains, and vegetables. Since the dam is capable of storing sufficient water for two years' use, the surrounding region is practically secure against drouth.

When preliminary work started, it was necessary to excavate to a depth of 175 feet below bedrock and to fill in with concrete. The huge structure rests on this foundation, spreading fan-wise from the bottom to meet the sloping gorge walls until it attains a span of 835 feet. The Owyhee Dam rises 405 feet from bedrock, with a thickness of 255 feet at the base and 30 feet at the crest. Its construction required 540,000 cubic yards of concrete, incorporated with a very white gravel. It has a storage capacity of 1,120,000 acre-feet of water, of which 715,000 acre-feet represent live storage or usable water.

The Owyhee Dam was authorized by an act of Congress in 1924, begun in 1926, and finished in 1932, at a cost of $6,000,000. The completed Owyhee Project will cost about $18,000,000. Before construction of the dam could begin, it was necessary to divert the river from its channel through a tunnel 25 feet in diameter and 1,500 feet long. The bore was through solid rock, from a point above the dam to a point below. Upon completion of the dam, the upper end of the tunnel was sealed, reserving a hole into the tunnel to act as a spillway. The water seeping through this "glory hole" as through a huge funnel, is an interesting feature of the dam. The Owyhee Dam is the first to be equipped with a freight and passenger elevator, which has a lift of 271 feet.

The Owyhee River was named in 1826 by Peter Skene Ogden, explorer for the Hudson's Bay Company, because two of his men, from the Hawaiian or Owyhee Islands, had been murdered on the river bank by Indians.

ADRIAN, **20.1** *m.* (2,190 alt., 60 pop.) (*service station and stores*), gateway to the Owyhee Dam, is in a farming district where pea-raising is extensively followed.

South of Adrian is a region of extensive sage plains, rolling hills, and rocky defiles. The SUCKER CREEK CANYON, **32.5** *m.,* is a cavernous gulch with walls that rise sheer for 300 feet and then slope upward to the height of a thousand feet. At certain points the canyon is so deep and narrow that stars are visible in the daytime. The overhanging rocks of the cliff are the natural abode of eagles. Southward of the canyon is an almost trackless expanse of sagebrush, the only human life observable an occasional sheepherder keeping vigil on hills grey-white with the wool of moving flocks.

ROCKVILLE, **57.8** *m.,* a hamlet, gets its name from fossil-bearing rocks in the vicinity. MALLOY RANCH, **63.9** *m.* (R), is one of the largest sheep ranches in the region and was one of the oldest cattle ranches in Oregon, dating back to the 1870's.

Left from the ranch, an improved road leads northwesterly across the Idaho Line, **2.3** *m.,* and into the valley of the Snake River. This is part of a projected Federal Aid highway, known as the I.O.N. (Idaho, Oregon, Nevada) Highway, which will follow the general course of the route as far as Rome (*see below*) then southerly across the Nevada Line, at McDermitt, and to Nevada and California points.

SHEAVILLE, **72.7** *m.,* is the center of a sheep-raising district.

JORDAN VALLEY, **83.2** *m.* (4,389 alt., 306 pop.), a Basque settlement, keeps its old world atmosphere. According to one account, a Basque sea captain came to San Francisco in the 1870's and found his way to Winnemucca by the new railroad. He remained in the grazing section, made his fortune, and then returned to Spain to spread the tidings of a great sheep country in the New World. Another story is that ambitious young men came from the Basque country by way of Ellis Island and drifted across the continent in search of a promised land which they found in this region adapted to a people that have loved liberty and solitude for centuries.

Among the early Basque settlers of the Jordan Creek Valley was Augustine B. Azcuenaga, who arrived about 1880 and took up sheep growing on a large scale.

The Basque houses of Jordan Valley have brightly painted rooms and are built of native stone in the Pyrenean manner to insure warmth in winter and coolness in summer. Huge piles of sagebrush in the dooryards are reminders that wood is scarce.

Names of the residents add to the feeling that one is very remote from all things American. Among them are Carmen Guerricagoitia, Thomas Corta, Pilar Eisaguirre, Alfonso Acordogoitia, Emilia Chertudi, Jesus Arristola, Damaso Cortabitarte, the pronunciation of which few persons attempt.

As descendants of a people that inhabited Spain before the Celts, the Basques claim to be the oldest unmixed race in Europe. The typical Basque has a remarkably clear skin, sparkling dark or blue eyes, and a warm smile. The women are noted for their dark beauty, which is heightened by the bright colors of their native dress and the graceful lace mantillas, intriguingly draped over high combs in the Spanish fashion.

The Basque herder carries his blanket roll on his back; slung at his side is his desert water bag, and in his hand his staff. During summer, distant fires on the hills tell of his solitary watch. Perhaps for many weeks no one comes near him but the camp tender, who brings supplies from the home ranch on the back of a burro.

Away from their work the Basques are a gay people, dancing, playing the guitar, accordion, or harp; they are likely to gather around the plaza in pastimes that bring the color of Old Spain to the wilderness. Among their folk dances are the arreska, the fandango and farandole. Their primitive dances, some of which were taken over by the Romans, are related to the Egyptian ritual. Among them are the vintage dance, the sword dance, and the weaving dance, from which we take our maypole dance. An organization with headquarters at Boise, Idaho, has for one of its purposes the preservation of the old Basque dances, customs, and music.

The pioneer generation of Oregon has kept alive these racial traditions, engaging in their old festivities on such occasions as their three important holidays—Christmas, New Year's and Three King's Day. The latter is observed on January 6, a festival honoring the eastern Kings who visited the Christ Child. In holiday mood, while the musicians play their native instruments, the others stand in a circle with their hands on one another's shoulders and sing. Plaintive Spanish songs, melodious Basque airs, and old French folk songs echo over the rimrock. A traveler to Jordan Valley thus pictures a modern occasion: "After a Basque dinner the entire population assembled in the community hall and gave a Basque dance in our honor. The snapping fingers, gaiety, merry-making, and frequent bursts of song that accompanied the dances flowed from the deep roots of their ancient heritage."

The Basques have brought their national game of handball, *pelota*, to the new world. It is a game played by two, four, or six players, in which the ball is thrown by hand against a stone wall, somewhat after the manner of American handball. The HANDBALL COURT is near the Jordan Valley Hotel.

The language spoken by the Basques is an ancient tongue; the characters are Roman and some of the words betray an Egyptian likeness. It is a smoothly flowing language with many final vowels, and it is said to be an enigma to philologists. The verb may contain allied parts of speech and sometimes uses 50 forms for one person. It is little wonder that French peasants said that the devil studied the Basque language for seven years and learned only two words. He was therefore unable to interfere in their religious faith.

At Jordan Valley the Basques have their own church and priest who conducts the services in the Basque language. The entire Basque family attends the service, all the little girls in spotless and stiffly starched white. It is told that the first marriage ceremony performed in Oregon could not be conducted until the ritual was forwarded from Salt Lake, since the couple, to their way of thinking, could be married only by their own rites. Since the Basque men out-number the women, the Basque men intermarry with American women, but the Basque girls rarely marry outside their own race.

In a Basque settlement dogs are nearly as important as the people. In southeastern Oregon the favored type is the Australian sheep dog, a small agile animal, with gray, nondescript coat and unmatched eyes; insignificant appearing, but in reality highly intelligent and highly trained. Without them the bands of sheep could not be handled.

"Every Basque a noble," is a saying that is not questioned by those who have known these people in their adopted land. Their devotion to a tradition has helped build a great industry. They have replaced one romantic epoch with another and have added their own color to landscapes that would be bleak without them. A racial ideal is preserved in one of their old songs:

> Far nobler on our mountains is he that yokes the ox,
> And equal to a monarch, the shepherd of the flocks.

West of Jordan Valley the route follows the newly constructed I.O.N. Highway, paralleling JORDAN CREEK, named for Michael M. Jordan, leader of a party that found gold on the banks of the stream in 1863, and the first settler of the district.

At 88 m. is a junction with the old Oregon Central Military Road, a section of the stage route that formerly ran from San Francisco to Idaho City.

R. on this rough and rocky road that is probably much as it was in the early stagecoach days, to an old STONE FORT, 8.6 m., once a stage stop and place of refuge from Indian attacks. DANNER, 9.6 m. (50 pop.), originally named Ruby for the old Ruby Cattle Ranch, is the nearest point to the JORDAN CRATERS (difficult of access; inquire at Danner for directions). These craters and an adjacent lava area of 60 square miles have been of extraordinary interest to the few scientists and tourists who have visited them. From recently extinct volcanoes, they have not been changed by erosion and they support no vegetation. The area is said to be comparable in extent, geologic interest, and scenic value to the Craters of the Moon in Idaho.

ROME, 115 m. (3,381 alt., 100 pop.), (service station, store), was named for imposing and fantastic formations of fossil-bearing clay, called the "Walls of Rome," which are southeast of the village. They are about five miles long and two miles wide, and rise to a height of 100 feet. Gloomy ravines penetrate the mounds and buttes. Among the most interesting of the formations are great solitary clay blocks that appear to have been shaped by the chisel of a giant sculptor. At dusk these mesas are weird and sinister in appearance, and moonlight dusts their symmetrical contours with an uncanny splendor.

Tour 7

Vale — Burns — Bend — Sisters — Albany; 370 m. State 54. Santiam Highway.

Paved or gravel roadbed. Between Burns and Bend route traverses 138 miles of almost uninhabited country. Sufficient gas and water should be provided.

Service stations at Hampton, and a few other points. Snow occasionally blocks road at Santiam Pass on the summit of the Cascades. Sudden winter blizzards in the desert country an added hazard.

Union Pacific Railroad parallels the route between Vale and Juntura; Oregon Short Line between Juntura and Burns; Southern Pacific Railroad between Albany and Lebanon. Motor stage service between Burns and Bend, also Bend and Sisters; summer stage service over the Cascades.

Tourist accommodations range from excellent to very limited; hotels in cities; tourist camps.

Through central Oregon State 54 crosses a comparatively unsettled country, about which cluster the traditions of the Old West, when the range was free, herds uncounted, and ranches small principalities, with the latch-string out for strangers. But the cowboy of tradition has vanished, and a modern, less picturesque type has taken his place. The red men who drove off the cattle and burned the buildings of the ranchers, doze on the reservations, and the rustlers live only in memory or on the picture screen. The open spaces are tamed by the invading homesteader. The cattle kings of the Old West are gone, and their vast empires lost in a mesh of barb wire.

Between Burns and Bend lies the High Desert, graveyard of homesteaders' hopes. When the better lands of Oregon had been taken up, land-hungry settlers swarmed into this, one of the most inhospitable regions of continental United States. High, arid, treeless, and chill, the country baffled the utmost labors of the homesteaders and destroyed their dream of a new wheat empire. It has reverted to what it was before the unhappy pioneers went down to defeat. Beyond the Cascades is the more densely settled Willamette Valley.

State 54 follows approximately the route of the old central Oregon Emigrant Trail. In 1845, a wagon train piloted by Stephen H. L. Meek, brother of the famous Col. Joe Meek, came through this region, in an attempt to find a short cut to the Willamette Valley, instead of following the established route of the Oregon Trail. The country was unknown to any of the party other than Meek. Bewildered by the maze of similar ridges, canyons, and washes of the region, he was soon lost. For weeks the migrants struggled across the sagebrush desert, suffering intensely from the lack of water and food, but finally won through to the Deschutes, which they descended to The Dalles. More than 70 members of the train died from hardship and exposure in this the greatest disaster met by a wagon train in Oregon. Other trains followed, hardy bands that profited from the knowledge of the country obtained by the first adventurers, and the Central Route became established as one of the three main trails into western Oregon.

The old Willamette Valley and Cascade Mountain Military Road, laid out from Albany to Ontario, and built between 1864 and 1868, followed the Emigrant Trail. It was an important factor in the development of the Willamette Valley and the interior. Wagon trains, some of them a half-mile long, brought wool and livestock from the range country and returned with fruit, vegetables, and other food supplies. Stagecoaches, carrying mail and passengers, added a dramatic chapter to this historic road. Every settlement on the route drew all or a part of its livelihood from this source. Seventy years ago a reverse flow of homesteaders entered central Oregon by the road. The first automobile to cross the United States was driven over this road in June, 1905.

Section a. Vale to Bend, 246.7 m. State 54

State 54 branches southwest from its junction with US 28 at VALE, 0 m. (2,243 alt., 922 pop.), the seat of Malheur County, headquarters for the VALE IRRIGATION PROJECT, and shipping point for a wide agricultural and range country. (*Hotel; tourist camps; natatorium.*) In 1864, Jonathan Keeney built a small house on the bank of the Malheur River, where he offered accommodations to west-bound migrants and miners on their way to the Powder River and Boise mines. To the migrants this arid country appeared a land devoid of hope or promise, and they pushed on hurriedly to other fields. Stockmen saw its possibilities, and eventually it became a typical frontier cattle town and trading center for a large expanse of range country. Stages left Vale each day heavily laden with mail and passengers for the tedious journey over the barren hills to Burns, 140 miles away. Two days and a night were required for the trip, which was continuous, with a change of horses every 15 miles.

The Vale Reclamation Project combined with the great Owyhee Project (*see TOUR 6A*), the largest irrigation development in Oregon, has been constructed by the United States Bureau of Reclamation. The Project comprises more than 30,000 acres of irrigable land to the north of the Malheur River, with an average elevation of 2,370 feet above sea level. It gets its water supply from the natural flow of the river, and from the Warm Springs Reservoir, on the Middle Fork about 80 miles southwest of Vale, and another reservoir with a capacity of 6,000 acre-feet on the North Fork (*see below*). A diversion dam about 60 miles down-stream from the main dam carries the water through a main canal to the Jamieson district. The major portion of the project is sagebrush benchland, surrounded by a large hilly region, covered with sagebrush and native grasses, which furnishes a summer grazing range for thousands of sheep and cattle. The irrigated lands, which produce heavily, are devoted to a wide variety of crops, with alfalfa predominating. In portions of the area, apple, peach, and pear orchards yield abundantly.

Vale has an asset in the numerous hot springs at the eastern edge of the city, the water serves a sanitarium and a laundry. The springs were known in pioneer days and it is said the women of the emigrant trains stopped at this point to do their laundering.

El Campo Rugeinte (Sp. The Roaring Camp), commemorating gold rush days, is an annual winter festival of the Vale Fire Department.

West of Vale are irrigated farmlands, beyond which are fold upon fold of arid sage-covered hills, treeless except for scattered junipers. The country is impressive for the immensity of the barren reaches and the vast horizons. In small valleys along the creeks are ranches marked by the characteristic tall Lombardy poplars. State 54 for 60 miles follows the course of the MALHEUR RIVER, named, in 1826 by Peter Skene Ogden, who left a cache of furs and supplies hidden on the river. When he returned with his fur brigade he found that the cache had been rifled by Indians and the stream became the River au Malheur (*evil hour*).

HARPER (R), **22.6** *m.* (2,514 alt., 50 pop.), was named for the Harper Ranch of the Pacific Livestock Company, which in turn was named for an early settler along the Malheur River. The lands of the Vale Irrigation Project extend to the right. The town is the headquarters of the Harper Unit of the Project (*see TOUR 6a*).

Right from Harper on an unimproved road 1 *m.* to the QUARRIES and MILL used for the development of diatomaceous silica deposits that underlie the region. The extreme toughness and absence of lamination in the product render it suitable for insulating brick and for other forms subject to crushing loads. This white substance is chemically inert, insoluble in water, and practically indestructible, since it easily sustains a temperature of more than 2,000 degrees without cracking or shrinking.

Left from Harper on a country road leading southwest between the Steens and the Cedar mountains, into the heart of the great eastern Oregon range country, and to the Basque settlements of Harney and Malheur counties. COYOTE WELLS, 20 *m.*, was named for the ubiquitous little wolf of the high country. At 32 *m.* is SKULL SPRINGS (4,420 alt.), where water pours out of a solid rock shaped like a skull.

FOLLYFARM, 75 *m.* (4,068 alt.), was so named because of an unsuccessful attempt to irrigate land under adverse conditions (*see TOUR 5A*).

West of Harper the valley narrows to the confines of the deep gash of MALHEUR CANYON which the river has cut through the volcanic strata.

At **44.3** *m.*, is the site of one of the older cattle ranches, known as Jonesborough, from the founder, William Jones, whose original log cabin is still standing (L) near the ranch house.

JUNTURA, **56.8** *m.* (2,953 alt., 136 pop.), is the trade center of a large sheep-raising and wool region. At this point, the North Fork of the Malheur River joins with the South Fork, to give the town its name. The poplar-shaded village lies in a small valley, where vivid green alfalfa fields are in striking contrast with the surrounding barren gray hills. It is a shipping point for sheep and cattle. Extensive lambing sheds lie to the L. across the railroad tracks.

A hot spring flows from a hillside at the edge of town. It is owned by the town and is used to supply the water for a community bath house.

This entire valley and the surrounding range country were once dominated by Henry Miller, the most powerful cattle baron of eastern Oregon. The valley was then known as the Juntura Ranch (*see TOUR 5b*).

Right from Juntura on a gravel road is BEULAH, (3,277 alt., 26 pop.), 15.8 *m.*, just north of which is the AGENCY DAM, a part of the Vale Irrigation Project. About 2,000 acres of the surrounding area were known as Agency Valley because of the Indian reservation established here in the early 1880's. Here the Indians were made to work with plow and scraper, constructing irrigation canals. They could not understand why the white man wanted to take the rivers away and put them in other places, and before long they not only refused to work but openly revolted. They stole horses and cattle and ravaged the countryside, murdering settlers and burning houses. When troops were sent against them they would not surrender and were killed. This left an improved reservation but no one to benefit by it.

One day Henry Miller (*see TOUR 5b*) was inspecting his corrals in California when he saw a fine bunch of steers belonging to T. M. Overfelt, an Oregon cattleman. When he learned from Overfelt of the quality of the grazing grasses in Oregon, Miller bought a partnership with him, and together they rapidly acquired land and cattle. The apple of their eyes was Agency Ranch in the reservation, vacant but for the agent who kept up the canals; they visualized the verdant pasturage that would result from proper handling of the water. Overfelt was in the Silvies Valley when he was informed at the last moment of the government land sale of the ranch being held at Lakeview. He jumped on his horse and by relaying to fresh mounts at the ranches along the way he covered the distance of nearly 200 miles in less than 24 hours, arriving in time to outbid two competitors. His draft on the company, known as a "Bull's Head" because of the picture of the head of a bull on it, was refused. These drafts were honored in all communities where the company was known, and when Miller appealed to the General Land Office the commissioner held that the draft was good. Shortly afterwards Overfelt was dragged to death when the saddle slipped from the horse he was riding.

Left from Juntura, on a country road to a SHEARING AND DIPPING PLANT, 4 *m.*, equipped with mechanical shearing devices. During the season, many wagons leave this plant piled high with bags of wool.

RIVERSIDE, 22 *m.* (3,330 alt., 48 pop.), is a small but typical frontier town, which has gone through four phases of development. It was established as a trading center for cattlemen of the old regime. As the sheep men encroached on the cattle barons, it became a wool and shearing center. With the building of the railroad, it took on the dynamic life of a railroad construction camp. Finally it was the scene of the building of the WARM SPRINGS DAM, a part of the Vale Project, which brought agriculture to the range country.

Above Riverside is the WARM SPRINGS RESERVOIR, with a storage capacity of 190,000 acre-feet, forming a lake about 12 miles long.

At **66.3** *m.* State 54 enters Harney County, the largest county of Oregon, exceeding in size the combined areas of Massachusetts and Rhode Island. It was created February 25, 1889, and named for William S. Harney, a veteran of three Indian wars, the Mexican and Civil wars, and the Commander of the Department of Oregon in 1858. Over this wide, sparsely-populated expanse grazed the herds of the former cattle barons, and its wide boundaries still include a number of the largest individually-owned cattle ranches in Oregon. Great stretches remain in their primitive state, with herds of antelope roaming the sage plains, and bear, deer, and other large game abundant in the wilder mountain regions.

(At the county line change is made between Mountain and Pacific Standard Times.)

At **32.2** *m.* is a junction with an unimproved road.

Right on this road to DREWSEY, 3 *m.* (3,516 alt., 66 pop.), a town on the old stage route from Vale to Burns. This village was the scene of highly-colored drama of the Old West, when cattlemen, bad men, gamblers, miners, and adventurers quickened the pulse-beat of frontier life.

Abner Robbins started a store at this place in the summer of 1883, and called it Gouge Eye, from the frontier method of settling disputes. For a number of years the settlement was known by this unpleasant name. Postal authorities refused to adopt it, and it was called Drewsey in honor of Drewsey Miller, daughter of a rancher.

West of Drewsey is the STINKING WATER MOUNTAIN (4,848 alt.) named from the disagreeable fumes of mineral springs along a creek of the same name. The route climbs the slopes of this elevation through juniper, and occasional pine to the summit, winds along the crest of the mountain, and at **89.4** *m.* overlooks the sweeping expanses of the great Harney Valley, lost in a haze of color.

The old BUCHANAN STAGE STATION (L), **91.6** *m.,* was on the run from Vale to Burns; it was kept by Thomas Buchanan, who took up this homestead in the 1880's.

On the level Harney Valley floor is a junction with a dirt road, **102.6** *m.*

Right on this road to HARNEY, 2 *m.,* on Rattlesnake Creek. It was once the center of all the varied life of Harney Valley; it is a ghost town with only one occupied house and two or three inhabitants. Rabbit brush and sage flatten in the wind about its tottering walls; jack-rabbits leap along the one street, and rattlesnakes sun on the deserted steps of the store, whose counters and showcases are still standing.

North of the town is the SITE OF FORT HARNEY, 2 *m.,* established in 1867, whose troops under Gen. O. O. Howard, fought in the Bannock-Paiute war of 1878 (*see TOUR 1C*). Near the Post was a cemetery; the remains of soldiers buried there have been removed.

At **112.5** *m.* is a junction with US 395 (*see TOUR 5a*), with which State 54 is united for about 30 miles.

BURNS, **115** *m.* (4,155 alt., 2,599 pop.), the seat of Harney County, is one of the key cities of interior Oregon, and one of the most remote, serving a larger trade area than many eastern states. Burns was the capital of the old cattle empire.

Located on the cattle ranch of Pete Stinger, the town was named paradoxically for Robert Burns, the poet. In 1889, Burns was still a straggling frontier village of one dusty main street bordered by frame shacks. Because of its desert location many of the later buildings are native stone which give an air of solidity to the city. Indians in moccasins and gaudy blankets add a dress-rehearsal touch of the primitive to the modern street scene of Burns.

For more than 50 years the settlers waited for the railroad, and it was a colorful throng that saw the first train arrive in September, 1924. The sombreroed cattlemen were there, and the cowboys, with spurs jingling on high-heeled boots, and the Indians, in native splendor.

The designation of Burns as the administrative headquarters of the Taylor Grazing Act, 1936, made it the modern livestock center of Oregon.

In striking contrast to the modern and progressive Burns is the Paiute Indian village within the city boundaries. This settlement constitutes the only independent unit of Indian life in Oregon and is said to be the largest permanent Indian settlement outside a reservation in the United States. It is probable that a small number of Paiutes who engaged in the Bannock War of 1878, returned to the Burns country after the Indian princess, Winnemucca, secured their release from the close confinement of the Reservation at Yakima, Wash., where they were herded after Gen. Howard defeated them at Willow Springs (*see TOUR 5a*). Since this uprising and the dissolution of the Malheur Reservation the Indians in this vicinity who could make their own living, have been allowed to do so. Many find employment in the lumber mills. Because of the squalor of the old village a new one has been recently built to which the families have moved. The second village, with its small but rather individual white houses, is more cleanly and more comfortable if less picturesque than the native patchwork village.

HINES, 117.4 *m.,* is the $4,000,000 development of the Edward Hines Lumber Company. The town is built about a huge electrically operated plant erected in 1930, which has the most modern machinery, loading facilities, and 40 dry-kilns. The mill is located on the margin of a small lake, fed by warm springs, of such even temperature that it does not freeze over even in the coldest weather, and makes an ideal log-storage pond. Twenty acres are under cover in the units comprising the manufacturing and shipping departments. Storage sheds, a half-mile in length, protect the lumber. Three large band and resaws have a capacity cut of 400,000 feet of lumber daily, with an annual output of 100,000,000 feet. Logging headquarters are at Seneca, at the edge of the Malheur National Forest, containing one of the largest stands of ponderosa pine yet remaining in the West (*see TOUR 5a*).

West of Hines is the high desert, a land of isolated sagebrush flats, alkali depressions, dry lake beds, and creek bottoms. In late spring, the region is briefly green with grasses springing to new life. Clusters of golden-belled flowers and patches of purple lupine give vivid touches of color. As summer advances the vividness fades and low-toned grays return. This country, constantly changing under the changing light, has a grim allure. Fleeting mirages often add a mysterious beauty to the landscape, and in the evening haze, the buttes and distant heights take on softer tones. The region is made memorable in Oregon literature by Charles Erskine Scott Wood in *The Poet in the Desert,* and Ada Hastings Hedges, in her *Desert Poems.*

LOCKER CASTLE (L), **120.1** *m.,* is a curious structure built in crude imitation of a German castle. It is a weird labyrinth of rooms, passages, and underground chambers which were never habitable with the exception of one room in which the owner lived until his death. It was built about 1912 by an old German eccentric named Locker.

At **141.9** *m.* US 395 leaves State 54 and turns southward (*see TOUR 5b*).

M. M. Brown's GAP RANCH (R), **155.7** *m.,* now deserted, once nurtured large herds of prize horses and cattle. The SQUAW BUTTE LIVESTOCK EXPERIMENT STATION has been established near the Gap Ranch by the U. S. Department of Agriculture in cooperation with the Oregon State College Experiment Station.

Between **164** *m.* and **175** *m.* extend (L) the great GLASS BUTTES (6,385 alt.), rising 2,000 feet above the surrounding country. These Buttes are said to be the largest obsidian outcropping in the world, and probably the largest occurrence of iridescent obsidian known. This volcanic substance, formed from rapid cooling of the lava, fractures to form sharp edges. It furnished the Indians with material for their arrow-head and spear points, skin scrapers, axes, chisels, and numerous other implements. At this place are the one-time arrow-head factories and tons upon tons of chipped obsidian left by the red men and perhaps by their predecessors. These buttes and the outcroppings of Yellowstone Park furnished the obsidian arrow-heads for the primitive Americans at least as far east as Ohio. Arrow-heads found in the Ohio mounds have been identified as having come from the Glass Buttes of Oregon. The identifying characteristic of this obsidian is its varied coloring and its iridescence reaching to a quarter of an inch in thickness. The Yellowstone obsidian is in two colors only, white and black, and is opaque. The glistening ebony and iridescent blocks, cubistic in outline, are sometimes as large as houses; others of weirdly carved shapes resemble Epstein sculptures.

The Klamath Rim, stretching for the next 50 miles, is the great ridge between the north and south drainage of eastern Oregon. In this region, known as the Imperial Valley, are many abandoned shacks, the sole evidence of an innocent trust in unscrupulous land promoters, and the disillusionment of the homesteaders when the promised Vale of Cashmere proved to be only a desert.

HAMPTON, **183.2** *m.* (4,416 alt., 31 pop.), at the base of Cougar Butte (R), was named for the distant Hampton Butte (6,333 alt.), (R). Both buttes are the results of volcanic eruptions which probably formed the extended tufa sheets over the surface of much of the adjacent country. Fossils, both flora and fauna, minerals, and curious rock formations are found in this section. (*Limited supplies and accommodations.*)

BROTHERS, **204.1** *m.* (4,650 alt., 55 pop.), is a supply station named in contradistinction to Sisters (*see below*). An interesting collection of rocks, minerals and fossils is on exhibit at an agate shop at this point.

MILLICAN, **220.7** *m.* (4,255 alt., 10 pop.), is often called the "one man town," because it was named for George Millican, its single citizen and mayor. This pioneer cattleman was one of the first to raise stock in the region, and at one time, was connected with the operation of a toll road through McKenzie Pass in the Cascade Mountains.

At 224.2 *m.* is a junction with an unimproved road.

Left on this road along the south slope of HORSE RIDGE to a junction with another dirt road at 13 *m.* Left along this latter spur 3 *m.* to ARNOLD ICE CAVES, the floors of which are covered with ice the year around.

On the rugged bluffs of the bed of DRY RIVER (R), 224.6 *m.*, is one of the largest collections of INDIAN PICTOGRAPHS in Oregon. These crude, prehistoric paintings of varying heights, are applied to the canyon walls with colors that have grown dim with the ages. (*Not visible from the highway, reached by foot-trail that leads to the base of the cliffs,* 0.2 *m.*) Dry River is a geological wonder in itself, and can be traced across the central Oregon plateau for 50 miles. Formerly, it was a large river rising in the prehistoric lake region of central Oregon, and flowing northeast to empty into an ancient stream which followed in general the course of the John Day River. The summit of Horse Ridge, 225.7 *m.*, (4,304 alt.), commands a wide panorama. Along the western horizon Mount Hood, Mount Jefferson, Broken Top, and the Sisters rear their crests above the blue ramparts of the Cascade Range.

At the northern entrance to the TERRANCE H. FOLEY STATE PARK, 245.5 *m.* is PILOT BUTTE, (3,400 alt.), a cinder cone towering 511 feet above the plain. It was by this eminence that the emigrants charted their course across the desert stretches to the crossing of the Deschutes River at Farewell Bend. From its summit, reached by a winding road, no less than a dozen snow-capped mountains are visible.

BEND, 246.7 *m.* (3,628 alt., 8,848 pop.) (*see BEND*).

Points of Interest: Drake Park, Harmon Park, Home of Klondike Kate, lumber camps and others.

Bend is at the intersection of US 97 (*see TOUR 4a*).

Section b. Bend to Albany, 123.3 *m.* State 54

West of BEND, 0 *m.*, the highway winds down through lava and juniper to the DESCHUTES RIVER BRIDGE, 5.6 *m.* (*see TOUR 4a*). At 7.1 *m.* is TUMALO (Ind., *tumallowa*, icy water), (3,183 alt., 50 pop.), an important supply and trading center, during construction of the Tumalo Irrigation Project a quarter of a century ago.

At 21.3 *m.* is a junction with US 28 (*see TOUR 6b*), with which State 54 unites. At 22.6 *m.* State 54 runs through an open forest of ponderosa pine. The highway enters the Deschutes National Forest, 25.8 *m.;* mile after mile are tall sepia-barked pines rising in columnar ranks.

At 29.6 *m.* BLACK BUTTE (6,415 alt.) appears (R) through the pine forest.

At 31.5 *m.* is a junction with a forest road.

Right on this road to CAMP SHERMAN, 5 *m.,* in the METOLIUS RIVER RECREATIONAL AREA. (*Commercial resorts with modern accommodations; cabins and tents for rent; golf course; postoffices; saddle and pack horses; supplies.*) The river springs full bodied from a rock cliff on the north slope of Black Butte at a temperature slightly above freezing, and winds through a park-like growth of pines in its upper reaches, to enter a gorge more than 1,500 feet deep at points, through which it flows into the Deschutes River (*see TOUR 4a*), immediately north of the mouth of Crooked River. The Metolius is noted for excellent fishing.

SUTTLE LAKE, 35.4 *m.* (3,433 alt.), is a beautiful body of water that rests in a forest of tall evergreens (L). (*Resort; forest camp; tourist facilities; bathing beach; boats for rent.*) At the east end of the lake is a FOREST GUARD STATION (*free telephone, campfire permits, information*). The lake teems with trout.

BLUE LAKE (L), 37.3 *m.,* a blue crater lake, cradled in rocky, timbered walls, with MOUNT WASHINGTON (7,769 alt.), rising above it (L), lies far below the highway.

SANTIAM PASS, 41.6 *m.* (4,817 alt.), marks the boundary between the Deschutes and the Willamette National Forests, and the summit of the Cascade Range. Santiam Pass was formerly called Hogg Pass, for Col. T. E. Hogg, who dreamed of a transcontinental railroad which would make Yaquina a small coast city (*see TOUR 3a*), the rival of San Francisco and Portland as a world port. The road was built from Yaquina to Corvallis, in the 1880's, and later extended toward the Cascade Mountains. Colonel Hogg met financial reverses, but to keep his franchise alive he constructed a mile of road through the pass and carried in, piecemeal, a box car which was moved periodically by mule power across the divide. The company finally went bankrupt, but near HOGG BUTTE (R), the old railroad grade is visible and a hundred yards of rails still lie on the rotted ties. Appealed to a few years ago to decide the correct name of the pass, the U. S. Board of Geographic Names, ruled in favor of Santiam.

At 42.6 *m.* the highway crosses the Pacific Crest Trail.

Right on the Pacific Crest Trail to MARION LAKE, 12.7 *m.,* a mile-long indigo pool in a jagged cup of lava. (*Forest Guard Station; improved camp; boating; fishing; bathing; feed for pack animals.*)

In the MOUNT JEFFERSON PRIMITIVE AREA, is the austere and lofty BINGHAM RIDGE, 18.4 *m.,* and green-wooded HUNT'S COVE, 21.2 *m.* Small lakes shimmer like scattered jewels. Rustic bridges sway above streams that rush through gorges or shallow canyons.

The still waters of PAMELIA LAKE, 23.8 *m.,* are sufficiently warm to permit bathing during the middle hours of summer days. (*Forest Guard Station; improved camp; good fishing, angling limited to shore casting, since there are no boats on the lake.*)

Right from Pamelia Lake, 14 *m.,* on a trail crossing ravines and creeks, passing waterfalls and small lakes, and traversing glaciers and snowfields, to the summit of MOUNT JEFFERSON (10,495 alt.).

West of the pass the open stands of yellow pine give way to dense woods of Douglas fir, mountain hemlock, and cedar, with thick growths of underbrush.

LOST LAKE (R), 46.3 *m.* (4,000 alt.), a small lake in a picturesque meadow, lies in a lava region, and though a stream flows into it, there is no visible outlet, as the water disappears into subterranean channels.

Near Lost Lake are gloomy craters and lava fields of the McKenzie flow (*see TOUR 6b*), great clots of lava in fantastic shapes.

At **47.5** *m.* is a junction with State 222 (*see TOUR 7A*).

SAWYER CAVE (L), **50.4** *m.* (3,400 alt.), was formed by a bubble in the lava crust at the time of cooling, when the molten matter congealed about a pocket of volcanic gas.

At **51.6** *m.* is a junction with a forest road.

Left on this road to FISH LAKE, 1 *m.* (*Forest Camp; Forest Ranger Station; free telephone and information about trips; fishing; and points of interest.*) Varying with the season, it may be a lake with a wide shore line, or an almost dry depression. The old tavern at Fish Lake was a popular stopping place on the pioneer toll road.

CLEAR LAKE (*campsite*), 4 *m.* (3,030 alt.), is a geological curiosity. It lies in a depression 2,000 feet deep, and was formed by the damming of the old Santiam Valley by the great McKenzie lava flow. It is fed by springs, the largest called Giant Spring, which gushes from the northeast shore. Clear Lake is the coldest in the Cascades, its temperature remaining about 41 degrees, the water of such crystal clearness that articles on the bottom, at a depth of 40 feet, can readily be distinguished. The lake is of so recent a formation that tree trunks, well preserved, and with bark still clinging to the trunks, stand on the sloping bottom.

West of the junction is TOMBSTONE PRAIRIE, **58.8** *m.* (4,252 alt.), named for the grave of the victim of an accidental shooting in an emigrant train.

At **59.5** m. is the RABBIT SPRINGS FOREST GUARD STATION.

Right from the station on a forest trail to IRON MOUNTAIN LOOKOUT, 2 *m.* (5,476 alt.). Iron Mountain is easy to climb and the reward is an inspiring view of endless virgin forests with the snow-caps of Mount Hood, Mount Jefferson, Mount Washington, and the Three Sisters looming in bold relief against the sky.

At **70.4** *m.* on State 54 is a junction with a forest road.

Right on this road to UPPER SODA SPRINGS, 0.5 *m.*, a mineral water resort.

At **71.3** *m.* is FERN VIEW CAMP, a spacious, free camp ground on the banks of the South Santiam River.

Right from Fern View Camp on a trail to ROOSTER ROCK LOOKOUT, 3 *m.*, which is plainly visible from the highway. It can be scaled by a series of ladders.

TROUT CREEK CAMP (*picnic grounds*), is at **73.9** *m.*, and at **79.3** *m.* is the western boundary of the Willamette National Forest.

CASCADIA, **81.3** *m.* (800 alt., 77 pop.), (*hotel, mineral springs*), is one of Oregon's leading mountain resorts. In earlier days it was a popular recreation spot for the Willamette Valley. The old livery barn, built of hewn logs, which played an important part in the transportation system of the stagecoach days of the old Wagon Road is an interesting relic of Cascadia.

Right from Cascadia to the CASCADIA RESORTS, 0.5 *m.* (*Privately owned medicinal soda springs, hotel and cabins.*)

Right from Cascadia Resorts 1 *m.* to the INDIAN CAVES, with prehistoric heiroglyphics scrawled upon the walls.

Right from Cascadia Resorts 4 *m.* on a trail to HIGH DECK MOUNTAIN LOOKOUT, with a fine view of the mid-Willamette Valley.

The RANGER STATION, **82.7** *m.*, serves a district of the Willamette National Forest. (*Fire permits and camping equipment checked.*) The Hill fire patrol has its large main plant a short distance from the Ranger Station.

FOSTER, **92.4** *m.* (586 alt., 85 pop.), is in the foothills bordering the Willamette Valley, near the confluence of the Santiam and the South Santiam rivers. The town is the center of a number of mountain roads and is a trading post for a wide sweep of thinly populated country.

Right from Foster on a mountain road to the QUARTZVILLE GOLD MINES, **30** *m.* In Civil War days gold miners flocked from California and southern Oregon to wash the gold out of QUARTZVILLE CREEK, and to pick nuggets of free gold out of the quartz hills. The region quickly became netted with mining claims. A British syndicate established a large gold-milling plant and for several years received substantial returns. When the free gold was exhausted the mill was closed. Since that time smaller activities have been carried on.

SWEET HOME, **95.4** *m.* (537 alt., 189 pop.), named by the pioneer Lowell Ames, who took up a donation land claim in the valley in the 1840's, is a center for small logging outfits in the surrounding hills.

At **106.3** *m.* is a junction with a gravel road.

Left on this road to SODAVILLE, 1 *m.* (77 pop.), named for the cold mineral-water spring in the SODAVILLE SPRINGS STATE PARK.

LEBANON, **109.3** *m.* (333 alt., 1,851 pop.), on the South Santiam River, is the second largest city in Linn County. Its typical pioneer dwellings are symbolic of the era when it was an important stopping place on the Cascade Wagon Road, and the outfitting of wagon trains was a profitable enterprise. Jeremiah Ralston surveyed and platted the town, in 1851, and named it for a town in Tennessee. In 1854, the Santiam Academy, founded by the Methodists, was chartered by the Territorial Legislature and established at Lebanon. Suspended in 1907, its building and grounds were acquired by the Lebanon School District. An interesting feature of the historic building, no longer standing, was the bell, brought around Cape Horn by sailing vessel, in 1864, and still in use. In 1935, a monument to perpetuate the memory of the Academy was dedicated by a number of old settlers who had secured their education in the ancient hall. At the intersection of Main and Tangent streets, Linn County Chapter of the Daughters of the American Revolution has erected a bronze tablet on a large boulder in honor of The Pioneers of the Oregon Trail. Lebanon is a fruit, nut, and farming area, and is known as a leading strawberry production center. The opening of the picking season is celebrated each year by a Strawberry Festival, with a shortcake, 15 feet in diameter and 12 feet high. The Lebanon paper mill, built in 1890, is an important industry.

ALBANY, **123.3** *m.* (210 alt., 5,325 pop.), is at a junction with US 99E (*see TOUR 2a*).

Tour 7A

Little Nash Crater Junction—Detroit—Mill City—Stayton—Sublimity —Salem; 87.3 m. State 222.

Road largely rock-surfaced; between Mill City and Salem, paved; impassable east of Detroit in winter.

Branch of Southern Pacific Railroad parallels the route between Detroit and Lyons.

Stages between Salem and Mill City; during summer months only between Mill City and Detroit.

Tourist camps in summer; improved camp sites.

State 222 traverses a region principally interesting for its scenic beauty. For thirty miles it cuts through a heavily forested area, until recent years known only to trappers, forest rangers, and adventurous hikers. For half this distance it follows the cliffs flanking a turbulent river. The western end of the route runs through the foothills of the Cascades and then the Willamette Valley.

State 222 branches northwest from State 54 (*see TOUR 7b*) at LITTLE NASH CRATER JUNCTION, 0 *m.* LITTLE NASH CRATER (L) is a small sister of Nash Crater and just north of the great lava flow that long ago poured from Belknap and Nash craters (*see TOUR 6b*). The route crosses a forested tableland, nearly a mile above sea level broken here and there by grassy meadows. In the main range of the Cascade Mountains the principal eminence visible (R) is imposing THREE-FINGERED JACK (7,848 alt.). Its perpendicular spires of snow-dusted rock defeat the ambitions of many alpinists, though skilled climbers have conquered it. There are good views of this peak from the highway.

At 5.9 *m.* is a junction with a foot-trail.

Right on this trail into the MOUNT JEFFERSON PRIMITIVE AREA, the boundary of which is at 2.5 *m.* The wilderness reserve extends across the Cascade divide. Near its northern end rises snow-capped MOUNT JEFFERSON (10,495 alt.). HUNT'S COVE, the most frequent starting point for a climb of Mount Jefferson, is one of a series of charming valleys studded with lakes; it is just south of the peak.

DUFFY LAKE (*forest camp*), 5 *m.,* is at the center of a labyrinth of trails.

North of the junction with the trail State 222 proceeds through mountain meadows and forests to the North Fork of the Santiam River, 6 *m.,* which sweeps westward to its confluence with the South Fork.

At 15.3 *m.,* by a junction with the Marion Forks Forest Road, is a Forest Service campsite and Forest Ranger Station.

Right on this road to GATCH FALLS, 2.5 *m.,* a crystalline torrent from melting glacial ice, dropping like a veil over rocks polished brown.

Lovely MARION LAKE (4,170 alt.), **2.9** *m.,* shimmering under a rim of mountains, provides excellent fishing. On the western side of the lake is a Forest Service shelter for campers.

The WHITEWATER FOREST CAMP is at **20.2** *m.*

IDANHA, **27.4** *m.* (1,717 alt., 60 pop.), is a hamlet struggling for a foothold in the midst of forested mountains not far from the eastern terminus of the old Corvallis & Eastern Railroad, now part of the Southern Pacific. A few farms break the loneliness of valleys among heavy timber. This area is increasingly popular for winter sports.

DETROIT, **31.8** *m.* (1,458 alt., 105 pop.) (*fishing and hunting supplies; gas and oil; pack and saddle horses for hire*), a shipping and marketing center for the scattered farm population of several valleys, was named by immigrants from Michigan who settled here in early days. Detroit has long been the chief outfitting point for sportsmen fishing and hunting in the nearby mountains, for those on their way to climb Mount Jefferson, and for campers in the many beautiful spots in the vicinity. Here is the WILLAMETTE NATIONAL FOREST DISTRICT RANGER STATION (*information; campfire permits, maps*).

One of the earliest settlers here was John Outerson, who was untiring in his efforts to acquaint the world with the beauties of the Mount Jefferson Primitive Area. Outerson opened a store in the early nineties and after a while, began to rent pack trains to mountain climbers and other sportsmen.

In Detroit is a junction with the Breitenbush-Olallie Lake Road (*see TOUR 4A*).

NIAGARA, **43.4** *m.* (1,103 alt., 20 pop.), was so named because of its proximity to a turbulent, white-water section of the Santiam River.

GATES, **48.9** *m.* (936 alt., 50 pop.), is another old community on the Albany branch of the Southern Pacific. In earlier years there was considerable mining activity in the vicinity.

For many years MILL CITY, **51.7** *m.* (826 alt., 775 pop.), has been a lumber camp. Extensive logging operations are carried on in the vicinity. There is a big sawmill here.

LYONS, **59.3** *m.* (661 alt., 100 pop.), is a farmers' post office and supply point among undulating green hills.

State 222 turns north to MEHAMA, **60.6** *m.* (628 alt., 102 pop.), in a prosperous dairying, farming and fruit-growing district.

STAYTON, **69.6** *m.* (447 alt., 797 pop.), named for Drury S. Stayton, whose donation land claim lay north of the town, was platted in 1872. There was already a small grocery store here, but the owners in 1876 erected a grist mill. Near Stayton were quarried the flagstones used in the ski lounge of Timberline Lodge (*see MOUNT HOOD*).

In SUBLIMITY, **71.6** *m.* (547 alt., 214 pop.), another quiet farm town, was established Sublimity College. One of the first teachers at this school, which was charted in 1858 and whose faculty was authorized to "suspend or expel any student for misconduct . . . to grant and confer degrees in the liberal arts and sciences," was Milton Wright, who became the father of Orville and Wilbur Wright, inventors of the first successful airplane. Tuition was five dollars for a twelve weeks' term.

AUMSVILLE, 75.6 *m.* (363 alt., 153 pop.), in the heart of an area producing fruit, nuts and milk, became a town in the late 1860's and was named for Amos Davis, son-in-law of Henry L. Turner, on whose donation land claim the town was laid out. The Turners and Davis erected a flour mill there.

Through lowlands of the broad Willamette Valley, State 222 continues northwesterly.

The OREGON STATE HOSPITAL FARM (L), 82 *m.*, has a comfortable group of buildings on an extensive farm tract.

The OREGON STATE PENITENTIARY (R) is at 86.1 *m.*

At N. Capitol and Court Streets in SALEM, 87.3 *m.* (159 alt., 26,266 pop.) (*see SALEM*), is a junction with US 99E (*see TOUR 2a*).

Tour 8

Portland — Beaverton — Hillsboro — Forest Grove — Glenwood — Tillamook; 76.7 m. State 8. Wilson River Route.

Paved road.
Limited hotel and tourist camp accommodations.
Stage service between Portland and Forest Grove.

Part of this route has been in use for nearly a century. About 30 miles is new, having been constructed to shorten the distance between Portland and the coast by 40 miles.

After an easy ascent of the Portland hills, State 8 crosses the Tualatin Valley, with its rolling countryside, clustered houses, groves and orchards. A few miles west are the rugged, forest-clad Coast Mountains, gashed with ravines and canyons, through which the Wilson River road makes its way to the ocean.

From the corner of SW. Morrison Street and SW. Sixth Avenue, in PORTLAND, 0 *m.*, the route turns south on SW. Sixth Avenue, into SW. Jefferson Street, and westward on SW. Canyon Road, through a deep canyon, to the crest of the west-side hills.

The first road from Portland to the Tualatin Valley led through what is now Washington Park, and over the heights, by way of Barnes

Road. Because of the steep grades and sharp curves, it became necessary to find a less difficult route into the valley. D. H. Lownsdale superintended construction of the first Canyon Road, in 1849. In 1850, the Portland and Valley Plank Road Company was organized with Mr. Lownsdale as president. The first plank of the second road was laid with appropriate ceremonies near the present Art Museum, in Portland, on Sept. 21, 1851. The rapid growth of Portland has been attributed to this comparatively easy gateway to the rich Tualatin Plains.

SYLVAN, 3.7 *m.,* (625 alt.), is an old settlement, from which roads radiated to different sections of the Tualatin Valley.

At 4.1 *m.* the Wolf Creek super-highway (under construction in 1940) diverges (R) to NORTH PLAINS, 14 *m.* (*see TOUR* 9). At this point, State 8 enters Washington County and leads almost directly west. This broad busy highway is the "Main Street" of Washington County, passing through all of its larger towns, and a score of villages and settlements, and intersecting a gridiron of lateral feeder roads.

The Tualatin Valley is a great spoon-shaped depression between low mountains. Across the mottled terrain, the Tualatin River wanders for 75 miles to cover an airline distance of 25 miles from its source to its confluence with the Willamette. In one quarter section, it travels toward all points of the compass. Dairying, market-gardening, fruit and berry growing, and filbert and English walnut culture are the chief industries of the lowlands, while lumbering and logging are carried on extensively in the foothills and mountains. The Valley has no large cities, but from early days, it has been in the front rank educationally, since it saw the organization of the first official school district of Territorial Oregon, and the second oldest college in the Northwest.

The Tualatin Valley contains over one-third of the area of Washington County, historically important, because under the name of Tualaty, it was one of the four original districts of the old Oregon of pre-territorial days. Then it comprised all of northwestern Oregon and western Washington. But the county's far-flung confines have contracted as the region developed, until today, its area is 731 square miles. Before 1830, the valley was alive with brown beaver, a rich field for the Hudson's Bay men. The trappers in their quests through the region noted its rich soil. A few years later, when men of fashion abandoned the beaver-fur hats they had put on by a king's decree, many of the trappers came to the valley with their Indian wives and settled down to an agricultural routine. Several of the trapper-farmers lived to become influential figures in Oregon's Territorial epoch.

BEAVERTON, 7.5 *m.* (188 alt., 1,138 pop.), established in 1868, as a shipping point on the Oregon Central Railroad, derives its name from the rich beaver-dam lands in the district.

Left from Beaverton on State 208 which crosses HARRIS BRIDGE, 8.9 *m.,* a modern concrete structure dedicated to Philip Harris, a settler of 1845; it is on the site of the Harris-Landess Ferry, first operated in 1845. West of the bridge is FARMINGTON, 9.1 *m.,* one of the oldest settlements in the valley. It

attained prominence as a milling and grain-shipping point when Tualatin River
steamers were the principal means of transporting crops to the Willamette River
markets.

At 7.8 *m.* near the west edge of Beaverton, is a junction with a
macadam road that leads north, into a section made especially interesting
by the many pioneer churches scattered along its by-ways.

Right on this road 0.6 *m.* to the BERNARD AIRPORT (L), privately owned.
At 1 *m.* the route crosses the Walker Road near the site of the village of Osceola,
now only a name on old maps. CEDAR MILL, 3.3 *m.*, in a section formerly
heavily timbered with cedar; here in 1848 Elam Young established a sawmill
on Cedar Creek. Soon the settlement of Cedar Mill grew up nearby.

At Cedar Mill is the WESLEY (METHODIST) CHAPEL. Its congregation
had its beginning in 1852 when the settlers held services in their log-cabin
homes. The first building was erected in 1865. In 1891, it was replaced by the
present structure, a picturesque example of old rural churches.

West of Cedar Mill at 4.2 *m.*, the route branches R. from the Cornell Road
and winds northward over low ridges to the FIRST GERMAN BAPTIST
CHURCH OF BETHANY, 6 *m.*, whose congregation was organized at Cedar
Mill in the late 1870's by Swiss and German families. In 1881 a small chapel
was erected here; it still stands in the rear of the present structure. The Bethany
Baptist Church, recently remodeled, has a carrillon tower in the modified Spanish
colonial style.

The congregation of the BETHANIAN PRESBYTERIAN CHURCH, 7.1 *m.*,
at the crossing of the Springville Road, was founded in 1873, and its membership is largely of Swiss and German extraction. Services are held in both
English and German on alternate Sundays. The church stands snowy white
against forest trees.

The Springville Road continues to BETHANY, 9.1 *m.* Although at present
no more than a cross-road with a store, garage, mill, and blacksmith shop,
Bethany, a half century ago, was a town of several hundred inhabitants.

Right from Bethany across Rock Creek to WEST UNION, 10.9 *m.*, at a
junction with the Germantown Road; L. here to WEST UNION BAPTIST
CHURCH, 11.5 *m.*, the oldest Protestant church building still standing west of
the Rocky Mountains, dedicated on Christmas day, 1853. The first Baptist Church
in the Oregon country was organized in the home of Elder David T. Lennox,
in May, 1844, by "a few of us who have been thrown together in the wilds of
the West," and the first Baptist sermon was preached in the home of Peter H.
Burnett, by the Reverend Vincent Snelling, in 1845. The lumber for the building,
measuring 30 by 40 feet, was hauled from the mills at Milwaukie by ox-team.
The rafters are cedar poles, the joists of fir poles, and the sills of hand-hewn
fir logs. The well preserved building resembles the small rural New England
churches.

Members of the congregation came on foot, on horseback, and by ox-team
for many miles, and for a quarter of a century the old church was the spiritual
center of the region. For now-forgotten reasons, the congregation was dissolved
about 1878, and no regular services have since been held. The church structure
is owned by the Oregon State Baptist Convention and an annual memorial meeting is held here because of its historical significance. Surrounding the building
is a churchyard in which lie the remains of many who were prominent in
pioneer annals.

At West Union, also was organized on Sept. 21, 1851, School District No. 1,
Washington County, the first in the Oregon Country established under the school
law adopted by the Territorial Legislature in 1850. The building was torn down
about 1900. The present structure dates from 1891.

Westward on the Germantown Road are the North Tualatin Plains, one of
the earliest settled sections of the state, where a party of six former "mountain
men" or Rocky Mountain free trappers, came to live with their Indian wives
on Christmas day, 1840. This party consisted of Col. Joseph L. Meek (*see TOUR*

2B), "Squire" George Ebberts, Caleb Wilkins, William Black, William Doughty, and Joseph Gale.

The first settler of GLENCOE, 18.7 *m.,* was Charles McKay, a Hudson's Bay man who came to the Oregon Country with the Red River emigrants of 1841. He built a mill on McKay Creek, and before 1850, had laid out a town here which he named for his old home in Scotland. For more than a half century the village was the center of activity for the North Plains country. Stores and warehouses were built, and wheat was shipped over the Cornelius Pass Wagon Road to the wharves at Linnton and St. Helens. When the United Railways built into the country, in 1910, a depot was established on a high flat about a mile from Glencoe, and a town laid out and named North Plains. All that remains of the old Glencoe is the blacksmith shop, several deserted store buildings, and a few residences. The rest of the town was moved to the new town on the hill, leaving old Glencoe a ghost in the valley.

At 20.8 *m.* is a junction with a gravel road; L. here **0.5** *m.* to the TUALATIN PLAINS PRESBYTERIAN CHURCH, the "Old Scotch Church" of local fame. Its congregation was organized at Columbia Academy, two miles to the northwest, on November 16, 1873. The first settled pastor was the Reverend George Ross, who came from Scotland to the pastorate. The little white structure displays the fine workmanship frequently found in early Oregon churches. Almost surrounded by a secluding grove of fir, oak, and maple, it stands among white gravestones of its churchyard, which contains the GRAVE OF JOSEPH MEEK and of many others associated with Oregon's history.

South of the Scotch Church cross-road, the route runs through a highly improved farming district to rejoin State 8 at HILLSBORO, 25 *m.* (*see below*)

On State 8 is ST. MARY'S OF THE VALLEY, 8.7 *m.* (L), a Roman Catholic boarding and day school for girls. The large three-story, cream brick building, with copper dome, is conspicuous. ST. MARY'S BOYS' SCHOOL (R), 9.9 *m.,* is a home and school for orphan boys. The school consists of a large concrete main building, a gymnasium, a group of cottages, and other buildings. It maintains a farm that is worked largely by the boys.

ALOHA, **10.6** *m.* (212 alt.), is a settlement of commuters, who are for the most part, employed in Portland. Nearly 2,000 people live within a mile of the post office. Aloha is the home of Verne Bright, magazine writer and poet.

REEDVILLE, **12.1** *m.* (230 alt., 75 pop.), is the point at which the county's dairy industry had its start. In 1871, Ladd & Reed, Portland merchants, acquired several hundred acres, and stocked them with purebred cattle, sheep and horses imported from England. In order to supply stock raisers in the Valley with good stock, they added other importations from the choicest herds of the British Isles and of the eastern United States. The old buildings of the Ladd & Reed farm, just south of the railroad at the west edge of town, are in excellent condition. The original house, constructed in 1852, has retained all the simplicity and beauty of line that caused it to be known as the show place of the county. It is one of the best existing examples of early Oregon architecture. The central part, with full length porch, is flanked by symmetrical one-story wings. The fenestration is beautifully proportioned.

WITCH HAZEL, **13.4** *m.,* was the site of the Witch Hazel farms, owned in the 1880's by Van DeLashmutt, mayor of Portland. It was here that he kept one of the finest strings of race horses in the North-west. Across the tracks (L), are the tumble-down remnants of the once pretentious buildings. In the flat field, beyond the oak grove that shelters the buildings, was one of the best race tracks in America, and, in the early 1880's, many of the country's fastest horses sped to victory on its turfed oval.

SHUTE PARK (R), **16.8** *m.,* in the edge of Hillsboro is the site of the annual Washington County Fair. The Park is situated in a handsome grove of young fir and white oak (*picnic tables; no overnight camping*).

HILLSBORO, **17.2** *m.* (178 alt., 3,039 pop.), seat of Washington County, was the first seat of the Tualaty District. At its settlement in 1841 the neighborhood was known as East Tualaty Plains, but David Hill, who settled here in 1842 named the new village Columbia. Later it was changed by the first County Court to Hillsboro. Many of the men who participated in the formation of a civil government for the Oregon Country, resided in or near this community.

Hillsboro is a commercial center, and a shipping point for both wheat and milk products. It has two chief industries, a milk condensing plant, and one of the largest canneries and fruit processing plants in the state. Thirteen churches are supported by this small city.

In CALVARY CEMETERY, **18** *m.* are buried David Hill, the founder of Hillsboro, and the Reverend John S. Griffin, who established the first Congregational Church in Oregon (1842-1845), on the North Tualatin Plains near Glencoe.

CORNELIUS, **20.7** *m.* (176 alt., 487 pop.), named for its most prominent citizen, Col. T. R. Cornelius, is one of the older towns of the county. For many years, Colonel Cornelius maintained a commercial establishment, a grist mill, and sawmill at this point. The surrounding country supports prosperous farms from which much grain, fruit, milk, and other produce is shipped. A pickle and vinegar factory is the chief industrial establishment.

The MASONIC HOME, **22.1** *m.* has extensive and well-kept premises. The institution is owned and operated by the Grand Lodge of Oregon and the Order of the Eastern Star.

At **23.2** *m.* is a junction with an improved road.

Right on this road to the former PORTER NURSERY, **1.3** *m.,* where many redwood trees (*Sequoia sempervirens*) were propagated. Porter went to California to seek gold, but finding none, returned home with two gunnysacks filled with cones of the redwood tree. Two long rows of redwoods mark the nursery site. Many others are in various parts of Washington County.

VERBOORT, **2.2** *m.,* is a Dutch colony, whose settlers came from Wisconsin in 1875 under John Verboort. Reverend William A. Verboort, one of his sons, founded the Verboort Catholic Church, which, as the colony spread, established missions at Hillsboro, Cornelius, Forest Grove, and Roy, all of which became self-supporting parishes. The Verboort church conducts a grammar school and a high school.

FOREST GROVE, **23.4** *m.* (195 alt., 1,869 pop.), lies on a commanding elevation at the western border of the Tualatin Plains. Because of its grove of white oaks, with fir forests as a background, the town's founders gave it the name it bears. As the seat of PACIFIC UNIVERSITY, one of the oldest institutions of higher learning in the Northwest, the town has a distinctly academic atmosphere. The college traces its origin to a log cabin school established in 1845 by the Reverend Harvey Clark and Alvin T. Smith. Mr. Clark and Mr. Smith had started a school in the rude log churchhouse of the settlement. A year later they were joined in their efforts by Mrs. Tabitha Moffet Brown, who at the age of 66, accompanied by an aged relative, had driven her own ox-team across the plains. Entirely alone, she and her uncle had crossed the Cascades by the difficult Applegate route and had reached her goal practically penniless. Later, when she was visiting at Tualatin Plains, the idea of a boarding school occurred to her. In 1847, with the aid of her friends, she opened classes in the log church. Her original idea was to establish a school for orphans. Soon her boarding school was attended by the children of settlers, and the idea became an institution.

The building erected in 1850 to house the Tualatin Academy is still in use and is now SCIENCE HALL (R), across the campus. The building has a charming exterior design. In spite of the necessary frugality of the period, the designer surmounted it with a graceful bell-tower, marking it as an institutional building. Its hand-hewn timbers gave it permanence and it is known as the oldest structure still in active use for educational purposes west of the Mississippi River.

The first "class," graduated in 1863, was Harvey W. Scott, later for half a century editor of the Portland *Oregonian*. The Academy's existence is due to the interest taken in it by some of America's most outstanding men, who gave to it both time and money. In the list were Henry Ward Beecher, Edward Everett Hale, Edward Everett, Rufus Choate, and Sidney and Samuel F. B. Morse.

In the southern part of town near the sawmill of the Carnation Lumber Company, is the early home of Alvin T. Smith, who assisted in the establishment of Pacific University.

Left from Forest Grove on State 47 along the foothills of the Coast Range Mountains and up the main valley of the Tualatin. This road is part of the Portland-McMinnville Loop (*see TOUR* 10).

The Chehalem Mountains (L), a narrow range, was named for a small band of the Tualatin Indians who made their home in this vicinity.

GASTON, 6.9 *m.* (182 alt., 227 pop.), was the farm home of Joseph Gaston, early-day railroad promoter, who laid out the town as a station on the Oregon Central Railroad, of which he was president. He projected and started work on the Oregon Central and Ben Holladay, also an early railroad promoter, completed it as far as St. Joe on the Yamhill River in 1872; Henry Villard pushed it on to Corvallis in 1878.

YAMHILL, 15.1 *m.* (212 alt., 390 pop.), on the North Yamhill River, half hidden in orchards and groves, is one of the oldest agricultural centers of the Willamette Valley. At present, it has a bank, a tile factory, a planing mill, and a grain elevator, but, in the 1840's, it was one of the most important trading points of the Oregon Country.

CARLTON, 18.3 *m.* (225 alt., 749 pop.), has broad paved streets, parks, comfortable homes, a modern creamery, a flour mill, and a large sawmill. It was

the home of William Anderson Howe, inventor of the baseball catcher's mask.
At 23.3 *m.* is a junction with US 99W (*see TOUR* 10), at a point 2.2 miles
north of McMinnville.

Northwest of Forest Grove, the route is the old Forest Grove-Vernonia highway, up Gales Creek Valley to the little town of GALES
CREEK, **30.8** *m.,* formerly Gales City, the eastern terminus of the
old Wilson River Stage Road. This village, nearby Gales Creek, and
Gales Peak, the highest point in Washington County, were named for
Joseph Gale, captain of the *Star of Oregon,* first sailing vessel built in
Oregon. With several others, as little experienced on the sea as himself,
he sailed the tiny vessel to San Francisco, where he traded it for cattle
and sheep. They brought the stock overland from California, in 1842,
losing remarkably few on the long journey. Gale established the first
sawmill and the first grist mill in Washington County. In 1844, he became a member of the first governing commission under the Provisional
Government.

Near the logging town of GLENWOOD, **36.7** *m.,* (475 alt., 20
pop.), the route diverges L. to the new Wilson River Road. This road,
now (1940) nearing completion, is under construction by the W.P.A.

The highway passes through a 500-foot tunnel, **39.5** *m.* and at
44.1 *m.,* crosses the Coast Range (1,586 alt.) into an area heavily
timbered until August of 1933 when in a single week a forest fire
swept over 290,000 acres of woodland. The route cuts through this
wilderness of burned trees.

The confluence of the South Fork of Wilson River and Devil's Lake
Creek, at **49** *m.,* is the beginning of Wilson River, named for a man
who in 1851 drove the first cows into the country, thus establishing
dairying, which has become its chief resource. Construction of a route
up the Wilson River to the Tualatin Valley was projected from early
days. In 1890, the Wilson River Boom, Toll Road & Improvement
Company, began construction of a toll road, and spent over $50,000 on
the undertaking.

The highway reaches the coastal valleys at BLACK BRIDGE,
71.2 *m.,* and after traversing a section of the great dairy district of
Tillamook County, reaches TILLAMOOK, **76.7** *m.,* on US 101 (*see
TOUR* 3*a*).

Tour 9

Junction with State 8 — North Plains — Manning — Sunset Camp —
Elsie — Necanicum Junction; 62.3 m. State 2.

The Wolf Creek Highway, State 2, is open (1940) from Banks to the Coast.
It is under construction (1940) between Sylvan and Banks. At present travelers
should take State 8 (*see TOUR* 8) to Forest Grove, thence to Banks.
Stages between Portland, Necanicum Junction, and Seaside.
Accommodations limited.

The Wolf Creek Highway, being developed by the W.P.A., and
shortening the distance by 46 miles, is the most direct route between
Portland and the sea. It proceeds across the Tualatin Valley, up the
West Fork of Dairy Creek, through a short tunnel in the Sunset Summit
of the Coast Range, into the Nehalem Valley, follows Wolf Creek, to
the coast.

Slanting obliquely into the charming Tualatin Valley (*see TOUR* 8),
the route traverses lush prairies and green woodlands, where once fed
elk, deer, bear, beaver, and other wild animals. In the region, dwelt the
Atfalati (Tualatin) tribe, later subjected to the tyranny of the fierce
Klickitats, who in turn gave way to the advancing whites. Keen axes
hewed the trees into new homes, sharp-shared plows sliced the grassy
plains into fertile fields. Now they are yellow with grain or green with
umbrageous corn blades. Everywhere, wild animals have been replaced
by grazing herds of horses, cattle and sheep.

The new highway branches R. from State 8, **0** *m.* at a point 4.1
miles west of Portland, on an overcrossing. In its straight progress over,
through, and under obstacles, the highway claimed as right-of-way the
burial-ground of the Pointer family, who settled in this vicinity in
1848. Coffins were disinterred from graves a half-century old and re-
buried nearby.

At NORTH PLAINS, **14** *m.* (190 alt., 145 pop.), in a highly developed farming section, is a junction with the Wilson River Highway
(*see TOUR* 8). MANNING, **23.5** *m.* (275 alt., 100 pop.), on the
West Fork of Dairy Creek is a trading center in an agricultural and
dairying region.

SUNSET SUMMIT (1,370 alt.), **30.2** *m.,* is pierced by a tunnel
(1,180 alt.), through which the highway enters the Pacific drainage
area of the Coast Range. The NEHALEM RIVER, **33** *m.,* named
for a coast tribe, might be likened to Paul Bunyan's Round River, as it
rises but a short distance from its ocean outlet, and in its passage
describes an almost complete circle. One of the fine fishing streams of
the state, it abounds with rainbow, cutthroat and steelhead trout, and
silverside salmon.

SUNSET CAMP, 33.4 *m.* (770 alt.), is at the intersection of the Forest Grove-Vernonia Road.

Right on the Forest Grove-Vernonia Road, down the winding Nehalem Valley to a junction with State 47, **10** *m.* (*see TOUR 1c*).
Left over a high, logged-off plateau to the lumber town of TIMBER, **4** *m.,* and the Wilson River Road to GLENWOOD, **10** *m.,* on Gales Creek (*see TOUR 8*).

West of Sunset Camp, the highway passes up the denuded valley of Wolf Creek, traversing for the next 20 miles a land made desolate by fire and the axe of the logger. Tumbled hills stretch away to a jagged horizon bristling with dead forest growths. Green groves that have escaped the general destruction rise here and there like islands.

BEAR CREEK SPRING, 41 *m.,* gushes from beneath a massive fir stump and pours its sparkling flood down the rocky declivity to a creek bordered by vine-maple, willow and balm. Bear Creek veers between ridges of green timber that escaped the destructive fire of 1933. Deer and elk feed in the thickets, and occasionally a bear feasting on autumn berries makes his appearance in the forest tangles.

QUARTZ CREEK BRIDGE, 48.3 *m.* (1,135 alt.), spanning a precipitous-walled canyon, is of steel-towed construction, 900 feet long and 140 feet high, with six piers and seven suspended arches. West of the bridge, is an area densely wooded with forest trees and undergrowth. The trees that cover the steep slopes are principally Douglas fir, cedar and spruce, with a sprinkling of hemlock, pine and other conifers. Beneath them are masses of syringa, salmonberry and salal. In spring, white dogwood blossoms star the leafy firmament; in autumn, vine-maple crimsons the mountainsides.

The Nehalem River is crossed for the second time at 50.8 *m.* (503 alt.). This section of the Nehalem Valley is an excellent dairying region, favored by green pasturage, mild winters, and cool summers. The winds from the Pacific bring a continual moisture to fields and meadows, and vegetation is almost tropical in its profusion.

ELSIE, 52.2 *m.* (507 alt., 68 pop.), in the midst of a small farming area, was first established as Mishawaka post office, in 1876.

North of Elsie looms the ragged crest of SADDLE MOUNTAIN (3,266 alt.), known in Indian legends as *Swol-la-la-chast,* home of the Thunder Bird that dwelt in two caves in the volcanic cliffs (*see TOUR 3a*).

Through a country of virgin forest and newly-logged land, the highway swerves upward to Humbug Mountain Summit, 58.7 *m.* (1,310 alt.), from which it quickly descends the North Fork of the Necanicum River to join US 101 at NECANICUM JUNCTION, 63.3 *m.* (395 alt.) (*see TOUR 3a*).

Tour 10

Portland—Newberg—McMinnville—Monmouth—Corvallis—Junction City; 108.6 m. US 99W.

Paved road.

Stage service between Portland and Junction City.

Hotels and tourist camps.

US 99W, the main highway south of Portland on the west side of the Willamette Valley, is an alternate route to US 99E. Like US 99E, this route serves one of Oregon's most populous areas. For a score of miles it skirts low ridges, spans narrow valleys, or winds through rolling hills, a kaleidoscopic pattern of suburban homes, small farms, orchards, and rural settlements, interspersed with the ever-present firs, and the groves of native oak. Then leaving the hills, it traverses the wider reaches of the west side of the valley, past well-kept and productive farms, rustic hamlets, and attractive small cities.

The route is rich in significant events of early settlement. Along its course, trading centers were established, educational institutions founded, industries born, and civil governments launched.

South of the junction of SW. Fourth Avenue and SW. Sheridan Streets in PORTLAND, 0 *m.*, US 99W follows Barbur Boulevard. Below the roadway (L) is a residential and industrial district, built to the edge of the Willamette. Wooded canyons and hillsides tiered with homes rise R. Near the summit of the heights (R) is Portland's medical center (*see PORTLAND*). The road continues through the Tualatin Valley whose name, of Indian origin, has had many variations in spelling such as Twalaity, Quality, Falatin, Nefalatine. Translated the name is said to mean "slow river," indicative of the sluggishness of the Tualatin.

Except for French Prairie near Champoeg (*see TOUR 2a*), the Tualatin Valley was the first section in Oregon settled by white men. The first settlers were six "mountain men" who arrived on Christmas Day in 1840 (*see TOUR 8*). The Valley lies between the main Coast Range and one of its eastern spurs, both covered with valuable stands of timber. To the north, a narrow range of hills skirts the Columbia and Willamette rivers, and extends southward. To the south, rise the Chehalem Mountains, whose most conspicuous eminence is Bald Peak. Tualatin Valley is given over to specialized farming, including nut and onion growing, truck gardening, berry and fruit farming, as well as dairying.

TIGARD, **7.9** *m.* (169 alt., 276 pop.), was named for Wilson M.

Tigard, who took up a donation land claim near the present site of the town.

NEWBERG, 22.4 m. (172 alt., 2,951 pop.), was named in November, 1869, by Sebastian Brutscher, who gave it the English spelling of his native Nauberg, Germany. One block left on River Street is the old MINTHORN HOUSE (*private*), 115 River Street, where Herbert Hoover lived as a boy with his uncle, Dr. H. J. Minthorn.

The Quakers founded Newberg as their first settlement west of the Rocky Mountains, and an atmosphere of prim simplicity still clings to the little city. Wide streets, with spreading shade trees and comfortable homes, make it a typical valley community. PACIFIC ACADEMY was founded by the Society of Friends in 1885. Today it is PACIFIC COLLEGE and remains a Quaker institution with high scholastic standards. Herbert Hoover was a member of the first class and was graduated from there just before his uncle moved to Salem in 1888.

Right from First Street in Newberg on Main Street (*State* 240) through the older section of Newberg, where buildings have weather-beaten walls and rambling galleries. Approximately three blocks from First is the SAMUEL HICKS FACTORY (R), which manufactures wooden utensils, and supplied the first Byrd Antarctic Expedition with equipment.

At the end of the pavement, 1.9 m., on a dirt road that crosses a bridge and becomes the Chehalem Valley Road. Farmlands and foothills merge into the Chehalem Mountains (R). Right at 4.6 m. to the EWING YOUNG DONATION LAND CLAIM. A pasture road leads to the deserted home site, 5.1 m. by which is EWING YOUNG'S GRAVE (R) under an old oak tree planted as an acorn after his burial. Young settled here in 1834. Since he was neither of the Hudson's Bay Company nor of the Mission, he was called an "independent settler." With Lieut. William S. Slacum, who had been sent by President Andrew Jackson to Oregon in 1836, to discover what the British were doing here, he organized a company to buy cattle in California for himself, for Hudson's Bay men who had retired, and for the company itself. The party returned in the spring with 600 head of Spanish longhorns. Though overland travel was difficult, three-fourths of the stock came through. Young acquired considerable property, and when he died intestate, the settlers from the United States used his roving cattle as an excuse to demand that their government step in and give them legal rights (*see HISTORY; also TOUR 2B*).

At DUNDEE, 24.8 m. (187 alt., 232 pop.), the nut center of Oregon, groves of English walnuts and filberts spread over the surrounding hills. Prune orchards also are extensive in this area. Four of the largest prune dryers in the Pacific Northwest as well as other facilities for the most scientific handling of these crops are in the vicinity.

The first plum popularly raised in Oregon to make prunes was the Petite variety, established in local orchards from grafts imported from France. The fruit is small and the Petite was soon supplanted by the Italian plum, a larger blue variety imported from Italy, with the proper amount of sugar to evaporate without fermentation. In August the harvest begins. At dawn the shakers set out with long poles with hooks in one end. The hooks are engaged in a fork of the tree and the tree vigorously jerked; a shower of plums thud to the ground, many bouncing off of the straw hat of the shaker. Sometimes he gets a "shiner" on his eye from looking up too soon. The pickers follow closely behind the shakers as it is not well to let the plums lie on the ground too long. Several pickers advance toward a tree, each squatting with a pail between his knees, sorting the good plums from the culls as he goes. When his pail is full the picker empties it into a bushel box near at hand, and when he has filled a box he shouts the fact to the checker, and he tallies it to the credit of the picker who is paid by the box. The full boxes are collected by truckers and transported to the dryer.

In the dryer the plums are first cleansed of surface dirt in water. They are then treated with a mild lye solution to kill spores of fermentation. After they have been cleansed again in water they are ready for drying. A prune dryer is generally a building so constructed as to permit the application of hot air to groups of screen-bottomed trays in which plums are placed for drying. The dehydrating process takes place slowly, requiring from twenty-four to forty-eight hours. Some small orchardists still dry their plums by the sun, but their output is a small proportion of the total Oregon prune production.

At **28.5** *m.* is a junction with State 221, the Dayton Highway.

Left on State 221 to DAYTON, 1.4 *m.* (162 alt., 375 pop.), founded in 1848 by Joel Palmer, first "Superintendent of Indian Affairs in Oregon." Tree-shaded streets, houses of the Victorian type on wide lawns, and an air of leisure distinguish the town.

In the Dayton City Park, stands the FORT YAMHILL BLOCKHOUSE, built on the Grand Ronde Indian Reservation in 1855, when Phil Sheridan, junior lieutenant in the United States Army, was stationed there (*see TOUR* 10A). The two-story structure is of hewn logs, its upper story projecting for purposes of defense. The blockhouse was brought to Dayton in 1911. On Sheridan Day, August 23, 1912, during a G.A.R. reunion, it was dedicated to Joel Palmer, founder of Dayton.

The DAYTON METHODIST CHURCH, founded in the 1850's, has logs under its clapboards.

The large JOEL PALMER HOUSE (*private*), built in 1852, has been much modernized. It now has a two-story portico and is surrounded with magnificent oaks. To this place came many notables of pre-Civil War times, including Capt. Ulysses S. Grant and Lieut. Phil H. Sheridan. Charming belles danced in the arms of buckskin-clad pioneers to the rollicking music of banjo and violin. In the house are various relics, including an autographed photograph of Dr. John McLoughlin.

State 221 continues to a junction with the Neck Road, 1.8 *m.*; L. here 2 *m.* to the DONATION LAND CLAIM OF LOUIS LA BONTE, the first (1929) retired Hudson's Bay Company trapper to settle in this area.

At 5.9 *m.* on State 221 is the ALDERMAN FARM (L), of about a thousand acres.

The marker at 7.4 *m.* calls attention to the DONATION CLAIM OF HENRY AND ELIZABETH MATHENY HEWITT, who arrived in 1843. The family has been prominent in Oregon History.

At 10.4 *m.* is a junction with a dirt road. L. here 1 *m.* to the site of the vanished town of WHEATLAND. At the end of the road is the Wheatland Ferry, still carrying light traffic across the Willamette River. In early riverboat days a town grew up here around Matheny's Ferry. The vast amount of grain shipped from this point gave it the name of Wheatland.

Right 0.5 *m.* up the east bank of the Willamette River from the ferry to the SITE OF THE JASON LEE MISSION, marked with a bronze plaque on a granite boulder. Here, in 1834 Lee and his band of missionaries established their mission (*see HISTORY*), later abandoned. The mission school held in a log cabin, one of nine, was the first south of the Columbia River. In 1842 the school was moved to Chemeketa, now Salem.

The GEORGE GAY DONATION LAND CLAIM (R) is indicated by a bronze marker at **11.9** *m.* The GAY HOUSE, reached through a gate and across the fields **0.5** *m.,* is the oldest brick structure and probably the oldest house in Oregon. Constructed in 1843, it was of course the scene of much early hospitality. The dilapidated structure is a story and a half high. Gay was one of the 52 men who voted with Meek at Champoeg (*see also TOUR 2B*).

At **15.9** *m.* is a junction with a dirt road. L. here **0.5** *m.* to the ghost town of LINCOLN, originally called Doak's Ferry. The town grew with riverboat transportation as a wheat shipping center. Grain was hauled from points as far distant as Willamina.

State 221 forms a junction with State 22 in WEST SALEM, **21.5** *m.* (*see TOUR 2C*).

Right from Dayton on State 233 to FARM FAMILY LABOR CAMP (L), 5 *m.* built by the Federal government "to provide temporary housing, sanitary, health and social facilities for part of the thousands of farm family workers engaged in seasonal and specialized crop sections such as fruits, berries, hops and sugar beets during a four to six months' season." A complete drainage system has been installed and buildings and seasonal shelters erected. Besides the 176 family shelters a community auditorium, utility building, first aid and child clinic, machine shop, manager's quarters, and 47 homestead units have been constructed. Besides the headquarters camp two portable units are maintained for use at points distant from the camp.

On US 99W is LAFAYETTE, **31.1** *m.* (150 alt., 350 pop.), first seat of Yamhill County, and, in the 1840's and 1850's, the principal trading center of the western Willamette Valley. More than 30 stores were in operation bartering with valley farmers, and dispatching their pack trains to the gold diggings of California and southern Oregon. Founded in 1847, by Joel Perkins, it remained the county seat until 1889, when it was supplanted by McMinnville. Lafayette was the site of the first Circuit Court held in Oregon (1846), and of the first United States Court held in the Pacific Northwest (1849). Lacking a suitable building, the first court of Yamhill County convened at Lafayette in 1846 under a large oak tree, afterwards called the "council oak." The Oregon supreme court now uses a gavel made from a part of that tree. It was known in the early days as the "Athens of Oregon," for the thundering eloquence of such Oregon lawyers as Judge Matthew Deady, Logan Pratt, and William Burnett. Lafayette Seminary, an educational institution of early days, continued for three decades, until it was united with La Creole Academy of Dallas in 1900. Lafayette was the home of Abigail Scott Duniway, editor, writer, and co-worker with Susan B. Anthony, in the cause of woman suffrage.

Yamhill Valley, south of Lafayette, is a rich agricultural area with orchards, dairy farms and many acres of grain and truck gardens. The past is preserved in a few pioneer homes, commonly with two-storied verandas indicative of the southern influence brought by the early settlers.

At **33.6** *m.* is a junction with State 47 (*see TOUR 8*).

McMINNVILLE, **36.3** *m.* (154 alt., 2,917 pop.), seat of Yamhill County, is the trading center of a prosperous agricultural area. It was named by William T. Newby, a native of McMinnville, Tenn., who came to Oregon in 1844, built a grist mill, and established the town. The town now has a large milk condensary plant, a sash and door factory, two sawmills, and a brick and tile factory. It was one of the first in the state to own and operate its water and light systems, and its record on public utility management is frequently cited.

LINFIELD COLLEGE (L), at the southern edge of town, is a Baptist institution established in 1857 as McMinnville College. The name was changed to honor George Fisher Linfield, whose widow gave the college a large endowment. The college has about 500 students. PIONEER HALL, built in 1857, and MELROSE HALL, a modern structure, are among the principal buildings.

At 37.7 m., the southern edge of McMinnville, is a junction with State 18 (see TOUR 10A).

AMITY, 43.5 m. (159 alt., 438 pop.), is the center of a prune and dairy country. The name was given as the result of an amicable settlement of a local school dispute and was first applied to the community school, in 1849, by Ahio S. Watt, pioneer of 1848, who was the first teacher.

Joseph Watt, his brother, settled on the donation land claim of which Amity is a part. He returned to the East and brought with him on his second trip across the plains a band of 400 sheep; also the cards, reeds, and castings for a loom and spinning wheel, which were set up in his home, and later became the nucleus of the first woolen mill in Oregon. He was also the first person to sell Oregon wheat in New York, and Liverpool, England. The grain was sent around the Horn and the excellence of the product led to financial loss. The wheat was so white and plump from Oregon's virgin fields, that an experienced miller in New York, said that it had been wet on the trip and had swelled. Under this damaging testimony, the cargo was put on the market at a loss of $8,000. Nothing daunted, Watt later profitably shipped a cargo of wheat to Liverpool. This was Oregon's first agricultural venture into foreign ports.

At 48.5 m. is a junction with Bethel Road.

Left on this road to the SITE OF BETHEL INSTITUTE (1856), 1.5 m., later merged with the Monmouth Christian College, now the Oregon College of Education at Monmouth. It was established by members of the Christian Church, locally called "Campbellites," with gifts of money and land. A modern high school and gymnasium now occupy the old school campus.

ZENA, 6 m., a ghost town, was first called Spring Valley, because of the numerous springs in the vicinity. It became Zena in 1866, when D. J. Cooper and his brother, on building the store and obtaining the post office, named it after the last syllables of their wives' names, Arvazena and Melzena Cooper. The pioneer ZENA CHURCH, 6.5 m., built in 1859, still stands without alteration. The church bell, widely known for its tone, was cast in England and came around the Horn.

RICKREALL, 56.7 m. (210 alt., 127 pop.), is an old town by Oregon standards. In 1845 John E. Lyle arrived from Illinois and almost immediately opened a school in the home of Nathaniel Ford, near the site of Rickreall.

In 1846, Lyle and others founded Jefferson Institute, in a log cabin on the farm of Carey Embree. The school equipment was modern for the time and place; it consisted of plank benches, puncheon desks, goose quill pens, ink made from oak galls and iron filings, bullets hammered to a point for pencils, and paper from the Hudson's Bay Company store. The textbooks were the Bible, and such books as the settlers had brought with them. The institute was also used for interdenominational religious service.

At Rickreall US 99W forms a junction with State 22 (*see TOUR 2C*).

In MONMOUTH, 62.7 m. (204 alt., 906 pop.), is the OREGON COLLEGE OF EDUCATION (*see above*). The buildings of brick and stone, and the campus of 11 acres at the north edge of the town, are shaded by firs. The former Christian College became a training institution for elementary teachers after it was acquired by the State in 1882. Monmouth is in a diversified farming area raising pure bred dairy cattle and sheep. The town has a large cooperative creamery and a tile factory.

Left on a paved road to INDEPENDENCE, 2.6 m. (172 alt., 1,248 pop.), on the Willamette River. Independence is an important hop-raising center, the contiguous territory embracing a part of the Willamette Valley, areas, which produce more than half of the hops grown in America. Many of the hop farms have vines 30 years old (*see TOUR 2a*).

HELMICK STATE PARK, 67.3 m., on the Luckiamute River was formerly a camping place of Indians. The park was named for Henry Helmick, who with his wife, Sarah, took up a land claim on the Luckiamute in 1846.

At 75.3 m. is a junction with a dirt road.

Right on this road to the SITE OF TAMPICO, 0.2 m., laid out by Greenberry Smith. At one time Tampico was a stage station on the Oregon-California Line, along which ran the first telegraph line to Portland from the south.

At 76.6 m. are the McDONALD FOREST and the PEAVY ARBORETUM, consisting of 1,600 acres, owned by Oregon State Agricultural College, and used for experimental purposes. In this area are specimens of forest and orchard trees and shrubs under scientific experimentation.

CORVALLIS, 83.4 m. (228 alt., 7,585 pop.) (*see CORVALLIS*).

Points of Interest: Oregon State Agricultural College, Court House, Old Millstones, and others.

MONROE, 100.5 m. (287 alt., 227 pop.), formerly Starr's Point, is a farmers' trading center in the Long Tom River valley. This usually sluggish stream often overflows its banks and hinders traffic during the rainy season. The townsite is a part of the donation land claim (1846) of Joseph White, who built a sawmill here in 1850.

WASHBURN STATE PARK (R), 104.2 m., is a summer amusement park.

JUNCTION CITY, 108.6 m. (326 alt., 922 pop.), is at the intersection with US 99E (*see TOUR 2a*).

Tour 10A

Junction US 99W—Sheridan—Willamina—Valley Junction—Grand Ronde—Otis Junction; 45.1 m., State 18.

Asphalt paved road.
Greyhound Stages serve towns on route.
Small hotels and tourist camps in town.

State 18, the Salmon River Cut-off, the most direct route between the upper Willamette Valley and the central part of the Oregon coast, follows what was first an Indian trail and then an artery of white travel. It was traveled by Jason Lee and his bride on their honeymoon trip to the seashore, by settlers driving oxcarts piled high with gear, and by army wagons laden with rations for Fort Yamhill.

For several miles the route follows the South Yamhill River, called by the Indians Yam-hel-as—Yellow River—because of the ochre color of the waters that are churned to a foam by the rocky bed. In the early days the Yamhill played a part in the development of Oregon. Warehouses and wharfs were built, saw a period of activity, then decayed along its banks. During the days of river transporation, quantities of wheat and other farm products were taken down-river from this district to Dayton. But even before the advent of the steamboat, the Yamhill knew the Hudson's Bay bateaux, manned by Klickitats and loaded with furs.

State 18 branches southwestward from US 99W (*see TOUR* 10), **0** *m.,* at a point at south edge of McMinnville. Skirting a grove of ash and oak, it cuts through a prosperous farm section where in late summer and autumn melons, pumpkins, and squashes lie plump and bright on the dry ground, or await purchasers in wayside stalls. The old white farm houses and big red barns of the Yamhill Valley give an impression of economic stability.

BELLEVUE, **7.7** *m.,* a crossroads hamlet, lost importance as a rural trading center, when good roads were constructed to carry farmers to places with larger stocks of goods.

The South Yamhill River is seen at **11.1** *m.,* crowded between abrupt hills. Recesses along the bluff (R) are still smoke-stained from the signal fires lighted at intervals by the Indians to announce that some of the maidens of the tribe had reached marriageable age.

SHERIDAN, **11.9** *m.* (189 alt., 1,008 pop.), divided by the South Yamhill River, was founded by Abe Faulkner and named for Phil Sheridan, who, as a young lieutenant, had been stationed at Fort Yamhill (*see below*). The village lives on the trade of farmers and also serves lumbermen and loggers. Each June the community celebrates Phil Sheridan Day.

At **13.6** *m.* is a junction with the Novitiate Road.

Right here to the JESUIT NOVITIATE, **2.5** *m.*, on the crest of an elevation that affords an extensive view of the Willamette Valley.

A part of the old Newby Ditch, begun in 1867 and never completed, is south (L) at **13.7** *m.* The depression that scars the roadside, overgrown with trees, was to convey water from the South Yamhill to McMinnville.

WILLAMINA, **16.8** *m.* (225 alt., 360 pop.), at the point where Willamina Creek enters Yamhill, was named for Willamina Williams, the first white woman in the neighborhood. Here, in an area where dairying, stock-raising, and fruit growing is of first importance. One of the largest brick and tile factories in the state and several sawmills are located here. A new industry of the town is the 30-acre veneer plant opened in 1939.

At **18.6** *m.* by Wallace Bridge is a junction with State 22 (*see TOUR 2C*).

VALLEY JUNCTION, **23.2** *m.* (299 alt.), is near the eastern limit of the old Grand Ronde Indian Reservation (*see above*). The original Indian dwellers in this mountain-locked valley were the *Yamel* tribe of the Calapooyas. Alexander Henry wrote in his diary: "The Yamhelas or Yamils are short of statute and altogether the most miserable, wild, and rascally looking tribe I have yet seen on this side of the Rocky Mountains." They lived chiefly by hunting and fishing. The camas and wapato roots were their principal winter food. A small private Zoo (*free*) at Valley Junction attracts considerable attention. (*Good tourist accommodations*).

Right from Valley Junction on State 14, which soon passes the SITE OF FORT YAMHILL, **0.5** *m.* This post, established in 1856, was one of three holding troops to protect settlers from the Indians the government was seeking to pen up in reservations near here. Construction of the little fort was begun under Lieutenant William Hazen and completed under Lieutenant Philip Sheridan. The buildings at the fort were crude structures of log and rough sawed lumber. "In those days," wrote Sheridan in his *Memoirs,* "the Government did not provide very liberally for sheltering its soldiers and officers, and men were frequently forced to eke out parsimonious appropriations by toilsome work, or go without shelter in most inhospitable regions. Of course this post was no exception to the general rule, and as all hands were occupied in its construction, and I the only officer present, I was kept busily employed in supervising matters, both as commandant and quartermaster until July, when Captain D. A. Russell . . was ordered to take command, and I was relieved from the first part of my duties."

The post consisted of officers' quarters, barracks, barns, and utility buildings, clustered about a central parade ground, with a block-house and flag-pole in the center. The old block-house has been removed to the city park in Dayton (*see TOUR 10*).

Lieutenant Sheridan served at Fort Yamhill, under Capt. D. A. Russell, until Russell was called east early in 1861, when Sheridan assumed full command. The young lieutenant remained in charge until September, 1861, chafing under the enforced absence from fighting. "On the day of the week," he wrote, "that our courier, or messenger, was expected back from Portland, I would go out early in the morning to a commanding point above the post, from which I could see a long distance down the road as it ran through the valley of the Yamhill, and there I would watch with anxiety for his coming, longing for good news." When he was finally called he left behind these words: "I am going into this war to win a captain's spurs, or die with my boots on. Goodbye, boys, I may never see you again."

GRAND RONDE AGENCY, 3 m., was the headquarters of the reservation, in charge of John F. Miller, "a sensible, practical man, who left the entire police control to the military, and attended faithfully to the duty of settling the Indians in the work of cultivating the soil. . . . On this reservation the Indians were compelled to cultivate their land, to attend church, and to send their children to school. When I saw them 15 years later, transformed into industrious and substantial farmers, with neat houses, fine cattle, wagons and horses carrying their grain, eggs and butter to market, and bringing home flour, sugar, coffee and calico in return, I found abundant confirmation of my early opinion that the most effectual measures for lifting them from a state of barbarism, would be a practical supervision at the outset, coupled with a firm control and mild discipline." One of the early store-keepers at the agency was Benjamin Simpson, father of the poet Sam Simpson, and it is said that a volume of Byron's poems given Sam by Sheridan inspired the boy to essay the writing of poetry.

Indians from all parts of western Oregon were placed on the reservation, which was continued until 1908, when its lands were divided among the remaining Indians. Many of their descendants still own farms in the vicinity. The old agency church, the agent's house, and several other buildings, deserted and falling to decay, still stand (R) near the highway.

West of the agency the country becomes more mountainous, with large areas of cut-over land from recent logging operations. A low pass marks the SUMMIT OF THE COAST RANGE, 11 m. (672 alt.).

DOLPH, 14.2 m. (549 alt.), is a resort centering about sulphur springs.

CASTLE ROCK CAMP (*fishing, tourist accommodations*), 20.6 m., is at a bend of the Three Rivers, with the weathered turrets of Castle Rock rising ruggedly behind it.

At STAYSA'S TAVERN, 22.4 m., is an exhibit of animals—deer, squirrels, bears, and monkeys.

CEDAR CREEK FISH HATCHERY, 23.3 m., is operated by the state game commission for the propagation of trout and salmon. THREE RIVERS RANGER STATION, 24.4 m., is at the edge of the Siuslaw National Forest.

HEBO, 24.7 m. (54 alt., 275 pop.), is at the junction with US 101 (*see TOUR 3a*).

NEW GRAND RONDE, 25.1 m. (335 alt., 350 pop.), on State 18, is the modern trading post for a few whites and the remnants of the Indian tribes once confined to the Grand Ronde Reservation. Log loading zone is at 25.3 m. Several trucks, each carrying a single huge log, or a half-dozen small ones, are frequently lined up beside the highway, waiting their turn at the spar tree, a massive boom used to lift the logs from the trucks to the cars.

At 31.7 m. is the site of the old BOYER TOLL GATE, operated from 1908 to 1920. An attempt was made to make the old trail a toll road as early as 1860. Other desultory attempts followed and in 1908, John Boyer improved the route, and established a toll road which he operated for 12 years. In winter it was almost impassable. Crossing the summit of the Coast Range at LENO HILL, 32.3 m. (820 alt.), the highway enters the Pacific watershed and begins the descent of the Salmon River, named for the abundance of salmon ascending the stream.

Groves of young alder and thickets of salmonberry line the stream. The old toll road is plainly visible at many points.

ROUND PRAIRIE is at 37 *m.,* and at 38.3 *m.,* the hills begin to recede. Narrow fields border the river, as it drains seaward in a series of diminutive cascades. The riffles were placed in the river, so the Alsea Indians said, by Se-Ku, so that they might the more easily snare the salmon.

THE SIUSLAW PROTECTED AREA is reached at **39.4** *m.* This Reserve is scattered in numerous small areas between Tillamook and Winchester Bays.

ROSE LODGE, **41** *m.,* was named for the rose garden owned by the first postmistress. Logging is the chief industry, but a small cheese factory has been in operation since 1907.

As the valley widens toward the sea, typical tideland growth becomes abundant. Willow, ash, and alder trees root in the marshy land, and in spring, the broad-leafed skunk cabbage lifts its yellow bloom.

OTIS JUNCTION, **45.1** *m.* (37 alt., 23 pop.), is at the junction with US 101 (*see TOUR 3a*).

Mount Hood Recreational Area

Season: Year round; July and August the most favored months. Open all year.
Administrative Offices: Mount Hood National Forest Headquarters, Terminal
Sales Building, 1220 SW. Morrison St., Portland; District Ranger Station, Zigzag,
12 m. W. of Government Camp on State 50.
Admission: Free.

Transportation: East side, State 35 (*see TOUR 1E*); south side, State 50 (*see
TOUR 4A*), served by two Portland-Bend buses daily, with extra buses to
Mount Hood during week-ends and holidays.
Guide Service and Horses: Usually available by arrangement through hotels at
Rhododendron.

Accommodations: Timberline Lodge (E. plan); Battle Axe Inn at Government
Camp; Cloud Cap Inn; Timberline Lodge open all year; make inquiries about
others.

Climate, Clothing, Equipment: Nights invariably cold at higher elevations even
in summer; usual seasonal clothing with heavy wraps needed by those staying
in hotels and fully-equipped camps; campers need woolen shirts and pants,
ponchos, several pairs of woolen socks, and a heavy jacket, with heavier gar-
ments in winter; light sleeping bag desirable, in addition to usual camping
equipment; small axe and canteen; alpenstock spiked shoes and dark glasses
needed on expeditions over snow fields and for peak climb.
Warnings: Black flies in woods as weather advances, particularly bad in September. Storms, infrequent but sudden in July and August, are much more
common in winter. Watch for landslides after heavy snow and during melting
seasons. Hikers should leave word at camps, inns, and Forest Guard Stations if
going on long hikes; should never leave marked trails without a guide; should
never attempt peak climb without guide. Peak climbers unless experienced
should not attempt to make round trip in one day; should not make start after
sun is well up; should not wander off from party nor attempt short cuts.
Medical Services: First aid station at Timberline Lodge, Summit Forest Guard
Station near Government Camp, and at Zigzag CCC camp; physician at Rhododendron.
Special Regulations: Permit from Forest Service required for building camp fires
outside designated camps. State licenses required for hunting and fishing. Certain areas closed to campers in summer months; these districts posted, as are
regular camps. Camping not allowed along highway except at designated campsites.

Summary of Attractions: Mount Hood National Forest, which surrounds mountain, in summer affords opportunities for camping, fishing, hunting, swimming,
mountain climbing, horseback riding, and hiking. Network of trails. Skiing and
tobogganing in winter near Timberline Lodge and Government Camp.
Ski Trails: Ski trails in the vicinity of Timberline are of three types: trails

easily negotiated by the novice, trails for the intermediate skier, and trails for the expert. Representative trails are:

West Leg Ski Trail, for beginners, starts at Poochie Glade below Timberline Lodge, ends at Loop Highway; six miles long with average eight per cent grade.

Glade Ski Trail, for intermediates, starts near Timberline Lodge, ends at Government Camp; four miles long.

Alpine Ski Trail, for intermediates, starts immediately west of Timberline Lodge, ends west of Summit Guard Station on Loop Highway; four miles long. (Midway of this run are Nanitch Ski Area and Mazama Hill practice slopes.)

Mazama Ski Trail, for intermediates, diverges from Alpine Ski Trail at Mazama Hill, extends to Mazama Lodge; one mile long.

Blossom Ski Trail, for experts, starts at Timberline Cabin, drops 2,200 feet in its four-mile length. Requires great skill to negotiate.

Lone Fir Ski Trail, for experts, starts at Lone Fir Lookout Station, ends at Timberline Lodge; one mile long.

National Downhill Championship Trail, starts at Crater Rock, descends to Salmon River canyon immediately east of Timberline Lodge. Extremely hazardous, requiring exceptional skiing ability; 2.75 miles long, more than 50 per cent grade. The ski-bowl and Multorpor Mt. ski jump are just S. of Government Camp. A chair ski lift extends a thousand feet above Timberline Lodge.

MOUNT HOOD (11,245 alt.), Oregon's highest peak, rises from the Cascade Range east of Portland. The perpetually snow-capped pyramid, visible for long distances because of its isolation, is particularly impressive when seen from city pavements. Since first sighted by the British Lieutenant Broughton in 1792 the great peak has held attention. It was a landmark for the emigrants who sought the green lands west of the Cascade Range; the last obstacle in their long journey.

In summer the snow cap rises above green forests; in winter evergreens on the slopes and underbrush are hidden under drifted snow. Close to timberline the snow melts late and icy water cascades down forested slopes already thickly carpeted with flowers and fragrant with the scent of pine *(see A GUIDE TO MOUNT HOOD)*.

The mountain once was an active volcano and still sends out sulphurous fumes through vents on its upper slope. Before the days of quick communication people frequently stated that they saw evidences of volcanic activity. The *Weekly Oregonian* of August 20, 1859, reported: "It became hot about midday . . . in the evening occasional flashes of fire were seen. On Thursday night fire was plainly visible . . . A large mass on the northwest side (of Mount Hood) had disappeared, and an immense quantity of snow on the south side was gone." On September 18 of the same year, the newspaper reported that a man driving cattle over the Barlow Road saw "intermittent columns of fire erupting from the crater for two hours." In June, 1865, a man at Vancouver Barracks wrote to the *Oregonian* that he had just seen "the top (of Mount Hood) enveloped in smoke and flame, accompanied by discharges of what appeared to be fragments cast up from a considerable depth with a rumbling noise not unlike thunder." Since then no spectacular eruption has been recorded.

The Mount Hood region is one of the most popular recreational areas in Oregon and its facilities are being developed by the state. Its slopes are gay in winter with the brilliantly colored clothing of hardy visitors, as ski experts soar over its drifts and tobogganists dip and glide at whirlwind speed down its steep inclines. A winter carnival with the inevitable crowning of a sports queen is held about February 20, sponsored by Portland business interests.

Joel Palmer, Territorial Commissioner of Indian Affairs, was a member of the party that in 1845 accomplished the first known climb above timberline. The first white men reached the summit of the peak in 1857. In 1887, seven men climbed almost to the top and set off a hundred pounds of red fire to celebrate the Fourth of July.

Since then climbing Mount Hood, though dangerous at certain times, has become a popular pastime. Although thousands have scaled the peak only a few lives have been lost; the victims having been persons who took unnecessary risks.

There are nine known routes to the summit, ranging from the comparatively easy South Side Route, beginning at Timberline Lodge, to the dangerous routes up the sheer north face. Two of the routes on the north, the Cooper Spur and the Eliot Glacier routes, both of which start from Cloud Cap Inn (*see TOUR 1E*), are dangerous.

Center of activities on the south slope is TIMBERLINE LODGE (*see GEN. INF. for rates*), reached by a one-way road branching from State 50 (*see TOUR 4A*) at a point 55 miles east of Portland. This hotel, resembling those in European mountain resorts, rises two-and-a-half stories on a high basement. The steep roofs of the wings are broken by dormers. The wings, one long and one short, branch at different levels from a hexagonal unit whose roof rises high to a weather-vane-topped cupola. Inside the finish is rough, in keeping with the rugged character of the exterior.

On the basement floor is a ski lounge and coffee-shop, on the main floor a large main lounge with three fireplaces. The stair treads, whole logs, are bound together with straps of iron. The furniture, of simple types, was designed for the building. Murals depict the history of the region, stair decorations and other woodwork have motifs belonging to the Cascade forests. This building, erected under sponsorship of Portland businessmen by the Works Progress Administration and opened in 1937, is one of the proudest achievements of the relief era in Oregon because people of so many crafts were inspired to contribute their skills to a structure that symbolizes Oregon to them. Native materials were used as far as possible, even the draperies being hand-loomed from Oregon wool and flax.

TRAILS AND CLIMBS

The Pacific Crest trail is divided between Timberline Lodge and Eden Park, passing around both sides of the mountain.

TRAIL TOUR 1

North from TIMBERLINE LODGE (6000 alt.), 0 *m.,* on the

East Trail, which is easier and offers more beautiful views than the West Trail. It climbs through forests and alpine meadows to IRON CREEK, 8 *m.,* circles around to GNARL RIDGE (*shelter*), **14.1** *m.,* and reaches CLOUD CAP INN (5,985 alt.), **18.3** *m.,* perched on the mountain side at the head of motor road (*see TOUR 1E*). This hotel, anchored to the mountain by cables to resist winter storms, was opened in 1889. It is of logs, with a design suitable to its rugged site just below Eliot Glacier. North of the inn the trail winds through forests to ELK COVE, **22.1** *m.,* and EDEN PARK, **25.1** *m.,* where it meets the West Trail (*see below*) in a broad flower-starred meadow within the MOUNT HOOD PRIMITIVE AREA. Here red Indian paintbrush, white avalanche lilies, and blue lupines form a patriotic carpet.

TRAIL TOUR 2

North from TIMBERLINE LODGE, 9 *m.,* on the West Trail, shorter but more difficult than the East Trail, to PARADISE PARK, 5 *m.,* a lovely alpine meadow broken by sharp rocky upthrusts and carpeted during the short summer with brilliant blooms. A junction here with a foot trail that winds around Zigzag Mountain (*see TOUR 4A*). The West Trail continues through gorges and forests to RAMONA FALLS (*campsite*), **10.5** *m.,* a rainbow-tinted cataract falling over moss-covered ledges. The trail mounts to YOCUM RIDGE (6,500 alt.), **15.5** *m.,* and descends to EDEN PARK, **18.5** *m.,* where it meets the East Trail (*see above*).

SOUTH SIDE CLIMB

(*Average climbing time* 8 *to* 10 *hours.*)

Timberline Lodge—Lone Fir Lookout—Palmer Glacier—Triangular Moraine—Make-up Rock—Hot Rocks—the Chute—Mount Hood Summit; **3.7** *m.* Accommodations in Timberline Lodge and summit Ranger cabin.

This route leads northward up the south slope of the mountain, across packed snow, glaciers, and rocks, cut at irregular intervals by canyons. In clear weather the peak looms above, massive and imposing; at other times veils of sun-touched mist wrap the slopes and forest.

The climb begins at MOUNT HOOD TIMBERLINE LODGE (6,000 alt.), 0 *m.,* just below snowline, on a well-defined trail leading to LONE FIR LOOKOUT (6,700 alt.), **0.8** *m.,* where during summer a Forest Service ranger maintains a constant watch for signs of fire.

Continuing due north, the route reaches PALMER GLACIER (7,500 alt.), **1.5** *m.,* an active ice field, a half mile wide. Rather flat and devoid of crevasses, it is not dangerous to cross. To the east, is WHITE RIVER GLACIER, the source of White River, a tributary of the Deschutes and to the west is ZIGZAG GLACIER, whose melting ice forms Zigzag River, which flows into the Sandy.

The trail crosses TRIANGULAR MORAINE (8,000 alt.), **2** *m.,* a high drift of rock left by White River Glacier which it parallels for half a mile. There are spectacular views of the mighty stream frozen in its steep wide gorge. Far below, appear the blue ice and the foaming waters of the river as it emerges from the glacier.

The ascent is steep, rising 1,500 feet in the half mile to MAKE-UP ROCK (9,500 alt.), **2.5** *m.* This rock, rising above a great snow plain, was so named because many climbers stop at this point to put on dark glasses and daub their faces with grease paint for protection against sun and snow burn. It is also known as Pack Rock.

The route continues steeply across crevasse-furrowed snow and around wind-scoured crags to CRATER ROCK (10,000 alt.), **3.1** *m.* The boulder, rising from a huge drift of snow, seems massive as a sky-scraper. (*A first aid toboggan, provided by the Wy'easters, a mountain climbing organization, is kept here for emergencies.*)

The route cuts sharply westward to HOT ROCKS (10,500 alt.), where sulphurous fumes come from hundreds of vents. At the center is the spot known as the DEVIL'S KITCHEN, where temperatures taken a few inches below the rocks register 200°F. STEEL CLIFF (R) is a great wall of rock named for Will G. Steel, a pioneer in developing Oregon's natural attractions. Not only did he call attention to Crater Lake (*see CRATER LAKE*), but he was one of the early Mount Hood enthusiasts. The wall extends to the summit, which is almost a thousand feet above the level of the southern end. A trail leads up the cliff, providing a route to the summit that challenges even the expert mountaineer. (*Not for any but experienced climbers.*)

The main route proceeds westward across a huge field of ice and snow to the southern end of the CHUTE (10,800 alt.), **3.3** *m.,* where the trail has a grade of 34 to 45 per cent. A supporting rope extends 1,000 feet up the Chute which is about 100 yards wide at the bottom and narrows towards the top.

From the NORTH END OF THE CHUTE (11,225 alt.), **3.6** *m.,* on the summit ridge of the main peak, is a spectacular view. The northern side of the mountain falls away in one great precipice. Below 3,000 feet tumble the ice falls of COE and LADD GLACIERS.

The route proceeds eastward along the narrow summit-ridge for about 400 feet to SUMMIT CABIN (11,245 alt.), **3.7** *m.,* an abandoned fire lookout. The squat structure with a cupola affords shelter from storms and provides bunks for campers. Lumber for the building was carried up the mountain on the shoulders of Elijah Coalman, a well-known guide. In the ranger cabin is a book, provided by the Mazamas, a Portland mountain-climbing organization, that has done much since 1894 to foster Hood's recreational development. In the register are the names of members of the Mazamas, the Wy'east Club, the Hood River Crag Rats, the Eugene Obsidians, and the Salem Chemeketans, mountaineers all, and of numerous amateurs who have scaled the peak.

The view from the summit is magnificent. To the south, in the foreground, is Mount Jefferson, Hood's slightly smaller sister, whose straight chimney-like top is conquered only by expert mountaineers; beyond rise the Three Sisters, and much farther is Diamond Mountain, a blur of bluish green. Along the slopes of the Cascades, between these towering peaks, is a sea of green forest. Directly eastward are the checkered wheatfields and deserts of central Oregon with the turquoise backdrop of the Blue Mountains. To the west is the Willamette Valley with the Coast Range behind it. To the north a chain of white peaks—Mount Adams, Mount St. Helens, and Mount Rainier—stretch nearly 200 miles. Much nearer is the deep Columbia River Gorge, and immediately below Mount Hood is Lost Lake, a silver mirror among the evergreens.

COOPER SPUR CLIMB (NORTH SLOPE)

Average climbing time 6 to 10 hours.

This is the second of the three most popular summit routes. While this climb is not without danger from falling rocks and snow slides, it is one of the shortest and is climbed by a large American Legion party each year under guidance of the Crag Rats.

Will and Douglas Langille were the first to use this route. It is made from CLOUD CAP INN (*see TRAIL TOURS above, also TOUR 1E*) or the TILLY JANE FOREST CAMP (*see TOUR 1E*) cabin. The trail begins at an elevation of 6,000 feet and rises to GHOST RIDGE (7,000 alt.), along the eastern margin of Eliot Glacier, largest ice mass on the mountain. The trail then mounts the sharp rocky ice-hung pitch of COOPER SPUR, 3 *m.* on the northeast shoulder of the mountain. Atop Cooper Spur (8,500 alt.) the way curves R. to climb rapidly over a steep snow slope to THE CHIMNEY, 3.3 *m.*, along which a thousand feet of thick rope guide climbers almost to the summit. (*Rope strung by the Hood River Crag Rats each May and removed after Labor Day.*)

NORTH SUMMIT, 3.8 *m.*, is the high rim of the old crater.

Crater Lake National Park

Season: Open all year; hotel, cabin, and cafeteria open June 10 to Sept. 20. (*Rates change slightly from season to season*). Under favorable weather conditions accommodations available before June 10. Summer most popular season for visiting park; in winter area used for winter sports.

Administrative Offices: Summer, in park; winter, Medford, Oregon.

Admission: Registration at entrance checking stations; admission fee $1 a car for calendar year. Amateur photographers need no permit; professional photographers must have one. Main entrance: Annie Spring, on State 62 (*see TOUR 4D*), open all year. Lost Creek Station controls traffic at the east entrance from State 232 (*see TOUR 4b*). Checking station at junction of State 209 and the Rim Drive controls traffic from the north.

Transportation and trails: Motor stages from Medford and Klamath Falls to Crater Lake Lodge. Principal centers from which trails radiate are Rim Village and points along Rim Road. Guided trips from Information Building in Rim Village free. Launch trip on lake.

Accommodations: Crater Lake Lodge in Rim Village, modern hotel, A. or E. plan; also in village housekeeping cabins, cafeteria, community house, public campground, public shower baths, auto service, emergency mechanical service. Other campgrounds: At Lost Creek, on State 232 (*see TOUR 4b*); White Horse Camp and Cold Spring Camp (*see TOUR 4D*).

Climate, clothing, equipment: Mountain climate with cold nights. Medium weight clothing for visitors who spend time in hotels and motor cars; usual hiking clothing sufficient for riding and tramping in daytime; medium weight clothing, and plenty of covers for camping out; equipment cannot be purchased or rented at park, available only at Medford and Klamath Falls.

Medical service: At Park Headquarters.

Special regulations: Fires and camping only in designated campgrounds; hunting is not permitted; fishing permitted with limit of five fish to a person daily.

Warnings: Remain always on trails; do not feed bears; observe regulations regarding smoking and campfires; visitors forbidden to go between guarding barrier and the rim.

The first white man to gaze on the ultramarine body of water that is now the world-famed Crater Lake named it Deep Blue Lake. Chaliced in the crater of an extinct volcano, walled by majestic cliffs, and miraculously blue, it is one of earth's most beautiful lakes. No one can stand without reverence in the presence of this sublime creation. A beholder becomes silent as the sea at his feet.

Not only the beauty of the lake and its utterly blue color, but its crater within a crater makes it unique among the world's great scenic features. Crater Lake has been named with the Grand Canyon of the Colorado and Victoria Falls of Africa as one of the three greatest scenic marvels of the globe. Set high in Mount Mazama's shattered crest, its rugged cliffs rise to imposing heights. These implacable walls of volcanic rock send their reflected color into the deep, still water, so blended that the reality and the image are one. The two perfectly mirrored islands that seem but illusions add to the mystical effect.

Prehistoric Mount Mazama towered to heights of more than 14,000 feet. No man ever beheld this mighty glacier-covered mountain, but it is thought to have surpassed any of the existing peaks of the Cascades. The lake was formed eons ago when this mountain exploded or burned itself out from within, forming the great crater. Seepage and precipitation filled the caldera with water, and as it rose, a point was reached at which precipitation and seepage were balanced by evaporation, to a level that has since held, forming a lake six miles in diameter and reaching to the impressive depth of 2,000 feet. No streams flow into the crater and there is no visible outlet. Three theories have been advanced as to the formation of the lake. Many geologists believe that the top of the mountain was blown off by a series of terrific explosions, leaving a cauldron 4,000 feet deep. The second and generally accepted theory is that the mountain collapsed or was engulfed, since the volume of mountain top which has disappeared, no man knows where, amounts to about 17 cubic miles and such a mass, if removed by explosion would have thickly covered the radiating slopes and produced a symmetrical, conical base. Closely associated with the collapse is the third surmise which holds that the seething mass of lava in the crater of the volcano fused and undermined the walls and gradually produced the wide caldera without violent explosions. The base of this great mountain remains, and until August 21, 1896, bore no name until it was christened in behalf of the Mazamas, mountain-climbing organization.

The Klamath Indians had many picturesque legends of the crater in their mythology, curiously allied to that of the ancient Greeks. They believed that the great lake, far away and deep in the high mountain, was an amphitheater where the gods, who dwelt on its rocky heights and in its mystic depths forever, played in its blue waters, and sometimes staged terrifying battles among themselves, sending up angry smoke columns and making the mountains echo with the thunder of the conflict. Though the lake was guarded by Llao, god of the underworld, and his fearful creatures, the young Indian tested his courage and endurance by descending to the water. He was purified and renewed in body and spirit by bathing in the blue waters. To the lake also came the medicine men of the ancient tribes seeking the knowledge and the secrets of the gods.

The first white men to view the lake were members of a party of prospectors searching for the "Lost Cabin" mine. They were led by John Hillman, who discovered the body of water in June, 1853. The argonauts drank deep of its beauty, named it Deep Blue Lake, and pushed on, leaving the fabulous place forgotten for a decade until it was rediscovered in 1862. Soldiers from Fort Klamath broke through the green forest growth around the crater in 1865. A trapper promptly named the ultramarine depths Lake Majesty, but the title did not endure. In that same year Annie Gaines made the descent to the water, the first woman to achieve this feat. In July, 1869, a party was formed in Jacksonville to visit the great Sunken Lake, and its lonely island crater on which the foot of white man had never trod. They brought with them a wooden boat, which, with infinite labor, they succeeded in lowering to the water. In this frail craft, J. B. Coats, James D. Fay, David Linn, James M. Sutton, and Lt. S. B. Thoburn visited Wizard Island, which with appropriate ceremony was so christened by James M. Sutton. He and David Linn gave the lake its present name.

Crater Lake National Park, created in 1902, is the only National Park in Oregon, and in a sense a monument to William Gladstone Steel, one of Oregon's most widely known writers and mountain lovers, who as a schoolboy had heard of the lake, and determined to visit it. He spent nine years in Oregon, it is said, before he could find anyone who had heard of the mysterious lake, now visited by more than 200,000 persons in one season. It was not until 1885 that he was able to finish his quest, and found the fulfillment more beautiful than the dream. That same year, 1885, he urged that the entire area around the lake be set aside as a National Park. When his efforts to awaken interest in Crater Lake caused President Cleveland to withdraw ten townships, including the water, from the public domain, and they became in time reserves of the National Parks, Mr. Steel became the Park's first superintendent. As long as he lived, the lake and surrounding region received his constant and devoted attention. His donation of a miscellany of photographs and records have made the lake a pioneer shrine.

When discovered, there was no sign of fish in the lake's waters. In 1888, Mr. Steel carried 600 Rogue River fingerlings from that stream over the rough mountain roads to the lake. It was a hard journey. At every stream he freshened the water, and part of the way he carried the bucket of fish in his own hands, releasing the little trout at the lake's edge. Only thirty-seven of them, so he told, had sufficient life to swim feebly away. Yet the survivors flourished, while subsequent plantings have increased until they number about 200,000 young fish annually.

Unscarred by the axes of man, the forests of Crater Lake National Park stand in towering splendor, covering the mounds left by the cataclysm. Species of trees include the yellow pine, madrona-tree, mountain hemlock, and Douglas fir. The hemlock with its feathery, blue-green foliage, and reddish brown bark, is perhaps the most arresting tree of the region and common to the inner wall of the lake. Clinging to the broken crests of the rim, the wind-smitten hemlocks, twisted into fantastic shapes, accent the lake's weird beauty.

On the slopes of Mount Mazama are lovely meadows and marshes, and in them grow more than 500 species of flowering plants and ferns. Avalanche lilies, asters, and other alpine blooms flourish. Meadows of scarlet-trumpeted mountain gilia, snow-white phantom orchid, Indian paintbrush and blue lupine cover the scarred slopes of the mountain. Farther down the crater's corrugated sides, ramble the gold of sunflowers, beard's tongue, purple mimulus, and bleeding-hearts. Beneath the surface in the deeply encrusted lava, the rocks have run ridges and crests along the mountain sides in which glacier-eroded and washed soils and moisture from the upper slopes have collected. These miniature terraces pour color over outcropping lava ridges not unlike the Hanging Gardens of ancient Babylon.

The park abounds with smaller game, of great interest to the visitor because of their friendly inquisitiveness. Squirrels are numerous and have become tame through feeding by the park visitors. Larger mammals, with the exception of bear, are represented but not numerous. Columbia blacktail deer is plentiful. The larger mule deer is sometimes seen; and occasionally, white-tail deer graze in grassy watered meadows. Elk have been seen along the eastern side of the park as far north as the base of Mount Scott.

More than 70 species of birds make the park their habitat, and their song is heard continuously. Many brilliantly colored birds flit about in the dark foliage of pine, fir, and hemlock. Eagle Crags have been the eyrie of the golden and the American bald eagle; Llao Rock is the home of falcons. Ospreys have been seen and the horned owl forages nightly. Black cormorants are known to have nested and raised their young on the craggy shores of the lake. The most striking bird in the park is the western tanager, with its red head, yellow body, and black wings with yellow bars; and the sweetest singer is the elusive hermit thrush.

TOUR 1

Rim Drive branches north from State 62 (*see TOUR 4D*), 0 *m.*, close to the Park Administration Headquarters.

RIM VILLAGE, 3.7 *m.*, is a resort community at the south end of the lake and the focal point for all park activities. (*See GENERAL INFORMATION for rates*). Prominent here is CRATER LAKE LODGE, a modern three-story hotel in a setting of great beauty. The RIM CAMPGROUND (*see GENERAL INFORMATION*), in a fine stand of mountain hemlock near by, is also close to the rim of the lake. Near the campground is the COMMUNITY HOUSE, around whose great stone fireplace visitors gather each night.

Left from RIM VILLAGE on a short foot trail to the SINNOTT MEMO-RIAL, an attractive stone structure on Victor Rock, erected in recognition of the services to Crater Lake National Park and the state by Congressman Nicholas J. Sinnott of Oregon. A large relief map of the Crater Lake region is on the parapet. High-powered field glasses are trained on important features to reveal the geologic formations.

From this point is an excellent view of WIZARD ISLAND (L), the symmetrical cinder cone, rising 763 feet above the surface of the lake. It has a crater 400 feet in diameter and approximately 80 feet deep. Soundings of the lake have revealed the presence of two submerged, lesser cones. Wizard Island is reached by launch (*see below*).

The PHANTOM SHIP (R) is a small volcanic island resembling an old double-masted sailing ship. The sharp pinnacles of lava are the masts, 175 feet tall, and the pine and fir trees blend into ropes and rigging.

Right from Rim Village on the spectacular Crater Wall Trail, six feet wide, which slopes steeply down to the edge of the lake, 1.6 *m.* (45 *minutes walking time down,* 1 *hour and* 15 *minutes back; saddle horses and mules available*).

From the foot of the Crater Wall Trail a 26-mile circle launch trip (*see GENERAL INFORMATION*) can be taken with the guidance of a ranger-naturalist. (*Regularly scheduled trips daily by launch to Phantom Ship and Wizard Island,* $2; *hourly trips to Wizard Island at* $1; *row boats* 50c *an hour for one person,* 25c *for each additional person*). The lake is stocked with rainbow and steelhead trout, and with a lesser number of other varieties. The trout average around two pounds in weight, and are readily caught even by the inexpert angler. Fly-casting is used extensively but trolling is the more popular method.

Right from Rim Village on a good foot trail with an easy grade to GARFIELD PEAK, 1.7 *m.* (8,060 alt.), one of the highest points on Crater Rim, it commands a wide view of the lake and the rugged terrain to the eastward. It was named by William G. Steel for James R. Garfield, at that time Secretary of the Interior and the first cabinet officer to visit Crater Lake.

Left from Rim Village on a foot trail to the beautiful LADY OF THE WOODS, 0.5 *m.*, a carved stone figure.

TOUR 2

Rim Village—Park Headquarters—Lost Creek Campground—Kerr Notch—Sentinel Point—Cloud Cap Viewpoint—Wineglass—Llao Rock—The Watchman—Discovery Point—Rim Village; 38.8 m. Rim Road.

Closed during winter. Automobiles invited to join daily party conducted by ranger-naturalist. Time of leaving and other details posted on park bulletin board. Not open during the winter.

The Rim Drive is one of the most delightful features of the area. This route, provided with observation points at the most impressive vantage spots, gives an opportunity to view the lake from every angle. The direction of the drive is usually planned for the best light values.

South from RIM VILLAGE, 0 *m.*, on the drive to PARK HEADQUARTERS, 3.7 *m.* From this point the road proceeds over a part of an old rim road, rough in spots, past pits (R), where at certain times of the day black bears forage for the food placed there for them.

At 4.5 *m.* is a junction with the Castle Crest Garden Trail.

Left on this trail, is the WILD-FLOWER GARDEN, 0.5 *m.*, a beautiful spot and ideal for the study of the Crater Lake flora.

The narrow dirt road winds through hemlock forests, with UNION PEAK (7,698 alt.) in view (R) across the valley. CRATER PEAK, 5.9 *m.* (7,625 alt.), is one of the prominent volcanic cones of the region, a high point in Crater Ridge (R). The road now skirts the edge of glacial U-shaped SUN CANYON, with a magnificent view of surrounding country (R).

VIDAE FALLS (L), 7.1 *m.*, are formed by a small stream that tumbles down the face of VIDAE CLIFF on the side of Sun Canyon.

SUN CREEK, **7.3** *m.,* is seen flashing through groves of hemlock and red fir on a long slope that climbs to a view (L) of APPLEGATE PEAK (8,135 alt.) At **8.3** *m.* is one of the route's most far-reaching views of the Klamath Basin unscrolled to the distant horizon. MOUNT SCOTT (8,938 alt.), the highest point in the park, is directly in the foreground.

WHEELER CREEK CROSSING is at **11.1** *m.* The Sand Pinnacles are in the canyon of this creek, reached by State 232 (*see below*).

The road proceeds through forests, over sharply rising mountains to LOST CREEK CAMPGROUND, **11.9** *m.,* (*checking station; see* GENERAL INFORMATION).

Right on State 232 to the SAND PINNACLES, **5** *m.,* striking formations, like the pipes of a giant organ, that rise to heights of 200 feet from the depth of the canyon of Wheeler Creek. These slender spires have been carved through the ages by erosion and are ever growing by the action of wind and water.

From this junction the highway is hard-surfaced and climbs steadily to the rim of the lake.

From the parapets of KERR NOTCH, **15.4** *m.* (6,700 alt.), a scenic promontory overlooking the unbelievably blue water, is the first and one of the most inspiring views of the lake. The Phantom Ship is in full view against DUTTON CLIFF near the south shore. Depending upon the mood of the lake the Phantom Ship may be mirrored on the water, it may be sharply defined, or it may seem to vanish magically against the rocky background. The illusion at dusk or in moonlight is impressive. Red fir and hemlock trees make a natural frame for this arresting picture.

Beyond Kerr Notch, the lowest point on the rim, an improved motor road leads around the lake's broken-crested margin. At **15.9** *m.* is another wide view of Klamath Basin (R), and at **16.5** *m.* a view of CLOUDCAP (8,070 alt.) in the foreground between Danger Bay and Cloudcap Bay. SENTINEL POINT, wedge-shaped rock bastion jutting over the shimmering water, **17.7** *m.,* is also between Danger Bay and Cloudcap Bay. Two of the lofty peaks of the Cascades, MOUNT THIELSEN (9,178 alt.), on the E., and MOUNT BAILEY (8,360 alt.), on the W., crown the skyline at **18** *m.* (R).

At **19.4** *m.* DIAMOND LAKE is visible, deep in the somber-green forest under the jagged pinnacle of Mount Thielsen.

At **20.2** *m.* is a junction with a trail.

Right on this excellent trail to the summit of MOUNT SCOTT, **2.5** *m.* (10,083 alt.), where a fire lookout is situated.

CLOUDCAP VIEWPOINT, **20.3** *m.* (8,070 alt.), because of its elevation of 2,000 feet above the eastern rim affords the most spectacular view of the entire Rim Drive. Through gaps in white-barked, wind-buffeted pines are discernable the blue and ever-changing water, tumbled foothills, snow-capped peaks, and somber forests beyond, with Klamath Lake, an expanse of silver-blue in the vast green marshlands, south of the park area. Across the lake (L) are Dutton Cliff, Applegate

Peak (8,135 alt.), Dyor Rock, and Garfield Peak (8,060 alt.). To the NW. is Llao Rock. To the N. lies the Pumice Desert, formed by volcanic activity, showering the region with pumice and ash. Mount Scott to the E., and Mount McLoughlin and Mount Shasta to the S. are likewise in view from Cloudcap.

TIMBER CRATER (7,360 alt.), a low timbered cone, is visible at **21.6** *m.* SKELL HEAD, 24 *m.,* named for the Indian god of the upper world who vanquished Llao (*see below*), juts out into the lake between Cloudcap Bay and Grotto Cove.

The WINEGLASS, 25.3 *m.,* is a slide formation caused by erosion. When viewed from the opposite shore it resembles an enormous stem glass. This is said to be the point at which an 18-foot boat called the *Cleetwood,* used by members of the United States Geological Survey in making soundings of the lake in 1886, was lowered from the rim. Just NW. of the Wineglass and above the rim (R) is ROUND-TOP (6,069 alt.).

MAZAMA ROCK, 27.6 *m.,* is a single lava stone, 60 feet or more in height, yellow in color, and streaked with vermillion markings, which rises over brilliantly pigmented rock strata on the lake's rim. There is every indication, geologists assert, that this body of lava fell, or was literally blown out of the side of ancient Mount Mazama and hurled into space by some terrific force. This section of Rim Drive, known as Rugged Crest, is of particular interest to geologists. Left and right, in an all-encompassing view of the lake, are these points of special interest: Mount Scott, Cloudcap Viewpoint, Sentinel Point, Kerr Notch, Dutton Cliff, Sun Notch, Applegate Peak, Dyor Rock, Garfield Peak, Wizard Island, The Watchman, Hillman Peak, and Llao Rock.

PUMICE POINT, **29.1** *m.,* extends into Crater Lake at its northern extremity, between Cleetwood Cove and Steel Bay, and commands another excellent view. Sun Notch and Kerr Notch lie almost due south across the lake.

Passing huge rock formations (L), and occasionally meadows, the route climbs upward across the backbone of the lava flow of Llao Rock (*see below*). Pumice Desert lies far to the R.

At **31.6** *m.* (R) is RED CONE (7,372 alt.), and just west of RED CONE SPRING.

The junction with State 209, **33** *m.,* now the route (L), is a Park Checking Station.

Right from the junction on State 209, through windswept stretches of treeless pumice fields to the north entrance of the park, 4 *m.,* and a junction (L) with State 230 (*see TOUR* 4D).

State 209 continues north to DIAMOND LAKE, **7** *m.* (5,186 alt.), a village on the edge of the lake of the same name. Three miles wide and five miles long, this lake is one of the most charming of the many beautiful bodies of water in the Cascades. Beaches of yellow sand margin the nearer shores; dark forests fringe remoter borders. Mount Thielsen rises like a bared fang above it to the east. From the west, Mount Bailey casts its white reflection on the smooth water. (*Lodge; housekeeping cottages; other accommodations during season, if snow permits, to September 20. Free Forest camps throughout area.*

Excellent hiking trails, saddle horses; guides; post office). (For State 209 northward see TOUR 4b).

The Rim Drive proceeds S. from the junction with State 209, and reaches LLAO ROCK, 33.3 *m.* (8,046 alt.), a towering lava formation that rises nearly 2,000 feet above the water, the highest vertical precipice on the rim, and one of the most remarkable lava flows known to geologists. On its face may be traced the history of the mighty volcano. On this rock lived the mythical Indian god, Llao, invincible until overcome by Skell.

According to the legends of the Maklaks, ancestors of the Klamaths and the Modocs, the high mountain, La-o-Yaina, in the mystic land of Gaywas, known to us as Mount Mazama, was the home of Llao. His throne, in the infinite depths of the blue waters was surrounded by giant crawfish, his warriors, that were able to reach great claws out of the water and seize too venturesome enemies on the cliffs. Skell, who dwelt in the land east of the great marshes, was the upper-world god of sunlight and fertility and all things beautiful. The destruction of La-o-Yaina was the result of a terrible conflict between Llao and Skell. Skell came to the rescue of a great chief's daughter, with whom both had fallen in love, and whom the chief would not surrender. To prevent the maiden from being taken to realms of darkness within the center of the earth, Skell defied Llao. Llao summoned his creatures from their black caverns and caves of fire, and for five days thundered and threatened to destroy the land of the Maklaks with his fire-curse if the chief did not deliver the maiden to him. Lightning darted from the top of the mountain, thunder shook the world, winds tore at the forests, and dark smoke filled the sky. Skell hurled his spears of sunlight at Llao with all his might, piercing the darkness. The battle lasted seven days, and Llao's throne burst apart and rained fire over the land. Finally Llao aimed a flaming rock that struck Skell on the back of the head, and Skell died. Skell's heart, torn from his body and cast into the lake, had to be restored in order that he might live again. It was taken from Llao's creatures as they played ball with it at the feast of victory by Coyote, Skell's servant, passed to the Fox, and then seized in flight by the Golden Eagle, Skell's messenger. Once more Skell's body grew around his living heart and once more he was powerful and waged war until Llao was slain. From the highest cliff Llao's body was quartered and cast into the lake and eaten by his own monsters under the belief that it was Skell's body. When Llao's head was thrown into the water the monsters recognized it and would not eat it. Llao's head still lies in the lake, and men call it Wizard Island. The cliff on which Llao was quartered is named Llao Rock. The fire-curse never again came to La-o-Yaina but the spirit of Llao dwells in the great rock and comes forth to cause great storms on the lake.

At 34 *m.* a trail branches (L) to the DEVIL'S BACKBONE, 0.3 *m.*

The route continues S., passing (L) HILLMAN PARK, 34.7 *m.* (8,156 alt.), named for the lake's discoverer. The WATCHMAN,

35.1 *m.* (8,025 alt.), rising 2,000 feet above the lake, is reached by trail. It derives its name from the fact that it was an observation point used by the men of the United States Geological Survey while they were sounding the lake in 1886. The summit of this prominent peak commands one of the most impressive panoramic views of the entire park area. The eminence is surmounted by one of the finest fire lookout stations in the United States. It is glass enclosed, and completely insulated against the lightning storms, which occur frequently in the high altitudes of this region. (*Ranger in charge*).

At **35.8** *m.* is Watchman trail.

Left here **0.6** *m.* to the WATCHMAN.

DISCOVERY POINT, **36.3** *m.,* is a lava headland from which John Wesley Hillman peered over the rim and first beheld the awesome blue lake in its mammoth crater, June 12, 1853.

At **38.1** *m.* a viewpoint affords a splendid view (R) over the Umpqua-Rogue Divide. At about the same point Mount McLoughlin and Mount Shasta are in view (R).

At **38.8** *m.* is RIM VILLAGE.

National Forests

Season: Open all year, but impenetrable in higher elevations from early fall to midsummer; area in whole or in part subject to being closed for fire hazard by executive order; most satisfactory season, July, August, early September.

Administration Offices: North Pacific Regional Headquarters, in charge of all the forests, Post Office Building, Portland. Individual forest headquarters: Deschutes, Bend; Fremont, Lakeview; Malheur, John Day; Mount Hood, Terminal Sales Bldg., Portland; Ochoco, Prineville; Rogue River, Medford; Siskiyou, Grants Pass; Siuslaw, Eugene; Umatilla, Pendleton; Umpqua, Roseburg; Wallowa, Enterprise; Whitman, Baker; Willamette, Salem.

Admission: No registration at entrances, no fees, but all visitors are subject, within a forest, to rules and regulations of U. S. Forest Service (see below); photographers, amateur and professional, need no permits; forest rangers and guards give information.

Transportation: More than 7,600 miles of satisfactory major, secondary, and forest roads within the areas; improved trail mileage, 12,000; trail system so well developed that trails lead to all important points of interest.

Accommodations: No hotels under Federal or state control or ownership; forest camps, shelter, and private resorts are numerous.

Climate, clothing, equipment: Medium-weight clothing adequate for those who spend their time in private resorts and motorcars; ordinary hiking clothes sufficient for hikers who spend nights in equipped camps in lower areas; heavy clothing for hikers in greatest altitudes and heavy clothing and plenty of bedding for those who camp out; equipment not available within forests.

Medical service: Ordinarily at the CCC camps.

Special regulations: No campfire may be lighted without a permit from the supervisor or a forest ranger, except in improved camps, which are posted. Burning matches, tobacco, or lighted material of any kind may not be thrown away within the forest boundaries; smoking prohibited while traveling in forests in fire season except on paved or surfaced highways. Fire season begins on May 15 and ends Oct. 1, but may be extended at discretion of state authorities. Campers must extinguish all fires before breaking camp and may use only dead wood in campfires; growing trees must not be felled. Forest signs must not be defaced. State fish and game laws are enforced by forest rangers, all of whom are deputy game wardens. Sanitary rules must be observed. Campers should carry axe, shovel, and water container of a gallon or more capacity. Copies of state and Federal regulations relative to National Forests available from any forest supervisor.

Warning of danger: Always stay on trail while hiking; if lost wait quietly until rescued or follow water courses to lower country.

Attractions: Motoring, hiking, camping, fishing, hunting, mountain climbing; winter sports in season in high Cascade Mountains.

NEARLY one-half of the state's sixty million acres is forest, comprising one-fourth the standing timber remaining in the United States.

Oregon has more timbered area as well as more timber than any other State.

The woods of Oregon are a wonderland of overwhelming proportions. The eye, always drawn to the distant snow-capped peaks, sweeps over magnificent verdant blankets that cover the lower hills and spread back in tiers over higher hills and far up the mountainsides. From the heights, the forest far below is an undulating layer of dark green, sparkling with gem-like lakes and silvery streams, which stretches far off into a horizon serrated with the silhouette of distant trees. Within the forests is the beauty of loftiness, luxuriance, and symmetry, of tangles of wildwood and flowers, of green moss pendant from huge limbs, of grass-tapestried open spaces where solemn forest giants stand. Impressive in the red afterglow of the setting sun is a sentinel with one side shorn away by lightning, holding its own against the storms of a century. There is the grace of tree tops bowing in uniformity like a group of stately dancers, and pathos of a diminutive shoot on the top of a great crownless parent trunk. And there is the music and silence of solitude and peace.

Oregon's National forests profoundly affect the existence of the people of Oregon. They are the source of streams that produce the state's immense water-power; they provide pure water for three-fourths of the population and afford pasturage for hundreds of thousands of livestock. They perpetuate wild life and furnish recreation for vacationist, hunter, and fisherman. Source of much of Oregon's present timber supply, they conserve the timber for future generations. They also conserve moisture and snowfall, thus retarding run-off and consequent soil erosion. Without them, Oregon's fertile areas would become a desolation of torrential rains, shifting sands, and barren rocks.

Oregon has thirteen National forests, with a net total area of 13,701,834 acres. All but three lie wholly within its borders. With the exception of the Fremont Forest, on a high plateau extension of the great basin in central southern Oregon, they are supported by the state's three major mountain ranges, the Coast, Cascade, and Blue Mountains. The National forests are publicly owned timberlands, controlled by the Forest Service of the United States Department of Agriculture and set aside for the purpose of growing timber and conserving water supplies.

Each forest is administered by a supervisor, who is responsible for the protection and proper use of all its resources. Under the Government's sustained forest-yield policy, a perpetual supply of growing timber is assured and the control of the drainage waters of the high mountains guaranteed. An important part of forest conservation is fire prevention and the reforestation of cut or burned-over areas. The moist climate west of the Cascade summit assures prompt reforestation from seed stored in the forest floor; but east of the Cascades, the process of growing a new crop must be started from seedlings passed over by the logger or from cones borne on the seed trees that are left. Fire protection is a matter of eternal vigilance, and the forest authorities have established rigid regulations applicable to all visitors in the forests. Because of the 400 billion feet of standing timber in the forests, strict observance of the rules must be enforced.

The Forest Service has spent millions of dollars in the construction of roads and trails, both as fire protection and for recreational purposes, and in the establishment of recreation areas, camps, and campsites. It has surveyed summer-home sites along rivers and lakes for lease to responsible persons. As a result of these manifold activities, few parts of the forest area are inaccessible to the vacationist or sportsman. A number of the recreational areas may be reached by railroad; all are accessible by one or more of Oregon's major highways. In the recreational areas are to be found facilities for mountain climbing, hiking, and packing in summer; tobogganing, skiing, and snow shoeing in winter. Commercial accommodations within the forests take a wide range, both in matter of numbers and adequacy. There is the great Timberline Lodge on the slopes of Mount Hood, which has every accommodation of the modern hotel (*see MOUNT HOOD*).

The invitation of the Federal Government to the public to make use of the forests for vacation purposes is accompanied by cautionary advice which visitors should bear in mind. Lives have been forfeited because amateurs underestimated the hazards they faced. Safety precautions are insurance against danger and should be observed in making any excursion into the forests.

In the National forests of Oregon are six primitive areas, totaling 588,000 acres, set aside for the observation of trees and other growths in their native habitats. Trails have been cut through these areas and the public is permitted to enter them under restrictions. They are the Eagle Cap, in the Wallowa Mountains, the Ochoco Divide National Area, Mount Jefferson, Mountain Lakes (in the Klamath Mountains), Mount Hood, and the Three Sisters.

Wild life, both animals and birds, is extensive in Oregon, especially in the deep wilderness (*see FAUNA and FLORA*). In the National forests there are about 125,000 deer of different varieties, a number of antelope, and a few of the nearly extinct bighorn or Rocky Mountain sheep. There are about 4,000 bears, but the once plentiful beaver is reduced to about 10,000. There are large numbers of skunk, civet cat, weasel, and mink; and in less numbers, martens, badgers and coons. Predators in Oregon are coyotes, mountain lions, or cougars, bob cats, a few wolves and porcupines.

The forests are alive with birds. More than 300 varieties have been listed, largely non-game, although grouse and pheasants are plentiful, and there is a representation of sage hens and partridges (*see FAUNA and FLORA*).

The tree growth in the Oregon National forests is predominantly coniferous. The largest coverage is in Douglas fir and ponderosa pine, both of high commercial value. West of the Cascades summit, where the climate is moist, the volume of Douglas fir runs to 80 per cent. Other conifers are the red fir, amabilis (white or silver) fir, alpine fir, western hemlock, Sitka (tideland) spruce, and various cedars, among them almost all of the world's supply of Port Orford cedar. East of the summit, where the climate is dry to a point of aridity, the ponderosa pine stand is about 60 per cent of the whole. Douglas fir runs second, but it is stunted and not of high value. Other types in smaller volume are western larch, sugar pine, western white pine, lodgepole pine, hemlock and cedar.

The Deschutes National Forest, with a total net area of 1,347,653 acres, stretches its miles of lakes and streams, pine forests, and mountain peaks along the eastern slope of the Cascade Range from Mount Jefferson on the Jefferson County line to Mount Thielsen in Klamath County. Within this forest rises Newberry Crater, an extinct volcano with cinder cones, boiling sulphur springs, fields of yellow and black and red obsidian glass, and clear mountain lakes. The Metolius River, a famous fishing stream that spreads its fingers through groves of yellow pine, springs from the base of Black Butte near the Jefferson-Deschutes County line. Elk, Crescent, and Odell Lakes are among the more noted bodies of water in the area. (*see Tours 4, 6, and 7*).

The Fremont National Forest, in south central Oregon, has a total net area of 1,095,236 acres. Broken into many portions, the forest region extends over a high plateau in which jagged rimrock thrusts up sharp spires and ridges among swelling buttes and level mesas and vegetation varies from sagebrush and juniper to pine forests and lush meadowlands. Thousands of cattle and sheep graze upon the forest domain. A considerable amount of timber is cut annually under Government sale contract, but most of the forest is as primitive as it was when Capt. John C. Fremont explored the region in 1843. Duck and goose hunting is excellent, and deer are taken in certain parts of the forest (*see Tours* 5, 5C, *and* 5D).

Malheur National Forest, with a total net area of 1,071,425 acres, extends over the southern extremity of the Blue Mountains in eastern Oregon. The area, while not yet important as a recreational center, is being improved by the Forest Service, and the high peaks and mountain lakes of its scenic wonderland are already accessible by trail. Three of the peaks in the Malheur Forest tower above 7,000 feet, and several lakes beautiful in color and setting, afford good fishing as well. Although much timber is cut under Government sale contract, a great portion of the area is employed as grazing land for cattle and sheep (*see Tours* 5 *and* 6).

The Mount Hood National Forest, with a total net area of 1,098,022 acres, sweeps in a vast, superb panorama of peak and pine, river and lake and waterfall, from the banks of the Columbia River almost to the white bulk of Mount Jefferson, more than one hundred miles south of the forest's northern boundary. Mount Hood, monarch of Oregon's snow peaks, towers over lesser mountains as it casts its long shadow across dense forests, deep ravines, fields and alpine flowers, and lakes that reflect its splendor in their cold, tranquil depths. Five rivers—the Bull Run, the Sandy, the Clackamas, the Hood, and the White rise in the forest, and countless swift small watercourses race in white-capped frenzy down mountain and forest slope. Mount Hood is the center of recreational activities in the forest, but other portions of the area draw thousands of visitors annually. Lost Lake is among the attractive points of interest in the region (*see Tours,* 1, 1E, *and* 4A).

The Ochoco National Forest, in central Oregon, is divided into three sections and has a total net area of 728,934 acres. A great sheep and cattle range, the Ochoco has also a considerable amount of timber, and affords splendid opportunities for deer hunting in season. The Forest Service maintains three camps in the area (*see Tour* 6).

The Rogue River National Forest embraces a total net area of 849,568 acres in southern Oregon. Its northeast boundaries touch the famous Crater Lake National Park, and it is among the forest's heavily wooded hills that the mighty Rogue River rises. Famous as a fishing stream, the Rogue has many tributaries likewise beloved by anglers; and throughout the entire forest, clear watercourses trace a silver pattern through the perennial green of pine, fir, and spruce. Mount McLoughlin, one of the great snow-capped sentinels of the Cascades, rises to an elevation of 9,493 feet within the forest boundaries; the Lake of the Woods and the Dead Indian Soda Springs are scenic highlights of the region (*see Tours 2, 4, and 4D*).

The Siskiyou National Forest, in southern Oregon, has a total net area of 1,033,186 acres within the state and extends across the line into California, where there are more than 300,000 additional acres of forest domain. The peaks of the Siskiyou Range rise above great serene stretches of heavily wooded hills. It is in the Siskiyou Forest of Oregon that the state's few groves of redwood trees are found. The rare Brewer's spruce is also indigenous to the mountinous region. Ghost towns of the southwestern Oregon gold rush are scattered along the many streams which cut through the Siskiyou range. Rogue River, with its excellent fishing, flows westward through the forest; the wilderness area also offers bear, deer, and cougar hunting. Outstanding in this forest are the Oregon Marble Caves (*see Tours 2I, and 3*).

The Siuslaw National Forest, with a total net area of 500,877 acres, stretches along the Pacific Ocean from a point near Marshfield north almost to Tillamook and inland to the slopes of the Coast Range of mountains. Broken into many portions, the area embraces a number of Oregon's most famous beach resorts and fishing streams. Along the coast are great reaches of rolling surf, acres of golden sand, rocks sculptured into fantastic shapes by wind and pounding water; inland are dense forests, meadows carpeted with wild flowers, cultivated valleys, clear, swift rivers, and a multitude of small watercourses. Sea Lion Caves, Agate Beach, Seal Rock, and the promontory of Tillamook Head are among the many points of interest that are readily accessible to the Siuslaw Forest; Mount Hebo and other peaks of the Coast Range are within the forest boundary (*see Tours 2C, 2D, 2E, 2F, and 3*).

The Umatilla National Forest, with a total net area of 961,885 acres in northeastern Oregon, extends also into Washington where there are 313,359 additional acres. The area covers a region of mountain ridges and wooded uplands that furnish watershed protection for many streams; thousands of cattle and sheep graze upon the mountain slopes during the summer months. A large amount of timber is cut annually in the forest under Government sale contract. Residents of the intensely cultivated irrigated valleys adjacent to the forest find relief from summer heat at high elevation in the forest; a favorite recreation center in the area is Lake Langdon, on the old tollroad between Walla Walla, Washington, and La Grande, Oregon. Langdon is the only lake in the north spur of the Blue Mountains (*see Tour* 1a).

The Umpqua National Forest, which has a total net area of 984,566 acres, lies mainly within Douglas County, in southeastern Oregon. In it, as in the Siskiyou Forest, are great pine woods and mountains through which rivers and streams, noted for their fishing, roll down narrow ravines and valleys upon which civilization has left little trace. The Umpqua River rises among the darkly wooded slopes of the area. Big game abounds in the tangled forest thickets. Beautiful Diamond Lake, which reflects the snow-capped crest of Mount Bailey upon its smooth surface and looks forth across sharply rising hills at Mount Thielsen, is in the eastern part of the forest (*see Tour* 2).

The Wallowa National Forest, in northeastern Oregon, has a total net area of 969,016 acres. The grandeur of its scenery is perhaps unequaled in the entire Pacific Northwest. The great Snake River, winding through a gorge, breath-taking in its magnificence, forms the eastern boundary of the forest. Within the forest area are tall peaks, torrential streams, mountain waterfalls, and rivers that hurtle through precipitous canyons. Aneroid and Wallowa Lakes are among the bodies of water in a basin formed by a rim of towering peaks, more than 7,000 feet above sea level. There are more than 300 miles of trout streams within the forest. Sturgeon are taken in the Snake River, and grouse, mule deer, and bear are hunted in the heavy forests which cover the lower slopes of the mountains. The fast-vanishing elk are still fairly numerous. The few mountain sheep that remain in Oregon inhabit the mountains south of Wallowa Lake; they are protected by a permanent closed season (*see Tour* 1C).

The Whitman National Forest, south and west of the Wallowa Forest, has a total net area of 1,407,943 acres, and covers both the southern drainages of the Wallowa Range and portions of the Blue Mountains. The region has a wealth of timber and mineral resources, and the headwaters of the Powder, Burnt, and John Day rivers lie within its boundaries. Great herds of cattle and sheep graze under Government permit among its park-like pine groves (*see Tours* 1, 5, *and* 6).

The Willamette National Forest, with a total net area of 1,644,800 acres, is the largest National forest in Oregon. The region extends between the Mount Hood National Forest on the north, the Umpqua National Forest on the south, and along the western slopes of the

Cascade Range. It embraces several of the highest peaks in the mountain wall. Mount Jefferson, Mount Washington, and Three-Fingered Jack thrust their summits above luxuriant growths of Douglas fir; and the Mount Jefferson Primitive Area, one of Oregon's most notable recreation centers, is within its boundaries. The Santiam, the Calapooya, the Blue, and the McKenzie rivers rise among the Willamette highlands, and, with their tributaries, spread a network of watercourses throughout the entire area (*see Tour* 4C, 6, 7, *and* 7A).

PART IV.
Appendices

Chronology

1543 Juan Cabrillo's pilot, Bartolome Ferello, sails along the coast of Oregon, to 42 or 44 degrees N.

1579 Francis Drake passes Oregon coast; names region of southwest Oregon and northern California "New Albion."

1592 Apostolus Valerianos (alias Juan de Fuca), a Greek pilot, claims discovery of the Strait of Anian, the long-sought "Northwest Passage."

1602 Sebastian Vizcaino sights Cape Blanco. His lieutenant, Aguilar, sailing farther along the coast, not only finds and names Cape Blanco, but also discovers the mouth of a river near 43 degrees N., which may have been the Umpqua.

1728 Vitus Bering, Danish navigator, sent by Peter the Great of Russia, discovers the Bering Sea.

1741 Bering's second expedition reaches the Alaskan coast; as a result, a Russian fur-trading post is later established in Alaska, the Russians eventually extending their activities as far south as California.

1765 First known use of the territory's name "Oregon" by Major Robert Rogers, appears in petition asking permission of King George III to explore territory in search of Northwest Passage; the word is spelled "Ouragon."

1774 Juan Perez sails to 54 N. lat.; discovers Nootka Sound.

1775 Bruno Heceta and Bodega Y Quadra, Spanish navigators, sight but do not enter mouth of Columbia.

1778 Name "Oregon" appears for first time in published print in Carver's "Travels," which mentions "the River Oregon, or the River of the West." Gore and Ledyard, with Captain James Cook's expedition, sail along Oregon coast—the first Americans to visit Pacific Northwest.

1787 Captain Barkley reaches the Strait of Anian and names it *Juan de Fuca,* after its supposed discoverer of 1592.

1788 Captain Meares reaches the Strait of Anian and also names it *Juan de Fuca.*

1789 Spanish Naval force, under Estevan José Martinez, builds fort on Vancouver Island, expels English predecessors and takes possession for Spain.

1792 Captain Robert Gray, American, discovers and names Columbia River.

Lieutenant William Broughton, of the British Navy, reaches the Cascades after traveling up the Columbia River for about a hundred miles. Names Mount Hood.

1792- Captain George Vancouver (British commissioner) maps north-
'94 western coast.

1793 Sir Alexander Mackenzie completes first overland trip across Canada to Pacific coast, at 52 degrees 30 minutes lat., opening the Pacific Northwest to fur trappers.

1795 First British map bearing the name "Columbia River" is published.

1803 United States purchases Louisiana Territory—land west of Mississippi River and drained by it and its tributaries.

1804- Lewis and Clark, under orders from President Jefferson, lead
'06 an exploring expedition from St. Louis to mouth of Columbia River.

1810 Winship brothers attempt a settlement at Oak Point in lower Columbia, but fail.

1811 Astoria, first permanent American foothold in Pacific Northwest, founded as trading post by John Jacob Astor's Pacific Fur Company.

1812 Donald McKenzie explores the Willamette River.

1813 Astoria, renamed Fort George, comes under British rule during War of 1812.

1817 William Cullen Bryant's *Thanatopsis,* containing the lines "where rolls the Oregon and hears no sound save its own dashings," is published.

1818 Fort Walla Walla is built by North West Company. Astoria returned to United States. First Oregon joint occupancy treaty is made with Great Britain, permitting both nations to occupy for ten years disputed region between Columbia River and the present north boundary of the United States.

1819 Treaty with Great Britain is ratified, January 19. California-Oregon boundary fixed at 42° by treaty with Spain.

1824   Southern boundary of Russian possessions is fixed at 54° 40′ N. Dr. John McLoughlin, chief factor of the Hudson's Bay Company, arrives in Oregon and removes headquarters from Fort George to Fort Vancouver on north bank of Columbia.

1827   Second treaty with Great Britain extends provision for joint occupancy of Oregon Territory.

1828   Jedediah S. Smith and party of American trappers (first Americans to enter Oregon from California) are ambushed by Indians on the Umpqua River; Smith and two or three others survive.

1829   Hudson's Bay Company occupies location at Willamette Falls (Oregon City).

1832   McLeod and La Framboise build Fort Umpqua for Hudson's Bay Company.
       Nathaniel J. Wyeth reaches Vancouver overland and establishes a fishery on Sauvie Island at mouth of Willamette River.

1834   Reverend Jason Lee founds Methodist mission on French Prairie in Willamette Valley.

1836   Dr. Marcus Whitman and H. H. Spaulding establish missions in Walla Walla and Clearwater valleys.

1839   First American settlers, the "Peoria Party," come to Oregon from Illinois.

1841   Settlers meet, February 17-18, to make code of laws for settlements south of Columbia River.
       Lieut. Charles Wilkes, of the United States Navy, makes survey of Columbia River.
       American timbered *Star of Oregon* is launched from Swan Island and sails for San Francisco.

1842   Oregon Institute (Willamette University) is established at Salem.
       Marcus Whitman goes east and arouses interest in Oregon country.

1843   Influx of immigrants begins; first considerable wagon train west from Fort Hall.
       Provisional government is set up at meeting in Champoeg on May 2; this is first American government on Pacific coast.
       July 5, Oregon City becomes seat of government; code of laws adopted; executive governing committee constituted; and first districts established; Champoeg (Marion), Clackamas, Tualaty (Washington), and Yamhill.

1844　Indian Mission School on Chemeketa Plain is sold to the trustees of the Oregon Institute.

Salem is laid out.

1845　George Abernethy installed as first provisional governor on June 3.

Amended organic law approved by voters July 25.

1846　United States title to Oregon is established and northern boundary line fixed at 49° N. by treaty with Great Britain.

Publication of Oregon *Spectator* begins at Oregon City.

First mail contract in Oregon let to Hugh Burns.

1847　First regular mail service is established.

Cayuse Indians kill Dr. Whitman, his wife, and twelve other persons at Waiilatpu.

First school (private) is opened in Portland.

1848　Oregon Territory is established by Congress on August 14.

Pacific University and Tualatin Academy opened at Forest Grove.

1849　Gen. Joseph Lane is installed as first Territorial Governor on March 3.

Oregon Exchange Company coins and circulates five and ten-dollar gold pieces, known as beaver money.

Oregon's first school law is adopted.

First Territorial legislature meets at Oregon City on July 16.

1850　Population (U. S. Census) 13,294.

Legislature locates seat of government at Salem, the penitentiary at Portland, and the university at Corvallis.

Oregon Donation Act grants each missionary station 640 acres of land and to each settler a quantity to be apportioned according to length of residence and marital status.

1851　Major Philip Kearny fights Indians at Rogue River.

Territorial legislature incorporates Portland. First mayor, H. D. O'Bryant, is elected.

First public school under Oregon school law is organized September 21 at West Union as District No. 1, Washington County. A few weeks later District No. 2 is organized at Cornelius, and on December 15, District No. 3 at Portland.

Gold is discovered on Jackson Creek by James Cluggage and John R. Pool in December (or January, 1852).

1852　Jacksonville is founded, following gold discovery.

Congress decides state capital dispute, and seat of government is moved from Oregon City to Salem.

Great immigration takes place across plains into Oregon and northwest country.

1853- Indian Wars. Outbreaks of Rogue River tribes occur in south-
'59   ern Oregon.

1853   Willamette University is chartered at Salem.

Steamer *Gazelle* explodes while docked at Canemah; 24 lives lost. Treaty is made September 8, by which Indians sell the whole Rogue Valley for $60,000.

Washington Territory is organized, including all Oregon domain north of Columbia River.

1854   Charter granted to Pacific University and Tualatin Academy. Salem becomes a city. Statehouse is built.

1855   Astoria is chartered.

Legislature votes to locate state capital at Corvallis.

Legislature begins session in December at Corvallis.

Fire destroys statehouse at Salem, December 30.

1856   Legislature, meeting at Corvallis, votes to relocate seat of government at Salem.

1857   Constitutional convention held at Salem in August and September.

State constitution is ratified by popular vote, November 9; heavy vote against slavery; also free negroes are denied admission to state.

1858   Oregon State Educational Association is organized.

1859   Oregon admitted as free state to Union, February 14. John Whiteaker takes office as state governor on March 3. Steamer *Brother Jonathan* on March 15 reaches Oregon bringing news of statehood. May 16, organization of state government is completed.

1860   Population 52,465.

1861   Civil War begins. First Oregon Cavalry enlists for three years' service against Oregon Indians.

1862   Grande Ronde Valley is settled by immigrants. La Grande is founded.

Oregon receives Government grant of 90,000 acres for support of a state college.

1863   Idaho Territory is set off from Oregon.

1864   Fort Stevens is completed at mouth of Columbia River.

Through telegraph line extends from Portland to California points.

1865 First National Bank of Portland, first bank west of the Rocky Mountains, is organized.

Earthquake follows Mount Hood eruption.

1867 Oregon sends cargo of wheat directly to Australia in bark *Whistler.*

1868 Grading begins for two rival railroads.

First full cargo of wheat is shipped direct to Europe (Liverpool) in *Sally Brown.*

State agricultural college opens at Corvallis.

1869 Union Pacific and Central Pacific transcontinental railroads are connected May 10 at Promontory, Utah.

1870 Population 90,923.

1872 Legislature authorizes erection of permanent capitol.

Modoc War begins with night attack, November 29, on Captain Jack's camp.

1873 Modoc War ends with capture of Captain Jack's band.

Oregon State Woman's Suffrage Association meets in February for first time.

Public land grant for military road across Oregon is authorized.

Ground is broken for new capitol building at Salem.

1875 The Oregon and Washington Fish Propagating Company constructs hatching station near Oregon City.

1876 University of Oregon (chartered in 1872) opens at Eugene City October 18. (First class is graduated June 2, 1878).

Legislature meets for first time in new capitol at Salem.

1877 Chief Joseph's War. Nez Perce Indians are involved.

1880 Population 174,768.

1884 Legislative act creates Drain Normal School.

1885 Legislature passes "local option" bill.

State board of agriculture is created.

State takes over Corvallis College and establishes Oregon Agriculture College.

1888 Thomas Nast, famous cartoonist, lectures in Portland.

1890 Population 317,704.

1891 Legislature passes Australian Ballot law and creates state board of charities and corrections.

1893 State capitol is completed.

1894 Forty lives are lost in fire at Silver Lake.

1898 Second Volunteers depart for the Philippines.

1899 Resolution of legislature designates Oregon grape as the state flower.

Second Volunteers return.

1900 Population 413,536.

1902 Amendment to constitution providing for initiative and referendum is adopted.

1904 Direct primary law is passed.

1905 Centennial celebration of Lewis and Clark expedition takes place in Portland.

1906 City home rule law is passed.

1908 The Recall is adopted as a constitutional amendment.

1910 Population 672,765.

1911 Election of United States Senators by the people, indorsed by the Oregon Senate, calling upon Congress to submit to the states a constitutional amendment to carry out this reform.

1912 State legislature enacts woman suffrage law.

1913 Sarah Bernhardt, great French actress, makes first visit to Portland for three performances, January 28.

Workmen's Compensation Act and Widow's Pension Act are passed.

1916 Oregon troops are mobilized for Mexican border service.

1917 Oregon adopts modern highway program; imposes one cent per gallon tax on gasoline.

1917- Oregon contributes 44,166 to armed forces of United States '18 during World War, more than 1,000 dying in service; 350 Oregonians are cited for distinguished service.

1920 Population 783,369.

Special legislative session passes safety law and rehabilitation act and provides increased benefits under the compensation law.

Permanent state tax of two mills for elementary school purposes is approved by popular vote.

1921 Compulsory education law is passed.

1922 Indian Chiefs from Umpqua, Clackamas, and Rogue River tribes arrive in Portland January 17, to sue Federal Government for $12,500,000 for lands bought but not paid for.

KGW, the first commercial broadcasting station in the state, opens in March.

Astoria is almost wiped out by a $15,000,000 fire.

1923   The Shrine Hospital for Crippled Children is completed.

1925   Game preserve of ten million acres is created in Harney and Lake counties for antelope refuge.

1926   Queen Marie of Roumania visits Oregon November 3.

27,000 people attend dedication of Multnomah Civic Stadium.

1927   Western meadow-lark is chosen as state bird by popular vote of school children.

Legislature adopts state song "Oregon, My Oregon."

1929   State parks commission is organized.

1930   Population 953,786.

New $1,300,000 United States Veterans Hospital is dedicated on New Year's Day.

People's utility district law is passed.

1931   Department of state police begins operations.

1933   Erection of Bonneville Dam is begun.

1934   Works Progress Administration allocated $5,103,000 for construction of five Oregon coast bridges, January 6.

State operates liquor dispensaries, established for the first time.

First C.C.C. Camps are organized in Oregon.

Maritime strike lasts 82 days.

1935   Capitol building is destroyed by fire.

Cornerstone of burnt capitol building is opened.

1936   Second maritime strike begins.

Senator Steiwer makes keynote address at Republican convention.

Wolf Creek highway appropriations are granted by Works Progress Administration.

1937   Andre Gagnon "Father of Modern Saw Mills" and inventor of Gagnon Band Saw dies in Portland at the age of 93.

President Roosevelt visits Portland to inspect Federal projects; dedicates Timberline Lodge.

1938   First ocean-going vessel, the S. S. *Charles L. Wheeler,* passes through Bonneville Locks.

Portland newspapers suspend publication for five days because of strike.

1938   WPA begins clearing right of way for $1,000,000 power line for Bonneville transmission system.

Labor law, by referendum, makes picketing and strikes illegal.

1939   Opening of the new capitol building at Salem.

Selected Reading List

GENERAL INFORMATION

Oregon. Secretary of State. *The Oregon Bluebook,* 1939-1940. Compiled by Earl Snell, Secretary of State. Salem, 1939. Issued bi-yearly.

Emerson, Charles L. *This Is Oregon.* Portland, 1936. Guide, description, travel and game laws.

DESCRIPTION AND TRAVEL

Burg, Amos. "Rambles of a Native Son in Oregon. *National Geographic Magazine,* Feb. 1934, V. 65:173-233.

Cox. Ross. *Adventures on the Columbia.* New York, 1832. Description of life among the trappers and fur traders of the Astor expedition.

Eaton, Walter Prichard. *Skyline Camps.* Boston, 1922. Notebook of a wanderer in Northwest mountains.

Franchere, Gabriel. *Narrative of a Voyage to the Northwest Coast of America.* New York, 1854. By a clerk of the Astor company.

Furlong, Charles Wellington. *Let 'Er Buck.* New York, 1921. Descriptive of the Pendleton Round-up and of eastern Oregon.

Lyman, William D. *The Columbia River: Its History, its Myths, its Scenery, its Commerce.* New York, 1909.

Murphy, Thomas D. *Oregon, the Picturesque.* Boston, 1917. Description of an automobile trip through the State.

McArthur, Lewis A. *Oregon Geographic Names.* Eugene, 1928.

Putnam, George Palmer. *In the Oregon Country.* New York, 1915.

Ross, Alexander. *Adventures on the Oregon.* Chicago, 1923. Reprint of Ross' life with the Astorians.

Smith, Dr. Warren D. *Scenic Treasure-House of Oregon.* Portland, 1940.

Steel, W. G. *The Mountains of Oregon.* Portland, 1890.

Stevenson, E. N. *Nature Rambles in the Wallowas.* Portland, 1935.

Sharp, Dallas Lore. *Where Rolls the Oregon.* Boston and New York, 1914. Oregon through the eyes of a New England naturalist.

Wilkinson, Marguerite. *The Dingbat of Arcady.* New York, 1922. A boat trip down the Willamette.

GEOLOGY AND PALENONTOLOGY

Chaney, Ralph W. *Flora of the Eagle Creek Formation.* Chicago, University of Chicago Press, 1920.

Condon, Thomas. *Oregon Geology.* Portland, 1910. A revision of Dr. Condon's *Two Islands* published in 1902.

Hodge, Edwin T. *Mount Multnomah, Ancient Ancestor of the Three Sisters.* Eugene, University of Oregon Press, 1925.

Merriam, J. C. and Sinclair, William J. *Tertiary Fauna of the John Day Region.* Berkeley, University of California Press, 1907.

Schufeldt, Robert Wilson. *Review of the Fossil Fauna of the Desert Region of Oregon.* American Museum of Natural History, 1913. Bulletin 32, part 6.

Sternberg, Charles H. *Life of a Fossil Hunter.* New York, 1909. Expedition to the Oregon desert and John Day River region in 1878.

FLORA AND FAUNA

Bailey, Vernon. *The Mammals and Life Zones of Oregon.* Washington, D. C., 1936. (U.S. Department of Agriculture Bureau of Biology. Survey of North American Fauna No. 55).

Benson, Gilbert Theron. *The Trees and Shrubs of Western Oregon.* Stanford University, 1930.

Eliot, Willard Ayres. *Birds of the Pacific Coast.* New York, 1923. Illustrated with many paintings by R. Bruce Horsfall. *Forest Trees of the Pacific Coast.* New York, 1938.

Finley, William Lovell and Irene. *Wild Animal Pets.* New York, 1928.

Frye, Theodore C. *Ferns of the Northwest.* Portland, 1934.

Gabrielson, Ira N. *Western American Alpines.* New York, 1932.

Haskins, Leslie L. *Wild Flowers of the Pacific Coast.* Portland, 1934.

Howell, Thomas. *Flora of Northwest America.* Portland, 1903.

Lampman, Herbert Sheldon. *Northwest Nature Trails.* Portland, 1933.

Lord, William Rogers. *A First Book on the Birds of Oregon and Washington.* Portland, 1902.

Schultz, Leonard. *Checklist of Fresh-water Fishes of Oregon and Washington.* Seattle, 1929.

CONSERVATION AND NATURAL RESOURCES

Lewis, John H. *Water Resources of the State of Oregon, 1914-1924.* Compiled and prepared by the State Engineer in cooperation with the U. S. Geological Survey. Salem, 1925.

Lewis, Howard T. and Miller, Stephen L. *Economic Resources of the Pacific Northwest.* Seattle, 1923.

Treasher, Ray C. and Hodge, Edwin T. *Bibliography of the Geology and Mineral Resources of Oregon.* Portland, 1936. (Oregon. State Planning Board).

Winkenwerder, Hugo A. *Forestry in the Pacific Northwest.* Washington, 1928.

ARCHEOLOGY AND INDIANS

Bancroft, Hubert Howe. *Native Races of the Pacific States.* San Francisco, 1873.

Churchill, Claire Warner. *South of the Sunset.* New York, 1936. The story of Sacajawea.

Churchill, Claire Warner. *Slave Wives of Nehalem.* Portland, 1933. Stories based on the manners and customs of the Oregon coast Indians.

Curtiss, Edward S. *The North American Indians.* Seattle, 1907-31. 8 v. V. 8 treats of the Nez Perce, Walla Walla, Cayuse and Chinook tribes.

Fee, Chester A. *Chief Joseph: the Biography of a Great Indian.* New York, 1935.

Gatschet, A. S. *Klamath Indians of Southwestern Oregon.* Washington, 1893. (Smithsonian Institution. Bureau of American Ethnology Contributions to North American Ethnology, v. 2).

Meacham, A. B. *Wigwam and Warpath.* New York, 1873. The Modoc War.

Payne, Doris Palmer. *Captain Jack, Modoc Renegade.* Portland, 1938.

Victor, Frances Fuller. *The Early Indian Wars of Oregon.* Salem, 1894.

Thomas, Edward Harper. *Chinook: A History and Dictionary.* Portland, 1937.

HISTORY

Applegate, Jesse. *Recollections of My Boyhood.* Chicago, 1934.

Bancroft, Hubert Howe. *History of Oregon.* San Francisco, 1886. 2 v.

Carey, Charles H. *A General History of Oregon.* Portland, 1935. 2 v.

Clark, R. C. *History of the Willamette Valley.* Chicago, 1927.

Clarke, S. A. *Pioneer Days of Oregon History.* Portland, 1905.

Coe, Dr. Urling. *Frontier Doctor.* New York, 1939.

Davenport, Homer. *The Country Boy.* New York, 1910. The story of his early life in Oregon.

Dawson, Charles. *Pioneer Tales of the Oregon Trail.* Topeka, 1912.

Dobbs, Caroline E. *Men of Champoeg.* Portland, 1932. Short sketches of the men who voted for organization of a government at Champoeg on May 2, 1843.

Dunn, John. *History of the Oregon Territory.* London, 1844.

Dye, Eva Emery. *Conquest, The True Story of Lewis & Clark.* Chicago, 1902; Portland, 1938.

Dye, Eva Emery. *McLoughlin and Old Oregon.* Chicago, 1900; Portland, 1938.

Fuller, George W.   *A History of the Pacific Northwest.*   New York, 1931.

Gaston, Joseph.   *Centennial History of Oregon.*   Chicago, 1912.

Geer, T. T.   *Fifty Years in Oregon.*   New York, 1912.

Ghent, W. J.   *The Early Far West.*   New York, 1931.

Ghent, W. J.   *The Road to Oregon.*   New York, 1929.

Gray, W. H.   *History of Oregon, 1742-1849.*   Portland, 1870.

Greenhow, Robt.   *History of Oregon and California.*   Boston, 1848

Holman, F. V.   *Dr. John McLoughlin, the Father of Oregon.*   Cleveland, 1907.

Irving, Washington.   *Astoria and Captain Bonneville.*   Chicago, 1900.   Reprints of these two works on the fur trade, in one volume.

Judson, Katherine Berry.   *Early Days in Old Oregon.*   Chicago, 1916; Portland, 1935.

Lee, Daniel.   *Ten Years in Oregon.*   New York, 1844.

Lenox, E. H.   *Overland to Oregon.*   Oakland, 1904.

Lyman, Horace S.   *History of Oregon.*   New York, 1903.   4 v.

Montgomery, Richard G.   *The White Headed Eagle: John McLoughlin, the Builder of an Empire.*   New York, 1934.

Munford, Kenneth.   *John Ledyard, an American Marco Polo.*

Nash, Wallis.   *Two Years in Oregon.*   New York, 1882.

Parkman, Francis.   *The Oregon Trail.*   New York, 1933.

Parrish, Philip H.   *Before the Covered Wagon.*   Portland, 1931.

Powell, F. W.   *Hall J. Kelley, Prophet of Oregon.*   Portland, 1917.

Ross, Alexander.   *Fur Traders of the Far West.*   London, 1855.

Schafer, Joseph.   *Oregon Pioneers and American Diplomacy.*   New York, 1910.

Scott, Harvey W.   *History of the Oregon Country.*   Cambridge, 1924.   Edited and arranged by his son, Leslie M. Scott.

Simpson, Sir George.   *Fur Trade and Empire.*   Cambridge, 1931.   Hudson's Bay Company activities and description and travel in early Northwest.

Thwaites, Reuben Gold.   *Original Journals of Lewis and Clark.*   New York, 1905.   8 v.

Victor, Frances Fuller.   *River of the West.*   Hartford, 1870.   The story of Joe Meek, Rocky Mountain trapper, and Oregon's first U. S. Marshal.

Wagner, Henry R.   *Spanish Voyages to the Northwest Coast of America in the 16th Century.*   San Francisco, 1929.

Warren, Eliza Spalding.   *Memoirs of the West.*   Portland, 1916.   (*See also* Oregon Historical Society Quarterly, 1900—.)

POLITICS AND GOVERNMENT

Brown, J. Henry.   *Political History of Oregon.*   Portland, 1892.

Carey, Charles H.   *The Oregon Constitution and Proceedings and Debates of the Constitutional Convention of 1857.*   Salem, 1925-26.

Duniway, Abigail Scott. *Path Breaking: An Autobiographical History of the Equal Suffrage Movement in Oregon.* Portland, 1914.

Eaton, Allen H. *The Oregon System: The Story of Direct Legislation in Oregon.* Chicago, 1912.

Grover, Lafayette (compiler). *Oregon Archives.* Salem, 1853. Minutes of the proceedings of the Oregon Provisional Government.

Woodward, W. C. *Rise and Early History of Political Parties in Oregon,* 1843-1868. Portland, 1913.

AGRICULTURE

Haley, Lucia. *Oregon: A Preliminary List of Sources of Agricultural and Related Statistics of the State.* Washington, D. C., 1927.

Monroe, Anne Shannon. *Feelin' Fine: Bill Hanley's Book.* New York, 1930. The story of the cattle ranching era of southeastern Oregon.

Pratt, Alice Day. *A Homesteader's Portfolio.* New York, 1922. Experiences of a homesteader in central Oregon.

Stephens, Louise G., "Katharine". *Letters from an Oregon Ranch.* Chicago, 1905.

Treadwell, Edward F. *The Cattle King.* New York, 1931. The life and times of Henry Miller, Oregon cattle baron.

Works Progress Administration. *Flax in Oregon.* Portland, 1936. A history of the development of the flax industry in Oregon. Written by Margaret Clarke and revised in 1939 by Robert Wilmot.

INDUSTRY, COMMERCE, AND LABOR

Bonneville Commission. *Bonneville Power Development.* Salem, Oregon, 1934. Report of the Bonneville Commission on matters relating to Bonneville power development.

Hosmer, Paul. *Now We're Loggin'.* Portland, 1930. A picture of the logging industry and loggers of the Northwest.

Gilbert, James H. *Trade and Currency in Early Oregon.* New York, Columbia University Press, 1907. A study in the commercial and monetary history of the Pacific Northwest.

Holbrook, Stewart H. *Holy Old Mackinaw: A Natural History of the American Lumberjack.* New York, 1938.

Lomax, Alfred Lewis. *The Facilities, Commerce and Resources of Oregon's Coast Ports.* Eugene, Oregon, 1932.

Mitchell, Graham J. *Minerals of Oregon.* Salem, Oregon, 1916.

Stevens, James. *Homer in the Sagebrush.* New York, 1928. Short stories of Oregon lumberjacks, cowhands, miners, freighters, fishermen, etc.

TRANSPORTATION

Estes, George. *The Stage Coach.* Portland, 1925. The story of stage coaches and stage coaching in Oregon.

Hedges, James Blaine. *Henry Villard and the Railways of the Northwest.* New Haven, 1930.

Lancaster, Samuel C. *Columbia, America's Greatest Highway: Through the Cascade Mountains to the Sea.* Portland, 1915.

Laut, Agnes Christiana. *The Overland Trail, Epic Path of the Pioneers of Oregon.* New York, 1929.

Miller, Joaquin. *Overland in a Covered Wagon.* New York, 1930.

Miller, Joaquin. *A Royal Highway of the World.* Portland, 1932. Description of a stage trip from Burns to Canyon City.

Rucker, Maude A. *The Oregon Trail.* New York, 1930. Frontier and Oregon pioneer life. Includes recollections of Jesse Applegate.

Villard, H. H. *Memoirs of Henry Villard.* Boston, 1904.

Wright, Edgar W. *Marine History: Illustrated History of the Growth and Development of the Marine Industry of the Northwest.* Portland, 1895.

RACIAL ELEMENTS AND FOLKLORE

Harkness, Ione B. "Basque Settlement in Oregon." *Oregon Historical Quarterly.* Sept. 1933. V. 34:273-275.

Hendricks, Robert J. *Bethel and Aurora.* New York, 1933. An early Oregon experiment in communistic living.

Judson, Katherine Berry. *Myths and Legends of the Pacific Northwest* Chicago, 1910.

Stevens, James. *Paul Bunyan.* New York, 1925. Tales of the legendary hero of the lumber camps.

Turney, Ida Virginia. *Paul Bunyan Comes West.* Boston, 1928.

Wood, Charles Erskine Scott. *A Book of Indian Tales.* New York, 1929. Indian tales and myths of early Oregon.

EDUCATION AND RELIGION

Blanchet, F. N. *Historical Sketches of the Catholic Church in Oregon.* Washington, 1910.

de Smet, Pierre Jean. *Letters and Travels of Father de Smet, Missionary Labor and Adventures Among the Wild Tribes of North American Indians.* New York, 1905.

Drury, Clifford M. *Henry Harmon Spaulding, Pioneer of Old Oregon.* Caldwell, Idaho, 1936.

Drury, Clifford M. *Marcus Whitman, M.D., Pioneer and Martyr.* Caldwell, Ida., 1937.

Gay, Theressa. *Life and Letters of Mrs. Jason Lee: First Wife of Rev. Jason Lee of the Oregon Mission.* Portland, 1936.

Lee, Daniel, and Frost, J. H. *Ten Years in Oregon.* New York, 1844.

Nichols, Leona. *Joab Powell, Homespun Missionary.* Portland. 1935.

O'Hara, Edwin V. *Catholic History of Oregon.* Portland, 1916.

Schreibeis, C. D. *Pioneer Education in the Pacific Northwest, 1789 to 1847.*

Sheldon, H. D. *A Critical and Descriptive Bibliography of the History of Education in the State of Oregon.* Eugene, Oregon, 1929. (In Oregon University education series, v. 2. no. 1).

Sheldon, H. D. *History of the University of Oregon.* Portland, 1940.

PENOLOGY

Duncan, Lee. *Over the Wall.* By ex-convict No. 9256, Oregon State Prison. New York, 1936.

THE ARTS AND ARCHITECTURE

Harrison, Henry (editor). *Oregon Poets.* New York, 1935. Selected works from fifty writers, with foreword by Ethel Romig Fuller.

Ernst, Alice Henson. *High Country.* Portland, 1935. Four plays of the Pacific Northwest.

Merriam, H. G. (editor). *Northwest Verse, an Anthology.* Caldwell, Idaho, 1931. Representative work of poets of Oregon, Washington, Idaho and Montana.

Peterson, Martin Severin. *Joaquin Miller: Literary Frontiersman.* Palo Alto, Calif., Stanford University Press. 1937.

Powers, Alfred. *History of Oregon Literature.* Portland, 1936.

Rockwood, E. Ruth. *Books on the Northwest for Small Libraries.* n. p. 1923.

Skiff, Frederick W. *Adventures in Americana.* Portland, 1935. Contains many passages on Oregon life and writers.

Skiff, Frederick W. *Landmarks and Literature.* Portland, 1937. Contains several sketches of Oregon writers.

Smith, C. W. *Pacific Northwest Americana: A Checklist of Books and Pamphlets Relating to the Pacific Northwest.* New York, 1921.

Turnbull, George S. *History of Oregon Newspapers.* Portland, 1939. The essay on LITERATURE, DRAMA, MUSIC AND ART, lists numerous other works on the history, literature, and life of the State.

POINTS OF INTEREST

Churchill, Claire Warner. *Mount Hood Timberline Lodge.* Portland, 1936.

Lapham, Stanton C. *The Enchanted Lake.* Portland, 1931. History and Description of Crater Lake.

Watson, Chandler Bruer. *Prehistoric Siskiyou Island and the Marble Halls of Oregon.* Ashland, Oregon, 1909. History and description of Oregon Caves.

McNeil, Fred. H. *Wy-east, "THE Mountain."* A Chronicle of Mount Hood. Portland, 1937.

Federal Writers' Project. *The Oregon Trail.* New York, 1938.

Oregon Writers' Project. *A Guide to Mount Hood.* New York, 1940.

Work Projects Administration. *The Builders of Timberline Lodge.* Portland, 1937, 1940. Prepared by Claire Warner Churchill.

Work Projects Administration. *Timberline Lodge: Structure, art work, and furniture.* Portland, 1939. Prepared by Andrew S. Sherbert.

Index